NEVADA SCHOOL LAW
Cases and Materials

Second Edition

GERALD C. KOPS, J.D., Ph.D.
University of Nevada, Las Vegas

KENDALL/HUNT PUBLISHING COMPANY
4050 Westmark Drive   Dubuque, Iowa 52002

This edition has been printed directly from camera-ready copy.

Copyright © 1992, 1994 by Kendall/Hunt Publishing Company

Library of Congress Card Catalog Number: 93-80813

ISBN 0-8403-9176-5

Printed in the United States of America
10 9 8 7 6 5 4 3 2 1

CONTENTS

CHAPTER VI
HEALTH ISSUES

CHAPTER VII
EDUCATOR LIABILITY

CHAPTER VIII
CONCLUSION

PREFACE
SECOND EDITION

The primary purpose of the Second Edition of Nevada School Law is the description of the current Nevada school legal setting. It is appropriate to explore education law from a state perspective because under our system of government education still remains largely a state responsibility.

It is the goal of this text to contribute to the sound preparation of classroom and school leaders. It is also the authors hope that the work will assist practitioners to better understand the current school legal setting since a sound grounding in the school law is an essential ingredient of wise decisionmaking for children.

Change remains the theme of the second edition. The school legal setting has undergone dramatic restructuring. Governance responsibility has been dispersed and reordered. The legal relationships between school districts and their employees have been revised. The doctrine of 'in loco parentis' has been amended by incorporating certain constitutional protections for students in the school environment. Health issues, while not new to the school legal environment, present urgent social as well as legal problems for schools. The manner for resolving liability issues has not been subjected to major reform but understanding the conceptual framework for resolving allegations of negligent conduct remains a critical tool in pursuing the goal of safe schools. Nevada school law reflects national trends and provides a vehicle for analyzing the new challenges presented to school policymakers.

The second edition addresses significant Federal legislative action since the first edition and incorporates Nevada legislative actions taken during the 1993 session. The second edition also includes important judicial decisions of the United States Supreme Court, 9th Circuit Court of Appeals and Nevada supreme court through November 1993.

The book utilizes a combination of narrative and primary legal resources. Cases and other original source material are used to encourage independent analysis and develop critical thinking skills. After all, laws and decisions only express the current solution to school legal issues or disputes. The solutions will change and educators have a real stake in enlightened solutions. Hopefully, the study of this text will assist educators to assume an effective role in developing enlightened solutions to school legal problems.

The new edition addresses two major weakness of the initial volume. A Table of Cases and Subject Index have been added to assist the reader. This major step toward reader friendly use of the text could not have been accomplished without the excellent assistance of my graduate assistant, James M. Hayes, and his wife Cathy.

Of course, the second edition, as the initial effort, could not have been possible without the patient support and encouragement of my wife, Marilyn, and family.

I accept full responsibility for errors in content and presentation. I trust that my students and colleagues will continue to assist me in reaching for better understanding of the subject matter and in developing more effective communication skills to share it.

Now on to our Nevada school law journey!

TABLE OF CASES

CHAPTER I

FOUNDATION LEGAL PRINCIPLES OF SCHOOL GOVERNANCE IN THE UNITED STATES

A
INTRODUCTION

We begin our journey with a brief review of the key concepts which lie at the core of our system of self government:

1. LIMITED POWERS

Government possesses only those powers granted by the people. Those not granted to the federal or state governments are retained by the states and people respectively. The federal and state constitutions identify the powers granted and establish the structure within which governance issues are resolved.

2. FEDERALISM

Governmental authority is shared by or divided among the states and the Federal government. However, the Federal Constitution is the supreme law of the United States. States do not possess the power to adopt laws that are inconsistent with the Federal Constitution.

3. SEPARATION OF POWERS

State and Federal government power is divided among branches of government. (Judicial, Legislative, and Executive).

The President presides over the EXECUTIVE branch of the Federal government. The EXECUTIVE branch of state government is headed by a governor. These offices are filled by election. The primary function of the chief executive is to faithfully enforce or carry out government policy (law). Federal and state chief executives play an active role in the policy (law) making process.

LEGISLATIVE powers are vested with elected assembles. (Congress and the various state legislatures). The primary functions of these representative bodies are to investigate the need for policy change and actually make policy changes. When a legislature enacts a policy it is called a statute. Statutes (policy) enacted by the Congress are found in the United States Code Annotated (U.S.C.A.). The laws enacted by the Nevada legislature are published in the Nevada Revised Statutes (NRS) Legislative bodies are obviously active participants in the policy making process.

The JUDICIAL power is vested in Federal and state courts. Courts apply principles of law to factual situations, interpret law (statutes, case law), and determine the constitutionality of legislation. (measure laws adopted by legislatures against constitutions [judicial review]). The decisions of courts are called judge-made law, case law or common law. In the United States the doctrine of precedent or the rule of Stare Decisis, "let the decision stand," prevails. So past decisions are generally considered to be binding on subsequent cases that have the same or substantially the same factual setting. The rule of 'Stare Decisis' is rigidly followed by lower courts when applying authoritative decisions by higher courts in the same jurisdiction. Courts are passive participants in the policy making process because they must wait for a real dispute over the interpretation and application of law to be presented to them by adverse parties. Courts are only empowered to decide 'cases and controversies.' Courts are not concerned with hypothetical questions.

The United States Supreme Court presides over the Federal judiciary. Most education cases that reach the Supreme Court are taken there on Writs of Certiorari. A Writ of Certiorari is a petition filed with the Supreme Court arguing that the dispute in question is worthy of review and should be placed on the Court's calendar for decision.[1] If the Court agrees to hear the case it issues an order granting certiorari (cert granted). The Supreme Court is assisted by an intermediate court of appeal called the Circuit Court of Appeal. The United States is divided into 13 appellate circuits.[2] Nevada is part of the ninth (9th) circuit. In addition each state has at least one federal trial court called the federal district court.Federal District CourtThe boundaries of federal district courts do not extend beyond the boundaries of the state in which they are located. The district court is the point of entry for most litigation. All Federal Judges are appointed by the President with the advice and consent of the Senate. Federal judges are appointed for life or during good behavior.

Each state has adopted it's own system for organizing it's JUDICIAL branch. In Nevada Judges are elected. The Nevada judiciary is headed by a supreme court composed of 5 justices.[3] Unlike many states Nevada does not have an intermediate court of appeal. Nevada trial courts of general jurisdiction are called district courts. They are the primary point of entry for state education litigation in Nevada.

4. CHECKS AND BALANCES

The branches of government exercise governmental authority interdependently. For example, a law is enacted when a government chief executive signs a bill that has been adopted by a majority of both houses of the legislature. The law is subject to interpretation and judicial review by the courts to determine it's meaning and whether it is consistent with the constitution. Finally, all constitutions contain a procedure for amending the document. Amendments, of course, can reverse or vacate judicial interpretations.

Several key concepts of governance were illustrated in the December decision of the Nevada Supreme Court regarding implementation of a cost of living pay raise enacted by the legislature and signed into law by the governor. The raise was deferred by the (governor, attorney general, and secretary of state). The pay deferral provoked the State Employees Association to file a lawsuit challenging the legality of the action.

---

[1] The Supreme Court acts on 5,000 cases a year, and only about 150-200 are granted review. Four of the nine justices must agree to hear a case before the court will grant review and schedule an oral argument. Six members of the court--Chief Justice William Rehnquist, and Justices Byron White (since retired, participation of Justice Ginsburg unknown), Harry Blackmun, Sandra O'Connor, Antonin Scalia and Anthony Kennedy--now take part in a pooling arrangement to review petitions. One law clerk, chosen on a rotating basis among the 23 employed by the six justices, prepares a summary of each of the 5,000 cases and distributes it to all six offices. Some of the justices still review certain petitions on the basis of the summaries, while others rely on just the summaries. "Only Clerks May Be Screening Petitions To Supreme Court In Post Brennen Era", Wall Street Journal, Oct. 11, 1990 p. 8 B.

[2] See Outline of Federal Circuit courts of Appeal Fig. 1

[3] The Nevada Supreme Court decided a record 1,057 cases in 1990. Appeals filed also reached an all time high of 1,089. Filings and dispositions have been increasing steadily in the past 10 years. In 1981 court filings totaled 727 and dispositions 838. A supreme court committee has urged Nevada to join 37 other states and establish an intermediate court of appeals. For such a court to be established a resolution must be passed by the legislature at two sessions and then accepted by a vote of the people. "High Court Case Load Sets Record," Las Vegas Review Journal (Review Journal), January 4, 1990, p. 1 A.

STATE OF NEVADA EMPLOYEES ASSOCIATION
v.
DAINES
108 Nev. Advance Opinion No. 4 (1992)

PER CURIAM:

Petitioners in this original action seek a writ of mandamus compelling respondent Darrel Daines, Controller of the State of Nevada, to issue warrants for petitioners' salaries, including the four percent pay raise appropriated by the 1991 Nevada State Legislature to become effective October 1, 1991. 1991 Nev. Stat. ch. 496 at 1515 (approved June 30, 1991).

On December 13, 1991, following the oral arguments in this matter, this court directed the clerk of this court to issue a writ of mandamus compelling respondent forthwith to issue warrants sufficient to pay the salary increases provided to the classified employees of the state by the legislature. We specifically directed such salary increases to be paid retroactively from October 1, 1991, and we indicated that a formal opinion setting forth the grounds for our decision would be forthcoming. This opinion constitutes our final resolution of this proceeding.

FACTS

On June 30, 1991, the Nevada State Legislature passed a bill appropriating funds for a four percent salary increase for classified state employees. The salary increase was to become effective October 1, 1991. (Assembly Bill 815). The governor signed the bill (hereinafter "the act") into law.

On September 26, 1991, at a meeting of the Nevada State Board of Examiners, the clerk of the board of examiners, based on projected revenue shortfalls, recommended that "the Board of Examiners defer allocation and disbursement of the funds appropriated for salary adjustments for up to three months from the time the legislature contemplated their enactment." The board of examiners unanimously adopted the clerk's recommendation.

As a result of the action of the board of examiners, the respondent state controller refused to issue warrants sufficient to pay the authorized salary increases in the paychecks delivered to state employees beginning on October 11, 1991. This petition followed.

DISCUSSION

Petitioners contend that, pursuant to NRS §227.160, the state controller has a non-discretionary duty resulting from his office to pay the salary increases enacted by the legislature. We agree. This court has held that "[a]n appropriation of money to a specific object would be an authority to the proper officers to pay the money, because the auditor is authorized to draw his warrant upon an appropriation, and the treasurer is authorized to pay such warrant if he has appropriated money in the treasury." Thus, unless the act itself allows the board or the governor discretion in the payment of the salary increases, or the board or the governors are empowered by the constitution or by statute to defer payment of legislatively authorized salary increases, the controller has an absolute duty pursuant to NRS §227.160 to issue his warrants according to the legislative will.

Respondent essentially concedes this point and argues correctly that "the proper analysis of this matter begins and ends with the classified pay bill." Section 1(2) of the act provides:

> 2.   The state board of examiners, upon recommendation of the director of the department of administration, may allocate and

3

disburse to the various departments, commissions and agencies of the State of Nevada, out of the money appropriated by this section such sums of money as may from time to time be required, which when added to the money otherwise appropriated or available equals the amount of money required to pay the salaries of the classified employees of the respective departments, commissions and agencies under the adjusted pay plan.[4]

Respondent argues that the legislature's use of the word "may" rather than "shall" in sections 1(2), 2(2) and 3(3) indicates that allocation and disbursement of the appropriated amounts to pay salary increases is discretionary with the board of examiners and the Director of the Department of Administration. We disagree.

This court has stated that in statutes, "may" is permissive and "shall" is mandatory unless the statute demands a different construction to carry out the clear intent of the legislature. This court has also held, however, that the term "may" in a statute is conditional rather than permissive if the purpose of the statute requires that construction.("may" in the statute was not permissive; the statute created a duty to act upon the occurrence of a specified condition, leaving "no area for the exercise of discretion "). This construction of the word "may" has been recognized in numerous cases, especially where used to define the duties of a public officer.

Close examination of the language of the act in this case reveals that "may" in the act is conditional rather than permissive. Section 2(3) of the act provides that the state board of examiners "may allocate and disburse . . . out of the money appropriated such sums of money as "may from time to time be required" to "pay the salaries of the classified employees . . . under the adjusted pay plan."

The "pay plan" is the grade and step salary schedule for classified employees created by the Department of Personnel pursuant to NRS 284.175. Clearly, the legislature intended that the Department of Personnel would adjust the pay plan by approximately four percent.[5] The language of the act requires the board of examiners to allocate additional funds to state agencies to meet these pay increases upon the conditions set forth, i.e., when the funds previously appropriated for salaries are insufficient to pay the salaries required under the revised grade and step pay plan.[6] We conclude, therefore, that the governor and the board's decision to defer the legislatively enacted salary increases cannot be justified under the language of the act.

Respondent asserts, nevertheless, that an appropriation creates no duty that the appropriated money actually be spent. Respondent argues that because public officials are specifically prohibited from spending more than the amount appropriated but not specifically enjoined from spending less, it is permissible to spend less. See NRS 353.260(1). The instant case is not, however, a case of a public

---

[4] The language of sections 2(2) and 3(3) is identical to that of section 1(2) except that section 2(2) ,applies to employees of the department of motor vehicles and public safety, the public service commission, and the attorney general's office, and section 3(3) applies to the University of Nevada System.

[5] The act refers to a raise of approximately four percent, rather than four percent, because the grade and step pay schedule created by the Department of Personnel contains specific dollar figures derived by multiplying present amounts by 1.04. The resulting figures must be rounded to the nearest whole dollar amounts.

[6] In sections 6 and 7 of the act, dealing with potential pay raises in the second biennium, the act sets forth certain amounts that are "contingently appropriated" to provide additional salary increases depending on the projected balance. These provisions do not purport to give the board of examiners discretion to disburse or not disburse the amounts needed. Rather, they direct the board to implement certain pay raises if the projected balances support the increases. Notably, the legislature did not make the payment of the October 1, 1991, pay raises dependent on any revenue or state general fund projections. This supports our conclusion that the legislature enacted salary increases and provided a fund from which to pay the increases; the legislature did not, as contended by respondent, simply appropriate funds for discretionary distribution by the executive if it determined a pay raise was warranted.

official spending less than the amount appropriated by the legislature. In this case, the legislature enacted a pay raise, designated a date on which the raise would become effective, and appropriated funds to accomplish its purpose. The executive branch has attempted to impound the funds specifically appropriated for this salary increase in a manner that would defeat the legislative purpose and essentially rewrite the act. The executive is not empowered to disregard the mandate of the legislature that certain salaries be paid.

Respondent contends that the governor could order deferral of disbursement of the salary increases pursuant to the "supreme executive power" vested in him by article 5 section 1 of the Nevada Constitution.[7] Respondent has failed to cite any authority, however, for the proposition that the supreme executive power of the State of Nevada includes the power to disregard acts of the legislature. Indeed, the governor has a constitutional duty to see that the laws enacted by the legislature are faithfully executed. Nev. Const. art. 5, § 7; (executive power extends to carrying out and enforcing laws enacted by the legislature).

Further, it is well established that the power of controlling the public purse lies within legislative, not executive authority. ....Thus, the action of the governor was not authorized by his "supreme executive power." Similarly, the board of examiners had no constitutional authority to defer salary increases enacted by the legislature and signed into law by the governor. Article 5, section 21 of the Nevada Constitution provides:

> The Governor, Secretary of State and Attorney General . . . shall also constitute a Board of Examiners, with power to examine all claims against the State (except salaries or compensation of Officers fixed by law) and perform such other duties as may be prescribed by law, and no claim against the State (except salaries or compensation of Officers fixed by law) shall be passed upon by the Legislature without having been considered and acted upon by said "Board of Examiners."

This provision empowers the board of examiners to examine claims (except salaries or compensation of officers) against the state before the legislature passes upon such claims; there are no provisions in this section allowing the board to defer payment of a legislatively enacted salary increase after the act has been signed into law by the governor. Therefore, we conclude that there is no constitutional authority for the action of the board.

Respondent contends that the board's action was authorized by NRS §353.225, which provides for a reserve to meet emergencies. NRS §353.225 (emphasis added) provides:

> 1. In order to provide some degree of flexibility to meet emergencies arising during each fiscal year in the expenditures for the state distributive school account in the state general fund and for operation and maintenance of the various departments, institutions and agencies of the executive department of the state government, the chief, with the approval in writing of the governor, may require the state controller or the head of each such department, institution or agency to set aside a reserve in such amount as the chief may determine, out of the total amount appropriated or out of other funds available from any source whatever to the department, institution or agency.

---

[7] Article 5, §1 of the Nevada Constitution provides that "[t]he supreme executive power of this State, shall be vested in a Chief Magistrate who shall be Governor of the State of Nevada."

2. At any time during the fiscal year this reserve or any portion of it may be returned to the appropriation or other fund to which it belongs and may be added to any one or more of the allotments, if the chief so orders in writing.

This statute authorizes "the chief" of the Budget Division of the Department of Administration, with the approval of the governor, to require the controller of the heads of various agencies within the executive branch of government to set aside reserves to meet emergencies. We cannot conclude, however, that the legislature intended, when it enacted this statute, to endow the chief of the Budget Division of the Department of Administration or the governor with power to invalidate the acts of the legislature. Nor did the legislature intend NRS 353.225(2) to be construed as an authorization for a blanket executive repeal of a pay raise enacted by it. The provision was instead intended to provide a means for the executive and the individual agencies to provide flexibility to meet emergencies by utilizing available monies from the various budgets to fund a reserve for use at a later date. We conclude that this statute, at best, is irrelevant to this case. Accordingly, we decline to consider the constitutional challenges to the statute.

CONCLUSION

The governor and the board of examiners have no constitutional or statutory authority to defer the salary increases enacted by the legislature. Thus, the action of the board taken on September 26, 1991, was a nullity, and the state controller has an absolute duty to issue his warrants pursuant to the legislative mandate. A writ of mandamus may issue to compel the performance of an act which the law especially enjoins as a duty resulting from an office, trust or station and where there is no plain, speedy and adequate remedy at law. .

Accordingly, we grant this petition.

****

STUDY QUESTIONS

1. What key concepts of governance are illustrated in the Daines case?
2. How could the governor have legally secured a salary roll back?
3. What impact did the decision have on Nevada teacher salaries for the 1991- 92 school year?
4. Does the Daines decision illustrate the dynamic nature of the key concepts of governance?

B
SOURCES OF EDUCATION LAW

CONSTITUTIONS

A constitution is a body of precepts that provides a framework of law within which orderly government processes operate. Below are the provisions of the Federal Constitution which are of particular significance in understanding the governance of education. The articles and amendments reflect the key concepts reviewed earlier.

UNITED STATES CONSTITUTION
Relevant Articles
Article VI

Section 2 This Constitution,and the laws of the United States which shall be made, under the authority of the United States, shall be the supreme law of the land; and the judges in every state shall be bound thereby, anything in the Constitution or laws of any state to the contrary notwithstanding.

Relevant Amendments

Amendment I adopted 1791

Congress shall make no law respecting the establishment of religion, or prohibiting the free exercise thereof; or abridging the freedom of speech, or of the press; or the right of the people to peaceably to assemble, and to petition the government for a redress of grievances.

Amendment IV adopted 1791

The right of the people to be secure in their persons, houses, papers, and effects, against unreasonable searches and seizures, shall not be violated, and no warrants shall issue but upon probable cause, supported by oath or affirmation, and particularly describing the place to be searched, and the persons or things to be seized.

Amendment VIII adopted 1791

Excessive bail shall not be required, nor excessive fines imposed, nor cruel and un-usual punishments inflicted.

Amendment IX adopted 1791

The enumeration in the Constitution of certain rights shall not be construed to deny or disparage others retained by the people.

Amendment X adopted 1791

The powers not delegated to the United States by the Constitution, nor prohibited by it to the states are reserved to the states respectively, or to the people.

Amendment XIV adopted 1868

Section 1. All persons born or naturalized in the United States, and subject to the jurisdiction thereof, are citizens of the United States and of the state wherein they reside. No state shall make or enforce any law which shall abridge the privileges or immunities of citizens of the United States; nor shall any state deprive any person of life, liberty, or property, without due process of law; nor deny to any person within its jurisdiction the equal protection of the laws.

The United States Constitution does not mention education. Thus, under the 10th Amendment, reserved powers doctrine (see above) the primary governance authority over education appears to be vested with the various states or the people.[8] In fact every state constitution makes provision for establishing a system of free public schools. The provisions of the Nevada constitution dealing with education are as follows;

CONSTITUTION OF THE STATE OF NEVADA
ARTICLE 11
EDUCATION

Section: Table of Contents

1. Legislature to encourage education; appointment, term and duties of superintendent of public instruction.
2. Uniform system of common schools.
3. Pledge of certain property and money, escheated estates and fines collected under penal laws for educational purposes; apportionment and use of interest.
4. Establishment of state university; control by board of regents.
5. Establishment of normal schools and grades of schools; oath of teachers and professors.

---

[8] The legal model which places the states at the center of education policy has changed as the scope of the national government has expanded. Now federal statutes dealing with disabled students, records, and discrimination are part of the complex structure of Nevada school governance. It is important to note that in order for Congress to enact legislation impacting on education it must do so within the context of the powers granted by the U.S. Constitution. When Congress legislates without regard to the scope of its legislative authority it runs the risk of having the statute declared unconstitutional. The 'Gun Free School Zones Act of 1990' was recently declared unconstitutional because Congress failed to connect the law to any of its legislative powers. See U.S. v. Lopez, 2 F.3d 1342 (5th Cir. 1993).

In addition, the United States Supreme Court has insisted that state education laws pass constitutional scrutiny through incorporation of the Bill of Rights in the 14th Amendment due process clause. The extent of federal involvement in Nevada school governance will become clearer as our journey progresses.

In 1989, President Bush convened the nations's 50 Governors in Charlottesville, Virginia, where they agreed that the nation must set ambitious educational goals. The goals they jointly established included a pledge that by the year 2000 all American students would demonstrate competency in challenging subjects.

The National goals state that by the year 2000:
    1. All American children will start school ready to learn;
    2. At least 90 percent of our students will graduate from high school;
    3. Our students will demonstrate competency in challenging subject matter and will learn to use their minds well, so they may be prepared for responsible citizenship, further learning, and productive employment;
    4. American students will be first in the world in science and mathematics achievement;
    5. Every adult will be literate and have the knowledge and skills necessary to compete in a world economy and exercise the rights and responsibilities of citizenship; and
    6. Every school will be safe and drug-free and offer a disciplined environment conducive to learning.

The National Education Goals Panel was created soon after to monitor the nation's progress toward the goals.

In April 1991, President Bush announced the America 2000 strategy to reach the goals which called for the development of high standards and a national system of examinations. A few months later, Congress established the National Council on Education Standards and Testing, a bipartisan panel that recommended the creation of voluntary national standards and a voluntary national system of student assessment.

During the 1993 session the Nevada Legislature adopted Assembly Concurrent Resolution (ACR) No. 16 File No. 114 (1993) supporting the national education goals as modified for Nevada.

Nevada's goals provide that by the year 2000:
    1. All children in this state will start school ready to learn;
    2. The high school graduation rate in this state will be at least 90 percent;
    3. Students in this state will have demonstrated competency in challenging subject matter, and every school will ensure that students use their minds well ;
    4. Students in this state will he ranked in the top 10 percent of the nation in mathematics and science achievement;
    5. Every school in this state will be free of drugs and violence and offer a disciplined learning environment; and
    6. Every adult in this state will be literate and will possess the knowledge and skills necessary to compete in a global economy and exercise the rights and responsibilities of citizenship.

The National Education Goals Panel met on November 15, 1993 and issued its strongest and clearest statement yet that it was not in the business of dictating to local schools what they should and should not teach. The panel statement indicated that the standards being developed by national education groups in English, history and geography and those already issued in math and science should be flexible enough so that local schools could tailor their own curriculum within them. In issuing its guidelines to groups writing the standards, the panel said the benchmarks should be at least as challenging and rigorous as those found in other countries. "For these voluntary national education goals to be useful they must be relevant to each community using them. The panel has no intention of developing content standards on its own and would oppose any standards that were not developed through a broad-based, participatory process." See. Celis 3d, William, "No Federal Curriculum, Education Panel Says", New York Times, 11-26-93, p. 16 A.

Math standards were released in 1989 by the National Council of Teachers of Mathematics and have since been adopted by 41 states. Science standards were released three weeks ago by the American Association for the Advancement of Science. Work is continuing to develop standards in the teaching of English, history and geography. Ibid.

6. Support of university and common schools by direct legislative appropriation.
7. Board of regents: Election and duties.
8. Immediate organization and maintenance of state university.
9. Sectarian instruction prohibited in common schools and university.
10. No public money to be used for sectarian purposes.

Relevant Sections

Section 1. Legislature to encourage education; appointment, term and duties of superintendent of public instruction.

The legislature shall encourage by all suitable means the promotion of intellectual, literary, scientific, mining, mechanical, agricultural, and moral improvements, and also provide for the a superintendent of public instruction and by law prescribe the manner of appointment, term of office and the duties thereof.

Section 2. Uniform system of common schools.

The legislature shall provide for a uniform system of common schools,[9] by which a school shall be established and maintained in each school district at least six months in every year, and any school district which shall allow instruction of a sectarian character therein may be deprived of its proportion of the interest of the public school fund during such neglect or infraction, and the legislature may pass such laws as will tend to secure a general attendance of the children in each school district upon said public schools.[10]

Sec. 3. Pledge of certain property and money, escheated estates and fines collected under penal laws for educational purposes; apportionment and use of interest.

All lands granted by Congress to this state for educational purposes, all estates that escheat to the state, all property given or bequeathed to the state for educational purposes, and the proceeds derived from these sources, together with that percentage of the proceeds from the sale of federal lands which has been granted by Congress to this state without restriction or for educational purposes and all fines collected under the penal laws of the state are hereby pledged for educational purposes and the money therefrom must not be transferred to other funds for other uses. The interest only earned on the money derived from these sources must be apportioned by the legislature among the several counties for educational purposes, and, if necessary, a portion of that interest may be appropriated for the support of the state university, but any of that interest which is unexpended at the end of any year must be added to the principal sum pledged for educational purposes.

Sec. 5. Establishment of normal schools and grades of schools; oath of teachers and professors.

---

[9]The Nevada Constitution makes clear that the legislature has the primary authority for establishing the states framework for education governance. The legislature possesses broad discretion in constructing the framework. However, any governance framework must be consistent with the U.S. Constitution. Moreover, the framework established at a particular point in time is subject to change at the discretion of the legislature.

[10] a. Nevada statute refusing admittance to public schools based on race was declared unconstitutional. Stoutmeyer v. Duffy, 7 Nev. 342 (1872).
b. Legislature may maintain school for period longer than required 6 months. Cutting v. Westerfield, 24 Nev. 29, 49 Pac. 554 (1897).
c. **Doctrine of Enumerated Powers.** School districts are creatures of the legislative acts by which they are brought into existence with such powers as they may exercise conferred upon them. Hard v Depaoli 56 Nev. 19, 41 P.2d 1054 (1935)

The Legislature shall have power to establis [establish] Normal schools, and such different grades of schools, from the primary department to the University, as in their discretion they may deem necessary, and all Professors in said University, or Teachers in said Schools of whatever grade, shall be required to take and subscribe to the oath as prescribed in Article Fifteen of this Constitution. No Professor or Teacher who fails to comply with the provisions of any law framed in accordance with the provisions of this Section, shall be entitled to public monies set apart for school purposes.

Sec. 6. Support of university and common schools by direct legislative appropriation.

In addition to other means provided for the support and maintenance of said university and common schools, the legislature shall provide for their support and maintenance by direct legislative appropriation from the general fund, upon the presentation of budgets in the manner required by law.
Amended in 1889, 1938 and 1954. The third amendment was proposed and passed by the 1951 Iegislature; agreed to and passed by the 1953 Iegislature; and approved and ratified by the people at the 1954 general election. See: Statutes of Nevada 1951. p. 591; Statutes of Nevada 1953, p. 716.

Sec. 9. Sectarian instruction prohibited in common schools and university.

No sectarian instruction shall be imparted or tolerated in any school or University that may be established under this Constitution.[11]

Sec.10. No public money to be used for sectarian purposes.

No public funds of any kind or character whatever, State, County or Municipal, shall be used for sectarian purpose.

STATUTES

Statutes are another source of school law. A statute is an act of the legislative branch of government expressing its will and constituting a law of a state or the United States. Throughout the balance of our journey we will be studying federal and Nevada statutes which impact on the school setting.

Public schools in the United States are in large part governed by statutes enacted by state legislatures. However, federal statutes also impact on school governance.

School districts and school boards are creatures of the state legislature. They have no inherent (independent) powers. Their authority to govern must be found in either express or necessarily implied terms of state statutes. This legal principle, which establishes the subservient relationship of local school districts to state authority, is entitled the Doctrine of Enumerated Powers.

Rules and regulations of federal and state administrative agencies and local school boards come within the category of statutory sources of school law. However, the rules and regulations adopted by these bodies must be rooted in specific legislatively granted powers within limits established by the legislature.

Nevada statutes addressing education are found in Title 34 of the Nevada Revised Statutes (NRS). Title 34 is divided into a series of chapters as follows;

---

[11] Primary purpose of section to prevent sectarian religious instruction in public schools. AGO(Attorney General Opinion) 67 (9-5-63)

TITLE 34 NEVADA REVISED STATUTES
EDUCATION
CHAPTER HEADINGS OF NEVADA REVISED STATUTES DEALING WITH
EDUCATION:

385	State Administrative Organization
386	Local Administrative Organization
387	Financial Support of School System
388	System of Public Instruction
389	Courses of Study
390	Textbooks
391	Personnel
392	Pupils
393	School Property
394	Private Educational Institutions and Establishments
395	Education of Handicapped Persons

JUDICIAL DECISIONS

A third source of school law is judicial decisions.[12] Rulings of administrative agencies and arbitrators after contested proceedings also fall into this category. This text contains a number of such decisions which impact on school operations and help establish the legal framework within which a teachers pursue their professional responsibilities.

C
CHAPTER SUMMARY

As we proceed to explore the nature of the Nevada school legal environment it will become apparent that the key concepts of governance play an important role in developing a sophisticated perspective of the legal setting. Further, during our journey we will study materials gathered from all the sources of school law outlined above.

---

[12]A word is in order on finding and reading case opinions. Legal citations are quiet simple. Cases are given the names of the parties to the lawsuit. Civil cases usually carry the names of two persons or entities with the appellants name appearing first. The numbers following the name of the case refer to the volume and page in that order. The letters between the numbers refer to the title of the book where the opinion may be found. Many times the identical opinion can be found in more than one book. The official report of the case is always cited first. Thus in Pierce v. Society of Sisters, (infra) the citation is to volume 268 of the official United States Reports where the opinion is printed beginning at page 510; it also refers you to volume 45 of the Supreme Court Reporter (cited S.Ct.), a publication of the West Publishing Company, where the identical opinion is printed at page 517. Finally, (1925) is the date (court term) when the case was decided. The citations to state cases are reported in a similar manner. Court decisions are reported (published) in various sets of books. The official reporter for Supreme Court decisions is entitled the United States Reports(U.S.). Federal circuit decisions are found in the Federal Reporter (F.2d). Federal district court decisions are published in the Federal Supplement (F.Supp.).

When reading opinions you should look for the following: a statement of the facts the court assumes; a statement of the precise way the question has come before the court -- including what the plaintiff wanted from the lower court, and what the trial court and\or other lower appellate courts did that is complained of ; then the outcome on appeal, the judgment; and finally the reason(s) the court gives for doing what it did.

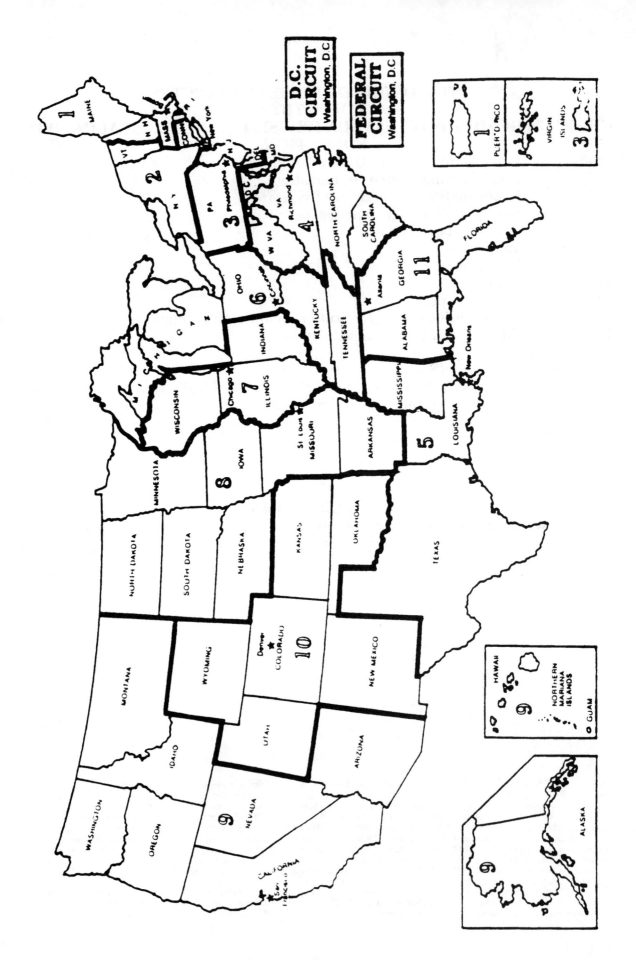

CHAPTER II

NEVADA SCHOOL GOVERNANCE FRAMEWORK[13]
"LOCAL LAYPERSON CONTROL OF SCHOOLS" MYTH OR REALITY?

A
STATE ADMINISTRATIVE ORGANIZATION[14]

The Nevada constitution directs the legislature to establish a uniform system of common schools [15] and authorizes it to pass such laws as will tend to secure general attendance of the children in each school district at said public schools.

The legislature has chosen to introduce the Chapter entitled State Administrative Organization with three General Provisions. These provisions affirm the legislatures intent that public education in Nevada is essentially a matter of local control[16] by local school districts and that the provisions of the Education Title are intended to reserve to the boards of trustees of local school districts within the state those rights and powers as are necessary to maintain control of the education of the children within their respective districts **limited only by other specific provisions of law.**[17]

The General provisions further indicate that the responsibility for establishing a statewide policy of integration or desegregation of public schools is reserved to the legislature and the responsibility for local integration policy rests with the respective boards of trustees of local school districts.[18]

In addition the legislature reminds state and local school officials of their responsibility to advise the legislature regarding action to insure equality of educational opportunity for the states children.[19]

---

[13]Senate Concurrent Resolution (SCR) No. 52 File No. 166 (1993) directs the Legislative Commission to conduct an interim study to examine the structure and financing of public elementary and secondary education in Nevada. The study will be performed by four members of the Nevada legislature, the superintendent of public instruction, and the dean of the College of Education for the University of Nevada Reno, or his designee. Although the Resolution was never formally amended the membership of the study group has been expanded to include the dean of the College of Education at UNLV and a representative of the state teachers association. The results of the study and recommended legislation are due to be submitted to the 68th session of the Nevada legislature.

[14] Chapter 385 NRS (1993)

[15]The Nevada Constitution makes clear that the legislature has the primary authority for establishing the states framework for education governance. The legislature possesses broad discretion in constructing the framework. However, any governance framework must be consistent with the U.S. Constitution. Moreover, the framework established at a particular point in time is subject to change at the discretion of the legislature.

[16]A frequent complaint of local school districts has been the number of mandates imposed by Federal and State legislatures unaccompanied by the resources necessary to achieve compliance with the dictates. Chapter 419 Laws of Nevada (1993) appears to be a nod in the direction of those making such complaints. The Chapter amends Sec. 354.599 NRS (1991) providing that if the legislature directs local governments to establish a program or provide a service, or to increase a program or service already established which requires additional funding, a specified source for the additional revenue to pay the expense must be authorized by a specific statute. The additional revenue must be used to pay expenses directly related to the program or service. However, if the local government has money from any other source available to pay such expenses, that money must be applied to the expenses before any money from the revenue source specified by statute. What revenue source was identified in order to install safety arms on school busses? What new funding source was identified or established in order to accomplish the legislative direction to establish programs in suicide and child abuse prevention? What can local school districts do to see that the legislature complies with Chapter 419?

[17] Sec. 385.005 1 NRS (1993) As you study Nevada school governance structure consider whether the legislature has carried out the intention expressed in this general provision.

[18] Sec. 385.005 2 NRS (1993)

[19] Sec. 385.005 3 NRS (1993)

A brief definition section concludes the General Provisions section. The term "Department" refers to Department of Education,[20] "State Board" means state board of education.[21] Finally the term "Public schools" is defined as:

> "all kindergartens and elementary schools, junior high schools and middle schools and any other schools, classes and educational programs which receive their support through public taxation and whose textbooks and courses of study are under the control of the state board.[22]

The legislature has created a Department of Education to lead the state education system. The Department consists of the State Board of Education, State Board for Occupational Education[23] and the Superintendent of Public Instruction.[24] In 1987 the legislature created the Commission on Professional Standards in Education.[25] The attorney general is required to give written legal opinions without fee to the State Board, Superintendent of Public Instruction and the Commission on Professional Standards on matters related to the powers and duties of the department.[26] Nevada's system of public instruction also includes a Board for the Education and Counseling of Displaced Homemakers appointed by the governor.[27]

STATE BOARD OF EDUCATION

The 1990 census results required that the legislature redraw state board electoral districts to reflect the constitutional principle of "one man one vote." As a consequence, the legislature not only changed electoral district boundaries but increased the size of the state board from 9 to 11 members. The state was divided into three districts. District 2, including Clark County, is the most populous and elects 7 of the 11 members of the state board. District 1 is primarily Washoe County and elects 2 members. District 3 consists of the rest of the state and elects 2 members.[28]

The term of office is four years[29]. If a vacancy occurs the governor is required to appoint a member to fill the vacancy until the next general election.[30] No member may be elected to the office more than three times.[31]

At its first meeting [32] after each election and qualification of newly elected members the board is obligated to organize by electing one of its members as

---

[20] Sec. 385.007 1 NRS (1993)

[21] Sec. 385.007 3 NRS (1993)

[22] Sec. 385.007 2 NRS (1993)

[23] This board consists of members of the state board. The state superintendent serves as the executive director of the board. He/she is required to report the board's activities to the governor on a biennial basis. The provisions outlining the duties and responsibilities of this board are located in Chapter 388. See Sec. 388.330-400 NRS (1993)

[24] Sec. 385.010 NRS (1993)

[25] The Commission is charged with the authority to enact educator certification rules and regulations.

[26] Sec. 385.014 NRS (1993)

[27] Sec. 388.605-655 NRS (1993)

[28] Sec. 385.021 NRS (1993)

[29] Ibid.

[30] Ibid.

[31] Ibid.

[32] The meetings of the State Board and Commission are subject to the Nevada Open Meetings Law. See Chapter 241 NRS. Chapter 210 Laws of Nevada (1993) amends Sec. 241.035 (2) NRS (1991) mandating permanent retention of public meeting minutes. After at least 5 years of retention by the public body minutes may be transferred for archival preservation. See Sec. 239.080 to 239.125 NRS (1993). Chapter 629 Laws of Nevada (1993) amends Chapter 241 adding provisions which forbid a public body from holding a closed meeting to consider the character alleged misconduct, professional competence, or physical or mental health of an elected member of the public body. The new law also prohibits a public body from holding a meeting to consider the character, alleged misconduct, professional competence, or physical or mental health of any person unless it has given written notice to that person of the time and place of the meeting. The notice must be either personally delivered to the person at least five working days before the meeting or sent certified mail to the last known address of that person at least 21 working days before the meeting. Proof of service is a precondition for holding the meeting. A copy of any record of such a closed meeting must be provided to

president. The president serves at the pleasure of the board.[33] The Superintendent of Public Instruction is the secretary of the board and serves without additional salary.[34]

The board is authorized to hold at least 4 regular meetings at the state capital. The secretary is required to call all regular meetings. Special meetings may be scheduled by the board at other times and places upon the written request of the president or any three members of the board. A majority of the board constitutes a quorum for the transaction of business. However, no action of the board is valid unless that action receives the approval of a **majority of all** board members at a legally called meeting.[35]

Each member of the board is entitled to receive compensation of not more than $80 per day, as fixed by the board, for attending each meeting of the board not to exceed 12 meetings in any calendar year.[36] While engaged in the business of the board each member and employee of the board is entitled to receive the per diem allowance and travel expenses provided for state officers and employees generally.[37] Claims for compensation and expenses must be approved by the Superintendent of Public Instruction and the state board of examiners.[38]

An official seal has been adopted and is used by the board in authentication of its acts.[39]

The board is required to establish policies to govern the administration of all functions of the state relating to supervision, management and control of public schools not conferred by law on some other agency.[40] For example, in 1993 the legislature adopted a bill which directs the state board to establish a pilot program to evaluate the feasibility of increasing opportunities for transferring the responsibility for managerial decisions regarding public schools to staff members, administrators and parents.[41] This program seeks to provide more flexibility in the operation of public schools and increase the accountability of educational personnel.

This general power is supplemented by specific grants of authority. For example, the state board is authorized and directed to make the final selection of all textbooks used in the public schools of Nevada.[42] Furthermore, textbooks must not be selected for literature, history or social studies courses unless they accurately portray the cultural and racial diversity of our society, including lessons on the contributions made to our society by men and women from various racial and ethnic backgrounds.[43]

---

the person discussed upon his/her request. Chapter 629 also provides that if a public body elects to record a public meeting any portion of the meeting which is closed must also be recorded and be retained.

[33] 385.030 NRS (1993)

[34] Ibid.

[35] Sec. 385.040 NRS (1993)

[36] Sec. 385.050 NRS (1993)

[37] Ibid.

[38] Ibid.

[39] Sec. 385.060 NRS (1993)

[40] Sec. 385.075 NRS (1993)

[41] Chapter 667 Laws of Nevada Sec. 1 (1993). Under the program the state board is required to designate 10 public schools to participate. Eligibility to participate is determined through an application process. The schools application must be accompanied by evidence of support for participation in the pilot program. The law fruther obligates the state board to prepare and submit a report contanining its findings, conclusions and recommendations regarding the program to the director of the legislative counsel bureau no later tha January 10, 1995. No additional funding to accomplish the task was provided by the legislature.

[42] Sec. 390.140 (1) NRS (1993)

[43] Sec. 390.140 (2) NRS (1993)

Another specific power includes the duty to prescribe and cause to be enforced courses of study for the public schools of the state.[44] The state requires instruction in American government[45] and American history.[46] Satisfactory completion of those courses is required for graduation.[47] The state also mandates that schools set aside one hour each week for patriotic exercises.[48] Courses which provide instruction in the economics of the American syatem of free enterprise[49] and physical training designed to prepare students for the duties of citizenship in times of war and peace are also required.[50] Health instruction is also mandated.[51]

The legislature has also established a program to encourage local districts to establish driver education programs.[52]

Environmental education is another course of instruction imposed on local districts.[53] The state superintendent is directed to coordinate the efforts of the various disciplines within the educational system that are concerned with environmental education under the course of study designed by the legislature.[54]

The statutes direct the state superintendent in coordination with American Indian tribes to establish programs and curricula addressing special educational needs of Nevada Native Americans.[55] Another curricular requirement established by the legislature includes a procedure for obtaining credit toward graduation from high school for courses taken at a community college or university.[56]

The 1993 legislature expanded the responsibility of the state board beyond establishing courses of study in technology[57] and occupational guidance and counseling.[58] Chapter 384 requires the state board to establish, by regulation, a course of study in adult roles and responsibilities.[59] The legislature also obliged the state board to establish a program of instruction concerning the prevention of suicide[60]

---

[44]Sec. 389.010 NRS (1993)

[45] Sec. 389.020 NRS (1993)

[46] Sec. 389.030 NRS (1993)

[47] Sec. 389.035 NRS (1993)

[48] Sec. 389.040 NRS (1993)

[49]Sec. 389.080 NRS (1993)

[50] Sec. 389.040 NRS (1993)

[51] Sec. 389.060 NRS (1993) The attorney general has rendered an opinion concluding that school districts should excuse a child from classes in physiology and hygiene if a parent requests based on religious reasons. AGO 110 (9-22-55)

[52] 389.085-100 NRS (1993)

[53] 389.110-130 NRS (1993)

[54] Sec. 389.140 NRS (1993)

[55] Sec. 389.150 NRS (1993)

[56] Sec. 389.160 NRS (1991). The 1993 legislature amended this section of the statutes (Chapter 60 Laws 1993) to allow students to apply (versus 'substitute') credits received in approved university and community college courses toward the total number of credits required for high school graduation.

[57] Sec. 389.170 NRS (1993)

[58] Sec. 389.180 NRS (1993)

[59]Chapter 384 Laws of Nevada (1993) adding a new section to Chapter 389 requiring the state board to establish a course of study in adult roles and responsibilities. The course of study must be designed to prepare pupils for their potential roles as parents and as members of family groups. Local boards of each district are mandated to establish the curriculum for the course of study in that district. Curriculum development must be accomplished with the assistance of teachers, administrators, licensed school counselors, pupils and parents. Instruction must include: (a) personal and family management, including identifying values, setting goals, understanding oneself, developing personal assets and balancing the responsibilities of work and family; (b) skills for daily living and coping with stress, including problem solving, decision making, positive communication and conflict resolution; (c) money management, including identifying personal assets, financial goals and effective consumer practices relating to credit, taxes, savings and investments; (d) establishing and maintaining relationships, including marriage. relationships at a job and within the community, and relationships with friends, peers, family and extended family; and (e) skills and knowledge relating to the relationship between a parent and a child, including the growth and development of children, skills needed to be, an effective parent, and the responsibilities of parenthood. The instruction required by this section must be made available to each pupil at some time after his completion of grade 5 and before his completion of grade 12. The content may be included as part of an existing course of study or presented as a separate course of study.

[60]Chapter 385 Laws of Nevada (1993) adding a new section to Chapter 389 requiring the state board to establish a program of instruction in the prevention of suicide. The instruction must be provided to each pupil by the completion of grade 12 as a part of a required course of study.

Furthermore, the legislature has directed the state board in cooperation with district trustees to develop programs designed to reduce the number of drop outs and prevent the abuse of alcohol and controlled substances.[61]

Local high schools may have modified courses of study as long as the state board approves. In addition any high school offering courses normally accredited as being beyond the level of the 12th grade must have the approval by the board prior to offering the courses.[62]

The statutes also vest the board with authority to adopt standard plans and specifications for the construction of school buildings by the boards of trustees of the various school districts. If the board adopts such plans they must be approved by the state public works board. However, local school districts are given discretion to determine whether to utilize the plans.[63]

The legislature further has directed the board to cooperate with the aging services division or the department of human resources in the planning of programs whereby school districts may prepare hot lunches for persons 60 years of age or older utilizing the procedures and systems already developed for use and operation of school lunch programs.[64]

Furthermore, the board must cooperate with the attorney general in the establishment in the school of programs of information about missing children and adopt regulations containing guidelines for such programs.[65]

Moreover, it may also adopt regulations for its own government and as necessary for the execution of the other powers and duties conferred upon it.[66] This includes the power to adopt regulations for the approval of programs for the education of teachers which are accredited by the National Council of Accreditation of Teacher Education.[67]

The legislature has also empowered the board to form a nonprofit corporation for the acquisition of money and personal property, for awards in recognition of exceptional teachers, pupils and public schools and for special projects regarding educational enhancement [68] If the board receives a gift for educational purposes outside the nonprofit corporate framework it is required to deposit the money in a permanent trust fund in the state treasury. The money available in the fund must be used only for the purpose specified by the donor.[69]

Another duty given to the board is prescribing regulations under which contracts, agreements or arrangements may be made with agencies of the federal government. School districts,School Districtswith limited exceptions, are required to comply with the regulations when entering such contracts.[70]

The legislature has also authorized the establishment of a higher education student loan program. The program is administered by the state superintendent. However, he/she may choose to withdraw from administration of the program if proper notice is given. If the state superintendent gives the required notice the state

---

[61] Sec. 388.532 NRS (1993)

[62] Sec. 385.110 NRS (1993)

[63] Sec. 385.125 NRS (1993)

[64] Sec. 385.109 NRS (1993). Chapter 659 Laws of Nevada (1993) amends Chapter 387 expanding eligible participants in progams of nutrition provided through school to adults.

[65] Sec. 385.115 NRS (1993)

[66] Sec. 385.080 NRS (1993)

[67] Ibid.

[68] Sec. 385.091-093 NRS (1993)

[69] Sec. 385.095 NRS (1993)

[70] Sec. 385.110 NRS (1993)

board and the governor are required to designate another public agency to continue the program. The program was established to provide loans to further the educational goals of Nevada residents who are admitted to and attending institutions of higher education.[71]

SUPERINTENDENT OF PUBLIC INSTRUCTION

The superintendent of public instruction is appointed by the board for a term of three years. This state office is in the unclassified service of the state. The state board is also empowered to fill any vacancy in the office.[72]

There are two qualifications for holding the office. The appointee must be 21 years old and possess a master's degree in the field of education or school administration.[73] Once appointed the superintendent is forbidden from pursuing any other business or occupation or holding any other office for profit without the approval of the state board.[74]

A number of general duties and responsibilities have been conferred on the superintendent by the legislature.[75] The superintendent is directed to supervise all administrative, technical and procedural activities of the department in accordance with the policies prescribed by the state board,[76] employ personnel for the positions approved by the state board,[77] organize the department in a manner which will assure efficient operation and service,[78] maintain liaison and coordinate activities with other state agencies performing educational functions [79] and perform such other duties prescribed by law.[80] The account may only be used for health education and is administered by the state superintendent of public instruction.

His\her responsibilities also include issuing proper and necessary regulations for making reports to the department and for conducting all necessary proceedings in which he\she is involved.[81]

Specific duties conferred by the legislature include visiting each county in the state at least once each school year, conducting institutes, visiting schools, consulting with school officers, and addressing public assemblies on subjects pertaining to the schools. The superintendent is also directed to consult and study with school officers and educators in Nevada and other states on topics of school

---

[71] Sec. 385.102-108 NRS (1993)

[72] Sec. 385.150 NRS (1993)

[73] Sec. 385.160 NRS (1993)

[74] Sec. 385.170 NRS (1993). Chapter 536 Laws of Nevada (1993) concerns ethics in government. It amends Chapter 281 adding a new section establishing rules for determining conflict of interest when a public officer or employee is considering bidding on a contract with a public agency.

[75] Sec. 385.175 NRS (1993)

[76] Sec. 385.175 (1) NRS (1993)

[77] Sec. 385.175 (2) NRS(1993)

[78] Sec. 385.175 (3) NRS (1993)

[79] Sec. 385.175 (4) NRS (1993)

[80] Sec. 385.175 (5) NRS (1993). Chapter 336 Laws of Nevada (1993) directs the state superintendent of public instruction and the director of the department of human resources to appoint a task force to study the feasibility of establishing course work in American Sign Language in secondary and post-secondary schools for credit as a foreign language and as a special course in elementary schools. The legislation directs the superintendent to provide clerical support for the task force. A majority of the task force shall be deaf or related to a deaf person. Specific members representing groups with knowledge regarding the issue are designated in the law. The task force is charged with compiling and analyzing legislation of other states, identifying effect of course work in American Sign Language on availability of teachers and interpreters for deaf Nevadans, determining impact of course work on employment opporitunties for deaf persons, determining the interest of pupils and students for course work, identifying existing curricula on American Sign Language, providing recommendations for necessary legislation, and ascertaining the costs related to carrying out the various levels of course work recommended by the task force. The findings and recommendations of the task force are due for submission to the director of the legislative counsel brueau no later than November 15, 1994.

Chapter 651 Laws of Nevada (1993) amending Chapter 202 NRS. Violations of the statute entail both criminal and civil penalties. A health authority where the violation occurs may commence a civil proceeding to collect the penalty. Money collected is deposited with the state treasurer for credit to the account for health education for minors. The superintendent of public instruction is empowered to adiminister the account and may expend money in the account only for programs of health education for minors.

[81] Sec. 385.200 NRS (1993)

administration, school methods and school law.[82] Further, the superintendent or his designee is charged with convening teacher and administrator conferences in various sections of the state. However, these conferences are subject to a budget limitation of $8,500 per year.[83]

He\she is obligated to prescribe a convenient form of register for the purpose of securing accurate returns from the teachers of public schools, prepare pamphlet copies of the school law, and, if directed by the board, publish a bulletin as the official publication of the department.[84]

Specific duties also include reporting to the governor biennially on or before December 1, in the year immediately preceding a regular session of the legislature.

The 1993 Legislature added another specific duty. Pursuant to Chapter 404 the state superintendent is obligated to establish programs to develop internships in businesses for pupils enrolled in grades 11 and 12 for the 1994-95 school year.[85] The superintendent is directed to cooperate with county school districts and the State Apprenticeship Council in establishing the programs. The internships are to be designed to prepare and train the students to serve as apprentices and allow students to earn academic credit for their work.[86] The superintendent is directed to make quarterly reports after October 1, 1993, on the progress being made in establishing the pilot programs to the state board and the director of the legislative counsel bureau for transmittal to the members of the legislative commission.[87]

The superintendent is also charged with approving or disapproving lists of books for use in public school libraries.[88] The superintendents actions regarding the lists are subject to review by the state board.

He\she and members of the professional staff within the department, designated by the superintendent, may administer oaths relating to schools.[89]

Finally, the statutes require that the superintendent deliver immediately to his\her successor in office all property and effects belonging to the office.[90]

DEPUTY SUPERINTENDENTS, PROFESSIONAL STAFF AND OTHER PERSONNEL

The superintendent may appoint two deputy superintendents. One deputy is responsible for instructional, research and evaluative services (IRE deputy). The other is responsible for administrative and fiscal services (AF deputy).[91] Both positions are in the unclassified service of the state. Appointees are required to

---

[82] Sec. 385.180 NRS (1993)

[83] Sec. 385.190 NRS (1993)

[84] Sec. 385.210 NRS (1993)

[85] Chapter 404 Laws of Nevada (1993)

[86] Chapter 404 Laws of Nevada Sec. 1 (1) (1993)

[87] Chapter 404 Laws of Nevada Sec. 1 (2) (1993)

[88] Sec. 385.230, 240 NRS (1993) The book lists must not include books containing or including any story in prose or poetry which would be to influence the minds of children in the formation of ideals not in harmony with truth and morality or the American way of life, or not in harmony with the Constitution and laws of the United States or of the State of Nevada.
See also Gallant, John "Educators Debating Lurid Stories," Review Journal, January 10, 1993, p. 1 B. The Gallant article describes a complaint brought to the state board of education regarding the publication 'Rolling Stone.' The issue in question, which the protesters found in the Virginia City School library, contained graphic descriptions of various sexual acts available in the streets and bars of Bangkok. As a result of the complaint the state board adopted new rules pursuant to which the state superintendent will review and approve county school district library selection practices.

[89] Sec. 385. 220 NRS (1993)

[90] Sec. 385.250 NRS (1993)

[91] Sec. 385.290-300 NRS (1993)

devote their entire time and attention to the business of their office and not pursue any other business or occupation or hold any other office for profit.[92]

The IRE deputy must hold a master's degree in school administration or a related subject from an accredited college or university and have a minimum of 3 years of administrative experience including supervision and evaluation of staff, development of and administration of budgets and development of curriculum. The IRE deputy is empowered to perform any duty required of the superintendent when he/she is absent from the state and such other work as the superintendent may direct under the laws of the state.[93]

In order to be appointed AF deputy the candidate must be a graduate from a 4-year accredited college or university and have familiarity with the field of education as evidenced by sufficient college credits in education to qualify for a license to teach in a high school in Nevada. Participation in recognized educational research and study may be substituted for education credits. In addition, the appointee must have familiarity with the general field of public administration and budgeting [94] The AF deputy is required to determine the apportionment of all state school money to schools of the state, develop a uniform system of budgeting and accounting which is mandatory for all public schools in the state, carry on continuing study of school finance in the state and make recommendations deemed advisable to the board, perform statistical and financial duties pertaining to the administration and finances of the schools as directed by the superintendent, and prepare biennial budgets of the department under the direction of the superintendent for submission to board and the governor.[95] In addition to his/her other duties, the AF deputy is required to investigate any claims whenever a written protest is filed with the county auditor, inspect the record book and accounts of boards of trustees, enforce the uniform method of keeping school district financial records, inspect school fund accounts of the county auditors and report the condition of the funds of any school district to the board of trustees, and inspect separate accounts established by boards of trustees.[96]

In 1987 the legislature created a position of state library coordinator. The duties of the position include advising school districts on proper use of libraries, development of new materials, and coordinating use of public libraries in local school districts.[97]

Other state department professional staff and personnel are members of the classified service (civil service system). Their qualifications must be fixed by the state department of personnel. The duties of classified staff are assigned by the superintendent.[98]

---

[92] Sec. 385.320 NRS (1993)
[93] Sec. 385.290 NRS (1993)
[94] Sec. 385.300 NRS (1993)
[95] Sec. 385.310 NRS (1993)
[96] Sec. 385.315 NRS (1993)
[97] Sec. 385.345 NRS (1993)
[98] Sec. 385.330-340 NRS (1993)

SCHOOL FINANCE;[99] THE NEVADA PLAN[100]

The Nevada Plan is the means used to finance elementary and secondary education in the state's public schools. The process involves the state developing a guaranteed amount of funding for each of the local school districts. The revenue which provides the guaranteed funding is derived both from state and local sources.[101] The guaranteed funding includes approximately 85% of the General Fund resources available to the school districts of the state. The Nevada Plan funding for the districts consists of state support received through the Distributive School Account[102] and locally collected revenues from the 1.5 cent Local School

---

[99]Senate Concurrent Resolution (SCR) No. 52 File No. 166 (1993) directs the Legislative Commission to conduct an interim study to examine the structure and financing of public elementary and secondary education in Nevada. The study will be performed by four members of the Nevada legislature, the superintendent of public instruction, and the dean of the College of Education for the University of Nevada Reno, or his designee. Although the Resolution was never formally amended the membership of the study group has been expanded to include the dean of the College of Education at UNLV and a representative of the state teachers association. The results of the study and recommended legislation are due to be submitted to the 68th session of the Nevada legislature.

The school finance debate has always included arguments over the impact of increased spending on the quality of schools. A recent article is worthwhile reading for those pondering the issue. See Ferguson, Ronald F. "Paying for Public Education: New Evidence on How and Why Money Matters," Harvard Journal on Legislation, Vol 28, p. 465 (1992).

The imposition of impact fees on new residential construction for new school facilities will probably be discussed by the committee. Florida has approved such fees. See Murray, Kenneth T., "Impact Fee on New Residential Construction to be Used for New School Facilities Approved by Florida Supreme Court," 70 Ed.Law Rep. [273] (December 19, 1991).

Public and Private school enrollment was 57.4 million students in 1983. Enrollment is estimated to jump to 63.9 million students in 1993. Average teacher salaries in 1993 dollars were $31,637 in 1983. The 1993 estimate is $36,700. Per pupil spending in public schools was $4,577 in 1983. The 1993 estimate is $5,920. See National Center for Education Statistics, U.S. Department of Education as reported in "A New School Year: Getting Younger, and Costlier," New York Times, September 8, 1993, p. 8 B.

[100] "The Nevada Plan", State Department of Education document, Carson City, Nevada April 2, 1992.

THE NEVADA PLAN -- AN EXAMPLE**

Following is an example which illustrates the guarantee process based on the revenue of a hypothetical district and, in addition, shows other revenue outside of the guarantee, making up total resources included in an operating budget.

BASIC SUPPORT GUARANTEE	DISTRICT EXAMPLE
1. Nunber of pupils (weighted enrollment)***	5,500
2. x Basic Support Per Pupil	$3,000
3. = Guaranteed Basic Support	$ 16,500,000
4. + Special Education Allocation (35 units @ $26,000 per unit)	$910,000
5. + Adult High School Diploma Program (capped amount determined by Department of Education	$4,000
6. = Total Guaranteed Support	$ 17,414,000
7. - Local resources	
2.25 cent Local School Support (sales) Tax	($ 7,500,000)
25 cent Ad Valorem (property) tax	($ 2,000,000)
8. = State Responsibility	$ 7,914,000
RESOURCES IN ADDITION TO BASIC SUPPORT	
9. 50 Cent Ad Valorem (Property) Tax	$ 4,000,000
10. Motor Vehicle Privilege Tax	$ 200,000
11. Federal Revenues	$ 150,000
12. Miscellaneous Revenues	$ 10,000
13. Opening Fund Balance	$ 150,000
14. Total Resources in Addition to Basic Support	$ 4,510,000
15. Total Resources Available (line 6 + line 14)	$ 21,924,000

**State Department of Education Document Dated April 1, 1992
***Weighted enrollment includes six-tenths the count of pupils enrolled in kindergarten, six-tenths of the count of handicapped 3 and 4 year olds, a full count of pupils enrolled in grades 1 through 12, and a full count of handicapped minors age 5 and over receiving special education.

The 'Nevada Plan' addresses the school district operating budget. Captial improvements requiring issuance of general obligation bonds are addressed in Sec. 387.328-591 NRS (1993) and other public finance statutes. For example Chapter 442 Laws of Nevada (1993) amends certain public finance statutes (Sec. 349.015 NRS (1991)) requiring the inclusion of an estimate of the annual cost to operate, maintain and repair any buildings, structures or other facilities or improvements to be constructed or acquired with bond proceeds.

[101]NEVADA GENERAL FUND REVENUES ACTUAL BY SOURCE FISCAL YEAR 1991-92; Gaming Taxes 40.5%, Sales Tax 31.6%, Insurance Premium Tax 7.3%, Non Tax Revenues 5.7%, Business License Tax 5.3%, Cigarette Tax 3.6%, Casino Entertainment Tax 2.4%, Mining Tax 2.0%, Other Taxes 1.6%. NEVADA GENERAL FUND EXPENDITURES BY FUNCTIONAL AREA FISCAL YEAR 1991-92; Education (Pre-K-12 and Higher Education) 58.7%, Human Resources 21.4%, Public Safety 10.1%, General Government 4.4%, Regulatory 2.4%, Conservation / Agriculture 2.0%, Miscellaneous 0.6%, Transportation 0.4%. Source: State of Nevada Fiscal Analysis Division Document dated April 22, 1993.

[102] The Distributive School Account (See Sec. 387.030 NRS (1993) is financed by legislative appropriations from the state's General Fund and other revenues, including a 2.25 cent tax on out-of-state sales, a slot machine tax, mineral land lease income, and interest from investments of the Permanent School Fund. Chapter 85 Laws of Nevada (1993) implements budget savings realized by cuts requested by the governor reduceing the estimated weighted average basic per pupil guarantee from $3,312 to $3,231 for the 1992-93 school year. The adjusted basic support guarantee for the respective school districts ranges from a low of $100 for Eureka County to a high of $5,871.49 for Esmeralda County. The 1992-93 adjusted basic support guarantee for Clark County is $3,150.98 and $2,970.86 for Washoe County. Chapter 85 also reduces the 1992-93 appropriation for adult high school diploma programs by $1.1 million.

Support Tax (Sales tax) and the 25 cent Ad Valorem Tax (property tax). In addition, revenue from fines for violation of air pollution control regulations, above administrative expenses, must also be deposited to the county school district fund of the county where the violation occurred.[103]

In order to determine the level of funding for the districts, a Basic per Student Support Rate is established. This rate is determined by a formula that considers the demographic characteristics of the districts. In addition the districts' transportation costs are equalized by including 85% of the actual historical costs adjusted for inflation according to the Consumer Price Index. A Wealth Adjustment, based on a district's ability to generate revenues in addition to the guaranteed funding, is also included in the formula.

The Basic per Student Support Rate is then applied to the number of students enrolled in the districts. The official count for apportionment purposes is taken in each of the districts on the last day of the first school month. The total number of kindergarten children and children under the age of five enrolled in special programs for the handicapped is reduced to 60%, and then added to the total number of all other enrolled children in each of the districts, creating the Weighted Enrollment. The Basic per Student Support is multiplied by the Weighted Enrollment to determine the guaranteed level of funding.

In order to protect districts from decreases in enrollment, the Nevada Revised Statutes contain a Hold Harmless Provision. If a district's enrollment decreases, the guaranteed level of funding for the current year is based on the immediate past year' enrollment.

An additional provision applies to districts that experience significant growth within the school year. If a district grows by more than 3% but less than 6% after the first school month, a growth increment consisting of an additional 2% is added to the guaranteed level of funding. If a district grows more than 6%, the growth increment is 4%.

Special Education is funded on a "unit" basis, with the amount per unit established by the state legislature.[104] A "unit" includes the full-time services of one licensed professional providing a program of instruction in accordance with minimum standards prescribed by the State Board of Education. The Special Education funding is separate from and in addition to the Basic per Student Support. The 1993 legislature amended Chapter 387 adding a new section regarding the method of accounting for funds distributed to school districts for education of children with disabilities. The new law requires establishment of a separate accounting system for money expended for special education and related services.[105]

The local districts also receive funding through the Nevada Plan for Adult High School Diploma Program. One adult taking one class toward a high school

Chapter 447 Laws of Nevada (1993) apportions the state distributive school account in the state general fund for the 1993-95 biennium. The basic support guarantee weighted average for 1993-94 is $3,320 and $3,323 for 1994-95. Clark County basic support guarantee per pupil is $3,224 for 1993-94 and $3,227 for 1994-95. Washoe County basic support guarantee per pupil in $3,069 for 1993-94 and $3,069 for 1994-95.

[103]Sec. 445.546 NRS (1993)

[104]Chapter 447 Laws of Nevada Sec. 8 (1993) Clark County is accorded 876 units for 1993-94 and 923 units for 1994-95. Washoe County is granted 309 and 325 respectively. The state board of education reserved 40 units to meet unforseen need.

[105]Chapter 447 Laws of Nevada Sec. 1 (1993). The separate accounting must include the amount of money provided to the school district for special education for basic support and transfers of money from the school district's general fund needed to balance the special revenue fund. The accounting system must also include the cost of instruction provided by licensed special education teachers and supporting staff, related services, including, but not limited to, services provided by psychologists, therapists, and health-related personnel, transportation of handicapped students to and from school, the direct supervision of educatonal and supporting prpgrams and the supplies and equipment needed for providing special education. Money received from federal sources must be accounted for separately and excluded from the state accounting system established by the new legislation.

diploma is counted as one-quarter student for apportionment purposes. The number of students is determined by multiplying the average of the highest three months of attendance in adult classes by 25%. the result is multiplied by the district's Basic per Student Rate to calculate the regular Adult High School Diploma program funding. The maximum funding for the Adult High School Diploma Program in the State's prisons is established by the Legislature.

It is important to remember that under the Nevada Plan of school finance, local school districts have not been accorded the power to levy a tax to support their school operations.

In 1991 the legislature authorized the Board of County Commissioners to levy a tax of no more than 3 cents on each $100 of assessed valuation of taxable property within a county for enhancing the safety and security of the public schools.[106] The tax could only be imposed after voter approval. The law forbid levying the tax after the 1994-95 fiscal year. The Clark County School District sought voter approval for the tax in June 1993. The measure was defeated.[107]

The Security Tax Authorization Law was renewed during the 1993 legislative session.[108] extending the sunset for collecting the tax to June 30, 1997. However, the reauthorization reduces the maximum levy to 2 cents on each $100 of assessed valuation of taxable property in the county.

Educational foundations may also provide special financial assistance to local school districts.[109] A new section was added to the statutes by the 1993 legislature addressing educational foundations.[110]

---

[106]Sec. 387.197 NRS (1993). The legislature adopted this measure following the slaying of a student the first day of school 1990 at Eldorado High School in Clark County. (See"Trial Delayed For Teen Charged In Slaying At High School," Review Journal, June 10, 1991, p. 1 A.

[107]On June 7, 1993, the day before the vote, a school librarian was brutally attacked while she loaded her car outside J.D. Smith Junior High School. Voters were greeted with news of the stabbing in bold newspaper headlines, radio and T.V. coverage the day of the vote. In spite of the tragic reminder of school safety problems voters turned down authorization for a tax to by a large margin. The assailant was apprehended and pleaded guilty to the stabbing. He was sentenced to 20 years in prison instead of the maximum 40 years requested by the prosecutor and the teachers relatives. See Geer, Carri, "Teen Gets 20-Year Term For Stabbing Librarian," Review Journal, November 10, 1993, p. 1 B.
See also Gallant, John , "Students Packing Weapons," Review Journal, January 24, 1993, p. 1 B. Mr. Gallant's story discusses the 1991-92 school year in Clark County. The toll of weapons incidents on Clark County school campuses reached a record 342 by June 1992. Knives and guns topped the list of confiscated weapons. The list also included lead pipes, brass knuckles, spiked bands, razors and Mace.
******
Excerpts from the story by John Gallant follow:
"There were 20 incidents at Rancho High School in North Las Vegas, but also 16 incidents at the new Cimarron-Memorial High School near the affluent Desert Shores community according to school district figures.
The district's elementary schools reported 17 incidents involving guns, including nine where a gun was discharged on a campus.
The number of weapons incidents appears to have stopped climbing, but not before reaching a record high during the last school year. In the 1989-90 school year, there were some 30 incidents involving guns. The number doubled the following year and climbed to 105 in the 1991-92 school year.
"Kids who are normally never in trouble are bringing Mace to school," said the junior high school principal who asked to remain anonymous.
But the history of stepped up school security can be traced to Aug. 27, 1990, the day 16-year-old Donnie Lee Bolden was gunned down in the Eldorado High School cafeteria on the first day of school. Two weeks later, a second 16-year-old boy was stabbed at Western High School, but survived.
Shocked by the crimes, school district officials hired more school police, began installing video surveillance cameras at the high schools and mandated the use of metal detectors at sporting events.
Jack Lazzarotto, the school district's security director, said the increased police presence and video surveillance may be responsible in part for the higher number of weapons incidents reported last year.
"We have more officers out there who can spot these things (7B) before something happens," he said. "Our goal is to be preventive."
"It just becomes a way of life anymore" Edwards said. "You talk about mathematics out of one side of your mouth and school security out of the other "" (Gallant, John, see above)
[108]Chapter 544 Laws of Nevada (1993)
[109]See GALLANT, JOHN, "Business, Community Groups Raise Money To Help Education," Review Journal, January 5, 199, p. 3 B.
..."A group of business and community leaders is raising funds to aid Clark County's public education system. The group, which includes former Gov. Grant Sawyer, Las Vegas Mayor Jan Laverty Jones and developer Ernest Becker Jr., formed the Clark County Education Foundation Inc. last fall and expects to begin a major fund-raising effort early this year.
The group hopes to raise a $3 million endowment by year's end to fund education programs in local schools, said Karen Galatz, a vice president with First Interstate Bank and president of the foundation's board of directors.
Galatz said the idea of a private foundation modeled along the lines of a university foundation was hatched two years ago by School Superintendent Brian Cram, Trustee Lois Tarkanian and Becker.
It arose out of the concern, he said, "that youngsters are not necessarily graduating with all the requirements that the business community wanted."

Captial improvements requiring issuance of general obligation bonds are addressed in Sec. 387.328-591 NRS (1993) and other public finance statutes.[111]

B
LOCAL ADMINISTRATIVE ORGANIZATION[112]

Pursuant to constitutional authority and direction, the legislature has created county school districts.[113] The boundaries of each school district are coterminous with the state's county boundaries. However, the state legislature has also created the Carson City School District and directed that it be considered as a county school district. Each county school district is a political subdivision of the State of Nevada whose purpose is to administer the state system of public education.[114] Each school district is vested with the power to sue and be sued.[115]

The trustees of a school district constitute a board, which is designated a body corporate.[116] Trustees are allowed a salary, and living and travel expenses while in actual attendance at board meetings. The living and travel allowances are

---

The foundation will give the private sector a say in school curriculum while providing teachers with the programs and equipment the district can't afford, she said.

"The district with the tremendous growth it has experienced can't fund everything it needs. For example, they may not be able to link all the schools by computer so the foundation will take that on," Galatz said Tuesday.

Although the real fund-raising push hasn't started, the foundation has received seed money from the Summa Corp., First Interstate Bank, Chaisson Motors and from Becker, said Judi Steele, special projects director for the school district and the foundation's executive director.

Summa Corp. created a $500,000 investment fund in which interest earnings will be used for programs at two schools in the Summerlin housing development and two of the district's "at risk" schools, Steele said.

In addition to targeting areas of need in the schools, the foundation will make grants available to teachers and principals, Galatz said.

"We're looking to fund programs directly in classrooms. If teachers say they want to make students more computer literate, but don't have computers, we want to help," she explained.

Steele said other foundation efforts being considered include the sponsorship of education think tanks to address and seek solutions to problems facing Clark County educators.

"Basically, we want to help with policy issues. We are thinking this can have a great impact," Steele said.

In addition, a foundation committee is studying ways to forge a partnership between community services such as the United Way, Girl Scouts and juvenile court system and the school system. The hope is to establish a computer information network at schools to provide parents with access to such programs, she said.

"If we're asking school people to be creative and innovative, the foundation by model and example also wants to be innovative and creative" Steele said."

[110]Chapter 561 Laws of Nevada (1993). The law defines 'educational foundation' as a nonprofit corporation, association, or institution organized and operated exclusively for the purpose of supporting one or more kindergarten, elementary schools, junior high or middle schools or high schools or a combination thereof. The law requires that educational foundations comply with Chapter 241 NRS. Further, records of the foundation are made subject to the public records laws (Sec. 239.010 NRS (1993)). However, an educational foundation is not required to disclose the names of contributors or the amount of their contributions. Educational foundation records related to contributors are open to inspection by such contributor during regular business hours.

[111]For example, Chapter 442 Laws of Nevada (1993) amends certain public finance statutes (Sec. 349.015 NRS (1991)) requiring the inclusion of an estimate of the annual cost to operate, maintain and repair any buildings, structures or other facilities or improvements to be constructed or acquired with bond proceeds.

Chapter 637 Laws of Nevada (1993) requires school districts to submit a written statement of its the debt management policy . The policy must include a complete statement of current and contemplated general obligation debt and associated matters. The policy must also address its ability to afford existing and future general obligation debt, capacity to incur future general obligation debt without exceeding the applicable debt limit, general obligation debt per capita as compared with the average for such debt of local governments in this state, general obligation debt as a percentage of assessed valuation of all taxable property within the boundaries of the political subdivision , the effective buying income of all persons who reside within the pollitical subdivision, a polcy statement regarding the manner in which the local government expects to sell its debt, sources of money projected to be available to pay existing and future general obligation debt and operational costs and revenue sources associated with each project.

Assembly Concurrent Resolution (ACR) No 38 File No. 174 (1993) directs the Legislative Commission to conduct an interim study of the laws relating to the financing of infrastructure which accompany residential, commercial and industrial development in the state. The results of the study are due for consideration during the 68th session of the legislature.

For additional background see Bittle, Edgar H., "School Building Programs, Equipment Acquisitions and Cash Flow: The Anatomy of School Debt Finacing," 73 Ed Law Rep. [593] (June 4, 1992).

[112] For additional background regarding the local school governance see First & Walberg, "School Boards: Changing Local Control," McCutchan Publishing Corporation, Berkeley, CA. (1992), Chubb & Moe, "Politics Markets and America's School," The Brookings Institution, Washington, D.C., (1991) and Mawdsley, Ralph D. & Drake, Daniel, "Involving Parents in Public Schools: Legal and Policy Issues," 76 Ed.Law Rep. [299] (October 8, 1992).

[113] The legislature reorganized the local school governance framework following a study of Nevada schools by the Peabody School of Education of Vanderbilt University completed December 1954. See "Public Education in Nevada Survey Report", State Document Library, December 1954. Prior to the adoption of a County school district system of school governance Nevada had 100 school districts.

[114] Sec. 386.010 NRS (1993)

[115] Ibid.

[116] Sec. 386.110 NRS (1993)

limited to the rates authorized by law for state officers.[117] Effective July 1, 1992 the clerk and president of school boards with an enrollment of less than 1,000 pupils may each receive $85 dollars for each meeting attended not to exceed $170 per month. Other trustees in the district may each receive $80 per meeting not to exceed $160 per month. The president and clerk of school districts enrolling more than 1,000 students may receive $85 per meeting not to exceed $340 per month. Other trustees may receive $80 per meeting not to exceed $320 per month.[118] Since the board may acquire membership in county, state and national school board associations trustees are also authorized to receive pay for travel expenses and per diem allowances while attending meetings of these organizations.[119]

School District boards are composed of either 5 or 7 members elected by district residents. If the school district enrolls less than 1000 pupils in the school year immediately preceding a general election, the board consists of 5 members. Districts enrolling more than 1000 pupils have 7 members. Trustees are elected for 4 year terms and must be qualified electors and reside in the election district which they represent. Elections occur on even numbered years. The election scheme applicable to each district depends on the number of pupils enrolled.[120] For example, in each school district with more than 75,000 pupils the 7 trustees are required to establish 7 election districts which are as nearly equal in population as practicable and composed of contiguous territory. Four trustees stand for election on one even numbered year and the remaining trustees on the next even numbered year. Regular terms commence on the 1st Monday in the January following the November general election.[121] They are required to take and subscribe the official oath which must be filed with the superintendent of public instruction. Vacancies occurring in a board of trustees are filled by appointment by the remaining members at a public meeting. The appointee serves until the next general election, at which time an individual is elected for the balance of the unexpired term.[122]

Following the election, the board is required to meet and organize by electing one of its members president. The board is also directed to elect one of its members as clerk or select some other qualified person to hold that office. Immediately after the organization the clerk must file the names of the officers and members with the Department of Public Instruction and the county auditor.[123] The duties of the clerk also include keeping minutes of all meeting and transactions of the board. In addition the clerk is charged with drawing all orders for the payment of monies belonging to the district.[124]

Regular meetings [125] of the board must be held at least once each month at a place and time determined by the board. Special meetings may be called by the

[117] Sec. 386.290 NRS (1993)

[118] Sec. 386.320 NRS (1993) In order to receive the salary authorized individual school trustee must request payment and the board of trustees must approve payment because payment of any salaries is within discretion of the board. AGO 161 (1-30-1974)

[119] Sec. 386.345 NRS (1993)

[120] Sec. 386.120-190 NRS (1993) The legislature has also provided an alternate manner for creating areas for the election of trustees in districts with enrollment of less than 25,000 pupils.Sec. 386.200-225 NRS (1991)

[121] Sec. 386.300 NRS (1993)

[122] Sec. 386.270 NRS (1993)

[123] Chapter 197 Laws of Nevada (1993) amends Sec. 386.310 NRS (1991) repealing duplicate and obsolete provisions concerning funds maintained by school districts.

[124] Sec. 386.325 NRS (1993)

[125] Board of Trustee meetings are subject to the Nevada open meeting law. See Chapter 241 NRS (1993). Chapter 210 Laws of Nevada (1993) amends Sec. 241.035 (2) NRS (1991) mandating permanent retention of public meeting minutes. After at least 5 years of retention by the public body minutes may be transferred for archival preservation. See Sec. 239.080 to 239.125 NRS (1993). Chapter 629 Laws of Nevada (1993) amends Chapter 241 adding provisions which forbid a public body from holding a closed meeting to consider the character alleged misconduct, professional competence, or physical or mental health of an elected member of the public body. The new law also prohibits a public body from

president whenever there is sufficient business to come before the board or upon the written request of three members of the board. The clerk is obligated to give written notice of each special meeting either by personal delivery of the notice at least 1 day before the meeting or by mail at least 4 days before the meeting. The notice must specify the time, place and purpose of the meeting. However, if all members are present at a special meeting lack of notice shall not invalidate the proceedings of the board.[126] A majority of the members constitute a quorum for the transaction of business. But, no action of the board is valid unless it receives approval of a **majority of all the members of the board** at a regularly called meeting.[127]

Each board may prescribe and enforce rules for its own government and the government of the schools [128] under its charge as long as those rules are consistent with law [129] or the rules prescribed by the state board of education.[130]

---

holding a meeting to consider the character, alleged misconduct, professional competence, or physical or mental health of any person unless it has given written notice to that person of the time and place of the meeting. The notice must be either personally delivered to the person at least five working days before the meeting or sent certified mail to the last known address of that person at least 21 working days before the meeting. Proof of service is a precondition for holding the meeting. A copy of any record of such a closed meeting must be provided to the person discussed upon his/her request. Chapter 629 also provides that if a public body elects to record a public meeting any portion of the meeting which is closed must also be recorded and be retained.

Sec. 241.020 2 (c) (3) NRS (1993) requires that each public meeting agenda include a period of time devoted to comments by the general public and discussion of those comments. No action may be taken on a matter raised under this item of the agenda until the matter itself has been specifically included on an agenda as an item upon which action will be taken.

[126] Sec. 386.330 NRS (1993)

[127] Sec. 386.330 4 NRS (1993)

[128] Chapter 664 Laws of Nevada (1993) amends Chapter 386 authorizing local boards to prescribe rules relating to the creation and administration of a program of school-based decision making. The law dictates that the rules must provide for the creation of a school council, involvement of parents and other members of the community on and with the school council, the requirements for recordkeeping by the council, the procedure for appealing a decision of the council, the procedure for a school to obtain a waiver of the requirements of regulations of the board of trustees or the state board, a method for reporting the progress of a pupil to the pupil, his parents or guardians, the board of trustees and the state board, plans for improving the schools within the district, a method for allocating money to schools that have adopted a program and the procedure which a school council or board of trustees may use to withdraw from the program.

The board of trustees may waive the requirements of regulations of the board of trustees and the state board for a public school within the district that adopts a program of school-based decision making. However, the board of trustees may not waive statutory requirements.

The state board may waive a course of study otherwise required by statute upon application of the board of trustees of a school district on behalf of a school council created pursuant to a program of school-based deision making.

The law expires on June 30, 1997

Assembly Concurrent Resolution No. 17 File No. 58 (1993) reminds school districts of the Nevada School Improvement Project established in 1986 and urges school trustees to encourage all public schools to participate in the voluntary program.

[129] Chapter 239 NRS (1993)entitled 'Public Records' is one example of a state law which must be considered when a board of trustees is making rules for its own government and the government of the schools under its charge.

The law provides that all public books and public records of a "governmental subdivision" (school district) the contents of which are not otherwise declared by law to be confidential must be open at all times during office hours to inspection by any person, and the books and records may be fully copied or an abstract or memorandum prepared therefrom. See Sec. 239.010 NRS (1993).

Chapter 393 Laws of Nevada (1993) amends Chapter 239 NRS (1991) by substituting civil enforcement proceedings for access to public books and records for a criminal penalty for denial of access. Under the new legislation a requester denied inspection or copying of a public record may apply to the district court in the county in which the book or record is located for an order permitting him to inspect or copy it. District courts are required to give the matter priority over other civil matters accorded no other priority by statute. If the requester prevails, he/she is entitled to recover his costs and reasonable attorney's fees in the proceeding from the agency whose officer has custody of the book or record.

The new law also confers immunity from damages upon public officers or employees who act in good faith in disclosing or refusing to disclose public information either to the requester or the person whom the information concerns. The public employer is also shielded from liability by the good faith action or inaction of their officers or employees.

[130] Sec. 386.360 NRS (1993). Each board is directed to prescribe rules for granting permission to carry of possess a weapon on school grounds under this section. See Sec 202.265 NRS (1993).

General Powers of Local Boards

General powers have been conferred on local boards by the legislature.[131] These include reasonable and necessary powers, not conflicting with the constitution and the laws of Nevada as may be requisite to attain the ends for which the public schools are established and to promote the welfare of the school children, including the establishment and operation of schools and classes deemed necessary and desirable.[132] The power to employ school personnel is also vested with the board of trustees.[133]

Special procedural rules govern adoption, repeal or amendment of specific policies and regulations in districts whose population is at least 100,000 are subject to special procedural rules.[134] In such districts, the board must give 15 days' notice of its intention to adopt, repeal, or amend policy concerning attendance rules, zoning, grading, district staffing patterns, curriculum and program, pupil discipline, and personnel. The required notice includes a description of the subject or subjects involved and must state the time and place of the meeting at which the matter will be considered by the board. The board is obligated to mail the notice to the principal, president of the PTA or similar and the president of the classroom teachers' organization from each of the schools affected. Furthermore, a copy of the notice and the terms of the proposed policy must be made available for inspection by the public in the office of the superintendent of schools at least 15 days before its adoption. All persons interested in a proposed policy or regulation change must be afforded a reasonable opportunity to submit data, views or arguments orally or in writing. The board is obligated to consider all written and oral submissions respecting the proposal or change before taking final action.[135] However, the statute allows the board to adopt emergency policies or regulations based on the board's determination that an emergency exists.[136]

Specific Powers of Local Boards

Local Boards have also been granted specific powers.

---

[131] Sec. 386.350 NRS (1993)

[132] Ibid., It is well settled general law that school officers only have such powers as are vested in them by statute AGO 320 (2-3-1954); Although school trustees had power under Sec. 386.350 etc. to order closure of a rural high school and transport student to another school, decision to close school and bus students 80 miles per day to larger school was abuse of discretion where the only evidence before the board supporting closure was a 15-year-old study which was not relevant to current circumstances and expert testimony indicated busing of students would have negative effect on their education. Bartlett v. Board of Trustees, 92 Nev. 347, 550 P.2d 416 (1976); Boards of trustees of school districts have authority to prescribe reasonable rules respecting dress of students in attendance at schools. AGO 288 (5-25-1962)

[133] Sec. 391.100 NRS (1993). Sec. 391.110 NRS (1993) deals specifically with employment of a superintendent of schools. Chapter 536 Laws of Nevada (1993) concerns ethics in government. It amends Chapter 281 adding a new section establishing rules for determining conflict of interest when a public officer or employee is considering bidding on a contract with a public agency.

[134] Sec. 386.365 NRS (1993)

[135] Ibid.

[136] Ibid.

School Property

Local Boards are charged with the management and control [137] of school property including records.[138] and financial resources.[139] Of course the control exercised by local boards for school sponsored events must be consistent with the U. S. Constitution.

This principle was a key factor in determining the outcome in the recent case entitled **Lee v. Weisman**.[140]

In **Lee,** decided June, 24 1992, the Court reaffirmed its precedents banning state sponsored prayer in public schools. A closely divided Court held that prayer by a member of the clergy at a public school graduation ceremony violates the The First Amendment Establishment clause. The majority opinion was written by Justice Kennedy. Justice's Blackmun and Souter filed concurring opinions. The opinion of the four dissenting Justices was written by Justice Scalia.

LEE
v.
WEISMAN
505 U.S.____, 112 S.Ct. 2649 (1992)[141]

JUSTICE KENNEDY for the Court

School principals in the public school system of the city of Providence, Rhode Island, are permitted to invite members of the clergy to offer invocation and

---

[137]Sec. 393.010 NRS (1993). Chapter 517 Laws of Nevada Sec. 1 (1993) amends Chapter 393 adding a new section prohibiting any kind of surreptitious electronic surveillance by a person on any property of a public school "without the knowledge of the person being observed." (How can surveillance be surreptitious and be with the knowledge of the person being observed? What if any responsibility does a school district have for policing video taping on school property by individuals other than its employees?)The prohibition does not apply to any electronic surveillance authorized by a court order, by a law enforcement agency pursuant to a criminal investigation, that which is necessary as part of a system of security used to protect and ensure the safety of persons on school property or of a class or laboratory when authorized by the teacher of the class or laboratory. (Does this law forbid use of electronic means and methods for teacher evaluation purposes without the teachers consent? Does the law forbid electronic surveillance of a classroom for safety or law enforcement purposes without the teachers consent?) This legislation is the result of the furor caused by the secret video taping of a UNLV basketball conditioning class. The motivation for the taping was determining whether the class was being conducted in violation of NCAA regulations. See Gallant, John, "Legislative Probe Of UNLV Ends," Review Journal, December 15, 1992, p. 1 B.

[138]Chapter 239 NRS entitled 'Public Records' regulates school district record keeping and access. disclosure and safekeeping. Chapter 393 Laws of Nevada (1993) amends Chapter 239 substituting a civil procedure for a criminal penalty for improper handling of public records. Chapter 102 Laws of Nevada (1993) amending Sec. 239.125 NRS (1991) providing local governments adopt a program for management of records including schedules for retention and microfilming.

[139]Chapter 121 Laws of Nevada (1993) amending Sec 355.170 NRS (1991) specifies the type of investments that can be made by county school districts. Reports of receipts and expenditures for the fiscal year must be reported to the department of taxation within 4 months of June 30. See Chapter 123 Laws of Nevada (1993) amending Sec. 354.602 NRS (1991)

[140]Lee v. Weisman, 505 U.S.____, 112 S.Ct. 2649 (1992).

[141]See also Jones v. Clear Creek Independent School Dist., 930 F.2d 416 (5th Cir. 1991) (JONES I), vacated and remanded in the light of Lee 505 U.S. ____, 112 S.Ct. 3020 (1992). On remand the court of appeals reinstated its prior decision concluding that Lee did not render Clear Creek's invocation policy unconstitutional, and again affirmed the district courts summary judgment in Clear Creek's favor. Jones v. Clear Creek Independent School Dist., 977 F.2d 963 (5th Cir. 1992) (Jones II). Parents again filed a petition for a writ of certiorari. The Supreme Court denied the petition on June 7, 1993. (See USSC Case No. 92-1564). The school board resolution dealing with graduation invocations found constitutional by the court in the Clear Creek reads as follows:

> **1. The use of an invocation and/or benediction at high school graduation exercise shall rest within the discretion of the graduating senior class, with the advice and counsel of the senior class principal;**
>
> **2. The invocation and benediction, if used, shall be given by a student volunteer; and**
>
> **3. Consistent with the principle of equal liberty of conscience, the invocation and benediction shall be nonsectarian and nonproselytizing in nature." JONES II, p. 964.**

The 5th Circuits most recent opinion addressing prayer in public schools is entitled Doe v. Duncanville School Dist., 994 F.2d 160 (5th Cir. 1993). In the Doe case the Fifth Circuit decided that when teachers and coaches led the girls' junior high basketball team in prayer, they violated the Establishment Clause.

For three mornings in November 1993 the president of the student government of Wingfield High School in Jackson, Mississippi, began the school day by reading a nonsectarian prayer over the school's P.A. system. The prayer read as follows:

> **"Almighty God, we ask that you bless our parents, teachers and country throughout the day. In your name, we pray. Amen."**

The reading was authorized by the school principal. He was suspended and then fired. Was the action of the school board consistent with the holdings in Lee, Doe and Clear Creek? See "Mississippi Prays," Wall Street Journal, Editorial, December 6, 1993, p. 14 A.

benediction prayers as part of the formal graduation ceremonies for middle schools and for high schools. The question before us is whether including clerical members who offer prayers as part of the official school graduation ceremony is consistent with the religion clauses of the First Amendment.

****

Deborah Weisman graduated from Nathan Bishop Middle School, a public school in Providence, at a formal ceremony in June 1989.... For many years it has been the policy of the Providence School Committee and the Superintendent of Schools to permit principals to invite members of the clergy to give invocations and benedictions at middle school and high school graduations.... Acting for himself and his daughter, Deborah's father, Daniel Weisman, objected to any prayers at Deborah's middle school graduation, but to no avail. The school principal petitioner Robert E. Lee, invited a rabbi to deliver prayers at the graduation exercises for Deborah's class. Rabbi Leslie Gutterman, of the Temple Beth El in Providence, accepted.

It has been the custom of Providence school officials to provide invited clergy with a pamphlet entitled "Guidelines for Civic Occasions," prepared by the National Conference of Christians and Jews.... The principal gave Rabbi Gutterman the pamphlet before the graduation and advised him the invocation and benediction should be nonsectarian.

Rabbi Gutterman's prayers were as follows:

Invocation:

God of the Free, Hope of the Brave, for the legacy of America where diversity is celebrated and the rights of minorities are protected, we thank You. May these young men and women grow up to enrich it.

For the liberty of America, we thank You. May these new graduates grow up to guard it.

For the political process of America in which all its citizens may participate, for its court system where all may seek justice we thank You. May those we honor this morning always turn to it in trust.

For the destiny of America we thank You. May the graduates of Nathan Bishop Middle School so live that they might help to share it.

May our aspirations for our country and for these young people, who are our hope for the future, be richly fulfilled. Amen.

Benediction:

O God we are grateful to You for having endowed us with the capacity for learning which we have celebrated on this joyous commencement. Happy families give thanks for seeing their children achieve an important milestone.

Send Your blessings upon the teachers and administrators who helped prepare them. The graduates now need strength and guidance for the future, help them to understand that we are not complete with academic knowledge alone. We must each strive to fulfill what You require of us all: To do justly, to love mercy, to walk humbly.

We give thanks to You, Lord, for keeping us alive, sustaining us and allowing us to reach this special, happy occasion.
Amen.

The school board (and the United States, which supports it as amicus curiae) argued that these short prayers and others like them at graduation exercises are of profound meaning to many students and parents throughout this country who consider that due respect and acknowledgement for divine guidance and for the deepest spiritual aspirations of our people ought to be expressed at an event as important in life as a graduation. We assume this to be so in addressing the difficult case now before us, for the significance of the prayers lies also at the heart of Daniel and Deborah Weisman's case....

Deborah and her family attended the graduation, where the prayers were recited. In July 1989, Daniel Weisman filed an amended complaint seeking a permanent injunction barring petitioners, various officials of the Providence public schools, from inviting the clergy to deliver invocations and benedictions at future graduations . . .

The District Court held that petitioners' practice of including invocations and benedictions in public school graduations violated the establishment clause of the First Amendment, and it enjoined petitioners from continuing the practice. The court applied the three-part establishment clause test set forth in Lemon v. Kurtzman (1971). Under that test as described in our past cases, to satisfy the establishment clause a governmental practice must (1) reflect a clearly secular purpose; (2) have a primary effect that neither advances nor inhibits religion, and (3) avoid excessive government entanglement with religion. The District Court held that petitioners' actions violated the second part of the test, and so did not address either the first or the third.... The court determined that the practice of including invocations and benedictions, even so-called nonsectarian ones, in public school graduations creates an identification of governmental power with religious practice, endorses religion, and violates the establishment clause....

On appeal, the United States Court of Appeals for the First Circuit affirmed....

Precedents as they relate to prayer and religious exercise in primary and secondary public schools compel the holding here that the policy of the city of Providence is an unconstitutional one. We can decide the case without reconsidering the general constitutional framework by which public schools' efforts to accommodate religion are measured. .. The government involvement with religious activity in this case is pervasive, to the point of creating a state-sponsored and state-directed religious exercise in a public school. Conducting this formal religious observance conflicts with settled rules pertaining to prayer exercises for students, and that suffices to determine the question before us.

The principle that government may accommodate the free exercise of religion does not supersede the fundamental limitations imposed by the establishment clause. It is beyond dispute that, at a minimum, the Constitution guarantees that government may not coerce anyone to support or participate in religion or its exercise, or otherwise act in a way which "establishes a (state) religion or religious faith, or tends to do so." The State's involvement in the school prayers challenged today violates these central principles.

That involvement is as troubling as it is undenied. A school official, the principal, decided that an invocation and a benediction should be given; this is a choice attributable to the State, and from a constitutional perspective it is as if a state statute decreed that the prayers must occur. The principal chose the religious participant, here a rabbi, and that choice is also attributable to the State.

****

The State's role did not end with the decision to include a prayer and with the choice of clergyman. Principal Lee provided Rabbi Gutterman with a copy of the

"Guidelines for Civic Occasions," and advised him that his prayers should be nonsectarian. Through these means the principal directed and controlled the content of the prayer . . .

****

The First Amendment's religion clauses mean that religious beliefs and religious expression are too precious to be either proscribed or prescribed by the State. The design of the Constitution is that preservation and transmission of religious beliefs and worship is a responsibility and a choice committed to the private sphere, which itself is promised freedom to pursue that mission.

These concerns have particular application in the case of school officials, whose effort to monitor prayer will be perceived by the students as inducing a participation they might otherwise reject. .

The lessons of the First Amendment are as urgent in the modern world as in the 18th century when it was written. One timeless lesson is that if citizens are subjected to state-sponsored religious exercises, the State disavows its own duty to guard and respect that sphere of inviolable conscience and belief which is the mark of a free people. To compromise that principle today would be to deny our own tradition and forfeit our standing to urge others to secure the protections of that tradition for themselves.

As we have observed before, there are heightened concerns with protecting freedom of conscience from subtle coercive pressure in the elementary and secondary public schools....

Finding no violation under these circumstances would place objectors in the dilemma of participating, with all that implies or protesting. We do not address whether that choice is acceptable if the affected citizens are mature adults, but we think the State may not, consistent with the establishment clause, place primary and secondary school children in this position. Research in Psychology supports the common assumption that adolescents are often susceptible to pressure from their peers towards conformity, and that the influence is strongest in matters of social convention....

There was a stipulation in the District Court that attendance at graduation and promotional ceremonies is voluntary. Petitioners and the United States, as amicus, made this a center point of the case arguing that the option of not attending the graduation excuses any inducement or coercion in the ceremony itself. The argument lacks all persuasion. Everyone knows that in our society and in our culture high school graduation is one of life's most significant occasions

The importance of the event is the point the school district and the United States rely upon to argue that a formal prayer ought to be permitted but it becomes one of the principal reasons why their argument must fail. Their contention, one of considerable force were it not for the constitutional constraints applied to state action, is that the prayers are an essential part of these ceremonies because for many persons an occasion of this significance lacks meaning if there is no recognition, however brief, that human achievements cannot be understood apart from their spiritual essence. We think the Government's position that this interest suffices to force students to choose between compliance or forfeiture demonstrates fundamental inconsistency in its argumentation. It fails to acknowledge that what for many of Deborah's classmates and their parents was a spiritual imperative was for Daniel and Deborah Weisman religious conformance compelled by the State. While in some societies the wishes of the majority might prevail, the establishment clause of the First Amendment is addressed to this contingency and rejects the balance urged upon us. The Constitution forbids the State to exact religious conformity from a student as the price of attending her own high school graduation.

JUSTICE SCALIA dissenting
In holding that the establishment clause prohibits invocations and benedictions at public school graduation ceremonies, the Court, with nary a mention that it is doing so, lays waste a tradition that is as old as public school graduation ceremonies themselves and that is a component of an even more longstanding American tradition of nonsectarian prayer to God at public celebrations generally . . . Today's opinion shows more forcefully than volumes of argumentation why our Nation's protection, that fortress which is our Constitution, cannot possibly rest upon the changeable philosophical predilections of the Justices of this Court, but must have deep foundations in the historic practices of our people.
****
In addition to this general tradition of prayer at public ceremonies, there exists a more specific tradition of invocations and benedictions at public-school graduation exercises....
****
The narrow context of the present case involves a community's celebration of one of the milestones in its young citizens' lives, and it is a bold step for this Court to seek to banish from that occasion, and from thousands of similar celebrations throughout this land, the expression of gratitude to God that a majority of the community wishes to make.
I dissent.
****

Specific Powers--School Property Cont.
This power to control and manage school property vested with school trustees includes the the responsibility for custody and safekeeping of schools, their sites[142] and equipment.[143] The real property (land & buildings) is held by the trustees as a corporation.[144] Persons who damage school property, commit any nuisance in a school, loiter on or near school property or maliciously trespass on school grounds are guilty of a public offense no less than a misdemeanor.[145]

The use of school property is also subject to board regulation. In fact the board is authorized and directed to make all necessary regulations for the use of school buildings and grounds.[146] However, the board is prohibited from granting the use and occupancy of school property which would be inconsistent with or interfere with its use for school purposes.[147] The board is also prohibited from granting a use which would constitute a monopoly for the benefit of any person [148]

---

[142] Trustees are empowered to prohibit or regulate the use of motor vehicles on school property. The rules promulgated by the board may be enforced by any peace officer. See Sec. 393.051 NRS (1993).
[143] Sec. 393.010 NRS (1991)
[144] Sec. 393.030 NRS (1991)
[145] Sec. 393.070 NRS (1991) In a case entitled A Minor Girl v. Clark County Juvenile Court Services, 87 Nev. 544, 490 N.2d 1248 (1971) the Nevada supreme court determined that the purpose of the statute was to protect children from molestation and prevent damage to school property. The case was also cited in Junior v. State, 89 Nev. 121 at 122, 507 P.2d 1037 (1973), Turpin v. State, 89 Nev. 518, at 520, 515 P.2d 1271 (1971)
[146] Sec. 393.0717 NRS (1993)
[147] Sec. 393.0711 NRS (1993)
[148] Sec. 393.0712 NRS (1993)

or for a term exceeding one year.[149] Granting use of school property for a program or movement whose purpose is violent overthrow of the United States or the state is also forbidden.[150] Persons granted the use of school property are required to reimburse the board for expenses incurred as a result of their use.[151]

It is important to note that the regulations adopted by the board regrading the use of school facilities by students and community groups must be consistent with the United States Constitution and other applicable federal statutes. This principle is well illustrated by the recent decision of the United States Supreme Court in **Westside Community Schools v. Mergens.**[152]

BOARD OF EDUCATION OF THE WESTSIDE COMMUNITY SCHOOLS
v.
MERGENS[153]
496 U.S. 226, 110 S.Ct. 2356 (1990)

JUSTICE O'CONNOR delivered the opinion of the Court, except as to Part III.

This case requires us to decide whether the Equal Access Act, 98 Stat. 1302, 20 U. S. C. §§4071-4074, prohibits Westside High School from denying a student religious group permission to meet on school premises during noninstructional time, and if so, whether the Act, so construed violates the Establishment Clause of the First Amendment.

I

Respondents are current and former students at Westside High School, a public secondary school in Omaha, Nebraska. At the time this suit was filed, the school enrolled about 1,450 students and included grades 10 to 12; in the 1987-1988 school year, ninth graders were added. Westside High School is part of the Westside Community School system, an independent public school district. Petitioners are the Board of Education of Westside Community Schools (District 66)(and other individuals).

Students at Westside High School are permitted to join various student groups and clubs, all of which meet after school hours on school premises. The students may choose from approximately 30 recognized groups on a voluntary basis. A list of student groups, together with a brief description of each provided by the school, appears in the appendix to this opinion.

School Board Policy 5610 concerning "Student Clubs and Organizations" recognizes these student clubs as a "vital part of the total education program as a

---

[149] Sec. 393.0713 NRS (1993)

[150] Sec. 393.0715 NRS (1993)

[151] Sec. 393.0719 NRS (1993)

[152] ___U.S.___, 110 S.Ct. 2356 (1990).

[153] Renton School District No. 403 v. Garnett, 987 F2d. 641 (9th Cir. 1993), Case No. 92-1890, Cert. Denied, 10-4-93 USSC, No. 92- 1890. Below. School officials denied students permission to form a religious club or to meet on school premises although other student groups were allowed to do so. Students claimed this violated the Equal Access Act, 20 U.S.C. 4071-4074 (1988) (EAA). The district court found the Equal Access Act did not apply because the school did not have a "limited open forum," and the Washington State Constitution barred religious groups from meeting on school property. The decision was upheld on appeal. The Supreme Court vacated and remanded for reconsideration in light of Board of Education v. Mergens, 496 U.S. 226 (1990). Upon reconsideration, the Ninth Circuit Court reversed the district court's decision, holding that the EAA preempts state law, which cannot abridge rights granted by federal law. The students have a right to meet on School property on the same basis as other noncurriculum-related clubs. See also Bjorklun, Eugene C., "implementing the Equal Access Act and State Constitutional Provisions," 74 Ed.Law Rep. [1] (July 2, 1992). See also Collins v. Chandler Unified Sch. Dist., 644 F.2d 759 (9th Cir.) cert denied, 454 U.S. 863, 102 S.Ct. 322 (1981) & Bartlett, Larry D. "The Equal Access Act v. State Constitutions: The Supremacy Clause Question," 71 Ed.Law Rep. [983] (March 12, 1992).

33

means of developing citizenship, wholesome attitudes, good human relations, knowledge and skills.". Board Policy 5610 also provides that each club shall have faculty sponsorship and that "clubs and organizations shall not be sponsored by any political or religious organization, or by any organization which denies membership on the basis of race, color, creed, sex or political belief.". Board Policy 6180 on "Recognition of Religious Beliefs and Customs" requires that "[s]tudents adhering to a specific set of religious beliefs or holding to little or no belief shall be alike respected." In addition, Board Policy 5450 recognizes its students' "Freedom of Expression," consistent with the authority of the Board.

There is no written school board policy concerning the formation of student clubs. Rather, students wishing to form a club present their request to a school official who determines whether the proposed club's goals and objectives are consistent with school board policies and with the school district's "Mission and Goals"—a broadly worded "blueprint" that expresses the district's commitment to teaching academic, physical, civic, and personal skills and values.

In January 1985, respondent Bridget Mergens met with Westside's principal, Dr. Findley, and requested permission to form a Christian club at the school. The proposed club would have the same privileges and meet on the same terms and conditions as other Westside student groups, except that the proposed club would not have a faculty sponsor. According to the students' testimony at trial, the club's purpose would have been, among other things, to permit the students to read and discuss the Bible, to have fellowship, and to pray together. Membership would have been voluntary and open to all students regardless of religious affiliation.

Findley denied the request, as did associate superintendent Tangdell. In February 1985, Findley and Tangdell informed Mergens that they had discussed the matter with superintendent Hanson and that he had agreed that her request should be denied. The school officials explained that school policy required all student clubs to have a faculty sponsor, which the proposed religious club would not or could not have, and that a religious club at the school would violate the Establishment Clause. In March 1985, Mergens appealed the denial of her request to the Board of Education, but the Board voted to uphold the denial.

Respondents, by and through their parents as next friends, then brought this suit in the United States District Court for the District of Nebraska seeking declaratory and injunctive relief. They alleged that petitioners' refusal to permit the proposed club to meet at Westside violated the Equal Access Act, 20 U. S. C. §§ 4071-4074, which prohibits public secondary schools that receive federal financial assistance and that maintain a "limited open forum" from denying "equal access" to students who wish to meet within the forum on the basis of the content of the speech at such meetings, §4071(a). Respondents further alleged that petitioners' actions denied them their First and Fourteenth Amendment rights to freedom of speech, association, and the free exercise of religion. Petitioners responded that the Equal Access Act did not apply to Westside and that, if the Act did apply, it violated the Establishment Clause of the First Amendment and was therefore unconstitutional.

The District Court entered judgment for petitioners. The court held that the Act did not apply in this case because Westside did not have a "limited open forum" as defined by the Act—all of Westside's student clubs, the court concluded, were curriculum-related and tied to the educational function of the school.

****

The United States Court of Appeals for the Eighth Circuit reversed. The Court of Appeals held that the District Court erred in concluding that all the existing student clubs at Westside were curriculum-related. The Court of Appeals noted that the "broad interpretation" advanced by the Westside school officials "would make the [Equal Access Act] meaningless" and would allow any school to "arbitrarily deny access to school facilities to any unfavored student club on the basis of its speech content," which was "exactly the result that Congress sought to prohibit by enacting the [Act]."

****

The Court of Appeals then rejected petitioners' contention that the Act violated the Establishment Clause.

****

We granted certiorari, ...and now **affirm.**

II

A

In Widmar v. Vincent, 454 U. S. 263 (1981), we invalidated, on free speech grounds, a state university regulation that prohibited student use of school facilities " 'for purposes of religious worship or religious teaching. '" In doing so, we held that an "equal access" policy would not violate the Establishment Clause under our decision in Lemon v. Kurtzman, 403 U. S. 602, 612-613 (1971). In particular, we held that such a policy would have a secular purpose, would not have the primary effect of advancing religion, and would not result in excessive entanglement between government and religion. We noted, however, that "[u]niversity students are, of course, young adults. They are less impressionable than younger students and should be able to appreciate that the University's policy is one of neutrality toward religion."

In 1984, Congress extended the reasoning of Widmar to public secondary schools. Under the Equal Access Act, a public secondary school with a "limited open forum" is prohibited from discriminating against students who wish to conduct a meeting within that forum on the basis of the "religious, political, philosophical, or other content of the speech at such meetings." 20 U. S. C. §§4071(a) and (b). Specifically, the Act provides:

> **"It shall be unlawful for any public secondary school which receives Federal financial assistance and which has a limited open forum to deny equal access or a fair opportunity to, or discriminate against,any students who wish to conduct a meeting within that limited open forum on the basis of the religious, political, philosophical, or other content of the speech at such meetings." 20 U. S. C. §4071(a). (emphasis add)**

A "limited open forum" exists whenever a public secondary school "grants an offering to or opportunity for one or more noncurriculum related student groups to meet on school premises during noninstructional time." §4071(b). "Meeting" is defined to include "those activities of student groups which are permitted under a school's limited open forum and are not directly related to the school curriculum." §4072(3). "Noninstructional time" is defined to mean "time set aside by the school before actual classroom instruction begins or after actual classroom instruction ends." § 4072(4). Thus, even if a public secondary school allows only one "noncurriculum related student group" to meet, the Act's obligations are triggered and the school may not deny other clubs, on the basis of the content of their speech, equal access to meet on school premises during noninstructional time.

The Act further specifies that "[s]chools shall be deemed to offer a fair opportunity to students who wish to conduct a meeting within its limited open forum" if the school uniformly provides that the meetings are voluntary and student-initiated; are not sponsored by the school, the government, or its agents or employees; do not materially and substantially interfere with the orderly conduct of educational activities within the school; and are not directed, controlled, conducted, or regularly attended by "nonschool persons." §§4071(c)(1), (2), (4), and (5). "Sponsorship" is defined to mean "the act of promoting, leading, or participating in a meeting. The assignment of a teacher, administrator, or other school employee to a meeting for custodial purposes does not constitute sponsorship of the meeting." §4072(2). If the meetings are religious, employees or agents of the school or government may attend only in a "nonparticipatory capacity." §4071(c)(3). Moreover, a State may not influence the form of any religious activity, require any person to participate in such activity, or compel any school agent or employee to attend a meeting if the content of the speech at the meeting is contrary to that person's beliefs. §4071(d)(1), (2), and (3).

Finally, the Act does not "authorize the United States to deny or withhold Federal financial assistance to any school," §4071(e), or "limit the authority of the school, its agents or employees, to maintain order and discipline on school premises, to protect the well-being of students and faculty, and to assure that attendance of students at the meetings is voluntary," § 4071(f).

B

The parties agree that Westside High School receives federal financial assistance and is a public secondary school within the meaning of the Act. The Act's obligation to grant equal access to student groups is, therefore, triggered if Westside maintains a 'limited open forum"— i. e., if it permits one or more "noncurriculum related student groups" to meet on campus before or after classes.

Unfortunately, the Act does not define the crucial phrase "noncurriculum related student group. " Our immediate task is, therefore, one of statutory interpretation. We begin, of course, with the language of the statute. The common meaning of the term "curriculum" is "the whole body of courses offered by an educational institution or one of its branches." Webster's Third New International Dictionary 557 (1976).

****

Any sensible interpretation of "noncurriculum related student group" must therefore be anchored in the notion that such student groups are those that are not related to the body of courses offered by the school. The difficult question is the degree of "unrelatedness to the curriculum" required for a group to be considered "non-curriculum related."

The Act's definition of the sort of "meeting[s]" that must be accommodated under the statute, § 4071(a), sheds some light on this question. "[T]he term 'meeting' includes those activities of student groups which are . . . not directly related to the school curriculum." §4072(3) (emphasis added). Congress' use of the phrase "directly related" implies that student groups directly related to the subject matter of courses offered by the school do not fall within the "noncurriculum related" category and would therefore, be considered "curriculum related."

36

The logic of the Act also supports this view, namely, that a curriculum-related student group is one that has more than just a tangential or attenuated relationship to courses offered by the school. Because the purpose of granting equal access is to prohibit discrimination between religious or political clubs on the one hand and other noncurriculum-related student groups on the other, the Act is premised on the notion that a religious or political club is itself likely to be a noncurriculum-related student group. It follows, then, that a student group that is "curriculum related" must at least have a more direct relationship to the curriculum than a religious or political club would have.

Although the phrase "noncurriculum related student group" nevertheless remains sufficiently ambiguous that we might normally resort to legislative history, we find the legislative history on this issue less than helpful.

****

We think it significant, however, that the Act, which was passed by wide, bipartisan majorities in both the House and the Senate, reflects at least some consensus on a broad legislative purpose. The committee reports indicate that the Act was intended to address perceived widespread discrimination against religious speech in public schools, see H. R. Rep. No. 98-710, p. 4 (1984); S. Rep. No. 98-;357, pp. 10-11 (1984), and, as the language of the Act indicates, its sponsors contemplated that the Act would do more than merely validate the status quo.

****

In light of this legislative purpose, we think that the term "noncurriculum related student group" is best interpreted broadly to mean any student group that does not directly relate to the body of courses offered by the school. In our view, a student group directly relates to a school's curriculum if the subject matter of the group is actually taught, or will soon be taught, in a regularly offered course; if the subject matter of the group concerns the body of courses as a whole; if participation in the group is required for a particular course; or if participation in the group results in academic credit. We think this limited definition of groups that directly relate to the curriculum is a commonsense interpretation of the Act that is consistent with Congress' intent to provide a low threshold for triggering the Act's requirements.

For example, a French club would directly relate to the curriculum if a school taught French in a regularly offered course or planned to teach the subject in the near future. A school's student government would generally relate directly to the curriculum to the extent that it addresses concerns, solicits opinions, and formulates proposals pertaining to the body of courses offered by the school. If participation in a school's band or orchestra were required for the band or orchestra classes, or resulted in academic credit, then those groups would also directly relate to the curriculum. The existence of such groups at a school would not trigger the Act's obligations.

On the other hand, unless a school could show that groups such as a chess club, a stamp collecting club, or a community service club fell within our description of groups that directly relate to the curriculum, such groups would be "noncurriculum related student groups" for purposes of the Act. The existence of such groups would create a "limited open forum" under the Act and would prohibit the school from denying equal access to any other student group on the basis of the content of that group's speech. Whether a specific student group is a "noncurriculum related student group" will therefore depend on a particular school's curriculum, but such determinations would be subject to factual findings well within the competence of trial courts to make.

Petitioners contend that our reading of the Act unduly hinders local control over schools and school activities, but we think that schools and school districts nevertheless retain a significant measure of authority over the type of officially recognized activities in which their students participate. First, schools and school districts maintain their traditional latitude to determine appropriate subjects of instruction. To the extent that a school chooses to structure its course offerings and existing student groups to avoid the Act's obligations, that result is not prohibited by the Act. Second, the Act expressly does not limit a school's authority to prohibit meetings that would "materially and substantially interfere with the orderly conduct of educational activities within the school." §4071(c)(4). The Act also preserves "the authority of the school, its agents or employees, to maintain order and discipline on school premises, to protect the well-being of students and faculty, and to assure that attendance of students at meetings is voluntary." §4071(f). Finally, because the Act applies only to public secondary schools that receive federal financial assistance, §4071(a), a school district seeking to escape the statute's obligations could simply forgo federal funding. Although we do not doubt that in some cases this may be an unrealistic option, Congress clearly sought to prohibit schools from discriminating on the basis of the content of a student group's speech, and that obligation is the price a federally funded school must pay if it opens its facilities to noncurriculum-related student groups.

****

C

The parties in this case focus their dispute on 10 of Westside's approximately 30 voluntary student clubs: Interact (a service club related to Rotary International); Chess; Subsurfer; (a club for students interested in scuba diving); National Honor Society; Photography; Welcome to Westside (a club to introduce new students to the school); Future Business Leaders of America; Zonta (the female counterpart to Interact); Student Advisory Board (student government); and Student Forum (student government). Petitioners contend that all of these student activities are curriculum-related because they further the goals of particular aspects of the school's curriculum. Welcome to Westside, for example, helps "further the School's overall goal of developing effective citizens by requiring student members to contribute to their fellow students." The student government clubs "advance the goals of the school's political science classes by providing an understanding and appreciation of government processes." Subsurfers furthers "one of the essential goals of the Physical Education Department—enabling students to develop lifelong recreational interests." Chess "supplement[s] math and science courses because it enhances students' ability to engage in critical thought processes." Participation in Interact and Zonta "promotes effective citizenship, a critical goal of the WHS curriculum, specifically the Social Studies Department_"

To the extent that petitioners contend that "curriculum related" means anything remotely related to abstract educational goals, however, we reject that argument. To define "curriculum related" in a way that results in almost no schools having limited open fora, or in a way that permits schools to evade the Act by strategically describing existing student groups, would render the Act merely hortatory.

****

See ...Garnett v. Renton School Dist. No. 403, 874 F. 2d 608, 614 (CA9 1989) ("Complete deference [to the school district] would render the Act meaningless because school boards could circumvent the Act's requirements simply by asserting that all student groups are curriculum related").

Rather, we think it clear that Westside's existing student groups include one or more "noncurriculum related student groups." Although Westside's physical education classes apparently include swimming, counsel stated at oral argument that scuba diving is not taught in any regularly offered course at the school. Based on Westside's own description of the group, Subsurfers does not directly relate to the curriculum as a whole in the same way that a student government or similar group might. Moreover, participation in Subsurfers is not required by any course at the school and does not result in extra academic credit. Thus, Subsurfers is a "noncurriculum related student group" for purposes of the Act. Similarly, although math teachers at Westside have encouraged their students to play chess, chess is not taught in any regularly offered course at the school, and participation in the chess club is not required for any class and does not result in extra credit for any class. The chess club is therefore another "noncurriculum related student group" at Westside. Moreover, Westside's principal acknowledged at trial that the Peer Advocates program—a service group that works with special education classes—does not directly relate to any courses offered by the school and is not required by any courses offered by the school. Peer Advocates would therefore also fit within our description of a "noncurriculum related student group." The record therefore supports a finding that Westside has maintained a limited open forum under the Act.

****

The remaining statutory question is whether petitioners' denial of respondents' request to form a religious group constitutes a denial of "equal access" to the school's limited open forum. Although the school apparently permits respondents to meet informally after school, App. 315-316, respondents seek equal access in the form of official recognition by the school. Official recognition allows student clubs to be part of the student activities program and carries with it access to the school newspaper, bulletin boards, the public address system, and the annual Club Fair. Given that the Act explicitly prohibits denial of "equal access . . . to . . . any students who wish to conduct a meeting within [the school's] limited open forum" on the basis of the religious content of the speech at such meetings, §4071(a), we hold that Westside's denial of respondents' request to form a Christian club denies them "equal access" under the Act.

III

Petitioners contend that even if Westside has created a limited open forum within the meaning of the Act, its denial of official recognition to the proposed Christian club must nevertheless stand because the Act violates the Establishment Clause of the First Amendment, as applied to the States through the Fourteenth Amendment. Specifically, petitioners maintain that because the school's recognized student activities are an integral part of its educational mission, official recognition of respondents' proposed club would effectively incorporate religious activities into the school's official program, endorse participation in the religious club, and provide the club with an official platform to proselytize other students.

39

We disagree. In <u>Widmar</u>, we applied the three-part <u>Lemon</u> test to hold that an "equal access" policy, at the university level, does not violate the Establishment Clause. We concluded that "an open-forum policy, including nondiscrimination against religious speech, would have a secular purpose," and would in fact avoid entanglement with religion. ("[T]he University would risk greater 'entanglement' by attempting to enforce its exclusion of religious worship' and 'religious speech"). We also found that although incidental benefits accrued to religious groups who used university facilities, this result did not amount to an establishment of religion. First, we stated that a university's forum does not "confer any imprimatur of state approval on religious sects or practices." Indeed, the message is one of neutrality rather than endorsement; if a State refused to let religious groups use facilities open to others, then it would demonstrate not neutrality but hostility toward religion. "The Establishment Clause does not license government to treat religion and those who teach or practice it, simply by virtue of their status as such, as subversive of American ideals and therefore subject to unique disabilities."

****

Because the Act on its face grants equal access to both secular and religious speech, we think it clear that the Act's purpose was not to " endorse or disapprove of religion."

****

We think that secondary school students are mature enough and are likely to understand that a school does not endorse or support student speech that it merely permits on a nondiscriminatory basis.

****

...[W]e note that the Act expressly limits participation by school officials at meetings of student religious groups, §§ 4071(c)(2) and (3), and that any such meetings must be held during "noninstructional time," § 4071(b). The Act, therefore, avoids the problems of "the students' emulation of teachers as role models" and "mandatory attendance requirements," To be sure, the possibility of student peer pressure remains, but there is little if any risk of official state endorsement or coercion where no formal classroom activities are involved and no school officials actively participate. Moreover, petitioners' fear of a mistaken inference of endorsement is largely self-imposed, because the school itself has control over any impressions it gives its students. To the extent a school makes clear that its recognition of respondents' proposed club is not an endorsement of the views of the club's participants, students will reasonably understand that the school's official recognition of the club evinces neutrality toward, rather than endorsement of, religious speech.

...[T]he broad spectrum of officially recognized student clubs at Westside, and the fact that Westside students are free to initiate and organize additional student clubs, counteract any possible message of official endorsement of or preference for religion or a particular religious belief.

****

Petitioners' final argument is that by complying with the Act's requirement, the school risks excessive entanglement between government and religion. The proposed club, petitioners urge, would be required to have a faculty sponsor who would be charged with actively directing the activities of the group, guiding its leaders, and ensuring balance in the presentation of controversial ideas. Petitioners claim that this influence over the club's religious program would entangle the

40

government in day-to-day surveillance of religion of the type forbidden by the Establishment Clause.

Under the Act, however, faculty monitors may not participate in any religious meetings, and nonschool persons may not direct, control, or regularly attend activities of student groups. §4071(c)(3) and (5). Moreover, the Act prohibits school "sponsorship" of any religious meetings, §4071(c)(2), which means that school officials may not promote, lead, or participate in any such meeting. § 4072(2). Although the Act permits "[t]he assignment of a teacher, administrator, or other school employee to the meeting for custodial purposes," such custodial oversight of the student-initiated religious group, merely to ensure order and good behavior, does not impermissibly entangle government in the day-to-day surveillance or administration of religious activities. Indeed, as the Court noted in Widmar, a denial of equal access to religious speech might well create greater entanglement problems in the form of invasive monitoring to prevent religious speech at meetings at which such speech might occur.

Accordingly, we hold that the Equal Access Act does not on its face contravene the Establishment Clause. For the foregoing reasons, the judgment of the Court of Appeals is **affirmed**.

JUSTICE STEVENS, dissenting.

The dictionary is a necessary, and sometimes sufficient, aid to the judge confronted with the task of construing an opaque act of Congress. In a case like this, however, I believe we must probe more deeply to avoid a patently bizarre result. Can Congress really have intended to issue an order to every public high school in the nation stating, in substance, that if you sponsor a chess club, a scuba diving club, or a French club—without having formal classes in those subjects—you must also open your doors to every religious, political, or social organization, no matter how controversial or distasteful its views may be? I think not. A fair review of the legislative history of the Equal Access Act (Act), 20 U. S. C. §§4071-4074, discloses that Congress intended to recognize a much narrower forum than the Court has legislated into existence today.

****

STUDY QUESTIONS

1. What test did the court adopt to determine whether secondary students could use school facilities
2. Does the ruling of the court apply to elementary student groups?
3. Does the Court's decision indicate that schools can now establish a course which provides sectarian instruction?

****

The Supreme Court addressed the constitutionality of school facility use by community sectarian groups in the in the **Lamb's Chapel** case.[154]

---

[154]Prior to the Supreme Court decision in the Lambs Chapel case the Nevada Attorney General issued its opinion No. 93-2 (OAG 93-2 March 16, 1993) relating to use of school facilities by sectarian groups. The opinion, which appears consistent with the Court holding the Lamb's Chapel case, concludes as follows:

"CONCLUSION

The Nevada Constitution does not prohibit the use of a school facility by sectarian groups for occasional worship services outside of normal school hours if the school board of trustees has created a limited public forum and the cost associated with the use is reimbursed to the school district. While it is our conclusion that the Nevada Constitution does not prohibit occasional sectarian use of public school facilities, this conclusion does not require school boards of trustees to create a limited public forum or permit sectarian activity.

This opinion reverses Op. Nev. Atty Gen. 316 (Feb. 19, 1954) insofar as it prohibited use of school facilities for a sectarian purpose with or without the payment of a rental fee." (OAG 93-2 March 16, 1993, p. 5).

LAMB'S CHAPEL ET AL
V.
CENTER MORICHES UNION FREE SCHOOL DISTRICT
___ U.S.___, 113 S Ct. 2141 (1993)

JUSTICE WHITE delivered the opinion of the Court.

Section 414 of the New York Education Law (McKinney 1988 and Supp. 1993), authorizes local school boards to adopt reasonable regulations for the use of school property for lO specified purposes when the property is not in use for school purposes. Among the permitted uses is the holding of "social, civic and recreational meetings and entertainments, and other uses pertaining to the welfare of the community; but such meetings, entertainment and uses shall be non-exclusive and open to the general public." §414(c).[155] The list of permitted uses does not include meetings for religious purposes, and a New York appellate court in Trietley v. Board of Ed. of Buffalo, 409 N. Y. S. 2d 912, 915 (App. Div. 1978), ruled that local boards could not allow student bible clubs to meet on school property because "[r]eligious purposes are not included in the enumerated purposes for which a school may be used under section 414." In Deeper Life Christian Fellowship, Inc. v. Sobol, 948 F. 2d 79, 83-94 (1991), the Court of Appeals for the Second Circuit accepted Trietley as an authoritative interpretation of state law. Furthermore, the Attorney General of New York supports Trietley as an appropriate approach to deciding this case.

Pursuant to §414's empowerment of local school districts, the Board of Center Moriches Union Free School District (District) has issued rules and regulations with respect to the use of school property when not in use for school purposes. The rules allow only 2 of the 10 purposes authorized by §414: social, civic, or recreational uses (Rule 10) and use by political organizations if secured in compliance with §414 (Rule 8). Rule 7, however, consistent with the judicial interpretation of state law, provides that "[t]he school premises shall not be used by any group for religious purposes." App. to Pet. for Cert. 57a. The issue in this case is whether, against this background of state law, it violates the Free Speech Clause of the First Amendment, made applicable to the States by the Fourteenth Amendment, to deny a church access to school premises to exhibit for public viewing and for assertedly religious purposes, a film dealing with family and child-rearing issues faced by parents today.

I

Petitioners (Church) are Lamb's Chapel, an evangelical church in the community of Center Moriches, and its pastor John Steigerwald. Twice the Church applied to the District for permission to use school facilities to show a six-part film series containing lectures by Doctor James Dobson.[156] A brochure provided on request of the District identified Dr. Dobson as a licensed psychologist, former associate clinical professor of pediatrics at the University of Southern California, best-selling author, and radio commentator. The brochure stated that the film series

---

See also Wallace v. Washoe County School Dist., 701 F. Supp. 187 (1988) and Wallace V. Washoe County School Dist., Case No. CV-N-88-302-BRT.

[155]Section 414(e) authorizes the use of school property "[f]or polling places for holding primaries and elections and for the registration of voters and for holding political meetings. But no meetings sponsored by political organizations shall be permitted unless authorized by a vote of a district meeting, held as provided by law, or, in cities by the board of education thereof."

[156]Shortly before the first of these requests, the Church had applied for permission to use school rooms for its Sunday morning services and for Sunday School. The hours specified were 9 a.m. to 1 p.m. and the time period one year beginning in the next month. Lamb's Chapel v. Center Moriches Union Free School Dist., 959 F. 2d 381, 383 (CA2 1992). Within a few days the District wrote petitioner that the application "requesting use of the high school for your Sunday services" was denied, citing both the State Education Law § 414 and the District's Rule 7 barring uses for religious purposes. The Church did not challenge this denial in the courts and the validity of this denial is not before us.

would discuss Dr. Dobson's views on the undermining influences of the media that could only be counterbalanced by returning to traditional, Christian family values instilled at an early stage. The brochure went on to describe the contents of each of the six parts of the series.[157] The District denied the first application, saying that "[t]his film does appear to be church related and therefore your request must be refused." App. 84. The second application for permission to use school premises for showing the film, which described it as a "Family oriented movie—from the Christian perspective," App. 91, was denied using identical language.

The Church brought suit in District Court, challenging the denial as a violation of the Freedom of Speech and Assembly Clauses, the Free Exercise Clause, and the Establishment Clause of the First Amendment, as well as the Equal Protection Clause of the Fourteenth Amendment. As to each cause of action, the Church alleged that the actions were undertaken under color of state law, in violation of 42 U. S. C. §1983. The District Court granted summary judgment for respondents, rejecting all of the Church's claims. With respect to the free-speech claim under the First Amendment, the District Court characterized the District's facilities as a"limited public forum." The court noted that the enumerated purposes for which §414 allowed access to school facilities did not include religious worship or instruction, that Rule 7 explicitly proscribes using school facilities for religious purposes, and that the Church had conceded that its showing of the film would be for religious purposes. 770 F. Supp. 91, 92, 98-99 (EDNY 1991). The District Court stated that once a limited public forum is opened to a particular type of speech, selectively denying access to other activities of the same genre is forbidden. Id., at 99. Noting that the District had not opened its facilities to organizations similar to Lamb's Chapel for religious purposes, the District Court held that the denial in this case was viewpoint neutral and, hence, not a violation of the Freedom of Speech Clause. Ibid. The District Court also rejected the assertion by the Church that denying its application demonstrated a hostility to religion and advancement of nonreligion not justified under the Establishment of Religion Clause of the First Amendment. 736 F. Supp. 1247, 1253 (EDNY 1990).

The Court of Appeals affirmed the judgment of the District Court "in all respects." Lamb's Chapel v. Center Moriches Union Free School Dist., 959 F. 2d 381, 389 (CA2 1992). It held that the school property, when not in use for school purposes, was neither a traditional nor a designated public forum; rather, it was a limited public forum open only for designated purposes, a classification that "allows it to remain non-public except as to specified uses." Id., at 386. The court observed

---

[157]"Turn Your Heart Toward Home is available now in a senes of six discussion-provoking films:

"1) A FATHER LOOKS BACK emphasizes how swiftly time passes and appeals to all parents to 'turn their hearts toward home' during the all-important child-rearing years. (60 minutes.)

"2) POWER IN PARENTING: THE YOUNG CHILD begins by exploring the inherent nature of power, and offers many practical helps for facing the battlegrounds in child-rearing—bedtime, mealtime and other confrontations so familiar to parents. Dr. Dobson also takes a look at areas of conflict in marriage and other adult relationships. (60 minutes.)

"3) POWER IN PARENTING: THE ADOLESCENT discusses father/daughter and mother/son relstionships, and the importance of allowing children to grow to develop as individuals. Dr. Dobson also encourages parents to free themselves of undeserved guilt when their teenagers choose to rebel. (45 minutes.)

"4) THE FAMILY UNDER FIRE views the family in the context of today's society, where a "civil war of values" is being waged. Dr. Dobson urges parents to look at the effects of governmental interference, abortion and pornography, and to get involved. To preserve what they care about most—their own families! (52 minutes

Note: This film contains explicit information regarding the pornoraphy industry. Not recommended for young audiences.

"5) OVERCOMING A PAINFUL CHILDHOOD includes Shirley Dobson's intimate memories of a difficult childhood with her alcoholic father. Mrs. Dobson recalls the influences which brought her to a loving God who saw her personal circumstances and heard her cries for help. (40 minutes)

"6) THE HERITAGE presents Dr. Dobson's powerful closing remarks. Here he speaks clearly and convincingly of our traditional values which, if properly employed and defended, can assure happy, healthy strengthened homes and family relatlonships in the years to come. (60 minutes)" App. 87-88.

43

that exclusions in such a forum need only be reasonable and viewpoint neutral, ibid., and ruled that denying access to the Church for the purpose of showing its film did not violate this standard. Because the holding below was questionable under our decisions, we granted the petition for certiorari, 506 U. S. _ (1992), which in principal part challenged the holding below as contrary to the Free Speech Clause of the First Amendment.[158]

II

There is no question that the District, like the private owner of property, may legally preserve the property under its control for the use to which it is dedicated. Cornelius v. NAACP Legal Defense and Ed. Fund, Inc., 473 U. S. 788, 800 (1985); Perry Ed. Assn. v. Perry Local Educators' Assn., 460 U. S. 37, 46 (1983); United States Postal Service v. Council of Greenburgh Civic Assns., 453 U. S. 114, 129-130 (1981); Greer v. Spock, 424 U. S. 828, 836 (1976); Adderley v. Florida, 385 U. S. 39, 47 (1966). It is also common ground that the District need not have permitted after-hours use of its property for any of the uses permitted by §414 of the state education law. The District, however, did open its property for 2 of the 10 uses permitted by §414. The Church argued below that because under Rule 10 of the rules issued by the District, school property could be used for "social, civic, and recreational" purposes, the District had opened its property for such a wide variety of communicative purposes that restrictions on communicative uses of the property were subject to the same constitutional limitations as restrictions in traditional public fora such as parks and sidewalks. Hence, its view was that subject-matter or speaker exclusions on District property were required to be justified by a compelling state interest and to be narrowly drawn to achieve that end. See Perry, supra, at 45; Cornelius, supra, at 800. Both the District Court and the Court of Appeals rejected this submission, which is also presented to this Court. The argument has considerable force, for the District's property is heavily used by a wide variety of private organizations, including some that presented a "close question," which the Court of Appeals resolved in the District's favor, as to whether the District had in fact already opened its property for religious uses. 959 F. 2d, at 387.[159] We need not

---

[158]The petition also presses the claim by the Church, rejected by both courts below, that the rejection of its application to exhibit its film violated the Establishment Clause because it and Rule 7's categorical refusal to permit District property to be used for religious purposes demonstrate hostility to religion. Because we reverse on another ground, we need not decide what merit this submission might have.

[159]In support of its case in the Distnct Court, the Church presented the following sampling of the uses that had been permitted under Rule 10 in 1987 and 1988:

    A New Age religious group known as the 'Mind Center'
    Southern Harmonize Gospel Singers
    Salvation Army Youth Band
    Hampton Council of Churches' Billy Taylor Concert
    Center Moriches Co-op Nursery School's Quilting Bee
    Manorville Humane Society's Chinese Auction
    Moriches Bay Power Squadron
    Unkechaug Dance Group
    Paul Gibson's Baseball Clinic
    Moriches Bay Civic Association
    Moriches Chamber of Commerce's Town Fair Day
    Center Moriches Drama Club
    Center Moriches Music Award Associations' 'Amahl & the Night Visitors'
    Saint John's Track and Field Progrnm
    Girl Scouts of Suffolk [C]ounty
    Cub Scouts Pack 23
    Boy Scout Troop #414[.]" 770 F. Supp. 91, 93, n.4 (EDNY 1991).

    The Church claimed that the first three uses listed above demonstrated that Rule IO actually permitted the District property to be used for religious purposes as well as a great assortment of other uses. The first item listed is particularly interesting and relevant to the issue before us. The District Court referred to this item as "a lecture series by the Mind Center, purportedly a New Age religious group." 770 F. Supp., at 93. The Court of Appeals described it as follows:

"The lecture series,'Psychology and TheUnknown,'by Jerry Huck,was sponsored by the Center Moriches Free Public Library. The library's newsletter characterized Mr. Huck as a psychotherapist who would discuss such topics as parapsychology, transpersonal psychology, physics and metaphysics in his 4-night series of lectures. Mr. Huck testified that he lectured principally on parapsychology, which he defined by

rule on this issue however, for even if the courts below were correct in this respect—and we shall assume for present purposes that they were—the judgment below must be reversed.

With respect to public property that is not a designated public forum open for indiscriminate public use for communicative purposes, we have said that "[c]ontrol over access to a nonpublic forum can be based on subject matter and speaker identity so long as the distinctions drawn are reasonable in light of the purpose served by the forum and are viewpoint neutral." Cornelius, supra, at 806, citing Perry Education Assn., supra, at 49. The Court of Appeals appeared to recognize that the total ban on using District property for religious purposes could survive First Amendment challenge only if excluding this category of speech was reasonable and viewpoint neutral. The court's conclusion in this case was that Rule 7 met this test. We cannot agree with this holding, for Rule 7 was unconstitutionally applied in this case.[160]

The Court of Appeals thought that the application of Rule 7 in this case was viewpoint neutral because it had been and would be applied in the same way to all uses of school property for religious purposes. That all religions and all uses for religious purposes are treated alike under Rule 7, however, does not answer the critical question whether it discriminates on the basis of viewpoint to permit school property to be used for the presentation of all views about family issues and child-rearing except those dealing with the subject matter from a religious standpoint.

There is no suggestion from the courts below or from the District or the State that a lecture or film about child- rearing and family values would not be a use for social or civic purposes otherwise permitted by Rule 10. That subject matter is not one that the District has placed off limits to any and all speakers. Nor is there any indication in the record before us that the application to exhibit the particular film involved here was or would have been denied for any reason other than the fact that the presentation would have been from a religious perspective. In our view, denial on that basis was plainly invalid under our holding in Cornelius, 473 U. S., at 806, that

> "[a]lthough a speaker may be excluded from a non-public forum if he wishes to address a topic not encompassed within the purpose of the forum . . . or if he is not a member of the class of speakers for whose special benefit the forum was created . . . the government violates the First Amendment when it denies access to a speaker solely to suppress the point of view he espouses on an otherwise includible subject."

The film involved here no doubt dealt with a subject otherwise permissible under Rule 10, and its exhibition was denied solely because the film dealt with the subject from a religious standpoint. The principle that has emerged from our cases "is that the First Amendment forbids the government to regulate speech in ways that favor some viewpoints or ideas at the expense of others." City Council of Los Angeles v. Taxpayers for Vincent, 466 U. S. 789, 804 (1984). That principle applies in the

---

'reference to the human unconscious, the mind, the unconscious emotional system or the body system.' When asked whether his lecture involved matters of both a spiritual and a scienhfic nature, Mr. Huck responded: 'It was all science. Anything I speak on based on parapsychology, analytic, quantum physicists [sic].' Although some incidental reference to religious matters apparently was made in the lectures, Mr. Huck himself characterized such matters as 'a fascinating sideline' and 'not the purpose of the [lecture.]'" 959 F. 2d, at 388.

[160]Although the Court of Appeals apparently held that Rule 7 was reasonable as well as viewpoint neutral, the court uttered not a word in support of its reasonableness holding. If Rule 7 were to be held unreasonable, it could be held facially invalid, that is, it might be held that the rule could in no circumstances be applied to religious speech or religious communicative conduct. In view of our disposition of this case, we need not pursue the issue.

circumstances of this case; as Judge Posner said for the Seventh Circuit Court of Appeals, to discriminate "against a particular point of view . . . would . . . flunk the test . . . [of] Cornelius, provided that the defendants have no defense based on the establishment clause." May v. Evansville Vonderburgh School Corp., 787 F. 2d 1105, 1114 (1986).

The District, as a respondent, would save its judgment below on the ground that to permit its property to be used for religious purposes would be an establishment of religion forbidden by the First Amendment. This Court suggested in Widmar v. Vincent, 454 U. S. 263, 271 (1981), that the interest of the State in avoiding an Establishment Clause violation "may be [a] compelling" one justifying an abridgment of free speech otherwise protected by the First Amendment; but the Court went on to hold that permitting use of University property for religious purposes under the open access policy involved there would not be incompatible with the Court's Establishment Clause cases.

We have no more trouble than did the Widmar Court in disposing of the claimed defense on the ground that the posited fears of an Establishment Clause violation are unfounded. The showing of this film would not have been during school hours, would not have been sponsored by the school, and would have been open to the public, not just to church members. The District property had repeatedly been used by a vide variety of private organizations. Under these circumstances, as in Widmar, there would have been no realistic danger that the community would think that the District was endorsing religion or any particular creed, and any benefit to religion or to the Church would have been no more than incidental. As in Widmar, supra, at 271-272, permitting District property to be used to exhibit the film involved in this case would not have been an establishment of religion under the three-part test articulated in Lemon v. Kurtzman, 403 U. S. 602 (1971): The challenged governmental action has a secular purpose, does not have the principal or primary effect of advancing or inhibiting religion, and does not foster an escessive entanglement with religion.[161]

The District also submits that it justifiably denied use of its property to a "radical" church for the purpose of proselytizing, since to do so would lead to threats of public unrest and even violence. Brief for Respondent Center Moriches Union Free School District, et al. 4-5,11-12, 24. There is nothing in the record to support such a justification, which in any event would be difficult to defend as a reason to deny the presentation of a religious point of view about a subject the District otherwise makes open to discussion on District property.

We note that the Attorney General for the State of New York, a respondent here, does not rely on either the Establishment Clause or possible danger to the public peace in supporting the judgment below. Rather, he submits that the exclusion is justified because the purpose of the access rules is to promote the interests of the public in general rather than sectarian or other private interests. In light of the variety of the uses of District property that have been permitted under Rule 10, this approach has its difficulties. This is particularly so since Rule 10 states that District property may be used for social, civic, or recreational use "only if it can be non-exclusive and open to all residents of the school district that form a

---

[161]While we are somewhat diverted by JUSTICE SCALIA'S evening at the cinema, post, at 1-3, we return to the reality that there is a proper way to inter an established decision and Lemon, however frightening it might be to some, has not been overruled. This case, like Corporation of Presiding Bishop of Church of Jesus Christ of Latter-day Saints v. Amos 483 U. S. 327 (1987), presents no occasion to do so. JUSTICE SCALIA apparently was less haunted by the ghosts of the living when he joined the opinion of the Court in that case.

homogeneous group deemed relevant to the event." App. to Pet. for Cert. 57a. At least arguably, the Rule does not require that permitted uses need be open to the public at large. However that may be, this was not the basis of the judgment that we are reviewing. The Court of Appeals, as we understand it, ruled that because the District had the power to permit or exclude certain subject matters, it was entitled to deny use for any religious purpose, including the purpose in this case. The Attorney General also defends this as a permissible subject-matter exclusion rather than a denial based on viewpoint, a submission that we have already rejected.

The Attorney General also argues that there is no express finding below that the Church's application would have been granted absent the religious connection. This fact is beside the point for the purposes of this opinion, which is concerned with the validity of the stated reason for denying the Church's application, namely, that the film sought to be shown "appeared to be church related."

For the reasons stated in this opinion, the judgment of the Court of Appeals is
Reversed.

JUSTICE KENNEDY, concurring in part and concurring in the judgment.

Given the issues presented as well as the apparent unanimity of our conclusion that this overt, viewpoint-based discrimination contradicts the Speech Clause of the First Amendment and that there has been no substantial showing of a potential Establishment Clause violation, I agree with JUSTICE SCALIA that the Court's citation of Lemon v. Kurtzman, 403 U. S. 602 (1971), is unsettling and unnecessary. The same can be said of the Court's use of the phrase "endorsing religion," see ante, at 10 which, as I have indicated elsewhere, cannot suffice as a rule of decision consistent with our precedents and our traditions in this part of our jurisprudence. See Allegheny County v. American Civil Liberties Union, Greater Pittsburgh Chapter, 492 U. S. 573, 655 (KENNEDY, J., concurring in judgment in part and dissenting in part). With these observations, I concur in part and concur in the judgment.

JUSTICE SCALIA, with whom JUSTICE THOMAS joins, concurring in the judgment.

I join the Court's conclusion that the District's refusal to allow use of school facilities for petitioners' film viewing, while generally opening the schools for community activities, violates petitioners' First Amendment free-speech rights (as does N. Y. Educ. Law §414 (McKinney 1988 and Supp. 1993), to the extent it compelled the District's denial, see ante, at 1-2). I also agree with the Court that allowing Lamb's Chapel to use school facilities poses "no realistic danger" of a violation of the Establishment Clause, ante, at 10, but I cannot accept most of its reasoning in this regard. The Court explains that the showing of petitioners' film on school property after school hours would not cause the community to "think that the District was endorsing religion or any particular creed," and further notes that access to school property would not violate the three-part test articulated in Lemon v. Kurtzman, 403 U. S. 602 (1971). Ante, at 10.

As to the Court's invocation of the Lemon test: Like some ghoul in a late-night horror movie that repeatedly sits up in its grave and shuffles abroad, after being repeatedly killed and buried, Lemon stalks our Establishment Clause jurisprudence once again, frightening the little children and school attorneys of Center Moriches Union Free School District. Its most recent burial, only last Term, was, to be sure, not fully six-feet under: our decision in <u>Lee</u> v. <u>Weisman,</u> 505 U. S.___, ___ (1992) (slip op., at 7), conspicuously avoided using the supposed "test" but also declined the invitation to repudiate it. Over the years, however, no fewer than five of the currently sitting Justices have, in their own opinions, personally driven pencils through the creature's heart (the author of today's opinion repeatedly), and a sixth has joined an opinion doing so.... (citations omitted)

The secret of the Lemon test's survival, I think, is that it is so easy to kill. It is there to scare us (and our audience) when we wish it to do so, but we can command it to return to the tomb at will. See, e.g., <u>Lynch</u> v. <u>Donnelly</u>, 465 U. S. 668, 679 (1984) (noting instances in which Court has not applied Lemon test). When we wish to strike down a practice it forbids, we invoke it, see, e.g., <u>Aguilar</u> v. <u>Felton</u>, 473 U S 402 (1985) (striking down state remedial education program administered in part in parochial schools); when we wish to uphold a practice it forbids, we ignore it entirely, see <u>Marsh</u> v. <u>Chambers,</u> 463 U. S. 783 (1983) (upholding state legislative chaplains). Sometimes, we take a middle course, calling its three prongs "no more than helpful signposts," <u>Hunt</u> v. <u>McNair,</u> 413 U. S. 734, 741 (1973). Such a docile and useful monster is worth keeping around, at least in a somnolent state; one never knows when one might need him.

For my part, I agree with the long list of constitutional scholars who have criticized Lemon and bemoaned the strange Establishment Clause geometry of crooked lines and wavering shapes its intermittent use has produced....(citations omitted)... I will decline to apply Lemon—whether it validates or invalidates the government action in question—and therefore cannot join the opinion of the Court today.[162]

I cannot join for yet another reason: the Court's statement that the proposed use of the school's facilities is constitutional because (among other things) it would not signal endorsement of religion in general. Ante, at 10. What a strange notion, that a Constitution which itself gives "religion in general" preferential treatment (I refer to the Free Exercise Clause) forbids endorsement of religion in general. The Attorney General of New York not only agrees with that strange notion, he has an explanation for it: "Religious advocacy," he writes, "serves the community only in the eyes of its adherents and yields a benefit only to those who already believe." Brief for Respondent Attorney General 24. That was not the view of those who adopted our Constitution, who believed that the public virtues inculcated by religion are a public good. It suffices to point out that during the summer of 1789, when it was in the process of drafting the First Amendment, Congress enacted the famous Northwest Territory Ordinance of 1789, Article III of which provides, "Religion, morality, and knowledge, being necessary to good government and the happiness of mankind, schools and the means of education shall forever be encouraged." 1 Stat. 52 (emphasis added). Unsurprisingly, then, indifference to "religion in general" is not what our cases, both old and recent, demand. See, e.g., <u>Zorach</u> v. <u>Clauson,</u> 343 U. S. 306, 313-314 (1952) (When the state encourages religious instruction or cooperates with religious authorities by adjusting the schedule of public events to sectarian needs, it follows the best of our traditions"); <u>Walz</u> v. <u>Tax</u> <u>Comm'n</u> <u>of</u> <u>New</u> <u>York</u> <u>City</u>, 397 U. S. 664 (1970) (upholding property tax exemption for church

---

[162]The Court correctly notes, ante, at 10-11, n. 7, that I joined the opinion in <u>Corporation of Presiding Bishop of Church of Jesus Christ of Latter-day Saints v. Amos</u>, 483 U. S. 327 (1987), which considered the Lemon test. Lacking a majority at that time to abandon Lemon, we necessarily focused on that test, which had been the exclusive basis for the lower court's judgment, Here, of course, the lower court did not mention Lemon, and indeed did not even address any Establishment Clause argument on behalf of respondents. Thus, the Court is ultimately correct that Presiding Bishop provides a useful comparison: it was as impossible to avoid Lemon there, as it is unnecessary to inject Lemon here.

property); <u>Lynch</u>, 465 U. S., at 673 (the Constitution "affirmatively mandates accommodation, not merely tolerance, of all religions .... Anything less would require the 'callous indifference' we have said was never intended" (citations omitted)); id., at 683 ("our precedents plainly contemplate that on occasion some advancement of religion will result from governmental action"); Marsh, supra; Presiding Bishop, supra (exemption for religious organizations from certain provisions of Civil Rights Act).

For the reasons given by the Court, I agree that the Free Speech Clause of the First Amendment forbids what respondents have done here. As for the asserted Establishment Clause justification, I would hold, simply and clearly, that giving Lamb's Chapel nondiscriminatory access to school facilities cannot violate that provision because it does not signify state or local embrace of a particular religious sect.

I Concur in the Judgment

****

Specific Powers--School Property Cont.

Local school boards are further empowered to build,[163] purchase or rent schoolhouses, change the location of schools, and close [164] a school or change its use. But if the trustees propose to change a schools location, close or change the use of a school building they must give 30 days written notice to the principal and teachers of the affected school and to the parents of the children attending that school.[165] Any resident aggrieved by a decision to close or change the use of a school may request reconsideration. Upon the receipt of such a request the board must schedule a hearing on the matter. Any resident aggrieved by the reconsideration decision may appeal to the state board. The decision of the state board on the matter is final subject to judicial review as provided by law.[166]

Library books, textbooks, and other school supplies must be purchased by the board. The materials purchased must be loaned to the students while pursuing their course of study. Parents are responsible for lost or damaged school property.[167]

The board is empowered to sell, lease or rent property owned by the district if the board finds such action is necessary for the best interest of the district.[168] The legislature has specified procedures applicable to sale, lease or exchange transactions.[169]

---

[163]Chapter 314 Laws of Nevada (1993) amends Chapter 338 NRS (1991) relating to public works authorizing alternative financing for the retrofitting of buildings occupied by state or local governmental entities to make use of energy in the buildings more efficient.

Chapter 539 Laws of Nevada (1993) amends Chapter 338 relating to public works contracts. The law disqualifies persons that have had an administrative penalty imposed from receiving public works contracts. Chapter 602 Laws of Nevada (1993) is only applicable to Mineral County. The Board of Trustees of the Mineral County School District has been unable to find a means of replacing a school for 23 years since its condemnation. The district also needs to build and renovate other school facilities since the pupil population has grown 20% per year the last two years. The legislation authorizes the board of county commissioners to hold a special election for the purpose of seeking permission to issue bonds for replacing the Schurz school and other facilities.

Chapter 546 Laws of Nevada (1993) requires school districts to comply with the requirements of the building code of a city or county in which the school building is located.

Chapter 577 Laws of Nevada (1993) amends Sec. 393.080 NRS (1991) authorizing the board of trustees of a school district to supervise and inspect certain construction work performed for the school district. (Liability considerations should be carefully considered before adopting this option)

[164] Prior to the notice statutes discussed infra., the Nevada supreme court decided <u>Bartlett</u> v. <u>Board</u> of <u>Trustees</u>, 92 Nev. 347, 550 P.2d 416 (1976). In that case the court held that an order of the trustees to close a rural high school was an abuse of the discretion.

[165] Sec. 393.080 NRS (1991)

[166] Sec. 393.085 NRS (1991)

[167] Sec. 393.170 NRS (1991)

[168] Sec. 393.220 NRS (1991)

[169] Sec. 393.240-3293 NRS (1991)

Other Specific Powers of Local Boards

In 1993 the legislature empowered school districts to establish alternative programs for the education of pupils at risk of dropping out of high school.[170] Operation of the alternative program developed by the local board is subject to approval of the state board.

When any school district has and maintains more than one school offering instruction in the same grade the board is authorized to zone the district to determine which pupils shall attend each school.[171] The trustees are also empowered, with the consent of the juvenile court and the county commissioners, to provide instruction in detention homes, juvenile forestry camps and training camps.[172]

Boards are specifically empowered to accept Federal assistance if their district is affected by federal activities,[173] administer oaths,[174] accept gifts,[175] employ private legal counsel,[176] form a nonprofit association composed of all school districts for the purposes of controlling, supervising and regulating all interscholastic athletic events and other interscholastic events in the public schools [177] operate and provide programs of nutrition for children and adults.[178]

---

[170]Chapter 215 Laws of Nevada (1993) creates a new section in Chapter 388 NRS (1993) The legislation is focused on pupils who because of extenuating circumstances, such as being pregnant, parents, chronically ill or self-supporting are not able to attend the classes of instruction regularly provided in high school; are deficient in the amount of academic credit necessary to graduate with pupils their same age; are chronically absent from high school; or require instruction on a more personal basis than that regularly provided in high school. (Chapter 215 Laws of Nevada (1993) Chapter 388 Sec. 1) An alternative program may include: a shorter school day, and an opportunity for pupils to attend a longer school day, than that regularly provided in high school, an opportunity for pupils to attend classes of instruction during any part of the calendar year, a comprehensive curriculum that includes elective classes of instruction and occupational education, a comprehensive curriculum that includes elective classes of instruction and occupational education, an opportunity for pupils to obtain academic credit through experience gained at work or while engaged in other activities, an opportunity for pupils to satisfy either the requirement for a regular high school diploma or a diploma for adults, the provision of child care for the children of pupils, the transportation of pupils to and from classes of instruction and the temporary placement of pupils for independent study, if there are extenuating circumstances which prevent those pupils from attending the alternative program on a daily basis. (Chapter 215 Laws of Nevada (1993) Chapter 388 Sec. 2)

[171] Sec. 388.040 NRS (1993). Zoning decisions are subject to scrutiny under the equal protection clause of the 14th amendment. See Brown v. Board of Education infra.

[172] Sec. 388.550-570 NRS (1993)

[173] Sec. 386.355 NRS (1993)

[174] Sec. 386.380 NRS (1993)

[175] Sec. 386.390 NRS (1993)

[176] Sec. 386.410 NRS (1993)

[177] Sec. 386.420-470 NRS (1993)

[178] Sec. 386.415 NRS (1993). See also Sec. 385.109 NRS (1993). Chapter 659 Laws of Nevada (1993) amends Chapter 387 expanding eligible participants in programs of nutrition provided through school to the adult population.

Local Board Duties

The legislature has directed that school boards adopt a program providing for the accountability to the residents of the district for the quality of the schools and the educational achievement of the pupils in the district.[179] Associations recognized as representing education personnel in the district must be involved in development of the program. A bill revising the program of accountability was adopted during the 1993 legislative session.[180]

Now the program must require the board of trustees to report to district residents and the state board regarding the quality of district schools and the achievement of the pupils in the district. The report to residents is due each March. The contents of the report must include:

> (a) The educational goals and objectives of the school district;
>
> (b) A comparison of pupil achievement for each school in the district and the district as a whole at each age and grade level for the current school year with that of previous school years;
>
> (c) The ratio of pupils to teachers at each grade level for each school in the district and the district as a whole and other data concerning licensed and unlicensed employees of the school district;
>
> (d) A comparison of the types of classes that each teacher has been assigned to teach with the qualifications and licensure of the teacher for each school in the district and the district as a whole;
>
> (e) The total expenditure per pupil, set forth individually for each source of funding for each school in the district and the district as a whole;
>
> (f) The curriculum used by the school district, including any special programs for pupils at an individual school;
>
> (g) Records of the attendance and advancement of pupils in all grades, for each school in the district and the district as a whole, and of graduation rates for pupils in high school; and
>
> (h) Efforts made by the school district and by each school in the district to increase communication with the parents of pupils in the district;
>
> (i) such other information as is directed by the superintendent of public instruction.[181]

The report must be submitted to the state board on or before April 15 of each year.[182]

In addition, on or before June 15 of each year the board of trustees must submit a separate report summarizing the effectiveness of the district's program of accountability during the school year and a description of the efforts the district has made to correct deficiencies identified in the effectiveness report.[183]

The state superintendent is given specific responsibilities regarding implementation of district accountabillty programs.[184] The superintendent is directed to prescribe the forms to be utilized by the respective school districts for reporting to school district residents and provide statistical information and

---

[179] Sec. 385.347 NRS (1993).

[180] Chapter 644 Laws of Nevada (1993) amending Sec. 385.347 NRS (1991).

[181] Sec. 385.347 3 NRS (1993).

[182] Chapter 644 Laws of Nevada (1993) adding Sec. 385.347 4 NRS (1993).

[183] Chapter 644 Laws of Nevada (1993) adding Sec. 385.347 4 NRS (1993).

[184] Chapter 644 Laws of Nevada (1993) adding Sec. 385.347 3 NRS (1993).

technical assistance to the school districts to ensure that the reports provide comparable information with respect to each school in each district and among the districts. He/she is also directed the consult with the Nevada State Education Association, the Nevada Association of School Boards the Nevada Association of School Administrators and the Nevada Parents Teachers Association regarding the accountability program.

School Curriculum

Duties imposed by the state may restrict the local board's control of curriculum. For example, the Trustees are required to enforce the courses of study prescribed and adopted by the state board.[185]

In 1993 the legislature adopted a statute requiring local boards to establish a program of instruction relating to child abuse for pupils in kindergarten and grades 1 to 6 inclusive.[186] The law provides that the program must include, without limitation, instruction relating to the types of child abuse and the methods used to recognize, report, prevent and stop child abuse.[187]In addition, the legislature urged each school district to develop alternative programs of education for pupils who have been suspended or expelled or who are otherwise dangerous to other pupils.[188] If such programs are established the law requires that the school district submit a report to the next legislative session evaluating the program including any recommended legislation.[189]

Another specific provision addresses instruction on acquired immune deficiency syndrome (AIDS), human reproductive system, related communicable diseases and sexual responsibility.[190] The statute reads as follows:

1. The board of trustees of a school district shall establish a course or unit of a course of:

(a) Factual instruction concerning acquired immune deficiency syndrome;

(b) Instruction on the human reproductive system, related communicable diseases and sexual responsibility.

2. Each board of trustees shall appoint an advisory committee consisting of;

(a) Five parents of children who attend schools in the district; and

(b) Four representatives, one from each of four of the following professions or occupations:

(1) Medicine or nursing;

(2) Counseling;

(3) Religion;

---

[185] Sec.389.010 NRS (1993)

[186]Chapter 223 Laws of Nevada (1993) adds a new section to Chapter 389. Chapter 223 Laws of Nevada Sec. 1 (1993)

[187]Chapter 223 Laws of Nevada Sec. 2 (1993). Implementation of this statute poses some difficult questions for local boards. What process should the board use to develop the program? Should a committee composed of diverse interests professional expertise and experience be established to make recommendations to the board? What interests should be represented on such a committee; law enforcement experts, juvenile authorities, medical professionals, mental health workers, educators, child psychologists, religious leaders, parents, others? How do you instruct kindergarten, first and second students to recognize, report, prevent and stop child abuse? How much school time should be devoted to the issue? What staff development should precede implementation of the program? Unlike instruction in AIDS, the human reproductive system and related communicable diseases (see Sec. 389.065 (1993) the legislature has not required parental notice or consent prior to instruction. Should the board make an effort to share the nature and content of the curriculum with parents prior to all children (K-6) receiving the instruction? Note the legislature has not appropriated any financial assistance for local boards to accomplish the statutory directive.

[188]Chapter 561 Laws of Nevada Sec. 10 (1) (a) (1993)

[189]Chapter 561 Laws of Nevada Sec. 10 (2) (1993)

[190] Sec. 389.065 NRS (1993)

(4) Pupils who attend schools in the district; or
(5) Teaching.
This committee shall advise the district concerning the content of and materials to be used in a course of instruction established pursuant to this section, and the recommended ages of the pupils to whom the course is offered. The final decision on these matters must be that of the board of trustees.
3. The subjects of the courses may be taught only by a teacher or school nurse whose qualifications have been previously approved by the board of trustees.
4. The parent or guardian of each pupil to whom a course is offered must first be furnished written notice that the course will be offered. The notice must be given in the usual manner used by the local district to transmit written material to parents, and must contain a form for the signature of the parent or guardian of the pupil consenting to his attendance. Upon receipt of the written consent of the parent or guardian, the pupil may attend the course. If the written consent of the parent or guardian is not received, he must be excused from such attendance without any penalty as to credits or academic standing. Any course offered pursuant to this section is not a requirement for graduation.
5. All instructional materials to be used in a course must be available for inspection by parents or guardians of pupils at reasonable times and locations before the course is taught, and appropriate written notice of the availability of the material must be furnished to all parents and guardians.[191]

****

School Curriculum-Cont.

Boards must also enforce the use of basic textbooks prescribed and adopted by the state board.[192] Supplemental textbooks may be purchased by school districts upon the approval of the state superintendent. Temporary use of textbooks is also subject to approval by the state board.[193] School personnel that violate the textbook requirements are subject to a fine of not more than $250.

Another specific duty imposed by the legislature is the establishment of kindergartens if 15 children or more petition for admission.[194]

Testing

School districtsSchool Districts:Duties:School Curriculum:Achievement/proficiency testsmust administer state prepared reading, writing and math examinations to determine the achievement and proficiency of students.[195] The examinations must be administered before completion of the 4th,

---

[191] Sec. Ibid., Compare this approach to the policy recently adopted by the school board of New York City which allows condoms to be distributed upon student request. Parent wishes are disregarded under the New York policy. A court challenge to the policy proved unsuccessful. See Alfonso v. Fernandez, 584 N.Y.S.2d 406 (1992).

[192] Sec. 390.220.NRS (1993)

[193] Sec. 390.230.(2) (b)-(c) NRS (1993)

[194] Sec. 388.060 NRS (1991)

[195] Chapter 213 Laws of Nevada (1993) amends Sec. 389.015 NRS (1991) changing the grades during which examinations for achievement and proficiency are administered replacing grades 3, 6, 9 and 12 with 4, 8 and 11. Chapter 424 Laws of Nevada (1993) amemds Chapter 213 Laws of

8th and 11th grades.[196] A student who fails to meet proficiency standards for 4th and 8th grade may be promoted to the next grade but the examination results must be assessed to determine what remedial study is appropriate. If a student fails to pass the proficiency examination adinistered before grade 11 he/she must not be graduated until able, through remedial study to pass the examination.[197] However, a certificate attendance may be granted in the place of a diploma if the student has reached the age of 17. Different standards of competence may be adopted for pupils with diagnosed learning disabilities. Results of the tests are reported to the state superintendent.[198]

School Day\Year

Another specific duty is the requirement that local boards maintain their schools for an equal length of time and with equal rights and privileges as far as practicable.[199]

The school year and minimum number of school days are prescribed by the state.[200] The minimum number of days is set at 180. The number of days may be reduced by up to 10 if the trustees can show that the students are receiving equivalent hours of instruction. Three contingent days must be scheduled to be used in case the schools are closed due to natural disaster or inclement weather. Schools must be closed on legal holidays. However, any board may elect to keep school open on October 31 or other day observed as Nevada Day.[201]

The school day is also regulated by legislative direction.[202] Every school district must set aside a period at the beginning of the school day, during which all persons must be silent for voluntary individual meditation, prayer or reflection.[203]

Class Size Reduction

In 1989 the legislature embarked on an ambitious class size reduction program applicable in selected Kindergartens and grades 1 and 2. Under the program school districts were directed to reduce the pupil-teacher ratio in classes where the core curriculum was taught to no more than 15 to 1. A trust fund was established administered by the state superintendent and state board to finance the program.

In 1991 the legislature extended local district responsibility under the program to grade 3 to be effective at the beginning of the 1992-93 school year.[204] The legislature again utilized a trust fund and appropriated resources to achieve the mandate.[205] The responsibility for distributing the funds was given to the state

---

Nevada (1993) at the time of the amendment known as Senate Bill 67 requiring school districts to administer proficiency tests to 9th graders in the 1993-94 school year and report the results to the state department.

[196] Chapter 213 Laws of Nevada (1993) amends Sec. 389.015 NRS (1991) changing the grades during which examinations for achievement and proficiency are administered replacing grades 3,6,9 and 12 with 4, 8 and 11. For an excellent discussion of the testing process in schools see Oakes, Jeannie , "Keeping Track", Yale University Press, New Haven and London, 1985.

[197] Phillips, S.E., "Legal Issues in Performance Assessment," 79 Ed.Law Rep. [709] (March 11, 1993).

[198] Chapter 213 Laws of Nevada (1993) amends Sec. 389.017 NRS (1991) changing the reporting obligation of local boards regarding examinations for achievement and proficiency administered before completion of grades 4, 8 and 11.

[199] Sec. 388.070 NRS (1993)

[200] Sec. 388.090 NRS (1993)

[201] Sec. 388.110 NRS (1993)

[202] Assembly Concurrent Resolution (ACR) No. 18 File No. 75 (1993). ACR's are not binding on local school districts but merely offer advice as to the sense of the legislature regarding issues addressed in the ACR. ACR 18 urges boards of trustees of all county school districts to adopt daily class schedules for public elementary schools which include a fixed period of uninterrupted teaching time during each school day.

[203] Sec. 388.075 NRS (1993). The attorney general has issued his opinion concluding that the period of silence law does not violate the establishment clause of the 1st Amendment under the Lemon test. infra. AGO 85-15 (10-1-1985)

[204] Sec. 388.700-730 NRS (1993)

[205] See Reviser's Note Ch.518 Stats 1991 for provisions not included in NRS.

superintendent. However, the legislation was unhappily worded. The initial section of the law was clear enough. It mandated achievement of class size reduction.[206] District boards were directed to prepare plans for achieving the reduction for submission to the state board.[207] The state and local boards were further directed to determine the data to be used to measure the effectiveness of the plans developed by each district.[208] Yet, a district could be relieved of its duty to comply with the mandate by the state board for good cause.[209] Furthermore, the legislature created a procedure pursuant to which the state board of examiners (see Daines case) could divert the class size reduction appropriation to fund existing or future obligations of the state.[210] It follows that thoughtful planning by school districts was difficult, if not impossible, because program funding was subject to revocation depending on the states fiscal vitality.

The economic recession became more apparent after the adjournment of the 1991 legislature. It motivated the Governor to call on school districts to postpone implementation of class size reduction for third grade.[211] The tactic was successful.[212] Local districts requested relief from the implementation of class size reduction for third grade from the state board of education because of the states fiscal problems. The Governors' indirect approach of dealing with the state fiscal crisis caused some confusion in local districts.[213] It also placed educators in the curious position of asking for relief from a mandate most believed important to achieving academic excellence in the states schools.

The legislature revisited the class size reduction issue during the 1993 session.[214] The legislature left the original mandate reducing class sizes to 15 pupils per teacher in selected kindergarten classrooms and grades 1, 2 and 3 in place. However, money merely sufficient to reduce class sizes to 16 pupils per teacher in selected kindergarten classrooms and grades 1 and 2 was appropriated to the class size reduction trust fund for 1993-94 and 1994-95.[215] The law also places additional reporting responsibilities upon the department of education. On or before December 15 of each year the department must report the number of teachers employed, the number of teachers employed in order to attain class size reduction, the number of pupils enrolled and the number of teachers assigned to teach in the same classroom

---

[206] Sec. 388.700 (1) NRS (1993).

[207] Sec. 388.720 NRS (1993).

[208] Sec. 388.710 NRS (1993).

[209] Sec. 388.700 (3) NRS (199). Lack of available financial support specifically set aside for the reduction is designated as good cause.

[210] Sec. 388.730 (3) NRS (1993).

[211] The Governor never requested the board of examiners to divert the class size reduction trust fund resources to other state purposes instead relying on school district petitions to the state board for relief from the legislative mandate.

[212] The Governor was able to secure the cooperation of the states school districts without having to personally seek diversion of class size reduction resources to other state purposes.

[213] Whaley, Sean, "Nevada's Finances Take Turn For Worse", Review Journal, June 10, 1992, p. 1 B.; Gallant, John, "Schools Consider Class-size Cuts". Review Journal, June 10, 1992, p. 5 B. ; Gallant, John, "State Officials Question School Board", Review Journal, June 11, 1992, p. 3 A. Why should a school district assume the money will be diverted if the board of examiners has not recommended that the money be diverted to other uses?

[214] Chapter 423 Laws of Nevada (1993) The preamble of the legislation recites the goals of the legislature regarding class size reduction to be a pupil teacher ratio of no more that 15 pupils per teacher or 30 pupils per two teachers in kindergarten and grades 1,2 and 3 where core curriculum is taught. However, available money was estimated to provide only enough teachers to achieve a ratio of 16 pupils per teacher in selected kindergarten classrooms in which pupils were most at risk of failure and in grades 1 and 2.

Future Legislative intentions regarding class size reduction are also addressed in the preamble of Chapter 423. A class size of 15 pupils to per class in grade 3, 22 pupils per class in grades 4, 5 and 6 and 25 pupils per class in grades 7 to 12 are specified as the intended goal of the legislature.

[215] Chapter 423 Laws of Nevada Sec. 2 (1993). The money appropriated must be used to meet class size reduction first in schools and classes with pupils considered most at risk of failure. It must be accounted for separately from any other money received by the school districts and used only to pay the salaries and benefits of teaching positions required to be added by the law. It cannot be used to settle or arbitrate disputes between a recognized organization representing employees of the school district or to settle any negotiations. The funds cannot be used to adjust district-wide schedules of salaries and benefits of the employees of the school district. The money cannot be distributed to a school district whose plan for achieving class size reduction has not been received by the department of education. See Chapter 423 Laws of Nevada Sec. 4 (1993)

for kindergarten and grades 1, 2 and 3 for each school district.[216] Finally, the class size reduction legislation also continues to fund 90 scholarships for qualified students pursuing degrees in teaching.[217]

Other Specific Duties

Specific board duties also include making reports to the superintendent of public instruction in the manner and form prescribed by the superintendent.[218]

School district review and revision of specifications for procuring goods and products for the schools to eliminate discrimination against recycled products is also mandated by the legislature.[219]

C
CHAPTER SUMMARY

The Nevada legislature has created a uniform system of common schools pursuant to the state constitution. Does the system created by the state give local school districts sufficient authority to govern their schools? Does the state retain substantial control of schools through the state department? What role does the federal government play in school governance? Is the principle of 'Local Layperson Control of Schools' a myth or reality?

Nevada school law is a complex mix of local, state, and federal statutes, case law and regulations. Nevada school governance is a complex mix of layperson and professional control of schools. The recipe for effective governance is always being reconsidered. By the end of our journey you should have some understanding of where we have been, where we are and where we are heading in our efforts to find a more effective school governance framework.[220]

---

[216]Chapter 423 Laws of Nevada Sec. 1 (1993) amending Sec. 388. 700 NRS (1991) subsection 5.

[217]Chapter 423 Laws of Nevada Sec. 2 (2) (a) (1993)

[218] For example, Examination reports supra. See also Sec. 387.303 NRS (1993) Budget Reports. Chapter 447 Laws of Nevada (1993) amends Sec. 387.303 NRS (1991) requiring school districts to submit the number of employees eligible for health insurance within the school district for the current and preceeding fiscal years and the amount paid by the district for health insurance for each employee during those years, the rates for fringe benefits, excluding health insurance, paid by the school district for its licensed employees in the preceding and current fiscal years and the amount paid for extra duties, supervision of extracurricular activities and supplemental pay, and the number of employees receiving that pay in the preceding and current fiscal years. Do such reporting requirements divert resources from the classroom?

[219] Sec. 386.416-418 NRS (1993)

[220] On May 23, 1991 The legislature adopted Assembly Concurrent Resolution (ACR) No. 85. The resolution directs the Legislative Commission to conduct an interim study on public elementary and secondary education in Nevada. The resolution reads as follows:

"WHEREAS, Public education is a fundamental responsibility of state government; and

WHEREAS, Public education plays a crucial role in producing well- informed, educated and productive members of society; and

WHEREAS, Public education is an important factor in maintaining the excellent quality of life enjoyed by the people of this state; and

WHEREAS. Public education is critically important in the state's plan for economic diversification; now, therefore, be it

RESOLVED BY THE ASSEMBLY OF THE STATE OF NEVADA, THE SENATE CONCURRING, That the Legislative Commission is hereby directed to conduct an interim study on public elementary and secondary education in this state; and be it further

RESOLVED, That the study must emphasize an evaluation of:

1. The effects of allowing parents the right to choose which school their child attends;

2. Alternative teaching methods to that of "tracking" pupils in particular courses of study;

3. The feasibility and desirability of lengthening the school year;

4. Cost-effective ways of reducing the ratio of pupils to teachers in the classroom;

5. Flexible hours for a school day;

6. Any new teaching methods and procedures currently being used successfully in other states;

7. The present and long-term effects of using certain drugs to treat pupils who are hyperactive or inattentive; and

8. The problems of providing alternative housing and educational opportunities for pupils who are suspended or expelled from public schools for the commission of violent acts or the possession of dangerous weapons; and be it further

RESOLVED, That the committee appointed by the Legislative Commission to study public elementary and secondary education in this state must meet at least seven times during the interim and must consult with such experts in the field of education as the committee deems appropriate to obtain information necessary for the study; and be it further

RESOLVED. That the results of the study and any recommended legislation be reported to the 67th session of the Nevada Legislature."

The Legislative Commission appointed a nine member panel to conduct the study. The panel was assisted by the Legislative Counsel Bureau. The subcommittee held six meetings between October 1991 and June 1992, in Carson City, Reno and Las Vegas. The subcommittee received presentations and testimony concerning the 12 topics mentioned in the resolution. All meeting minutes and supporting documents are available from the Legislative Counsel Bureau's Research Library. The subcommittee adopted 18 recommendations.

"SUMMARY OF RECOMMENDATIONS

1. Adopt a subcommittee resolulion urging the 1993 Nevada Legislature to continue the Class-Size Reduction Program.

2. Adopt a resolution urging the State Department of Education to conduct a study concerning the prevalence of "tracking" students in Nevada's public school system, and report the results and recommendations to the 1995 Legislative Session. The study should include, but not be limited to:

    a. The need for additional teacher training (and the associated funding) to enable teachers to use the innovative teaching methods offered as alternatives to tracking;

    b. The need to measure the extent of ability grouping and monitor the effectiveness of specific forms of tracking; additional data may need to be collected;

    c. How equity matters are addressed, including the quality of instruction and resources in "low-track" classes, along with racial/ethnic inequity;

    d. Parental attitudes toward tracking and "detracking";

    e. The use of "gifted" pupils as role models for other students; potential impact upon existing programs for gifted students; and

    f. The impact of tracking upon student behavior and teacher expectations.
(BDR R-417)

3. Include a statement in the final report recommending that Nevada's school districts expand the magnet school concept from its current occupational education emphasis to include additional curricular areas (for example, fine arts, languages, mathematics and science). The districts are encouraged to publicize the differences among the magnet schools and establish an accountability system.

4. Include in the subcommittee's final report a statement concluding that school choice voucher system involving private schools is not feasible in the State of Nevada at this time.

5. Make an appropriation to the State Treasury to the special fund for the enhancement of occupational education in Grades 9 to 12. The money is to be used to establish classes in Grades 9 and 10 on occupations in general, and to improve occupational classes for pupils in Grades 10,11 and 12. The money shall be distributed to the districts according to; formula using a base allocation and proportional enrollment. Funding in the amount of $2,252,781 for each year of the next biennium is appropriated from the State General Fund for this purpose. (BDR 34-425)

6. Require, by statute, a one-time appropriation, that the State Board Education adopt regulations to establish a course of study relating to home and occupational skills. The course would be offered in the 7th and/or 8th Grade, and would instruct students in skills relating to making decisions, solving problems, and management and leadership. Students would learn to apply these skills in all areas of daily living. Funding in the amount of $1,376,340 for Fiscal Year 1994 only is appropriated from the State General Fund for this purpose.
(BDR 34-426)

7. Adopt a resolution, directed to all public schools, urging participation in the State Department of Education's Nevada School Improvement Project.
(BDR R-419)

8. Adopt a resolution, directed to Nevada's school district boards of trustees, urging the adoption of a daily class schedule in each public elementary school that includes a fixed period of uninterrupted teaching time during each school day.
(BDR R-421)

9. Adopt a resolution, directed to the State Board of Education, supporting the following for Nevada's public schools:

    a. Implementing the National Council of Teachers of Mathematics curriculum and evaluation standards;

    b. Implementing the Nevada State Course of Study for Mathematics;

    c. Aligning assessment with the revised Nevada State Course of Study for Mathematics and the National Council of Teachers of Mathematics curriculum and evaluation standards;

    d. Promoting equity in mathematics education for all students; and

    e. Using technology and concrete materials for instruction as well as assessment.
(BDR R-420)

10. Include in the subcommittee's final report a statement directed to the State Board of Education, expressing support for statewide reform in mathematics education, and support for State matching funds to obtain possible Federal grant money. Include in the statement that Nevada currently supports education reform in general, and mathematics reform indirectly, through its current program of class-size reduction. Such a declaration is expected to facilitate applications for Federal funds for statewide mathematics initiatives.

11. Include a statement in the subcommittee's final report expressing support for implementing and funding the reform of mathematics education in Nevada through a systematic program of staff development designed to implement the revised "Nevada State Course of Study for Mathematics." Such a program would include instructional strategies, content knowledge and alternative/authentic assessment. The program is designed to improve students' understanding and achievement in mathematics.

12. Include a statement in the subcommittee's final report expressing support for implementing and funding the development of forms of alternative assessment, including portfolio assessments, to expand and align mathematics assessment with the revised "Nevada State Course Study for Mathematics."

13. Require, by statute, that a physician obtain an informed consent form signed by a parent before a child is placed on Class II drug therapy. The form shall be prepared by the State Board of Health in Department of Human Resources and should include, but not be limited to, a list of potential side effects of the drug, a description of the need for continuous monitoring by a physician, and a description of alternative therapies.
(BDR 40-422)

14. Require, by statute, that the State Board of Education adopt regulation to establish a diagnostic referral network to ensure that children suspected of having Attention Deficit Hyperactivity Disorder evaluated and diagnosed by a physician who is an expert in screening such cases on a regular basis. (BDR 34-424)

15. Adopt a resolution urging the State Board of Education to adopt a policy of cooperation with medical facilities, educators, physicians and psychologists, school counselors, social workers, marriage and family therapists, and parents to facilitate the diagnosis and treatment of Attention Deficit Hyperactivity Disorder and Attention Deficit Disorder.
Further resolve that proper classroom placement, physical education programs, behavior modification strategies, counseling, and concurrent drug treatment be attempted.
(BDR R-423)

16. Adopt a resolution, directed to the State Board of Education, supporting the National Education Goals. The six goals, modified for Nevada specify that by the year 2000:

    a. All children in Nevada will start school ready to learn;

    b. The high school graduation rate will be at least 90 percent;

    c. Nevada students will have demonstrated competency in challenging subject matter, and that every school will ensure that students use their minds well;

CHAPTER III

COMPULSORY ATTENDANCE
A
GENERAL RULE
SCOPE OF COMPULSORY ATTENDANCE AUTHORITY

Historical Background

At the time of the American Revolution education was a matter of private concern. The question of whether to acquire the ability to read, write and compute was a determination left primarily to family judgment or individual initiative. The evolution of a complex social, political and economic structure raised questions about the wisdom of relying on individuals and families to determine the wisdom of pursuing education. What, if any, role government should play in providing an opportunity for all citizens to learn was a question being hotly debated at about the time that Nevada statehood was being considered by Congress and the United States was about to engage in Civil War.[221]

Some delegates to the Nevada constitutional convention contended it was improper to authorize state government to compel school attendance.

> Mr. Hawley. I know that the provision of the former constitution, making it compulsory on parents to send their children to school, met with a great deal of opposition. And for myself, I certainly consider it entirely at variance with the spirit of our institutions.[222]
> **********
> Mr. Warwick. ...[W]e are living in a Republic, that a man's house is his castle, and that in it he has a perfect right to exercise full authority and control over his children--- to send them to school, or to keep them at home, just as he pleases. The very character of our free institutions forbids this proposed interference with the private rights of the citizen....[223]

---

d. Nevada students will be ranked among the top 10 percent of the Nation in mathematics and science achievement;

e. Every school in Nevada will be free of drugs and violence and offer a disciplined learning environment; and

f. Every adult in Nevada will be literate and will possess the knowledge and skills necessary to compete in a global economy and exercise the rights and responsibilities of citizenship.

(BDR R-427)

17. Include in the subcommittee's final report a statement supporting funding to allow school districts to offer tuition-free summer school for certain youths from financially needy families. Such a program would, among other things, assist students needing additional units to satisfy requirements to graduate from high school.

18. Include in the subcommittee's final report a recommendation that each school district review requirements for graduation, including the State's requirements, to ensure that students have sufficient time to accumulate the units needed to graduate within 4 years. School districts should consider lengthening the school day, if necessary, to accomplish this objective. Further, recommend that the Legislature review the total units required for graduation from high school." "Study of Public Elementary and Secondary Education," Legislative Counsel Bureau Bulletin No. 93-3 September 1992 p. v-ix.

Senate Concurrent Resolution (SCR) No. 52 File No. 166 (1993) directs the Legislative Commission to conduct another interim study to examine the structure and financing of public elementary and secondary education in Nevada. The study will be performed by four members of the Nevada legislature, the superintendent of public instruction, and the dean of the College of Education for the University of Nevada Reno, or his designee. Although the Resolution was never formally amended the membership of the study group has been expanded to include the dean of the College of Education at UNLV and a representative of the state teachers association. The results of the study and recommended legislation are due to be submitted to the 68th session of the Nevada legislature.

[221] See Kaestle, Carl F. "Pillars of the Republic Common Schools and American Society," 1780-1860, Hill and Wang, New York, 1983; Tyack, David etc. "Law and the Shaping of Public Education, 1785-1954," The University of Wisconsin Press, Madison, Wisconsin 1987.

[222] "Debates and Proceedings in the Constitutional Convention on Nevada Assembled at Carson City, July 4, 1864 to form a Constitution and State Government , Andrew J. Marsh Official Reporter, Frank Eastman Printer, San Francisco, California, 1866 p.567

[223] Ibid., p. 571.

But, arguments to the contrary, which sound familiar even today, carried the day.

> Mr. Collins. ....There are many children who are daily squandering their time, and what is far worse, contracting habits which will ultimate in crime in some form, and if we shall adopt some provision by which the authorities can exact their attendance upon the schools, they may be saved from an evil destiny, and the State will certainly be the better for it....[224]
>
> ******************
>
> Mr. Collins. ....Suppose a boy brought up in ignorance, in consequence of such breeding, commits a felony. If he is convicted, his imprisonment of course involves a charge to the State. Now which is the better investment for the State, to instruct him or to imprison him?[225]
>
> ******************
>
> Mr. Dunne ....Ours being a Democratic form of government, every person upon arriving at mature age who was born in the country or has been naturalized according to law, who has not been convicted of crime, etc., has a voice in the administration of the public affairs of the country-- in the making and administering of the laws-- and I consider it only a fair proposition that he should not have that privilege unless he has some knowledge of the nature of the duties which devolve upon him. Therefore, when the State has provided a system of public instruction, a means of obtaining education, it should also require that all who are to become its citizens, and take part in the formation of its laws, shall avail themselves of those means, and go so far at least as to know how to read and write.[226]

Now, as in the past, three major arguments provide major support for compulsory attendance laws First, proponents contend that compulsory school attendance is essential because education is a critical element for ensuring a sound and vital system of self government. Second, educated citizens are more likely to be self-sufficient and contribute to the economic well-being of the country. Third, education provides individuals with the opportunity to recognize and realize their human potential and thereby maximize their personal growth and development.

Today, all states have adopted laws requiring school attendance.

Nevada Compulsory Attendance Law

Nevada requires parents, guardians or other persons having control of or charge of any child between the ages of 7 and 17 years to send the child to a public school during all the time the school is in session in the school district in which the child resides.[227] A child that will arrive at the age of 6 years by September 30 must

---

[224] Ibid., p. 567

[225] Ibid., p. 571

[226] Ibid., p. 569

[227] Sec. 392.040 NRS (1991) Nevada is required to make programs available for disabled students prior to and subsequent to the statutory compulsory attendance requirement under the Individuals with Disabilities Education Act see Infra.See also Attorney General Opinions; Attendance at school of pupils who marry cannot be barred by school authorities only for reason that such pupils are married. AGO 44 (4-18-

be admitted to a regular school program, and may be admitted to the first grade at the beginning of the school year. If a child will not reach his\her 6th birthday by September 30, the child must not be admitted to the first grade until the beginning of the school year following his sixth birthday.[228]

Compulsory attendance may be excused when satisfactory written evidence is presented to the board of trustees of the school district that the physical or mental condition or attitude is such as to prevent of render inadvisable the childs attendance at school. A certificate in writing from any reputable physician is deemed satisfactory evidence by the legislature.[229] Attendance may also be excused upon completion of 12 grades of course work[230], if the childs residence is at such a distance from the nearest public school as to render attendance unsafe or impractical[231], upon order of the district court if a child has completed the eighth grade[232], and if the child is 14 years of age or older and must support himself or his parent.[233] Further a child between the ages of 14 and 17 who has completed the eighth grade may be excused from full-time attendance for employment or apprenticeship by the written authority of the board of trustees. Employers are forbidden from employing such children unless the child presents a written permit. Employers are required to keep the permit on file during the childs employment.[234]

In 1956, Nevada became the first state to pass legislation authorizing parents to teach their children at home.[235] The state treats home schooling as another exception to the compulsory attendance law. Parents may home school when satisfactory written evidence is presented to the board of trustees of the school district of residence that the child is receiving at home **equivalent instruction** of the kind and amount approved by the State Board of Education.[236] The legislature has given local school boards the primary responsibility for determining legislative intent, establishing substantive standards and creating procedural requirements for parents seeking to use the law.[237]

Enforcement of Nevada Compulsory Attendance Laws

A pupil absent from school without a valid excuse acceptable to his teacher or the principal is truant. Absence for any part of the day is deemed to be for the entire day by statute. The teacher, truant officer, or other school official shall deliver or cause to be delivered a notice of truancy to the parent, guardian or other person having charge of the child.[238] A child truant three or more times within the school year is an habitual truant. Once a child has been declared an habitual truant

---

1951) Parents of a pupil suspended for failure to submit to discipline is not required to send their child to another school outside their district of residence. AGO 204 (1-27-1965).

[228] Sec. 392.040 (1) NRS (1993)

[229] Sec. 392 050 NRS (1993)

[230] Sec. 392.060 NRS (1993)

[231] Sec. 392.080 NRS (1993)

[232] Sec. 392.090 NRS (1993)

[233] Sec. 392.100 NRS (1993)

[234] Sec. 392.110 NRS (1993)

[235] Mayberry & Gerdes, "Home Schooling in Nevada," Inter Alia Journal of the State Bar of Nevada, Nov.1989 p. 16. See also Davis, Michael A., "The Constitutional Right to Home School," Inter Alia-Journal of the State Bar of Nevada, October 1990, p.14.

[236] Sec. 392.070 NRS (1991)

[237] Mayberry & Gerdes supra., at p. 16. However, administrative regulations have been promulgated by the state board of education and can be found in the Nevada Administrative Code (NAC). See Sec. 392.015-075 NAC (1991)

[238] Sec. 392.130 NRS (1993)

he\she may be declared such in the next school year after one absence without a valid excuse.[239]

The board of trustees are empowered to appoint an attendance officer, fix his\her compensation, prescribe his\her duties and adopt regulations consistent with law for the performance of those duties.[240] Peace officers, attendance and any other school officer is required to take into custody, without a warrant, any child between the ages of 7 and 17 who has been reported as an absentee from instruction without a valid excuse.[241] Children apprehended during school hours must be delivered to school authorities. After school hours such children are to be returned to the parent or guardian of the child.[242] In addition, the school district may enter an agreement with a counseling agency and permit delivery of truants for counseling.[243]

Upon written complaint of any person the board of trustees is required to make a full and impartial investigation of all charges against individuals having control of any child for violation of compulsory attendance laws.[244] A written report of the investigation is to be filed in the records of the board. If it appears upon investigation that persons having control or charge of a child have violated the compulsory attendance statutes the clerk of the board of trustees must make and file a criminal complaint against such person and see that the charge is prosecuted by the proper authorities.[245] If the school district employs an attendance officer, that person assumes the responsibility of the clerk.[246] In addition, the statutes authorize any taxpayer or school officer to file a criminal complaint against a parent or guardian violating the compulsory attendance law.[247]

Persons given notice of their childs truancy who fail to prevent subsequent truancy within the school year are guilty of a misdemeanor.[248] Persons making false statements, presenting false documents concerning a students age or school attendance with the intent to defeat the compulsory attendance law are also guilty of a misdemeanor.[249]

Persons who induce students to be absent from school unlawfully or knowingly harbor or employ truants while school is in session are guilty of a misdemeanor.[250] Attendance officers are entitled to visit places of employment in order to determine if the compulsory attendance laws are being obeyed. They may also demand from all employers a list of children employed with their names and ages.[251]

Finally, Nevada law makes it unlawful for any person to beat, whip, detain or otherwise interfere with a pupil while he\she is on their way to and from school.[252] Violation of the section is a misdemeanor.[253]

---

[239] Sec. 392.140 NRS (1993)
[240] Sec. 392.150 NRS (1993)
[241] Sec. 392.160 NRS (1993)
[242] Sec. 392.160 (2) NRS (1993)
[243] Sec. 392.160 (3) NRS (1993)
[244] Sec. 392.170 NRS (1993)
[245] Sec.392.180 NRS (1993)
[246] Sec.392.190 NRS (1993)
[247] Sec.392.200 NRS (1993)
[248] Sec.392.210 NRS (1993)
[249] Sec. 392.215 NRS (1993)
[250] Sec. 392.220 NRS (1993)
[251] Sec. 392.220 (2) NRS (1993)
[252] Sec. 392.470 NRS (1993)
[253] Ibid.

In spite of compulsory attendance laws many children drop out of school. A recent Federal Department of Education report indicated that Nevada ranked 31st among the fifty states with a graduation rate of 72.1%.[254] So, how effective is the compulsory attendance statute? School officials have complained that a lack of manpower and facilities at Clark County Juvenile Court Services leaves that entity unable to compel attendance except in cases involving hard core truants. Officials claim the school district and the court services work to encourage students to attend, but often there is little that can be done beyond that.[255] It follows that creative ways to encourage children to stay in school must be found to supplement compulsory attendance legislation.[256]

The Clark County School District has a number of experiments in progress to encourage attendance. Special assistance for at-risk students in elementary school as well as alternative nontraditional high school programs are being provided by the district.[257] Furthermore, a pilot project at two Clark County schools provides an excellent illustration of how the private sector can help improve school attendance. Students at Dell Robinson Junior High School and Valley High School who achieve good grades, have high attendance or earn excellent citizenship ratings are awarded 'smart cards'. The cards entitle students to discounts at a local mall. Hundreds of 'smart cards' have been issued which provide up to 20% discounts on items offered at the Meadows Mall.[258] Preliminary results of the program have been so encouraging that other district schools are considering adoption of the program.

Grade Promotion and Retention and Compulsory Attendance

Another dimension of the power to compel attendance is the authority to determine whether a student should be promoted to the next higher grade. Nevada law provides that before any pupil may be retained in the same grade rather than promoted to the next grade for the succeeding school year, the pupils teacher and principal must make a reasonable effort to arrange a meeting with the parents of the child to discuss the reasons and circumstances for a proposed retention.[259] The law further vests the teacher and the principal, in joint agreement, with the final authority to retain a pupil in the same grade for the succeeding school year.[260] However, no pupil may be retained more than one time in the same grade.[261] In the 1989-90 school year a total of 1,013 students were retained by the Clark County School District. The number represented .9% of the Clark County School District student population.[262]

Nevada law may allow retention and establish a procedure which vests educators with the final authority to retain students but is it wise educational

---

[254] Hinds, Michael, "Cutting the Dropout Rate: High Goal But Low Hopes", New York Times, February 17, 1990 p. 1 A at p. 10 A. See also Kominski, Robert, "School Enrollment--Social and Economic Characteristics of Students." US Census Bureau Released in Washington D.C., June 5, 1992, Reported in Review Journal article entitled "One- Third Of High-Schoolers Falling Behind, Dropping Out," June 6, 1992, p. 6 A. The report, based on census data, states that 40% of boys and 29% of girls ages 15-17 were either one or more grades behind in school or had left school without graduating. The study also determined that the 34.8% overall rate of laggers and dropouts was up from 29.1% in 1980. The overall rate increased in spite of a decline in the annual dropout rate from 6% in 1980 to 4% in 1990.

[255] Pappa, Erik "Clinics For Failing Truants", Las Vegas Sun, March 5, 1990, p. 1 B.

[256] Experiments currently underway in other school districts outside Nevada include suspension of driving privileges if the student fails to attend school, reduction of AFDC payments if children fail to attend school (Learnfare), paying children to stay in school and paying parents to keep their children in school.

[257] Ibid., p. 1 B.

[258] "'Smart Cards' a Good Idea to Motivate U.S. Students, Las Vegas Sun, March 21, 1990 p. 3 A.

[259] Sec. 392.125 (1) NRS (1993)

[260] Sec. 392.125 (2) NRS (1993)

[261] Sec. 392.125 (3) NRS (1993)

[262] Special Edition Reporter, prepared by the Clark County School District 1990.

practice? Few educational causes get more popular applause than refusing to promoteCompulsory attendance:Promotionstudents just because they are a year older, yet few current policies have been shown to be as ineffective.[263]

> There is probably no widespread practice in education today that has been as thoroughly discredited by research according to Roy P. Doyle, a professor of education at Arizona State University.[264]

At the heart of the arguments for and against 'social promotion' are very different philosophies of education. Advocates of retention view promotion as something to be earned. Opponents emphasize the student's self image and social needs. They also claim that retention assumes, sometimes improperly, that the child did not work hard enough, when in fact the teaching was deficient [265]or that the student was learning disabled.

The issue surfaced recently in Nevada. On July 7, 1991 a large color photo of a student and his father on the first page of the second section of the Sunday Las Vegas Review Journal was accompanied by the headline **"F Student Heads For High School."**[266]. The article indicated that the students parents were upset with school officials because their son was being 'socially promoted' to high school. Follow-up stories and letters to the editor reported public concern that the school district had embraced a policy of 'social promotion.' School district authorities responded to the controversy stating that the decision on passing or retaining students is made on an individual basis. Moreover, the superintendent was reported as stating he was opposed to automatically passing students from grade to grade.[267] However, the principal of the junior high school involved was quoted as saying that he ordered all flunking eighth-graders be promoted to high school.[268] The Review Journal entered the fray with an editorial expressing concern about 'social promotions' but worried more about the districts apparent failure to keep records of how many flunking students were promoted to the next grade and how many were held back.

> This information would seem to be highly relevant to policy-making....The school board should insist that the school district administration begin keeping records on and observing the progress of students who have flunked. And on the basis of that information, the school board should formulate a policy-- one with flexibility covering social promotions."[269]

On February 17, 1992 the Review Journal presented the following headline above a followup story; **"Once-Failing Student Doing Well At Cheyenne High School."**[270] The article reported that the student who was promoted to high school despite failing grades was doing well in high school according to his father.

---

[263] Fiske, Edward B., "Lessons", New York Times , January 24, 1990 p. 9 B.

[264] Ibid., p. 9 B.

[265] Ibid., p. 9 B.

[266] Papinchak, Steve, "F Student Heads For High School", Review Journal, July 7, 1991, p. 1 B.

[267] Papinchak, Steve, "Grade-Promotion Practice Defended", Review Journal July 9, 1991, p. 1 B.

[268]Ibid., p. 1 B.

[269] "A Flexible Policy on Failing Students" Review Journal Editorial July 10, 1991, p. 9 B. The Editorial did not address whether the Review Journal would support hiring additional non teaching personnel to keep the statistics. Is this information to be collected as part of the program of accountability required of each school district? supra.; On October 26, 1991 the Review Journal carried a small story indicating that the California State Superintendent of Public instruction sent memos to the states 1009 school districts recommending against retaining students. "School Chief Against Flunking" Review Journal, October 26, 1991, p. 14 A.

[270] Gallant, John ,"Once-Failing Student Doing Well At Cheyenne High School" Review Journal, February 17, 1992, p. 1 B.

"The reason: High school officials tested Tommy and discovered he had a learning disability.

Now Tommy is in a special class and his grades have vastly improved, said Tom Stroud.

'What a difference,' he said....

In his final semester at junior high, Tommy Stroud received a D in industrial art and F's in reading, English, geography\history and math.

It was the discovery this year of the learning disability that made the difference, Tommy's father said.

He should have been tested earlier.

Its something we tried to get Brinley to do and [they] wouldn't ," he said."[271]

What lessons does this incident teach us about the interrelationship between law, educational research, and educational practice?

CONSTITUTIONAL LIMITS ON A STATES GENERAL POWER TO COMPEL ATTENDANCE

The authority of states to enact compulsory education laws is beyond question. However, there are limits on a states' authority to compel school attendance. We now turn to an examination of two landmark cases where the Supreme Court determined that a states' compulsory attendance laws were unconstitutional on their face or as applied.

Can A State Require That All Normal Children ONLY Attend Public Schools?

PIERCE
v.
SOCIETY OF SISTERS[272]
268 U.S. 510, 45 S.Ct. 571 (1925)

Mr. JUSTICE McREYNOLDS delivered the opinion of the Court.

These appeals are from decrees, based upon undenied allegations, which granted preliminary orders restraining appellants from threatening or attempting to enforce the Compulsory Education Act[273] adopted November 7, 1922 (Laws Or. 1923, p. 9), under the initiative provision of her Constitution by the voters of Oregon. They present the same points of law; there are no controverted questions of

---

[271] Ibid., p. 1 B.

[272] Although the Nevada compulsory attendance statute requires attendance at 'public school' the Attorney General has rendered an opinion concluding that it is well settled that attendance at private school may constitute sufficient attendance under the compulsory statute. AGO 320 (1-3-1954)

[273] Be it enacted by the people of the state of Oregon:

Section 1. That section 5259, Oregon Laws, be and the same is hereby amended so as to read as follows:

Sec. 5259. Children Between the ages of Eight and Sixteen Years.—Any parent, guardian or other person in the state of Oregon. having control or charge or custody of a child under the age of sixteen years and of the age to eight years or over at the commencement of a term to public school of the district in which said child resides, who shall fail or neglect or refuse to send such child to a public school for the period to time a public school shall he held during the current year in said district, shall be guilty of a misdemeanor and each day's failure to send such child to a public school shall constitute a separate offense; provided, that in the following cases, children shall not be required to attend public schools:

(a) Children Physically Unable.—Any child who is abnormal, subnormal or physically unable to attend school. etc.
****
This act shall take effect and be and remain in force from and after the first day of September, 1926.

fact. Rights said to be guaranteed by the federal Constitution were specially set up, and appropriate prayers asked for their protection.

The challenged act, effective September 1, 1926, requires every parent, guardian, or other person having control or charge or custody of a child between 8 and 16 years to send him "to a public school for the period of time a public school shall be held during the current year" in the district where the child resides; and failure so to do is declared a misdemeanor. There are exemptions—not specially important here—for children who are not normal or who have completed the eight grade. or whose parents or private teachers reside at considerable distances from any public school. or who hold special permits from the county superintendent. The manifest purpose is to compel general attendance at public schools by normal children between 8 and 16 who have not completed the eighth grade. And without doubt enforcement of the statute would seriously impair, perhaps destroy, the profitable ventures of appellees' business and greatly diminish the value of their property.

Appellee, the Society of Sisters, is an Oregon corporation organized in 1880 with power to care for orphans, educate and instruct the youth, establish and maintain academies or schools, and acquire necessary real and personal property. It has long devoted its property and effort to the secular and religious education and care of children, and has acquired the valuable good will of many parents and guardians. It conducts interdependent primary and high school and junior colleges, and maintains orphanages for the custody and control of children between 8 and 16. In its primary schools many children between those ages are taught the subjects usually pursued in Oregon public schools during the first eight years. Systematic religious instruction and moral training according to the tenets of the Roman Catholic Church are also regularly provided. All courses of study. both temporal and religious, contemplate continuity of training under appellee's charge: the primary schools are essential to the system and the most profitable. It owns valuable buildings especially constructed and equipped for school purposes. The business is remunerative—the annual income from primary schools exceeds $30,000— and the successful conduct of this requires long time contracts with teachers and parents. The Compulsory Education Act of 1922 has already caused the withdrawal from its schools of children who would otherwise continue and their income has steadily declined. The appellants public officers have proclaimed their purpose strictly to enforce the statute,

After setting out the above facts the Society's bill alleges that the enactment conflicts with the right of parents to choose schools where their children will receive appropriate mental and religious training, the right of the child to influence the parents' choice of a school, the right of schools and teachers therein to engage in a useful business or profession, and is accordingly repugnant to the Constitution and void. And, further, that unless enforcement of the measure is enjoined, the corporation's business and property will suffer irreparable injury.

****

No answer was interposed in either cause, and after proper notices they were heard by three judges on motions for preliminary injunctions upon the specifically alleged facts. The court ruled that the Fourteenth Amendment guaranteed appellees against the deprivation of their property without due process of law consequent upon the unlawful interference by appellants with the free choice of patrons, present and prospective. It declared the right to conduct schools was property and that parents and guardians, as a part of their liberty, might direct the education of children by selecting reputable teachers and places. [It also decalred], that appellees' schools were not unfit or harmful to the public, and that enforcement of the challenged statute would unlawfully deprive them of patronage and, thereby destroy appellees' business and property. Finally [it stated] that the threats to enforce the act would continue to cause irreparable injury and the suits were not premature

No question is raised concerning the power of the state reasonably to regulate all schools, to inspect, supervise and examine them, their teachers and pupils; to require that all children of proper age attend some school, that teachers shall be of good moral character and patriotic disposition, that certain studies plainly essential to good citizenship must be taught, and that nothing be taught which is manifestly inimical to the public welfare.

The inevitable practical result of enforcing the act under consideration would he destruction of appellees' primary schools. and perhaps all other private primary schools for normal children within the state of Oregon. Appellees are engaged in a kind of undertaking, not inherently harmful, but long regarded as useful and meritorious. Certainly there is nothing in the present records to indicate that they have failed to discharge their obligations to patrons, students, or the state. And there are no peculiar circumstances or present emergencies which demand extraordinary measures relative to primary education.

Under the doctrine of <u>Meyer</u> <u>v.</u> <u>Nebraska</u>, 262 U. S. 390, we think it entirely plain that the Act of 1922 unreasonably interferes with the liberty of parents and.guardians to direct the upbringing and education of children under their control. As often heretofore pointed out, rights guaranteed by the Constitution may not be abridged by legislation which has no reasonable relation to some purpose within the competency of the state. The fundamental theory of liberty upon which all governments in this Union repose excludes any general power of the state to standardize its children by forcing them to accept instruction from public teachers only. The child is not the mere creature of the state; those who nurture him and direct his destiny have the right, coupled with the high duty, to recognize and prepare him for additional obligations.

The courts of the state have not construed the act, and we must determine its meaning for ourselves. Evidently it was expected to have general application and cannot be construed as merely intended to amend the charters of certain private corporations. No argument in favor of such view has been advanced.

****

Appellees asked protection against arbitrary, unreasonable, and unlawful interference with their patrons and the consequent destruction of their business and property. Their interest is clear and immediate, within the rule approved by this court and many other cases where injunctions have been issued to protect business enterprises against interference with the freedom of patrons or customers.

The suits were not premature. The injury to appellees was present and very real, not a mere possibility in the remote future. If no relief had been possible prior to the effective date of the act, the injury would have become irreparable. Prevention of impending injury by unlawful action is a well recognized function of courts of equity.

The decrees below are affirmed.

When Must State Compulsory Attendance Laws Yield To The First Amendment Right to Free Exercise Of Religion?

WISCONSIN
v.
YODER
406 U.S. 205, 92 S.Ct. 1526 (1972)

MR. CHIEF JUSTICE BURGER delivered the opinion of the Court.

On petition of the State of Wisconsin, we granted the writ of certiorari in this case to review a decision of the Wisconsin Supreme Court holding that respondents' convictions of violating the State's compulsory school-attendance law were invalid under the Free Exercise Clause of the First Amendment to the United States Constitution made applicable to the States by the Fourteenth Amendment. For the reasons hereafter stated we affirm the judgment of the Supreme Court of Wisconsin

Respondents Jonas Yoder and Wallace Miller are members of the Old Order Amish religion, and respondent Adin Yutzy is a member of the Conservative Amish Mennonite Church. They and their families are residents of Green County, Wisconsin. Wisconsin's compulsory school-attendance law required them to cause their children to attend public or private school until reaching age 16 but the respondents declined to send their children, ages 14 and 15, to public school after they completed the eighth grade.[274] The children were not enrolled in any private school, or within any recognized exception to the compulsory-attendance law, and they are conceded to be subject to the Wisconsin statute

On complaint of the school district administrator for the public schools, respondents were charged, tried, and convicted of violating the compulsory-attendance law in Green County Court and were fined the sum of $5 each. Respondents defended on the ground that the application of the compulsory-attendance law violated their rights under the First and Fourteenth Amendments.[275] The trial testimony showed that respondents believed, in accordance with the tenets of Old Order Amish communities generally, that their children's attendance at high school, public or private, was contrary to the Amish religion and way of life. They believed that by sending their children to high school, they would not only expose themselves to the danger of the censure of the church community, but, as found by the county court, also endanger their own salvation and that of their children. The state stipulated that respondents' religious beliefs were sincere.

In support of their position, respondents presented as expert witnesses scholars on religion and education whose testimony is uncontradicted. They expressed their opinions on the relationship of the Amish belief concerning school attendance to the more general tenets of their religion, and described the impact that compulsory high school attendance could have on the continued survival of Amish communities as they exist in the United States today. The history of the Amish sect was given in some detail, beginning with the Swiss Anabaptists of the 16th century who rejected institutionalized churches and sought to return to the early, simple, Christian life de-emphasizing material success, rejecting the

---

[274] The children, Frieda Yoder, aged 15, Barbara Miller, aged 15, and Vernon Yutzy, aged 14, were all graduates of the eighth grade of public school.

[275] The First Amendment provides: "Congress shall make no law respecting an establishment of religion, or prohibiting the free exercise thereof

competitive spirit, and seeking to insulate themselves from the modern world. As a result of their common heritage, Old Order Amish communities today are characterized by a fundamental belief that salvation requires life in a church community separate and apart from the world and worldly influence. This concept of life aloof from the world and its values is central to their faith.

A related feature of Old Order Amish communities is their devotion to a life in harmony with nature and the soil, as exemplified by the simple life of the early Christian era that continued in America during much of our early national life. Amish beliefs require members of the community to make their living by farming or closely related activities. Broadly speaking, the Old Order Amish religion pervades and determines the entire mode of life of its adherents. Their conduct is regulated in great detail by the Ordnung, or rules, of the church community. Adult baptism, which occurs in late adolescence, is the time at which Amish young people voluntarily undertake heavy obligations, not unlike the Bar Mitzvah of the Jews, to abide by the rules of the church community.[276]

Amish objection to formal education beyond the eighth grade is firmly grounded in these central religious concepts. They object to the high school, and higher education generally, because the values they teach are in marked variance with Amish values and the Amish way of life; they view secondary school education as an impermissible exposure of their children to a "worldly" influence in conflict with their beliefs. The high school tends to emphasize intellectual and scientific accomplishments, self-distinction, competitiveness, worldly success, and social life with other students. Amish society emphasizes informal learning-through-doing; a life of "goodness," rather than a life of intellect; wisdom, rather than technical knowledge; community welfare, rather than competition; and separation from, rather than integration with, contemporary worldly society.

Formal high school education beyond the eighth grade is contrary to Amish beliefs, not only because it places Amish children in an environment hostile to Amish beliefs with increasing emphasis on competition in class work and sports and with pressure to conform to the styles, manners, and ways of the peer group, but also because it takes them away from their community, physically and emotionally, during the crucial and formative adolescent period of life. During this period, the children must acquire Amish attitudes favoring manual work and self-reliance and the specific skills needed to perform the adult role of an Amish farmer or housewife. They must learn to enjoy physical labor. Once a child has learned basic reading, writing, and elementary mathematics, these traits, skills, and attitudes admittedly fall within the category of those best learned through example and "doing" rather than in a classroom. And, at this time in life, the Amish child must also grow in his faith and his relationship to the Amish community if he is to be prepared to accept the heavy obligations imposed by adult baptism. In short, high school attendance with teachers who are not of the Amish faith---and may even be hostile to it— interposes a serious barrier to the integration of the Amish child into the Amish religious community. Dr. John Hostetler, one of the experts on Amish society, testified that the modern high school is not equipped, in curriculum or social environment, to impart the values promoted by Amish society.

---

[276] See generally J. Hostetler, Amish Society (1968); J. Hostetler G. Huntington. Children in Amish Society (1971); Littell, Sectarian Protestantism and the Pursuit of Wisdom: Must Technological Objectives Prevail?, in Public Controls for Nonpublic Schools 61 (D. Erickson ed. 1969).

The Amish do not object to elementary education through the first eight grades as a general proposition because they agree that their children must have basic skills in the "three R's" in order to read the Bible, to be good farmers and citizens, and to be able to deal with non-Amish people when necessary in the course of daily affairs. They view such a basic education as acceptable because it does not significantly expose their children to worldly values or interfere with their development in the Amish community during the crucial adolescent period. While Amish accept compulsory elementary education generally, wherever possible they have established their own elementary schools in many respects like the small local schools of the past. In the Amish belief higher learning tends to develop values they reject as influences that alienate man from God.

On the basis of such considerations, Dr. Hostetler testified that compulsory high school attendance could not only result in great psychological harm to Amish children, because of the conflicts it would produce, but would also, in his opinion, ultimately result in the destruction of the Old Order Amish church community as it exists in the United States today. The testimony of Dr Donald A. Erickson, an expert witness on education, also showed that the Amish succeed in preparing their high school age children to be productive members of the Amish community. He described their system of learning through doing the skills directly relevant to their adult roles in the Amish community as "ideal" and perhaps superior to ordinary high school education. The evidence also showed that the Amish have an excellent record as law-abiding and generally self-sufficient members of society.

Although the trial court in its careful findings determined that the Wisconsin compulsory school-attendance law "does interfere with the freedom of the Defendants to act in accordance with their sincere religious belief", it also concluded that the requirement of high school attendance until age 16 was a "reasonable and constitutional" exercise of governmental power and therefore denied the motion to dismiss the charges. The Wisconsin Circuit Court affirmed the convictions. The Wisconsin Supreme Court however sustained respondents' claim under the Free Exercise Clause of the First Amendment and reversed the convictions. A majority of the court was of the opinion that the State had failed to make an adequate showing that its interest in "establishing and maintaining an educational system overrides the defendants' right to the free exercise of their religion."

I

There is no doubt as to the power of a State having a high responsibility for education of its citizens to impose reasonable regulations for the control and duration of basic education. See e.g. Pierce v. Society of Sisters, 268 U. S. 510 534 (1925). Providing public schools ranks at the very apex of the function of a State. Yet even this paramount responsibility was in Pierce, made to yield to the right of parents to provide an equivalent education in a privately operated system.

****

. ...[A] State's interest in universal education, however highly we rank it, is not totally free from a balancing process when it impinges on fundamental rights and interests, such as those specifically protected by the Free Exercise Clause of the First Amendment, and the traditional interest of parents with respect to the religious upbringing of their children so long as they, in the words of Pierce, "prepare [them] for additional obligations." 268 U. S., at 535.

It follows that in order for Wisconsin to compel school attendance beyond the eighth grade against a claim that such attendance interferes with the practice of a legitimate religious belief, it must appear either that the State does not deny the free exercise of religious belief by its requirement, or that there is a state interest of sufficient magnitude to override the interest claiming protection under the Free Exercise Clause. Long before there was general acknowledgment of the need for universal formal education, the Religion Clauses had specifically and firmly fixed the
right to free exercise of religious beliefs, and buttressing this fundamental right was an equally firm, even if less explicit, prohibition against the establishment of any religion by government. The values underlying these two provisions relating to religion have been zealously protected, sometimes even at the expense of other interests of admittedly high social importance.

****

The essence of all that has been said and written on the subject is that only those interests of the highest order and those not otherwise served can overbalance legitimate claims to the free exercise of religion. We can accept it as settled, therefore, that, however strong the State's interest in universal compulsory education, it is by no means absolute to the exclusion or subordination of all other interests.

II

We come then to the quality of the claims of the respondents concerning the alleged encroachment of Wisconsin's compulsory school-attendance statute on their rights and the rights of their children to the free exercise of the religious beliefs they and their forebears have adhered to for almost three centuries.

****

...[W]e see that the record in this case abundantly supports the claim that the traditional way of life of the Amish is not merely a matter of personal preference, but one of deep religious conviction, shared by an organized group, and intimately related to daily living. That the Old Order Amish daily life and religious practice stem from their faith is shown by the fact that it is in response to their literal interpretation of the Biblical injunction from the Epistle of Paul to the Romans, "be not conformed to this world ...." This command is fundamental to the Amish faith. Moreover, for the Old Order Amish, religion is not simply a matter of theocratic belief. As the expert witnesses explained, the Old Order Amish religion pervades and determines virtually their entire way of life, regulating it with the detail of the Talmudic diet through the strictly enforced rules of the church community.

The record shows that the respondents' religious beliefs and attitude toward life, family, and home have remained constant—perhaps some would say static—in a period of unparalleled progress in human knowledge generally and great changes in education.[277] The respondents freely concede, and indeed assert as an article of faith, that their religious beliefs and what we would today call "life style" have not altered in fundamentals for centuries. Their way of life in a church-oriented community, separated from the outside world and "worldly" influences, their attachment to nature and the soil, is a way inherently simple and uncomplicated, albeit difficult to preserve against the pressure to conform. Their rejection of

---

[277] See generally R. Butts & L. Cremin, A History of Education in American Culture (1953); L. Cremin, The Transformation of the School (1961).

telephones, automobiles, radios, and television, their mode of dress, of speech, their habits of manual work do indeed set them apart from much of contemporary society; these customs are both symbolic and practical.

****

...As the record so strongly shows, the values and programs of the modern secondary school are in sharp conflict with the fundamental mode of life mandated by the Amish religion; modern laws requiring compulsory secondary education have accordingly engendered great concern and conflict [278] The conclusion is inescapable that secondary schooling, by exposing Amish children to worldly influences in terms of attitudes, goals, and values contrary to beliefs, and by substantially interfering with the religious development of the Amish child and his integration into the way of life of the Amish faith community at the crucial adolescent stage of development, contravenes the basic religious tenets and practice of the Amish faith, both as to the parent and the child.

****

In sum, the unchallenged testimony of acknowledged experts in education and religious history, almost 300 years of consistent practice, and strong evidence of a sustained faith pervading and regulating respondents' entire mode of life support the claim that enforcement of the State's requirement of compulsory formal education after the eighth grade would gravely endanger if not destroy the free exercise of respondents' religious beliefs.

III

Neither the findings of the trial court nor the Amish claims as to the nature of their faith are challenged in this Court by the State of Wisconsin. Its position is that the State's interest in universal compulsory formal secondary education to age 16 is so great that it is paramount to the undisputed claims of respondents that their mode of preparing their youth for Amish life, after the traditional elementary education, is an essential part of their religious belief and practice. Nor does the State undertake to meet the claim that the Amish mode of life and education is inseparable from and a part of the basic tenets of their religion—indeed, as much a part of their religious belief and practices as baptism, the confessional, or a Sabbath may be for others.

****

We turn, then, to the State's broader contention that its interest in its system of compulsory education is so compelling that even the established religious practices of the Amish must give way. Where fundamental claims of religious freedom are at stake, however, we cannot accept such a sweeping claim; despite its admitted validity in the generality of cases, we must searchingly examine the interests that the State seeks to promote by its requirement for compulsory education to age 16, and the impediment to those objectives that would flow from recognizing the claimed Amish exemption.

The State advances two primary arguments in support of its system of compulsory education. It notes, as Thomas Jefferson pointed out early in our history, that some degree of education is necessary to prepare citizens to participate effectively and intelligently in our open political system if we are to preserve

---

[278] Hostetler, supra, n. 5, c. 9; Hostetler & Huntington, supra, n. 5.

freedom and independence. Further, education prepares individuals to be self-reliant and self-sufficient participants in society. We accept these propositions.

However, the evidence adduced by the Amish in this case is persuasively to the effect that an additional one or two years of formal high school for Amish children in place of their long-established program of informal vocational education would do little to serve those interests. Respondents' experts testified at trial, without challenge, that the value of all education must be assessed in terms of its capacity to prepare the child for life. It is one thing to say that compulsory education for a year or to beyond the eighth grade may be necessary when its goal is the preparation of the child for life in modern society as the majority live, but it is quite another if the goal of education be viewed as the preparation of the child for life in the separated agrarian community that is the keystone of the Amish faith.

The State attacks respondents' position as one fostering "ignorance" from which the child must be protected by the State. No one can question the State's duty to protect children from ignorance but this argument does not square with the facts disclosed in the record. Whatever their idiosyncrasies as seen by the majority, this record strongly shows that the Amish community has been a highly successful social unit within our society, even if apart from the conventional "mainstream." Its members are productive and very law-abiding members of society; they reject public welfare in any of its usual modern forms. The Congress itself recognized their self-sufficiency by authorizing exemption of such groups as the Amish from the obligation to pay social security taxes.[279]

It is neither fair nor correct to suggest that the Amish are opposed to education beyond the eighth grade level. What this record shows is that they are opposed to conventional formal education of the type provided by a certified high school because it comes at the child's crucial adolescent period of religious development. Dr. Donald Erickson, for example, testified that their system of learning-by-doing was an "ideal system" of education in terms of preparing Amish children for life as adults in the Amish community, and that "I would be inclined to say they do a better job in this than most of the rest of us do." As he put it, "These people aren't purporting to be learned people, and it seems to me the self-sufficiency of the community is the best evidence I can point to— whatever is being done seems to function well." [280]

****

Insofar as the State's claim rests on the view that a brief additional period of formal education is imperative to enable the Amish to participate effectively and intelligently in our democratic process, it must fall. The Amish alternative to formal secondary school education has enabled them to function effectively in their day-to-day life under self-imposed limitations on relations with the world, and to survive and prosper in contemporary society as a separate, sharply identifiable and highly self-sufficient community for more than 200 years in this country. In itself this is

---

[279] Title 26 U. S. C. §1402 (h) authorizes the Secretary of Health, Education, and Welfare to exempt members of "a recognized religious sect," existing at all times since December 31, 1950, from the obligation to pay social security taxes if they are, by reason of the tenets of their sect, opposed to receipt of such benefits and agree to waive them, provided the Secretary finds that the sect makes reasonable provision for its dependent members The history of the exemption shows it was enacted with the situation of the Old order Amish specifically in view H R Rep. No 213, 89th Cong, 1st Sess, l0I-102 (1965)

The record in this case establishes without contradiction that the Green County Amish had never been known to commit crimes, that none had been known to receive public assistance, and that none were unemployed

[280] Dr Erickson had previously written: any public educators would be elated if their programs were as successful in preparing students for productive community life as the Amish system seems to be. In fact, while some public schoolmen strive to outlaw the Amish approach, others are being forced to emulate many of its features " Erickson, Showdown at an Amish Schoolhouse: A Description and Analysis of the Iowa Controversy, in Public Controls for Nonpublic Schools.15, 53 (D. Erickson ed. 1969) . And see Littell,.supra. n. 5, at 61.

strong evidence that they are capable of fulfilling the social and political responsibilities of citizenship without compelled attendance beyond the eighth grade at the price of jeopardizing their free exercise of religious belief.[281] When Thomas Jefferson emphasized the need for education as a bulwark of a free people against tyranny, there is nothing to indicate he had in mind compulsory education through any fixed age beyond a basic education. Indeed, the Amish communities singularly parallel and reflect many of the virtues of Jefferson's ideal of the "sturdy yeoman" who would form the basis of what he considered as the ideal of a democratic society.[282] Even their idiosyncratic separateness exemplifies the diversity we profess to admire and encourage.

...The independence and successful social functioning of the Amish community for a period approaching almost three centuries and more than 200 years in this country are strong evidence that there is at best a speculative gain, in terms of meeting the duties of citizenship, from an additional one or two years of compulsory formal education. Against this background it would require a more particularized showing from the State on this point to justify the severe interference with religious freedom such additional compulsory attendance would entail

****

...There is no intimation that the Amish employment of their children on family farms is in any way deleterious to their health or that Amish parents exploit children at tender years. Any such inference would be contrary to the record before us. Moreover, employment of Amish children on the family farm does not present the undesirable economic aspects of eliminating jobs that might otherwise be held by adults.

IV

Finally, the State, ... argues that a decision exempting Amish children from the State's requirement fails to recognize the substantive right of the Amish child to a secondary education, and fails to give due regard to the power of the State as parens patriae to extend the benefit of secondary education to children regardless of the wishes of their parents.

****

This case, of course, is not one in which any harm to the physical or mental health of the child or to the public safety, peace, order, or welfare has been demonstrated or may be properly inferred. The record is to the contrary, and any reliance on that theory would find no support in the evidence.

Contrary to the suggestion of the dissenting opinion of MR JUSTICE DOUGLAS, our holding today in no degree depends on the assertion of the religious interest of the child as contrasted with that of the parents. It is the parents who are subject to prosecution here for failing to cause their children to attend school, and it is their right of free exercise, not that of their children, that must determine

---

[281] All of the children involved in this case are graduates of the eighth grade. In the county court, the defense introduced a study by Dr. Hostetler indicating that Amish children in the eighth grade achieved comparably to non-Amish children in the basic skills. Supp App. 9-11. See generally Hostetler & Huntington, supra, n. 5, at 88-96.

[282] While Jefferson recognized that education was essential to the welfare and liberty of the people, he was reluctant to directly force instruction of children "in opposition to the will of the parent." Instead he proposed that state citizenship be conditioned on the ability to "read readily in some tongue, native or acquired." Letter from Thomas Jefferson to Joseph Cabell, Sept. 9, 1817, in 17 Writings of Thomas Jefferson 417, 423-24 (Mem. ed. 1904). And it is clear that, so far as the mass of the people were concerned, he envisaged that a basic education in the "three R's" would sufficiently meet the interests of the State. He suggested that after completion of elementary school, "those destined for labor will engage in the business of agriculture, or enter into apprenticeships to such handicraft art as may be their choice." Letter from Thomas Jefferson to Peter Carr, ,Sept. 7, 1814, in Thomas Jefferson and Education in a Republic 93-106 (Arrowood ed. 1930). See also id., at 60-64, 70, 83, 136-137.

Wisconsin's power to impose criminal penalties on the parent. The dissent argues that a child who expresses a desire to attend public high school in conflict with the wishes of his parents should not be prevented from doing so. There is no reason for the Court to consider that point since it is not an issue in the case. The children are not parties to this litigation The State has at no point tried this case on the theory that respondents were preventing their children from attending school against their expressed desires, and indeed the record is to the contrary.[283] The State's position from the outset has been that it is empowered to apply its compulsory-attendance law to Amish parents in the same manner as to other parents— that is, without regard to the wishes of the child. That is the claim we reject today.

Our holding in no way determines the proper resolution of possible competing interests of parents, children, and the State in an appropriate state court proceeding in which the power of the State is asserted on the theory that Amish parents are preventing their minor children from attending high school despite their expressed desires to the contrary. Recognition of the claim of the State in such a proceeding would, of course, call into question traditional concepts of parental control over the religious upbringing and education of their minor children recognized in this Court's past decisions. It is clear that such an intrusion by a State into family decisions in the area of religious training would give rise to grave questions of religious freedom comparable to those raised here and those presented in Pierce v. Society of Sisters. On this record we neither reach nor decide those issues.

The State's argument proceeds without reliance on any actual conflict between the wishes of parents and children. It appears to rest on the potential that exemption of Amish parents from the requirements of the compulsory-education law might allow some parents to act contrary to the best interests of their children by foreclosing their opportunity to make an intelligent choice between the Amish way of life and that of the outside world. The same argument could, of course, be made with respect to all church schools short of college. There is nothing in the record or in the ordinary course of human experience to suggest that non-Amish parents generally consult with children of ages 14-16 if they are placed in a church school of the parents' faith.

Indeed, it seems clear that if the State is empowered, as parens patriae, to "save" a child from himself or his Amish parents by requiring an additional two years of compulsory formal high school education, the State will in large measure influence, if not determine, the religious future of the child. Even more markedly than in Prince, therefore, this case involves the fundamental interest of parents, as contrasted with that of the State, to guide the religious future and education of their children. The history and culture of Western civilization reflect a strong tradition of parental concern for the nurture and upbringing of their children. This primary role of the parents in the upbringing of their children is now established beyond debate as an enduring American tradition.

****

In the face of our consistent emphasis on the central values underlying the Religion Clauses in our constitutional scheme of government, we cannot accept a

---

[283] The only relevant testimony in the record is to the effect that the wishes of the one child who testified corresponded with those of her parents. Testimony of Frieda Yoder, Tr. 92-94, to the effect that her personal religious beliefs guided her decision to discontinue school attendance after the eighth grade. The other children were not called by either side.

parens patriae claim of such all-encompassing scope and with such sweeping potential for broad and unforeseeable application as that urged by the State.

V

For the reasons stated we hold, with the Supreme Court of Wisconsin, that the First and Fourteenth Amendments prevent the State from compelling respondents to cause their children to attend formal high school to age 16. Our disposition of this case, however, in no way alters our recognition of the obvious fact that courts are not school boards or legislatures. and are ill-equipped to determine the "necessity" of discrete aspects of a State's program of compulsory education. This should suggest that courts must move with great circumspection in performing the sensitive and delicate task of weighing a State's legitimate social concern when faced with religious claims for exemption from generally applicable educational requirements. It cannot be overemphasized that we are not dealing with a way of life and mode of education by a group claiming to have recently discovered some "progressive" or more enlightened process for rearing children for modern life.

Aided by a history of three centuries as an identifiable religious sect and a long history as a successful and self-sufficient segment of American society, the Amish in this case have convincingly demonstrated the sincerity of their religious beliefs, the interrelationship of belief with their mode of life, the vital role that belief and daily conduct play in the continued survival of Old Order Amish communities and their religious organization, and the hazards presented by the State's enforcement of a statute generally valid as to others. Beyond this, they have carried the even more difficult burden of demonstrating the adequacy of their alternative mode of continuing informal vocational education in terms of precisely those overall interests that the State advances in support of its program of compulsory high school education. In light of this convincing showing, one that probably few other religious groups or sects could make, and weighing the minimal difference between what the State would require and what the Amish already accept, it was incumbent on the State to show with more particularity how its admittedly strong interest in compulsory education would be adversely affected by granting an exemption to the Amish.

Nothing we hold is intended to undermine the general applicability of the State's compulsory school-attendance statutes or to limit the power of the State to promulgate reasonable standards that, while not impairing the free exercise of religion, provide for continuing agricultural vocational education under parental and church guidance by the Old Order Amish or others similarly situated. The States have had a long history of amicable and effective relationships with church-sponsored schools, and there is no basis for assuming that, in this related context, reasonable standards cannot be established concerning the content of the continuing vocational education of Amish children under parental guidance, provided always that state regulations are not inconsistent with what we have said in this opinion.[284]

Affirmed.

****

---

[284] Several States have now adopted plans to accommodate Amish religious beliefs through the establishment of an "Amish vocational school." See n. 3, supra. These are not schools in the traditional sense of the word. As previously noted, respondents attempted to reach a compromise with the State of Wisconsin patterned after the Pennsylvania plan, but those efforts were not productive. There is no basis to assume that Wisconsin will be unable to reach a satisfactory accommodation with the Amish in light of what we now hold, so as to serve its interests without impinging on respondents' protected free exercise of their religion.

provided always that state regulations are not inconsistent with what we have said in this opinion.[284]

Affirmed.

****

B
COMPULSORY ATTENDANCE AND THE 14TH AMENDMENT RIGHT TO
EQUAL PROTECTION OF THE LAW

The Constitution was amended following the Civil War. Section 1 of the Fourteenth Amendment provides that "no State shall ... deny to any person within its jurisdiction the equal protection of the laws." Early Supreme Court interpretation of the Amendment concluded that the duty imposed by the provision was satisfied if the state provided "separate but equal" facilities. Pursuant to this interpretation public education was provided in racially segregated facilities by law in some states and through state practices in others.

Equal Protection Prohibits State Segregated Schools

Initially the doctrine of 'separate but equal' was successfully challenged in higher education. Then in 1954 the doctrine was successfully challenged at the elementary and secondary education level in the landmark case of **Brown v. Board of Education**.[285]

BROWN
v.
BOARD OF EDUCATION
347 U.S. 483, 74 S.Ct. 686 (1954)

CHIEF JUSTICE WARREN delivered the opinion of the Court.

These cases come to us from the states of Kansas, South Carolina, Virginia, and Delaware. They are premised on different facts and different local conditions, but a common legal question justifies their consideration together in this consolidated opinion.

In each of the cases, minors of the Negro race, through their legal representatives, seek the aid of the courts in obtaining admission to the public schools of their community on a nonsegregated basis. In each instance, they have been denied admission to schools attended by white children under laws requiring or permitting segregation according to race. This segregation was alleged to deprive the plaintiff of the equal protection of the laws under the Fourteenth Amendment. In each of the cases other than the Delaware case, a three-judge federal district court denied relief to the plaintiffs on the so-called "separate but equal doctrine" announced by this court in Plessy v. Ferguson, 163 U.S. 537. Under that doctrine, equality of treatment is accorded when the races are provided substantially equal facilities, even though these facilities be separate. In the Delaware case, the

---

[284] Several States have now adopted plans to accommodate Amish religious beliefs through the establishment of an "Amish vocational school." See n. 3, supra. These are not schools in the traditional sense of the word. As previously noted, respondents attempted to reach a compromise with the State of Wisconsin patterned after the Pennsylvania plan, but those efforts were not productive. There is no basis to assume that Wisconsin will be unable to reach a satisfactory accommodation with the Amish in light of what we now hold, so as to serve its interests without impinging on respondents' protected free exercise of their religion.

[285] 347 U.S. 483, 74 S.Ct. 686 (1954)

Reargument was largely devoted to the circumstances surrounding the adoption of the Fourteenth Amendment in 1868. It covered exhaustively consideration of the Amendment in Congress ratification by the states, then existing practices in racial segregation, and the views of proponents and opponents of the Amendment. This discussion and.our own investigation convince us that, although these sources cast some light, it is not enough to resolve the problem with which we are faced. At best, they are inconclusive. The most avid proponents of the post-War Amendments undoubtedly intended them to remove all legal distinctions among "all persons born or naturalized in the United States." Their opponents, just as certainly, were antagonistic to both the letter and the spirit of the Amendments and wished them to have the most limited effect. What others in Congress and the state legislatures had in mind cannot be determined with any degree of certainty.

An additional reason for the inconclusive nature of the Amendment's history, with respect to segregated schools, is the status of public education at that time. In the South, the movement toward free common schools, supported by general taxation, had not yet taken hold. Education of white children was largely in the hands of private groups. Education of Negroes was almost nonexistent, and practically all of the race were illiterate. In fact, any education of Negroes was forbidden by law in some states. Today, in contrast, many Negroes have achieved outstanding success in the arts and sciences as well as in the business and professional worlds. It is true that public school education at the time of the Amendment had advanced further in the North, but the effect of the Amendment on Northern States was generally ignored in the congressional debates. Even in the North, the conditions of public education did not approximate those existing today. The curriculum was usually rudimentary; ungraded schools were common in rural areas; the school term was but three months a year in many states; and compulsory school attendance was virtually unknown. As a consequence, it is not surprising that there should be so little in the history of the Fourteenth Amendment relating to its intended effect on public education

In the first cases in this court construing the Fourteenth Amendment, decided shortly after its adoption, the court interpreted it as proscribing all state-imposed discriminations against the Negro race. The doctrine of "separate but equal" did not make its appearance in this court until 1896 in the case of Plessy v. Ferguson, involving not education but transportation. American courts have since labored with the doctrine for over half a century. In this Court, there have been six cases involving the "separate but equal" doctrine in the field of public education. In Cumming v. County Board of Education, and Gong Lum v. Rice, the validity of the doctrine itself was not challenged. In more recent cases, all on the graduate school level, inequality was found in that specific benefits enjoyed by white students were denied to Negro students of the same educational qualifications. In none of these cases was it necessary to re-examine the doctrine to grant relief to the Negro plaintiff. And in Sweatt v. Painter, supra, the Court expressly reserved decision on the question whether Plessy v. Ferguson should be held inapplicable to public education.

In the instant cases, that question is directly presented. Here, unlike Sweatt v. Painter, there are findings below that the Negro and white schools involved have been equalized, or are being equalized, with respect to buildings, curricula, qualifications and salaries of teachers, and other "tangible" factors. Our decision, therefore, cannot turn on merely a comparison of these tangible factors in the Negro and white schools involved in each of the cases. We must look instead to the effect of segregation itself on public education.

In approaching this problem, we cannot turn the clock back to 1868 when the Amendment was adopted, or even to 1896 when Plessy v. Ferguson was written. We must consider public education in the light of its full development and its present place in American life throughout the Nation. Only in this way can it be determined if segregation in public schools deprives these plaintiffs of the equal protection of the laws.

Today, education is perhaps the most important function of state and local governments. Compulsory school attendance laws and the great expenditures for education both demonstrate our recognition of the importance of education to our democratic society. It is required in the performance of our most basic public responsibilities, even service in the armed forces. It is the very foundation of good citizenship. Today it is a principal instrument in awakening the child to cultural values, in preparing him for later professional training, and in helping him to adjust normally to his environment. In these days, it is doubtful that any child may reasonably be expected to succeed in life if he is denied the opportunity of an education. Such an opportunity, where the state has undertaken to provide it, is a right which must be made available to all on equal terms.

We come then to the question presented: Does segregation of children in public schools solely on the basis of race, even though the physical facilities and other "tangible" factors may be equal, deprive the children of the minority group of equal educational opportunities? We believe that it does.

In Sweatt v. Painter, supra, in finding that a segregated law school for Negroes could not provide them equal educational opportunities, this Court relied in large part on "those qualities which are incapable of objective measurement but which make for greatness in a law school." In McLaunn v. Oklahoma State Regents, supra, the Court, in requiring that a Negro admitted to a white graduate school be treated like all other students, again resorted to intangible considerations: ". . . his ability to study, to engage in discussions and exchange views with other students, and, in general, to learn his profession" Such considerations apply with added force to children in grade and high schools. To separate them from others of similar age and qualifications solely because of their race generates a feeling of inferiority as to their status in the community that may affect their hearts and minds in a way unlikely ever to be undone. The effect of this separation on their educational opportunities was well stated by a finding in the Kansas case by a court which nevertheless felt compelled to rule against the Negro plaintiffs:

> Segregation of white and colored children in public schools has a detrimental effect upon the colored children. The impact is greater when it has the sanction of the law; for the policy of separating the races is usually interpreted as denoting the inferiority of the Negro group. A sense of inferiority affects the motivation of a child to learn. Segregation with the sanction of law, therefore, has a tendency to retard the educational and mental development of Negro Children and to deprive them of some of the benefits they receive in a racially integrated school system

Whatever may have been the extent of psychological knowledge at the time of Plessy v. Ferguson this finding is amply supported by modern authority. Any language in Plessy v. Ferguson contrary to this finding is rejected.

Segregation with the sanction of law, therefore, has a tendency to retard the educational and mental development of Negro Children and to deprive them of some of the benefits they receive in a racially integrated school system

Whatever may have been the extent of psychological knowledge at the time of Plessy v. Ferguson this finding is amply supported by modern authority. Any language in Plessy v. Ferguson contrary to this finding is rejected.

We conclude that in the field of public education the doctrine of "separate but equal" has no place. Separated educational facilities are inherently unequal. Therefore we hold that the plaintiffs and others similarly situated for whom the actions have been brought are, by reason of the segregation complained of, deprived of the equal protection of the laws guaranteed by the Fourteenth Amendment. This disposition makes unnecessary any discussion whether such segregation also violates the Due Process Clause, of the Fourteenth Amendment.

Because these are class actions, because of the wide applicability of this decision, and because of the great variety of local conditions, the formulation of decrees in these cases presents problems of considerable complexity. On reargument, the consideration of appropriate relief was necessarily subordinated to the primary question—the constitutionality of segregation in public education. We have now announced that such segregation is a denial of the equal protection of the laws. In order that we may have the full assistance of the parties in formulating decrees, the cases will be restored to the docket, and the parties are requested to present further argument on Questions 4 and 5 (**appropriate remedy**) previously propounded by the Court for the reargument this term.. The Attorney General of the United States is again invited to participate. The Attorneys General of the states requiring or permitting segregation in public education will also be permitted to appear as amici curiae upon request to do so.

BROWN II
v.
BOARD OF EDUCATION
349 U. S. 294, 75 S. Ct. 753 (1955)

CHIEF JUSTICE WARREN delivered the opinion of the Court.

These cases were decided on May 17, 1954. The opinions of that date, declaring the fundamental principle that racial discrimination in public education is unconstitutional are incorporated herein by reference. All provisions of federal, state, or local law requiring or permitting such discrimination must yield to this principle. There remains for consideration the manner in which relief is to be accorded.

Because these cases arose under different local conditions and their disposition will involve a variety of local problems, we requested further argument on the question of relief.

These presentations were informative and helpful to the Court in its consideration of the complexities arising from the transition to a system of public education freed of racial discrimination. The presentations also demonstrated that substantial steps to eliminate racial discrimination in public schools have already been taken, not only in some of the communities in which these cases arose, but in some of the states appearing as amici curiae, and in other states as well.

whether the action of school authorities constitutes good faith implementation of the governing constitutional principles. Because of their proximity to local conditions and the possible need for further hearings, the courts which originally heard these cases can best perform this judicial appraisal. Accordingly, we believe it appropriate to remand the cases to those courts.

In fashioning and effectuating the decrees, the courts will be guided by equitable principles. Traditionally, equity has been characterized by a practical flexibility in shaping its remedies and by a facility for adjusting and reconciling public and private needs. These cases call for the exercise of these traditional attributes of equity power. At stake is the personal interest of the plaintiffs in admission to public schools as soon as practicable on a nondiscriminatory basis. To effectuate this interest may call for elimination of a variety of obstacles in making the transition to school systems operated in accordance with the constitutional principles set forth in our May 17, 1954, decision. Courts of equity may properly take into account the public interest in the elimination of such obstacles in a systematic and effective manner. But it should go without saying that the vitality of these constitutional principles cannot be allowed to yield simply because of disagreement with them.

While giving weight to these public and private considerations, the courts will require that the defendants make a prompt and reasonable start toward full compliance with our May 17, 1954, ruling. Once such a start has been made, the courts may find that additional time is necessary to carry out the ruling in an effective manner. The burden rests upon the defendants to establish that such time is necessary in the public interest and is consistent with good faith compliance at the earliest practicable date. To that end, the courts may consider problems related to administration, arising from the physical condition of the school plant, the school transportation system, personnel, revision of school districts and attendance areas into compact units to achieve a system of determining admission to the public schools on a nonracial basis, and revision of local laws and regulations which may be necessary in solving the foregoing problems. They will also consider the adequacy of any plans the defendants may propose to meet these problems and to effectuate a transition to a racially nondiscriminatory school system. During this period of transition, the courts will retain jurisdiction of these cases.

The judgments below, except that in the Delaware case, are accordingly reversed and the cases are remanded to the District Courts to take such proceedings and enter such orders and decrees consistent with this opinion as are necessary and proper to admit to public schools on a racially nondiscriminatory basis with **all deliberate speed** the parties to these cases. The judgment in the Delaware case-ordering the immediate admission of the plaintiffs to schools previously attended only by white children--is affirmed on the basis of the principles stated in our May 17, 1954, opinion, but the case is remanded to the Supreme Court of Delaware for such further proceedings as that court may deem necessary in light of this opinion.

****

Recent Cases

Decades of contentious litigation followed the <u>Brown</u> decision as the nation struggled to implement the principle of equal educational opportunity.[286]

---

[286]Jonathan Kozol concludes that the effort has been a failure. See Kozol, Jonathan, <u>Savage Inequalities</u>, Crown Publishers Inc., New York 1991. See also; First, Patricia F. & Miron, Louis F., "The Meaning of an Adequate Education," 70 Ed.Law Rep. [735] (January 2, 1992).

On January 15, 1991, in **BOARD OF EDUCATION OF OKLAHOMA CITY v. DOWELL,**[287] the Supreme Court reaffirmed the fundamental principles established by the Court in <u>Brown v. Board of Education</u> and other important school desegregation cases. In the Dowell decision the Court held that in order to be freed of court supervision of school desegregation decrees, a school district must show that **1)** it has complied in good faith with desegregation orders, **2)** that it is unlikely to return to its former ways and **3)** that the vestiges of segregation have been eliminated to the extent practicable. This determination insures that release from court supervision of school desegregation will continue to be made on a case-by-case basis by district courts. But the Supreme Court made clear that once the three criteria are met court supervision may end and outstanding injunctions may be lifted.

The <u>Dowell</u> case has special significance for Nevada because the first desegregation remedy adopted in Oklahoma City was similar to that adopted by the Clark County School District. Prior to 1954, the Oklahoma City public schools were segregated by law. In 1961, a group of black students and their parents sued the Board of Education of Oklahoma City to end segregation. The District Court found that officials in Oklahoma City had intentionally segregated both schools and housing. After a number of desegregation efforts, in 1972 the District Court ordered the Board of Education to adopt a desegregation plan involving significant student reassignments and increased transportation.

In 1977, the District Court found the School District "unitary"(desegregated) but did not lift the injunction requiring student reassignments. The plaintiffs did not appeal this order and the Board continued to implement the old busing plan.

In 1984, however, the School District adopted a new student assignment plan which discontinued busing for students in grades 1-4. The new neighborhood student assignment plan resulted in 11 elementary schools returning to enrollments of more than 90% black and 22 others exceeding 90% white enrollment. Minority students sought to reopen the case and challenge the new student assignment plan. The District Court upheld the School District's actions.

In 1989, after protracted proceedings, the Court of Appeals for the Tenth Circuit reversed the District Court. The Court of Appeals held that a desegregation decree remains in effect until a school district can show "grievous wrong evoked by new and unforeseen circumstances."

The Supreme Court reversed this decision, ruling that this onerous standard was not applicable to school desegregation cases. Rather, the Court concluded that if a school district has complied in good faith with a desegregation decree and eliminated the vestiges of past discrimination to the extent practicable, it is entitled to have a school desegregation decree terminated. When the decree is terminated, the Court explained, the school district can change the desegregation plan as long as it does not commit any new intentional act of discrimination.

The Court's holding was a reiteration of earlier Supreme Court doctrine. As the Court ruled earlier and restated in <u>Dowell</u>, in determining whether the effects of segregation have been eliminated as far as practicable, the lower courts should look "to every facet of school operations" including student assignment, faculty, staff, transportation, extra-curricular activities and facilities.

---

[287] __U.S.__, 111 S.Ct. 630 (1991). See also McCarthy, Martha M., "Elusive "Unitary Status,"" 69 Ed.Law Rep. [9] (October 24, 1991) & Vacca, Richard S. & Hudgins Jr., H.C. "The Supreme Court Charts a New Course for School Desegregation in the 1990's: Dowell's Pivotal Position," 75 Ed.Law Rep. [981] (Sept. 10, 1992).

A little over a month after Dowell, the Court agreed to decide a desegregation case from a school district that served suburban Atlanta. In Freeman v. Pitts the court of appeals determined that the Dekalb County School District, after more than 20 years of court supervision, had not yet erased the legacy of official segregation. In 1986 the school district asked the trial court to declare the district "unitary" (integrated) and end court supervision. The district court granted release from supervision in those areas where the school district had done everything that was reasonable to achieve maximum practical desegregation. The court of appeals reversed, holding that incremental release from supervision was improper. It held that a formerly segregated school district could not be considered "unitary" until it had achieved integration for a period of three years in six areas: student assignment, faculty and administrator assignments, transportation, physical facilities, extracurricular activities and allocation of resources. The Supreme Court reversed the court of appeals holding that school districts can be released from court supervision on a incremental basis.

FREEMAN
v.
PITTS
___U.S. ___, 112 S.Ct. 1430 (1992)

JUSTICE KENNEDY delivered the opinion of the Court.

DeKalb County, Georgia, is a major suburban area of Atlanta. This case involves a court-ordered desegregation decree for the DeKalb County School System (DCSS). DCSS now serves some 73,000 students in kindergarten through high school and is the 32nd largest elementary and secondary school system in the Nation.

DCSS has been subject to the supervision and jurisdiction of the United States District Court for the Northern District of Georgia since 1969, when it was ordered to dismantle its dual school system. In 1986, petitioners filed a motion for final dismissal. The District Court ruled that DCSS had not achieved unitary status in all respects but had done so in student attendance and three other categories. In its order the District Court relinquished remedial control as to those aspects of the system in which unitary status had been achieved, and retained supervisory authority only for those aspects of the school system in which the district was not in full compliance. The Court of Appeals for the Eleventh Circuit reversed, 887 F. 2d 1439 (1989), holding that a district court should retain full remedial authority over a school system until it achieves unitary status in six categories at the same time for several years. We now reverse the judgment of the Court of Appeals and remand, holding that a district court is permitted to withdraw judicial supervision with respect to discrete categories in which the school district has achieved compliance with a court-ordered desegregation plan. A district court need not retain active control over every aspect of school administration until a school district has demonstrated unitary status in all facets of its system.

****

Justice Kennedy's majority opinion also accepted the district court's conclusion that the resegregation of the school population was the result not of official action but of private choices and uncontrollable demographic shifts for which the school system had no continuing constitutional responsibility. "Racial balance is not to be achieved for its own sake." "Once the racial imbalance due to the de jure violation (segregation by law or other intentional state action) has been remedied, the school district is under no duty to remedy imbalance that is caused by demographic factors."

****

The Nevada Federal District Court recently rendered a decision involving a complaint charging that the Clark County School District was unlawfully segregated. The Clark County School District desegregation effort began in 1972.

<u>ARMSTRONG; LAS VEGAS ALLIANCE OF BLACK SCHOOL EDUCATORS, INC., et al.,</u>
<u>v.</u>
<u>THE BOARD OF TRUSTEES OF CLARK COUNTY ,et al.</u>
CV-S-89-418-LDG(LRL)
SLIP OPINION
DATED 11\15\91
UNPUBLISHED

ORDER

This matter is before the court on defendants' motion for summary judgment.

1. Background

In 1968 a federal class action complaint was filed in this court against the Clark County Board of Trustees, see <u>Kelly</u> v. <u>Mason</u>/CV-LV-1146 (D. Nev. 1968). The plaintiffs in that action alleged that the Clark County School District ("CCSD") was operating a racially segregated school system, in violation of the Equal Protection clause of the Fourteenth Amendment to the United States Constitution.

In an order issued on December 3, 1970, Judge Bruce R. Thompson of this court held in Kelly that the secondary schools within the CCSD were fully integrated, but that the elementary schools were not. Judge Thompson found that the CCSD's "neighborhood school" policy of enrolling elementary school students in schools close to their homes had produced a number of racially identifiable "black schools" in the Westside area of town. Accordingly, Judge Thompson ordered the Board to develop a plan to insure that no grade level in any elementary school had a black student enrollment of more than fifty (50) percent.[288]

To comply with that order, the CCSD adopted the "Sixth Grade Center Plan," under which the traditionally "black" elementary schools of the Westside were attended only by neighborhood children in kindergarten and members of a racially mixed sixth grade class, most of whom were bussed in from different areas of Las Vegas. The students in grades 1-5 who lived near the Westside elementary schools were thereafter bussed to other, more racially diverse schools.

The Sixth Grade Center Plan was challenged before Judge Thompson at the time of its implementation as unfairly burdensome to the Westside students, who would be bussed, under the plan, for five years while other children in the school district would only be bussed for one year. Judge Thompson rejected this challenge and the Ninth Circuit Court of Appeals affirmed that decision, ruling that no

---

[288]This order was later modified to permit up to sixty (60) percent black enrollment in any one school.

showing had been made that Judge Thompson had exceeded his broad discretion in approving the Sixth Grade Center Plan.[289]

In 1977 Judge Thompson terminated the court's jurisdiction over the Kelly case based upon his findings that the CCSD had fully complied with its affirmative duty to desegregate Clark County elementary schools. No appeal was taken from that decision. The CCSD has continued to implement the Sixth Grade Center Plan to date, with a few slight modifications.

2. This suit

In 1989 this suit was filed. Originally, the plaintiffs asserted claims based on alleged discriminatory practices at the CCSD that related to specific employment-related actions. In 1990, however, the plaintiffs filed a substantially revised amended complaint containing very sweeping allegations of pervasive institutional racism at the CCSD involving students, faculty, administration and staff. The plaintiffs claim that the CCSD Board of Trustees and Superintendent have intentionally taken specific steps to create, maintain and operate a racially segregated public school system within Clark County. Specifically, the plaintiffs have alleged that CCSD officials have intentionally created and/or maintained a segregated school system through site selection, school construction, facility management and utilization, drawing and re-drawing of attendance boundaries, the establishment and changing of grade structures and feeder patterns, recruitment, employment, assignment, promotion and demotion of staff at all levels throughout the system, selection and utilization of textbooks and other curricular materials, student discipline policies, academic tracing, the establishment, utilization and abandonment of optional attendance zones, use of zoning variances, placement and utilization of portable classrooms, additions, double sessions, year-round schools, and the development and use of extra-curricular activities.

3. Law

To prevail the plaintiffs must prove, essentially, two elements: 1) that the Clark County School District is operating a "dual" school system of distinct and identifiable "white" and "black" schools, and 2) that CCSD officials have intentionally discriminated against blacks to achieve this result. The defendants have moved for summary judgment, arguing that the plaintiffs have failed to produce sufficient evidence in support of their claims to create a genuine issue of material fact to be resolved at trial with respect to either element..

In support of their claims, the plaintiffs have submitted the following evidence: 1) two "preliminary reports" from school desegregation experts who have begun to review CCSD statistical data provided to them by the plaintiffs, 2) an affidavit from their own paralegal employee alleging that, statistically, blacks are underrepresented among CCSD administrators and 3) a series of affidavits from black CCSD employees (four total) who claim to have been passed over for promotion or demoted on the basis of their race. The plaintiffs have provided absolutely no evidence to support their allegations concerning CCSD curriculum, site selection, school construction, attendance boundaries, grade structures, feeder patterns or recruitment and disciplinary procedures, although plaintiff's experts

---

[289] Kelly v. Guinn, 456 F.2d 100, 110-11 (9th Cir. 1972), cert. denied, 413 U.S. 919, 93 S.Ct. 3048 (1973).

make a few oblique references to these subjects in the reports of their preliminary findings. The court will review each of plaintiffs' pieces of evidence.

A. The experts' reports

The plaintiffs have submitted two reports from retained desegregation experts. In these reports the plaintiffs' experts represent that a dual system of "white" and "black" schools is being operated by the CCSD. The conclusions reached by these experts must be reviewed against the undisputed statistical data made available by the parties with respect to the racial make-up of the CCSD students and faculty.

i) Elementary schools[290]

School desegregation cases usually involve schools within a district which are overwhelmingly black or Hispanic. The plaintiffs concede that there are no schools of this type within the CCSD. However, of the 107 elementary schools in the District as a whole, the plaintiffs' experts have labeled some 43 schools within metropolitan Las Vegas and 9 rural schools as schools intentionally opened and/or kept "white" by the practices and policies of the CCSD during the last twenty years. In order to assess whether these schools are identifiably white, the court must look both to the student body and the faculty:

> [E]xisting policy & practice with regard to faculty, staff, transportation, extracurricular activities, and facilities [are] among the most important indicia of a segregated system . . . . Independent of student assignment, where it is possible to identify a "white school" or a "Negro school" simply by reference to the racial composition of teachers and staff, the quality of school buildings and equipment, or the organization of sports activities, a prima facie case of violation of substantive constitutional rights under the Equal Protection Clause is shown.

If identifiably "white" or "black" schools exist within the CCSD as a result of CCSD policy and practice with respect to student and/or faculty assignment, an inference of discrimination might possibly be drawn.

However, the present undisputed statistical make-up of the schools the plaintiffs' experts have identified as "white" is as follows:

// // //

---

[290]The plaintiffs have apparently abandoned their claim that any of the District's high schools or junior highs are identifiable as "white" or "black." Rather, they focus on the elementary schools, including the sixth-grade centers.

School	Students[3] Black	White	Hisp.	Teachers Black	White	Hisp.
Lv-average	14%	69%	13%	8%	85%	4%
Beatty	2%	87%	7%	6%	91%	3%
Christen.	4%	86%	5%	3%	92%	3%
David Cox	2%	90%	4%	3%	95%	0%
Culley	13%	76%	7%	2%	88%	7%
Decker	14%	74%	6%	10%	88%	2%
Derfelt	7%	83%	6%	16%	75%	6%
Diskin	13%	68%	13%	4%	94%	2%
Dondero	10%	79%	5%	7%	80%	5%
Dooley	.25%	92%	5.5%	9%	91%	0%
Ferron	11%	67%	20%	7%	84%	7%
Ira Earl	13%	67%	14%	5%	91%	2%
Eisenberg	8%	86%	4%	3%	94%	3%
French	9%	83%	3%	3%	89%	5%
Galloway	1%	93%	4%	7%	90%	0%
Gragson	14%	60%	22%	7%	87%	4%
Gray	19%	72%	5%	5%	95%	5%
Harris	19%	73%	5%	10%	85%	3%
Hill	2%	88%	4%	7%	79%	7%
Hinman	3%	80%	13%	3%	85%	3%
Jacobson	6%	88%	5%	3%	86%	3%
Fong	18%	75%	6%	4%	93%	4$
Kim	9%	78%	6%	4%	86%	6%
Lake	11%	59%	20%	4%	87%	2%
Lincoln	43%	30%	22%	14%	86%	0%
Long	14%	71%	9%	5%	89%	3%
Mack	2%	91%	4%	2%	96%	0%
Manch	27%	62%	6%	10%	84%	2%
M. Earl	5%	88%	5%	10%	83%	2%
McDoniel	1%	92%	4%	7%	90%	2%
McWilliams	14%	73%	8%	5%	87%	0%
Paradise	12%	47%	35%	9%	83%	6%
Park	6%	40%	49%	2%	78%	20%
Red Rock	23%	67%	7%	9%	89%	0%
Ronnow	15%	63%	16%	8%	90%	3%
Ronzone	20%	72%	7%	5%	92%	3%
Sewell	5%	81%	13%	0%	93%	2%
Smith	16%	78%	4%	3%	95%	0%
Taylor	9%	74%	15%	2%	85%	7%
Tobler	14%	80%	4%	3%	92%	0%
Treem	6%	82%	9%	10%	77%	3%
Ward	12%	69%	13%	7%	93%	0%
Wasden	18%	69%	10%	2%	93%	0%
Whitney	1%	92%	7%	14%	86%	0%
Rural-avg.	1%	88%	8%	.25%	100%	.2%
Blue Diamond	0%	91%	7%	0%	100%	0%
Bowler	1%	87%	11%	0%	100%	0%
Indian Springs	2%	82%	9%	0%	100%	0%
Laughlin	2%	83%	11%	3%	86%	11%
Mt. Charleston	0%	95%	5%	0%	100%	0%
Perkins	0%	51%	27%	0%	92%	0%
Sandy Valley	1%	99%	0%	0%	100%	0%
Searchlight	05	100%	0%	0%	100%	00%
V. Valley	.25%	87%	12.7%	0%	100%	0%

Clearly these statistics fail to support the plaintiffs' allegations. There has been no pattern of demonstrably "white" schools established within the CCSD. The only area in which there is a fairly uniform disparity between the racial populations is among the rural school students and faculty. This disparity can be easily explained by demographics; no inference of intentional discrimination on the part of the CCSD arises from it alone.

If these are the schools that the plaintiffs have identified as the "worst" examples of segregation in Clark County, the court must assume that the remaining 82 CCSD elementary schools have racial mixes which are satisfactory to all parties. Under these circumstances, the court is compelled to conclude that the elementary schools within the CCSD are not segregated by race, notwithstanding the opinions expressed by the plaintiffs' experts.

---

[3] These statistics are derived from the official statistics submitted by the CCSD in support of its motion for summary judgment. They have not been challenged by the plaintiffs. Therefore, the court will accept them as accurate. The percentages have been rounded to the nearest whole number.

ii) The sixth grade centers

In addition, the plaintiffs' experts have identified several sixth grade centers as identifiably "black" schools. The relevant statistics are as follows:

	Students			Teachers		
School	Black	White	Hisp.	Black	White	Hisp.
Average	15%	73%	8%	23%	73%	1%
Booker	13%	77%	6%	10%	88%	2%
Carson	14%	71%	9%	29%	58%	0%
Gilbert	16%	75%	5%	20%	78%	0%
Hoggard	20%	71%	6%	33%	63%	0%
Kelly	14%	76%	6%	12%	87%	0%
Mackey	14%	73%	8%	36%	61%	0%
Madison	15%	67%	13%	33%	68%	0%
McCall	12%	72%	11%	11%	74%	3%

Again, these statistics compel a finding that the general racial make-up of the sixth grade centers represents the success of the CCSD to create a racially diverse, integrated school district. Even if plaintiffs' experts testify to the contrary, the statistics stand by themselves and effectively prevent the plaintiffs from proving the existence of a "dual" school system of either de facto or de jure segregation in Clark County.

B. The Hubbard affidavit

The plaintiffs have submitted an additional affidavit from their own employee who states that, according to her research, 72 elementary schools (out of 107), 17 junior highs (out of 25) and 9 senior high schools (out of 16) did not have a black principal or assistant principal during 1990. This statistic does not support an inference of intentional discrimination against blacks in view of the undisputed fact that 1) many elementary schools have only one "administrator" and 2) blacks comprise approximately 13 (13) percent of the total number of CCSD administrators, nine (9) percent of CCSD teachers, and eighteen (18) percent of CCSD staff. These numbers demonstrate that blacks are well represented within the CCSD at all levels, relative to their proportion to the general population.

With respect to proving actual segregation, the Supreme Court has ruled as follows:

> The constitutional command to desegregate schools does not mean that every school in every community must always reflect the racial composition of the school system as a whole,
>
> . . .
>
> Neither school authorities or district courts are constitutionally required to make year-by-year adjustments of the racial composition of student bodies once the affirmative duty to desegregate has been accomplished & racial discrimination through official action is eliminated from the system.

This case presents the situation of a school district that was found in 1977 to have accomplished desegregation and has an ongoing policy to maintain an acceptable level of integration among students and teachers. The statistics above, despite slight variances from the norm within individual schools, demonstrate that the goal of integration is still being actively pursued and met by the CCSD.

C. The employee affidavits

Finally, the plaintiffs have submitted four affidavits sworn by four black CCSD employees who allege that they were passed over for promotion and/or demoted for discriminatory reasons. These affidavits are made up almost entirely of conclusory allegations and unsupported accusations; they cannot, by themselves, create an inference of pervasive racial discrimination by the officials of the CCSD. The court has no doubt that these declarants believe, as they state, that they were the victims of racial discrimination. However, that belief, even if sincerely held, cannot take the place of specific facts which give rise to an inference of district-wide discrimination. The court finds no such facts identified in any of these affidavits.

D. Plaintiff's remaining arguments

The plaintiffs have submitted no additional evidence. They do, however, make a number of additional arguments on the basis of uncontested facts to demonstrate discrimination within the CCSD. For example, they claim that the fact that Henderson and Boulder City students have been excluded from participation in the Sixth Grade Center Program favors the students from those locales and gives rise to an inference of discrimination. They also complain that no schools have been built on the Westside since 1971 and make the very bold assertion that this is the result of the CCSD's intent to punish Westside families and the black community. Both of these arguments can be readily disposed of if examined in light of the geography and current demographics of Clark County.

First, Henderson and Boulder City are municipalities independent of Las Vegas proper and located at a considerable distance from the sixth grade centers in Las Vegas. It is, in the view of the court, disingenuous of the plaintiffs to suggest that these areas are excluded from the Sixth Grade Center Plan as a result of racial discrimination. It is much more easily inferable that these areas are excluded from the Sixth Grade Center Plan due to the extreme inconvenience and wastefulness that would be the result of bussing students from those locales in and out of Las Vegas, and of bussing students from Las Vegas in and out of those locales, every day.

Secondly, with respect to the placement of schools on the Westside, the Supreme Court has held,

> [i]n the absence of a showing that either the school authorities or some other agency of the State has deliberately attempted to fix or alter demographic patterns to affect the racial composition of the schools, further intervention by a district court should not be necessary.

No such deliberate attempt has been shown here. The undisputed facts before the court demonstrate that, between 1970 and the present, Clark County experienced an unprecedented population influx. During this period, the general county population increased by some one hundred seventy-five (175) percent. However, during the same period the population of the Westside area of town decreased by twenty (20) percent. Student populations have traced general population trends during this period. As a result, the black population (making up approximately nine and one half (9.5) percent of the general population) has become much more broadly dispersed throughout Clark County than it was twenty years ago. It makes perfect sense that the CCSD would endeavor to place schools where the population of Clark County was growing and hesitate to place schools in areas where the population base was diminishing, without regard to the racial make-up of either area. The fact that the CCSD has chosen to do this is undisputed and does not, in the view of the court, support any inference of discrimination.

4. Conclusion

The Supreme Court has summarized the two elements necessary to be proven in a school desegregation case as follows:

> It is understood that to prevail the plaintiffs [are] required to prove not only that segregated schooling exists but also that it was brought about or maintained by intentional state action. . ., that is, that the school officials had intended to segregate.

Here the plaintiffs have produced grossly insufficient evidence to prove either actual segregation or the intention to segregate. Instead, they have attempted to rely mainly on conclusory allegations. Under these circumstances, the case does not merit a trial and may be disposed of on a motion for summary judgment.

Accordingly, for the reasons above stated,

IT IS ORDERED that defendants' motion for summary judgment is granted.

****

Clark County School Board Action Outside Legal Arena

The decision of Judge George was appealed to the 9th Circuit Court of Appeals.

While the appeal was pending parents of black children continued to raise fairness issues regarding the 6th grade center plan at school board meetings.[291] It appeared that the parents primary complaint was directed at the busing policy which dated back to the original desegregation lawsuit in 1972.

In June 1992, the superintendent established the Educational Opportunities Committee(EOC) to make recommendations to him for the enhancement of educational opportunities for Clark County students, with particular attention to students living in West Las Vegas. In the course of its work, the EOC considered modifying the desegregation plan. The first report to the superintendent was delivered in late August 1992. The report consisted of two belief statements, one addressing funding formulas an the other discussing the sixth grade centers.

Following an emotionally charged school boycott at the beginning of the 1992-93 school year the school board, pursuant to a request by the superintendent, directed that certain aspects of the EOC's belief statements be implemented beginning with the 1993-94 school year.

Prior to the decision of the 9th Circuit which affirmed [292] the decision of Judge George the school board adopted the Prime 6 Educational Proposal.[293] Under

---

[291]Gallant, John, "Racism Charges Hurled at Board," Review Journal, June 10, 1992, p. 1B.

[292]The decision of the court is referenced in a "Table of Decisions Without Reported Opinions" appearing n the Federal Reporter. See Armstrong; The Las Vegas Alliance Of Black School Educators, Inc., v. The Board Of Trustees Of Clark County, Et Al., 990 F. 2d 1255 (9th Cir. 1993). The unpublished slip opinion which follows is not precedential and should not be cited except when relevant under the doctrine of the case, res judicata, or collateral estoppel.
Argued and Submitted March 9, 1993. Decided April 19, 1993. Appeal from the United States District Court for the District of Nevada; Lloyd D. George, District Judge, Presiding. D.Nev. **AFFIRMED.**
Before NORRIS, HALL and FERNANDEZ, Circuit Judges
MEMORANDUM [FN*]
"Appellants contend that the Clark County School Board ("Board") has created and maintained a segregated school system in violation of the Fourteenth Amendment's Equal Protection Clause. The district court granted summary judgment for the Board. We affirm.
To prevail on their Fourteenth Amendment claim, appellants must prove that the Board is operating a dual school system with racially identifiable "white" and "black" schools, and that the Board acted with discriminatory intent in achieving this result. Diaz v. San Jose Unified School Dist., 733 F.2d 660, 662 (9th Cir.1984) (en banc), cert. denied, 471 U.S. 1065 (1985). Furthermore, to survive summary judgment

the plan the district reconstituted 6th grade center schools as new elementary prime 6 schools. Beginning in the 1993-94 school year these schools would provide innovative educational programs which have a multiclutural focus and are developmentally appropriate for students in prekindergarten through grade three and sixth grade. Mabel Hoggard was designated a math and science special emphasis school. In addition, Fitzgerald Elementary School was constructed in the westside area to assist in the successful implementation of the plan. So, for the first time since the implementation of the 6th grade center desegregation plan in 1972 residents of the Westside have the option of sending their children to a neighborhood school begining with the 1993-94 school year. Prime 6 schools will accommodate fourth-graders in 1994-95 and fifth-graders the following year.[294]

Equal Protection Forbids Exclusion of Disabled Students From School.

In 1972 the Federal District Courts in Pennsylvania and the District of Columbia rendered decisions holding that exclusion of disabled students from public schools violated the equal protection clause of the 14th amendment.[295] These decisions played an important role in securing adoption of the Education for All Handicapped Children Act in 1975.[296]

C
COMPULSORY ATTENDANCE
AND THE
SCHOOL CURRICULUM

State and local school authorities have broad discretion to determine the scope and content of school curriculum.[297] This discretion is subject to constitutional

---

appellants must present "significant probative evidence" in support of the allegations of their complaint. Anderson v. Liberty Lobby, 477 U.S. 242, 249 (1986) (quoting First Nat'l Bank of Arizona v. Cities Service Co., 391 U.S. 253, 290 (1968)). If the evidence viewed in the light most favorable to appellants would fail to support a verdict in their favor, summary judgment for the Board is required. Appellants have not met their burden. While they make a plethora of claims regarding the appellees' segregative practices, they have no significant probative evidence to support these claims. First, in support of their claim of segregative student assignments, appellants submitted a preliminary report prepared by school desegregation expert William D. Lamson. The Lamson report, however, shows only that many of the new schools and new portable classrooms built between 1969 and 1990 were identifiably white, and that no new schools were built in the neighborhood in which the largest single cluster of black students lived. The report fails, however, to demonstrate that any of the decisions were made with an intent to discriminate. Because "[w]here resegregation is a product not of state action but of private choices, it does not have constitutional implications," Freeman v. Pitts, 112 S.Ct. 1430, 1448 (1992), we conclude that the Lamson report, without more, fails to support an inference that the Board acted with discriminatory intent in school siting or student assignments.

Nor does appellants' evidence regarding faculty and administrative assignments support the conclusion that the Board operates a segregated system. Appellants offer the declaration of school desegregation expert Marvin B. Scott to support their claim of segregative faculty assignments. Scott found that in 1991, thirty-five of the 107 elementary schools in the district had teaching staffs that were at least 90% white, whereas the teaching staffs at the historically black schools ranged from 8% to 33% black. In a school district in which 10% of the population is black, it is not statistically significant that one-third of the schools have faculties that are less than 10% black. Standing alone, these statistics fail to prove segregation. Appellants' evidence of segregative assignment of administrators is similarly deficient. Appellants' paralegalsubmitted a declaration stating there are no black administrators in 72 (out of 107) elementary schools, 17 (out of 25) junior high schools and 9 (out of 16) senior high schools. Again, these statistics do not prove segregation in light of the fact that blacks comprise 10% of the population and 13% of the total number of administrators. Nor is there any evidence that any statistical imbalance stems from intentional discrimination by appellees.

Finally, appellants have submitted affidavits from four black school district employees who allege that they were treated in a discriminatory fashion. Even if we assume that these highly conclusory employment discrimination claims have some basis, they are insufficient to support a claim that the Board intentionally created a segregated school system. Viewing the evidence in the light most favorable to the appellants, we hold that it fails to support the conclusion that appellees are operating a segregated school system in violation of the Fourteenth Amendment. **AFFIRMED.**

FN* This disposition is not appropriate for publication and may not be cited to or by the courts of this circuit except as provided by Ninth Circuit Rule 36-3."

[293]"Prime 6 Educational Proposal," Clark County School District, State of Nevada, proposal for discussion / action at the December 1, 1992 meeting of the Clark County Board of Trustees.

[294]Ibid., See also "Fitzgerald Elementary School Making Prime 6 Work," Review Journal, November 15, 1993, p. 1 B.

[295] See Mills v Board of Education 348 F.Supp. 866 (D.D.C. 1972) PARC v. Commonwealth of Pa. 334 F.Supp. 1257 (E.D. Pa. 1971) and PARC v. Commonwealth of Pa. 343 F.Supp. 279 (E.D. Pa. 1972)

[296] P.L 94.142, 20 USCS §§ 1400 et seq.

[297]See Steirer by Steirer v. Bethlehem Area School Dist. 987 F.2d 989 (3rd Cir. 1993). In Steirer pupils and parents sought court determination of whether a public high school could constitutionally require students to complete 60 hours of community service before graduation. The court upheld the requirement finding no merit in the 1st and 13th Amendment arguments raised by the students. See also Sherman v. Community

constitutional limitations. The scope of state power over school curriculum has been addressed in a series of Supreme Court cases starting with the landmark decision entitled **Meyer v. State Of Nebraska**[298]

MEYER[299]
v.
STATE OF NEBRASKA
262 U.S. 390, 43 S.Ct. 625 (1923)

JUSTICE McREYNOLDS delivered the opinion of the Court.

Plaintiff in error was tried and convicted in the district court for Hamilton county, Nebraska, under an information which charged that on May 25, 1920, while an instructor in Zion Parochial School he unlawfully taught the subject of reading in the German language to Raymond Papart, a child of 10 years who had not attained and successfully passed the eighth grade. The information is based upon "An act relating to the teaching of foreign languages in the state of Nebraska," approved April 9, 1919 (Laws 1919, c. 249), which follows:

"Sec. 1. No person, individually or as a teacher, shall, in any private, denominational, parochial or public school, teach any subject to any person in any language than the English language.

"Sec. 2. Languages, other than the English language, may be taught as languages only after a pupil shall have attained and successfully passed the eighth grade as evidenced by a certificate of graduation issued by the county superintendent of the county in which the child resides.

"Sec. 3. Any person who violates any of the provisions of this act shall be deemed guilty of a misdemeanor and upon conviction, shall be subject to a fine of not less than twenty-five dollars , nor more than one hundred dollars ($100,) or be confined in the county jail for any period not exceeding thirty days for each offense.

"Sec. 4   Whereas, an emergency exists, this act shall be in force from and after its passage and approval."

The Supreme Court of the state affirmed the judgment of conviction. It declared the offense charged and established was "the direct and intentional teaching of the German language as a distinct subject to a child who had not passed the eighth grade," in the parochial school maintained by Zion Evangelical Lutheran Congregation, a collection of Biblical stories being used therefor. And it held that the statute forbidding this did not conflict with the Fourteenth Amendment, but was a valid exercise of the police power. The following excerpts from the opinion sufficiently indicate the reasons advanced to support the conclusion:

"The salutary purpose of the statute is clear. The Legislature had seen the baneful effects of permitting foreigners, who had taken residence in this country, to rear and educate their children in the language of their native land. The result of that condition was found to be inimical to our own safety. To allow the children of foreigners, who had emigrated here, to be taught from early childhood the language of the country of their parents was to rear them with that language as their mother tongue. It was to educate them so that they must always think in that language,

---

Sherman v. Community Consol. Dist. 21, 980 F.2d 437 (7th Cir. 1992) upholding the power of the state to require that the public schools to lead the Pledge of Allegiance daily. The practice is consistent with the First Amendment so long as pupils were free not to participate.

[298] 262 U.S. 390, 43 S.Ct. 625 (1923).

[299] Compare Lau v. Nichols 414 U.S. 563, 94 S.Ct. 786 (1974) infra.

and, as a consequence, naturally inculcate in them the ideas and sentiments foreign to the best interests of this country. The statute, therefore, was intended not only to require that the education of all children be conducted in the English language, but that, until they had grown into that language and until it had become a part of them, they should not in the schools be taught any other language. The obvious purpose of this statute was that the English language should be and become the mother tongue of all children reared in this state. The enactment of such a statute comes reasonably within the police power of the state.

****

The problem for our determination is whether the statute as construed and applied unreasonably infringes the liberty guaranteed to the plaintiff in error by the Fourteenth Amendment:

"No state .....shall deprive any person of life, liberty or property without due process of law."

While this court has not attempted to define with exactness the liberty thus guaranteed, the term has received much consideration and some of the included things have been definitely stated. Without doubt, it denotes not merely freedom from bodily restraint but also the right of the individual to contract, to engage in any of the common occupations of life, to acquire useful knowledge, to marry, establish a home and bring up children, to worship God according to the dictates of his own conscience, and generally to enjoy those privileges long recognized at common law as essential to the orderly pursuit of happiness by free men. The established doctrine is that this liberty may not be interfered with, under the guise of protecting the public interest, by legislative action which is arbitrary or without reasonable relation to some purpose within the competency of the state to effect. Determination by the Legislature of what constitutes proper exercise of police power is not final or conclusive but is subject to supervision by the courts.

The American people have always regarded education and acquisition of knowledge as matters of supreme importance which should be diligently promoted. The Ordinance of 1787 declares:

"Religion, morality and knowledge being necessary to good government and the happiness of mankind, schools and the means of education shall forever be encouraged."

Corresponding to the right of control, it is the natural duty of the parent to give his children education suitable to their station in life; and nearly all the states, including Nebraska, enforce this obligation by compulsory laws.

Practically, education of the young is only possible in schools conducted by especially qualified persons who devote themselves thereto. The calling always has been regarded as useful and honorable, essential, indeed, to the public welfare. Mere knowledge of the German language cannot reasonably be regarded as harmful. Heretofore it has been commonly looked upon as helpful and desirable. Plaintiff in error taught this language in school as part of his occupation. His right thus to teach and the right of parents to engage him so to instruct their children, we think, are within the liberty of the amendment.

The challenged statute forbids the teaching in school of any subject except in English; also the teaching of any other language until the pupil has attained and successfully passed the eighth grade, which is not usually accomplished before the age of twelve. The Supreme Court of the state has held that "the so-called ancient or dead languages" are not "within the spirit or the purpose of the act.". Latin,

Greek, Hebrew are not proscribed; but German, French, Spanish, Italian, and every other alien speech are within the ban. Evidently the Legislature has attempted materially to interfere with the calling of modern language teachers, with the opportunities of pupils to acquire knowledge, and with the power of parents to control the education of their own.

It is said the purpose of the legislation was to promote civic development by inhibiting training and education of the immature in foreign tongues and ideals before they could learn English and acquire American ideals, and "that the English language should be and become the mother tongue of all children reared in this state." It is also affirmed that the foreign born population is very large, that certain communities commonly use foreign words, follow foreign leaders, move in a foreign atmosphere, and that the children are thereby hindered from becoming citizens of the most useful type and the public safety is imperiled.

That the state may do much, go very far, indeed, in order to improve the quality of its citizens, physically, mentally and morally, is clear;but the individual has certain fundamental rights which must be respected. The protection of the Constitution extends to all, to those who speak other languages as well as to those born with English on the tongue. Perhaps it would be highly advantageous if all had ready understanding of our ordinary speech, but this cannot be coerced by methods which conflict with the Constitution—a desirable end cannot be promoted by prohibited means.

****

The desire of the Legislature to foster a homogeneous people with American ideals prepared readily to understand current discussions of civic matters is easy to appreciate. Unfortunate experiences during the late war and aversion toward every character of truculent adversaries were certainly enough to quicken that aspiration. But the means adopted, we think, exceed the limitations upon the power of the state and conflict with rights assured to plaintiff in error. The interference is plain enough and no adequate reason therefor in time of peace and domestic tranquility has been shown.

The power of the state to compel attendance at some school and to make reasonable regulations for all schools, including a requirement that they shall give instructions in English, is not questioned. Nor has challenge been made of the state's power to prescribe a curriculum for institutions which it supports. Those matters are not within the present controversy. Our concern is with the prohibition approved by the Supreme Court. ...No emergency has arisen which renders knowledge by a child of some language other than English so clearly harmful as to justify its inhibition with the consequent infringement of rights long freely enjoyed. We are constrained to conclude that the statute as applied is arbitrary and without reasonable relation to any end within the competency of the state.

As the statute undertakes to interfere only with teaching which involves a modern language, leaving complete freedom as to other matters, there seems no adequate foundation for the suggestion that the purpose was to protect the child's health by limiting his mental activities. It is well known that proficiency in a foreign language seldom comes to one not instructed at an early age, and experience shows that this is not injurious to the health, morals or understanding of the ordinary child.

The judgment of the court below must be reversed and the cause remanded for further proceedings not inconsistent with this opinion. **Reversed.**

What is the current test for determining whether a state or school board has exceeded its authority to determine the content of school curriculum in matters unrelated to the Establishment Clause of the 1st Amendment?

As we know, in Nevada, the State Board of Education is vested with the power to adopt textbooks and establish courses of study which local districts are required to enforce. The following case illustrates criteria courts find persuasive when reviewing a challenge to the exercise of state or local district discretion regarding textbook [300] selection and course content.[301]

---

[300]The Oakland California school district rejected state adopted textbooks. A series of articles regarding the dispute appeared the 'Phi Delta Kappan'. The articles offer insight into the process of developing enlightened policy in the school curriculum arena. See Epstein, Kitty & Ellis, William F. " Oakland Moves to Create Its Own Multicultural Curriculum," Phi Delta Kappan, April 1992, p. 635+; Berenson, Edward, "Getting the Story Straight," Phi Delta Kappan, October 1992, p. 160+; and Ellis, William F. & Epstein, Kitty Kelly, "Who Needs Defending--Textbook Publishers or Students?," Phi Delta Kappan, October 1992, p. 163+

[301]See Steirer by Steirer v. Bethlehem Area School Dist. 987 F.2d 989 (3rd Cir. 1993). In Steirer pupils and parents sought court determination of whether a public high school could constitutionally require students to complete 60 hours of community service before graduation. The court upheld the requirement finding no merit in the 1st and 13th Amendment arguments raised by the students.

Additional background information on school curriculum and book censorship is available. Each year the People For the American Way, a self described constitutional liberties organization, prepares a report entitled "Attacks on Freedom to Learn." The 1992-93 edition was the organization's eleventh annual survey of censorship and other challenges to public education. The report provides two kinds of information. First, the study draws a general outline of the problem of censorship and other challenges to public education. Second, in a "50 Sate Report," summaries of individual incidents are presented.

The executive summary of the report outlines major 1992-93 findings.

"Attacks continue to rise: Challengers were more active in the 1992- 93 school year than at any time in the eleven-year history of this report. Three hundred ninety-five (395) incidents were reported in 44 states in all regions of the country this year. These include 347 cases of attempted censorship—where demands were made to remove or restrict curricular or library materials for all students. The five states with the highest number of incidents were California, Pennsylvania, Oregon, Texas and Washington. The least active states, where no challenges were reported, include: Hawaii, Rhode Island, South Dakota, Utah, Vermont, and Wyoming.

Censors succeed in 41 percent of challenges: The success rate of censorship challenges was disturbingly high. In fully 41 percent of the reported cases, challenged materials were removed or restricted in some fashion.

Broad range of targets: The range of challenges was extremely broad this year, with self-esteem guidance programs the most frequent target. Also challenged were classic novels; sex-education and drug-abuse-prevention; plays; films; student newspapers; school reform initiatives and more.

Religious Right and Far Right on the offensive: More than 20% of all incidents were the handiwork of right-wing political organizations and individuals working at the national or local level. Further, in an additional 18% of the challenges, targets and rhetoric were clearly inspired by these groups. Often casting their efforts as a defense of "parents ' rights," the movement continues to be at the forefront of censorship efforts in the public schools.

Library censorship attempts high: Challenges to library materials —books no child is required to read—were high for the second year in a row. Nearly half of all reported censorship challenges were to library books.

Religious objections most frequent: The most frequent rationale for challenges was that materials were perceived to be at odds with religion. Second most common were those in which treatment of sexuality was found to be offensive. Third most common were challenges in which materials were deemed to be profane or to contain otherwise objectionable language.

Teachers fired, harassed in the wake of attacks: In an unprecedented number of incidents, teachers were fired or otherwise harassed in the wake of challenges to educational materials." "Attacks on the Freedom to Learn 1992-93 Report," People for the American Way 2000 M Street, N.W. Suite 400 Washington D.C. 20036 (1993) p. 5-6.

Nevada is ranked 33rd on a 44 state ranking scale. Two Nevada incidents are reported in the State summary.

"In one of Nevada's two challenges, an objector charged that James Giblin's "The TruthAbout Unicorns" maligned the Catholic Church, promoted "Hindu religious ideas," and treated unicorns, "a symbol for Jesus Christ," sacrilegiously. In a second incident, the Eagle Forum assisted an objector's challenge to "Rolling Stone" magazine, specifically an article on prostitution in Bangkok.

1. INCIDENT: In Gardnerville, objections to "The Truth About Unicorn's" by James Giblin, available in an elementary school library for being sacrilegious in its use of a unicorn, a "symbol for Jesus Christ," for using "Hindu religious ideals" and for allegedly maligning the Roman Catholic Church. Removal requested

OBJECTOR: Grandparent.

RESOLUTION: Following a formal complaint, a school-level review committee decided to retain the book. School officials informed the objector of her option to appeal the decision to the school district level; she declined. "The Truth About Unicorns" remains on library shelves.

2. INCIDENT: In Storey County, objections to "Rolling Stone" magazine, available in district high school libraries for profanity and, in particular, for an article on prostitution in Bangkok. District-wide and statewide removal requested

OBJECTOR: Parents assisted by representatives from the Eagle Forum

RESOLUTION: A district review committee refused to remove the magazine. citing the school board's adoption of the American Library Association s Bill of Rights Objectors then appealed to the Nevada state Board of Education, calling for the state board to ban "Rolling Stone" from all public school libraries in the state. The appeal has been referred to the state superintendent of schools. At the time of the appeal the state board was considering new selection guidelines for public school libraries in the state. Objectors asked that the state guidelines not include the A L A 's Bill of Rights. The board declined, approving the new selection guidelines with the A L A.'s Bill of Rights included. Rolling Stone remains available in district high school libraries. The state superintendents decision on the proposed statewide ban of the magazine is pending." "Attacks 1992-93" p. 110-11.

VIRGIL[302]
v.
SCHOOL BOARD OF COLUMBIA COUNTY
862 F.2d 1517 (11th Cir. 1989)

Before TJOFLAT, ANDERSON and COX, Circuit Judges.
ANDERSON, Circuit Judge:

This case presents the question of whether the first amendment prevents a school board from removing a previously approved textbook from an elective high school class because of objections to the material's vulgarity and sexual explicitness. We conclude that a school board may, without contravening constitutional limits, take such action where, as here, its methods are "reasonably related to legitimate pedagogical concerns." Accordingly, we affirm the judgment of the district court.

I. FACTS

The essential facts were stipulated by the parties to this dispute. Since about 1975 the educational curriculum at Columbia High School has included a course entitled "Humanities to 1500" offered as part of a two-semester survey of Western thought, art and literature. In 1985 the school designed the course for eleventh-and twelfth-grade students and prescribed as a textbook Volume I of The Humanities: Cultural Roots and Continuities.[303] This book contained both required and optional readings for the course.

Among the selections included in Volume I of Humanities which were neither required nor assigned are English translations of Lysistrata, written by the Greek dramatist Aristophanes in approximately 411 B.C., and The Millers Tale, written by the English poet Geoffrey Chaucer around 1380-1390 A D. During the fall semester of the 1985-86 school year, a portion of Lysistrata was read aloud in class during a session of the Humanities course.

In the spring of 1986, after the first semester had ended, the Reverend and Mrs. Fritz M. Fountain, the parents of a student who had taken the class in the fall of 1985, filed a formal complaint concerning Volume I of Humanities with the School Board of Columbia County. The Fountains also submitted a Request for Examination of School Media. Their objections centered upon Lysistrata and The Miller's Tale.

In response to this parental complaint, the School Board on April 8,1986, adopted a Policy on Challenged State Adopted Textbooks to address any complaints regarding books in use in the curriculum. Pursuant to the new policy, the School Board appointed an advisory committee to review Volume I of Humanities. Upon examination, the committee recommended that the textbook be retained in the curriculum, but that Lysistrata and The Miller's Tale not be assigned as required reading.

---

[302] See also Mozert v. Hawkins County Board of Education, 827 F.2d 1058 (1987). The Supreme Court addressed the issues of removal of books from the school library in the case entitled Island Trees Union Free School Dist. 26 v. Pico, 457 U.S. 853, 102 S.Ct. 2799 (1982) Although there are a number of opinions in the Pico case it appears all the justices agreed that books could not be removed from a school library merely because the board members disagreed with the ideas contained in them.

[303] M. Witt, et al., eds. (1980) (hereinafter Humanities). Virgil v. School Board of Columbia County, 677 F.Supp. 1547, 1548 (M.D.Fla.1988). Volume II of Humanities was used in the second semester course, Humanities Since 1500. At all times relevant to this litigation Humanities has been the only approved humanities textbook in the Florida Department of Education's Catalog of State-Adopted instructional materials.

At its April 22,1986 meeting the School Board considered the advisory committee's report. Silas Pittman, Superintendent of the Columbia County School System, offered his disagreement with the committee's conclusion, and recommended that the two disputed selections be deleted from Volume I or that use of the book in the curriculum be terminated. Adopting the latter proposal, the School Board voted to discontinue any future use of Volume I in the curriculum.

Pursuant to the Board decision, Volume I of Humanities was placed in locked storage and has been kept there ever since. Volume II was used as the course textbook for the rest of the second semester of the 1985-86 academic year, as well as for both semesters of the "Humanities" course during the 1986-87 term. Since the Board's removal decision, both Volumes I and II have been available in the school library for student use, along with other adaptations and translations of Lysistrata and The Miller's Tale.

On November 24, 1986 parents of students at Columbia High School filed an action against the School Board and the Superintendent seeking an injunction against the textbook removal and a declaration that such action violated their first amendment rights. ...On January 29, 1988 the district court ...granted the defendants-appellees' motion for summary judgment.

The district court found that the two principal factors giving rise to the School Board's decision were "the sexuality in the two selections" and their "excessively vulgar . . . language and subject matter."... [T]he court held that the deferential standard recently established in Hazelwood School District v. Kuhlmeier, had been met, as the removal decision was "reasonably related" to the "legitimate pedagogical concern" of denying students access to "potentially sensitive topics" such as sexuality.

On February 19, 1988 plaintiffs-appellants filed notice of appeal to this court.

II. DISCUSSION

It has long been clear that public school students do not "shed their constitutional rights to freedom of speech or expression at the schoolhouse gate." At the same time, the Supreme Court has held that the rights of students in public schools are not automatically coextensive with the rights of adults...

****

In matters pertaining to the curriculum, educators have been accorded greater control over expression than they may enjoy in other spheres of activity.

****

The most direct guidance from the Supreme Court is found in the recent case of Hazelwood School District v. Kuhlmeier, [where the] authority of a high school principal to excise two pages from a school-sponsored student newspaper on the grounds that articles concerning teenage pregnancy and divorce were inappropriate for the level of maturity of the intended readers, the privacy interests of the articles' subjects were insufficiently protected, and the controversial views contained therein might erroneously be attributed to the school [was upheld]. Hazelwood established a relatively lenient test for regulation of expression which "may fairly be characterized as part of the school curriculum." Such regulation is permissible so long as it is "reasonably related to legitimate pedagogical concerns." [304]

---

[304] Tinker v Des Moines Independent School District, 393 U.S. 503, 509, 89 S.Ct. 733, 738 21 LEd.2d 731 (1969), held that school authorities may not prohibit student expressive activity unless it is shown "that engaging in the forbidden conduct would materially and substantially

In applying that test the Supreme Court identified one such legitimate concern which is relevant to this case: "a school must be able to take into account the emotional maturity of the intended audience in determining whether to disseminate student speech on potentially sensitive topics . . . [e.g.] the particulars of teenage sexual activity."

****

In applying the <u>Hazelwood</u> standard to the instant case, two considerations are particularly significant. First, we conclude that the Board decisions at issue were curricular decisions. The materials removed were part of the textbook used in a regularly scheduled course of study in the school. Plaintiffs argue that this particular course was an elective course, and not a required course. However, common sense indicates that the overall curriculum offered by a school includes not only the core curriculum (i.e., required courses) but also such additional, elective courses of study that school officials design and offer. Each student is expected to select from the several elective courses which school officials deem appropriate in order to fashion a curriculum tailored to his individual needs.

One factor identified in <u>Hazelwood</u> as relevant to the determination of whether an activity could fairly be characterized as part of the curriculum is whether "the public might reasonably perceive [the activity] to bear the imprimatur of the school." It is clear that elective courses designed and offered by the school would be so perceived. Moreover, we can take judicial notice that the journalism class which was considered in <u>Hazelwood</u> itself to be part of the curriculum was surely an elective course.

Plaintiffs further point out that the materials removed in this case not only were part of an elective course, but were optional, not required readings. For the reasons just mentioned, we conclude that the optional readings removed in this case were part of the school curriculum. Just as elective courses are designed by school officials to supplement required courses, optional readings in a particular class are carefully selected by the teacher as relevant and appropriate to supplement required readings in order to further the educational goals of the course. This is especially true in the instant circumstances, where the optional readings were included within the text itself, and thus had to accompany the student every time the text was taken home. Such materials would obviously carry the imprimatur of school approval.

The second consideration that is significant in applying the <u>Hazelwood</u> standard to this case is the fact that the motivation for the Board's removal of the readings has been stipulated to be related to the explicit sexuality and excessively vulgar language in the selections. It is clear from <u>Hazelwood</u> and other cases that this is a legitimate concern. School officials can "take into account the emotional maturity of the intended audience in determining .. . [the appropriateness of potentially sensitive topics" such as sex and vulgarity.

Since the stipulated motivation of the School Board relates to legitimate concerns, we need only determine whether the Board action was reasonably related thereto. It is of course true, as plaintiffs so forcefully point out, that Lysistrata and The Miller's Tale are widely acclaimed masterpieces of Western literature. However, after careful consideration, we cannot conclude that the school board's actions were not reasonably related to its legitimate concerns regarding the

interfere with the requirements of appropriate discipline in the operation of the school." In <u>Hazelwood,</u> the Court expressly declined to employ the more stringent <u>Tinker</u> standard. ___ U.S. at ___, 108 S.Ct. at 570.

appropriateness (for this high school audience) of the sexuality and vulgarity in these works. Notwithstanding their status as literary classics, Lysistrata and The Miller's Tale contain passages of exceptional sexual explicitness, as numerous commentators have noted.[305] In assessing the reasonableness of the Board's action,

[305] The textbook's introduction to the Lysistrata selection explains as follows: "Aristophanes, the only Greek classical comic author whose works survive, composed 'old comedies.' In his comedies, many of the old ritual features of the komos—the big phalluses, padding, animal costumes, grotesque masks, colloquial speech, and obscene jokes—are retained.... Because of its explicitness about sex, Lysistrata was forbidden reading in schools for a long time. Most modern readers, however. with less puritanical attitudes, find it extremely funny." M. Witt et al., eds. The Humanities: Cultural Roots and Continuities Vol. 1(1980) at 68. Evidently, the attitudes of some "modern readers" have been slower to change than this assessment suggests. Excerpts from Lysistrata which might reasonably be termed sexually explicit or vulgar include the following-.
LYSISTRATA: Darling Lampito, how pretty you are today!
What a nice color! Goodness, you look as though you could strangle a bull!
LAMPITO: Ah think Ah could! It's the workout in the gym every day; and, of co'se that dance of ahs where y'kick yo' own tail.
LYSISTRATA: What lovely breasts!
LAMPITO: Lawdy, when y'touch me lahk that, Ah feel lahk a heifer at the altar!
Humanities Volume I, at 70.
LYSISTRATA: I WILL HAVE NOTHING TO DO WITH MY HUSBAND OR LOVER
KALONIKE: I will have nothing to do with my husband or lover
LYSISTRATA: THOUGH HE COME TO ME IN PITIABLE CONDITION
KALONIKE: Though he come to me in pitiable condition (Oh, Lysistrata! This is killing me!)
LYSISTRATA: I WILL STAY IN MY HOUSE UNTOUCHABLE
KALONIKE: I will stay in my house untouchable
LYSISTRATA: IN MY THINNEST SAFFRON SILK
KALONIKE: In my thinnest saffron silk
LYSISTRATA: AND MAKE HIM LONG FOR ME
KALONIKE: And make him long for me
LYSISTRATA: I WILL NOT GIVE MYSELF
KALONIKE: I will not give myself
LYSISTRATA: AND IF HE CONSTRAINS ME
KALONIKE: And if he constrains me
LYSISTRATA: I WILL BE AS COLD AS ICE AND NEVER MOVE
KALONIICE: I will be as cold as ice and never move
LYSISTRATA: I WILL NOT LIFT MY SLIPPERS TOWARD THE CEILING
KALONIKE: I will not lift my slippers toward the ceiling
LYSISTRATA: OR CROUCH ON ALL FOURS LIKE THE LIONESS IN THE CARVING
KALONIICE: Or crouch on all fours like the lioness in the carving .
Id at 72
OLD WOMEN: Strip, strip, my women: we've got the veterans on the move! Tangle with me, Gramps, And you'll have cramps For the rest of your days! No more beans! No more cheese! My two legs Will scramble your eggs! Id at 80-81.
LYSISTRATA: Oh, quick, girls. quick! Come here!
FEM CHORAGOS: What is it?
LYSISTRATA: A man! A man simply bulging with love! ...
KINESIAS: Oh God! Oh my God! I'm stiff for lack of exercise. All I can to do stand up!
MYRRHINE: There we are. Ups-a-daisy!
KINESIAS: So we are. Well, come to bed....
MYRRHINE: Here we are. Up you go!
KINESIAS: Up? I've been up for ages! ...
MYRRHINE: At last! The right bottle!
KINESIAS: I've got the rightest bottle of all. and it's right here waiting for you. Darling, forget everything else. Do come to bed! ... Id at 83-85.
AN ATHENIAN: Let's take off our clothes and plow our fields.
A SPARTAN: Ah'll fertilize mahn first, by the Heavenly Twins! Id at 89.
    The editors of Humanities characterize The Miller's Tale as "Courtly Love in a Bawdy Version." Id at 207. Chaucer, the reader is told, "was interested in a wide range of people and topics, among them the comedy of sex.... The situation of the piece is one typically ripe for sexual hanky-panky...." Id
    Other scholars have characterized The Miller's Tale as one of several examples in The Canterbury Tales "of the genre of fabliau, which is capable of quite strict definition as a comic tale of low or bourgeois life, involving trickery, often obscene, with a coarse sexual motive." Derek Pearsall, ed., The Canterbury Tales (1985) at 166. The world of The Miller's Tale, it has been said, is one "in which men are aware of the compulsions of the flesh." Derek Traversi, The Canterbury Tales: A Reading (1983) at 70. "The presence of the obscene in The Miller's Tale," observes another writer, "has caused critical problems from the earliest times.... [I]t is evident from the beginning that Chaucer's readers have been reluctant to deal in print with its bold diction and its forthright descriptions of body functions." Thomas W. Ross, A Variorum Edition of the Works of Geoffrey Chaucer, Vol 11, The Canterbury Tales, Part III, The Miller's Tale (1983) at 12-13. "[N]o poet in the whole literary tradition of England," writes a biographer, "can write more titillating poetry than Chaucer's ... as in the Miller's Tale " John Gardner, The Life and Times of Chaucer (1977) at 119.
    The Miller's Tale contains the following passages which might be found vulgar or sexually explicit:
    "And he slyly caught her by the crotch and said, 'Unless I have my will, through my secret longing for you, I'll die!' And he held her hard by the buttocks, and said. 'Sweetheart, make love to me right now, or, by God, I'll die!'
Humanities, Volume 1, at 208.
    "Absolon wiped his mouth dry. The night was as dark as pitch, black as coal: and out the window she thrust her hole. And Absolon, as Fortune had in store for him, with his mouth kissed her naked ass with relish before he knew what was happening. He started back and thought something was wrong, for he knew well that women do not have beards and he had felt something rough and long-haired." Id at 212.
    "Nicholas had gotten up to piss and thought he could improve on the joke. He would have Absolon kiss his ass before he left. He quickly raised the window up and slyly thrust his ass far out, buttocks and all, even to the haunches. Then Absolon said, 'Speak, sweet bir. I don't know where you are.' Nicholas at once let fly a fart as great as a thunder clap, that almost blinded Absolon. But he was ready with his hot iron and smote Nicholas in the middle of his ass."
Id. at 213.

we also take into consideration the fact that most of the high school students involved ranged in age from fifteen to just over eighteen, and a substantial number had not yet reached the age of majority. We also note that the disputed materials have not been banned from the school. The Humanities textbook and other adaptations of Lysistrata and The Miller's Tale are available in the school library. No student or teacher is prohibited from assigning or reading these works or discussing the themes contained therein in class or on school property. ...Under all the circumstances of this case, we cannot conclude that the Board's action was not reasonably related to the stated legitimate concern.

We decide today only that the Board's removal of these works from the curriculum did not violate the Constitution. Of course, we do not endorse the Board's decision. Like the district court, we seriously question how young persons just below the age of majority can be harmed by these masterpieces of Western literature. However, having concluded that there is no constitutional violation, our role is not to second guess the wisdom of the Board's action.

The judgment is **Affirmed .**

STUDY QUESTIONS

1. Are the chances of reaching a national consensus on curricular matters advanced by the ruling in this case?

2. How would the decision regarding the use of the textbook involved in this case be made under Nevada law?

3. Does the outcome of this case support those who contend that locally elected school boards should not have the power to determine the nature and content of the school curriculum?

What is the test for determining whether state or local school district curriculum collides with the Establishment Clause of the 1st Amendment?[306]

EPPERSON
v.
ARKANSAS
393 U.S. 97, 89 S.Ct. 266 (1968)

MR. JUSTICE FORTAS delivered the opinion of the Court.
I

This appeal challenges the constitutionality of the "anti-evolution" statute which the State of Arkansas adopted in 1928 to prohibit the teaching in its public schools and universities of the theory that man evolved from other species of life. The statute was a product of the upsurge of "fundamentalist" religious fervor of the twenties. The Arkansas statute was an adaptation of the famous Tennessee "monkey law" which that State adopted in 1925. The constitutionality of the

---

"Thus was the carpenter's wife screwed in spite of all his care and jealousy; and Absolon kissed her lower eye; and Nicholas was burned in the rump."
Id.
[306]See Bjorklun, Eugene C., "Evolution and Creationism in the Public School Curriculum: The Academic Freedom Issue," 70 Ed.Law Rep. [277] (December 19, 1991). See also Berger v. Rensselaer Cent. School Corp., 982 F.2d 1160 (7th Cir. 1993) finding that classroom distribution of Gideon Bibles to fifth grade public school students violated the Establishment Clause.

Tennessee law was upheld by the Tennessee Supreme Court in the celebrated Scopes case in 1927.

The Arkansas law makes it unlawful for a teacher in any state-supported school or university "to teach the theory or doctrine that mankind ascended or descended from a lower order of animals," or "to adopt or use in any such institution a textbook that teaches" this theory. Violation is a misdemeanor and subjects the violator to dismissal from his position.[307]

The present case concerns the teaching of biology in a high school in Little Rock. According to the testimony, until the events here in litigation, the official textbook furnished for the high school biology course did not have a section on the Darwinian Theory. Then, for the academic year 1965-1966, the school administration, on recommendation of the teachers of biology in the school system, adopted and prescribed a textbook which contained a chapter setting forth "the theory about the origin . . . of man from a lower form of animal."

Susan Epperson, a young woman who graduated from Arkansas' school system and then obtained her master's degree in zology at the University of Illinois, was employed by the Little Rock school system in the fall of 1964 to teach 10th grade biology at Central High School. At the start of the next academic year, 1965, she was confronted by the new textbook (which one surmises from the record was not unwelcome to her). She faced at least a literal dilemma because she was supposed to use the new textbook for classroom instruction and presumably to teach the statutorily condemned chapter; but to do so would be a criminal offense and subject her to dismissal.

She instituted the present action in the Chancery Court of the State, seeking a declaration that the Arkansas statute is void and enjoining the State and the defendant officials of the Little Rock school system from dismissing her for violation of the statute's provisions. H. H. Blanchard, a parent of children attending the public schools, intervened in support of the action.

The Chancery Court, in an opinion by Chancellor Murray O. Reed, held that the statute violated the Fourteenth Amendment to the United States Constitution. The court noted that this Amendment encompasses the prohibitions upon state interference with freedom of speech and thought which are contained in the First Amendment. Accordingly, it held that the challenged statute is unconstitutional because, in violation of the First Amendment, it "tends to hinder the quest for knowledge, restrict the freedom to learn, and restrain the freedom to teach." In this perspective, the Act, it held, was an unconstitutional and void restraint upon the freedom of speech guaranteed by the Constitution.

On appeal, the Supreme Court of Arkansas reversed.... It sustained the statute as an exercise of the State's power to specify the curriculum in public schools. It did not address itself to the competing constitutional considerations.

---

[307] Initiated Act No. 1, Ark. Acts 1929; Ark. Stat. Ann. §§ 80-1627, 80-1628 (1960 Repl. Vol.). The text of the law is as follows:
"§80 1627.—Doctrine of ascent or descent of man from lower order of animals prohibited.—It shall be unlawful for any teacher or other instructor in any University, College, Normal, Public School, or other institution of the State, which is supported in whole or in part from public funds derived by State and local taxation to teach the theory or doctrine that mankind ascended or descended from a lower order of animals and also it shall be unlawful for any teacher, textbook commission, or other authority exercising the power to select textbooks for above mentioned educational institutions to adopt or use in any such institution a textbook that teaches the doctrine or theory that mankind descended or ascended from a lower order of animals.
"§8-1628.—Teaching doctrine or adopting textbook mentioning doctrine—Penalties—Positions to be vacated.—Any teacher or other instructor or textbook commissioner who is found guilty of violation of this act by teaching the theory or doctrine mentioned in section 1 hereof, or by using, or adopting any such textbooks in any such educational institution shall be guilty of a misdemeanor and upon conviction shall be fined not exceeding five hundred dollars; and upon conviction shall vacate the position thus held in any educational institutions of the character above mentioned or any commission of which he may be a member."

Appeal was duly prosecuted to this Court... Only Arkansas and Mississippi have such "anti-evolution" or "monkey" laws on their books. There is no record of any prosecutions in Arkansas under its statute. It is possible that the statute is presently more of a curiosity than a vital fact of life in these States. Nevertheless, the present case was brought,...and it is our duty to decide the issues presented.

II
****

...[W]e do not rest our decision upon the asserted vagueness of the statute. On either interpretation of its language, Arkansas' statute cannot stand. It is of no moment whether the law is deemed to prohibit mention of Darwin's theory, or to forbid any or all of the infinite varieties of communication embraced within the term "teaching." Under either interpretation, the law must be stricken because of its conflict with the constitutional prohibition of state laws respecting an establishment of religion or prohibiting the free exercise thereof. The overriding fact is that Arkansas' law selects from the body of knowledge a particular segment which it proscribes for the sole reason that it is deemed to conflict with a particular religious doctrine; that is, with a particular interpretation of the Book of Genesis by a particular religious group.[308]

III

The antecedents of today's decision are many and unmistakable. They are rooted in the foundation soil of our nation. They are fundamental to freedom.

Government in our democracy, state and national, must be neutral in matters of religious theory, doctrine, and practice. It may not be hostile to any religion or to the advocacy of no-religion; and it may not aid, foster, or promote one religion or religious theory against another or even against the militant opposite. The First Amendment mandates governmental neutrality between religion and religion, and between religion and nonreligion.

****

Judicial interposition in the operation of the public school system of the Nation raises problems requiring care and restraint. Our courts, however, have not failed to apply the First Amendment's mandate in our educational system where essential to safeguard the fundamental values of freedom of speech and inquiry and of belief. By and large, public education in our Nation is committed to the control of state and local authorities. Courts do not and cannot intervene in the resolution of conflicts which arise in the daily operation of school systems and which do not directly and sharply implicate basic constitutional values. On the other hand, "[t]he vigilant protection of constitutional freedoms is nowhere more vital than in the community of American schools." As this Court said in Keyishian v. Board of Regents, the First Amendment "does not tolerate laws that cast a pall of orthodoxy over the classroom."

The earliest cases in this Court on the subject of the impact of constitutional guarantees upon the classroom were decided before the Court expressly applied the specific prohibitions of the First Amendment to the States. But as early as 1923, the Court did not hesitate to condemn under the Due Process Clause "arbitrary" restrictions upon the freedom of teachers to teach and of students to learn. In that year, the Court, in an opinion by Justice McReynolds, held unconstitutional an Act

---

[308] In Scopes v. State, 154 Tenn 105, 126, 289 S. W. 363, 369 (1927), Judge Chambliss, concurring, referred to the defense contention that Tennessee's anti-evolution law gives a "preference" to "religious establishments which have as one of their tenets or dogmas the instantaneous creation of man."

of the State of Nebraska making it a crime to teach any subject in any language other than English to pupils who had not passed the eighth grade. The State's purpose in enacting the law was to promote civic cohesiveness by encouraging the learning of English and to combat the "baneful effect" of permitting foreigners to rear and educate their children in the language of the parents' native land. The Court recognized these purposes, and it acknowledged the State's power to prescribe the school curriculum, but it held that these were not adequate to support the restriction upon the liberty of teacher and pupil. The challenged statute, it held, unconstitutionally interfered with the right of the individual, guaranteed by the Due Process Clause, to engage in any of the common occupations of life and to acquire useful knowledge. Meyer v. Nebraska, 262 U. S. 390 (1923). See also Bartels v. Iowa, 262 U. S. 404 (1923).

****

...Today's problem is capable of resolution in the narrower terms of the First Amendment's prohibition of laws respecting an establishment of religion or prohibiting the free exercise thereof.

There is and can be no doubt that the First Amendment does not permit the State to require that teaching and learning must be tailored to the principles or prohibitions of any religious sect or dogma.

****

While study of religions and of the Bible from a literary and historic viewpoint, presented objectively as part of a secular program of education, need not collide with the First Amendment's prohibition, the State may not adopt programs or practices in its public schools or colleges which "aid or oppose" any religion. This prohibition is absolute. It forbids alike the preference of a religious doctrine or the prohibition of theory which is deemed antagonistic to a particular dogma. As Mr. Justice Clark stated, "the state has no legitimate interest in protecting any or all religions from views distasteful to them ...." The test was stated as follows in Abington School District v. Schempp: "[W]hat are the purpose and the primary effect of the enactment? If either is the advancement or inhibition of religion then the enactment exceeds the scope of legislative power as circumscribed by the Constitution ."

These precedents inevitably determine the result in the present case. The State's undoubted right to prescribe the curriculum for its public schools does not carry with it the right to prohibit, on pain of criminal penalty, the teaching of a scientific theory or doctrine where that prohibition is based upon reasons that violate the First Amendment. It is much too late to argue that the State may impose upon the teachers in its schools any conditions that it chooses, however restrictive they may be of constitutional guarantees.

In the present case, there can be no doubt that Arkansas has sought to prevent its teachers from discussing the theory of evolution because it is contrary to the belief of some that the Book of Genesis must be the exclusive source of doctrine as to the origin of man. No suggestion has been made that Arkansas' law may be justified by considerations of state policy other than the religious views of some of its citizens. It is clear that fundamentalist sectarian conviction was and is the law's reason for existence.

****

Arkansas' law cannot be defended as an act of religious neutrality. Arkansas did not seek to excise from the curricula of its schools and universities all discussion of the origin of man. The law's effort was confined to an attempt to blot out a particular theory because of its supposed conflict with the Biblical account, literally read. Plainly, the law is contrary to the mandate of the First, and in violation of the Fourteenth, Amendment to the Constitution .

The judgment of the Supreme Court of Arkansas is **Reversed.**

EDWARDS
v.
AGUILLARD
482 U.S. 578, 107 S.Ct. 2573 (1987)

JUSTICE BRENNAN delivered the opinion of the Court.[**]

The question for decision is whether Louisiana's "Balanced Treatment for Creation-Science and Evolution-Science in Public School Instruction" Act (Creationism Act), La. Rev.Stat. Ann. §§17:286.1-17:286.7 (West 1982), is facially invalid as violative of the Establishment Clause of the First Amendment.

I

The Creationism Act forbids the teaching of the theory of evolution in public schools unless accompanied by instruction in "creation science." No school is required to teach evolution or creation science. If either is taught, however, the other must also be taught. The theories of evolution and creation science are statutorily defined as "the scientific evidences for [creation or evolution] and inferences from those scientific evidences."

Appellees, who include parents of children attending Louisiana public schools, Louisiana teachers, and religious leaders, challenged the constitutionality of the Act in District Court, seeking an injunction and declaratory relief. Appellants, Louisiana officials charged with implementing the Act, defended on the ground that the purpose of the Act is to protect a legitimate secular interest, namely, academic freedom. Appellees attacked the Act as facially invalid because it violated the Establishment Clause and made a motion for summary judgment. The District Court granted the motion. The court held that there can be no valid secular reason for prohibiting the teaching of evolution, a theory historically opposed by some religious denominations. The court further concluded that "the teaching of 'creation-science' and 'creationism,' as contemplated by the statute, involves teaching 'tailored to the principles' of a particular religious sect or group of sects." The District Court therefore held that the Creationism Act violated the Establishment Clause either because it prohibited the teaching of evolution or because it required the teaching of creation science with the purpose of advancing a particular religious doctrine.

The Court of Appeals affirmed. The court observed that the statute's avowed purpose of protecting academic freedom was inconsistent with requiring, upon risk of sanction, the teaching of creation science whenever evolution is taught. The court found that the Louisiana Legislature's actual intent was "to discredit evolution by counterbalancing its teaching at every turn with the teaching of creationism, a religious belief." Because the Creationism Act was thus a law furthering a

---

[**] JUSTICE O'CONNOR joins all but Part II of this opinion.

particular religious belief, the Court of Appeals held that the Act violated the Establishment Clause.... We noted probable jurisdiction,... and now affirm.

II

The Establishment Clause forbids the enactment of any law "respecting an establishment of religion."[309]

In this case, the Court must determine whether the Establishment Clause was violated in the special context of the public elementary and secondary school system. States and local school boards are generally afforded considerable discretion in operating public schools. "At the same time . . . we have necessarily recognized that the discretion of the States and local school boards in matters of education must be exercised in a manner that comports with the transcendent imperatives of the First Amendment."

The Court has been particularly vigilant in monitoring compliance with the Establishment Clause in elementary and secondary schools. Families entrust public schools with the education of their children, but condition their trust on the understanding that the classroom will not purposely be used to advance religious views that may conflict with the private beliefs of the student and his or her family. Students in such institutions are impressionable and their attendance is involuntary. The State exerts great authority and coercive power through mandatory attendance requirements, and because of the students' emulation of teachers as role models and the children's susceptibility to peer pressure. Furthermore, "[t]he public school is at once the symbol of our democracy and the most pervasive means for promoting our common destiny. In no activity of the State is it more vital to keep out divisive forces than in its schools ...."

Consequently, the Court has been required often to invalidate statutes which advance religion in public elementary and secondary schools. See, e. g., Grand Rapids School Dist. v. Ball, supra (school district's use of religious school teachers in public schools); Wallace v. Jaffree, supra (Alabama statute authorizing moment of silence for school prayer); Stone v. Graham, 449 U. S. 39 (1980) (posting copy of Ten Commandments on public classroom wall); Epperson v. Arkansas, 393 U. S. 97 (1968) (statute forbidding teaching of evolution); Abington School Dist. v. Schempp, supra (daily reading of Bible); Engel v. Vitale, 370 U. S. 421, 430 (1962) (recitation of "denominationally neutral" prayer).

Therefore, in employing the three-pronged Lemon test, we must do so mindful of the particular concerns that arise in the context of public elementary and secondary schools. We now turn to the evaluation of the Act under the Lemon test.

III

Lemon's first prong focuses on the purpose that animated adoption of the Act. "The purpose prong of the Lemon test asks whether government's actual purpose is to endorse or disapprove of religion." A governmental intention to promote religion is clear when the State enacts a law to serve a religious purpose. This intention may be evidenced by promotion of religion in general, or by advancement of a particular religious belief. ...If the law was enacted for the purpose of endorsing religion, "no consideration of the second or third criteria [of Lemon] is necessary " In this case, appellants have identified no clear secular purpose for the Louisiana Act.

---

[309] The First Amendment states: "Congress shall make no law respecting an establishment of religion ...." Under the Fourteenth Amendment, this "fundamental concept of liberty" applies to the States. Cantwell v. Connecticut, 310 U. S. 296, 303 (1940).

True, the Act's stated purpose is to protect academic freedom. This phrase might, in common parlance, be understood as referring to enhancing the freedom of teachers to teach what they will. The Court of Appeals, however, correctly concluded that the Act was not designed to further that goal. We find no merit in the State's argument that the "legislature may not [have] use[d] the terms 'academic freedom' in the correct legal sense. They might have [had] in mind, instead, a basic concept of fairness; teaching all of the evidence." Even if "academic freedom" is read to mean "teaching all of the evidence" with respect to the origin of human beings, the Act does not further this purpose. The goal of providing a more comprehensive science curriculum is not furthered either by outlawing the teaching of evolution or by requiring the teaching of creation science.

A

While the Court is normally deferential to a State's articulation of a secular purpose, it is required that the statement of such purpose be sincere and not a sham. ...."It is not a trivial matter, however, to require that the legislature manifest a secular purpose and omit all sectarian endorsements from its laws. That requirement is precisely tailored to the Establishment Clause's purpose of assuring that Government not intentionally endorse religion or a religious practice."

It is clear from the legislative history that the purpose of the legislative sponsor, Senator Bill Keith, was to narrow the science curriculum. During the legislative hearings, Senator Keith stated: "My preference would be that neither [creationism nor evolution] be taught." Such a ban on teaching does not promote— indeed, it undermines— the provision of a comprehensive scientific education.

It is equally clear that requiring schools to teach creation science with evolution does not advance academic freedom. The Act does not grant teachers a flexibility that they did not already possess to supplant the present science curriculum with the presentation of theories, besides evolution, about the origin of life. Indeed, the Court of Appeals found that no law prohibited Louisiana public school teachers from teaching any scientific theory. As the president of the Louisiana Science Teachers Association testified, "[a]ny scientific concept that's based on established fact can be included in our curriculum already, and no legislation allowing this is necessary." The Act provides Louisiana schoolteachers with no new authority. Thus the stated purpose is not furthered by it.

****

Furthermore, the goal of basic "fairness" is hardly furthered by the Act's discriminatory preference for the teaching of creation science and against the teaching of evolution. While requiring that curriculum guides be developed for creation science, the Act says nothing of comparable guides for evolution. Similarly, resource services are supplied for creation science but not for evolution. Only "creation scientists" can serve on the panel that supplies the resource services. The Act forbids school boards to discriminate against anyone who "chooses to be a creation-scientist" or to teach "creationism," but fails to protect those who choose to teach evolution or any other noncreation science theory, or who refuse to teach creation science.

If the Louisiana Legislature's purpose was solely to maximize the comprehensiveness and effectiveness of science instruction, it would have encouraged the teaching of all scientific theories about the origins of humankind. But under the Act's requirements, teachers who were once free to teach any and all

105

facets of this subject are now unable to do so. Moreover, the Act fails even to ensure that creation science will be taught, but instead requires the teaching of this theory only when the theory of evolution is taught. Thus we agree with the Court of Appeals' conclusion that the Act does not serve to protect academic freedom, but has the distinctly different purpose of discrediting "evolution by counterbalancing its teaching at every turn with the teaching of creationism ...."

B

Stone v. Graham invalidated the State's requirement that the Ten Commandments be posted in public classrooms. "The Ten Commandments are undeniably a sacred text in the Jewish and Christian faiths, and no legislative recitation of a supposed secular purpose can blind us to that fact." As a result, the contention that the law was designed to provide instruction on a "fundamental legal code" was "not sufficient to avoid conflict with the First Amendment."

****

These ... historic and contemporaneous antagonisms between the teachings of certain religious denominations and the teaching of evolution are present in this case. The pre-eminent purpose of the Louisiana Legislature was clearly to advance the religious viewpoint that a supernatural being created humankind. The term "creation science" was defined as embracing this particular religious doctrine by those responsible for the passage of the Creationism Act.

****

Furthermore, it is not happenstance that the legislature required the teaching of a theory that coincided with this religious view. The legislative history documents that the Act's primary purpose was to change the science curriculum of public schools in order to provide persuasive advantage to a particular religious doctrine that rejects the factual basis of evolution in its entirety.

****

The legislation, therefore sought to alter the science curriculum to reflect endorsement of a religious view that is antagonistic to the theory of evolution.

In this case, the purpose of the Creationism Act was to restructure the science curriculum to conform with a particular religious viewpoint. Out of many possible science subjects taught in the public schools, the legislature chose to affect the teaching of the one scientific theory that historically has been opposed by certain religious sects. As in Epperson, the legislature passed the Act to give preference to those religious groups which have as one of their tenets the creation of humankind by a divine creator. ...[T]he Creationism Act is designed either to promote the theory of creation science which embodies a particular religious tenet by requiring that creation science be taught whenever evolution is taught or to prohibit the teaching of a scientific theory disfavored by certain religious sects by forbidding the teaching of evolution when creation science is not also taught. The Establishment Clause, however, "forbids alike the preference of a religious doctrine or the prohibition of theory which is deemed antagonistic to a particular dogma." Because the primary purpose of the Creationism Act is to advance a particular religious belief, the Act endorses religion in violation of the First Amendment.

We do not imply that a legislature could never require that scientific critiques of prevailing scientific theories be taught. Indeed, the Court acknowledged in Stone that its decision forbidding the posting of the Ten Commandments did not mean that no use could ever be made of the Ten Commandments, or that the Ten

Commandments played an exclusively religious role in the history of Western Civilization. In a similar way, teaching a variety of scientific theories about the origins of humankind to schoolchildren might be validly done with the clear secular intent of enhancing the effectiveness of science instruction. But because the primary purpose of the Creationism Act is to endorse a particular religious doctrine, the Act furthers religion in violation of the Establishment Clause.[310]

****

V

The Louisiana Creationism Act advances a religious doctrine by requiring either the banishment of the theory of evolution from public school classrooms or the presentation of a religious viewpoint that rejects evolution in its entirety. The Act violates the Establishment Clause of the First Amendment because it seeks to employ the symbolic and financial support of government to achieve a religious purpose. The judgment of the Court of Appeals therefore is **Affirmed** .

JUSTICE SCALIA, with whom THE CHIEF JUSTICE joins, dissenting.

Even if I agreed with the questionable premise that legislation can be invalidated under the Establishment Clause on the basis of its motivation alone, without regard to its effects, I would still find no justification for today's decision. The Louisiana legislators who passed the "Balanced Treatment for Creation-Science and Evolution-Science Act" each of whom had sworn to support the Constitution,[311] were well aware of the potential Establishment Clause problems and considered that aspect of the legislation with great care. After seven hearings and several months of study, resulting in substantial revision of the original proposal, they approved the Act overwhelmingly and specifically articulated the secular purpose they meant it to serve. Although the record contains abundant evidence of the sincerity of that purpose (the only issue pertinent to this case), the Court today holds, essentially on the basis of "its visceral knowledge regarding what must have motivated the legislators," that the members of the Louisiana Legislature knowingly violated their oaths and then lied about it. I dissent. Had requirements of the Balanced Treatment Act that are not apparent on its face been clarified by an interpretation of the Louisiana Supreme Court, or by the manner of its implementation, the Act might well be found unconstitutional; but the question of its constitutionality cannot rightly be disposed of on the gallop, by impugning the motives of its supporters.

****

STUDY QUESTIONS

1. What interest is at the heart of the requirement that government refrain from passing laws or engaging in other activity respecting an establishment of religion.
2. What are the elements of the Lemon test?
3. Is the test helpful for the purpose of guiding curriculum decisions? How?

---

[310] Neither the District Court nor the Court of Appeals found a clear secular purpose, while both agreed that the Creationism Act's primary purpose was to advance religion. "When both courts below are unable to discern an arguably valid secular purpose, this Court normally should hesitate to find one." Wallace v. Jaffree, 472 U. S., at 66 (POWELL, J., concurring).

[311] Article VI, cl. 3, of the Constitution provides that "the Members of the several State Legislatures . . . shall be bound by Oath or Affirmation, to support this Constitution."

4. Do advances in biotechnology raise curriculum issues similar and more complex curricular than those raised by the theory of evolution?
5. Does the Establishment Clause prevent private schools from teaching creationism?
6. Is creation science a science? Why? Why not

D
CHAPTER SUMMARY

Nevada, has enacted a compulsory attendance statute. Attendance at a private school[312] or equivalent home instruction satisfies the duty imposed by the law.

The power to mandate compulsory attendance must be exercised in a manner which is consistent with the Constitution. Actions regarding the school curriculum are subject to scrutiny under the 1st and 14th Amendments.

Equal protection of the laws requires that the state refrain from action which results in segregated schools. Equal protection also means that disabled students may not be excluded from the regular school setting.

Furthermore, the ability of state authorities to compel school attendance is related to its power to control the scope and content of the public school curriculum. Mandated school courses of study must have a rational basis. States must also take care to avoid adopting laws mandating a curriculum which endorses or denigrates religion.

---

[312] Nevada statutes regulating private schools can be found in Chapter 394 NRS (1991) Specific provisions dealing elementary and secondary education are located at Sec. 394.005-394.351 NRS (1991).

CHAPTER IV

LEGAL ASPECTS OF THE
SCHOOL DISTRICT \ TEACHER EMPLOYMENT RELATIONSHIP

RULES FOR TEACHERS [313]
1872

1. TEACHERS EACH DAY WILL FILL LAMPS, CLEAN CHIMNEYS.

2. EACH TEACHER WILL BRING A BUCKET OF WATER AND SCUTTLE OF COAL FOR THE DAY'S SESSION.

3. MAKE YOUR PENS CAREFULLY. YOU MAY WHITTLE NIBS TO THE INDIVIDUAL TASTE OF THE PUPILS.

4. MEN TEACHERS MAY TAKE ONE EVENING EACH WEEK FOR COURTING PURPOSES, OR TWO EVENINGS A WEEK IF THEY GO TO CHURCH REGULARLY.

5. AFTER TEN HOURS IN SCHOOL, THE TEACHERS MAY SPEND THE REMAINING TIME READING THE BIBLE OR OTHER GOOD BOOKS.

6. WOMEN TEACHERS WHO MARRY OR ENGAGE IN UNSEEMLY CONDUCT WILL BE DISMISSED.

7. EVERY TEACHER SHOULD LAY ASIDE FROM EACH PAY A GOODLY SUM OF HIS EARNINGS FOR HIS BENEFIT DURING HIS DECLINING YEARS DO THAT HE WILL NOT BECOME A BURDEN ON SOCIETY.

8. ANY TEACHER WHO SMOKES, USES LIQUOR IN ANY FORM, FREQUENTS POOL OR PUBLIC HALLS OR GETS SHAVED IN A BARBER SHOP WILL GIVE GOOD REASON TO SUSPECT HIS WORTH, INTENTION, INTEGRITY AND HONESTY.

9.THE TEACHER WHO PERFORMS HIS LABOR FAITHFULLY AND WITHOUT FAULT FOR FIVE YEARS WILL BE GIVEN AN INCREASE OF TWENTY - FIVE CENTS PER WEEK IN HIS PAY, PROVIDING THE BOARD OF EDUCATION APPROVES.

A
TEACHER CERTIFICATION[314]

Each state has enacted its own teacher licensing standards and procedures. In 1987 the Nevada Legislature created the Commission on Professional Standards in Education.[315] The commission is composed of 9 members appointed by the governor. Members are appointed for 3 year terms. No member of the commission who is a teacher, counselor, administrator or representative of the general public may serve more than two terms. Four members of the commission must be teachers

---

[313]DeMitchell, Todd A., "Private Lives: Community Control vs. Professional Autonomy ," 78 Ed.Law Rep. [187] (January 14, 1993).

[314] See Scannell, Andersen & Gideonse, "Who Sets the Standards: The Need for State Professional Standards Boards," Association of Colleges and Schools of Education in State Universities and Land Grant Colleges and Affiliated Private Universities. July, 1989. and Goodlad, John H., "Teachers for Our Nations Schools," Jossey-Bass Publishers, San Francisco, CA., 1990. A national certification effort is underway see "Toward High and Rigorous Standards for the Teaching Profession," National Board for Professional Teaching Standards 3rd Edition, Washington, D.C. (1991)

[315] Chapter 433, Stats. 1987 Sec. 391.005-032 NRS (1991).

who teach in the classroom (A secondary teacher, a middle school or junior high school teacher, an elementary school teacher and a special education teacher). Three members must include a counselor or psychologist employed by a school district and two administrators of schools, at least one of which must be a principal of a school. The remaining members are the dean of either the UNLV or UNR College of Education and member of the general public. One of the members must be employed by a private school licensed by the state.

Teacher and counselor members are appointed from lists of three submitted to the governor by the employee organization representing the majority of counselors and\or teachers in Nevada.[316] Administrators are appointed from lists of three submitted to the governor by an organization of school administrators in which the majority of administrators of schools in Nevada have membership.

The Legislature [317] has vested the commission with the power to adopt regulations prescribing the qualifications for licensing teachers and other educational personnel and the procedures for the issuance and renewal of such licenses.[318]

In 1993 the legislature adopted amendments requiring the commission to adopt regulations setting forth the educational standards needed for teachers to obtain endorsements in fields of specialization and requiring the state board of education to provide to an applicant, upon request, the course of study required to qualify for an endorsement.[319]

Prior to 1987 the State Board of Education possessed that responsibility. When the legislature transferred the power to the commission it reserved to the state board the authority to veto any regulation adopted by the commission if the regulation threatened the efficient operation of the public schools or created an undue financial hardship for any teacher, administrator or other educational personnel or any county school district. A regulation is deemed approved if the state board does not disapprove it within 90 days after it is adopted by the commission.

The standards, regulations and procedures adopted by the commission are published in the Nevada Administrative Code.(NAC).

Individuals wishing to teach in Nevada must possess a valid Nevada teachers license in order to be employed by one of the state's school districts. The purpose of licensing laws is to protect the general welfare. After all, parents are required to send their children to school and licensing is a means of insuring that those who stand in the shoes of the parent have sound professional training and appropriate character.   The state Superintendent of Public Instruction is charged with issuing teacher licenses.[320] Applicants for a license must submit a complete set of fingerprints and written permission authorizing the superintendent to forward the fingerprints to the FBI for its report.[321] Upon receipt of the FBI report and a determination by the superintendent that the applicant is qualified a license must

---

[316]Sec. 391.011 (2) - (3) NRS (1993).

[317]On occassion the legislature adopts laws which reflect a concern for teacher competency. For example, Chapter 399 Laws of Nevada (1993) adds a new section to Chapter 396 entitled 'University of Nevada System' mandating that the board of regents establish a program of student teaching and practicum which requires a division of the University of Nevada System to enter into agreements with the school districts in the state for the assignment of university students for training purposes as student teachers, counselors or trainees in a library.

[318]The legal aspects of teacher competency tests were the subject of a recent federal appeals court decision. Frazier v. Garrison I.S.D., 980 F.2d 1514 (5th Cir. 1993).

[319]Chapter 204 Laws of Nevada (1993) amending Sec. 391.019 NRS (1991).

[320] Sec. 391.033 NRS (1991).

[321] Sec. 391.033 NRS (1991).

be issued.[322] The application is confidential. The applicants file is available for his\her inspection during regular business hours.[323]

It is unlawful for the superintendent to issue a license or for a school district to employ any teacher or instructor who is not 1) a citizen of the United States, 2) a person who has filed a valid declaration to become a citizen or valid petition for naturalization, 3) or who is not a lawful permanent resident of the United States.[324] Teachers are also required to take and subscribe to the constitutional oath before commencing their teaching duties.[325] In addition persons granted a license to teach must show adequate knowledge of the origin, history, provisions and principles of the Constitution of the United States and the constitution of the State of Nevada.[326]

The license to teach is a revocable privilege.[327] The state board is vested with the authority to suspend or revoke the license of any teacher, administrator or other licensed employee.[328] Grounds for suspension are listed in the statutes.[329] Specific sections of the law also allow revocation for falsely reporting pupil attendance [330] and breach of an employment contract.[331]

The state board with the assistance of the attorney general developed rules for the conduct of license suspension and revocation hearings.

The rules were utilized in a 1989 revocation proceeding brought against a Las Vegas teacher who belonged to a white supremacist group.[332] Angelo E Stefanelli, a teacher employed by the Clark County School District, was placed on administrative leave in December 1987. He was a member of the paramilitary Committee of the States, a white supremacist organization that believed taxes were illegal and claimed its legitimacy from the Articles of Confederation. Stefanelli was originally charged with a 10 count federal felony indictment, but as the result of a plea bargain, in which he agreed to testify against other members of the Committee, he pleaded guilty and was convicted in November 1987 of four misdemeanor counts charging efforts to obstruct enforcement of the tax laws. He served a one-year jail sentence.

---

[322] Sec. 391.033 (3) NRS (1991). Recently an issue arose concerning a license issued on the basis of Mexican bachillerato degree earned when the applicant was 18 years old. The department awarded her an elementary certificate in 1982 and professional and administrative endorsements in 1987 based on the applicants masters degree. Should the department attempt to revoke the teachers license because she does not possess the required undergraduate degree? See Pappa, Erik, "Accommodation sought for teacher with Mexico degree" Las Vegas Sun, February 6, 1989, p. 2 B.

[323] Sec. 391.035 NRS (1993).

[324] Sec. 391.060 NRS (1993).

[325] Sec. 391.080 NRS (1993).

[326] Sec. 391.090 NRS (1993).

[327] Sec. 391.051 NRS (1993).

[328] Sec. 391.320 NRS (1993). Chapter 294 Laws of Nevada (1993) amends Sec. 391.330 NRS (1991) expanding the jurisdiction of the state board to all licensed education personnel.

[329] Sec. 391.330 NRS (1993) Grounds for suspension or revocation of teacher's or administrator's license. The state board of education may suspend or revoke the license of any teacher or administrator, after notice and an opportunity for hearing before the state board, for:
1. Immoral or unprofessional conduct.
2. Evident unfitness for service.
3. Physical or mental incapacity which renders the teacher or administrator unfit for service.
4. Conviction of a felony or crime involving moral turpitude.
5. Conviction of a sex offense under NRS 200.366 (Sexual Assault), 200.368 (Statutory sexual seduction), 201.190 (Crime against nature; sexual act between consenting adults of the same sex), 201.220 (Indecent or obscene exposure), 201.230 (Lewdness with a child under 14 years)or 207.260 (Annoyance or molestation of a minor) in which a student enrolled in a school of a Nevada public school district was the victim.
6. Knowingly advocating the overthrow of the Federal Government or of the State of Nevada by force, violence or unlawful means.
7. Persistent defiance of or refusal to obey the regulations of the state board of education, the commission or the superintendent of public instruction, defining and governing the duties of teachers and administrators.

[330] Sec. 391.340 NRS (1993).

[331] Sec. 391.350 NRS (1993).

[332] Pappa, Erik, "State Board to Consider Revoking Teacher's License," Las Vegas Sun, September 28, 1989, p. 1 B.

Following his release from prison the state department sought to revoke Stefanelli's license on two grounds--"immoral or unprofessional conduct" and "knowingly advocating the overthrow of the government."[333]

The revocation hearing was conducted before attorney MichaelCherry, Michael, attorneyCherry. He rendered the following decision and recommendation to the state board.

BEFORE THE NEVADA STATE BOARD OF EDUCATION

EUGENE T. PASLOV vs.ANGELO E. STEFANELLI
License No. 219-42-4844,
CASE NO. 88-2
HEARING OFFICERS REPORT
Dated this 30th day of June, 1989.

SCOPE OF HEARING
On May 1, 1988, EUGENE T. PASLOV,Superintendent of Public Instruction, Department of Education, State of Nevada, filed a Complaint for the Revocation of the Nevada Teacher's License of ANGELO E. STEFANELLI.

On July 18, 1988, RICHARD SEGERBLOM, ESQ., attorney for ANGELO STEFANELLI, requested in writing a hearing in accordance with N.R.S. 391.355.

On September 16, 1988 MICHAEL A CHERRY, ESQ., was notified of his selection as Hearing Officer in the above-entitled matter.

Due to the Hearing Officer's congested court calendar the hearing in this matter was set and held on May 5, 1989, at the office of the State Board of Education.

Counsel for Petitioner and Counsel for Respondent both submitted excellent trial briefs and exhibits that were thoroughly reviewed by the Hearing Officer. Numerous witnesses were called and testified for both Petitioner and Respondent. Although a transcript of the proceedings was not prepared, the Hearing Officer was given cassette tapes of the entire hearing for his use and review in preparing this written report.

FINDINGS OF FACT AND CONCLUSIONS OF LAW
1. That Petitioner made and filed the Amended Complaint herein on September 16, 1988, in his official capacity as Superintendent of Public Instruction, Department of Education, State of Nevada.

2. That at all times since September 1973 , Respondent has been and is now the holder of a Nevada teacher's license issued by the Superintendent of Public Instruction, Department of Education, State of Nevada, pursuant to the provisions of Chapter 391 of Nevada Revised Statutes.

3. That N.R.S. 391.330 provides in pertinent part that the Nevada State Board of Education may suspend or revoke any state license of any teacher or administrator, after notice and an opportunity for hearing, for immoral or unprofessional conduct and knowingly advocating the overthrow of the Federal Government by force, violence of unlawful means. N.R.S. 391.290 and 391.330(1) and (6).

---

[333]Ibid., p. 1 B.

4. That respondent has subjected his teacher's license number 219-42-4484 to revocation or suspension by the Nevada State Board of Education pursuant to N.R.S. 391.320 and 391.330(1) and (6) by his conviction on November 6, 1987, in the United States District Court of the District of Nevada, Las Vegas, of attempting to interfere with the administration of the Internal Revenue laws a violation of 26 U.S.C. §7212(a), and aiding and abetting, a violation of 18 U.S.C. §2. Respondent's conviction stemmed from his activities as a member of a group known as the Committee of the States.

5. That although Respondent was originally charged in a 10 count Federal Indictment with misdemeanor and felony counts, Respondent struck a plea bargain with the United States Government and was allowed to plead guilty to four (4) misdemeanor counts in exchange for his testimony and full cooperation with the Government against his Co-Defendants at their trial which was held in approximately September and October,1987. A copy of the Judgement of conviction is attached hereto as Hearings Officer Exhibit "1" and is incorporated herein by reference. (omitted from this document)

6. That although Respondent was convicted of misdemeanor offenses, and not felony offenses, he did serve a prison sentence in the Federal facility located in Boron, California.

7. That Respondent is presently on probation under the supervision of the United States Department of Parole and Probation.

8. That Respondent has been on a leave of absence from the Clark County School District from December, 1987, through the present time.

9. That the evidence presented by Petitioner was insufficient to sustain the charge of immoral and unprofessional conduct, N.R.S. 391.330(1).

10. That the evidence presented by Petitioner was sufficient to sustain the charge of knowingly advocating overthrow of the government by force, violence or unlawful means N.R.S. 391.330(6).

RECOMMENDED COURSE OF ACTION

N.R.S. 391.320 states that the State Board of Education may suspend or revoke the license of any teacher for any cause specified by law. N.R.S. 391.330 (1) through (7) states the specific grounds for suspension or revocation of a teacher's or administrator's license. Petitioner alleged two grounds to revoke Respondent's license, to-wit: N.R.S. 391.330(1) Immoral or Unprofessional Conduct and N.R.S. 391.330(6) Knowingly advocation the overthrow of the Government by force, violence and unlawful means.

Although the evidence presented was insufficient to show the Respondent conducted himself immorally or unprofessionally, there was an abundance of evidence that Respondent knowingly advocated the overthrow of the government by force, violence of unlawful means by his participation in the Committee of the States. However, the fact that Petitioner successfully proved a ground for revocation of license does not automatically mean revocation of license since N.R.S. 391.320 is framed in terms of "may revoke" which is discretionary or permissive, rather than "shall revoke" which is mandatory or automatic.

The Hearing Officer, after giving a great deal of thought and study to the entire record finds that society will best be served, by not revoking the teacher's license of Respondent.

This finding is based on the following factors:

(1) Although Respondent joined and participated in the Committee of the States he was most interested in being a tax protestor rather than an advocate of overthrowing the government. Respondent's insensitivity and ignorance is not being condoned but rather Respondent is being forgiven and given a second chance due to the punishment already handed down by the United States District Court.

(2) Respondent fully cooperated with the United States government and testified truthfully against his Co-Defendants at their trial. Having reviewed Respondent's trial testimony it can only be concluded that without Respondent's testimony the other Defendants may not have been convicted. The FBI was satisfied that Respondent testified truthfully and that Respondent was instrumental in the Government obtaining convictions and prison sentences for members of the Committee of the States.

(3) Respondent has been punished severely by being sentenced to Federal prison and Respondent is presently on probation having to adhere to strict conditions and being monitored by a probation officer.

(4) Respondent is married and has an infant child and seems to have a stable life and lifestyle.

(5) Respondent has previously taught Band and Physical Education and should again be allowed to share his skill and training with the students of the Clark County School District.

(6) Respondent's previous record with the Clark County School District is more than satisfactory.

(7) Dr. Rebecca H. Hechter of Counseling Association of Nevada has evaluated Respondent on July 30, 1988, and in her report of August 3, 1988, states "There was no evidence at this time that would indicate his unsuitability to return to the classroom. He knows to keep his personal opinions and beliefs separate from his teaching."

(8) Former students, parents of former students, fellow teachers and administrators favor Respondent being allowed to return to the classroom. Their support for Respondent was sincere and convincing.

For the above reasons the Hearing Officer finds in favor of Respondent, ANGELO STEFANELLI, and recommends that his teaching license not be revoked or suspended.
Michael A. Cherry Hearing Officer

****

State Board Action Following Decision

On September 29, 1989 the state board of education by a 6-2 vote accepted the recommendations of hearing officer Cherry allowing Mr Stefanelli to keep his teaching license. Prior to the vote, state superintendent Paslov told the board he believed Stefanelli was an "outstanding teacher" and that he had paid for his crimes.[334]

1993 Legislative Activity Regarding License Revocation

In 1993 the Legislature amended Chapter 391 revising the procedure for license revocation and suspension.[335] The new law specifies that a license suspension or revocation proceeding may be initiated by the board of trustees of a

---

[334] McKinnon, Shaun, "Education Board Votes To Let Veteran Teacher Keep His License," Review Journal, September 30, 1989, p. 1 A.

[335] Chapter 294 Laws of Nevada (1993) adding language to Chapter 391 addressing license suspension and revocation procedure.

school district or the state Superintendent of Public Instruction. The proceeding is started by submitting a recommendation for suspension or revocation to the state board.[336] Upon receipt of a recommendation the state board is required to give written notice of the to the person holding the license subject to challenge. The notice must contain a statement of the charge upon which the recommendation is based, a copy of the recommendation received by the board, a statement that the licensee is entitled to hearing before a hearing officer if a written request is submitted, and a statement that the grounds and procedure for the proceeding are set forth in Chapter 391 NRS(1993).[337] A written request for a hearing before a hearing officer must be filed with the state superintendent within 15 days after receipt of the notice by the licensee.[338]

If a timely request is received, the law obligates the state superintendent to ask the American Arbitration Association [339] for a list of seven potential arbitrators to act as hearing officers.[340] The selection of the hearing officer is accomplished by the state superintendent and licensee alternately striking names from the list until only one remains. The superintendent is accorded the first strike under the law.[341]

Within 30 days after his/her selection the hearing officer is mandated to conduct a hearing on the recommendation filed with the state board.[342] Within 15 days after the conclusion of the hearing the arbitrator is obliged to prepare and submit a report to the Superintendent of Public Instruction.[343] The contents of the report must include a recommendation as to whether the license of the licensee should be suspended or revoked.[344] The report must also include findings of fact and conclusions of law which support the recommendation.[345]

The state board is empowered to accept or reject the arbitrators recommendation. They may also refer the matter back to the arbitrator for further evidence recommendations. Written notice of its decision must be given to the licensee. The decision of the state board is accorded the status of a final decision in a contested case.[346]

B
EMPLOYMENT
GENERAL PROVISIONS

School districts are required to recruit and select employees in conformity with equal employment opportunity principles.[347]

---

[336]Chapter 294 Laws of Nevada (1993) Sec. 2 (1).

[337]Chapter 294 Laws of Nevada (1993) Sec. 2 (2) (a), (b), (c), (d).

[338]Chapter 294 Laws of Nevada (1993) Sec. 2 (3). Failure to file a timely written request for a hearing frees the state board to suspend, revoke or take no action regarding the license recommendation on file. Chapter 294 Laws of Nevada (1993) Sec. 2 (5).

[339]Chapter 294 Laws of Nevada (1993) Removes the option of selecting a Nevada attorney from a list of hearing officers appointed by the state board. See Chapter 294 Laws of Nevada (1993) Sec. 6 amending Sec. 391.355 4 NRS (1991) See also Sec. 391.3161 NRS (1991) regarding state board hearing officer list appointment, qualifications, term, vacancies, and duties.

[340]Chapter 294 Laws of Nevada (1993) Sec. 2 (4).

[341]Chapter 294 Laws of Nevada (1993) Sec. 2 (4).

[342]Chapter 294 Laws of Nevada (1993) Sec. 3 (1). The law requires the state board to adopt rules of procedure for the conduct of the hearings. Chapter 294 Laws of Nevada (1993) Sec. 6 amending Sec. 391.355 1.NRS (1991). The hearing officer is granted power to issue subpenas to compel attendance of witnesses and production of records to be used as evidence in hearings. Chapter 294 Laws of Nevada (1993) Sec. 6 amending Sec 391.355 3 NRS (1991).

[343]Chapter 294 Laws of Nevada (1993) Sec. 3 (1).

[344]Chapter 294 Laws of Nevada (1993) Sec. 3 (1) (a).

[345]Chapter 294 Laws of Nevada (1993) Sec. 3 (1) (b).

[346]Chapter 294 Laws of Nevada (1993) Sec. 3 (2).

[347] Civil Rights Act of 1964,42 USCA §2000E-E-2, Americans with Disabilities Act 1990, 42 USCA § 12101, Age Discrimination Act 29 USC § 621-623.

When Boards of trustees employ teachers or other licensed personnel [348] the conditions agreed upon by the parties must be embodied in a written contract or notice of employment to be approved by the board and accepted and signed by the employee.[349] A copy of the contract or notice of reemployment must be delivered to each teacher or other licensed employee not later that the opening of the term of school. The board may not employ teachers for any school year commencing after the expiration of the time for which any member of the board was elected of appointed.[350]

It is unlawful for the board to employ any teacher who is not legally qualified to teach all the grades which the teacher is engaged to teach.[351] Teachers must file a copy of their license to teach with the school district superintendent and the superintendent must acknowledge the receipt of the credential and make a proper record thereof. Notice of a teachers employment must be given to the department before a teacher may perform under the terms of the contract.[352] Discrimination between male and female employees on matters of salary is prohibited.[353]

The Nevada legislature has required county school districts to give teachers credit for prior Nevada service and sick leave accumulated in another Nevada school district. Specifically, when determining the salary of a teacher a school district is required to give full credit for previous service in another Nevada school district.[354] This obligation does not require a school district to allow more credit for previous Nevada teaching service than the maxumum credit for teaching experience provided for in the schedule of salaries established by it for its licensed personnel.[355] However, it does include service for which a teacher received credit from his prior Nevada employer at the beginning of his former employment.[356]

Teachers transferring from one Nevada school district to another carry all sick leave that was accumulated in the former district to the new district.[357] However, the amount of sick leave transferred may not exceed the maximum amount of sick leave which may be carried forward from one year to the next according to the applicable negotiated agreement [358] or the policy of the district into which the employee transferred. Furthermore, unless otherwise specified in a negotiated agreement or district policy the employee is required to use sick leave credited from the district into which he/she transferred before using any of the transferred sick leave.[359] Moreover, the employee is not entitled to compensation for any sick leave transferred.[360]

---

[348] Sec. 391.100 NRS (1993).

[349] Sec. 391.120 NRS (1993). Chapter 536 Laws of Nevada (1993) concerns ethics in government. It amends Chapter 281 adding a new section establishing rules for determining conflict of interest when a public officer or employee is considering bidding on a contract with a public agency.

[350] Ibid.

[351] Ibid.

[352] Ibid. Principles governing contracts generally are applicable to contracts for employment of teachers AGO B954 (10-6-50)

[353] Sec. 391.160 NRS (1993).

[354] Sec. 391.160 (2) NRS (1993). This provision was added during the 1991 session of the legislature. Will this new law encourage or discourage recruitment of Nevada teachers by state school districts? Does the law encourage Nevada school districts to recruit teachers from outside the state instead of those already employed within the state?

[355] Chapter 200 Laws of Nevada (1993) amending Sec. 391.160 NRS (1991).

[356] Chapter 200 Laws of Nevada (1993) creating Sec. 391.160 (4) NRS (1993).

[357] Sec. 391.180 (6) NRS (1993). Sick leave accumulated in the receiving district shall be used first. Further, when transferred sick leave is used the employee is not entitled to compensation. Does the law encourage Nevada school districts to recruit teachers from outside the state instead of those already employed within the state?

[358] Chapter 414 Laws Nevada (1993) amends Sec. 391. 180 by adding subsection 9 providing that any subject referred to in the section entitled 'Absenses of employee: Compensation; deductions; intermission and extension of days of school' (Sec. 391. 180 NRS 1993) included in a an agreement negotiated by the board of trustees under Chapter 288 supersede any conflicting provisions of the section.

[359] Sec. 391.180 (6) (a) NRS (1993).

[360] Sec. 391.180 (6) (b) NRS (1993).

All newly employed full time teachers serve a one-year probationary period.[361] A probationary employee who has received a notice of reemployment from the school district is entitled to be postprobationary in the ensuing year of employment. A school district which has not given notice of reemployment to a probationary employee may offer a contract for a trial year.[362]

The trustees may direct licensed personnel to exercise such powers and authority in the schools as the board possesses under the education laws of the state.[363] Teachers are required to keep a true, full and correct register of all pupils attending school.[364] In addition, teachers are directed to enforce the course of study, use legally authorized textbooks and follow rules and regulations prescribed for them.[365]Finally, teachers are obligated to hold their students of a strict account of their conduct on and in close proximity to the school grounds.[366]

Generally speaking, unlicensed personnel of a school district must be directly supervised by licensed personnel in all duties which are instructional in nature. The law also provides that to the extent practicable, the direct supervision must be such that the unlicensed personnel are in the immediate location of the licensed personnel and are readily available during such times when supervision is required.[367]

SUSPENSIONS, DEMOTIONS, DISMISSALS AND REFUSALS TO REEMPLOY

Nevada statutes list specific grounds upon which a teacher may be subjected to employment discipline and the procedure that applies when discipline is invoked.[368] These statutes (Nevada Professional Practices Act) do not apply to substitute teachers, or adult education teachers.[369]

Substantive Aspects of Teacher Discipline
Nevada Statutes

The grounds for discipline are found in Section 391.312 NRS (1991) and read as follows;

1. A teacher may be suspended, dismissed or not reemployed ...for the following reasons:
    (a) Inefficiency;
    (b) Immorality;[370]

---

[361] Sec. 391.3197 NRS (1993). Any postprobationary employee of a Nevada school district employed by another Nevada district must be allowed to continue as a postprobationary employee. Sec 391.31965 NRS (1993).

[362] Sec. 391.3197 NRS (1993).

[363] Sec. 391.210 NRS (1993).

[364] Sec. 391.240 NRS (1993).

[365] Sec. 391.260 NRS (1993). The superintendent of public instruction may suspend a teachers license for a period not to exceed 1 year if the employee has an unexcused absence from any educational conference he\she is required to attend Sec. 391.285 NRS (1993)

[366] Sec. 391.270 NRS (1993) When children enter school, jurisdiction during school hours passes from parents to school authorities. Dual jurisdiction could mean destruction of school discipline. AGO 79 (11-22-1921); AGO 684 (10-4-1948).

[367] Sec 391.273 NRS (1993). Could this law interfere with distance learning programs?

[368] Sec. 391.311-3197 NRS (1993).

[369] Sec. 391.3115 NRS (1993).

[370] Immorality is defined in Sec. 391.311 (4) NRS (1991). It includes sexual assault, statutory sexual seduction, battery with intent to commit a crime, abuse, neglect or endangerment of a child, incest, crime against nature (**Chapter 236 Laws of Nevada (1993) limits application of the criminal statute to public sexual activity; See also Burton v. Cascade School Dist. Union High Sch. No. 5. 512 F.2d 850 (9th Cir. 1975) cert denied 423 U. S. 839 (1976) teacher dismissed because of admission she was 'practicing homosexual' awarded damages, attorney fees and costs along with an order that the school expunge from its board meeting records and personnel files all references to the teachers dismissal. Failure to order reinstatement found to be within sound discretion of court.**), open and gross lewdness, indecent or obscene exposure, lewdness with a child under 14 years, sale, display etc. of obscene material to a minor and annoyance or molestation of a minor.

(c) Unprofessional conduct;

(d) Insubordination;

(e) Neglect of duty;

(f) Physical or mental incapacity;

(g) A justifiable decrease in the number of positions due to decreased enrollment or district reorganization;

(h) Conviction of a felony or of a crime involving moral turpitude;

(i) Inadequate performance;

(j) Evident unfitness for service;

(k) Failure to comply with such reasonable requirements as a board may prescribe;

(I) Failure to show normal improvement and evidence of professional training and growth;

(m) Advocating overthrow of the Government of the United States or of the State of Nevada by force, violence or other unlawful means, or the advocating or teaching of communism with the intent to indoctrinate pupils to subscribe to communistic philosophy;

(n) Any cause which constitutes grounds for the revocation of a teacher's license;

(o) Willful neglect or failure to observe and carry out the requirements of this Title; or

(p) Dishonesty.

2. In determining whether the professional performance of a licensed employee is inadequate, consideration must be given to the regular and special evaluation reports prepared in accordance with the policy of the employing school district and to any written standards of performance which may have been adopted by the board.

Nevada Case Law

The Nevada Supreme Court has interpreted and applied the general terms of the statute outlining the grounds for teacher employment discipline in several important cases.

MEINHOLD
v.
CLARK COUNTY SCHOOL DISTRICT BD. OF ED.
89 NEV. 56, 506 P.2d 420 (1973)

By the Court, BATJER, J.

This appeal is taken from an order of the district court dismissing appellant's petition for a writ of certiorari. That order of the district court had the effect of affirming the action of the Clark County Board of School Trustees (hereinafter referred to as the "board") in refusing to renew an employment contract for the appellant, a teacher in the Clark County School District.

See also Mawdsley, Ralph D. & Hampton, Frederick M., "Sexual Misconduct by School Employees Involving Students 73 Ed.Law Rep. [883] (June 18, 1992) & Regotti, Terri L., "Negligent Hiring and Retaining Sexually Abusive Teachers," 73 Ed.Law Rep. [333] (May 21, 1993)

For several alleged reasons, including unprofessional conduct, insubordination, inadequate performance and failing to comply with such reasonable requests as the board may prescribe, the appellant was notified in March of 1971 that his contract with the Clark County School District would not be renewed for the 1971-72 school year. The notice of dismissal was given pursuant to the requirements of NRS 391.312 to 391.3196, inclusive.

The appellant requested a hearing before a panel of the professional review committee (NRS 391.316-391.3195). That panel upheld the recommendation that the appellant's contract not be renewed. The appellant then sought relief from the board and the board also approved the recommendation.

The district court in reviewing the determination of the board was limited to a review of the record of the evidence presented to the board to determine if it had exceeded its jurisdiction and whether there was cause to refuse to rehire the appellant.

...[T]his is an appeal from an order of the district court denying certiorari. When the determination of an inferior tribunal, in this case the board of trustees, is challenged by certiorari, the function of this court is identical to that of the district court.

The appellant does not contend that there was any defect in the notice of non-renewal of his contract, given pursuant to NRS 391.312-391.319,[371] ...

****

The appellant participated fully in the hearing before the board, and the alleged procedural errors were never raised at that hearing but were raised for the first time in his brief filed with the district court. It must be deemed that they have been waived if in fact they ever existed. In any event, none of the alleged errors go to the question of jurisdiction or cause.

****

...[T]he appellant contends that the evidence presented to the board did not, as a matter of law, support a finding of cause for non-renewal of his contract.

The exhibits, together with some testimony by the school district's witnesses, and the testimony of the appellant before the board clearly revealed that appellant had informed his daughters, who were students at the school where he taught, that they need not attend school if they were not so inclined and as a result they were absent a substantial part of the time, resulting in action by the civil authorities.[372]

---

[371] No contention has been raised by the appellant that the provisions of NRS 391.311 to 391.3197 are not applicable to him because he had entered into a contract with the board as a result of the Local Government-Employee-Management Relations Act providing separate provisions relating to the board's right to dismiss or refuse to employ him. See NRS 391.3197(2).

[372]Mr. Meinhold]: I am perfectly glad we are going into all the evidence Mr. Schnepp has presented, but I did want to read a statement, what you call an opening statement, with regard to the findings of the Professional Review Panel, and the Professional Review Panel supported Mr. Schnepp on all of his charges beginning with the first one, unprofessional conduct. I would like to read that charge so that everyone in the audience can hear. Unprofessional conduct: Mr. Meinhold stated to the Panel his children had been given permission by him to remain out of school whenever they so desired. He also stated several times publicly and to the Panel that school was harmful to children and should be discontinued. There was a transcript of this meeting of the Professional Review Panel. I would be willing to stand corrected, but those are not my words with regard to this 'should be discontinued,' since that says—I stated that I am being misquoted. I have, though, on a number of occasions stated that schools are harmful for children and I did so state to the Professional Review Panel....

[Cross-examination] By Mr. Petroni [Attorney for the school district]:

Q. Getting back to your children not being in school, it is your belief or statement that you did not believe in obeying the law in the school attendance?

[Mr. Meinhold] A. No, I never said that. I am afraid I am going to have to go into some detail on this with regard to the school attendance of my daughters. Two of them are Garside students, as he mentioned earlier. My daughters know that on those days they choose not to go to school they are not going to be forced to go to school. I am in total disagreement with the compulsory school attendance law. I was somewhat remiss with regard to the law. I didn't know how stringent it was. I really didn't realize the wording of the law until, it must have been Mr. Schnepp or one of the people at Garside, started some kind of truancy action against my oldest daughter and we were required, as he stated earlier, to go to a hearing, and at that time I was presented with the fact with regard to the law. Since then that particular daughter has quite regular attendance, but again I don't force her. She was quite put out by the whole procedure, including the hearing with the gentleman out at Bonanza road, and attended school fairly regularly from there on.

Q. I am not quite clear—

119

In support of his position that, as a matter of law, the evidence did not support the board's conclusion and recommendation, the appellant relies on Richardson v. Board of Regents and Boswell v. Bd. Med. Ex., 72 Nev. 20, 293 P.2d 424 (1956). Although the Richardson case tends to support the appellants contention with reference to some of the other charges levied against him, it does not support his position in regards to the charge of unprofessional conduct because Richardson was not accused of unprofessional conduct. In Boswell v. Bd. Med. Ex., supra, Boswell was charged with unprofessional conduct, but that case can be distinguished because the charge was based entirely upon extremely harsh criticism levied against other doctors and members of the medical profession in his community. There this Court said: "It has never been held that the public health, safety or morals requires protection through the suppression of criticism of individual doctors or criticism of the medical profession as a whole, no matter how harsh the terms in which such criticism is expressed." See Pickering v. Board of Education, infra. Here the unprofessional conduct was based in part upon the appellant's conduct in refusing to require his daughters to attend school in defiance of the laws of this state. We believe this to be sufficient cause to support the board's finding of unprofessional conduct. Without citing any authority the appellant contends that the grounds for dismissal specifically charged against the appellant are without defined standards and guidelines and are constitutionally vague and in violation of fundamental due process. In Moore v. Board of Trustees this court adopted with approval the language from In re Mintz, 378 P.2d 945, 948 (Ore. 1963): ". . . [T]he variety of forms which unprofessional conduct may take makes it infeasible to attempt to specify in a statute or regulation all of the acts which come within the meaning of the term. The fact that it is impossible to catalogue all of the types of professional misconduct is the very reason for setting up the statutory standard in broad terms and delegating to the board the function of evaluating the conduct in each case...."

Teachers may not be compelled to relinquish the First Amendment rights that they would otherwise enjoy as citizens to comment on matters of public interest in connection with the operation of public schools in which they work, absence of proof of false statements knowingly or recklessly made. Pickering v. Board of Education (1968). Here, however, the appellant persisted in authorizing and encouraging his daughters not to attend school and he indicated that he would continue to allow his daughters to be truant in violation of the law.[373] It was this

---

A. I am not advocating breaking the law for anyone else.
Q. You say you are not familiar with the law. Aren't you required to take Nevada School Law to receive a certificate?
A. We took a test which is about like all other tests. We came in Saturday morning, because I wasn't a resident, you see, and I passed with fairly high scores, which doesn't mean I know Nevada School Law. There is a great deal to it....
[Mr. Cantor of the board, questioning Mr. Meinhold]: On unprofessional conduct I am not especially concerned about what you believe, but I am concerned about what you advocate, in a certain contest. Now, you advocate that children or parents—let me rephrase it. Do you advocate that children should not attend school or parents should not send them to school?
[Mr. Meinhold] THE WITNESS: No.
MR. CANTOR: Then I take it, then, the amount of your advocacy is limited to the law should be changed somehow?
THE WITNESS: The compulsory school attendance law. I think they should have a choice, is what I am saying.
MR. CANTOR: As long as it is law do you go along with the idea it has got to be obeyed?
THE WITNESS: I can't answer that question.
MR. CANTOR: All right. Now, as I understand it. you did not have any children in Garside; is that correct?
THE WITNESS: Two.
MR. CANTOR: I am sorry.
THE WITNESS: Two daughters.
MR. CANTOR: You have two children of your own there?
THE WITNESS: Right."
[373] In Vance v. Board of Ed. of Pekin Com. H. Sch. Dist. No. 303, 277 N.E.2d 337 (llI App. 1971), the dismissal of a teacher was upheld when he advised teenage students to demonstrate and walk out of school in order to obtain "student power," and where he indicated that in the future under like circumstances he would conduct himself as he had in the past.

conduct and not any statements he made which were productive of harmful disorganization and chaos among the students, teachers and administrators not only at Garside Junior High School but throughout the entire school system.

The appellant expressed disagreement with the laws requiring compulsory attendance at school and his carrying of that attitude into effect was a prerogative he was entitled to indulge but with it went the price that he might not be rehired. This conduct on the part of the appellant evidenced a lack of professional fitness and responsibility to the teaching profession and to the school system.

A teacher's influence upon his pupils is not limited to what he says and does in the schoolroom and a teacher's right to teach cannot depend solely upon his conduct in the schoolroom. In Johnson v. Taft School Dist. (Cal.App. 1937), unprofessional conduct was established by evidence showing a long drawn out course of conduct on the part of the teacher that produced serious friction in the school and showed insubordination on her part and a refusal to conform to the instructions and requirements of her superiors. In Robel v. Highline Public Schools, District No. 401 (Wash. 1965), it was held that classroom organization, control and discipline are so vital to the success of a teaching program that failure of a teacher in this area was sufficient cause for non-renewal of a contract.

The trial court found, as a matter of law, that the evidence presented to the board was sufficient to sustain any or all of the enumerated grounds for dismissal. The board had the right to weigh the evidence, resolve conflicts in the evidence, to judge the credibility of witnesses and to find the facts relevant to the issues. The appellant was not rehired for cause, a cause which he and he alone created. The evidence is sufficient to sustain the charge of unprofessional conduct. (NRS 391.312(1)(c).) That finding is sufficient to support the judgment and a consideration of the remaining charges becomes unnecessary.

Affirmed. [374]

---

[374]**The Las Vegas Sun recently published an article providing some additional information regarding the case.**

""I pledge allegiance to the flag .. "

Twenty-six years have gone by and a lot has changed since social studies teacher Alvin Meinhold stood silently with his arms at his sides as his students recited those words during an assembly in the auditorium at Frank Garside Junior High School.

It was February 1966. As the war was waged in Vietnam, tempers raged in the United States.

Meinhold, a favorite among his students, did not believe in the war. He chose not to salute the flag during the Pledge of Allegiance as a form of passive resistance.

But in the eyes of some Las Vegas residents, Meinhold may as well have torn up an American flag and scattered the pieces over the Tomb of the Unknown Soldier.

They called him the "warhating teacher," a "scumbag," and those were some of the nicer things they said. At UNLV (then Nevada Southern University) angry students hanged Meinhold in effigy.

"My daughter Elizabeth, when she was 9 years old, was stopped on the street and threatened by a guy in a car," the 60-year-old Meinhold remembers. "I still get riled up when I think of that."

But such moments of anger are rare, even though his protest cost him his livelihood and, arguably, his standing in the community. It also caused his family - especially his wife, Letty - a great deal of pain.

For the most part, he bears no grudges and he has no regrets.

But, looking back, would he do it again?

"You bet I would," Meinhold says firmly. "I have a right not to salute the flag. I stood there with the rest of the class "

But others didn't think he had that right. American Legion Post 8 sought an injunction to bar Meinhold from working in the local school system.

The local branch of the American Federation of Teachers voted to oust Meinhold from the union. Months later, after national AFT officials pressured the local chapter to reinstate Meinhold, members voted to secede rather than accept the ruling.

The vote followed an hour of debate "marked by frequent boos, hisses and catcalls directed at Meinhold," according to a newspaper account.

Meanwhile, Clark County School District officials informed Meinhold that his contract was not being renewed.

The social studies teacher won a reprieve in late 1966, when the School Board voted that it was unconstitutional to terminate a teacher for refusing to salute the Flag.

But at the end of the 1971 school year, Meinhold was again discharged - this time on grounds of insubordination, inadequate performance, unprofessional conduct and failure to comply with board teaching requirements.

In other words, he says, refusing to salute the flag.

Meinhold took his case to the Nevada Supreme Court, but the justices voted unanimously to reject his appeal. Undaunted, Meinhold appealed to the U.S. Supreme Court, but a majority of the court decided against hearing the case.

"Only two justices wanted to hear. It They were William O. Douglas and Thurgood Marshall," Meinhold says. "Douglas, he was so aggravated, he wrote a dissenting opinion. I still have it."

RUST I
v.
CLARK COUNTY SCHOOL DISTRICT
100 Nev. 372, 683 P.2d 23 (1984)

By the Court, MOWBRAY, J.:

Appeal from judgment of district court affirming administrative termination of employment; Eighth Judicial District Court, Clark County; J. Charles Thompson, Judge.

Appellant Dayle K. Rust (Rust) was an employee of the Clark County School District for over twenty years. For seventeen of those years he served as assistant principal, or principal, of elementary schools in the district, the last three years as principal of Vegas Verde Elementary School. In the fall of 1979, Rust took a long-planned leave of absence of ten school days in order to meet his son, who was completing a religious mission in Europe. Because his request for such leave was denied, on the basis of a recently-enacted district policy severely curtailing school administrators' ability to use previously accumulated leave days, Rust was suspended from his duties on his return, and ultimately dismissed from the employ of the Clark County School District, on the ground of "insubordination." Because we find that under the particular circumstances presented by this case the action of the respondent Clark County School District Board of Trustees in dismissing appellant after twenty years of service was arbitrary and capricious, we reverse the judgment of the district court affirming the decision of the board.

Meinhold had some supporters in Las Vegas. And as the years went by and American casualties grew into the tens of thousands, more and more Las Vegans began to question U.S. involvement in the war. "

A lot of people were sympathetic. They offered me support, and when I got fired they wrote letters," Meinhold says.

In the early '70s, as others began to listen to the Vietnam protesters, Meinhold found himself without a job and with three children to support.

His wife went to work.

He took a job as a runner for the Las Vegas SUN. The pay was $85 a week. Later, he worked as a mental health technician for the state Department of Mental Health. The pay wasn't much better.

"My wife and I paid the bills all those years. I guess we did it the hard way."

Meinhold retired on April 22, 1978.

"It was a glorious day. I remember that day well," he says.

But not so glorious, perhaps, as the day he challenged the establishment and made a lot of enemies simply by keeping his mouth shut and his arms to his sides.

"I don't think a lot of these people will accept to this day what I did," Meinhold says.

Today, the Vietnam War is a distant memory to most Americans Meinhold's children are grow, and Elizabeth, now 35, graduated with honors from Harvard.

Meinhold spends much of his time reading political biographies or new fiction. One of his favorite authors is iconoclast Gore Vidal. Meinhold also enjoys spending as much time a possible with his two young grandchildren.

He encourages them to speak up for what they believe in - and to look forward to a time when American leaders will think long and hard before they order young men and women into battle." Shemeligian, Bob, "Meinhold Fought His Own War," Las Vegas Sun, Nov. 22, 1992, p. 1 D.

The Clark County School District Legal counsel is quoted in an article, published the same day, regarding the District's current policy

"If a teacher or student refused to salute the flag, his First Amendment rights would be protected by the Clark County School District, and these righls were protected 26 years ago, according to a school official.

"If this happened today, the same thing would happen that would happen in 1966," says Donald Haight, general counsel for the school district. "It's unconstitutional to discharge someone for exercising his First Amendment rights to not salute the flag."

Haight notes that the School Board in late l966 voted that it was unconstitutional to terminate a teacher for refusing to salute the flag, and says that social studies teacher Alvin Meinhold was terminated five years later for other reasons.

Meinhold and some of his supporters believe that the teacher's political views were in the backs of the minds of school officials who discharged him in 1971 on grounds of insubordination.

The precedent-setting case that protects students and teachers who refuse to salute the flag was decided long before Meinhold made his moral stand.

The case was West Virginia State Board of Education v Barnette and the year was 1943. The U.S. Supreme Court ruled that students could not be compelled to salute the flag if doing so conflicts with their rights of free speech and religion as protected by the First Amendment.

In recent years, several students have indicated they do not want to salute the flag, according to school officials.

"They say it's their right, and sometimes the principal calls the office, and we tell the principal that the students don't have to salute the flag if they don't want to," Haight says." Shemeligian, Bob, "Students Can't Be Forced To Salute," Las Vegas Sun, Nov. 22, 1992, p. 6 D.

But See Palmer v. Board of Education City of Chicago dismissal for failure to offer valid portion of curriculum upheld. infra. (patriotic matters pledge, songs and national holidays)

In the fall of 1977, appellant's son left on a two year mission abroad, under the auspices of a church of which Rust is also a member. At that time Rust made a commitment to his son that at the conclusion of his mission, Rust would join him in Europe and accompany him home. Rust's plans were predicated upon a long-standing district policy which allowed liberal use of earned leave days.

Rust proceeded to make preparations to effectuate his plans, including arranging with his church to meet its requirements by becoming a missionary himself for the period of the trip, and purchasing the required tickets. Rust made no secret of his plans, and indeed discussed them with the Associate Superintendent for Personnel some eight months before his departure. He spent evenings and weekends making the necessary preparations so that the school would run smoothly during his absence.

Unfortunately for Rust, sixteen days before his planned departure on October 3, 1979, the district, following inconclusive collective bargaining on the issue with district administrators, unilaterally changed its leave policy by limiting administrators' use of earned leave to no more than five school days per year, or two days in succession, except in cases of "emergency." Rust then had accumulated over forty days of leave, of which he sought to use ten days in succession. Rust's request for leave was denied by his supervising administrator on September 25, as was his request for reconsideration. Rust indicated that he nevertheless intended to fulfill his commitment by completing the trip as planned, and preparations were made for administration of the school in his absence. On October 1, the district presented Rust with a formal admonishment repeating the denial of the request for leave and specifying that "defiance of this directive may result in your immediate demotion, dismissal or nonrenewal of contract," on the ground of insubordination, or failure to comply with reasonable board requirements, citing NRS 391.312(1)(d) and (k).[375]

On October 3, Rust left for Europe as planned. When he returned to school on October 18, he was presented with a Notice of Suspension, announcing the district's decision to suspend Rust immediately from his position as principal of Vegas Verdes Elementary School and as an administrator with the Clark County School District, "in the best interests of the children of the district." The Notice further announced the intent of the district to initiate dismissal proceedings.

Such proceedings were subsequently undertaken, and the respondent Board of Trustees on July 10, 1980, upon recommendation of a hearing officer, issued its decision dismissing Rust from its employ. The district court affirmed.

On appeal, Rust raises a number of procedural statutory and constitutional issues, many of which we find without merit. However, we do agree that under the circumstances presented, appellant's conduct did not warrant the drastic remedy of dismissal.

This Court has long taken seriously its duty to review the evidence before the findings of administrative boards on cases involving dismissal of public employees to determine whether legal cause for removal has been shown. As we have consistently reiterated, legal cause is "not any cause which the officer authorized to make such removal may deem sufficient." Rather such cause "must be one which

---

[375] NRS 391.312 provides in pertinent part:
    (1) [A]n administrator may be demoted, suspended, dismissed or not reemployed for the following reasons:
       . . . .
       (d) Insubordination;
       . . . .
       (k) Failure to comply with such reasonable requirements as a board may prescribe;
       . . . .

specifically relates to and affects the administration of the office, and must be restricted to something of a substantial nature directly affecting the rights and interests of the public. The cause must be one touching the qualifications of the officer or his performance of his duties, showing that he is not a fit or proper person to hold the office."

In this case the district has predicated its action upon a charge of "insubordination." We have defined this term as "a willful disregard of express or implied directions, or such a defiant attitude as to be equivalent thereto. 'Rebellious,' 'mutinous,' and 'disobedient' are often quoted as definitions or synonyms of 'insubordinate.'" We suggested that the authority of the superior to promulgate the order, or the "reasonableness of the order in question" might also be considered in an appropriate case. *Id.*

"Insubordination" has elsewhere been defined as "'constant or continuing intentional refusal to obey a direct or implied order, reasonable in nature, and given by and with proper authority.'" Board of Trustees v. Holso (Wyo. 1978). The Wyoming court also noted that "[t]he better-reasoned decisions place emphasis on the presence of a persistent course of willful defiance." . Thus, a number of courts have refused to find cause supporting dismissal in a single instance of being absent without prior permission of school authorities. .

In Beverlin the Court found that dismissal for an unauthorized absence, on the ground of insubordination, was arbitrary and capricious. The court stressed that the pupils did not suffer in his absence, and that the reason for his absence was laudable. Here, the district does not claim that the students or the school were detrimentally affected by Rust's absence, for which he apparently made dutiful advance preparation. Further, the reason for his absence, while personal, is deserving at least of consideration and respect. As the court said of Beverlin, his "unexcused absence best might be described as an error of judgment, resulting in no harm to his employer".

It appearing that the penalty is excessive, we reverse the judgment of the district court and remand the case with instruction to return the matter to the school district Board of Trustees for imposition of a penalty consistent with the views expressed in this opinion. **Reversed and remanded**[376]

---

[376] Rust II v. Clark County School District, 103 Nev. 686 (1987)

This is the second time this case has come before this court on appeal. The facts of this case are reported in our prior opinion in this matter. In Rust, we concluded that, although appellant had been guilty of misconduct, the penalty imposed for his single unexcused absence was so severe that it amounted to an abuse of discretion. We therefore reversed the prior judgment of the district court, and remanded the case to the Board of Trustees "for imposition of a penalty consistent with the views expressed in [our prior] opinion." On remand, the Board of Trustees reinstated appellant, but reduced him from a principal to an assistant principal. The Board imposed an additional penalty of suspension of his pay and benefits during the period between his dismissal and his reinstatement. Appellant petitioned the district court for judicial review of the Board's decision .

On January 11, 1985, following a hearing, the district court stated its intention to affirm the decision of the Board of Trustees and also announced that it would not file a written decision. Appellant filed a notice of appeal on January 16, 1985. Thereafter, on March 6, 1985, the district court entered a written judgment affirming the decision of the Board of Trustees. Respondents served written notice of entry of this judgment on appellant on March 21, 1985. Appellant, however, failed to file a new notice of appeal. Respondents contend, therefore, that appellant's notice of appeal was premature, and that the premature notice failed to vest jurisdiction in this court. We agree.

Generally, a premature notice of appeal fails to vest jurisdiction in this court. There are sound reasons for this rule. First, the proper and timely filing of a notice of appeal is jurisdictional. Jurisdictional rules go to the very power of this court to act. They must, accordingly, be clear and absolute in order to give all fair notice of what is required to bring a matter properly before this court. Indeed, a timely notice of appeal divests the district court of jurisdiction to act and vests jurisdiction in this court. Prior to the entry of a final judgment the district court remains free to reconsider and issue a written judgment different from its oral pronouncement. The point at which jurisdiction is transferred must, therefore, be sharply delineated .

Appellant contends that the district court misled appellant and induced him to file a premature notice of appeal by announcing that it did not intend to enter a written judgment, and that respondents caused confusion by causing a written judgment to be entered. This argument is unpersuasive. An oral pronouncement of judgment is not valid for any purpose, NRCP 58(c); therefore, only a written judgment has any effect, and only a written judgment may be appealed. The district court's oral pronouncement from the bench. the clerk's minute order, and even an unfiled written order are ineffective for any purpose and cannot be appealed. Appellant, rather than filing a premature notice of appeal. should have requested a written judgment from the district court. At the very least, appellant should have filed an amended notice of appeal after the written judgment was entered on March 6, 1985. Further, we are not persuaded that counsel for respondents acted improperly in any

The Nevada supreme court rendered its decision in the case entitled **KONEWKO v. DOUGLAS COUNTY SCHOOL DISTRICT in June 1992. (Unpublished)**.[377] The case involved Mrs Karen Konewko, who had worked for the Douglas County School District for 12 years. She was a high school trigonometry teacher.

During the 1988-89 school year, Mrs. Konewko taught trigonometry at Douglas High School. Cameron Alder was one of her students. Cameron was in his junior year at high school. He celebrated his 17th birthday on January 11, 1989.

Mrs. Konewko also served as faculty advisor to the school debate team and traveled with the team to out-of town tournaments several times during the school year. Cameron Alder was not a member of the debate team.

During the 1988/89 school year Mrs. Konewko sent several written messages to Cameron Alder. In her letters to Cameron she called him "snookums" and "Honey bun" and told him "...I do consider you to be love material..." One letter said, "If you and I were less restrained you would no longer be in your virginal prime (if indeed you still are) and I would be very pregnant with your child." She also telephoned him at home as many as three times a week.[378]

Cameron Alder served as the student teacher for the trigonometry class taught by Mrs Konewko. When Mrs Konewko could not meet her classes she left messages for Cameron in a folder containing instructions to student teachers. One of the messages was discovered by a substitute teacher on April 6, 1989, while she was looking through the instructions Mrs. Konewko left for substitute teachers and student teachers.[379] She transmitted the information to school authorities.

The school board sought to dismiss Mrs Konewko citing immorality as the grounds. In the decision to dismiss Mrs Konewko the district said the letters "exhibited an unquenchable need for companionship with a minor."

Mrs Konewko appealed her dismissal and a hearing officer was appointed to consider her appeal.

---

way by seeking a written order from the district court. Nothing precluded appellant from filing an amended notice of appeal after written notice of entry of the written judgment was served on him.

Finally, it has been suggested that appellant's premature notice of appeal should be excused as a technical defect pursuant to Knox v. Dick. We disagree. Unlike the circumstances present in Knox. this case involves a notice of appeal that is truly premature. There is nothing technical about it. In Knox, a written judgment was appealed in a timely fashion; there was nothing wrong with the judgment other than the fact that the district court had not certified it as final pursuant to NRCP 54(b). Also, the judgment in Knox was unquestionably certifiable as final pursuant to NRCP 54(b). We concluded, therefore, that the prematurity of the notice of appeal in that case was purely technical. Contrarily. in this case, no written judgment was entered by the district court; and, consequently, there was no judgment to appeal from at the time appellant's notice of appeal was filed. As a result, appellant's premature notice of appeal did not divest the district court of jurisdiction to act at that time.

Allowing a premature notice of appeal to be valid under the facts of this case would impose an unnecessary burden on this court to determine on an ad hoc basis whether we have power to act and would so obscure rules of jurisdiction as to be detrimental to the judicial process. For example, if notices of appeal filed after the oral rendition of judgment, but before a final written judgment is entered, are held to be valid, it would become difficult, if not impossible, to determine when or if a final oral judgment has been rendered. Under such circumstances, this court would be required to issue numerous orders, and to grapple with fine and nonexistent distinctions between valid and invalid premature notices of appeal. Also, it would be difficult to determine when the thirty-day appeal period began to run under NRAP 4(a), whether postjudgment motions were timely and whether they would toll the appeal period that may or may not have commenced to run. Such a rule would render uncertain the validity of findings of fact, conclusions of law and a written judgment filed after a "timely" notice of appeal had been filed. Also, such a rule would ignore the possibility (and the possibility is not remote) that no judgment would ever be properly entered. In addition, questions would arise as to when a notice of cross-appeal would be due under such a flexible rule of jurisdiction. In light of these and other considerations, we decline to adopt such a rule in this state.

Other states have held that a premature notice of appeal is ineffective to vest jurisdiction in an appellate court to review a subsequently entered final judgment. Also, in analogous cases, where a notice of appeal was filed during the pendency of a timely post trial motion, the notices have been held to be premature and of no effect. We conclude that the result of these authorities is sound.

We conclude that we lack jurisdiction to entertain this appeal. Accordingly, we dismiss this appeal.

Justice Mowbray filed a strong dissent.

[377] Nevada supreme court case No. 21657 decided June 30, 1992. Unpublished.

[378] See Ryan, Cy ,"Judge Studies Case Of Fired Teacher", Las Vegas Sun, August 29, 1990, p. 2 B. See Also Hearing Officer's Report and Recommendation, Dated October 23, 1989, Hearing Officer Steven P. Elliott. Exhibits A, B, C, D, and E. .

[379] Ibid., p. 2.

The hearing officer determined that the activity engaged in by the teacher constituted immorality. The content of the letters, said the hearing officer, indicated that Mrs. Konewko found Cameron to be an attractive, intelligent and helpful young man and that she would enjoy sexual relations with him. He continued,

> "the impropriety of such communication from a teacher to a student is obvious. Teachers must maintain sufficient emotional distance from students so that discipline and fairness is maintained. A teacher holds great power over a student whose future may be affected by a grade given in a class taught by the teacher. Thus, the issue of consent versus compulsion for sexual favors is inherently raised in a student-teacher relationship. Teachers are also models influencing the values of their students. The advocacy of extra-marital sexual relations is contrary to the values of many Americans, including the Alder family."[380]

The hearing examiner determined that Mrs. Konewko should be disciplined. He found her actions unprofessional and in violation of the School District's sexual harassment policy. He also found that she was well aware that her actions were prohibited, since she discussed the destruction of the messages with Cameron and requested such destruction in the messages themselves. He determined that "Her relationship with Cameron will severely undermine her effectiveness as a teacher at Douglas High School as long as the memory and rumors of her actions survive."[381]

Since the cause for dismissal which the School District presented against Mrs. Konewko was immorality,[382] it assumed the burden of proving that Mrs. Konewko had been convicted of one of the offenses listed in § 391-311 (4) NRS or that she otherwise committed acts forbidden by such criminal statutes. The hearing examiner determined that the criminal statute which best applied to the facts in the case was § 207.260 NRS, "Annoyance or Molestation of a Minor." He held that Mrs. Konewko had annoyed or molested Cameron Alder within the meaning of the statute and recommended dismissal by the school board.[383]

The district court affirmed the decision of the hearing officer.[384]

An appeal was taken and the case was submitted for decision to the Nevada supreme court on the record and briefs of counsel October 21, 1991.[385] The Nevada supreme court affirmed the district court decision on September 23, 1993. This is the only reported case in Nevada on concerning annoyance and\or molestation of a minor.[386]

Summary-Substantive Aspects of Discipline

The substantive grounds for teacher discipline are stated in broad terms. However, the vague terms have been restricted by holding that school boards must

---

[380] Ibid., p. 2

[381] Ibid. p.3.

[382] A licensed employee is subject to immediate dismissal or refusal to reemploy according to the statutory procedures without admonition on grounds of immorality. Sec. 391.313 (3) NRS (1993).

[383] Ibid., p. 8. He made this finding in spite of testimony from the 17-year-old that he found the letters "flattering and humorous." He also testified that he had a girlfriend and "did not consider the teacher as a potential sexual partner." Ryan article p. 2 B.

[384] Konewko v. Douglas County School District, Case No. 89-01705A First Judicial District, Carson City, Judge Michael R. Griffin, September 19, 1990.

[385] Should writing steamy love letters to a student constitute immorality for which immediate dismissal is appropriate or is it merely an indication of unprofessional conduct (c) or evident unfitness for service (j) or inadequate performance (i) which require an admonition prior to dismissal. See Sec. 391.313 NRS (1993). Should a teacher have to be warned that the activity engaged in by Mrs Konewko is inappropriate? Should Mrs Konweko be returned to the classroom because she was not admonished that her conduct was inappropriate?

[386] Sec. 207.260 NRS (1993), Annoyance and Molestation of a Minor.

not only be prepared to show grounds exist for discipline but also that there is a nexus between the grounds for discipline and proper performance of a teachers professional responsibilities.[387]

---

[387] See **RUST** I supra., However, thv nexus requirement may be defeated by outlandish public activity. See for example, **Wishart v. Mcdonald,** 500 F.2d 1110 (1st Cir. 1974) LEVIN H. CAMPBELL, Circuit Judge.

D. Franklin Wishart, a tenured sixth grade teacher in Easton, Massachusetts, was dismissed from his job for conduct unbecoming a teacher, following a hearing before the school committee on, charges that be had carried in public view on his property located in the town where he taught, in a lewd and suggestive manner, a dress mannequin that he had dressed, undressed and caressed.

He has alleged that the individual defendants, among them the superintendent of schools Paul J. McDonald and the members of the Easton school committee, deprived him of constitutional rights by removing him arbitrarily and capriciously, by penalizing "private" conduct which did not interfere with his teaching duties, and by applying an unconstitutionally vague statute. He sought an injunction, an order directing reinstatement and payment of damages, and a declaratory judgment that the phrase "conduct unbecoming a teacher" was unconstitutionally vague. [T]he district court ruled against Wishart. We affirm.

The evidence in the district court disclosed the following: Wishart, who taught for several years in another school system, was employed by the Easton system in September, 1968. He subsequently acquired tenure by operation of law. A tenured teacher "shall not be dismissed, except for inefficiency, incapacity, conduct unbecoming a teacher or superintendent, insubordination or other good cause, ..." That same section provides numerous procedural safeguards, none of which Wishart claims were denied to him. ...

In the Easton schools Wishart received from his superiors ratings of slightly above average. In his last evaluation, in March 1972, his principal wrote that "Mr. Wishart is an excellent teacher. He has a genuine enthusiasm for pupils and teaching, making him a valuable member of the Middle School staff."

Sometime about the fall of 1971 Wishart began to engage in unusual conduct which his psychiatrist testified was symptomatic of a personality disorder characterized by the displacement of sexual interest into a dress. Occasionally until the spring of 1972, and weekly on Thursday evening thereafter until March of 1973, Wishart took a mannequin outdoors and moved about his yard. The mannequin, according to Wishart, was a camera tripod to which he had strapped a pillow and covered with his wife's dress. His immediate neighbors, three of whom testified in court, thought the contraption was an actual mannequin, and that it was draped in a negligee. In any event, Wishart could be observed readily from nearby houses handling the mannequin at different places on his lot, including in his well illuminated front yard. Neighbors testified that they observed him caressing the mannequin in the area of the breast, and that once he had placed it on top of a car. One neighbor observed him lifting the skirt and placing it between his legs. Two neighbors thought they observed masturbation: he denied it. There was no testimony of actual exposure. Wishart testified that he did not think he was observed , but conceded that possibility. In fact he was regularly observed by the neighbors who paid considerable attention to, these evening activities. Wishart's testimony to a desire to keep the conduct private was offset by testimony of neighbors that, in their opinion, he acted as if he wished to be seen. He did not stay inside; his property fronted on a well-travelled street; he carried out the activity in illuminated places; on one occasion he entered a neighbor's lot. There was abundant evidence from which it might be concluded both that he was observed and that he should have expected to be observed. There was also evidence that besides the three nearby neighbors who testified, other persons in Easton, a small town, became aware of the conduct. Superintendent McDonald testified that it had become such public knowledge that even prior to the dismissal it was being discussed among his wife's friends in another area of Easton. The school psychologist told Wishart in mid-December 1972 that she had been made aware of strange conduct taking place on his property. She offered help, which he refused. After stopping for two weeks, he recommenced the conduct.

One of Wishart's neighbors informed McDonald via a school committee member of Wishart's behavior. After speaking with another neighbor, McDonald went to Spooner Street one night and observed the conduct for himself from both across the street and the house next door. He observed from both locations as Wishart carried the contraption to the front, side and rear of his house.

McDonald met with Wishart after school on March 9, 1973, informing him orally and by letter that he was relieved of classroom duties and transferred to nonteaching duties; his compensation was continued pending a meeting of the school committee to decide whether he should be fired. Prior to March 9 McDonald had not advised Wishart that his conduct would be viewed as a cause for discharge. On,May 16, 1973, McDonald formally notified Wishart that he had been charged with "conduct unbecoming a teacher". pursuant to § 42, and that a discharge hearing would be held before the school committee. The letter made two particularized charges of "unbecoming" conduct:

"a. That you have on various occasions displayed and carried a dress mannequin in the public view on your Spooner Street property, have dressed said mannequin in feminine attire, and have on occasion caressed said mannequin.

"b. That your actions in the public view on your Spooner Street property in regard to the dressing and undressing of said dress mannequin in feminine attire have been on various occasions of a suggestive or lewd nature."

Wishart and his counsel attended the meeting on June 18 at which the school committee, after hearing the recommendation and testimony of McDonald, several neighbors, Wishart, and a police officer who had accompanied McDonald on his sojourn, voted unanimously to discharge Wishart. Wishart received his salary for' the entire 1972-73 school year. ...The school committee gave no reasons, other than those;in the May 16 letter, for the discharge. McDonald testified at trial that he recommended Wishart's dismissal on the grounds that his conduct had become notorious in the town and that this would impair his ability to function as a sixth grade teacher, and, moreover, that Wishart's conduct indicated possible emotional instability unbefitting a teacher. Wishart's psychiatrist testified that Wishart's conduct was unrelated to his performance as a teacher and would not affect classroom conduct.

...The court found that under the standards set out [in another case] the action of the school committee was not arbitrary or capricious. Because Wishart admitted engaging in the conduct with which he was charged, the district court reasoned, the only open question was whether the reasons given were related to the educational process. The court noted the uncontradicted testimony of Wishart's psychiatrist that his personality disorder would have no effect on classroom performance, and observed that Wishart's teacher evaluations (including one filed after his public conduct had commenced), rated him generally above average to excellent. But the court wrote:

"Even if the Court were to agree (which it is not altogether prepared to do), that plaintiff's problem would in no way reflect on his performance in the classroom, there is still the problem of notoriety and its effect on 'relationships within the educational process.' The extent of the pre-March notoriety of plaintiff's conduct is uncertain as is the extent of the notoriety to date. ...

The Court feels that there was a basis, if somewhat meager, for McDonald's belief that the conduct had, or certainly would in the future, gain a degree of notoriety which would damage plaintiff's effectiveness as a teacher in the school system and his working relationships within the educational process. It cannot be said that the school committee acted arbitrarily or capriciously in sharing in that opinion and following the recommendation to dismiss. Whether or not some of the notoriety was caused by the defendants' investigations and hearings cannot change that result."

The court also rejected Wishart's contention that the school committee was punishing him for constitutionally protected "private" conduct. The court agreed with plaintiff that the conduct occurred on his "private property" but refused to equate "on private property" with " in private". The district court was correct on this point. The right of privacy, even as advocated in Warren & Brandeis, may be surrendered by public display. The right to be left alone in the home extends only to the home and not to conduct displayed under the street lamp on the front lawn.

127

Procedural Aspects of Teacher Discipline
Nevada Statutes

The procedural requirements of the Nevada Professional Practices Act applicable to an employee depend on whether the employee's status is probationary or postprobationary.

The legislature has ordered each school district, following consultation with and involvement of elected representatives of the teachers or their designees, to develop a policy for objective evaluations in a narrative form.[388] The policy must set forth a means by which an employee's over-all performance may be determined to be satisfactory or unsatisfactory and include evaluations by the teacher, pupils, administrators or other teachers or any combination thereof. Counselors, librarians and other licensed personnel must be evaluated on forms developed specifically for their respective specialities. Evaluations, while not the sole criterion, must be used in the dismissal process. A copy of the policy adopted by each board must be filed with the state department.

Other specific requirements of the evaluation policy include a conference and a written evaluation for a probationary employees no later that December 1, February 1, and April 1, of the school year. Probationary teachers assigned to year-round schools must be evaluated at least 3 times during each 12 months of employment. Whenever an administrator charged with the evaluation of a

---

Finally, the district court declined to decide Wishart's contention that the standard of "conduct unbecoming a teacher " is unconstitutionally vague. The court wrote:

"Whether or not this a determination which can be made by a single judge is questionable and whether or not it belongs in the federal court at all in the first instance is even more questionable. The statute could easily be interpreted by the state court to refer only to conduct which is job related. Such a construction would most probably save the statute from being attacked as vague."

There are,then, three issues for our decision:...second, was the dismissal arbitrary or capricious within the meaning of Drown; and third, was the dismissal predicated on a statute too vague to afford notice of the prohibited conduct?

ARBITRARY AND CAPRICIOUS ACTION

The most persuasive argument that the dismissal was arbitrary or capricious is that the reasons for the dismissal are "unrelated to the educational process or [the] working relationships within the educational institution." But we think fair minded men could reasonably dispute whether public conduct and a "personality disorder" of the sort described by Wishart's psychiatrist are "related" to the educational process, especially in the case of a small town elementary school teacher. Precisely because the question could be disputed, we should not overturn the action of the school committee on constitutional grounds, whatever our own preferences. We have no doubt that the conduct would seem sufficiently bizarre and threatening so that, in the minds of many, it would destroy his ability to serve as a role-model for young children. This may be an overly strict view, and it may be that Wishart's abilities and future could both be preserved by a more tolerant and understanding course. But this is the sort of judgment a school committee is elected to make, and the committee is entitled to prevail unless plainly wrong. If the cause for dismissal were speech or some other constitutionally protected activity, the matter would he entirely different.

VAGUENESS

Wishart's vagueness challenge is foreclosed by Arnett v. Kennedy.

...

If the conduct had been so inoffensive —such as not wearing a tie ---that a teacher might not be aware of the prevailing standard, we would require evidence that the required standard had been communicated, and that the teacher had nonetheless refused to adhere. In such a case, persistent failure to wear a tie would be less itself conduct unbecoming a teacher than it would be evidence of a more serious refusal to follow a reasonable and express rule. But we cannot say that Wishart's behavior was not fairly identifiable in advance as conduct unbecoming a teacher. True it was probably not criminal, nor was it seriously disruptive. But we think it was sufficiently odd and suggestive that the ordinary person would know, in advance, that his image as an elementary school teacher would be gravely jeopardized. ...Humanly it is perhaps unfortunate that there was no warning; on the other hand, the message of the school psychologist in December can be described as a guarded warning which Wishart chose to ignore or at least was unable to do anything about.

The choice between specific rules and general standards is a difficult one; each has its unique costs. The real safeguard under a general standard is the common-law adjudicatory process coupled with judicial review. That administrative and adjudicatory process is present here and we hold that the statutory standard is not unconstitutional.

Affirmed.

Another situation raising similar issues (Outrageous public activity impacting on the nexus requirement) is unfolding in New York City. There, a physics teacher at the Bronx High School of Science has been reassigned pending a dismissal hearing because of his activities in an organization of pedophiles. School district officials say this makes him unfit to teach. Peter Melzer, the teacher, is a leader of the North American Man-Boy Love Association. Mr Melzer stands accused of encouraging child abuse, child pornography and child prostitution in a newsletter published by the group. The teachers name appeared on the masthead of the publication when one of the articles in the newsletter offered graphic tips on how to make that special boy feel good. Mr Melzer opposes laws against sex between children and adults, but he denies promoting law-breaking. And he says that in 31 years in the classroom, he has never mentioned sex or done anything inappropriate. Should membership in such an organization be an automatic disqualification for teaching? Does the First Amendment have any application to such activity? Henneberger, Melinda, "A Pedophile's Rights," New York Times, October 3, 1993, Sec. 4, p. 6.

[388] Sec. 391.3125 NRS (1991) Note this section applies to all licensed employees, probationary and postprobationary. See also Sperry, David J., Pounder, Diana G. & Drew, Clifford J., "Educator Evaluation and the Law: A Case Study of Common Statutory Problems," 75 Ed.Law Rep. [965] (Sept. 10, 1992).

probationary employee believes the employee will not be reemployed for the next school year, he\she is obligated to bring the matter to the employee's attention in a written document which is separate from the evaluation no later than February 15. The notice must include the reasons for the potential decision not to reemploy or refer to the evaluation in which the reasons are stated. Such notice is not required if the probationary employee has received a letter of admonition during the current school year.

Postprobationary teachers must be evaluated at least once each year.

Evaluations of probationary and postprobationary teachers must, if necessary, include recommendations for improvement in their performance. Moreover, reasonable efforts must be made to assist the teacher to correct any deficiencies noted in the evaluation. A copy of each evaluation must be provided to the teacher not later than 15 days following the evaluation. A copy of the evaluation and the teacher's response are placed in the teacher personnel file.

Nevada law supplements the evaluation provisions with a section dealing with admonition[389] of licensed employees.[390] The provision states that whenever an administrator of a licensed employee believes it is necessary to admonish the employee for a reason that he\she believes may lead to demotion, dismissal or cause the employee not to be reemployed he\she shall bring the matter to the attention of the employee involved in writing. The written statement should include the reasons for the admonition and that it may lead to the employees demotion, dismissal or nonrenewal. The administrator is obligated to make a reasonable effort to assist the employee to correct whatever appears to be the cause of the potential discipline and, except where immediate removal is appropriate,[391] allow a reasonable time for improvement. The time allowed cannot exceed 3 months for the first admonition. If improvements occur within the time granted, the admonition must be removed from the employee's records together with all notations and indications of its having been issued. In any event, the admonition must be removed from the records of the employee not later that 3 years after it was issued.

An administrator need not admonish an employee if his\her contract will be terminated under the law dealing with probationary employees.[392] However, if a probationary employee does not receive a written notice of potential nonrenewal before February 15 [393] he\she must receive an admonition before any such decision is taken.[394]

A licensed employee is subject to immediate dismissal, without admonition on grounds contained in paragraphs (b), (f), (g), (h) and (p) of Section 391.312 (1) NRS (1991).[395]

If a superintendent has reason to believe that cause exists for the dismissal of a licensed employee and he\she is of the opinion that the immediate suspension of the employee is in the best interests of the students in the district, the statutes authorize him\her to suspend the staff member without notice and without a

---

[389] Admonish is defined as to reprove gently; to instruct or direct or rebuke. New Websters Dictionary, Book of Essentials,Inc. New York , New York (1991).

[390] Sec. 391.313 NRS (1993).

[391] See Sec. 391.314 NRS (1993).

[392] Sec. 391.313 (2) NRS (1993). See also Sec. 391.3197 NRS (1991).

[393] Sec. 391.3125 (4) NRS (1993).

[394] Sec. 391.313 (2) NRS (1993).

[395] Sec. 391.313 (3) NRS (1993). See Sec. 391.312 (1) supra. (b) Immorality, (f) Physical or Mental Incapacity, (g) Decreased number of positions due to decreased enrollment, (h) Conviction of a felony or a crime involving moral turpitude, (p) Dishonesty.

hearing.[396] Furthermore, the superintendent may suspend a licensed employee who has been officially charged but not yet convicted of a felony or a crime involving moral turpitude or immorality.[397] The superintendent is required to notify the employee of the suspension in writing. If the charge is dismissed or the staff member is found not guilty, he\she is entitled to reinstatement with back pay, plus interest and normal seniority.

Within 5 days after a suspension becomes effective, the superintendent is required to begin dismissal proceedings. During the dismissal process the staff member may continue to receive his salary as long as he\she furnishes a bond or other security as a guarantee that he\she will repay any amounts paid if the dismissal is upheld.

The statutes specify the procedural requirements for considering recommendations for dismissal,[398] and against reemployment.

At least 15 days before recommending to the school board that it dismiss or not reemploy a postprobationary employee or dismiss a probationary employee the superintendent is required to give written notice to the employee, by registered or certified mail, of his intention to make the recommendation.[399] The law also specifies the contents of the notice. It must inform the employee of the grounds for the recommendation, specify that if the employee files a written request within 10 days of receiving the notice he\she is entitled to a hearing before a hearing officer indicate that the employee may request appointment of a hearing officer [400] and refer to chapter 391 of the statutes.

If a request for a hearing is untimely or no hearing request is received the superintendent is obligated to file his\her recommendation with the board of trustees. The board may then act on the recommendation as it deems appropriate.[401]

If a request for a hearing is made, the superintendent's recommendation is held in abeyance pending the report of the hearing officer.[402]

Requests for appointment of a hearing officer are forwarded to the state superintendent. Within 10 days of receiving a request, the superintendent must designate seven attorneys from the state panel. After designation the staff member and the district superintendent strike [403] one member from the list until only one

---

[396] Sec 391.314 (1) NRS (1993).

[397] A licensed employee who is convicted of a crime which requires registration as a sex offender and\or Abuse, neglect or endangerment of a child, a Crime against Nature, Sale or loan of obscene material to a minor or Annoynance of molestation of a minor forfeits all rights of employment from the date of his\her arrest. Sec. 391.314 (5) NRS (1993) An employee charged with the aforementioned crimes who waives his right to a speedy trial while suspended may receive no more than 12 months of back pay and seniority upon reinstatement. Sec. 391.314 (7) A licensed employee convicted of any crime and who is sentences to and serves any sentence of imprisonment forfeits all rights of employment. Sec. 391.314 (6) NRS (1993).

[398] The procedure applies to probationary teachers facing dismissal.

[399] Sec. 391.317 NRS (1993).

[400] The State Board of Education maintains a list of hearing officers. Appointment to the panel is limited to residents of the state recommended by the State Bar of Nevada and the Nevada Trial Lawyers Association. Each nominee appointed to the list must have completed a course of instruction in administrative law relating to the provisions of the education personnel chapter of the statutes. (See Sec. 391.3161 NRS (1993)). The hearing officer may be appointed from a list provided by the American Arbitration Association if the number of names on the list of qualified, trained hearing officers falls below 10 (Chapter 109 Laws of Nevada 1993 amending Sec. 391.3161 (3) NRS (1991)) and the superintendent agrees. Sec 391.317 (2) (c).NRS (1991). If a AAA hearing officer is used the law requires that the employee and the board share the costs of the hearing (Is there a potential Due Process problem with this provision). Sec 391.3161 (3) NRS (1993) If the superintendent refuses to use a AAA list a panel of hearing officers created by the state board is utilized. Sec. 391.3161 NRS (1991). The superintendent and employee may challenge not more than five of the list of hearing officers on the state panel. Those challenged may not be appointed as the hearing officer by the state superintendent. The existence of the state board hearing officer list and the AAA arbitrator option does not preclude the employee and the superintendent from selecting a mutually acceptable attorney who is a resident of Nevada to serve as a hearing officer to conduct a particular hearing. (See Chapter 109 Laws of Nevada 1993 amending Sec 391.3161 NRS (1991)).

[401] Sec. 391.318 (1) NRS (1993).

[402] Sec. 391.318 (2) NRS (1993).

[403] The person entitled to strike first is determined by lot.

remains. The person remaining after the striking process is completed is designated the hearing officer to decide the employment issue.[404]

As soon as possible after designation, the hearing officer is required to hold a hearing to determine whether the grounds for the recommendation are substantiated. The hearing officer may require witnesses to give testimony under oath and require production of evidence relevant to his\her decision.[405] The law provides that the employee and superintendent may be represented by an attorney and call witnesses.[406] The statute further provides that the employee and the school board are equally responsible for the expense and compensation of the hearing officer including an official transcript.[407] The technical rules of evidence do not apply to the hearing.[408]

Within 30 days after the time of his\her designation the law requires that the hearing be completed and a written report filed with the parties not later than 15 days after the conclusion of the hearing.[409] The report must contain an outline of the scope of the hearing, findings of fact and conclusions of law, and recommend a course of action to be taken by the board.[410] The report is final and binding on the employee and the board if the employee and the superintendent have so agreed before the selection of the hearing officer was begun.[411] Judicial review of a final and binding report may be requested by either party.[412]

Within 5 days of receiving a non-binding report from the hearing officer the superintendent may withdraw the recommendation or file his recommendation with the school board. Within 15 days of receiving the superintendents recommendation the board is mandated to accept, reject or remand the case for further evidence and recommendations. The board must inform the employee of its decision in writing. The board decision is subject to judicial review.

The superintendent may also discipline an employee by suspending him\her with loss of pay at any time after a hearing has been held which affords due process.[413] Grounds for suspension are the same as those listed for dismissal. An employee may be suspended more than once during a contract year but the total number of days of suspension may not exceed 20 in one contract year. Suspension used as discipline should be progressive unless circumstances dictate otherwise.[414]

School boards are required to notify postprobationary staff members in writing concerning their reemployment for the ensuing year on or before May 1.[415] Employees so notified must notify the board in writing of their acceptance of employment by May 10.[416] Failure to notify the board on a timely basis is conclusive evidence of rejection of the contract.

---

[404] Sec. 391.31915 NRS (1993).

[405] Sec. 391.3192 (2) NRS (1993).

[406] If the employee is disabled he\she is entitled to an interpreter at the hearing. Sec. 391.31925 NRS (1993).

[407] Sec. 391.3192 (6) NRS (1993). Is there any due process issue present because the employee is made jointly responsible for hearing expenses? Isn't the employer solely responsible for providing a fair hearing?

[408] Sec. 391.3192 (7) NRS (1993).

[409] The time limits are subject to waiver by mutual agreement. Sec. 391.3193 (4) NRS (1993).

[410] Sec. 391.3193 (2) NRS (1993).

[411] Ibid.

[412] Sec. 391.3194 (4) NRS (1993). See Sec. 38.145 or 38.155 NRS (1993).

[413] Sec. 391.314 (8) NRS (1993).

[414] Ibid.

[415] Sec. 391.3196 NRS (1993).

[416] Collective Bargaining Agreements negotiated by the recognized employee organization and the school board become a part of the contract of employment between the board and the employee. Sec 391.3196 (4) NRS (1993).

Probationary employees are employed on an annual basis and have no right to employment after the probationary year. Teachers employed after June 30 for the ensuing school year must be notified whether they will be reemployed for the following school year on or before May 1. Teachers employed in year-round schools must be notified of their employment status no later than 45 days before the last day of work under their contract. Those employees notified of reemployment must accept or reject the offer of employment within 10 days of the reemployment notice. Failure to submit a timely acceptance is constitutes a rejection of the contract. A probationary teacher who receives a notice of reemployment is entitled to postprobationary status in the ensuing school year. A school district may offer a trial year to a teacher it has not given a regular notice of reemployment. A teacher who receives a trial year employment offer may request a supplemental evaluation by another administrator in the school district selected by the teacher and the superintendent.[417] The notice of refusal to reemploy must include a statement of the reasons for the decision.[418]

Case Law

The Nevada Supreme Court and the 9th Circuit Court of Appeals have rendered a number of decisions which address procedural aspects of the employment relationship. These decisions help deepen our understanding of the current statutory protections outlined above.[419]

The federal decision is presented first because it addresses a question regarding determination of probationary status. The Nevada cases are then presented in chronological order so that the reader can perceive changes in the procedural statutes which have occurred since 1976.

---

[417] Sec. 391.3197 NRS (1993).
[418] Ibid.
[419] Please note that the statutes have changed since many of the cases were decided.

Federal Case Law

CAIN
v.
McQUEEN
580 F.2d 1001 (9th Cir. 1978)

Before TRASK and ANDERSON, Circuit Judges, and GRANT, District Judge.

TRASK, Circuit Judge:

This appeal is taken by both plaintiff and defendants from an order of the district court denying defendants' motion to dismiss and granting limited summary judgment to plaintiff.

...Appellant in her amended complaint also alleged that the defendant-trustees violated her rights under the First and Fourteenth Amendments to the Constitution of the United States and under Nev.Rev.Stat. § 391.3197 as it existed in March 1973.

Plaintiff was employed in November 1972 as a substitute teacher for the Washoe County School District in Reno, Nevada. In January 1973, she was given a full-time teaching position which was created by another teacher who had resigned. At that time she was given a standard employment contract, the same as that of any other teacher in the school district, except that it contained the following notation: "Contract starts January 16, 1973 and is for the remainder of the school year only."

Defendants contend that this notation placed plaintiff in a different status than other teachers, and made her merely a "short-term" employee. The fact is, however, that all teachers' contracts expire at the end of the school year. All such contracts, including plaintiff's, are expressly made subject "to the laws of the state of Nevada regarding public schools" whose laws give teachers certain rights to continued employment.

Nevada law (Nev.Rev.Stat. § 391.3197) provides that new teachers are put on probation annually for three years, provided their services are satisfactory, or they may be dismissed at any time at the discretion of the board.

The practice of the school district had been generally to provide a teacher with notice and a hearing before the nonrenewal of his or her contract. However, the district had recently adopted the practice of denominating certain teachers' contracts as "short-term" or "one year only," and consequently, claimed that §391.3197 NRS did not apply to such employees. Defendants maintain that plaintiff was one of these "short-term" teachers and, therefore, was not entitled to the protection of the statute.

On March 19, 1973, plaintiff was notified by letter signed by the administrative assistant in charge of personnel that her contract would not be renewed. No reasons were given for the nonrenewal. Plaintiff then wrote a letter to the President of the Board of Trustees, defendant Pine, requesting a hearing before the board. Her request was denied.

While the plaintiff's request was pending before the board, some students and teachers wrote letters to the board requesting that plaintiff be retained. Defendant McQueen, a member of the board, indicated that he considered such action an organized "letter writing campaign rather than an out-pouring of spontaneous support," and it caused him to become "disenchanted" with plaintiff. He also indicated that he was "turned off" by her own request for a hearing. He expressed these views at a board meeting where plaintiff was discussed and informed the principal of Reno High School, where plaintiff was employed, that he would not be enthused about hiring her on a full-time basis.

In spite of this, the principal recommended plaintiff to fill a position to be left by a retiring teacher. At a board meeting held in August 1973, however, plaintiff's employment was discussed and the board determined not to employ her. At that time, defendants Pine and McQueen apparently expressed the view that plaintiff's husband made too much money and, since he was the dean of the college of education at the University of Nevada, Reno, it would be wrong to hire his wife while there were so many graduates of that college who would not get jobs. An informal vote was taken, and only two members favored hiring plaintiff

McQueen telephoned the principal of Reno High School reminding him of his opposition to the hiring of plaintiff. In addition, Superintendent Picollo met with the principal and encouraged him to fill any vacancies with teachers who had "one year only" contracts or who requested transfer from other schools. When vacancies finally did become available, plaintiff was not recommended.

Defendants have never alleged that those selected were more qualified than plaintiff. On the contrary, Superintendent Picollo informed plaintiff that she "had received excellent recommendations" and that her "capability as a teacher had never been questioned." Both the head of the English department and the principal praised her teaching ability.

Plaintiff brought this action against the trustees in their official capacity and two of the trustees, Pine and McQueen, as individuals, claiming she was deprived of her job in violation of procedural due process and her substantive constitutional rights under the First and Fourteenth Amendments.

Defendants' motion to dismiss was based on their claim that plaintiff was a substitute teacher and therefore according to the express provisions of § 391.3115 NRS, she was not entitled to the non-employment provisions of § 391.3197 NRS. In addition, they claimed the action should have been dismissed because plaintiff's complaint alleges that no more than two of the seven board members were motivated by constitutionally impermissible reasons.

The district court denied defendants' motion to dismiss and granted limited summary judgment for the plaintiff. The court held that § 391.3197 NRS applied to plaintiff and that this statute gave her a "property" interest within the meaning of the Fourteenth Amendment and that she was entitled to a hearing as a matter of due process and under Nevada law. A hearing was consequently ordered. Plaintiff thereupon filed a motion to amend the judgment urging that her termination should be considered null and void and that she should be granted reinstatement and back pay. Plaintiff's motion was denied.

I

For the procedural rights of plaintiff under the due process clause of the Fourteenth Amendment to have been violated, she must have possessed a property interest as contemplated by the Fourteenth Amendment. Board of Regents v. Roth (1972). A teacher has a property interest in his or her job not only when he or she has formal tenure under an express provision of a statute or contract, but also when

134

applicable rules or practices establish a "clearly implied promise of continued employment."

Plaintiff claims that such a property interest was created by § 391.3197 NRS.[420] Under that statute a "probationary" teacher, although lacking formal tenure, is entitled to be reappointed from year to year unless specific "reasons" are found for non-renewal. The court below accordingly held that § 391.3197 NRS, as it existed in 1973, "gave to probationary teachers a form of limited tenure and a right to know and reply to the reasons for termination."

Defendants contend that plaintiff was not a probationary teacher and therefore not entitled to the benefits and protections of §391.3197 NRS. Rather, it is their position that she was a substitute teacher. They base this on the fact that the statute states that teachers are on "probation annually." From this, they conclude that a teacher becomes a probationary employee when granted an annual contract, rather than one for only a portion of a year as the plaintiff had in this case.

We find no merit in defendants' contention. It cannot be said that merely because plaintiff was hired after the school year started that she did not have an annual contract.

We agree with the district court which held that defendants' contention that plaintiff was a substitute teacher is erroneous as a matter of law. The court found:

> "The undisputed facts show unequivocally that plaintiff was not a substitute teacher. She was a substitute teacher in the Washoe County School District from November 10,1972, until sometime in December or January, 1972 [sic], hired on a day-to-day basis as needed. On January, 29, 1973, plaintiff entered into a contract with the Washoe County School District to serve as a teacher from January 16, 1973, 'for the remainder of the 1972-1973 school year only.' The contract is in the standard form then in use for teachers and expressly provides: 'The initial three years of service for the certificated employee shall constitute a probationary period during which time the employee may be dismissed at the discretion of the Board of Trustees pursuant to NRS 391.3197.' Plaintiff thus became a probationary employee of the School District subject to all the rights of every probationary employee. The fact that she was hired to perform the services of another certificated teacher who had resigned does not place her in the category of substitute teacher."

Irrespective of the procedural safeguards afforded by the Fourteenth Amendment due process, plaintiff was at least entitled to those procedural protections mentioned in § 391.3197 NRS. The statute provides for an advance notice of "the reasons for the recommendation to dismiss or not to renew the contract" and an "opportunity to reply." The district court determined that the phrase "opportunity to reply" must be construed as contemplating a hearing since a "statement of reasons for termination and an opportunity to reply are meaningless unless there is some sort of hearing to resolve any issues which may be presented."

Nev.Rev.Stat. §391.3197 was amended on July 1, 1973, to provide that "prior to dismissal or nonrenewal, the teacher may obtain a due process hearing . ..." With regard to this amendment, which occurred after plaintiff's contract had not been renewed, the district court stated:

---

[420] Plaintiffs employment contract contained a specific reference to this statute.

> "As we interpret the law, the amendments made by the 1973 legislature with respect to NRS §391.3197 were clarifying in character and did not materially change the rights of a probationary teacher."

In <u>McGee</u> v. <u>Humbolt</u> <u>County</u> <u>School</u> <u>Dist.</u>, 561 P.2d 458 (Nev.1977), the Supreme Court of Nevada determined that a probationary teacher "received all the process due" her when she "received notification of the reasons respondent [school district] was not rehiring her and was given an opportunity to reply at a public hearing."

II

Plaintiff contends that in addition to a hearing, she is entitled to reinstatement and back pay. This contention presents a difficult issue in which "a careful weighing of all facts and circumstances" must take place. <u>Burton</u> v. <u>Cascade</u> <u>School</u> <u>Dist.</u> <u>Union</u> <u>High</u> <u>School</u> <u>No. 5</u>, 512 F.2d 850, 853 (9th Cir. 1975). There must be a balancing of plaintiff's interests in her wrongfully terminated teaching position against the possible disruption which her reinstatement may cause the school district.

The <u>Burton</u> case points out that reinstatement and back pay are appropriately granted in situations involving racial discrimination and the legal exercise of free expression in a manner critical of the employer. It is also an appropriate form of relief when used to discourage school systems from taking similar action against other teachers in the future. In this case, plaintiff claims that her termination was partially the result of her request for a hearing. If so, this situation is strikingly similar to the situation where the employee is terminated because of the legal exercise of free expression in a manner critical of the employer.

Plaintiff argues that a court-ordered hearing held years after her employment was terminated does not "make good the wrong done." This argument is especially valid in light of §391.3197 NRS which expressly requires that the notice of reasons and opportunity to reply be provided "prior to formal action by the board." This court has affirmed an order of a district court mandating officials to reinstate a college English instructor because his termination was in violation of his procedural due process rights under the Fourteenth Amendment.

The Third Circuit has noted that a post-termination hearing is not an adequate substitute for a pre-termination hearing:

> "But there is substantial difference in the position of the parties once termination has actually occurred. First, the employee, cut-off from the payroll, is greatly disadvantaged in his ability to pursue the hearing remedy. He may be forced by the necessity for survival to seek other employment which will foreclose the pursuit of reinstatement. Second, the institution will have made substitute teaching arrangements, thus introducing into the hearing consideration of the interests of other faculty members. This inevitability will increase whatever tendency may already exist for the hearing officials to defer to the administration's decision. We agree with the district court, therefore, that a hearing after the fact is not the due process equivalent of the pre-termination hearing required by <u>Perry</u> v. <u>Sinderman</u>.

An important consideration is the time lag between the wrongful termination and the hearing. In the Skehan case, supra, the Third Circuit noted that there is probably a greater likelihood that the original termination decision will be upheld if the hearing is held long after the event than if a hearing is held before the termination becomes effective. The Eighth Circuit recently held that a post-termination hearing held two years after the termination did not satisfy the requirements of due process. In that case, plaintiff, a former high school teacher, was terminated without a hearing when defendants discovered that she, a single woman, had become pregnant. In the court-ordered hearing held more than two years after she was terminated, defendants voted to confirm their earlier action.

Not all cases that have found violations of procedural due process and where hearings have been ordered have granted reinstatement and back pay, however. The disadvantage to the school district should be carefully considered.

The district court's order was as follows:

"1. Defendants' motion to dismiss is denied.

"2. A summary judgment will be entered in favor of plaintiff and against defendants requiring that defendants shall, within a reasonable time, accord to plaintiff the due process hearing contemplated by the foregoing opinion. The Court reserves jurisdiction to make such further orders in the premises as may be required to accord to plaintiff the full benefit of the rights to which she is entitled and will entertain supplemental pleadings if they should become necessary. It is the view of the Court that plaintiff's rights and remedies are primarily to be worked out by plaintiff and the Board of Trustees of the Washoe County School District except to the extent that the Court has been required to interject itself into the situation in order to recognize and enforce plaintiff's rights to due process of law.

"Dated: December 31, 1975." C.T. at 276.

We affirm that judgment.

Judgment accordingly.

****

Nevada Case Law

TRUSTEES OF THE CLARK COUNTY SCHOOL DISTRICT
v.
RATHBUN
92 Nev. 651, 556 P.2d 548 (1976)

Per Curiam:

Appellant dismissed respondent from a teaching position with the Clark County School District for alleged unprofessional conduct. On review, the district court ordered respondent reinstated because admonishments required by NRS 391.313 had not been given for certain conduct specified as grounds for dismissal and other conduct, properly admonished, did not constitute legal cause for dismissal. Here, appellant contends the district court erred in ruling (1) admonishments must be given for each diverse and dissimilar act relied upon as grounds for disciplinary action, and (2) there was no legal cause for respondent's dismissal. We disagree.

As a condition precedent to the dismissal of a certificated teacher for unprofessional conduct, NRS 391.313 requires an admonishment be given the teacher to enable him to remedy the cause for potential dismissal.[421] No such

---

[421] NRS 391.313(1) provides:

"1. Whenever an administrator charged with supervision of a certificated employee believes it is necessary to admonish a certificated employee for a reason that he believes may lead to demotion, dismissal or cause the certificated employee not to be reemployed under the provisions of NRS 391.312, he shall:

admonishments were given for each diverse and dissimilar type of conduct relied upon by appellant as grounds for dismissing respondent. Thus, the district court correctly ruled this conduct could not be considered in the disciplinary action against respondent.

The only conduct admonished in accordance with NRS 391.313 consisted of data respondent placed in an article concerning an incident which occurred at his school. This article, which was prepared for a university class attended by respondent, did not produce any harmful disorganization or chaos among students, teachers, or administrators; and it did not adversely affect respondent's ability to perform his duties. As such, it did not constitute a legal cause for dismissal

Affirmed.

McGEE
v.
HUMBOLDT COUNTY SCHOOL DISTRICT
93 Nev. 171, 561 P.2d 458 (1977)

Per Curiam:

Appellant brought suit against respondent for its alleged unlawful failure to renew her teaching contract. The district court granted respondent's motion for summary judgment and denied appellant's motion for partial summary judgment. Appellant here contends (1) she was a post-probationary teacher and, therefore, entitled to the procedural mandates of NRS 391.111 to 391.3196, and (2) her proprietary and liberty interests were impaired without due process. We disagree.

Pursuant to statutes then in force, the procedures of NRS 391.111 to 391.3196, concerning the dismissal of or refusal to reemploy teachers, were applicable only to post-probationary teachers.[422] Such status was achieved after a teacher had been employed for two consecutive contract periods. 1969 Nev. Stats. 271-72. Prior to appellant's completion of the second contract period, but subsequent to the execution of an employment contract for her third teaching term, the legislature amended NRS Ch. 391 by extending the probationary period from two to three years. 1971 Nev. Stats. 379-82. The amendment also provided that, prior to formal action, ". . . the probationary teacher shall be given the reasons for the recommendation to dismiss or not to renew the contract and be given the opportunity to reply." 1971 Nev. Stats. 382.

Even though she had not completed two consecutive contract periods, appellant contends she became a post-probationary teacher upon the execution of her third year contract. The clear statutory mandate then in effect required employment for two consecutive contract periods, and the mere fact of executing a contract for a third term did not alter this requirement. Appellant was a probationary teacher at the time of the amendment and, pursuant to that amendment, remained a probationary teacher during her third year when she received notification of the school district's intention not to reemploy her. Therefore, the procedural mandates of NRS 391.111 to 391.3196 were not available to her.

Affirmed.

"(a) Bring the matter to the attention of the certificated employee involved, in writing, and make a reasonable effort to assist the employee to correct whatever appears to be the cause for potential dismissal or failure to reemploy; and

"(b) Except as provided in NRS 391.314, allow reasonable time for improvement, which shall not exceed 3 months for the first admonishment."

[422] NRS Ch. 391 has since been amended to give probationary teachers the right to a hearing before a hearing officer or hearing commission as set out in NRS 391.111 to 391.3196. NRS 391.3197(3).

CARSON CITY SCHOOL DISTRICT
v.
BURNSEN
96 Nev. 315, 608 P.2d 507 (1980)

By the Court, THOMPSON, J.:

For twelve years Vivian Burnsen was employed by the Carson City School Board as a teacher. During that time her performance had been continuously evaluated. Her personnel file containing such evaluations shows her inability to discipline the students, poor lesson planning, and the ineffective use of materials. She was notified of her deficiencies on many occasions. She was offered assistance to improve her performance as a teacher, but rejected such offers. The file also contains many requests from parents that their children be removed from her classroom and taught by someone else. Finally, on February 3, 1978, the principal of Fremont School gave Burnsen a letter informing her that she would not be recommended for a teaching contract for the year 1978-79. On February 7, 1978, the Superintendent of the Carson City School District mailed a notice of intent to recommend non-reemployment for inefficiency, inadequate performance and the failure to show normal improvement and evidence of professional training and growth. Those reasons for non-reemployment are among those specified by NRS 391.312. The notice included a statement that Burnsen had ten days to request a hearing before a commission pursuant to NRS 391.317. She did not timely request a hearing. Instead, she submitted a letter of resignation which was acknowledged on February 17, 1978. Subsequently, on March 10, 1978, she rescinded her resignation.

Burnsen petitioned the district court for a writ of mandamus and at the conclusion of the hearing the court ordered that she be reinstated as a teacher. Statute requires that when an admonition is made for a reason that may lead to dismissal or cause the employee not to be reemployed, the matter shall be brought to the attention of the employee, in writing, and a reasonable time for improvement given.[423] The February 3 letter from the principal of Fremont School did not advise her of the particular deficiencies in her performance as a teacher, nor did it notify her that she would have a reasonable time within which to improve. It was mainly for this reason that the district court directed reinstatement. This appeal by the school board followed. We reverse.

Although admonishment and a reasonable time for improvement should precede a recommendation that a teacher not be reemployed, the failure to do so is unimportant when the teacher, after being notified that she would not be recommended for a contract, does not timely request a hearing, and voluntarily submits her resignation. Vivian Burnsen resigned her position as a teacher. Her resignation was acknowledged. In these circumstances the failure fully to comply

---

[423] NRS 391.313(1) Whenever an administrator charged with supervision of a certificated employee believes it is necessary to admonish a certificated employee for a reason that he believes may lead to demotion, dismissal or cause the employee not to be reemployed under the provisions of NRS 391.312, he shall:

(a) Bring the matter to the attention of the employee involved, in writing and make a reasonable effort to assist the employee to correct whatever appears to be the cause for potential dismissal or failure to reemploy, and

(b) Except as provided in NRS 391.314, allow reasonable time for improvement, which shall not exceed 3 months for the first admonition. An admonition issued to a certificated employee who, within the time granted for improvement, has met the standards set for him by the administrator who issued the admonition shall be removed from the records of the employee together with all notations and indications of its having been issued. The admonition shall be removed from the records of the employee not later than 3 years after it is issued.

with NRS 391.313 must be considered meaningless. To hold otherwise exalts form over substance. This we decline to do.

Reversed .

MOWBRAY, C. J., and MANOUKIAN and BATJER, JJ., concur.

GUNDERSON, J., dissenting:

The district court determined that the requirements of NRS 391.313 had not been met in admonitions made to Burnsen before her discharge. NRS 391.313(1) provides that when an admonition is made for a reason which may lead to dismissal, or cause the employee not to be reemployed, the matter shall be brought to the employee's attention, in writing, and a reasonable time for improvement given. Although recommendations for improvement had been given to Burnsen, it had not been suggested to her that such admonitions could lead to non-reemployment. The letter of February 3, 1978, was the first such indication Burnsen received. On February 7, she was informed that she would not be recommended for reemployment.

We have previously held that the statutory admonitions must be "given the teacher to enable him to remedy the cause for potential dismissal." It follows that the admonitions should be given in such a fashion that the teacher knows that dismissal or non-reemployment may result.

As a result of appellant's lack of compliance with the statutory requirements, all proceedings subsequent to the invalid letter of non-reemployment were prematurely taken and the statutory ten-day limitation period for requesting a hearing was never invoked. Because Burnsen's resignation clearly resulted from the invalid letter of non- reemployment, it should not stand.

The district court's granting of the petition for a writ of mandamus should be affirmed.

EUREKA COUNTY SCHOOL DISTRICT
v.
HOLBO
101 Nev. 372, 705 P.2d 640 (1985)

Per Curiam:

In August 1981, plaintiff-respondent Phillip Holbo contracted with defendant-appellant Board of Trustees of Eureka County School District for employment as a probationary teacher for the 1981-1982 school year. Respondent's responsibilities were to teach social studies and government at the secondary level, to coach football, and to act as senior class advisor.

Pursuant to NRS 391.3125(3),[424] appellants evaluated respondent's performance as a probationary teacher on schedule. In October 1981, the first teacher evaluation revealed respondent's performance was either "good" or "superior" in all areas. In November, respondent ordered a student to arrange for

---

[424] NRS 391.3125 provides, in part:
        3. The probationary period must include a conference and a written evaluation for the probationary employee no later than:
            (a) November 1;
            (b) January 1;
            (c) March 1; and
            (d) May 1, of the school year.
        4. Each postprobationary teacher shall be evaluated at least once each year.
        5. The evaluation of a probationary teacher or a postprobationary teacher shall, if necessary, include recommendations for improvements in teaching performance. A reasonable effort shall be made to assist the teacher to correct deficiencies noted in the evaluation. The teacher shall receive a copy of each evaluation not later than 15 days after the evaluation . . . ."

disciplinary detention after the student repeatedly used the term "ain't." When the student failed to arrange for detention, respondent referred the student to Principal Selway Mulkey. The principal thereafter conferred with respondent and offered suggestions for less punitive means to handle disciplinary incidents; the principal's report of that conference criticized respondent for requiring strict adherence to the disciplinary system and offered respondent suggestions and help in becoming more effective in handling disciplinary incidents.

Respondent's second evaluation in December, 1981 indicated that he needed to improve classroom management. Respondent then wrote a letter to Superintendent Ted Jackson challenging the accuracy of the second evaluation report and requesting a conference. During the ensuing conference, the principal advised respondent that the best recommendation he could make for reemployment would be a "trial year." The principal requested permission from the superintendent to issue respondent an admonition pursuant to NRS 391.313(1).[425] The principal testified the superintendent denied him permission to admonish respondent. Respondent's third evaluation, in February, showed that some areas previously needing improvement were now satisfactory.

By letter dated March 30, 1982, the principal, now acting superintendent, notified respondent that his contract would not be renewed for the ensuing academic year. The reasons given for the decision not to renew employment were inadequate performance, unprofessional conduct, insubordination, and failure to show both normal improvement and professional growth. Holbo was unable to obtain employment for the 1982-1983 school year and filed this action for breach of contract for failure to admonish him pursuant to NRS 391.313, seeking a declaratory judgment, damages and reinstatement. Following trial, the district court decided the admonition requirement was applicable to non-reemployment of probationary teachers and the contract was breached by the failure to give the admonition. The court ordered one year's salary as damages but refused to order reinstatement. Appellants appeal from the order assigning several aspects of the decision as error.

Appellants contend that the NRS 391.313(1) admonition is inapplicable to probationary employees and thus the court erred in finding a breach of contract by the failure to admonish respondent. We agree.

We conclude the application of the admonition provision to probationary teachers would render useless the existing evaluation schedule and reemployment notification provisions of the statute. NRS 391.3125(3) establishes a detailed teacher evaluation schedule for probationary employees. NRS 391.3197(2) entitles the probationary employee to a written notification of whether he is to be reemployed for the next school year prior to April I of the school year.[426] Any

---

[425] NRS 391.313(1) provides in part:

Whenever an administrator charged with supervision of a certified employee believes it is necessary to admonish a certified employee for a reason that he believes may lead to demotion, dismissal or cause the employee not to be reemployed under the provisions of NRS 391.312, he shall:

(a) Bring the matter to the attention of the employee involved, in writing, and make a reasonable effort to assist the employee to correct whatever appears to be the cause for potential demotion, dismissal or failure to reemploy; and

(b) Except as provided in NRS 391.314, allow reasonable time for improvement, which must not exceed 3 months for the first admonition.

[426] NRS 391.3197 provides:

1. A probationary employee is employed on an annual basis and has no right to employment after a probationary contract year

2. ... the board of trustees shall notify him in writing on or before April I of the school year whether he is to be reemployed for the next school year....

****

evaluation and reemployment notification after the issuance of an admonition would serve little purpose. The purpose for the admonition, as expressed in NRS 391.313(1)(b), is to permit the employee an opportunity to improve his or her work performance. Conferences were held between respondent and the principal in addition to those required by NRS 391.3125(3), and the principal offered suggestions for corrections of respondent's deficiencies which fulfilled the purpose of the admonition.

Additionally, NRS 391.3197(8) entitles the probationary employee to a hearing upon dismissal from employment, but not upon demotion or refusal to reemploy. NRS 391.3161(4), which is not expressly applicable to probationary employees. permits the employee a hearing in cases of demotion. dismissal or refusal to reemploy based on grounds contained in NRS 391.312. The application of the admonition to probationary employees would thus impermissibly imply the creation of a right to a hearing upon non-reemployment in addition to the existing statutory rights of probationary teachers.

...The conference and evaluation reports which occurred during the school year pursuant to NRS 391.3125(3) alerted respondent that grounds for non-reemployment existed. Respondent could not have had an objectively reasonable belief that his reemployment was assured. Respondent received written notice of non-reemployment before April I as required by 391.3197(2), and thus received all the process due him pursuant to the statute.

Accordingly, the order of the district court is reversed.

BOYLE
v.
TRUSTEES CLARK COUNTY SCHOOL DISTRICT
101 Nev. 591, 707 P.2d 1135 (1985)

Per Curiam:
Darleen Boyle, an elementary school teacher of 19 years experience. was dismissed by the school board from her tenured position with the Clark County School District. Boyle challenged the board's action in district court, and, after an adverse decision, brings this appeal.

After a long period of apparently satisfactory performance, charges attacking Boyle's competency to teach erupted in her nineteenth year of service. Whether adequate cause exists for her removal is not before us as Boyle's counsel acknowledges that there is evidence in the record, which, if believed, would provide cause for dismissal. Our task is limited to determining whether Boyle's dismissal was carried out in conformance with the procedure mandated by state law for dismissing a tenured teacher.

Boyle was first informed on September 30, 1981, that her performance as a teacher was unsatisfactory. Her principal gave her a written notice that she had failed to comply with lesson plan requirements, failed to supervise students in her charge and failed to report to her duty location on specified dates. Boyle was repeatedly notified that her failure to prepare lesson plans and to employ certain teaching skills and concepts was unsatisfactory.

---

5. If a probationary employee is notified that he will not be reemployed for the ensuing school year, his employment ends on the last day of the school year specified in the contract. The notice that he will not be reemployed must include a statement of the reasons for that decision.

8. Before dismissal, the probationary employee is entitled to a due process hearing....

On December 2, 1981, Boyle was warned that unless she demonstrated improvement by March 3, 1982, she would be recommended for non-renewal of her contract or for dismissal. On December 7, 1981, a special assistance team was formed to aid Boyle in improving her performance and to evaluate her progress. Throughout December and January evaluations of Boyle's work continued to he unfavorable. Because of a work-related injury Boyle was absent from work from February 18, 1982, through April 26, 1982. Although she had been given only until March 3 to improve her performance, no recommendation regarding Boyle's reemployment was made until after she returned to work in April.

On June 1, 1982, the special assistance team, in accordance with NRS 391.314(1), recommended Boyle's dismissal. Boyle was afforded a hearing before a hearing officer who also concluded that she should be dismissed. The superintendent of schools concurred in the hearing officer's recommendation, and the board of trustees dismissed Boyle on January 27, 1983. The board gave retroactive effect to its decision by making it effective as of June 3, 1982, the last day of the 1981-82 school year.

As a result of the special assistance team's decision to forestall making its recommendation of dismissal until after Boyle's return to work from her injury related absence, the critical reemployment date of April 1 passed without Boyle's having received notice of her status for the upcoming year. NRS 391.3196 [427] categorically requires the board of trustees to notify teachers in writing on or before April I of each year concerning their employment for the ensuing year; failure to notify results in automatic reemployment. Because of the board of trustee's failure to act and to give Boyle notification of its decision prior to April 1, 1982, she had a statutory right to be employed by the Clark County School District for the "ensuing" year, which is to say the school year September, 1982 through June, 1983.

The school district relies on subparagraph 2 of NRS 391.3196 to support the validity of the dismissal processes which it followed. Subparagraph 2 contains two sentences. The first sentence makes the automatic April 1 renewal provisions of NRS 391.3196(1) inapplicable to a teacher who, on the April 1 date, has already been recommended to be dismissed. Since the recommendation of dismissal in this case did not come until June 3, 1982, this provision has no application to Boyle's right to reemployment for the 1982-83 school year.

The second sentence of subparagraph 2 provides that a teacher may be dismissed on statutory grounds "after he had been notified that he is to be reemployed for the ensuing year." We read that language to mean that even after receiving the April 1 notice of contract renewal a teacher may still be subject to dismissal proceedings. For example, a teacher who had been renewed on April 1 could still be subject to dismissal proceedings if found to be guilty of serious immoral or criminal conduct. NRS 391.312 expressly provides that a teacher may be subject to immediate dismissal for immorality, physical or mental incapacity or a

---

[427] NRS 391.3196 provides:

     391.196 Reemployment of postprobationary employees: Procedure

       1. On or before April 1 of each year. the board or trustees shall notify postprobationary employees in their employ, in writing, by certified mail or by delivery of the employee's contract, concerning their reemployment for the ensuing year. If the hoard, or the person designated by it, fails to notify a postprobationary employee who has been employed by a school district of his status for the ensuing year, the employee shall be deemed to be reemployed for the ensuing year under the same terms and conditions under which he is employed for the current year.

       2. This section does not apply to any certificated employee who has been recommended to be demoted. dismissed or not reemployed if such proceedings have commenced and no final decision has been made by the board. A certificated employee may he demoted or dismissed for grounds set forth in NRS :391.312 after he had been notified that he is to be reemployed for the ensuing year. (emphasis added.)

justifiable decrease in the number of positions due to a decreased student enrollment or district organization or conviction of a felony or of a crime involving moral turpitude. These "statutory" grounds of moral, physical and mental unfitness and economic exigency are clearly intended to be available at any time even, as stated in subparagraph 2, "after he has been notified that he is to be reemployed for the ensuing year." Because Boyle was not dismissed on any of these statutory grounds, this part of the statute has no application to her.

We must next consider what effect the January 27, 1983, decision of the board had on Boyle's right to employment after the 1982-83 school year. Notwithstanding its attempt at retroactivity, which we have held void above, that decision certainly constituted notice to Boyle that the school district no longer desired to retain her in its employ. In addition, Boyle had prior actual notice of that fact and had been afforded a hearing. The hearing adduced evidence which Boyle's counsel readily admits constitutes sufficient cause for non-renewal of her contract. We therefore conclude that Boyle was duly notified that she would not be rehired for the 1983-84 school year.

We hold that Boyle's dismissal was improper. We further hold that the decision of the board of trustees on January 27, 1983, not to rehire Boyle was effective to provide her with notice that she would not be rehired for the following year, 1983-84.

The judgment of the trial court is reversed and remanded with instructions that the appellant, Darleen Boyle, receive all salary and emoluments, including pension rights, due to her for the 1982-83 school year.

McCRACKIN
v.
ELKO CTY. SCHOOL DIST.
103 NEV. 655, 747 P.2d 1373 (1987)

By the Court, YOUNG, J.:

This is a case of first impression involving the 1985 amendments to the statutory provisions addressing evaluation and reemployment of probationary teachers. Pamela McCrackin appeals from the district court judgment that the Elko County School District had properly determined not to renew her employment.

In the school year 1985-86 appellant McCrackin was employed by respondent Elko County School District as a special education teacher at the Wells Junior-Senior High School. She was on a second probationary, or trial year. Miss McCrackin held the same position as a probationary teacher in the 1984-85 school year. That was her first year as a teacher. She was not made a regular, postprobationary teacher because her handling of certain required paperwork was not satisfactory. Miss McCrackin apparently corrected this problem; her October and December 1985 evaluations rated her performance of the paperwork as satisfactory. Neither evaluation gave Miss McCrackin any indication that she might not be reemployed, and both noted that her performance in some areas had improved.

On February 20, 1986, Mr. Harold Ridgway, the Elko County School District Director of Instructional Services, observed Miss McCrackin's classroom for fifteen minutes and discussed the observation with her. On February 26, 1986, Mr. Ridgway delivered the formal report of the February 20, 1986 observation to Miss

McCrackin and discussed it with her. On the afternoon of February 28, 1986, Mr. Weight, the school principal, discussed Mr. Ridgway's observation with Miss McCrackin. At this time she was informed that her prospects for reemployment were not good.

On Monday, March 3, 1986, Mr. Weight presented Miss McCrackin a letter stating that he would recommend to the school board that she not be reemployed due to inadequate performance. He also gave her an evaluation report detailing deficiencies in her performance. Mr. Weight advised Miss McCrackin to resign, and said her resignation would probably be accepted. Charles Knight, Superintendent for the Elko County School District, informed Miss McCrackin by a letter dated March 31, 1986, that he would recommend not reemploying her to the school board. The Elko County School Board did not renew Miss McCrackin's contract.

After completing her term, Miss McCrackin brought an action claiming that the school district and its employees had not complied with the relevant statutory provisions. The district court concluded that Miss McCrackin had received adequate notice under NRS 391.3125(4) and that the observation and evaluation reports for the school year 1985-86 constituted substantial compliance with NRS 391.3125(6). We disagree.

In 1985 the legislature amended the statutory provisions dealing with teacher contracts. A new provision requires that probationary teachers either receive an admonition or, by March 1, receive notice that they may not be reemployed and the reasons for their potential non-reemployment. NRS 391.3125(4). Enactment of the amendments followed this court's ruling in Eureka County v. Holbo, 101 Nev. 372, 705 P.2d 640 (1984) that probationary teachers were not entitled to an admonition under NRS 391.313 before non-renewal of their contracts.

All teachers must receive evaluations that include, if necessary, recommendations for improvements in performance. A reasonable effort must be made to assist teachers in correcting deficiencies. NRS 391.3125(6).

The statutory subsection addressing notice, NRS 391.3125(4), provides:

> Whenever an administrator charged with the evaluation of a probationary employee believes the employee will not be reemployed for the next school year, he shall bring the matter to the employee's attention in a written document which is separate from the evaluation no later than the third required evaluation. The notice must include the reasons for the potential decision not to reemploy or refer to the evaluation in which the reasons are stated. Such a notice is not required if the probationary employee has received a letter of admonition during the current school year.

The parties agree that the date of the notice, Monday, March, 3, was within the March 1 statutory decision deadline for the third evaluation, because March 1 was a Saturday.

The notice gave as the reason for non-renewal, "inadequate performance in your position as a teacher." Although the notice did not refer to it, Miss McCrackin received an evaluation which listed specific deficiencies.

The notice stated, "I am recommending . . . that you not be reemployed." The statute speaks of a "potential decision not to reemploy." Mr. Weight presented his decision as a final determination, at least on his part. It is true that Mr. Weight's decision represents a potential decision in the sense that the school board makes the final determination regarding employment. However, Miss McCrackin's acceptance of Mr. Weight's decision as a final determination of the matter seems justified by the written and oral communication she received from him, which included his advice that she should resign.

The March 3 notice and evaluation did not achieve the statute's purpose. Miss McCrackin received notice of the deficiencies because of which she was terminated on the last permitted day. However, she had no chance to improve her performance in those areas because her principal, who would have had to recognize that improvement, presented his decision as a final one.

Subsection six of NRS 391.3125 provides, in pertinent part:

> The evaluation of a probationary teacher or a postprobationary teacher must, if necessary, include recommendations for improvements in his performance. A reasonable effort must be made to assist the teacher to correct any deficiencies noted in the evaluation.

Miss McCrackin did not receive any assistance in improving her performance after receiving the March 3 notice and evaluation. Mr. Weight, her principal, testified that he did not give or offer her such assistance.

The evaluation which Miss McCrackin received on March 3, 1986, was not phrased in terms of the reasons for potential non-reemployment required by NRS 391.3125(4). Although it could have been interpreted as also setting out recommendations for improvement, the presentation of the decision as a final determination made efforts to improve on Miss McCrackin's part seem futile.

Implicit in the NRS 391.3125(6) requirement that school districts make "reasonable efforts" to assist teachers in correcting their deficiencies is a chance for the teachers to put such assistance to use, a chance to improve. NRS 391.3125(4) requires that probationary teachers be given notice of deficiencies so serious as to potentially cause their non-reemployment. Such notice must be given by March 1, forty-five days before the April 15 deadline for giving probationary teachers notice of non-renewal of their contracts under NRS 391.3197(2).

In determining the meaning of specific provisions of an act, the act should be read as a whole and meaning given to all its parts. Courts will avoid an unreasonable result. The legislature's requirement that probationary teachers be given notice of a potential decision not to reemploy them, and the reasons for such a decision, could serve no purpose if those teachers are not also given a chance to respond to that notice. In the absence of language specifying the contrary, the requirement that teachers be given recommendations for improvement and assistance in correcting deficiencies applies also to deficiencies so serious as to potentially cause non-reemployment. Miss McCrackin received neither a chance to correct the deficiencies mentioned in the March 3 notice nor any assistance in correcting those deficiencies.

As a probationary teacher, Miss McCrackin has only a unilateral expectation of employment and no claim or entitlement to it. However, school boards must follow the procedures required by statute in the non-renewal of a probationary teacher's contract. We find the district court's conclusion that the Elko County School Board's actions in the non-renewal of Miss McCrackin's contract complied with the relevant provisions of NRS 391.3125 to be in error as a matter of law.

Accordingly, we reverse the district court's judgment and remand these proceedings to that court for the fashioning of a remedy.

Reversed and remanded.

Nevada Public Sector Collective Bargaining Law

Nevada education statutes provide teachers with substantive and procedural employment protection. The Local Government Employee-Management Relations Act (EMRA) provides another vehicle for enhancing teacher employment security.[428] The law was enacted in 1969.[429]

The law recognizes the right of public employees (teachers) to join any employee organization or to refrain from such membership.[430] It also establishes a procedure by which an employee organization may be designated as the exclusive representative[431] of the employees for the purpose of collective bargaining with the employer.[432] If an exclusive bargaining representative has been recognized the employer (school district) is obligated to negotiate in good faith concerning mandatory subjects set forth in law.[433] Agreements reached are reduced to writing

---

[428] Chapter 288 NRS (1993).

[429] NRS 1376, 1377 (1969).

[430] Sec. 288.140 NRS (1993).

[431] The scope of the right of exclusive representation was addressed in Clark County Classroom Teachers Association v. Clark County School District & Las Vegas A.F.T..91 Nev. 143, 532 P.2d 1032 (1975).

    The appellant, Clark County Classroom Teachers Association petitioned the district court to enjoin the Las Vegas Federation of Teachers, Local 2170 A. F. T., and others from using Clark County school facilities to solicit memberships and distribute union information. Appellant has sought to prevent respondents' use of school bulletin boards, mail delivery service, teachers' mail boxes, meeting rooms, and payroll deductions of union dues. Such activities are encompassed by "exclusive use" provisions embodied in a Collective Bargaining Agreement between Clark County Classroom Teachers Association and the Clark County School District Board of Trustees, in effect since April 17, 1970.

    The trial court denied injunctive relief and declared the "exclusive use" provisions unconstitutional, insofar as they denied respondents an equal opportunity to use school facilities for membership solicitations and to dispense information. Appellant contends the trial court erred. We agree.

    After the Collective Bargaining Agreement was negotiated, respondent's predecessor, American Federation of Teachers, Pen local 1800, and its president, Al Triner, contested the agreement before Mark Smith, Taylor Wines and Clel Georgetta, the members of the Local Government Employee-Management Relations Board. The E. M. R. B. resolved the contest in favor of the Clark County Classroom Teachers Association by order, filed October 20, 1970, and a written decision, filed November 17, 1970. The decision was based on respectable authority.

    It has been held that the constitutional right of equal protection may be abridged, where shown necessary to promote a compelling governmental interest. Shapiro v. Thompson, 394 U.S. 618, 634 (1969). The E. M. R. B.'s decision found compelling Nevada's interest in allowing appellant, as the elected bargaining representative, the "exclusive uses" here challenged. This view accorded with the case of Local 858 of A.F.T. v. School D. No. 1 in Co. of Denver, wherein the court said: ". . . labor peace and stability in an area as vital as public education are indisputably a necessity to the attainment of that goal. Inter-union strife within the schools must be minimized. Unnecessary work stoppages and the consequent impairment of the educational process cannot be tolerated without significant injury to public education." Neither the union nor respondent Triner sought judicial review of the E. M. R. B.'s ruling then, as authorized by NRS 288.130, and they are precluded from doing so now.

    The order of the trial court is reversed and the case remanded with instructions to grant an injunction consistent with this opinion.

[432] Sec. 288.160 NRS (1991) Sixteen of the Seventeen Nevada school districts have recognized a teacher association for the purpose of collective bargaining.

[433] Sec. 288.150 NRS (1993).

...2. The scope of mandatory bargaining is limited to:

(a) Salary or wage rates or other forms of direct monetary compensation.
(b) Sick leave.
(c) Vacation leave.
(d) Holidays.
(e) Other paid or nonpaid leaves of absence.
(f) Insurance benefits.
(g) Total hours of work required of an employee on each workday or work week.
(h) Total number of days' work required of an employee in a work year.
(i) Discharge and disciplinary procedures.
(j) Recognition clause.
(k) The method used to classify employees in the bargaining unit.
(I) Deduction of dues for the recognized employee organization.
(m) Protection of employees in the bargaining unit from discrimination because of participation in recognized employee organizations consistent with the provisions of this chapter.
(n) No-strike provisions consistent with the provisions of this chapter
(o) Grievance and arbitration procedures for resolution of disputes relating to interpretation or application of collective bargaining agreements.
(p) General savings clauses.
(q) Duration of collective bargaining agreements.
(r) Safety of the employee.
(s) Teacher preparation time.
(t) Materials and supplies for classrooms.
(u) The policies for the transfer and reassignment of teachers.
(v) Procedures for reduction in work force.
3. Those subject matters which are not within the scope of mandatory bargaining and which are reserved to the local government employer without negotiation include:

and included in a collective bargaining agreement (CBA). The collective agreement is incorporated by reference in a teachers individual employment contract. A new school district employee should be provided with a copy of the district's CBA. If not, don't fail to request a copy. Familiarity with the contents of the collective agreement is an important element in understanding the legal aspects of the school employment setting.

The EMRA establishes a timetable for bargaining. It also creates a dispute resolution process should the parties be unable to reach agreement on the terms and conditions of the CBA through negotiations. In 1991 the Nevada legislature amended the law to provide for final and binding last best offer arbitration as the final step in the dispute resolution procedure.[434]

EMRA declares that all strikes by public employees are unlawful.[435]

The Local Government Employee Management Board is vested with jurisdiction to administer Chapter 288 and resolve disputes over the interpretation and application of the Act.[436] The board's authority includes resolving unfair labor practice complaints.[437]

All Nevada CBA's contain a grievance arbitration provision for resolving disputes over the interpretation and application of the terms of the agreement. The grievance procedure typically provides that unresolved disputes be referred to an arbitrator whose decision is final and binding on the parties subject to judicial review.[438]

Nevada law specifically allows the terms of a CBA to supersede the provisions of the Nevada Professional Practices Act (Sec.391.311-3197 NRS (1991)). Pursuant to this authorization school districts can negotiate their own teacher discipline policy and procedure.

Negotiated provisions normally prohibit school districts from invoking discipline except for just cause. The determination of whether discipline is supported by just cause is vested with an impartial arbitrator selected pursuant to

---

(a) Except as otherwise provided in paragraph (u) of subsection 2, the right to hire, direct, assign or transfer an employee, but excluding the right to assign or transfer an employee as a form of discipline.
(b) The right to reduce in force or lay off any employee because of lack of work or lack of money, subject to paragraph (v) of subsection 2.
(c) The right to determine:
(1) Appropriate staffing levels and work performance standards, except for safety considerations;
(2) The content of the workday, including without limitation work load factors, except for safety considerations;
(3) The quality and quantity of services to be offered to the public, and
(4) The means and methods of offering those services.
(d) Safety of the public.
4. Notwithstanding the provisions of any collective bargaining agreement negotiated pursuant to this chapter, a local government employer is entitled to take whatever actions may be necessary to carry out its responsibilities in situations of emergency such as a riot, military action, natural disaster or civil disorder. Those actions may include the suspension of any collective bargaining agreement for the duration of the emergency. Any action taken under the provisions of this subsection must not be construed as a failure to negotiate in good faith.
5. The provisions of this chapter, including without limitation the provisions of this section, recognize and declare the ultimate right and responsibility of the local government employer to manage its operation in the most efficient manner consistent with the best interests of all its citizens, its taxpayers and its employees.
6. This section does not preclude, but this chapter does not require the local government employer to negotiate subject matters enumerated in subsection 3 which are outside the scope of mandatory bargaining. The local government employer shall discuss subject matters outside the scope of mandatory bargaining but it is not required to negotiate those matters.
7. Contract provisions presently existing in signed and ratified agreements as of May 15, 1975, at 12 p.m. remain negotiable.
See also Clark County School District v. EMRB, 90 Nev. 442, 530 P.2d 114 (1974) where the supreme court upheld a Employment Management Relations Board (EMRB) determination that where a negotiation proposal significantly affects wages, hours and conditions of employment it is subject to mandatory negotiation. The items in dispute found negotiable included classroom preparation, class size, professional improvement, student discipline, school calendar, teacher performance, differentiated staffing, teacher load and instructional supplies.
[434] Sec. 288.217 NRS (1991). The decision of the arbitrator must address the financial ability of the public employer to grant monetary benefits demanded and also other normal criteria for assessing bargaining disputes. Sec. 391.200 (7) NRS (1991)
[435] Sec. 288.230-260 NRS (1993)
[436] Sec. 288.080-137 NRS (1993)
[437] Sec. 288.270-280 NRS (1993)
[438] The classic text treatment of labor arbitration is Elkouri & Elkouri, "How Arbitration Works," Fourth Edition, Bureau of National Affairs, Inc., Washington, D.C. (1985)

the terms of the grievance procedure. The decision of the arbitrator is normally final and binding on the parties.

For example, the State Board of Education accepted the recommendation of hearing examiner, Michael Cherry, allowing Angelo Stefanelli to retain his Nevada teachers license. However, the Clark County School District proceeded to take dismissal action against Mr Stefanelli and the matter was submitted to an arbitrator pursuant to the terms and conditions of the CBA between the school board and the Clark County Classroom Teachers Association. The arbitrator rendered the following decision:

In The Matter of Arbitration Between:
CLARK COUNTY. SCHOOL DISTRICT
and
CLARK CNTY. CLASSROOM TEACHERS ASSOCIATION
Grievance:Dismissal of Angelo Stefanelli
BEFORE IMPARTIAL ARBITRATOR DONALD A. ANDERSON
ISSUE

1. Did the District's dismissal of Angelo Stefanelli violate the parties Collective Bargaining Agreement and/or the Nevada Revised Statutes, and was there cause?
2. If so, what is the appropriate remedy?

BACKGROUND

Angelo Stefanelli, hereinafter referred to as the Employee, was primarily assigned teaching duties as a band director but also taught physical education from time to time in the Clark County School District for approximately ten (10) years. During certain years of that employment Grievant became involved in a federal and state tax evasion movement espoused by a Mr. Erwin Schiff. Basically the movement asserted that the collection of income taxes by government was unconstitutional because United States currency was invalid as a form of monetary exchange and had no specific value because it was not backed by gold or a commodity equal to the currency's stated value. According to Schiff, citizens were, therefore, permitted to refuse payment of taxes and to virtually defy government officials or documented demands for same.

The Employee's involvement was apparently moved by his belief that the movement was valid and he publicly expressed confirmation of its theory and philosophies. He discussed the subject with fellow teachers and also challenged school officials regarding its withholding of tax monies he believed were due him.

After several years of legal sparring with governmental officials in the Internal Revenue Service, and based on the fact that he had not acquiesced to the payment of taxes, the Employee was arrested, tried and convicted. He spent approximately six (6) months of a three (3) year term in federal penitentiary and/or at a halfway house.

During his involvement with the tax evasion movement the Employee also joined other organizations of similar tack in that they also espoused and exhibited a certain defiance of U.S. law and the social and political status quo. Of particular note in the District's case against him, it cited his membership and high ranking officer status in the "Organization of American States," (OAS) which was alleged to advocate ultra right wing political strategies and was allegedly associated with the "Aryan Nation," the alleged umbrella organization including the Ku Klux Klan.

According to the District, when it was apprised of Grievant's involvement with these organizations and his colleagues via his trial and that of alleged high members of the Aryan Nation/OAS, and after officially inspecting the final court records in this regard, it decided that his dismissal as a teacher in the District was appropriate. The District asserted that its dismissal was supported by numerous complaints from students, parents and school personnel who complained about his strict disciplinary approach, his belligerent behavior and his demands regarding the district's tax withholding procedure.

Also, the District contended that because of his unalterable philosophy on the tax issue and his association with organizations advocating violence and the overthrow of the United States Government he could not effectively carry out the District's educational policy and objectives. His dismissal was in the best interest of the pupils.

Grievant contended that his dismissal was inappropriate because while he may have been involved in activities of which the District was not fond, he did not carry their philosophies into the classroom nor did it interfere with any other professional teaching activities. He maintained that his teaching record was good which was corroborated not only by his personnel record but also by students and parents who testified on his behalf.

Grievant also pointed to the fact that a hearing before an impartial hearing examiner sanctioned by the State Board of Education resulted in a decision favoring his retainment of his teaching credential.

Furthermore, because he expressed remorse for those activities which he now claims were not in his best interest, and because he has since married and has a child his life has stabilized. Moreover, Grievant maintained that his philosophies and/or thoughts regarding his past affiliations have been greatly altered. He contended that he can still provide expert teaching and student guidance and provide a positive and productive educational service to the District's school program.

When the parties were unable to resolve the issue the Undersigned Arbitrator was selected to preside at hearings on November 7, and 8, 1989, at the office of the District where the parties stipulated that the issue was properly in arbitration. Witnesses were duly sworn and testified and the parties were afforded full opportunity to exhaust their respective evidence and proofs in the matter.

Post hearing briefs were exchanged through Mr. Gaylord Benz of the American Arbitration Association in Los Angeles, California and was received by the Arbitrator on or about January 17, 1990.

DISTRICT POSITION

The District contended that Grievant's voluntary actions of defying the U.S. Government and State of Nevada tax laws by joining and espousing the theory and philosophies of Erwin Schiff was clear evidence that he was not suitable for District employment. Grievant was belligerent in dealing with government officials and harassed not only federal and state personnel but school employees and officials as well by continuing to insist that taxes must not be taken from his pay. He clogged up the federal courts with what his constituency referred to as "at-law" and/or "common law" law suits designed to deliberately disrupt accepted social, legal and political procedure for the purpose of moving the United States toward a state of chaos.

The District also focused its presentation on Grievant's activities revolving around his association with known right wing radicals. His periodic visits to isolated and/or secret locations for the purpose of conspiring against the United States government were obviously activities directly opposed to the high standard of the teaching profession and not in keeping with a teacher's role model.

According to the District, during these secret meetings Grievant and his co-conspirators trained with firearms and other implements designed to harm, maim and/or kill human beings. Grievant and his cohorts made threats to government officials and publicly exhorted the beliefs of the general "white supremacists" ideology.

In addition, the district cited Grievant as being a member of and a high ranking officer in the "Unorganized Militia" within the OAS. This group is dedicated to carrying out death threats on American citizens particularly government officials. His voluntary association and active involvement in the OAS labeled him as being in favor of and actively promoting neo-Nazi, anti-semite and racist dogma designed to rid society of certain groups of people.

The District also pointed to the fact that Grievant was blatantly defiant of state vehicle laws and refused to properly license his automotive vehicles or to hold a valid drivers license. He also refused to properly insure himself and/or his vehicles and also defied speed laws. He had refused to honor traffic tickets he received and again defied the law by failing to appear in court for vehicle driving violations and the like. This conduct according to the District, was symptomatic of a thinking and lifestyle disassociated and incompatible with the teaching profession. With such an approach Grievant could not be allowed to continue in his teaching role.

The District also asserted that Grievant's marriage to co-conspirator Susan Kieffer was more than convenient relative to his trial as a member of the "Unorganized Militia" of the OAS and his association with radical right wing organizations and tax evasion groups. The District alleged that Grievant's convenient marriage allowed for his protection of possibly having his new wife testify against him. The District asserted that this nuptial relationship and the fact that he testified against his co-conspirators was instrumental in greatly reducing his prison term. The District maintained that it was another indication of the Employee's manipulative personality and approach to problems which it believed was not the type of teacher the District could tolerate.

In addition, according to the District, while his co-conspirators were sentenced to extensive prison terms the Employee received but a six (6) months term in federal prison because of his plea bargain and testimony against his former associates. He effectively admitted his guilt during his trial by saying that he was just as guilty as his co-conspirators. Even while in prison he was conveniently stricken with a mental illness and asked for and received counselling and drew two months sick pay which shortened his prison stay even more.

The District alleged that Grievant was a shrewd manipulator of people and somehow believed that he owed no particular allegiance to his employer, the state in which he lived and/or the United States Government. While on the one hand he used public funds to further his education and career and protect himself from punishment for crimes, on the other hand he defied the tax paying public by giving another oath of allegiance to "outlaws" in direct violation of his oath to protect and defend the U.S. Constitution and the laws of the State of Nevada.

Also, the District believed that he willingly sacrificed the good of the community for his own self interest. His voluntary acceptance of radical organizations' philosophies in place of community interests and accepted social norms and demands via criminal and dishonest conduct was also defiant of his professional obligation to the District to image a conduct conducive to maintaining a teacher's role model. His behavior of threatening the life of a judge in the court room was typical of his inability to sort out good from bad and the expected conduct of teachers.

Based on the foregoing and the numerous incidents showing him to be unfit as a teacher, the District solicited the Arbitrator to deny the grievance and uphold its decision of dismissal.

ASSOCIATION POSITION

The Association contended that the District was not justified in its decision to dismiss Grievant because the record was clear that despite his initial involvement with what the District referred to as radical organizations, he expressed and demonstrated true remorse regarding such decisions and involvements. He believed he was duped into joining such movements and voluntarily testified against the leaders of the organizations when he better understood his folly. Such an approach must be viewed as being remorseful and having gained a renewed insight into his own psyche.

Furthermore according to the Association, Grievant's teaching record was excellent which was verified by the fact that many of his former students and their parents testified on his behalf during the arbitration hearings. He is highly skilled at organizing and motivating groups of students into teams for the purpose of achieving pre-determined goals and objectives. His record as a band director and organizer was outstanding in the past and can continue to be so in the future.

The Association also maintained that Grievant should not be deprived of his employment in the District because he is an excellent teacher and because while he unfortunately had been part of questionable organizations, he did not allow their teachings and/or philosophies to enter into his teaching format. There was no evidence that he had expressed anything but socially healthy educative programs in the classroom.

In addition, the Association maintained that Grievant's conduct leading to his arrest trial and conviction does not warrant his dismissal because Nevada Revised Statutes 391.312 does not mandate same. The law is clearly discretionary and the District's dismissal decision was unwarranted under the circumstances.

The Association reminded the Arbitrator that in NRS 391.3193.(2) it allowed the Employee to bring his case before a State of Nevada sanctioned independent review to determine his fitness to hold a teaching license. When he received this review it resulted in the hearing officer's recommendation that he not be denied his teaching license.

Furthermore, such case law as Brewer v. United States Postal Service, 647 F.2d 093, 1093, 1098 (Ct. Ct. 1981), Rust v. Clark County School District, 100 Nev. 372, 683 p.2d 23 (19840, State Bar of Nevada v. Claiborne, 104 Nevada, Advance Opinion 22 (1988), each supported Grievant's contention that dismissal for the circumstances relevant in this case was inappropriate. Moreover, these decisions provide the foundational case law needed in this case because the circumstances were not necessarily dissimilar to that involved here. In each of these cases the appellant was upheld.

Finally, the Association asserted that the District's contention that Grievant could never atone for his previous conduct and continue to be a positively contributing employee in its education process is without foundation. Grievant was and remains an outstanding teacher and should be reinstated.

RELEVANT CONTRACTUAL LANGUAGE
Directly Relevant Collective Bargaining Agreement (1987-1989) language. (JX-1)
Article 36
DISCIPLINARY PROCEDURES
36-8: .

In implementing the suspension and dismissal procedures of NRS 391, the parties agree that the decision of the hearing officer shall be final and binding. The hearing officer shall be selected in accordance with the expedited arbitration procedures in Article 4 of this Agreement. The teacher or the teacher's representative shall, within ten (10) days of receiving the notice of suspension of dismissal that the matter be submitted to final and binding arbitration. Pursuant to the terms of NRS 391, the nonrenewal of a probationary teacher's contract shall not be subject to a hearing under the provisions of Article 36-8. Probationary teachers shall be entitled to a hearing under the terms of this Article for Suspensions and Dismissals."

4-12. "EXPEDITED ARBITRATION PROCEDURE:

The District and Association will jointly request a list of twenty-seven (27) arbitrators from which they will strike until nine (9) names remain. These nine (9) arbitrators will be the panel from which an arbitrator will be assigned for Expedited Arbitration. The list of nine (9) arbitrators will be sent to the American Arbitration Association and when an arbitrator is needed for the Expedited Arbitration Procedure, the District and the Association will request that AAA send the first available Arbitrator."

Directly Relevant Nevada Revised Statute(s)
NRS 391.312. "Grounds for suspension, demotion, dismissal and refusal to reemploy teachers and administrators; consideration of evaluations and standards of performance.

1.   A teacher may be suspended, dismissed or not reemployed and an administrator may be demoted, suspended, dismissed or not reemployed for the following reasons:
    (n)   Any cause which constitutes grounds for the revocation of a teacher's license.

NRS 391.314. Suspension of licensed employee; dismissal or reinstatement; salary during suspension; forfeiture of right of employment for certain offenses; period of suspension.

1.   If a superintendent has reason to believe that cause exists for the dismissal of a licensed employee and is of the opinion that the immediate suspension of the employee is necessary in the best interests of the pupils in the district, the superintendent may suspend the employee without notice

and without a hearing. Notwithstanding the provisions of NRS 391.312, a superintendent may suspend a licensed employee who has been officially charged but not yet convicted of a felony or a crime involving moral turpitude or immorality. If the charge is dismissed or if the employee is found not guilty, he must be reinstated with back pay, plus interest, and normal seniority. The superintendent shall notify the employee in writing of the suspension.

 2. Within 10 days after a suspension becomes effective, the superintendent shall begin proceedings pursuant to the provisions of NRS 391.312 to 391.3196, inclusive, to effect the employee's dismissal. The superintendent may recommend that an employee who has been charged with a felony or crime involving immorality be dismissed for another ground set forth in NRS 391.312.

 3. If sufficient grounds for dismissal do not exist, the employee must be reinstated with full compensation, plus interest."

NRS 391.315. "Recommendations for demotion, dismissal and against reemployment; request for appointment of hearing officer.

 1. A superintendent may recommend that a teacher be dismissed or not reemployed.. . ."

NRS 391.317. "Notice of intention to recommend demotion, dismissal or refusal to reemploy; rights of employee.

 1. Except as otherwise provided in NRS 391.31963, at least 15 days before recommending to a board that it demote, dismiss or not reemploy a postprobationary employee, or dismiss or demote a probationary employee, the superintendent shall give written notice to the employee, by registered or certified mail, of his intention to make the recommendation.

NRS 391.318. "Request for hearing: Action by superintendent

 2. If a request for a hearing is made, the superintendent shall not file his recommendation with the board until a report of the hearing is filed with him."

NRS 391.3192. "Hearing: Procedures; compensation and expenses of hearing officer; payment for expenses of hearing officer and transcript.

 1. As soon as possible after the time of his designation, the hearing officer shall hold a hearing to determine whether the grounds for the recommendation are substantiated.

NRS 391.3193. "Written report of hearing: Contents; final and binding if so agreed; time limited for filing.

 2. The report must contain the outline of the scope of the hearing, findings of fact and conclusion of law, and recommend a course of action to be taken by the board. The report of the hearing officer is final and binding on the employee and the board if the employee and the superintendent have so agreed before the selection of the hearing officer was begun.

NRS 391.330. "Grounds for suspension or revocation of teacher's or administrator's license. The state board of education may suspend or revoke

the license of any teacher or administrator, after note and an opportunity for hearing before the state board, for:
1.   Immoral or unprofessional conduct
2.   Evident unfitness for service
6.   Knowingly advocating the overthrow of the Federal Government or of the State of Nevada by force, violence or unlawful means."

NRS 391.355. "Procedure for conduct of hearings.
4.   A hearing officer, selected under NRS 391.3161 and selected according to the provision of NRS 391.3191 and 391.31915 shall conduct the hearing and report findings of fact and conclusions of law, along with recommendations to be state board of education. The state board may accept or reject recommendations or refer the report back to the hearing officer for further evidence and recommendations, and shall notify the teacher, administrator or other licensed person in writing of its decision.

FINDINGS & DISCUSSION
The parties to the instant arbitration pursued differing approaches in presenting their evidence and proofs in this matter. The District on the one hand focused the Arbitrator's attention on its reasons for dismissing the Employee as being based on conduct not in concert with what the District and the public had established as being appropriate. It concentrated its case on the fact that the Employee had exhibited public conduct challenging the United States Constitution, the State of Nevada laws, and established norms of good citizenship.

The Employee on the other hand contended that while he had in fact been active in some organizations not particularly accepted by the general public, he in effect rectified his mistake by testifying against his former colleagues which led to their imprisonment. In effect, Grievant apparently believed that he had paid his debt to society and his return to the classroom would help and not hinder the District's educational program.

The Arbitrator reviewed the numerous documentary evidence with particular attention given to the parties' contractual agreement and the Nevada Revised Statutes, (NRS) which held the controlling language leading to the final recommendation. It is no secret that an individual arbitrator's personal convictions and/or beliefs must be greatly tempered during the arbitration process and his/her final evidentiary deliberations so as not to taint the final ruling.

Notwithstanding the foregoing, the Arbitrator's role in this case was to determine from the evidence whether or not the District acted within its management prerogative as provided by the parties' collective bargaining agreement and therein doing, whether it was also within the relevant provisions of the Nevada Revised Statutes (NRS). In 391.314/15, it provides certain decisionary latitudes for a superintendent to dismiss employees if in his/her opinion the dismissal is in the best interest of the pupils of the district. It is a hearing officer's charter then to determine from the evidence whether the grounds for the recommendation were substantiated by the District in the hearings. (391.3192)

The Arbitrator was compelled to disagree with the Association that NRS 391.312 was to wholly provide adequate support for the reinstatement of the Employee as a teacher. Moreover, while the Employee asserted his right to reinstatement because of a hearing examiner's recommendation he not be denied his teaching license, it remained nonetheless that this arbitration did not deal with this issue.

Moreover, NRS 391.312, (n), reveals that grounds for dismissal of a teacher's license exists when there is, "Any cause which constitutes grounds for the revocation of a teacher's license." However, while the Employees teaching license is a preliminary requirement for teaching in the state, the issue before the Arbitrator in this case is whether the District's ". . . grounds for the recommendations (for dismissal) are substantiated." (391.3192) As this Arbitrator views it, the District was burdened to show that its decision to dismiss the Employee was, ". . . in the best interests of the pupils of the District, . . ." (391.314) Moreover, such a decision is that reserved for the district superintendent and, as the Employee's Counsel so aptly pointed out, dismissal decisions are discretionary. The District pointed out that its decision to dismiss the Employee was based on his behavioral record of engaging in activities which are contrary to its educational policies as well as that of the general public's educational expectations.

The evidence was clear that the Employee had in fact engaged in those activities as outlined by the District. The Employee did not deny them and it was true that at one time at least he espoused and believed in the supremacy of certain human groups and that violence was an apparently justifiable activity.

Notwithstanding the possible legal implications of the foregoing, the Arbitrator closely reviewed the evidence relative to Grievant's assertion of a change of lifestyle pursuant to his claim of remorse. While it was true that the Employee himself expressed his feelings that he had made mistake(s) of judgement in his past associations, the Arbitrator could find little if any substantive evidence upon which he could "hang his hat" to substantiate these claim(s).

Moreover, while there was testimony of former students, parents and friends reflecting certain positives as to the Employee's teaching abilities and character, it failed to effectively counter the District's witnesses who testified otherwise. Apparently to some he exhibited outstanding abilities and to others he was a dismal failure.

Also, the very guarded testimony of Susan Kiefer Stefanelli was not particularly impressive. Her response to many of the questions appeared to be geared toward saying the least possible rather than to volunteer information showing the claimed renewed lifestyle. While not forgetting normal witness anxieties while testifying, the Arbitrator's deliberations could only address the facts and evidence actually in the record and the record was something less than persuasive to adequately support such a summary judgement.

Moreover, the facts presented showed that the District made its dismissal decision based on what it believed was appropriate in carrying out its operating charter. The parties' contract as well as the relevant NRSs provides it the right to exercise discretion in matters such as this.

It was somewhat curious to the Arbitrator however regarding the District's decision to retain the Employee while he was undergoing legal matters in court. Albeit, while such an approach might be viewed as somewhat ludicrous given the Employee's apparent challenge of the District's authority, in the final analysis it was not of such an evidentiary weight as to offset more substantive constraints of the law and the parties' contract.

On the one hand the District could have suspended him without proof of his guilt or on the other hand it could retain him pending the final facts. While the

Arbitrator experienced lengthy deliberation on this point, in the final analysis the delayed decision could not be viewed as an incident necessarily prohibiting the District's final decision for dismissal. Moreover, there were various court appearances made by the Employee and the District's approach of waiting for the final verdicts was viewed as being understandable.

The District particularly focused the Arbitrator's attention on the incident revolving around the Employee's confrontation with Judge Earle W. White relative to his appearance in court over a traffic violation. In this instance the Employee apparently took exception to the Judge's approach in the court room and sent various threatening correspondence to him. In effect the Employee and his OAS associates sent documents to White which included threats of death, racial innuendos, indictments, etc. (DX-4 thru 11) The record showed that as a result of these mailings Judge White was compelled to alter his usual lifestyle for fear of his life by continually altering transportation and travel habits to and from his home. He also obtained police protection and had to generally become particularly attentive to possible threats to his life.

In his deliberations the Arbitrator likewise could not effectively discount the fact that the Employee had also had confrontations with IRS Agents, that he was a participant in the Cold Creek episodes, that he attended OAS meetings both at Mariposa, California and in the Las Vegas area, etc. He did not deny that the tenor of these meetings was to further the organizations' less than forthright objectives.

Grievant maintained that his case was not necessarily different than that of United States Nevada District Judge Harry Claiborne who despite impeachment from public office was not deprived of his attorney license. A review of the parties' respective evidence and argument on this point the Arbitrator was compelled to view it similarly to that as expressed previously, this case is not based on a deprivation of his teaching license but rather, on whether or not the District held substantive grounds to terminate his services.

Moreover, the Employee's claim that his position for reinstatement was significantly bolstered by the results of the Claiborne decision and/or the other case decisions offered on his behalf, was not persuasive enough for the Arbitrator to conclude that he held the preponderance of the matter (sic law) in the matter.

Based on the parties' respective evidence and argument, the Arbitrator was compelled to conclude that the State's consideration and a hearing officer's recommendation that the Employee be allowed to retain his teaching license was not directly applicable to the District's decision to dismiss him. While the State's decision protected Grievant's minimum qualifications for teaching, it did not go to mandating that he be reinstated to the District's faculty. The State's function as this Arbitrator understands it, is to act as the licensing agent assuring that teaching candidates hold minimum teaching qualifications as mandated by law. Subsequent to an affirmative decision to license such an individual it remains for the various school districts to decide on the employment of candidates or to reemploy current faculty.

The legal language controlling the Arbitrator's final decision in this case (391.3192), clearly requires that the District must make an evidentiary showing that its grounds for dismissal hold substance and are substantiated by facts and evidence. The District's concerns for Grievant's activities while in its employ could only be viewed as being reasonable concerns which were bolstered by the testimony of students, parents, and school employees.

The Employee's plea for his job, given his court testimony on behalf of the government and his self acclaimed remorse which was probed in depth by the Arbitrator with certain benevolence during his deliberations, was not found to have been persuasive enough to effectively counter the District's evidence and argument. It must be remembered that arbitrators do not sit to dispense their own brand of justice but, rather, are chartered to hear each parties evidence and therefrom to make a decision which does not disrupt the agreement between them nor controlling laws of the state and/or federal government. In this instance the District presented the preponderance of the evidence to compel the conclusion that it had met its burden of proof.

On the other hand, the Employee did not present substantive evidence to favor his position to significantly alter the District's case. In "How Arbitration Works," BNA, 3rd. Ed. by Elkouri & Elkouri, p.278, it states:

". . . ; after the party having the burden of persuasion presents sufficient evidence to justify finding in its favor on the issue, the other party has the burden of producing evidence in rebuttal."

In the instant case, Grievant did not present evidence of such a nature or persuasiveness as to significantly rebut the District's position. The Arbitrator is bound by basic arbitral procedure to rule on the facts of a case and his/her license for leniency based on personal convictions are not appropriate except under only rare circumstances where there is a showing of an employer's abuse of its management discretion. In this instance the evidence failed to show such an abuse as the evidence showed that its decision was finally made after all the facts and evidence was in.

While the Arbitrator honors the general arbitral notion that arbitrators should refrain from granting leniency except under rare circumstances, he found significant ambivalence nonetheless with Grievant's situation. Moreover, Grievant contended that he held remorse for his previous conduct and that he had turned over a new leaf so to speak what with his testimony against his former associates, his marriage and a baby daughter to fend for now. Frankly, had there been more significant evidence reflecting Grievant's alleged new lifestyle, perhaps the final conclusion in this case might well have been modified.

It is the District which is the employer here and not the Arbitrator and when an employer makes a management decision which is neither arbitrary, capricious and/or discriminatory, its judgement should not be overturned. It is the parties' contract and relevant law which controlled this matter and the preponderance of the evidence presented compelled the decision not to overrule the District.

CONCLUSION & RECOMMENDATION

The evidence was persuasive that the dismissal of Angelo Stefanelli did not violate the parties Collective Bargaining Agreement nor the Nevada Revised Statutes. It is therefore recommended that the District's dismissal decision in this instance be upheld.

Notwithstanding the foregoing conclusion and recommendation, and while this Arbitrator's review of the record in this case failed to currently reveal a convincing evidentiary record of the Employee's change of heart in the matters for which he was dismissed, it should not go unnoticed by the District that many of his witnesses, former students and their parents held him in high regard. Therefore the Arbitrator makes a secondary recommendation to the Board that it should not necessarily now and forever more ignore possible employment consideration for the employee.

Educator Employment Security and the U.S. Constitution

The employment security of teachers is the subject to substantive and procedural statutory provisions on Nevada law. Court interpretations have clarified the nature and scope of the statutory protection accorded. Nevada's public sector labor law also provides a vehicle for addressing teacher employment security issues. Moreover, the United States Constitution is another source of employment protection. Public employees have been accorded certain 1st, 14th and 4th amendment rights in the employment setting.

We begin our consideration of the impact of the Constitution on the public sector employment setting with a landmark decision holding that teachers have 1st Amendment rights at the workplace.

PICKERING
v.
BOARD OF EDUCATION[439]
391 U.S. 563, 88 S.Ct. 1731 (1968)

JUSTICE MARSHALL delivered the opinion of the Court.

Appellant Marvin L. Pickering, a teacher in Township High School District 205, Will County, Illinois, was dismissed from his position by the appellee Board of Education for sending a letter to a local newspaper in connection with a recently proposed tax increase that was critical of the way in which the Board and the district superintendent of schools had handled past proposals to raise new revenue for the schools. Appellant's dismissal resulted from a determination by the Board, after a full hearing, that the publication of the letter was "detrimental to the efficient operation and administration of the schools of the district" and hence, under the relevant Illinois statute, that "interests of the schools require[d] [his dismissal]."

Appellant's claim that his writing of the letter was protected by the First and Fourteenth Amendments was rejected. Appellant then sought review of the Board's action in the Circuit Court of Will County, which affirmed his dismissal on the ground that the determination that appellant's letter was detrimental to the interests of the school system was supported by substantial evidence and that the interests of the schools overruled appellant's First Amendment rights. On appeal, the Supreme Court of Illinois, two Justices dissenting, affirmed the judgment of the Circuit Court. We noted probable jurisdiction of appellant's claim that the Illinois statute permitting his dismissal on the facts of this case was unconstitutional as applied under the First and Fourteenth Amendments. For the reasons detailed below we agree that appellant's rights to freedom of speech were violated and we reverse.

---

[439]See Wagle v. Murray, 546 F.2d 1329 (9th Cir. 1976), vacated and remanded 97 S.Ct. 2645, affirmed in part and reversed in part 560 F.2d 401 (9th Cir. 1977) cert denied 98 S.Ct. 729 (1978). In Wagle, a teacher claimed he was dismissed because he exercised his 1st Amendment rights. A jury found for the plaintiff and awarded $50,000 damages. The award was ultimately affirmed. The teacher's speech activity included a letter to the local newspaper defending the ACLU's position favoring legalization of marihuana. He also made available to his students a pamphlet titled, "The Student as Nigger," which, in unrestrained language, analogized the student-teacher relationship to a system of slavery. In addition, there was evidence that the teachers employer was aware of the problem of sustaining a dismissal based upon the teacher's commnications and deliberately undertook to "build a record" to support dismissal on other grounds. Wagel 546 F.2d at p. 1335.

I

In February of 1961 the appellee Board of Education asked the voters of the school district to approve a bond issue to raise $4,875,000 to erect two new schools The proposal was defeated. Then, in December of 1961, the Board submitted another bond proposal to the voters which called for the raising of $5,500,000 to build two new schools. This second proposal passed and the schools were built with the money raised by the bond sales. In May of 1964 a proposed increase in the tax rate to be used for educational purposes was submitted to the voters by the Board and was defeated. Finally, on September 19, 1964, a second proposal to increase the tax rate was submitted by the Board and was likewise defeated. It was in connection with this last proposal of the School Board that appellant wrote the letter to the editor (which we reproduce in an Appendix to this opinion) that resulted in his dismissal.

Prior to the vote on the second tax increase proposal a variety of articles attributed to the District 205 Teachers' Organization appeared in the local paper. These articles urged passage of the tax increase and stated that failure to pass the increase would result in a decline in the quality of education afforded children in the district's schools. A letter from the superintendent of schools making the same point was published in the paper two days before the election and submitted to the voters in mimeographed form the following day. It was in response to the foregoing material, together with the failure of the tax increase to pass, that appellant submitted the letter in question to the editor of the local paper.

The letter constituted, basically, an attack on the School Board's handling of the 1961 bond issue proposals and its subsequent allocation of financial resources between the schools' educational and athletic programs. It also charged the superintendent of schools with attempting to prevent teachers in the district from opposing or criticizing the proposed bond issue.

The Board dismissed Pickering for writing and publishing the letter. Pursuant to Illinois law, the Board was then required to hold a hearing on the dismissal. At the hearing the Board charged that numerous statements in the letter were false and that the publication of the statements unjustifiably impugned the "motives, honesty, integrity, truthfulness, responsibility and competence" of both the Board and the school administration. The Board also charged that the false statements damaged the professional reputations of its members and of the school administrators, would be disruptive of faculty discipline, and would tend to foment "controversy, conflict and dissension" among teachers, administrators, the Board of Education, and the residents of the district. Testimony was introduced from a variety of witnesses on the truth or falsity of the particular statements in the letter with which the Board took issue. The Board found the statements to be false as charged. No evidence was introduced at any point in the proceedings as to the effect of the publication of the letter on the community as a whole or on the administration of the school system in particular, and no specific findings along these lines were made.

The Illinois courts reviewed the proceedings solely to determine whether the Board's findings were supported by substantial evidence and whether, on the facts as found, the Board could reasonably conclude that appellant's publication of the letter was "detrimental to the best interests of the schools." Pickering's claim that his letter was protected by the First Amendment was rejected on the ground that his acceptance of a teaching position in the public schools obliged him to refrain from making statements about the operation of the schools "which in the absence of such position he would have an undoubted right to engage in."

****

II

To the extent that the Illinois Supreme Court's opinion may be read to suggest that teachers may constitutionally be compelled to relinquish the First Amendment rights they would otherwise enjoy as citizens to comment on matters of public interest in connection with the operation of the public schools in which they work, it proceeds on a premise that has been unequivocally rejected in numerous prior decisions of this Court.. "[The theory that public employment which may be denied altogether may be subjected to any conditions, regardless of how unreasonable, has been uniformly rejected." At the same time it cannot be gainsaid that the State has interests as an employer in regulating the speech of its employees that differ significantly from those it possesses in connection with regulation of the speech of the citizenry in general. The problem, in any case, is to arrive at a balance between the interests of teacher, as a citizen, in commenting upon matters of public concern and the interest of the State, as an employer, in promoting the efficiency of the public services it performs through its employees.

III

The Board contends that "the teacher by virtue of his public employment has a duty of loyalty to support his superiors in attaining the generally accepted goals of education and that, if he must speak out publicly, he should do so factually and accurately, commensurate with his education and experience." Appellant, on the other hand, argues that the test applicable to defamatory statements directed against public officials by persons having no occupational relationship with them, namely, that statements to be legally actionable must be made "with knowledge that [they were] * * * false or with reckless disregard of whether [they were] * * * false or not," New York Times Co. v. Sullivan (1964), should also be applied to public statements made by teachers. Because of the enormous variety of fact situations in which critical statements by teachers and other public employee's may be thought by their superiors, against whom the statements are directed to furnish grounds for dismissal, we do not deem it either appropriate or feasible to attempt to lay down a general standard against which all such statements may be judged. However, in the course of evaluating the conflicting claims of First Amendment protection and the need for orderly school administration in the context of this ease, we shall indicate some of the general lines along which an analysis of the controlling interests should run

An examination of the statements in appellant's letter objected to by the Board reveals that they, like the letter as a whole, consist essentially of criticism of the Board's allocation of school funds between educational and athletic programs, and of both the Board's and the superintendent's methods of informing, or preventing the informing of, the district's taxpayers of the real reasons why additional tax revenues were being sought for the schools. The statements are in no way directed towards any person with whom appellant would normally be in contact in the course of his daily work as a teacher. Thus no question of maintaining either discipline by immediate superiors or harmony among co-workers is presented here. Appellant's employment relationships with the Board and, to a somewhat lesser extent, with the superintendent are not the kind of close working relationships for which it can persuasively be claimed that personal loyalty and confidence are necessary to their proper functioning. Accordingly, to the extent that the Board's position here can be taken to suggest that even comments on matters of public concern that are substantially correct, such as statements (1)-(4) of appellant's letter, see appendix, infra, may furnish grounds for dismissal if they are sufficiently critical in tone, we unequivocally reject it.

We next consider the statements in appellant's letter which we agree to be false. The Board's original charges included allegations that the publication of the letter damaged the professional reputations of the Board and the superintendent and would foment controversy and conflict among the Board,.teachers, administrators, and the residents of the district. However, no evidence to support these allegations was introduced at the hearing. So far as the record reveals, Pickering's letter was greeted by everyone but its main target, the Board, with massive apathy and total disbelief. The Board must, therefore, have decided, perhaps by analogy with the law of libel, that the statements were per se harmful to the operation of the schools.

However, the only way in which the Board could conclude, absent any evidence of the actual effect of the letter, that the statements contained therein were per se detrimental to the interest of the schools was to equate the Board members' own interests with that of the schools. Certainly an accusation that too much money is being spent on athletics by the administrators of the school system (which is precisely the import of that portion of appellant's letter containing the statements that we have found to be false, see Appendix, infra) cannot reasonably be regarded as per se detrimental to the district's schools. Such an accusation reflects rather a difference of opinion between Pickering and the Board as to the preferable manner of operating the school system, a difference of opinion that clearly concerns an issue of general public interest.

In addition, the fact that particular illustrations of the Board's claimed undesirable emphasis on athletic programs are false would not normally have any necessary impact on the actual operation of the schools, beyond its tendency to anger the Board. For example, Pickering's letter was written after the defeat at the polls of the second proposed tax increase. It could, therefore, have had no effect on the ability of the school district to raise necessary revenue, since there was no showing that there was any proposal to increase taxes pending when the letter was written.

More importantly, the question whether a school system requires additional funds is a matter of legitimate public concern on which the judgment of the school administration including the School Board, cannot, in a society that leaves such questions to popular vote, be taken as conclusive. On such a question free and open debate is vital to informed decision-making by the electorate. Teachers are, as a class, the members of a community most likely to have informed and definite opinions as to how funds allotted to the operation of the schools should be spent. Accordingly, it is essential that they be able to speak out freely on such questions without fear of retaliatory dismissal.

In addition, the amounts expended on athletes which Pickering reported erroneously were matters of public record on which his position as a teacher in the district did not qualify him to speak with any greater authority than any other taxpayer. The Board could easily have rebutted appellant's errors by publishing the accurate figures itself, either via a letter to the same newspaper or otherwise. We are thus not presented with a situation in which a teacher has carelessly made false statements about matters so closely related to the day-to-day operations of the schools that any harmful impact on the public would be difficult to counter because of the teacher's presumed greater access to the real facts. Accordingly, we have no occasion to consider at this time whether under such circumstances a school board could reasonably require that a teacher make substantial efforts to verify the accuracy of his charges before publishing them.[440]

What we do have before us is a case in which a teacher has made erroneous public statements upon issues then currently the subject of public attention, which are critical of his ultimate employer but which are neither shown nor can be presumed to have in any way either impeded the teacher's proper performance of his daily duties in the classroom [441] or to have interfered with regular operation of the schools generally. In these circumstances we conclude that the interest of the school administration in limiting teachers' opportunities to contribute to.public debate is not significantly greater than its interest in limiting a similar contribution by any member of the general public.

IV

The public interest in having free and unhindered debate on matters of public importance—the core value of the Free Speech Clause of the First Amendment— is so great that it has been held that a State cannot authorize the recovery of damages by a public official for defamatory statements directed at him except when such statements are shown to have been made either with knowledge of their falsity or with reckless disregard for their truth or falsity. The same test has been applied to suits for invasion of privacy based on false statements where a "matter of public interest" is involved. It is, therefore, perfectly clear that, were appellant a member of the general public, the State's power to afford the appellee Board of Education or its members any legal right to sue him for writing the letter at issue here would be limited by the requirement that the letter be judged by the standard laid down in New York Times.

This Court has also indicated, in more general terms, that statements by public officials on matters of public concern must be accorded First Amendment protection despite the fact that the statements are directed at their nominal superiors.

While criminal sanctions and damage awards have a somewhat different impact on the exercise of the right to freedom of speech from dismissal from employment, it is apparent that the threat of dismissal from public employment is nonetheless a potent means of inhibiting speech. We have already noted our disinclination to make an across-the-board equation of dismissal from public employment for remarks critical of superiors with awarding damages in a libel suit by a public official for similar criticism. However, in a case such as the present one, in which the fact of employment is only tangentially and insubstantially involved in the subject matter of the public communication made by a teacher, we conclude that

---

[440] There is likewise no occasion furnished by this case for consideration of the extent to which teachers can be required by narrowly drawn grievance procedures to submit complaints about the operation of the schools to their superiors for action thereon prior to bringing the complaints before the public.

[441] We also note that this case does not present a situation in which a teacher's public statements are so without foundation as to call into question his fitness to perform his duties in the classroom. In such a case, of course, the statements would merely be evidence of the teacher's general competence, or Iack thereof, and not an independent basis for dismissal.

it is necessary to regard the teacher as the member of the general public he seeks to be.

In sum, we hold that, in a case such as this, absent proof of false statements knowingly or recklessly made by him, a teacher's exercise of his right to speak on issues of public importance may not furnish the basis for his dismissal from public employment. Since no such showing has been made in this case regarding appellant's letter, see Appendix, infra, his dismissal for writing it cannot be upheld and the judgment of the Illinois Supreme Court must, accordingly, be reversed and the case remanded for further proceedings not inconsistent with this opinion. It is so ordered.

Judgment reversed and case remanded with directions.
APPENDIX TO OPINION OF
THE COURT
A. Appellant's letter.
LETTERS TO THE EDITOR
**** Graphic Newspapers, Inc
Thursday, September 24, 1964, Page 4

Dear Editor:

I enjoyed reading the back issues of your paper which you loaned to me. Perhaps others would enjoy reading them in order to see just how far the two new high schools have deviated from the original promises by the Board of Education. First, let me state that I am referring to the February thru November, 1961 issues of your paper, so that it can be checked.

One statement in your paper declared that swimming pools, athletic fields, and auditoriums had been left out of the program. They may have been left out but they got put back in very quickly because Lockport West has both an auditorium and athletic field. In fact, Lockport West has a better athletic field than Lockport Central. It has a track that isn't quite regulation distance even though the board spent a few thousand dollars on it. Whose fault is that? Oh I forgot, it wasn't supposed to be there in the first place. It must have fallen out of the sky. Such responsibility has been touched on in other letters but it seems one just can't help noticing it. I am not saying the school shouldn't have these facilities, because I think they should, but promises are promises, or are they?

Since there seems to be a problem getting all the facts to the voter on the twice defeated bond issue, many letters have been written to this paper and probably more will follow, I feel I must say something about the letters and their writers. Many of these letters did not give the whole story. Letters by your Board and Administration have stated that teachers' salaries total $1,297,746 for one year. Now that must have been the total payroll, otherwise the teachers would be getting $10,000 a year. I teach at the high school and I know this just isn't the case. However, this shows their "stop at nothing" attitude. To illustrate further, do you know that the superintendent told the teachers, and I quote, "Any teacher that opposes the referendum should be prepared for the consequences." I think this gets at the reason we have problems passing bond issues. Threats take something away; these are insults to voters in a free society. We should try to sell a program on its merits, if it has any.

Remember those letters entitled "District 206 Teachers Speak," I think the voters should know that those letters have been written and agreed to by only five or six teachers, not 98%, of the teachers in the high school. In fact, many teachers didn't even know who was writing them. Did you know that those letters had to have the approval of the superintendent before they could be put in the paper? That's the kind of totalitarianism teachers live in at the high school, and your children go to school in.

In last week's paper, the letter written by a few uninformed teachers threatened to close the school cafeteria and fire its personnel. This is ridiculous and insults the intelligence of the voter because properly managed school cafeterias do not cost the school district any money. If the cafeteria is losing money, then the board should not be packing free lunches for athletes on days of athletic contests. Whatever the case, the taxpayer's child should only have to pay about 30¢ for his lunch instead of 35¢ to pay for free lunches for the athletes.

In a reply to this letter your Board of Administration will probably state that these lunches are paid for from receipts from the games. But $20,000 in receipts doesn't pay for the $200,000 a year they have been spending on varsity sports while neglecting the wants of teachers.

You see we don't need an increase in the transportation tax unless the voters want to keep paying $50,000 or more a year to transport athletes home after practice and to away games, etc. Rest of the $200,000 is made up in coaches' salaries, athletic directors' salaries, baseball pitching machines, sodded football fields, and thousands of dollars for other sports equipment.

These things are all right, provided we have enough money for them. To sod football fields on borrowed money and then not be able to pay teachers' salaries is getting the cart before the horse.

If these things aren't enough for you, look at East High. No doors on many of the classrooms, a plant room without any sunlight, no water in a first aid treatment room, are just a few of many things. The taxpayers were really taken to the cleaners. A part of the sidewalk in front of the building has already collapsed. Maybe Mr. Hess would be interested to know that we need blinds on the windows in that building also.

Once again, the board must have forgotten they were going to spend $3,200,000 on the West building and $2,300,000 on the East building.

As I see it, the bond issue is a fight between the Board of Education that is trying to push tax-supported athletics down our throats with education, and a public that has mixed emotions about both of these items because they feel they are already paying enough taxes, and simply don't know whom to trust with any more tax money.

I must sign this letter as a citizen, taxpayer and voter, not as a teacher, since that freedom has been taken from the teachers by the administration. Do you really know what goes on behind those stone walls at the high school?

Respectfully,
Marvin L. Pickering.

B. Analysis.

The foregoing letter contains eight principal statements which the Board found to be false. Our independent review of the record convinces us that Justice Schaefer was correct in his dissenting opinion in this case when he concluded that many of appellant's statements which were found by the Board to be false were in fact substantially correct. We shall deal with each of the statements found to be false in turn. (1) Appellant asserted in his letter that the two new high schools when constructed deviated substantially from the original promises made by the Board during the campaign on the bond issue about the facilities they would contain. The Board based its conclusion that this statement was false on its determination that the promises referred to were those made in the campaign to pass the second bond issue in December of 1961. In the campaign on the first bond issue the Board stated that the plans for the two schools did not include such items as swimming pools, auditoriums, and athletic fields. The publicity put out by the Board on the second bond issue mentioned nothing about the addition of an auditorium to the plans and also mentioned nothing specific about athletic fields, although a general reference to "state required physical education" facilities was included that was similar to a reference made in the material issued by the Board during the first campaign.

In sum, the Board first stated that certain facilities were not to be included in the new high schools as an economy measure, changed its mind after the defeat of the first bond issue and decided to include some of the facilities previously omitted, and never specifically or even generally indicated to the taxpayers the change. Appellant's claim that the original plans, as disclosed to the public, deviated from the buildings actually constructed is thus substantially correct and his characterization of the Board's prior statement as a "promise" is fair as a matter of opinion. The Board's conclusion to the contrary based on its determination that appellant's statement referred only to the literature distributed during the second bond issue campaign is unreasonable in that it ignores the word "original" that modifies "promises" in appellant's letter.

(2) Appellant stated that the Board incorrectly informed the public that "teachers' salaries" total $1,297,746 per year. The Board found that statement false. However, the superintendent of schools admitted that the only way the Board's figure could be regarded as accurate was to change the word "teachers" to "instructional" whereby the salaries of deans, principals, librarians, counselors and four secretaries at each of the district's three high schools would be included in the total. Appellant's characterization of the Board's figure as incorrect is thus clearly accurate.

(3) Pickering claimed that the superintendent had said that any teacher who did not support the 1961 bond issue referendum should be prepared for the consequences. The Board found this claim false. However, the statement was corroborated by the testimony of two other teachers, although the superintendent denied making the remark attributed to him. The Illinois Supreme Court appears to have agreed that something along the lines stated by appellant was said, since it relied, in upholding the Board's finding that appellant's version of the remark was false, on testimony by one of the two teachers that he interpreted the remark to be a prediction about the adverse consequences for the schools should the referendum not pass rather than a threat against noncooperation by teachers. However, the other teacher testified that he didn't know how to interpret the remark. Accordingly, while appellant may have misinterpreted the meaning of the remark, he did not misreport it.

(4) Appellant's letter stated that letters from teachers to newspapers had to have the approval of the superintendent before they could be submitted for publication. The Board relied in finding this statement false on the testimony by the superintendent that no approval was required by him. However, the Handbook for Teachers of the district specifically stated at that time that material submitted to local papers should be checked with the building principal and submitted in

triplicate to the publicity coordinator. In particular, the teachers' letters to which appellant was specifically referring in his own letter had in fact been submitted to the superintendent prior to their publication. Thus this statement is substantially correct.

The other four statements challenged by the Board, are factually incorrect in varying degrees. (5) Appellant's letter implied that providing athletes in the schools with free lunches meant that other students must pay 35¢ instead of 30¢ for their lunches. This statement is erroneous in that while discontinuing free lunches for athletes would have permitted some small decrease in the 35¢ charge for lunch to other students, the decrease would not have brought the price down to 30¢. (6) Appellant claimed that the Board had been spending $200,000 a year on athletics while neglecting the wants of teachers. This claim is incorrect in that the $200,000 per year figure included over $130,000 of nonrecurring capital expenditures. (7) Appellant also claimed that the Board had been spending $50,000 a year on transportation for athletes. This claim is completely false in that the expenditures on travel for athletes per year were about $10,000. (8) Finally, appellant stated that football fields had been sodded on borrowed money, while the Board had been unable to pay teachers' salaries. This statement is substantially correct as to the football fields being sodded with borrowed money because the money spent was the proceeds of part of the bond issue, which can fairly be characterized as borrowed. It is incorrect insofar as it suggests that the district's teachers had actually not been paid upon occasion, but correct if taken to mean that the Board had at times some difficulty in obtaining the funds with which to pay teachers. The manner in which the last four statements are false is perfectly consistent with good-faith error, and there is no evidence in the record to show that anything other than carelessness or insufficient information was responsible for their being made.

****

The United States Supreme Court revisited and refined the Pickering holding in **Connick v. Meyers**.

CONNICK
v.
MYERS
461 U.S. 138, 103 S.Ct. 1684 (1982)

JUSTICE WHITE delivered the opinion of the Court.

In Pickering v. Board of Education, 391 U. S. 563 (1968), we stated that a public employee does not relinquish First Amendment rights to comment on matters of public interest by virtue of government employment. We also recognized that the State's interests as an employer in regulating the speech of its employees "differ significantly from those it possesses in connection with regulation of the speech of the citizenry in general." The problem, we thought, was arriving "at a balance between the interests of the [employee], as a citizen, in commenting upon matters of public concern and the interest of the State, as an employer, in promoting the efficiency of the public services it performs through its employees." We return to this problem today and consider whether the First and Fourteenth Amendments prevent the discharge of a state employee for circulating a questionnaire concerning internal office affairs.

I

The respondent, Sheila Myers, was employed as an Assistant District Attorney in New Orleans for five and a half years. She served at the pleasure of petitioner Harry Connick, the District Attorney for Orleans Parish. During this period Myers competently performed her responsibilities of trying criminal cases.

In the early part of October 1980, Myers was informed that she would be transferred to prosecute cases in a different section of the criminal court. Myers was strongly opposed to the proposed transfer[442] and expressed her view to several of her supervisors, including Connick. Despite her objections, on October 6 Myers was notified that she was being transferred. Myers again spoke with Dennis Waldron, one of the First Assistant District Attorneys, expressing her reluctance to accept the transfer. A number of other office matters were discussed and Myers later testified that, in response to Waldron's suggestion that her concerns were not shared by others in the office, she informed him that she would do some research on the matter.

That night Myers prepared a questionnaire soliciting the views of her fellow staff members concerning office transfer policy, office morale, the need for a grievance committee, the level of confidence in supervisors, and whether employees felt pressured to work in political campaigns. Early the following morning, Myers typed and copied the questionnaire. She also met with Connick who urged her to accept the transfer. She said she would "consider" it. Connick then left the office. Myers then distributed the questionnaire to 15 Assistant District Attorneys. Shortly after noon, Dennis Waldron learned that Myers was distributing the survey. He immediately phoned Connick and informed him that Myers was creating a "mini-insurrection" within the office. Connick returned to the office and told Myers that she was being terminated because of her refusal to accept the transfer. She was also told that her distribution of the questionnaire was considered an act of insubordination. Connick particularly objected to the question which inquired whether employees "had confidence in and would rely on the word" of various superiors in the office, and to a question concerning pressure to work in political campaigns which he felt would be damaging if discovered by the press.

Myers filed suit under 42 U. S. C. §1983, contending that her employment was wrongfully terminated because she had exercised her constitutionally protected right of free speech. The District Court agreed, ordered Myers reinstated, and awarded backpay, damages, and attorney's fees. The District Court found that although Connick informed Myers that she was being fired because of her refusal to accept a transfer, the facts showed that the questionnaire was the real reason for her termination. The court then proceeded to hold that Myers' questionnaire involved matters of public concern and that the State had not "clearly demonstrated" that the survey "substantially interfered" with the operations of the District Attorney's office.

Connick appealed to the United States Court of Appeals for the Fifth Circuit, which affirmed on the basis of the District courts opinion. Connick then sought review in this Court by way of certiorari, which we granted.

---

[442] Myers' opposition was at least partially attributable to her concern that a conflict of interest would have been created by the transfer because of her participation in a counseling program for convicted defendants released on probation in the section of the criminal court to which she was to be assigned .

II

For at least 15 years, it has been settled that a State cannot condition public employment on a basis that infringes the employee's constitutionally protected interest in freedom of expression. Our task, as we defined it in Pickering, is to seek "a balance between the interests of the [employee], as a citizen, in commenting upon matters of public concern and the interest of the State, as an employer, in promoting the efficiency of the public services it performs through its employees." 391 U. S., at 568. The District Court, and thus the Court of Appeals as well, misapplied our decision in Pickering and consequently, in our view, erred in striking the balance for respondent.

A

The District Court got off on the wrong foot in this case by initially finding that, "[t]aken as a whole, the issues presented in the questionnaire relate to the effective functioning of the District Attorney's Office and are matters of public importance and concern." Connick contends at the outset that no balancing of interests is required in this case because Myers' questionnaire concerned only internal office matters and that such speech is not upon a matter of "public concern," as the term was used in Pickering. Although we do not agree that Myers' communication in this case was wholly without First Amendment protection, there is much force to Connick's submission. The repeated emphasis in Pickering on the right of a public employee "as a citizen, in commenting upon matters of public concern," was not accidental. This language, reiterated in all of Pickering's progeny,[443] reflects both the historical evolvement of the rights of public employees, and the common-sense realization that government offices could not function if every employment decision became a constitutional matter.

****

The Court cast new light on the matter in a series of cases arising from the widespread efforts in the 1950's and early 1960's to require public employees, particularly teachers, to swear oaths of loyalty to the State and reveal the groups with which they associated. In Wiemann v. Updegraff, (1952), the Court held that a State could not require its employees to establish their loyalty by extracting an oath denying past affiliation with Communists. In Cafeteria Workers v. McElroy (1961), the Court recognized that the government could not deny employment because of previous membership in a particular party. ...It was, therefore, no surprise when in Keyishian v. Board of Regents, the Court invalidated New York statutes barring employment on the basis of membership in "subversive" organizations, observing that the theory that public employment which may be denied altogether may be subjected to any conditions, regardless of how unreasonable, had been uniformly rejected.

In all of these cases, the precedents in which Pickering is rooted, the invalidated statutes and actions sought to suppress the rights of public employees to participate in public affairs. The issue was whether government employees could be prevented or "chilled" by the fear of discharge from joining political parties and other associations that certain public officials might find "subversive." The explanation for the Constitution's special concern with threats to the right of citizens to participate in political affairs is no mystery. The First Amendment "was

---

[443] See Perry v. Sindermann, 408 U. S. 593, 598 (1972); Mt. Healthy City Board of Ed. v. Doyle, 429 U. S. 274, 284 (1977); Givhan v. Western Line Consolidated School District, 439 U. S. 410, 414 (1979).

fashioned to assure unfettered interchange of ideas for the bringing about of political and social changes desired by the people. "[S]peech concerning public affairs is more than self-expression; it is the essence of self-government." Garrison v. Louisiana (1964). Accordingly, the Court has frequently reaffirmed that speech on public issues occupies the "'highest rung of the hierarchy of First Amendment values,'" and is entitled to special protection.

Pickering v. Board of Education, followed from this understanding of the First Amendment. ...Pickering's subject was "a matter of legitimate public concern" upon which "free and open debate is vital to informed decisionmaking by the electorate."

Our cases following Pickering also involved safeguarding speech on matters of public concern. The controversy in Perry v. Sindermann, 408 U. S. 593 (1972), arose from the failure to rehire a teacher in the state college system who had testified before committees of the Texas Legislature and had become involved in public disagreement over whether the college should be elevated to 4-year status—a change opposed by the Regents. In Mt. Healthy City Board of Ed. v. Doyle (1977), a public school teacher was not rehired because, allegedly, he had relayed to a radio station the substance of a memorandum relating to teacher dress and appearance that the school principal had circulated to various teachers. The memorandum was apparently prompted by the view of some in the administration that there was a relationship between teacher appearance and public support for bond issues, and indeed, the radio station promptly announced the adoption of the dress code as a news item. Most recently, in Givhan v. Western Line Consolidated School District (1979), we held that First Amendment protection applies when a public employee arranges to communicate privately with his employer rather than to express his views publicly. Although the subject matter of Mrs. Givhan's statements were not the issue before the Court, it is clear that her statements concerning the School District's allegedly racially discriminatory policies involved a matter of public concern.

Pickering, its antecedents, and its progeny lead us to conclude that if Myers' questionnaire cannot be fairly characterized as constituting speech on a matter of public concern, it is unnecessary for us to scrutinize the reasons for her discharge. When employee expression cannot be fairly considered as relating to any matter of political, social, or other concern to the community, government officials should enjoy wide latitude in managing their offices, without intrusive oversight by the judiciary in the name of the First Amendment. Perhaps the government employer's dismissal of the worker may not be fair, but ordinary dismissals from government service which violate no fixed tenure or applicable statute or regulation are not subject to judicial review even if the reasons for the dismissal are alleged to be mistaken or unreasonable.

...We hold only that when a public employee speaks not as a citizen upon matters of public concern, but instead as an employee upon matters only of personal interest, absent the most unusual circumstances, a federal court is not the appropriate forum in which to review the wisdom of a personnel decision taken by a public agency allegedly in reaction to the employee's behavior. Our responsibility is to ensure that citizens are not deprived of fundamental rights by virtue of working for the government; this does not require a grant of immunity for employee grievances not afforded by the First Amendment to those who do not work for the State.

Whether an employee's speech addresses a matter of public concern must be determined by the content, form, and context of a given statement, as revealed by the whole record. In this case, with but one exception, the questions posed by Myers to her co-workers do not fall under the rubric of matters of "public concern." We view the questions pertaining to the confidence and trust that Myers' co-workers possess in various supervisors, the level of office morale, and the need for a grievance committee as mere extensions of Myers' dispute over her transfer to another section of the criminal court. Unlike the dissent, we do not believe these questions are of public import in evaluating the performance of the District Attorney as an elected official. Myers did not seek to inform the public that the District Attorney's Office wasn't discharging its governmental responsibilities in the investigation and prosecution of criminal cases. Nor did Myers seek to bring to light actual or potential wrongdoing or breach of public trust on the part of Connick and others. Indeed, the questionnaire, if released to the public, would convey no information at all other than the fact that a single employee is upset with the status quo. While discipline and morale in the workplace are related to an agency's efficient performance of its duties, the focus of Myers' questions is not to evaluate the performance of the office but rather to gather ammunition for another round of controversy with her superiors. These questions reflect one employee's dissatisfaction with a transfer and an attempt to turn that displeasure into a cause celebre.[444]

To presume that all matters which transpire within a government office are of public concern would mean that virtually every remark—and certainly every criticism directed at a public official—would plant the seed of a constitutional case. While as a matter of good judgment, public officials should be receptive to constructive criticism offered by their employees, the First Amendment does not require a public office to be run as a roundtable for employee complaints over internal office affairs.

B

...Pickering unmistakably states, and respondent agrees, that the State's burden in justifying a particular discharge varies depending upon the nature of the employee's expression. Although such particularized balancing is difficult, the courts must reach the most appropriate possible balance of the competing interests.

C

The Pickering balance requires full consideration of the government's interest in the effective and efficient fulfillment of its responsibilities to the public. One hundred years ago, the Court noted the government's legitimate purpose in "promot[ing] efficiency and integrity in the discharge of official duties, and [in] maintain[ing] proper discipline in the public service."

****

We agree with the District Court that there is no demonstration here that the questionnaire impeded Myers' ability to perform her responsibilities. The District Court was also correct to recognize that "it is important to the efficient and successful operation of the District Attorney's office for Assistants to maintain close

---

[444] This is not a case like Givhan, where an employee speaks out as a citizen on a matter of general concern, not tied to a personal employment dispute, but arranges to do so privately. Mrs. Givhan's right to protest racial discrimination—a matter inherently of public concern—is not forfeited by her choice of a private forum. Here, however, a questionnaire not other vise of public concern does not attain that status because its subject matter could, in different circumstances, have been the topic of a communication to the public that might be of general interest. The dissent's analysis of whether discussions of office morale and discipline could be matters of public concern is beside the point—it does not answer whether this questionnaire is such speech.

working relationships with their superiors." Connick's judgment, and apparently also that of his first assistant Dennis Waldron, who characterized Myers' actions as causing a "mini-insurrection," was that Myers' questionnaire was an act of insubordination which interfered with working relationships.[445] When close working relationships are essential to fulfilling public responsibilities, a wide degree of deference to the employer's judgment is appropriate. Furthermore, we do not see the necessity for an employer to allow events to unfold to the extent that the disruption of the office and the destruction of working relationships is manifest before taking action.[446] We caution that a stronger showing may be necessary if the employee's speech more substantially involved matters of public concern.

****

Finally, the context in which the dispute arose is also significant. This is not a case where an employee, out of purely academic interest, circulated a questionnaire so as to obtain useful research. Myers acknowledges that it is no coincidence that the questionnaire followed upon the heels of the transfer notice. When employee speech concerning office policy arises from an employment dispute concerning the very application of that policy to the speaker, additional weight must be given to the supervisor's view that the employee has threatened the authority of the employer to run the office.

III

Myers' questionnaire touched upon matters of public concern in only a most limited sense; her survey, in our view, is most accurately characterized as an employee grievance concerning internal office policy. The limited First Amendment interest involved here does not require that Connick tolerate action which he reasonably believed would disrupt the office, undermine his authority, and destroy close working relationships. Myers' discharge therefore did not offend the First Amendment. We reiterate, however, the caveat we expressed in Pickering "Because of the enormous variety of fact situations in which critical statements by . . . public employees may be thought by their superiors . . . to furnish grounds for dismissal, we do not deem it either appropriate or feasible to attempt to lay down a general standard against which all such statements may be judged."

Our holding today is grounded in our longstanding recognition that the First Amendment's primary aim is the full protection of speech upon issues of public concern, as well as the practical realities involved in the administration of a government office. Although today the balance is struck for the government, this is no defeat for the First Amendment. For it would indeed be a Pyrrhic victory for the great principles of free expression if the Amendment's safeguarding of a public employee's right, as a citizen, to participate in discussions concerning public affairs were confused with the attempt to constitutionalize the employee grievance that we see presented here.

The judgment of the Court of Appeals is Reversed.

---

[445] Waldron testified that from what he had learned of the events on October 7, Myers "was trying to stir up other people not to accept the changes [transfers] that had been made on the memorandum and that were to be implemented." App. 167. In his view, the questionnaire was a "final act of defiance" and that, as a result of Myers' action, "there were going to be some severe problems about the changes." Ibid. Connick testified that he reached a similar conclusion after conducting his own investigation. "After I satisfied myself that not only wasn't she accepting the transfer, but that she was affirmatively opposing it and disrupting the routine of the office by this questionnaire. I called her in . . .[and dismissed her]." Id ., at 130.

[446] Cf. Perry Education Assn. v. Perry Local Educators' Assn., 460 U. S. 37, 52, n. 12 (1983) (proof of future disruption not necessary to justify denial of access to nonpublic forum on grounds that the proposed use may disrupt the property's intended function); Greer v. Spock, 424 U. S. 828 (1976) (same).

APPENDIX TO OPINION OF THE COURT
Questionnaire distributed by respondent on October 7, 1980.
PLAINTIFF'S EXHIBIT 2, App. 191

"PLEASE TAKE THE FEW MINUTES IT WILL REQUIRE TO FILL THIS OUT. YOU CAN FREELY EXPRESS YOUR OPINION WITH ANONYMITY GUARANTEED.
****

1. How long have you been in the Office?
2. Were you moved as a result of the recent transfers?
3. Were the transfers as they effected [sic] you discussed with you by any superior prior to the notice of them being posted?
4. Do you think as a matter of policy, they should have been?
5. From your experience, do you feel office procedure regarding transfers has been fair?
6. Do you believe there is a rumor mill active in the office?
7. If so, how do you think it effects [sic] overall working performance of A.D.A. personnel?
8. If so, how do you think it effects [sic] office morale?
9. Do you generally first learn of office changes and developments through rumor?
10. Do you have confidence in and would you rely on the word of:
> Bridget Bane
> Fred Harper
> Lindsay Larson
> Joe Meyer
> Dennis Waldron

11. Do you ever feel pressured to work in political campaigns on behalf of office supported candidates?
12. Do you feel a grievance committee would be a worthwhile addition to the office structure?
13. How would you rate office morale?
14. Please feel free to express any comments or feelings you have.
THANK YOU FOR YOUR COOPERATION IN THIS SURVEY."

JUSTICE BRENNAN, with whom JUSTICE MARSHALL, JUSTICE BLACKMUN, and JUSTICE STEVENS join, dissenting.

Sheila Myers was discharged for circulating a questionnaire to her fellow Assistant District Attorneys seeking information about the effect of petitioner's personnel policies on employee morale and the overall work performance of the District Attorney's Office. The Court concludes that her dismissal does not violate the First Amendment, primarily because the questionnaire addresses matters that, in the Court's view, are not of public concern. It is hornbook law, however, that speech about "the manner in which government is operated or should be operated" is an essential part of the communications necessary for self-governance the protection of which was a central purpose of the First Amendment. Mills v. Alabama, 384 U. S. 214, 218 (1966). Because the questionnaire addressed such matters and its distribution did not adversely affect the operations of the District Attorney's Office or interfere with Myers' working relationship with her fellow employees, I dissent.

FOWLER
v.
BOARD OF EDUCATION OF LINCOLN CNTY. KY.[447]
819 F.2d 657 (6th Cir. 1987)

Before MERRITT and MILBURN, Circuit Judges, and PECK, Senior Circuit Judge.
MILBURN, Circuit Judge.

Defendants, The Board of Education of Lincoln County, Kentucky, individual board members, and the Superintendent of the Lincoln County Schools, appeal from the judgment of the district court awarding reinstatement and damages to plaintiff Jacqueline Fowler on the ground that her employment was terminated in violation of her First Amendment rights. ...For the reasons that follow, we vacate the judgment of the district court and dismiss plaintiff's action.

I

Plaintiff Jacqueline Fowler was a tenured teacher employed by the Lincoln County, Kentucky, school system for fourteen years. She was discharged in July, 1984 for insubordination and conduct unbecoming a teacher. The basis for this action was that she had an "R" rated movie, Pink Floyd—The Wall, shown to her high school students on the last day of the 1983-84 school year. The students in Fowler's classes were in grades nine through eleven and were of the ages fourteen through seventeen.

The day on which the movie was shown, May 31, 1984, was a noninstructional day used by teachers for completing grade cards. A group of students requested that Fowler allow the movie to be shown while she was completing the grade cards. Fowler was unfamiliar with the movie and asked the students whether it was appropriate for viewing at school. Charles Bailey, age fifteen, who had seen the movie on prior occasions, indicated that the movie had "one bad place in it."

Fowler rented the video tape at a video store in Danville, Kentucky. The clerk who rented the "R" rated tape to Fowler told her that there was some nudity in the movie during a song called "Young Lust" and warned that she might wish to delete that section. However, Fowler did not preview the movie before having it shown to her morning class because the store did not have a tape compatible with her own VCR and because she did not have time to make other arrangements to preview the movie.

When Fowler had the movie shown on the morning of May 31,1984, she instructed Charles Bailey, the fifteen-year-old student who had seen the movie, to edit out any parts that were unsuitable for viewing at school. He did so by attempting to cover the 25" screen with an 8 1/2"by 11" letter-sized file folder.

There is conflicting testimony as to whether, or how much, nudity was seen by the students. At the administrative hearing, several students testified that they

---

[447] See also Miles v. Denver Public Schools 944 F.2d 773 (10th Cir. 1991) Ninth grade social studies class was not a public forum and therefore teachers expressions during class were properly considered as school sponsored for purposes of the 1st Amendment.The discipline action taken against the teacher for comments made during class were reasonably related to schools pedagogical interests.

saw no nudity. One student testified that she saw "glimpses" of nudity, but "nothing really offending."Assistant Principal Michael Candler, who observed the movie during part of the afternoon showing, testified that Charles Bailey's editing attempt was not sufficient to preclude the students from seeing the nudity. On cross-examination, Charles Bailey testified that Mrs. Fowler told him to open the file folder while editing after Candler entered the room. It is undisputed that the audio portion of the movie, which contained enough offensive language to mandate an automatic "R" rating under motion picture industry standards, was played through the entire movie.

There is also conflicting testimony regarding the amount of sexual innuendo existing in the "unedited" version of the film. Because some parts of the film are animated, they are susceptible to varying interpretations. One particularly controversial segment of scenes is animated in which flowers appear on the screen, are transformed into the shape of male and female sex organs and then engage in an act of intercourse. This segment of the film was shown in the morning session. Other segments involving a violent rape, nudity, a suggestion of oral sex, and a naked woman and naked man in bed engaging in foreplay and intercourse were also shown in the morning.

Once again, there is conflicting testimony concerning the effectiveness of the editing attempt. Moreover, there is testimony supporting the fact that more editing was done in the afternoon showing than in the morning showing.

In addition to the sexual aspects of the movie, there is a great deal of violence. One scene involves a bloody battlefield. Another shows police brutality. Another shows the protagonist cutting his chest with a razor. Another scene shows children being fed into a giant sausage machine.

On the afternoon of May 31,1984, Principal Jack Portwood asked Fowler to give him the video tape, and she did so. After the movie was viewed by the superintendent and members of the Lincoln County Board of Education, proceedings were instituted to terminate Fowler's contract.

Plaintiff Fowler received her termination notice on or about June 19, 1984. The notice advised her that a hearing would be held on July 10,1984, and she subsequently advised the board of her intention to appear at the hearing and contest the charges.

On July 10, 1984, plaintiff Fowler appeared with counsel at the administrative hearing. She testified that, despite the fact that she had never seen the movie before having it shown to her students, and despite the fact that she was posting grades on report cards and left the room several times while the movie was being shown, she believed it had significant value. She believed the movie portrayed the dangers of alienation between people and of repressive educational systems. She testified that she would show an edited version of the movie again if given the opportunity to explain it. She stated that she did not at any time discuss the movie with her students because she did not have enough time.

The board viewed the movie once in its entirety and once as it had been edited in the classroom. The board then retired into executive session. Following this executive session, the board returned to open session and voted unanimously to terminate plaintiff's employment for insubordination and conduct unbecoming a teacher.

Following her termination, plaintiff Fowler initiated her action in the district court alleging that her First and Fourteenth Amendment rights were violated by her discharge, and that the Kentucky statutes forming the basis for her discharge were unconstitutionally vague or overbroad. She also alleged that the factual findings made in support of her discharge were not supported by substantial evidence.

At the bench trial in the district court, Fowler repeated her contention that she believed the movie contained important, socially valuable messages. School officials testified that they objected to the movie because it promoted values which were described as immoral, anti-education, antifamily, anti-judiciary, and anti-police. They also found the movie objectionable because of its sexual content, vulgar language, and violence.

The district court concluded that Fowler's conduct was protected by the First Amendment, and that she was discharged for exercising her constitutionally protected rights. Consequently, it awarded her reinstatement, back pay with interest, reimbursement of funds necessary for her reinstatement with the Kentucky Teachers Retirement System, damages for emotional distress and damage to professional reputation, compensatory damages for costs incurred in seeking new employment, costs, and attorney's fees.

The district court concluded that Fowler was not insubordinate because she did not violate an established rule or regulation, and also found that plaintiff's due process rights were not violated by the procedures utilized at the administrative hearing.   In this appeal, defendants contend that the district court erred in its conclusion that plaintiff's discharge violated her First Amendment rights.

II
A

In its opinion, the district court relied upon the analytical framework provided by the Supreme Court in <u>Mt. Healthy City School District Board of Education v. Doyle</u> (1977). Under the the Healthy standard, a public employee establishes a prima facie case of a constitutional violation if she shows that she was engaged in protected activity, and that such activity was a substantial or motivating factor in the decision to terminate her employment. In order to defend itself against such a claim, the government must establish by a preponderance of the evidence that the decision to terminate would have been made in the absence of the exercise of the constitutionally protected right.

In the present case, it is undisputed that plaintiff's employment was terminated because she had the "R" rated movie shown to her students and because she said she would do it again. Consequently, the focus of our inquiry is whether Fowler's conduct was constitutionally protected.

The Supreme Court has consistently recognized the importance of the exercise of First Amendment rights in the context of public schools.

> "First Amendment rights, applied in light of the special characteristics of the school environment, are available to teachers and students. It can hardly be argued that either students or teachers shed their constitutional rights to freedom of speech or expression at the schoolhouse gate. This has been the unmistakable holding of this Court for almost 50 years.

Many courts have recognized that a teacher's First Amendment rights encompass the notion of "academic freedom" to exercise professional judgment in selecting topics and materials for use in the course of the educational process.

Among the "special circumstances" which must be considered in defining the scope of First Amendment protection inside the classroom is the "inculcat[ion] of] fundamental values necessary to the maintenance of a democratic political system."

Indeed, the "fundamental values necessary to the maintenance of a democratic political system" disfavor the use of terms of debate highly offensive or highly threatening to others. Nothing in the Constitution prohibits the states from insisting that certain modes of expression are inappropriate and subject to sanctions. The inculcation of these values is truly the "work of the schools."

The single most important element of this inculcative process is the teacher. "Consciously or otherwise, teachers ... demonstrate the appropriate form of civil discourse and political expression by their conduct and deportment in and out of class. Inescapably, like parents, they are role models" "To regard teachers—in our entire educational system, from the primary grades to the university—as the priests of our democracy is therefore not to indulge in hyperbole."

The accommodation of these sometimes conflicting fundamental values has caused great tension, particularly when the conflict arises within the classroom. In the final analysis,

[t]he ultimate goal of school officials is to insure that the discipline necessary to the proper functioning of the school is maintained among both teachers and students. Any limitation on the exercise of constitutional rights can be justified only by a conclusion, based upon reasonable inferences flowing from concrete facts and not abstractions, that the interests of discipline or sound education are materially and substantially justified.... "The problem in any case is to arrive at a balance between the interests of the teacher, as a citizen, in commenting upon matters of public concern and the interest of the State, as an employer, in promoting the efficiency of the public services it performs through its employees."

In the present case the district court concluded that Mrs. Fowler was entitled to the protection of the First Amendment while acting as a teacher. That a teacher does have First Amendment protection under certain circumstances cannot be denied. Likewise, a motion picture is a form of expression which may be entitled to the protection of the First Amendment.

However, I conclude that Fowler's conduct in having the movie shown under the circumstances present here did not constitute expression [448] protected by the First Amendment.[449] It is undisputed that Fowler was discharged for the showing of the movie, Pink Floyd—The Wall. Such conduct, under the circumstances involved, clearly is not "speech" in the traditional sense of the expression of ideas through use of the spoken or written word.

Nevertheless, the Supreme Court has long recognized that certain forms of expressive conduct are entitled to protection under the First Amendment.

---

[448] Whether a certain activity is entitled to protection under the First Amendment is a question of law.

[449] Plaintiff relies on Minarcini v. Strongsville City School District, 541 F.2d 577 (6th Cir.1976), for the proposition that students in a public school have a constitutionally protected right "to receive information which they and their teachers desire them to have." Id., at 583. In Minarcini, this court held that this "right to know" was violated by the removal of library books solely on the basis of the social and political tastes of the school board. The existence of such a "right to know" was considered by the Supreme Court in Board of Education, Island Trees Union Free School District No. 26 v. Pico, 457 U.S. 853, 102 S.Ct. 2799, 73 L.Ed.2d 435 (1982). Only three justices agreed that students possess a constitutionally protected entitlement to access to particular books in the school's library. Id, at 863-69, 102 S.Ct. at 2806 09. Moreover, even these three justices explicitly noted that the decision regarding this right did not extend to the classroom. Id, at 862. 869.102 S.Ct. at 2805-06, 2809. For similar reasons, plaintiff's reliance on Pratt v. Independent School District No. 831, 670 F.2d 771 (8th Cir.1982) is misplaced.

****

However, not every form of conduct is protected by the First Amendment right of free speech.

> To determine whether [plaintiff's] conduct is entitled to first amendment protection, "the nature of [plaintiff's] activity, combined with the factual context and environment in which it was undertaken" must be considered. If [plaintiff] shows "[a]n intent to convey a particularized message ... and in the surrounding circumstances the likelihood was great that the message would be understood by those who viewed it," the activity falls within the scope of the first and fourteenth amendments.

In the present case, it is undisputed that Fowler did not see the movie before she had it shown to her class on the morning of May 31, 1984, a noninstructional day.[450] Fowler agreed to allow the movie to be shown, at the students' request, because May 31 was "their treat type of day." It is also undisputed that she left the room on several occasions while the film was being shown. Under circumstances such as these, I cannot conclude that Fowler possessed "[a]n intent to convey a particularized message" to her students. The mere fact that at some point she may have developed an approval of the content of the movie is not, standing alone, a sufficient basis for the conclusion that her conduct in having the movie shown was a form of expression entitled to protection under the First Amendment.

If any sort of conduct that people wish to engage in is to be considered "speech" simply because those who engage in conduct are, in one sense, necessarily expressing their approval of it, the line between "speech" protected by the First Amendment and conduct not so protected will be destroyed.

Moreover, the surrounding circumstances in the present case indicate that there was little likelihood "that the message would be understood by those who viewed it." As we have noted, the "R" rated movie was shown on a noninstructional day to students in Fowler's classes in grades nine through eleven who were of ages ranging from fourteen through seventeen. Furthermore, Fowler never at any time made an attempt to explain any message that the students might derive from viewing the movie.

Thus, this case is distinguishable from those in which the Supreme Court has afforded First Amendment protection in cases involving expressive conduct.

****

The cases...demonstrate that conduct is protected by the First Amendment only when it is expressive or communicative in nature. In the present case, because plaintiff's conduct in having the movie shown cannot be considered expressive or communicative, under the circumstances presented, the protection of the First Amendment is not implicated.

B

Plaintiff argues that Ky.Rev.Stat. § 161.-790(1)(b), which proscribes "conduct unbecoming a teacher," is unconstitutionally vague as applied to her because the statute failed to give notice that her conduct would result in discipline. We find this argument to be without merit.

---

[450] Plaintiff's reliance upon cases grounded in the concept of "academic freedom, is misplaced. These cases are based upon the notion that teaching is a form of activity protected by the First Amendment. We do not intimate that a teacher is entitled to the protection of the First Amendment only when teaching. However, the fact that Fowler's conduct was unrelated to the educational process does remove it from the protection afforded by the concept of academic freedom.

The vagueness doctrine requires that a statute proscribing certain conduct must be drafted "with sufficient definiteness that ordinary people can understand what conduct is prohibited and in a manner that does not encourage arbitrary and discriminatory enforcement."

> The root of the vagueness doctrine is a rough idea of fairness. It is not a principle designed to convert into a constitutional dilemma the practical difficulties in drawing ... statutes both general enough to take to take into account a variety of human conduct and sufficiently specific to provide fair warning that certain kinds of conduct are prohibited. Colten v. Kentucky, 407 U.S. 104, 110 (1972).

The fundamental principles of due process are violated only when "a statute . . . either forbids or requires the doing of an act in terms so vague that men of common intelligence must necessarily guess at its meaning and differ as to its application."

****

In the present case, plaintiff Fowler had a fifteen-year-old student show a controversial, highly suggestive and somewhat sexually explicit movie to a group of high school students aged fourteen to seventeen. She did not preview the movie, despite the fact that she had been warned that portions were unsuitable for viewing in this context. She made no attempt at any time to explain the meaning of the movie or to use it as an educational tool. Rather, she had it shown for the purpose of keeping her students occupied during a noninstructional day while she was involved in posting grades on report cards. We conclude that the statute proscribing "conduct unbecoming a teacher" gave her adequate notice that such conduct would subject her to discipline. Accordingly, we conclude that the statute is not unconstitutionally vague as applied to Fowler's conduct.

C

Finally, we must determine whether plaintiff's conduct constituted "conduct unbecoming a teacher". ...Our analysis is guided by two recent decisions by the Kentucky Supreme Court.

In Board of Education v Wood (Ky.1986), two tenured teachers were discharged for conduct unbecoming a teacher under section 161.790(1)(b). The evidence in Wood established that the teachers had been smoking marijuana with two fifteen-year-old students in the teachers' apartment.

The court noted that "[t]he evidence indicates that there was serious misconduct of an immoral and criminal nature and a direct connection between the misconduct and the teachers' work." The court went on to view this conduct in light of the purpose for teacher tenure.

> The purpose of teacher tenure laws is to promote good order in the school system by preventing the arbitrary removal of capable and experienced teachers by political or personal whim.... A teacher is held to a standard of personal conduct which does not permit the commission of immoral or criminal acts because of the harmful impression made on the students. The school teacher has traditionally been regarded as a moral example for the students.

Under the circumstances present, the court concluded that a discharge for conduct unbecoming a teacher could be upheld.

****

In the present case, we conclude that plaintiff's conduct, although not illegal, constituted serious misconduct. Moreover, there was a direct connection between this misconduct and Fowler's work as a teacher. She introduced a controversial and sexually explicit movie into a classroom of adolescents without preview, preparation or discussion. In the process, she abdicated her function as an educator. Her having the movie shown under the circumstances involved demonstrates a blatant lack of judgment. Having considered the entire record, including the viewing of the movie, which we describe as gross and bizarre and containing material completely unsuitable for viewing by a classroom of students aged fourteen to seventeen, we conclude that such conduct falls within the concept of conduct unbecoming a teacher under Kentucky law.

III

Accordingly, for the reasons stated, the judgment of the district court is **Vacated**, and this cause is **Dismissed**.

****

Free Exercise of Religion[451]

PALMER
v.
BOARD OF EDUCATION OF CITY OF CHICAGO
603 F.2d 1271 (7th Cir. 1979)

Before PELL, SPRECHER, and WOOD, Circuit Judges.
HARLINGTON WOOD, Jr., Circuit Judge.

Plaintiff states the issue to be whether or not a public school teacher in her classes has the right to refuse to participate in the Pledge of Allegiance the singing of patriotic songs, and the celebration of certain national holidays when to do so is claimed to violate her religious principles. The issue is more correctly stated to be whether or not a public school teacher is free to disregard the prescribed curriculum concerning patriotic matters when to conform to the curriculum she claims would conflict with her religious principles.

Plaintiff, a member of the Jehovah's Witnesses religion, was a probationary kindergarten teacher in the Chicago public schools. After her appointment, but prior to the commencement of classes, plaintiff informed her principal that because of her religion she would be unable to teach any subjects having to do with love of country, the flag or other patriotic matters in the prescribed curriculum. Extraordinary efforts were made to accommodate plaintiffs religious beliefs at her particular school and elsewhere in the system, but it could not reasonably be accomplished.

The trial court allowed defendants' motion for summary judgment. As there is no substantive factual dispute, additional recitation of the factual details is not required. Plaintiff argues that the offended curriculum is so broad and vague as to be incomprehensible.

In Epperson v. Arkansas (1968), the Court held invalid as offending the First Amendment an Arkansas statute prohibiting the teaching of a particular doctrine of evolution considered contrary to the religious views of most citizens. The Court recognized, however, that the states possess an undoubted right so long as not restrictive of constitutional guarantees to prescribe the curriculum for their public

---

[451]See also; Reutter, Edmund, Jr., "Teachers' Religious Dress: A Century of Litigation," 70 Ed.Law Rep. [747] (January 2, 1992).

schools. Plaintiff would have us fashion for her an exception to that general curriculum rule. The issue is narrow.

Our decision in Clark v. Holmes (7th Cir. 1972), cert. denied, (1973), is of some guidance. In that case the complaint about a university teacher was that he ignored the prescribed course content and engaged in unauthorized student counseling. We held that the First Amendment was not a teacher license for uncontrolled expression at variance with established curricular content. The individual teacher was found to have no constitutional prerogative to override the judgment of superiors as to the proper content for the course to be taught. In Ahern v Board of Education (8th Cir. 1972), the court upheld a teacher dismissal for insubordination on the basis that the Constitution bestowed no right on the teachers to disregard the valid dictates of her superiors by teaching politics in a course on economics. In Adams v. Campbell County School District, 611 F.2d 1242 (10th Cir. 1975), the court stated that the Board and the principal had a right to insist that a more orthodox teaching approach be used by a teacher who was found to have no unlimited authority as to the structure and content of courses.

****

Plaintiff also cites Russo v. Central School District No. 1 (2d Cir. 1972), cert. denied (1978), as squarely considering the present issue, but it does not. The court held that a high school art teacher could not be dismissed for her silent refusal to participate in her school's daily flag ceremonies. She would only stand silently and respectfully at attention while the senior instructor led the program. Her job was not to teach patriotic matters to children, but to teach art. The court carefully indicated that through its holding it did not mean to limit the traditionally broad discretion that has always rested with local school authorities to prescribe curriculum.

The curriculum which plaintiff complains about is not spelled out in specific detail, but can be found in the Board of Education policy and the directives of plaintiff's principal and superiors. There is after all nothing innovative or unique in this phase of the curriculum. It is traditional. There was no misunderstanding about what was expected to be taught.

Plaintiff in seeking to conduct herself in accordance with her religious beliefs neglects to consider the impact on her students who are not members of her faith. Because of her religious beliefs, plaintiff would deprive her students of an elementary knowledge and appreciation of our national heritage. She considers it to be promoting idolatry, it was explained during oral argument, to teach, for instance, about President Lincoln and why we observe his birthday. However, it would apparently not offend her religious views to teach about some of our past leaders less proudly regarded. There would only be provided a distorted and unbalanced view of our country's history. Parents have a vital interest in what their children are taught. Their representatives have in general prescribed a curriculum. There is a compelling state interest in the choice and adherence to a suitable curriculum for the benefit of our young citizens and society. It cannot be left to Individual teachers to teach what they please. Plaintiff's right to her own religious views and practices remains unfettered, but she has no constitutional right to require others to submit to her views and to forego a portion of their education they would otherwise be entitled to enjoy. In this unsettled world, although we hope it will not come to pass, some of the students may be called upon in some way to defend and protect our democratic system and Constitutional rights, including plaintiff's religious freedom. That will demand a bit of patriotism.

****

We affirm the grant of summary judgment by the district court.

14th Amendment Protection
BOARD OF REGENTS
v.
ROTH[452]
408 U.S. 564, 92 S.Ct. 2701 (1972)

MR. JUSTICE STEWART delivered the opinion of the Court.

In 1968 the respondent, David Roth, was hired for his first teaching job as assistant professor of political Science at Wisconsin State University-Oshkosh. He was hired for a fixed term of one academic year. The notice of his faculty appointment specified that his employment would begin on September 1, 1968, and would end on June 30, 1969. The respondent completed that term. But he was informed that he would not be re-hired for the next academic year.

The respondent had no tenure rights to continued employment. Under Wisconsin statutory law a state university teacher can acquire tenure as a "permanent" employee only after four years of year-to-year employment. Having acquired tenure, a teacher is entitled to continued employment "during efficiency and good behavior." A relatively new teacher without tenure, however, is under Wisconsin law entitled to nothing beyond his one-year appointment.[453] There are no statutory or administrative standards defining eligibility for re-employment. State law thus clearly leaves the decision whether to rehire a nontenured teacher for another year to the unfettered discretion of university officials.

The procedural protection afforded a Wisconsin State University teacher before he is separated from the University corresponds to his job security. As a matter of statutory law, a tenured teacher cannot be "discharged except for cause upon written charges" and pursuant to certain procedures.[454] A nontenured teacher, similarly, is protected to some extent during his one-year term. Rules promulgated by the Board of Regents provide that a nontenured teacher "dismissed" before the end of the year may have some opportunity for review of the "dismissal." But the Rules provide no real protection for a nontenured teacher who simply is not re-employed for the next year. He must be informed by February 1 "concerning retention or non- retention for the ensuing year." But "no reason for non-retention need be given. No review or appeal is provided in such case."[455]

---

[452] In a companion case entitled Perry v. Sindermann 408 U.S. 593 (1972) the Supreme Court rendered a decision which has relevance to school employment not covered by tenure statutes. In Perry the court ruled that the customs and practices of the employer may create a reasonable expectation of continued employment requiring due process (notice and hearing) before nonrenewal of the employment relationship.

[453] Wis. Stat. §37.31 (1) (1967), in force at the time, provided in pertinent part that:
"All teachers in any state university shall initially be employed on probation. The employment shall be permanent, during efficiency and good behavior after 4 years of continuous service in the state university system as a teacher."

[454] Wis. Stat. § 37.31 (1) further provided that:
"No teacher who has become permanently employed as herein provided shall be discharged except for cause upon written charges. Within 30 days of receiving the written charges, such teacher may appeal the discharge by a written notice to the president of the board of regents of state colleges. The board shall cause the charges to be investigated, hear the case and provide such teacher with a written statement as to their decision."

[455] The Rules, promulgated by the Board of Regents in 1967 provide:
"RULE I—February first is established throughout the State University system as the deadline for written notification of non-tenured faculty concerning retention or non-retention for the ensuing year. The President of each University shall give such notice each year on or before this date."

In conformance with these Rules, the President of Wisconsin State University-Oshkosh informed the respondent before February 1, 1969, that he would not be rehired for the 1969-1970 academic year. He gave the respondent no reason for the decision and no opportunity to challenge it at any sort of hearing.

The respondent then brought this action in Federal District Court alleging that the decision not to rehire him for the next year infringed his Fourteenth Amendment rights. He attacked the decision both in substance and procedure. First, he alleged that the true reason for the decision was to punish him for certain statements critical of the University administration and that it, therefore, violated his right to freedom of speech. Second, he alleged that the failure of University officials to give him notice of any reason for nonretention and an opportunity for a hearing violated his right to procedural due process of law.

The District Court granted summary judgment for the respondent on the procedural issue, ordering the University officials to provide him with reasons and a hearing. The Court of Appeals, with one judge dissenting, affirmed this partial summary judgment. We granted certiorari. The only question presented to us at this stage in the case is whether the respondent had a constitutional right to a statement of reasons and a hearing on the University's decision not to rehire him for another year. We hold that he did not.

I

The requirements of procedural due process apply only to the deprivation of interests encompassed by the Fourteenth Amendment's protection of liberty and property. When protected interests are implicated, the right to some kind of prior hearing is paramount.[456] But the range of interests protected by procedural due process is not infinite.

****

...But, to determine whether due process requirements apply in the first place, we must look not to the "weight" but to the nature of the interest at stake. We must look to see if the interest is within the Fourteenth Amendment's protection of liberty and property.

"Liberty" and "property" are broad and majestic terms. They are among the "[g]reat [constitutional] concepts . . . purposely left to gather meaning from experience.... [T]hey relate to the whole domain of social and economic fact, and the statesmen who founded this Nation knew too well that only a stagnant society remains unchanged." For that reason, the Court has fully and finally rejected the wooden distinction between "rights" and "privileges" that once seemed to govern the applicability of procedural due process rights.[457] The Court has also made clear

---

"RULE II—During the time a faculty member is on probation, no reason for non-retention need be given. No review or appeal is provided in such case.

"RULE III—'Dismissal' as opposed to 'Non-Retention' means termination of responsibilities during an academic year. When a non-tenure faculty member is dismissed he has no right under Wisconsin Statutes to a review of his case or to appeal. The President may, however, in his discretion, grant a request for a review within the institution, either by a faculty committee or by the President, or both. any such review would be informal in nature and would be advisory only.

"RULE IV—When a non-tenure faculty member is dismissed he may request a review by or hearing before the Board of Regents. Each such request will be considered separately and the Board will, in its discretion, grant or deny same in each individual case."

[456] Before a person is deprived of a protected interest, he must be afforded opportunity for some kind of a hearing, "except for extraordinary situations where some valid governmental interest is at stake that justifies postponing the hearing until after the event." "While '[m]any controversies have raged about ... the Due Process Clause,' ... it is fundamental that except in emergency situations (and this is not one) due process requires that when a State seeks to terminate [a protected] interest ..., it must afford notice and opportunity for hearing appropriate to the nature of the case before the termination becomes effective."

[457] In a leading case decided many years ago, the Court of Appeals for the District of Columbia Circuit held that public employment in general was a "privilege," not a "right," and that procedural due process guarantees therefore were inapplicable. The basis of this holding has been

that the property interests protected by procedural due process extend well beyond actual ownership of real estate, chattels, or money. By the same token, the Court has required due process protection for deprivations of liberty beyond the sort of formal constraints imposed by the criminal process.

Yet, while the Court has eschewed rigid or formalistic limitations on the protection of procedural due process, it has at the same time observed certain boundaries. For the words "liberty" and "property" in the Due Process Clause of the Fourteenth Amendment must be given some meaning.

II

"While this Court has not attempted to define with exactness the liberty . . . guaranteed [by the Fourteenth Amendment], the term has received much consideration and some of the included things have been definitely stated. Without doubt, it denotes not merely freedom from bodily restraint but also the right of the individual to contract, to engage in any of the common occupations of life, to acquire useful knowledge, to marry, establish a home and bring up children, to worship God according to the dictates of his own conscience, and generally to enjoy those privileges long recognized . . . as essential to the orderly pursuit of happiness by free men." In a Constitution for a free people, there can be no doubt that the meaning of "liberty" must be broad indeed.

There might be cases in which a State refused to re-employ a person under such circumstances that interests in liberty would be implicated. But this is not such a case.

The State, in declining to rehire the respondent, did not make any charge against him that might seriously damage his standing and associations in his community. It did not base the nonrenewal of his contract on a charge, for example, that he had been guilty of dishonesty, or immorality. Had it done so, this would be a different case. For "[w]here a person's good name, reputation, honor, or integrity is at stake because of what the government is doing to him, notice and an opportunity to be heard are essential. In such a case, due process would accord an opportunity to refute the charge before University officials.[458] In the present case, however, there is no suggestion whatever that the respondent's good name, reputation, honor, or integrity" are at stake.

Similarly, there is no suggestion that the State, in declining to re-employ the respondent, imposed on him a stigma or other disability that foreclosed his freedom to take advantage of other employment opportunities. The State, for example, did not invoke any regulations to bar the respondent from all other public employment in state universities. Had it done so, this, again, would be a different case. For "[t]o be deprived not only of present government employment but of future opportunity for it certainly is no small injury ...." The Court has held, for example, that a state in regulating eligibility for a type of professional employment cannot foreclose a range of opportunities "in a manner . . . that contravene[s] . . . Due Process," and specifically, in a manner that denies the right to a full prior hearing. In the present case, however, this principle does not come into play.[459]

---

thoroughly undermined in the ensuing years. For, as MR. JUSTICE BLACKMUN wrote for the Court only last year, "this Court now has rejected the concept that constitutional rights turn upon whether a governmental benefit is characterized as a 'right' or as a "privilege."

[458] The purpose of such notice and hearing is to provide the person an opportunity to clear his name. Once a person has cleared his name at a hearing, his employer, of course, may remain free to deny him future employment for other reasons.

[459] The District Court made an assumption "that non-retention by one university or college creates concrete and practical difficulties for a professor in his subsequent academic career." And the Court of Appeals based its affirmance of the summary judgment largely on the premise that "the substantial adverse effect non-retention is likely to have upon the career interests of an individual professor" amounts to a limitation on future employment opportunities sufficient to invoke procedural due process guarantees. But even assuming, arguendo, that such a

****

Hence, on the record before us, all that clearly appears is that the respondent was not rehired for one year at one university. It stretches the concept too far to suggest that a person is deprived of "liberty" when he simply is not rehired in one job but remains as free as before to seek another.

III

The Fourteenth Amendment's procedural protection of property is a safeguard of the security of interests that a person has already acquired in specific benefits. These interests--property interest--may take many forms.

Thus the Court has held that a person receiving welfare benefits under statutory and administrative standards defining eligibility for them has an interest in continued receipt of those benefits that is safeguarded by procedural due process. Similarly, in the area of public employment, the Court has held that a public college professor dismissed from an office held under tenure provisions, <u>Slochower</u> v. <u>Board of Education,</u> and college professors and staff members dismissed during the terms of their contracts, <u>Wieman</u> v. <u>Updegraff</u>, have interests in continued employment that are safeguarded by due process. Only last year, the Court held that this principle "proscribing summary dismissal from public employment without hearing or inquiry required by due process" also applied to a teacher recently hired without tenure or a formal contract, but nonetheless with a clearly implied promise of continued employment.

Certain attributes of "property" interests protected by procedural due process emerge from these decisions. To have a property interest in a benefit, a person clearly must have more than an abstract need or desire for it. He must have more than a unilateral expectation of it. He must, instead, have a legitimate claim of entitlement to it. It is a purpose of the ancient institution of property to protect those claims upon which people rely in their daily lives, reliance that must not be arbitrarily undermined. It is a purpose of the constitutional right to a hearing to provide an opportunity for a person to vindicate those claims.

Property interests, of course, are not created by the Constitution. Rather, they are created and their dimensions are defined by existing rules or understandings that stem from an independent source such as state law—rules or understandings that secure certain benefits and that support claims of entitlement to those benefits. Thus, the welfare recipients in <u>Goldberg</u> v. <u>Kelly,</u> supra, had a claim of entitlement to welfare payments that was grounded in the statute defining eligibility for them. The recipients had not yet shown that they were, in fact, within the statutory terms of eligibility. But we held that they had a right to a hearing at which they might attempt to do so.

Just as the welfare recipients' "property" interest in welfare payments was created and defined by statutory terms, so the respondent's "property" interest in employment at Wisconsin State University-Oshkosh was created and defined by the terms of his appointment. Those terms secured his interest in employment up to June 30, 1969. But the important fact in this case is that they specifically provided that the respondent's employment was to terminate on June 30. They did not

---

"substantial adverse effect" under these circumstances would constitute a state-imposed restriction on liberty, the record contains no support for these assumptions. There is no suggestion of how non-retention might affect the respondent's future employment prospects. Mere proof, for example, that his record of nonretention in one job, taken alone, might make him somewhat less attractive to some other employers would hardly establish the kind of foreclosure of opportunities amounting to a deprivation of "liberty."

provide for contract renewal absent "sufficient cause." Indeed, they made no provision for renewal whatsoever.

Thus, the terms of the respondent's appointment secured absolutely no interest in re-employment for the next year. They supported absolutely no possible claim of entitlement to re-employment. Nor, significantly, was there any state statute or University rule or policy that secured his interest in re-employment or that created any legitimate claim to it. In these circumstances, the respondent surely had an abstract concern in being rehired, but he did not have a property interest sufficient to require the University authorities to give him a hearing when they declined to renew his contract of employment.

IV

Our analysis of the respondent's constitutional rights in this case in no way indicates a view that an opportunity for a hearing or a statement of reasons for nonretention would, or would not, be appropriate or wise in public colleges and universities.[460] For it is a written Constitution that we apply. Our role is confined to interpretation of that Constitution.

We must conclude that the summary judgment for the respondent should not have been granted, since the respondent has not shown that he was deprived of liberty or property protected by the Fourteenth Amendment. The judgment of the Court of Appeals, accordingly, is **reversed** and the case is remanded for further proceedings consistent with this opinion. It is so ordered.

Workplace Searches and the 4th Amendment

The Fourth Amendment to the U.S. Constitution prohibits unreasonable searches by government agents and generally requires that a warrant be issued pursuant to a showing of probable cause before a search may be conducted. In **O'CONNOR v. ORTEGA 480 U.S. 709, 107 S.Ct. 1492 (1987)**[461] the Supreme Court held that the 4th Amendment was applicable to workplace searches by public employers and adopted a reasonableness standard for determining the constitutionality of such searches.

The case involved Dr. Ortega, a physician and psychiatrist employed at a state hospital. When hospital officials became concerned that Ortega was involved in various work-related financial and sexual improprieties, they asked him to take a leave of absence during an investigation of the charges against him. While Ortega was on leave, hospital officials conducted a thorough search of his office. The official claimed the search was conducted in order to inventory and secure state property. Ortega contended that the purpose of the search was to obtain evidence for use against him in an administrative disciplinary proceeding. He also claimed that the search violated his fourth amendment rights.

The trial court decided that the warrantless search was reasonable because of the need to secure public property. It granted summary judgment to the hospital officials. The appellate court disagreed. It concluded that the search had violated the fourth amendment. The Supreme Court was widely split. Four justices joined in a plurality opinion expressing the judgment of the Court. Justice Scalia concurred

---

[460] See, e. g., Report of Committee A on Academic Freedom and Tenure, Procedural Standards in the Renewal or Nonrenewal of Faculty Appointments, 56 AAUP Bulletin No. 1, p. 21 (Spring 1970).
[461] See also Valente, William D., "Searches of Teacher Offices, Desks and Files in Public Schools", 39 Ed. Law Rep. 931 (August 20, 1987).

in this judgment, but took issue with some of the reasoning of the plurality. Four justices dissented.

In determining whether Ortega's fourth amendment rights had been violated, the plurality first addressed whether he had a legitimate expectation of privacy at his workplace. As the plurality noted, the fourth amendment protects only "an expectation of privacy that society is prepared to consider reasonable." The plurality defined workplace as those areas and items that are related to work and are generally within the employer's control." At the hospital. for example. the hallways, cafeteria, offices, desks, and file cabinets, among other things, were part of the workplace.

Acknowledging the great variety of work environments in the public sector, the plurality stated that whether an employee has a reasonable expectation of privacy must be evaluated on a case-by-case basis. Some offices and workstations may be so open to fellow employees or the public, the plurality noted. that no expectation of privacy is reasonable. In other workplaces, employees' expectations of privacy may be reduced by virtue of actual office practices and procedures or by the existence of rules or policies concerning the storage of private property on public premises. However, the plurality hastened to add that the absence of such a rule or policy does not create an expectation of privacy where one would not otherwise exist.

All the justices concluded that Ortega had a reasonable expectation of privacy in his office, desk and file cabinets. The following factors were significant: Ortega did not share these facilities with other employees; he had occupied his office for 17 years and consistently maintained personal items there; and the hospital had not established any policy discouraging employees from storing personal papers and effects in their desks or file cabinets. Thus. the justices agreed that the fourth amendment applied and that Ortega was therefore protected from unreasonable searches of his office.

Next, the plurality inquired whether the search conducted by the hospital officials was reasonable. "What is reasonable depends on the context within which a search takes place," the plurality stated. Balancing the invasion of an employee's legitimate expectation of privacy against a public employer's need for supervision, control, and efficiency in its operations, the plurality concluded that the warrant and probable cause requirements were impractical in the workplace—at least where the searches are undertaken for work-related reasons unrelated to illegal conduct or are part of administrative investigations of work-related employee misconduct.

To ensure proper operations, public employers must be given wide latitude to enter employee offices for work-related, noninvestigatory reasons, the plurality stated. Furthermore, public employees are entrusted with great responsibility, and the consequences of their misconduct or incompetence can be severe. The delay caused by a warrant requirement in investigating and correcting employee deficiencies would often result in irreparable damage to the public interest, the plurality concluded.

Compared with the special needs presented by public employment, the plurality found the intrusion on employee privacy "relatively limited." Public offices and workstations are provided to employees solely for the purpose of performing the public's work, the plurality emphasized. The employees may avoid exposing personal belongings simply by leaving them at home. Hence, the plurality adopted the standard of reasonableness under all the circumstances to determine whether workplace searches comport with the fourth amendment.

The standard requires a two-step inquiry. First, there must be reasonable grounds for believing that the search will turn up evidence that the employee is guilty of work-related misconduct or that the search is necessary for a noninvestigatory work-related reason such as to retrieving a document. Second, the search techniques adopted must be reasonably related.to the purpose of the search and not excessively intrusive in light of that purpose. Five of the justices concluded there was insufficient evidence to make these determinations, so they remanded the case for further consideration in light of the guidelines articulated in O'Connor.

The guidelines are not easy to discern. For example, to the four dissenting justices, the nature of public employment offers no compelling reason to dispense entirely with the warrant and probable cause requirements of the fourth amendment. They also disagree with the plurality about the extent to which the operational realities of the workplace may negate an employee's expectation of privacy. Together with Justice Scalia, they appear to form a majority for the view that workplaces should be entitled to fourth amendment protection except under extraordinary circumstances.

Thus, in O'Connor v. Ortega, the U.S. Supreme Court considered the constitutionality of employer-conducted searches of the workplace. The Court decided that public employees may have legitimate expectations of privacy in the workplace, which the Court defined as "those areas and items that are related to work and are generally within the employer's control." Employees that have such legitimate expectations of privacy are protected by the fourth amendment from unreasonable searches by school officials. Ordinarily, a search conducted without a warrant supported by probable cause is presumptively unreasonable. However, the O'Connor Court decided that the importance to the public of efficient operations called for a different standard. To be constitutional, employer-conducted workplace searches must simply be reasonable under all the circumstances both at their inception and in their scope.[462]

Employment Discrimination

Finally, public employers are required to abide by equal employment opportunity laws and refrain from actions which discriminate against employees based on race,[463] age, disability or sex. The following three cases involving age, sex and disability highlight the nature and scope of a school districts responsibility.

---

[462] However, the O'Connor opinion is almost as notable for what it didn't decide as for what it did. It provided little guidance regarding which employees have enforceable expectations of privacy. (This must be determined on a case-by-case basis.) It did not decide what standard applies to workplace searches conducted by or in concert with law enforcement officials. It did not decide what standard applies to the search of personal items like handbags or briefcases that are in the workplace but are not part of it.

Notably, in areas of substantial current interest. the O'Connor decision did not address the issue of drug and alcohol testing of employees. Nor did the opinion indicate whether individualized suspicion is an essential element of the reasonableness standard. Finally, the decision did not discuss whether school officials are entitled to qualified immunity from liability for damages if their search violates the civil rights of an employee.

[463] Title VII of the 1964 Civil Rights Act forbids employment discrimination on the basis of race. The rules regarding employment standards and tests are addressed in Griggs v.Duke Power Co.,401 U.S. 424, 91 S.Ct. 849 (1971); The Court determined that state use of the NTE for certification and as pay purposes met constitutional muster in United States v. South Carolina, 445 F.Supp. 1094, affirmed 343 U.S. 1026, 98 S.Ct. 756 (1978); In Wygant v. Jackson Board of Education, 476 U.S. 267, 106 S.Ct. 1842 (1986) the Court held that a school district layoff policy contained in the district's collective bargaining agreement that resulted in nonminority teachers with more seniority being laid off violated Equal Protection.

CLARKCOUNTY SCHOOL DISTRICT
v.
BEEBE
91 Nev. 165, 533 P.2d 161 (1975)
OPINION

By the Court, MOWBRAY, J.:

The principal issues presented on this appeal are whether the Nevada Fair Employment Practices Act as amended by chapter 577, Statutes of Nevada 1973, has nullified the Clark County School District's policy of forcing the involuntary retirement of its teachers on the sole basis of age, and, if so, when such nullification became effective.

William Beebe, the respondent, had been a teacher in Clark County since 1960. Beebe attained the age of 65 years during the fiscal year ending June 30, 1973. The policy of the Clark County School District, as set forth in District Policy and Regulation 4411, adopted June 25, 1964, provides for compulsory retirement of certified employees at the end of the fiscal year in which the age of 65 is attained.[465] Pursuant to this regulation, Beebe was notified by the District in November 1972 that he would be involuntarily retired in June 1973.

Beebe filed a grievance with the District, objecting to his retirement, on the ground that "[t]his policy, by contract or otherwise, will be against the public policy of the State of Nevada, and contrary to the law at the time grievance's discharge is to be effective."

The District rejected Beebe's grievance, and he filed a writ of review in the district court. The court below found that the District's Regulation 4411 was in direct conflict with the 1973 Nevada Fair Employment Practices Act and, consequently, void. The court ordered Beebe reinstated as a classroom teacher.

Assembly Bill 543 (amending NRS 281.370, among other statutes) was introduced in the Legislature on March 8, 1973. The bill was approved on April 25, 1973, effective July 1, 1973. Stats. Nev. 1973, ch. 577, § 2, at 980-981.[466]Section 2 of NRS 281.370 as amended provides that State, county, or municipal departments, agencies, boards, or appointing officers thereof shall not discharge from employment

---

[464]The Age Discrimination in Employment Act of (1967) (ADEA) 29 U.S.C.A. §621 was the subject of a recent teacher discharge dispute. See Lee v. Rapid City Area School Dist. 51-4, 981 F.2d 316 (8th Cir. 1992) upholding a determination that the school district violated the Act when it discharged the plaintiff teacher.

[465] CIark County School District Policy and Regulation 4411:
"Employees shall he retired at the end of the fiscal year in which age 65 is attained.
"In unique and unusual circumstances a principal or supervisor may submit a request for continuance of employment to the Associate Superintendent, Personnel Services. The request must be approved by the division head involved. Extensions may be granted on a year-by-year basis only."

[466] Stats. Nev. 1973, Ch. 577, § 2, at 980-981:
"SEC. 2. NRS 281.370 is hereby amended to read as follows:
"1. All personnel actions taken by state, county or municipal departments, agencies. boards or appointing officers thereof shall be based solely on merit and fitness.
"2. State, county or municipal departments, agencies, boards or appointing officers thereof shall not:
"(a) Refuse to hire a person because of such persons race, color creed, national origin [or sex,], sex or age, unless based upon a bona fide occupational classification.
"(b) Discharge or bar any person from employment because of such person's race, creed, color, national origin [or sex,], sex or age.
"(c) Discriminate against any person in compensation or in other terms or conditions of employment because of such person's race creed, color, national origin [or sex.], sex or age, except as provided in section 1 of this act

any person because of age. The district court ruled that the amendment nullified the District s Regulation 4411. We agree.

The District argues on appeal that, since NRS 281.370, subsection 2, fails to name specifically school districts as one of the agencies enumerated therein, District is not bound by the age discrimination proscription of the statute. We do not agree. The pertinent language of the statute barring age discrimination is directed to "State, county or municipal departments agencies, boards or appointing officers thereof . . ." (emphasis added). NRS 281.370(2), infra. Certainly, a school district may be considered a municipal department within the meaning of the statute, and the school board, a board within the statute. NRS 43.080 defines a municipality as follows: "'Municipality' means the State of Nevada, or any corporation, instrumentality or other agency thereof, or any incorporated city or town, any unincorporated city or town, or any county school district, . . ." (emphasis added).[467]

We conclude and so hold that District is bound by the mandate of the statute prohibiting age discrimination. Each school district, through its board of trustees, is given such reasonable and necessary powers as may be required to attain the ends for which the public schools are established. NRS 386.350.[468] However, no board of trustees may enforce a policy or rule that is inconsistent with the law. NRS 386.360.[469] This means that school districts may not retire school teachers and certified employees involuntarily on the basis of age. The district may, however, discharge any teacher, regardless of age, upon the grounds enumerated in NRS 391.312.

The court below found that Beebe's retirement began at the end of the fiscal year, on June 30, 1973, or "simultaneously" with the effective date of chapter 577, Statutes of Nevada 1973, July 1, 1973. We disagree. NRS 354.526 defines a fiscal year as the 12-month period beginning on the first day of July and ending on the last day of June.[470] Respondent Beebe suggests that his retirement commenced July 1, 12:00 a.m., and that, therefore, he is covered by the amendment to the statute barring age discrimination. We, however, construe "end of fiscal year" to be June 30, 1973. Otherwise, there would be constant conflict between policies in effect during one fiscal year and amended the following fiscal year.

There is nothing in the statute which indicates either expressly or impliedly that the Legislature intended that it be applied retrospectively. Unless the contrary plainly appears such statutes operate prospectively only.

Construing the applicable legislative pronouncements according to the normal acceptation of their words, we are constrained to hold erroneous the lower court's determination that Beebe's retirement and chapter 577, Statutes of Nevada 1973, were effective at the same moment. If the Legislature wishes to extend the

---

[467] NRS 43.080:
    "'Municipality' means the State of Nevada, or any corporation instrumentality or other agency thereof, or any incorporated city or Town, any unincorporated city or town, or any county, school district conservancy district, drainage district, irrigation district, general improvement district, other corporate district constituting a political subdivision of this state, housing authority, urban renewal authority, other type of authority the University of Nevada, the board of regents of the University of Nevada, or any other body corporate and politic of the State of Nevada, but excluding the Federal Government."

[468] NRS 386.350:
    "Each board of trustees is hereby given such reasonable and necessary powers, not conflicting with the constitution and the laws of the State of Nevada, as may be requisite to attain the ends for which the public schools are established and to promote the welfare of school children, including the establishment and operation of schools and classes deemed necessary and desirable."

[469] NRS 386.360:
    "Each board of trustees shall have the power to prescribe and enforce rules not inconsistent with law or rules prescribed by the state board of education for its own government and the government of public schools under its charge."

[470] NRS 354.526:
    "'Fiscal year' means the 12-month period beginning on the first day of July and ending on the last day of June."

benefits of its 1973 Act to those situated as Beebe, it may adopt appropriate legislation to do so during its current session.

On the basis of the statute as adopted, however, the judgment reinstating Beebe must be reversed.
GUNDERSON, C.J., and BATJER, ZENOFF, and THOMPSON, JJ., concur.

Sex Discrimination [471]

MERITOR SAVINGS BANK[472]
v.
VINSON
477 U.S. 57, 106 S.Ct. 2399 (1986)

JUSTICE REHNQUIST delivered the opinion of the Court.

This case presents important questions concerning claims of workplace "sexual harassment" brought under Title VII of the Civil Rights Act of 1964, 78 Stat. 253, as amended, 42 U. S. C. §2000e et seq.

I

In 1974, respondent Mechelle Vinson met Sidney Taylor, a vice president of what is now petitioner Meritor Savings Bank (bank) and manager of one of its branch offices. When respondent asked whether she might obtain employment at the bank, Taylor gave her an application, which she completed and returned the next day; later that same day Taylor called her to say that she had been hired. With Taylor as her supervisor, respondent started as a teller-trainee, and thereafter was promoted to teller, head teller, and assistant branch manager. She worked at the same branch for four years, and it is undisputed that her advancement there was based on merit alone. In September 1978, respondent notified Taylor that she was taking sick leave for an indefinite period. On November 1, 1978, the bank discharged her for excessive use of that leave.

Respondent brought this action against Taylor and the bank, claiming that during her four years at the bank she had "constantly been subjected to sexual harassment" by Taylor in violation of Title VII. She sought injunctive relief, compensatory and punitive damages against Taylor and the bank, and attorney's fees.

At the 11-day bench trial, the parties presented conflicting testimony about Taylor's behavior during respondent's employment. Respondent testified that during her probationary period as a teller-trainee, Taylor treated her in a fatherly way and made no sexual advances. Shortly thereafter, however, he invited her out to dinner and, during the course of the meal, suggested that they go to a motel to

---

[471]The Civil Rights Act of 1991 significantly expands the potential exposure of employers to discrimination suits by permitting those alleging intentional discrimination based on religion, sex, national origin or physical or mental disability access to jury trials and punitive and compensatory damages. The Act also permits prevailing plaintiffs to recover expert witness fees, extends certain statutes of limitation and for the first time, applies a variety of equal employment obligaitons to members of Congress. See Hotvedt, Richard, et al., "The Civil Rights Act of 1991," 71 Ed.Law Rep. [361] (February 13, 1992).

[472] In Cleveland Board of Education v. LaFleur 414 U.S. 632, 94 S.Ct. 791(1974), the Supreme Court declared unconstitutional a school board policy which required that all pregnant teachers cease teaching at the fourth or fifth month of pregnancy and forbid return to the classroom until three months after the child's birth. The Court determined that the conclusive presumptions of fitness included in the policy violated the due process clause of the 14th Amendment. A recent report assessing gender discrimination in education was just released. See "How Schools Shortchange Women: The AAUW Report," American Association of University Women Educational Foundation, (1992) discussed in Chira, Susan, "Bias Against Girls is Found Rife in Schools, with Lasting Damage," New York Times, February 12, 1992, p. 1 A.

have sexual relations. At first she refused, but out of what she described as fear of losing her job she eventually agreed. According to respondent, Taylor thereafter made repeated demands upon her for sexual favors, usually at the branch, both during and after business hours; she estimated that over the next several years she had intercourse with him some 40 or 50 times. In addition, respondent testified that Taylor fondled her in front of other employees, followed her into the women's restroom when she went there alone, exposed himself to her, and even forcibly raped her on several occasions. These activities ceased after 1977, respondent stated, when she started going with a steady boyfriend.

Respondent also testified that Taylor touched and fondled other women employees of the bank, and she attempted to call witnesses to support this charge. But while some supporting testimony apparently was admitted without objection, the District Court did not allow her "to present wholesale evidence of a pattern and practice relating to sexual advances to other female employees in her case in chief, but advised her that she might well be able to present such evidence in rebuttal to the defendants' cases." Respondent did not offer such evidence in rebuttal. Finally, respondent testified that because she was afraid of Taylor she never reported his harassment to any of his supervisors and never attempted to use the bank's complaint procedure.

Taylor denied respondent's allegations of sexual activity, testifying that he never fondled her, never made suggestive remarks to her, never engaged in sexual intercourse with her, and never asked her to do so. He contended instead that respondent made her accusations in response to a business-related dispute. The bank also denied respondent's allegations and asserted that any sexual harassment by Taylor was unknown to the bank and engaged in without its consent or approval.

The District Court denied relief... It found instead that

> "[i]f [respondent] and Taylor did engage in an intimate or sexual relationship during the time of [respondent's] employment with [the bank], that relationship was a voluntary one having nothing to do with her continued employment at [the bank] or her advancement or promotions at that institution." The court ultimately found that respondent "was not the victim of sexual harassment and was not the victim of sexual discrimination" while employed at the bank.

Although it concluded that respondent had not proved a violation of Title VII, the District Court nevertheless went on to address the bank's liability. After noting the bank's express policy against discrimination, and finding that neither respondent nor any other employee had ever lodged a complaint about sexual harassment by Taylor, the court ultimately concluded that "the bank was without notice and cannot be held liable for the alleged actions of Taylor."

The Court of Appeals for the District of Columbia Circuit reversed. Relying on its earlier holding in Bundy v. Jackson,... the court stated that a violation of Title VII may be predicated on either of two types of sexual harassment: harassment that involves the conditioning of concrete employment benefits on sexual favors, and harassment that, while not affecting economic benefits, creates a hostile or offensive working environment. The court drew additional support for this position from the Equal Employment Opportunity Commission's Guidelines on Discrimination Because of Sex, 29 CFR §1604.11(a) (1985), which set out these two types of sexual harassment claims. Believing that "Vinson's grievance was clearly of the [hostile environment] type," and that the District Court had not considered whether a violation of this type had occurred, the court concluded that a remand was necessary.

The court further concluded that the District Court's finding that any sexual relationship between respondent and Taylor "was a voluntary one" did not obviate the need for a remand. "[U]ncertain as to precisely what the [district] court meant" by this finding, the Court of Appeals held that if the evidence otherwise showed that "Taylor made Vinson's toleration of sexual harassment a condition of her employment," her voluntariness "had no materiality whatsoever." The court then surmised that the District Court's finding of voluntariness might have been based on "the voluminous testimony regarding respondent's dress and personal fantasies," testimony that the Court of Appeals believed "had no place in this litigation."

As to the bank's liability, the Court of Appeals held that an employer is absolutely liable for sexual harassment practiced by supervisory personnel, whether or not the employer knew or should have known about the misconduct. The court relied chiefly on Title VII's definition of "employer" to include "any agent of such a person," 42 U. S. C. § 2000e(b), as well as on the EEOC Guidelines. The court held that a supervisor is an "agent" of his employer for Title VII purposes, even if he lacks authority to hire, fire, or promote, since "the mere existence—or even the appearance—of a significant degree of influence in vital job decisions gives any supervisor the opportunity to impose on employees."

In accordance with the foregoing, the Court of Appeals reversed the judgment of the District Court and remanded the case for further proceedings. ...We granted certiorari, and now affirm but for different reasons.

II

Title VII of the Civil Rights Act of 1964 makes it "an unlawful employment practice for an employer . . . to discriminate against any individual with respect to his compensation, terms, conditions, or privileges of employment, because of such individual's race, color, religion, sex, or national origin." 42 U. S. C. §2000e-2(a)(1). The prohibition against discrimination based on sex was added to Title VII at the last minute on the floor of the House of Representatives. The principal argument in opposition to the amendment was that "sex discrimination" was sufficiently different from other types of discrimination that it ought to receive separate legislative treatment. This argument was defeated, the bill quickly passed as amended, and we are left with little legislative history to guide us in interpreting the Act's prohibition against discrimination based on "sex."

Respondent argues, and the Court of Appeals held, that unwelcome sexual advances that create an offensive or hostile working environment violate Title VII. Without question, when a supervisor sexually harasses a subordinate because of the subordinate's sex, that supervisor "discriminate[s]" on the basis of sex. Petitioner apparently does not challenge this proposition. It contends instead that in prohibiting discrimination with respect to "compensation, terms, conditions, or privileges" of employment, Congress was concerned with what petitioner describes as "tangible loss" of "an economic character," not "purely psychological aspects of the workplace environment." In support of this claim petitioner observes that in both the legislative history of Title VII and this Court's Title VII decisions, the focus has been on tangible, economic barriers erected by discrimination.

We reject petitioner's view. First, the language of Title VII is not limited to "economic" or "tangible" discrimination. The phrase "terms, conditions, or privileges of employment" evinces a congressional intent " 'to strike at the entire spectrum of disparate treatment of men and women'" in employment. Petitioner has pointed to nothing in the Act to suggest that Congress contemplated the limitation urged here.

Second, in 1980 the EEOC issued Guidelines specifying that "sexual harassment," as there defined, is a form of sex discrimination prohibited by Title VII. As an "administrative interpretation of the Act by the enforcing agency," these Guidelines, " 'while not controlling upon the courts by reason of their authority, do constitute a body of experience and informed judgment to which courts and litigants may properly resort for guidance.'" The EEOC Guidelines fully support the view that harassment leading to noneconomic injury can violate Title VII.

In defining "sexual harassment," the Guidelines first describe the kinds of workplace conduct that may be actionable under Title VII. These include "[u]nwelcome sexual advances, requests for sexual favors, and other verbal or physical conduct of a sexual nature." Relevant to the charges at issue in this case, the Guidelines provide that such sexual misconduct constitutes prohibited "sexual harassment," whether or not it is directly linked to the grant or denial of an economic quid pro quo, where "such conduct has the purpose or effect of unreasonably interfering with an individual's work performance or creating an intimidating, hostile, or offensive working environment."

In concluding that so-called "hostile environment" (i. e., non quid pro quo) harassment violates Title VII, the EEOC drew upon a substantial body of judicial decisions and EEOC precedent holding that Title VII affords employees the right to work in an environment free from discriminatory intimidation, ridicule, and insult. ...Courts applied this principle to harassment based on race, e. g., Firefighters Institute for Racial Equality v. St. Louis(1977); Gray v. Greyhound Lines, East, (1976), religion, (SD Ohio 1976), and national origin, Cariddi v. Kansas City Chiefs Football Club (CA8 1977). Nothing in Title VII suggests that a hostile environment based on discriminatory sexual harassment should not be likewise prohibited. The Guidelines thus appropriately drew from, and were fully consistent with, the existing case law.

Since the Guidelines were issued, courts have uniformly held, and we agree, that a plaintiff may establish a violation of Title VII by proving that discrimination based on sex has created a hostile or abusive work environment.

> "Sexual harassment which creates a hostile or offensive environment for members of one sex is every bit the arbitrary barrier to sexual equality at the workplace that racial harassment is to racial equality. Surely, a requirement that a man or woman run a gauntlet of sexual abuse in return for the privilege of being allowed to work and make a living can be as demeaning and disconcerting as the harshest of racial epithets."

Of course,... not all workplace conduct that may be described as "harassment" affects a "term, condition, or privilege" of employment within the meaning of Title VII. ("mere utterance of an ethnic or racial epithet which engenders offensive feelings in an employee" would not affect the conditions of employment to sufficiently significant degree to violate Title VII). For sexual harassment to be actionable, it must be sufficiently severe or pervasive "to alter the conditions of [the victim's] employment and create an abusive working environment." Respondent's allegations in this case—which include not only pervasive harassment but also criminal conduct of the most serious nature—are plainly sufficient to state a claim for "hostile environment" sexual harassment.

The question remains, however, whether the District Court's ultimate finding that respondent "was not the victim of sexual harassment," effectively disposed of respondent's claim.

****

...The gravamen of any sexual harassment claim is that the alleged sexual advances were "unwelcome." While the question whether particular conduct was indeed unwelcome presents difficult problems of proof and turns largely on credibility determinations committed to the trier of fact, the District Court in this case erroneously focused on the "voluntariness" of respondent's participation in the claimed sexual episodes. The correct inquiry is whether respondent by her conduct indicated that the alleged sexual advances were unwelcome, not whether her actual participation in sexual intercourse was voluntary.

Petitioner contends that even if this case must be remanded to the District Court, the Court of Appeals erred in one of the terms of its remand. Specifically, the Court of Appeals states that testimony about respondent's "dress and personal fantasies, which the District Court apparently admitted into evidence, "had no place in this litigation." Ibid. The apparent ground for this conclusion was that respondent's voluntariness vel non in submitting to Taylor's advances was immaterial to her sexual harassment claim. While "voluntariness" in the sense of consent is not a defense to such a claim, it does not follow that a complainant's sexually provocative speech or dress is irrelevant as a matter of law in determining whether he or she found particular sexual advances unwelcome. To the contrary, such evidence is obviously relevant. The EEOC Guidelines emphasize that the trier of fact must determine the existence of sexual harassment in light of "the record as a whole" and "the totality of circumstances, such as the nature of the sexual advances and the context in which the alleged incidents occurred." Respondent's claim that any marginal relevance of the evidence in question was outweighed by the potential for unfair prejudice is the sort of argument properly addressed to the District Court. In this case the District Court concluded that the evidence should be admitted, and the Court of Appeals' contrary conclusion was based upon the erroneous, categorical view that testimony about provocative dress and publicly expressed sexual fantasies "had no place in this litigation." While the District Court must carefully weigh the applicable considerations in deciding whether to admit evidence of this kind, there is no per se rule against its admissibility.

III
****

The EEOC, in its brief as amicus curiae, contends that courts formulating employer liability rules should draw from traditional agency principles. Examination of those principles has led the EEOC to the view that where a supervisor exercises the authority actually delegated to him by his employer, by making or threatening to make decisions affecting the employment status of his subordinates, such actions are properly imputed to the employer whose delegation of authority empowered the supervisor to undertake them. Thus, the courts have consistently held employers liable for the discriminatory discharges of employees by supervisory personnel, whether or not the employer knew, should have known, or approved of the supervisor's actions.

The EEOC suggests that when a sexual harassment claim rests exclusively on a "hostile environment" theory, however, the usual basis for a finding of agency will often disappear. In that case, the EEOC believes, agency principles lead to

> "a rule that asks whether a victim of sexual harassment had reasonably available an avenue of complaint regarding such harassment, and, if available and utilized, whether that procedure was reasonably responsive to the employee's complaint. If the employer has an expressed policy against sexual harassment and has implemented a procedure specifically designed to resolve sexual harassment claims, and if the victim does not take advantage of that procedure, the employer should be shielded from liability absent actual knowledge of the sexually hostile environment (obtained, e. g., by the filing of a charge with the EEOC or a comparable state agency). In all other cases, the employer will be liable if it has actual knowledge of the harassment or if, considering all the facts of the case, the victim in question had no reasonably available avenue for making his or her complaint known to appropriate management officials."

****

We, therefore, decline the parties' invitation to issue a definitive rule on employer liability, but we do agree with the EEOC that Congress wanted courts to look to agency principles for guidance in this area. While such common-law principles may not be transferable in all their particulars to Title VII, Congress' decision to define "employer" to include any "agent" of an employer, 42 U. S. C. §2000e(b), surely evinces an intent to place some limits on the acts of employees for which employers under Title VII are to be held responsible. For this reason, we hold that the Court of Appeals erred in concluding that employers are always automatically liable for sexual harassment by their supervisors. For the same reason, absence of notice to an employer does not necessarily insulate that employer from liability.

Finally, we reject petitioner's view that the mere existence of a grievance procedure and a policy against discrimination, coupled with respondent's failure to invoke that procedure, must insulate petitioner from liability. While those facts are plainly relevant, the situation before us demonstrates why they are not necessarily dispositive. Petitioner's general nondiscrimination policy did not address sexual harassment in particular, and thus did not alert employees to their employer's interest in correcting that form of discrimination. Moreover, the bank's grievance procedure apparently required an employee to complain first to her supervisor, in this case Taylor. Since Taylor was the alleged perpetrator, it is not altogether surprising that respondent failed to invoke the procedure and report her grievance to him. Petitioner's contention that respondent's failure should insulate it from liability might be substantially stronger if its procedures were better calculated to encourage victims of harassment to come forward.

IV

In sum, we hold that a claim of "hostile environment" sex discrimination is actionable under Title VII, that the District Court's findings were insufficient to dispose of respondent's hostile environment claim, and that the District Court did not err in admitting testimony about respondent's sexually provocative speech and dress. As to employer liability, we conclude that the Court of Appeals was wrong to

196

entirely disregard agency principles and impose absolute liability on employers for the acts of their supervisors, regardless of the circumstances of a particular case.

Accordingly, the judgment of the Court of Appeals reversing the judgment of the District Court is **affirmed,** and the case is remanded for further proceedings consistent with this opinion. It is so ordered.

****

The Supreme Court revisited the issue of sexual harrassment in the workplace in the case entitled **Harris v. Forklift Systems**.[473]

HARRIS
v.
FORKLIFT SYSTEMS INC.
___ U.S.___, 62 LW 4004 (1993)

JUSTICE O'CONNOR delivered the opinion of the Court.

In this case we consider the definition of a discriminatorily "abusive work environment" (also known as a "hostile work environment") under Title VII of the Civil Rights Act of 1964, 78 Stat. 253, as amended, 42 U. S. C. §2000e et seq. (1988 ed., Supp. III).

I

Teresa Harris worked as a manager at Forklift Systems, Inc., an equipment rental company, from April 1985 until October 1987. Charles Hardy was Forklift's president.

The Magistrate found that, throughout Harris' time at Forklift, Hardy often insulted her because of her gender and often made her the target of unwanted sexual innuendos. Hardy told Harris on several occasions, in the presence of other employees, "You're a woman, what do you know" and "We need a man as the rental manager"; at least once, he told her she was "a dumb ass woman." App. to Pet. for Cert. A-13. Again in front of others, he suggested that the two of them "go to the Holiday Inn to negotiate [Harris'] raise." Id., at A-14. Hardy occasionally asked Harris and other female employees to get coins from his front pants pocket. Ibid. He threw objects on the ground in front of Harris and other women, and asked them to pick the objects up. Id., at A-14 to A-15. He made sexual innuendos about Harris' and other women's clothing. Id., at A-15.

In mid-August 1987, Harris complained to Hardy about his conduct. Hardy said he was surprised that Harris was offended, claimed he was only joking, and apologized. Id., at A-16. He also promised he would stop, and based on this assurance Harris stayed on the job. Ibid. But in early September, Hardy began anew: While Harris was arranging a deal with one of Forklift's customers, he asked her, again in front of other employees, "What did you do, promise the guy . . . some [sex] Saturday night?" Id., at A-17. On October 1, Harris collected her paycheck and quit.

Harris then sued Forklift, claiming that Hardy's conduct had created an abusive work environment for her because of her gender. The United States District Court for the Middle District of Tennessee, adopting the report and

---

[473]Harris v. Forklift Systems Inc.,__ U.S.__, 62 LW 4004 (1993). The legal affairs editor of The New Republic, Jeffrey Rosen, was highly critical of the Courts decision. "Short, polemical, and hastily written, it reads like the worst sort of opinion journalism," he wrote. See Rosen, Jeffrey, "Fast Food Justice," New York Times, Nov. 11, 1993 p. 17 A. What is your reaction to the opinion?

recommendation of the Magistrate, found this to be "a close case," id., at A-31, but held that Hardy's conduct did not create an abusive environment. The court found that some of Hardy's comments "offended [Harris], and would offend the reasonable woman," id., at A-33, but that they were not

> "so severe as to be expected to seriously affect [Harris'] psychological well-being. A reasonable woman manager under like circumstances would have been offended by Hardy, but his conduct would not have risen to the level of interfering with that person's work performance.
>
> "Neither do I believe that [Harris] was subjectively so offended that she suffered injury .... Although Hardy may at times have genuinely offended [Harris], I do not believe that he created a working environment so poisoned as to be intimidating or abusive to [Harris]" Id., at A-34 to A-35.

In focusing on the employee's psychological well-being, the District Court was following Circuit precedent. See Rabidue v. Osceola Refining Co., 805 F. 2d 611, 620 (CA6 1986), cert. denied, 481 U. S. 1041 (1987). The United States Court of Appeals for the Sixth Circuit affirmed in a brief unpublished decision. We granted certiorari, 507 U. S.___(1993), to resolve a conflict among the Circuits on whether conduct, to be actionable as "abusive work environment" harassment (no quid pro quo harassment issue is present here), must "seriously affect [an employee's] psychological well-being" or lead the plaintiff to suffe[r] injury." Compare Rabidue (requiring serious effect on psychological well-being); Vance v. Southern Bell Telephone & Telegraph Co., 863 F. 2d 1503, 1510 (CA11 1989) (same); and Downes v. FAA, 775 F. 2d 288, 292 (CA Fed. 1985) (same), with Ellison v. Brady, 924 F. 2d 872, 877-878 (CA9 1991) (rejecting such a requirement).

Title VII of the Civil Rights Act of 1964 makes it "an unlawful employment practice for an employer . . . to discriminate against any individual with respect to his compensation, terms, conditions, or privileges of employment, because of such individual's race, color, religion, sex, or national origin." 42 U. S. C. §2000e-2(a)(1). As we made clear in Meritor Savings Bank v. Vinson, 477 U. S. 57 (1986), this language "is not limited to 'economic' or 'tangible' discrimination. The phrase 'terms, conditions, or privileges of employment' evinces a congressional intent 'to strike at the entire spectrum of disparate treatment of men and women' in employment," which includes requiring people to work in a discriminatorily hostile or abusive environment. Id., at 64, quoting Los Angeles Dept. of Water and Power v. Manhart, 435 U. S. 702, 707, n. 13 (1978) (some internal quotation marks omitted). When the workplace is permeated with "discriminatory intimidation, ridicule, and insult," 477 U. S., at 65, that is "sufficiently severe or pervasive to alter the conditions of the victim's employment and create an abusive working environment," id., at 67 (internal brackets and quotation marks omitted), Title VII is violated.

This standard, which we reaffirm today, takes a middle path between making actionable any conduct that is merely offensive and requiring the conduct to cause a tangible psychological injury. As we pointed out in Meritor, "mere utterance of an . . . epithet which engenders offensive feelings in a employee," ibid. (internal quotation marks omitted) does not sufficiently affect the conditions of employment to implicate Title VII. Conduct that is not severe or pervasive enough to create an objectively hostile or abusive work environment-an environment that a reasonable person would find hostile or abusive—is beyond Title VII's purview. Likewise, if the victim does not subjectively perceive the environment to be abusive, the conduct has not actually altered the conditions of the victim's employment, and there is no Title VII violation.

But Title VII comes into play before the harassing conduct leads to a nervous breakdown. A discriminatorily abusive work environment, even one that does not seriously affect employees' psychological well-being, can and often will detract from employees' job performance, discourage employees from remaining on the job, or keep them from advancing in their careers. Moreover, even without regard to these tangible effects, the very fact that the discriminatory conduct was so severe or pervasive that it created a work environment abusive to employees because of their race, gender, religion, or national origin offends Title VII's broad rule of workplace equality. The appalling conduct alleged in <u>Meritor</u>, and the reference in that case to environments "'so heavily polluted with discrimination as to destroy completely the emotional and psychological stability of minority group workers,'" supra, at 66, quoting <u>Rogers</u> <u>v.</u> <u>EEOC</u>, 454 F. 2d 234, 238 (CA5 1971), cert. denied, 406 U. S. 957 (1972), merely present some especially egregious examples of harassment. They do not mark the boundary of what is actionable.

We therefore believe the District Court erred in relying on whether the conduct seriously affect[ed] plaintiff's psychological well-being" or led her to "suffe[r] injury." Such an inquiry may needlessly focus the fact finder's attention on concrete psychological harm, an element Title VII does not require. Certainly Title VII bars conduct that would seriously affect a reasonable person's psychological well-being, but the statute is not limited to such conduct. So long as the environment would reasonably be perceived, and is perceived, as hostile or abusive, Meritor, supra, at 67, there is no need for it also to be psychologically injurious.

This is not, and by its nature cannot be, a mathematically precise test. We need not answer today all the potential questions it raises, nor specifically address the EEOC's new regulations on this subject, see 58 Fed. Reg. 51266 (1993) (proposed 29 CFR §§1609.1, 1609.2); see also 29 CFR §1604.11 (1993). But we can say that whether an environment is "hostile" or "abusive" can be determined only by looking at all the circumstances. These may include the frequency of the discriminatory conduct; its severity; whether it is physically threatening or humiliating, or a mere offensive utterance; and whether it unreasonably interferes with an employee's work performance. The effect on the employee's psychological well-being is, of course, relevant to determining whether the plaintiff actually found the environment abusive. But while psychological harm, like any other relevant factor, may be taken into account, no single factor is required.

II

Forklift, while conceding that a requirement that the conduct seriously affect psychological well-being is unfounded, argues that the District Court nonetheless correctly applied the Meritor standard. We disagree. Though the District Court did conclude that the work environment was not "intimidating or abusive to [Harris]," App. to Pet. for Cert. A-35, it did so only after finding that the conduct was not "so severe as to be expected to seriously affect plaintiff's psychological well-being," id., at A-34, and that Harris was not "subjectively so offended that she suffered injury," ibid. The District Court's application of these incorrect standards may well have influenced its ultimate conclusion, especially given that the court found this to be a "close case," id., at A-3 1.

We therefore reverse the judgment of the Court of Appeals, and remand the case for further proceedings consistent with this opinion. **So ordered**

JUSTICE SCALIA, concurring.

Meritor Savings Bank v. Vinson, 477 U. S. 57 (1986), held that Title VII prohibits sexual harassment that takes the form of a hostile work environment. The Court stated that sexual harassment is actionable if it is "sufficiently severe or pervasive 'to alter the conditions of [the victim's] employment and create an abusive work environment.'" Id., at 67 (quoting Henson v. Dundee, 682 F. 2d 897, 904 (CA 11 1982)). Today's opinion elaborates that the challenged conduct must be severe or pervasive enough "to create an objectively hostile or abusive work environment—an environment that a reasonable person would find hostile or abusive." Ante, at 4.

"Abusive" (or "hostile," which in this context I take to mean the same thing) does not seem to me a very clear standard—and I do not think clarity is at all increased by adding the adverb "objectively" or by appealing to a reasonable person's" notion of what the vague word means. Today's opinion does list a number of factors that contribute to abusiveness, see ante, at 5, but since it neither says how much of each is necessary (an impossible task) nor identifies any single factor as determinative, it thereby adds little certitude. As a practical matter, today's holding lets virtually unguided juries decide whether sex-related conduct engaged in (or permitted by) an employer is egregious enough to warrant an award of damages. One might say that what constitutes "negligence" (a traditional jury question) is not much more clear and certain than what constitutes "abusiveness." Perhaps so. But the class of plaintiffs seeking to recover for negligence is limited to those who have suffered harm, whereas under this statute "abusiveness" is to be the test of whether legal harm has been suffered, opening more expansive vistas of litigation.

Be that as it may, I know of no alternative to the course the Court today has taken. One of the factors mentioned in the Court's nonexhaustive list—whether the conduct unreasonably interferes with an employee's work performance—would, if it were made an absolute test, provide greater guidance to juries and employers. But I see no basis for such a limitation in the language of the statute. Accepting Meritor's interpretation of the term "conditions of employment" as the law, the test is not whether work has been impaired, but whether working conditions have been discriminatorily altered. I know of no test more faithful to the inherently vague statutory language than the one the Court today adopts. For these reasons, I join the opinion of the Court.

JUSTICE GINSBURG concurring.

Today the Court reaffirms the holding of Meritor Savings Bank v. Vinson, 477 U. S. 57, 66 (1986): "[A] plaintiff may establish a violation of Title VII by proving that discrimination based on sex has created a hostile or abusive work environment." The critical issue, Title VII's text indicates, is whether members of one sex are exposed to disadvantageous terms or conditions of employment to which members of the other sex are not exposed. See 42 U. S. C. §2000e-2(a)(1) (declaring that it is unlawful to discriminate with respect to, inter alia, "terms" or "conditions" of employment). As the Equal Employment Opportunity Commission emphasized, see Brief for United States and Equal Employment Opportunity Commission as Amici Curiae 9-14, the adjudicator's inquiry should center, dominantly, on whether the discriminatory conduct has unreasonably interfered with the plaintiff's work performance. To show such interference, "the plaintiff need not prove that his or her tangible productivity has declined as a result of the harassment." Davis v. Monsanto Chemical Co., 858 F. 2d 345, 349 (CA6 1988). It suffices to prove that a reasonable person subjected to the discriminatory conduct would find, as the plaintiff did, that the harassment so altered working conditions as to "ma[k]e it more difficult to do the job." See ibid. Davis concerned race-based discrimination, but that difference does not alter the analysis; except in the rare case in which a bona fide occupational qualification is shown, see Automobile Workers v. Johnson Controls, Inc., 499 U. S. 187, 200-207 (1991) (construing 42 U. S. C. §2000e-2(e)(1)), Title VII declares discriminatory practices based on race, gender, religion, or national origin equally unlawful.** The Court's opinion, which I join, seems to me in harmony with the view expressed in this concurring statement.

Disability Discrimination [474]

CHALK
v.
ORANGE COUNTY SUPERINTENDENT OF SCHOOLS
840 F.2d 701 (9th Cir. 1988)

Before SNEED, SKOPIL and POOLE, Circuit Judge .
POOLE, Circuit Judge:

Petitioner Vincent L. Chalk is a certified teacher of hearing-impaired students in the Orange County Department of Education. In February of 1987, Chalk was diagnosed as having Acquired Immune Deficiency Syndrome (AIDS). Subsequently, the Department reassigned Chalk to an administrative position and barred him from teaching in the classroom. Chalk then filed this action in the district court, claiming that the Department's action violated §504 of the Rehabilitation Act of 1973, 29 U.S.C.A. §794 (West Supp.1987), as amended, which proscribes recipients of federal funds from discrimination against otherwise qualified handicapped persons.

Chalk's motion for a preliminary injunction ordering his reinstatement was denied by the district court, and Chalk brought this appeal. After hearing oral argument, we issued an order reversing the district court and directing it to issue the preliminary injunction. In this opinion we now set forth in full the reasons underlying our reversal.

FACTS AND PROCEEDINGS BELOW

Petitioner Chalk has been teaching hearing-impaired students in the Orange County schools for approximately six years. In February 1987, Chalk was hospitalized with pneumocystis carinii pneumonia and was diagnosed as having AIDS. On April 20, after eight weeks of treatment and recuperation, he was found

---

** Indeed, even under the Court's equal protection jurisprudence, which requires "an exceedingly persuasive justification" for a gender-based classification, Kirchberg v. Feenstra, 450 U. S. 455, 461 (1981) (internal quotation marks omitted), it remains an open question whether "classifications based upon gender are inherently suspect." See Mississippi Univ. for Women v. Hogan, 458 U. S. 718, 724, and n. 9 (1982).

[474] Applicable Federal statutes include Sec. 504 of the Rehabilitation Act (1973) prohibiting discrimination by reason of handicap under any program or activity receiving Federal financial assistance. (Section 504 is patterned after Title VI of the Civil Rights Act of 1964, 42 USC §2000d [race discrimination], and Title IX of the Education Amendments of 1972, 29 USC §1681[sex discrimination]) and The Americans with Disabilities Act 42 USC §12101 et seq passed in 1990. ADA is a comprehensive nondiscrimination statute that prohibits various programs from discriminating on the basis of disability. Chapter 218 Laws of Nevada (1993) amends various Nevada statutes to bring them into conformity with The Americans with Disabilities Act. (Chapter 284 NRS, Chapter 245 NRS, Chapter 268 NRS)

fit for duty and released to return to work by his personal physician, Dr. Andrew Siskind. The Department, however, placed him on administrative leave pending the opinion of Dr. Thomas J. Prendergast, the Director of Epidemiology and Disease Control for the Orange County Health Care Agency. On May 22, Dr Prendergast informed the Department that "[n]othing in his [Chalk's] role as a teacher should place his students or others in the school at any risk of acquiring HIV infection."

Chalk agreed to remain on administrative leave through the end of the school year in June. On August 5, Chalk and representatives of the Department met to discuss his return to the classroom. The Department offered Chalk an administrative position at the same rate of pay and benefits, with the option of working either at the Department's offices or at his home, and informed him that if he insisted on returning to the classroom, it would file an action for declaratory relief. Chalk refused the offer.   On August 18, Chalk moved for a preliminary injunction ordering the Department to reinstate him to his classroom duties pending trial. At a hearing on September 8, the district court denied the motion. Following the ruling, the Department reassigned Chalk to an administrative position coordinating grant applications and educational materials for the hearing-impaired program. A panel of this court denied Chalk's emergency petition for an injunction pending appeal. We heard oral argument on November 10, and on November 18 we issued an order reversing the district court with this fuller statement of our reasons to follow.

STANDARD OF REVIEW

The grant of denial of a motion for a preliminary injunction lies within the discretion of the district court, and its order will be reversed only if the court relied on an erroneous legal premise or otherwise abused its discretion. To determine whether there has been an abuse of discretion the reviewing court must consider "whether the decision was based on a consideration of the relevant factors and whether there has been a clear error of judgment." An order is reversible for legal error if the court did not apply the correct preliminary injunction standard, of if the court misapprehended the law with respect to the underlying issues in the litigation. An abuse of discretion may also occur when the district court rests its conclusions on clearly erroneous findings of fact. A finding of fact is clearly erroneous when "the reviewing court on the entire evidence is left with the definite and firm conviction that a mistake has been committed."

APPLICATION OF THE PRELIMINARY INJUNCTION STANDARD

The basic function of a preliminary injunction is to preserve the status quo pending a determination of the action on the merits. The moving party may meet its burden by demonstration either (1) a combination of probable success on the merits and the possibility of irreparable injury or (2) that serious questions are raised and the balance of hardships tips sharply in its favor. "These are not separate tests, but the outer reaches 'of a single continuum.'" We will examine each of the elements in turn.

1.Probable Success on the Merits

Chalk bases his claim on section 504 of the Rehabilitation Act of 1973, 29 U.S.C.§794, as amended (the Act), which provides:

> No otherwise qualified individual with handicaps... shall, solely
> by reason of his handicap, be excluded from the participation in ... or be

subjected to discrimination under any program or activity receiving Federal financial assistance...

As the district court recognized, the Supreme Court recently held that section 504 is fully applicable to individuals who suffer from contagious diseases. School Bd. of Nassau County v. Arline ___U.S. ___,107 S.Ct. 1123 (1987). Arline involved a school teacher who was discharged after contracting tuberculosis. She sued the school authorities claiming unlawful discrimination in violation of section 504. ...The Court of Appeals for the Eleventh Circuit held that persons with contagious diseases were within the Act's coverage. The Supreme Court granted Certiorari and affirmed the court of appeals in an opinion by Justice Brennan.

In its opinion, the Court addressed the question which is of central importance to this case: under what circumstances may a person handicapped with a contagious disease be "otherwise qualified" within the meaning of section 504? Relying on its earlier opinion in Southeastern Community College v. Davis (1979) the Court said;

> An otherwise qualified person is one who is able to meet all of a program's requirements in spite of his handicap. In the employment context, an otherwise qualified person is one who can perform "the essential functions" of the job in question. When a handicapped person is not able to perform the essential functions of the job, the court must also consider whether any "reasonable accommodation" by the employer would enable the handicapped person to perform those functions. Accommodation is not reasonable if it either imposes "undue financial and administrative burdens" on a grantee, or requires a "fundamental alteration in the nature of [the] program."

In applying this standard to the facts before it the Court recognized the difficult circumstances which confront a handicapped person, an employer, and the public in dealing with the possibility of contagion in the workplace. The problem is in reconciling the needs for protection of other persons, continuation of the work mission, and reasonable accommodation--if possible ---of the afflicted individual. The court effected this reconciliation by formulating a standard for determining when a contagious disease would prevent an individual from being "otherwise qualified":

> A person who poses a significant risk of communicating an infectious disease to others in the workplace will not be otherwise qualified for his or her job if reasonable accommodation will not eliminate that risk. The Act would not require a school board to place a teacher with active, contagious tuberculosis in a classroom with elementary school children. Id. at 1131 n. 16.

The application of this standard requires, in most cases, an individualized inquiry and appropriate findings of fact, so that "§ 504 [may] achieve its goal of protection handicapped individuals from deprivations based on prejudice, stereotypes, or unfounded fear, while giving appropriate weight to such legitimate concerns of grantees as avoiding exposing others to significant health and safety risks." Specifically, Arline requires a trial court to make findings regarding four factors: "(a) the nature of the risk (how the disease is transmitted), (b) the duration of the risk (how long is the carrier infectious). (c) the severity of the risk (what is the potential harm to the third parties) and (d) the probabilities the disease will be transmitted and will cause varying degrees of harm." Findings regarding these factors should be based "on reasonable medical judgments given the state of medical knowledge," and the courts should give particular deference to the judgments of public health officials.

Chalk submitted in evidence to the district court, and that court accepted, more than 100 articles from prestigious medical journals and the declarations of five experts on AIDS, including two public health officials of Los Angeles county. Those submissions reveal an overwhelming evidentiary consensus of medical and scientific opinion regarding the nature and transmission of AIDS. AIDS is caused by infection of the individual with HIV, a retrovirus that penetrates chromosomes of certain human cells that combat infection throughout the body. Individuals who become infected with HIV may remain without symptoms for an extended period of time.[475] When the disease takes hold, however, a number of symptoms can occur, including swollen lymph nodes, fever, weight loss, fatigue and night sweats. Eventually, the virus destroys its host cells, thereby weakening the victim's immune system. When the immune system is in a compromised state, the victim becomes susceptible to a variety of so-called "opportunistic infections," many of which can prove fatal.[476]

Transmission of HIV is known to occur in three ways: (1) through intimate sexual contact with an infected person; (2) through invasive exposure to contaminated blood or certain other bodily fluids; or (3) through perinatal exposure (i.e., from mother to infant). Although HIV has been isolated in several body fluids, epidemiologic evidence has implicated only blood, semen, vaginal secretions, and possibly breast milk in transmission. Extensive and numerous studies have consistently found no apparent risk of HIV infection to individuals exposed through close, non-sexual contact with AIDS patients.

Based on the accumulated body of medical evidence, the Surgeon General of the United States has concluded:

> There is no known risk of non-sexual infection in most of the situations we encounter in our daily lives. We know that family members living with individuals who have the AIDS virus do not become infected except through sexual contact. There is no evidence of transmission (spread) of AIDS virus by everyday contact even though these family members shared food, towels, cups, razors, even toothbrushes, and kissed each other.

U.S. Public Health Service, Surgeon General's Report on Acquired Immune Deficiency Syndrome at 13 (1986) (Hereinafter Surgeon General's Report). The Surgeon General also specifically addressed the risk of transmission in the classroom setting:

> None of the identified cases of AIDS in the United States are known or are suspected to have been transmitted from one child to another in school, day care or foster care settings. Transmission would necessitate exposure of open cuts to the blood or other body fluids of the infected child, a highly unlikely occurrence. Even then, routine safety procedures for handling blood or other body fluids... would be

---

[475] It is not yet known what percentage of individuals who test positive for HIV will actually develop AIDS, but estimates range between 30 and 90 percent.

[476] The vast majority of opportunistic infections that prey upon AIDS patients are not transmissible to others with uncompromised immune systems. Some opportunistic infections, however, such as tuberculosis, may be communicable in a classroom setting. There is no evidence, nor does the Department contend, that Chalk is currently suffering from any opportunistic infections. If he should later develop a communicable infection, it would, of course, be proper for the Department to treat him as it would any other teacher with a communicable infection.

effective in preventing transmission from children with AIDS to other children in school...Casual social contact between children and persons infected with the AIDS virus is not dangerous.

Surgeon General's Report at 23-24.

These conclusions are echoed by such medical authorities as the United States Centers for Disease Control, the American Medical Association and the Institute of Medicine of the National Academy of Sciences. In its amicus brief in support of Chalk's appeal the American Medical Association summarized the medical evidence and concluded that "there is no evidence in the relevant medical literature that demonstrates any appreciable risk of transmitting the AIDS virus under the circumstances likely to occur in the ordinary school setting."

The only opposing medical opinion submitted by the Department was that of one witness, Dr. Steven Armentrout, that "there is a probability, small though it is, that there are vectors of transmission as yet not clearly defined." He elaborated on his opinion as follows:

I believe, sincerely believe that there is a significant even though it's small, potential for transmission of AIDS in ways which we have not yet determined and, therefore, may pose a risk...If they don't occur now, it is my firm belief that with the almost inevitable mutation to the virus, they will occur. And when that does occur, they certainly could be-- there can be a potential threat.

Asked whether there was a scientific basis for such a hypothesis, Dr. Armentrout indicated that he had "no scientific evidence that would enable me to answer that or to have an opinion...What we're saying is that we haven't proved scientifically a vector."

****

...Little in science can be proved with complete certainty, and section 504 does not require such a test. As authoritatively construed by the Supreme Court, section 504 allows the exclusion of an employee only if there is "a significant risk of communicating an infectious disease to others."[477] In addition, Arline admonishes courts that they "should defer to the reasonable medical judgments of public health officials." The district judge ignored these admonitions. Instead he rejected the overwhelming consensus of medical opinion and improperly relied on speculation for which there was no credible support in the record.

That Chalk demonstrates a string probability of success on the merits is supported by the three published opinions brought to our attention dealing with AIDS discrimination under section 504.

****

2. Irreparable Injury

Having demonstrated a strong probability of success on the merits, Chalk next had to demonstrate that he was threatened with the possibility of irreparable injury. ...In making its finding, the court focused on the monetary loss to Chalk and concluded that he was no worse off than before the reassignment. This approach failed to consider the nature of the alternative work offered Chalk. Chalk's original employment was teaching hearing-impaired children in a small-classroom setting, a job for which he developed special skills beyond those normally required to become a teacher. His closeness to his students and his participation in their lives is a source

---

[477] Where there is a significant risk, Arline further requires a court to determine if any reasonable accommodation will eliminate that risk. As no significant risk is posed here, this is not a case involving the standards or limits of accommodation and we do not reach those issues.

of tremendous personal satisfaction and joy to him and of benefit to them. The alternative work to which he is now assigned is preparing grant proposals. This job is "distasteful" to Chalk, involves no student contact, and does not utilize his skills, training or experience. Such non monetary deprivation is a substantial injury which the court was required to consider.

Several cases support petitioner's claim that his non-monetary deprivation is irreparable. The most striking parallel is E.E.O. C. v. Chrysler Corp., 546 F.Supp. 54 (E.D. Mich.1982), affd, 733 F.2d 1183 (6th Cir. 1984), where the court granted a preliminary injunction ordering reinstatement of employees terminated in violation of the Age Discrimination in Employment Act. The court acknowledged that the loss of income and its effects were compensable after trial and did not constitute irreparable harm. 546 F.Supp. at 69-70. Nonetheless, irreparable injury was found in the consequent emotional stress, depression and reduced sense of well-being, which constituted "psychological and physiological distress ... the very type of injury Congress sought to avert." ...Chalk's injury here is quite similar, and it likewise falls within the realm of non-compensable injury which Congress contemplated in enacting section 504. As stated by the Supreme Court in Arline:

> Congress acknowledged that society's accumulated myths and fears about disability and disease are as handicapping as are the physical limitations that flow from actual impairment. Few aspects of a handicap give rise to the same level of public fear and misapprehension as contagiousness. Even those who suffer or have recovered from such noninfectious diseases as epilepsy or cancer have faced discrimination based on the irrational fear that they might be contagious. The Act is carefully structured to replace such reflexive reactions to actual or perceived handicaps with actions based on reasoned and medically sound judgments.

...Here, plaintiff is not claiming future monetary injury; his injury is emotional and psychological—and immediate. Such an injury cannot be adequately compensated for by a monetary award after trial. An additional factor favoring a preliminary injunction here arises from the very nature of Chalk s affliction. Studies and statistics of etiology and terminus of AIDS show that although the time during which such a person may be quick and productive varies, the virus is fatal in all recorded cases. Presently Chalk is fully qualified and able to return to work; but his ability to do so will surely be affected in time. A delay, even if only a few months, pending trial represents precious, productive time irretrievably lost to him.

3. The Balance of Hardships

...[U]nder the balance of hardships standard, plaintiff's injury outweighs any harm to the defendant. Defendant's asserted injury is based entirely on the risk to others posed by plaintiff's return to the classroom. As discussed above, this theoretical risk is insufficient to overcome plaintiff's probability of success on the merits, and it is likewise insufficient to outweigh the injury which plaintiff is likely to suffer.

****

In denying the preliminary injunction, the district court concluded that Chalk's injury was outweighed by the fear that his presence in the classroom was likely to produce:

> The plaintiff desires to teach despite all these circumstances [i.e., that the results could be "so disastrous if ... by any chance the risk should prove to have been unjustified"]. Counsel has recognized that he doesn't have a constitutional right to do so. On the other hand, he has a statutory right not to be discriminated against. He has a statutory right to go back to the school if he is otherwise qualified.

But I think I have a right—in fact, an obligation to compare on the one hand the trauma on the plaintiff if he is held out from the school for a period of months until we can have a trial in this action. The trauma on him, on the one hand, with the trauma on the children and parents in being required to submit to what they are likely to conclude is an unacceptable risk. [478]

We recognize that the public interest is one of the traditional equitable criteria which a court should consider in granting injunctive relief. Here, however, there is no evidence of any significant risk to children or others at the school. To allow the court to base its decision on the fear and apprehension of others would frustrate the goals of section 504. "[T]he basic purpose of § 504 [is] to ensure that handicapped individuals are not denied jobs or other benefits because of the prejudiced attitudes or ignorance of others." The Supreme Court recognized in Arline that a significant risk of transmission was a legitimate concern which could justify exclusion if the risk could not be eliminated through reasonable accommodation; however, it soundly rejected the argument that exclusion could be justified on the basis of "pernicious mythologies" or "irrational fear." Id at 1129-30 & n. 12. See also Ray, 666 F.Supp. at 1535:

> The Court recognizes the concern and fear which is flowing from this small community, particularly from the parents of school age children in DeSoto County. However, the Court may not be guided by such community fear, parental pressure, and the possibility of lawsuits. "These obstacles, real as they may be, cannot be allowed to vitiate the rights ..." of [the Ray children].

Nonetheless, we recognize that the parties and the district court will have to deal with the apprehensions of other members of the school community, as well as with the inexorable progress of Chalk's disease. Although the time frame is unpredictable, given the current state of medical knowledge, the course of petitioner's condition is reasonably certain. Chalk's immune system will deteriorate over time, leaving him increasingly susceptible to opportunistic infections. These infections do not cause AIDS, nor do they increase the risk of transmission of the AIDS virus, but some of them may themselves be communicable to others in a classroom setting. The district court is in the best position, guided by qualified medical opinion, to determine what reasonable procedures, such as periodic reports from petitioner's doctors, will best give assurance to the Department, the community and the court that no significant risk of harm will arise in the future from Chalk's continued presence in the classroom.

CONCLUSION

We conclude that petitioner met all of the requirements necessary to receive a preliminary injunction. We therefore reverse the district court's order and remand

---

[478] The district court apparently miscalculated the reaction of at least some of Chalk's students and their parents. The mothers of five of Chalk's students joined amicus Disability Rights Education and Defense Fund in support of Chalk's appeal, and Chalk was greeted with hugs and homemade gifts upon his return to work following our order of November 18. See AIDS Teacher Returns Amid Hugs, Smiles, Los Angeles Times, November 24, 1987, p. 3.

this action with direction to enter a preliminary injunction ordering defendants forthwith to restore petitioner to his former duties as a teacher of hearing-impaired children in the Orange County Department of Education. This panel will retain jurisdiction over any subsequent appeal.

Reversed and remanded

****

Copyright

So far in this chapter we have concentrated on the nature, scope, and content of the legal setting from an employment relationship perspective. Our attention has been focused on exploring the protections accorded teachers in that setting. We conclude the chapter on the Legal Aspects of the Employment setting with a look at the some important rules which impact on the manner in which teachers carry out their professional responsibilities.

Compliance with federal copyright laws is a dual responsibility of the teacher and the district. The nature of the obligation imposed on teachers is illustrated by the case entitled Marcus v. Rowley[479]

MARCUS
v.
ROWLEY
695 F.2d 1171 (9th Cir. 1983)

Before POOLE and BOOCHEVER, Circuit Judges, and PFAELZER, District Judge

PFAELZER, District Judge:

This is an appeal from a dismissal on the merits of a suit for copyright infringement brought by a public school teacher who is the owner of a registered copyright to a booklet on cake decorating. The defendant, also a public school teacher, incorporated a substantial portion of the copyrighted work into a booklet which she prepared for use in her classes. Both parties moved the district court for summary judgment. The district court denied both motions and dismissed the action on the merits on the ground that defendant's copying of plaintiff's material constituted fair use. We reverse.

I. FACTUAL BACKGROUND

From September 1972 to June 1974, plaintiff, Eloise Toby Marcus was employed by the defendant, San Diego Unified School District ("District") as a teacher of home economics. Plaintiff resigned from the District's employ in 1974 and taught adult education classes intermittently from 1975 to 1980. Shortly after leaving her teaching position with the District, she wrote a booklet entitled "Cake Decorating Made Easy". Plaintiff's booklet consisted of thirty-five pages of which twenty-nine were her original creation. The remaining six pages consisted of material incorporated with the permission of the authors of the materials for which the authors were given appropriate credit.

---

[479] 695 F.2d 1171 (9th Cir. 1983)

Plaintiff properly registered the copyright for "Cake Decorating Made Easy" with the Register of Copyrights, and one hundred and twenty-five copies of the booklet were published in the spring of 1975. All of the copies of plaintiff's booklet contained a designation of copyright as evidenced by an encircled "c" followed by "1975 Eloise Marcus." This designation appeared on the table of contents page, the first page, and the page following the cover-title sheet.

Plaintiff sold all but six of the copies of her booklet for $2.00 each to the students in the adult education cake decorating classes which she taught. Plaintiff's profit was $1.00 on the sale of each booklet. Copies of plaintiff's booklet were never distributed to or sold by a bookstore or other outlet. Plaintiff never authorized anyone to copy or reproduce her booklet or any part of it.

Defendant, Shirley Rowley ("Rowley"), teaches food service career classes in the District. In the spring of 1975, she enrolled in one of plaintiff's cake decorating classes and purchased a copy of plaintiff's book. During the following summer, Rowley prepared a booklet entitled "Cake Decorating Learning Activity Package" ("LAP") for use in her food service career classes. The LAP consisted of twenty-four pages and was designed to be used by students who wished to study an optional section of her course devoted to cake decorating. Defendant had fifteen copies of the LAP made and put them in a file so that they would be available to her students. She used the LAP during the 1975,1976 and 1977 school years. The trial court found that sixty of Rowley's two hundred twenty-five students elected to study cake decorating. The trial court further found that neither Rowley nor the District derived any profit from the LAP.

Rowley admits copying eleven of the twenty-four pages in her LAP from plaintiff's booklet. The eleven pages copied consisted of the supply list, icing recipes, three sheets dealing with color flow and mixing colors, four pages showing how to make and use a decorating bag, and two pages explaining how to make flowers and sugar molds. Four additional pages in defendant's LAP also appear in plaintiff's booklet, but these pages primarily contain information collected by and used with the permission of the Consumer Service Department of the American Institute of Baking.[480] Twenty pages of plaintiff's booklet were not included in Rowley's LAP.[481] Rowley did not give plaintiff credit for the eleven pages she copied, nor did she acknowledge plaintiff as the owner of a copyright with respect to those pages.

Plaintiff learned of Rowley's LAP in the summer of 1977 when a student in plaintiff's adult education class refused to purchase plaintiff's book. The student's son had obtained a copy of the LAP from Rowley's class. After examining Rowley's booklet, the student accused plaintiff of plagiarizing Rowley's work. Following these events, plaintiff made a claim of infringement against Rowley and the District. Both denied infringement and the plaintiff filed suit.

...The trial court denied ...dismissed the case on the merits. The ground for dismissal was that the defendant's copying of the plaintiff's material for nonprofit educational purposes constituted fair use.

II. THE APPLICABLE COPYRIGHT ACT

Congress revised the statutory law of copyright on October 19,1976 in Public Law 94-553,17 U.S.C. § 101 et seq. (1976). The revised Copyright Act provides that

---

[480] 1. The other nine pages of defendant's booklet consisted of the cover, the introduction, and seven pages of lesson plans.

[481] These twenty pages consisted of the cover page, the table of contents, two pages on the technique of icing a cake, an explanation of how to make leaves, six pages of lettering designs eight pages of seasonal designs and one blank page for notes.

causes of action which arose prior to January 1, 1978 are governed by the Copyright Act in existence when the claim arose.

...Although it is therefore clear that the revised Copyright Act does not govern this action, which version of the Act applies would not affect the outcome of this case since its resolution turns entirely on the application of the doctrine of fair use.

The doctrine of fair use was a judicially articulated concept until Congress recognized its importance and incorporated it into section 107 of the revised Copyright Act. The legislative history states that "[s]ection 107 is a restatement of this judicially developed doctrine—it neither enlarges nor changes it in any way." Thus, the cases dealing with the doctrine of fair use under the common law and those under section 107 both give consideration to the same factors in analyzing whether the doctrine should apply. Section 107 codifies the factors developed under the prior case law.[482]

III. THE DOCTRINE OF FAIR USE

Fair use is most often defined as the "privilege in others than the owner of a copyright to use the copyrighted material in a reasonable manner without his consent, notwithstanding the monopoly granted to the owner ...." This doctrine was judicially created to "avoid rigid application" of the copyright laws when that application would defeat the law's original purpose which was the fostering of creativity. Because the doctrine was developed with a view to the introduction of flexibility and equity into the copyright laws, it has evolved in such a manner as to elude precise definition. It is, as Professor Nimmer has stated, a "most obscure doctrine." It is clear, however, that "assuming the applicable criteria are met, fair use can extend to the reproduction of copyrighted material for purposes of classroom teaching." Thus, a later House Report listed, among examples of fair use, the "reproduction by a teacher or student of a small part of a work to illustrate a lesson ...."

A. The Purpose and Character of the Use

The first factor to be considered in determining the applicability of the doctrine of fair use is the purpose and character of the use, and specifically whether the use is of a commercial nature or is for a nonprofit educational purpose. It is uncontroverted that Rowley's use of the LAP was for a nonprofit educational purpose and that the LAP was distributed to students at no charge. These facts necessarily weigh in Rowley's favor. Nevertheless, a finding of a nonprofit educational purpose does not automatically compel a finding of fair use.

This court has often articulated the principle that a finding that the alleged infringers copied the material to use it for the same intrinsic purpose for which the copyright owner intended it to be used is strong indicia of no fair use.

This same function test is addressed in the House of Representatives' 1967 Report, specifically in relation to classroom materials. The Report states that, with respect to the fair use doctrine, "[t]extbooks and other material prepared primarily

---

[482] Section 107, states in pertinent part:

[T]he fair use of a copyrighted work .. is not an infringement of copyright. In determining whether the use made of a work in any particular case is a fair use the factors to be considered shall include-

(1) the purpose and character of the use, including whether such use is of a commercial nature or is for non-profit educational purposes;

(2) the nature of the copyrighted work;

(3) the amount and substantiality of the portion used in relation to the copyrighted work as a whole; and

(4) the effect of the use upon the potential market for or value of the copyrighted work

for the school market would be less susceptible to reproduction for classroom use than material prepared for general public distribution."

In this case, both plaintiff's and defendant's booklets were prepared for the purpose of teaching cake decorating, a fact which weighs against a finding of fair use.[483]

Because fair use presupposes that the defendant has acted fairly and in good faith, the propriety of the defendant's conduct should also be weighed in analyzing the purpose and character of the use.[484]

Here, there was no attempt by defendant to secure plaintiff's permission to copy the contents of her booklet or to credit plaintiff for the use of her material even though Rowley's copying was for the most part verbatim.[485] Rowley's conduct in this respect weighs against a finding of fair use.

B. The Nature of the Copyrighted Work

The second factor to be weighed is the nature of the copyrighted work. ...[A]nalysis of this factor requires consideration of whether the work is "informational" or "creative." The court stated that "the scope of fair use is greater when informational type works, as opposed to more creative products, are involved." Here, plaintiff's booklet involved both informational and creative aspects. Some pages in her booklet undoubtedly contained information available in other cake decorating books or in recipe books. Other parts of her booklet contained creative hints she derived from her own experiences or ideas; certainly the manner in which plaintiff assembled her book represented a creative expression. Thus, on balance, it does not appear that analysis of this factor is of any real assistance in reaching a conclusion as to applicability of fair use.

C. The Amount and Substantiality of the Portion Used

The third factor to be considered is the amount and substantiality of the portion used in relation to the copyrighted work as a whole. Any conclusion with respect to this factor requires analysis of both the quantity and quality of the alleged infringement.

With respect to this factor, this court has long maintained the view that wholesale copying of copyrighted material precludes application of the fair use doctrine. Other courts are in accord with this principle, and two courts have specifically addressed the issue in relation to copying for educational purposes. ...[One case] involved alleged infringement by the defendant, a school teacher and church choir director, of a hymn entitled "My God and I". The defendant Crow incorporated plaintiff's original piano and solo voice composition into an arrangement for his choirs. He made forty-eight copies of his arrangement and had the piece performed on two occasions: once by the high school choir at the school chapel, and once in church on Sunday. The music was identified as "arranged Nelson E. Crow", but no reference was made to plaintiff as the original composer. The Eighth Circuit affirmed the trial court's finding that Crow had infringed plaintiff's copyright and in addressing the issue of whether Crow's copying

---

[483] Of course, this finding is not decisive on the issue of fair use. The fact that both works were used for the same intrinsic purpose carries less weight in a case such as this, because plainly the doctrine of fair use permits some copying of educational materials for classroom use. The critical issues here are the nature and the extent of defendant's copying.

[484] Runge v. Lee, 441 F.2d 579 (9th Cir.1971), cert. denied, 404 U.S. 887 (1971).

[485] Attribution is, of course, but one factor. Moreover, acknowledgement of a source does not excuse infringement when the other factors listed in section 107 are present.

constituted fair use, the court stated that "[w]hatever may be the breadth of the doctrine of 'fair use', it is not conceivable to us that the copying of all, or substantially all, of a copyrighted song can be held to be a 'fair use' merely because the infringer had no intent to infringe."

The court in Encyclopaedia Britannica Educational Corp. v. Crooks (W.D.N.Y.1978), also considered the issue of fair use in the educational context. In that case, three corporations which produced educational motion picture films sued the Board of Cooperative Educational Services of Erie County ("BOCES") for videotaping several of plaintiffs' copyrighted films without permission. BOCES distributed the copied films to schools for delayed student viewing. Defendants' fair use defense was rejected on the ground that although defendants were involved in noncommercial copying to promote science and education, the taping of entire copyrighted films was too excessive for the fair use defense to apply.[486]

In this case, almost 50% of defendant's LAP was a verbatim copy of plaintiff's booklet and that 50% contained virtually all of the substance of defendant's book. Defendant copied the explanations of how to make the decorating bag, how to mix colors, and how to make various decorations as well as the icing recipes. In fact, the only substantive pages of plaintiff's booklet which defendant did not put into her booklet were hints on how to ice a cake and an explanation of how to make leaves. Defendant argues that it was fair to copy plaintiff's booklet because the booklet contained only facts which were in the public domain. Even if it were true that plaintiff's book contained only facts, this argument fails because defendant engaged in virtually verbatim copying. Defendant's LAP could have been a photocopy of plaintiff's booklet but for the fact that defendant retyped plaintiff's material. This case presents a clear example of both substantial quantitative and qualitative copying.

D. The Effect of the Use Upon the Potential Market for or Value of the Copyrighted Work

The final factor to be considered with respect to the fair use defense is the effect which the allegedly infringing use had on the potential market for or value of the copyrighted work. The 1967 House Report points out that this factor is often seen as the most important criterion of fair use, but also warned that it "must almost always be judged in conjunction with the other three criteria." The Report explains that "a use which supplants any part of the normal market for a copyrighted work would ordinarily be considered an infringement." Here, despite the fact that at least one of plaintiff's students refused to purchase her booklet as a result of defendant's copying, the trial court found that it was unable to conclude that the defendant's copying had any effect on the market for the plaintiff's booklet. Even assuming that the trial court's finding was not erroneous, and that that finding must be accepted and weighed in Rowley's favor, it does not alter our conclusion. The mere absence of measurable pecuniary damage does not require a finding of fair use. Fair use is to be determined by a consideration of all of the evidence in the case. Thus, despite the trial court's finding, we conclude that the factors analyzed weigh decisively in favor of the conclusion of no fair use. This conclusion is in harmony with the Congressional guidelines which, as a final point,

---

[486] Contra Williams & Wilkins Co. v. United States, 487 F.2d 1345, 1352-1354 (Ct.Cl.1973),affd, 420 U.S. 376 (1975) (the existence of verbatim copying was not dispositive when the conduct encouraged scientific progress and did not cause plaintiff substantial monetary harm).

also merit consideration with respect to the issue of fair use in an educational context.

IV. THE CONGRESSIONAL GUIDELINES

The question of how much copying for classroom use is permissible was of such major concern to Congress that, although it did not include a section on the subject in the revised Act, it approved a set of guidelines with respect to it. The guidelines represent the Congressional Committees' view of what constitutes fair use under the traditional judicial doctrine developed in the case law. The guidelines were designed to give teachers direction as to the extent of permissible copying and to eliminate some of the doubt which had previously existed in this area of the copyright laws. The guidelines were intended to represent minimum standards of fair use. Thus, while they are not controlling on the court, they are instructive on the issue of fair use in the context of this case.

The guidelines relating to multiple copies for classroom use indicate that such copying is permissible if three tests are met. First, the copying must meet the test of "brevity" and "spontaneity." "Brevity" is defined, for prose, as "[e]ither a complete article, story or essay of less than 2,500 words, or an excerpt from any prose work of not more than 1,000 words or ... 10% of the work, whichever is less .... " Rowley's copying would not be permissible under either of these tests.

The guidelines also provide a separate definition of "brevity" for "special works." "Special works" are works "which often combine language with illustrations and which are intended sometimes for children and at other times for a more general audience." Plaintiff's booklet arguably would fall into this category. The guidelines provide that, notwithstanding the guidelines for prose, " 'special works' may not be reproduced in their entirety; however, an excerpt comprising not more than two of the published pages of such special work and containing not more than 10% of the words found in the text thereof, may be reproduced." Rowley's copying would not be permissible under this test.

Under the guidelines, "spontaneity" requires that "[t]he copying is at the instance and inspiration of the individual teacher, and . . . [t]he inspiration and decision to use the work and the moment of its use for maximum teaching effectiveness are so close in time that it would be unreasonable to expect a timely reply to a request for permission." Defendant compiled her LAP during the summer of 1975 and first used it in her classes during the 1975-76 school year. She also used the LAP for the following two school years. Rowley's copying would not meet this requirement either.

The second test under the guidelines is that of "cumulative effect". This test requires that the copied material be for only one course in the school. This aspect of the test would probably be met on these facts. The test also limits the number of pieces which may be copied from the same author and the number of times a teacher may make multiple copies for one course during one term. These latter two tests also appear to be met. The facts indicate that defendant copied only one piece of plaintiff's work. Defendant's conduct, therefore, would satisfy the second test under the guidelines.

The third test requires that each copy include a notice of copyright. As stated defendant's LAP did not acknowledge plaintiff's authorship or copyright and therefore would not meet this test.

In conclusion, it appears that Rowley's copying would not qualify as fair use under the guidelines.

We conclude that the fair use doctrine does not apply to these facts as that doctrine has been articulated in the common law, in section 107 of the revised Copyright Act, or in the special guidelines approved by Congress for nonprofit educational institutions. Rowley's LAP work, which was used for the same purpose as plaintiff's booklet, was quantitatively and qualitatively a substantial copy of plaintiff's booklet with no credit given to plaintiff. Under these circumstances, neither the fact that the defendant used the plaintiff's booklet for non-profit educational purposes nor the fact that plaintiff suffered no pecuniary damage as a result of Rowley's copying supports a finding of fair use.

The order of the district court is reversed, summary judgment is entered for the plaintiff, and the case is remanded for a determination of damages pursuant to the provisions of the Copyright Act.

Reversed and remanded.

****

STUDY QUESTIONS

1. What teaching methods and procedures are most vulnerable to copyright issues?
2. Does copyright protection extend to computer programs?
3. What resources are available to teachers that avoid copyright issues?

****

C

CHAPTER SUMMARY

This chapter has explored the legal aspects of the school district \teacher employment relationship. A license is a precondition to employment. The responsibility for development of rules and regulations concerning certification are vested with the Commission on Professional Standards in Education. The state superintendent issues licenses. A teaching license is a privilege subject to revocation by the state board. The grounds for revocation and procedure for issuance are outlined in state law.

School district recruitment practices are subject to statutes and case law guaranteeing equal employment opportunity.

Full time teachers are entitled to a written employment contract. New teachers serve a minimum of one year of probation.

State law outlines the grounds for employment discipline (substantive aspects of employment discipline). The Nevada Supreme Court has given meaning to the general words used in the statute in several decisions.

State law also specifies the procedural aspects of employment discipline. The procedure applicable depends on the teachers status (probationary or postprobationary) and the type of discipline being invoked (suspension, demotion, dismissal, contract nonrenewal).

Nevada's public sector labor law also impacts on the public school employment setting. Sixteen of seventeen Nevada school districts have recognized a teacher association for the purpose of collective bargaining. The terms and conditions of the Collective bargaining agreement are incorporated in the teachers individual employment contract. Disputes over the application and interpretation of the agreement are normally resolved by an impartial arbitrator. State labor law allows school districts and teacher associations to negotiate discipline procedures which supersede the Nevada Professional Practices Act.

During the 1991 legislative session the law was amended to provide for final and binding last best offer arbitration as the last step in the negotiation dispute resolution process.

The U.S. Constitution also affects the employment relationship. Public school teachers have certain 1st, 4th, and 14th Amendment rights at the workplace.

Schooldistricts are also bound by anti-discrimination laws regarding their employment practices.

Finally, teachers must be mindful of their obligation to comply with federal copyright law while carrying out their professional responsibilities.

CHAPTER V

STUDENT RIGHTS AND RESPONSIBILITIES

RULES
TO BE OBSERVED BY THE
PUPILS OF THE PUBLIC SCHOOLS
OF
MILWAUKEE
CODE IN FORCE IN MILWAUKEE PUBLIC SCHOOLS
1846

1. THE PUPILS MUST ALL APPEAR AT THE APPOINTED HOURS, WITH THEIR HANDS AND FACES CLEAN; AND HAIR COMBED, FREE FROM LICE, ITCH, SCALD HEAD AND OTHER CONTAGIOUS DISEASES; AND WITH THEIR CLOTHES CLEAN AND MENDED.

2. THEY MUST BE CAREFUL OF THEIR SCHOOL BOOKS; WHICH ARE NOT TO BE SOILED, TORN, OR SCRIBBLED IN.

3. THEY MUST BE REGULAR IN THEIR ATTENDANCE; AND NEVER LOITER TO OR FROM SCHOOL.

4. THE MUST OBEY THEIR INSTRUCTORS; AND STRICTLY OBSERVE THE RULES ADOPTED FOR THEIR GOVERNMENT.

5. THEY MUST ATTEND DILIGENTLY TO THEIR STUDIES.

6. THEY MUST NOT STUDY ALOUD, OR MAKE ANY IMPROPER GESTURES, OR UNNECESSARY NOISE.

7. THEY MUST NEITHER WRITE, TALK, NOR WHISPER TO EACH OTHER DURING SCHOOL HOURS.

8. THEY MUST NOT LEAVE THEIR SEATS WITHOUT PERMISSION; NOR REMAIN AT PLAY LONGER THAN THE TIME PRESCRIBED FOR THEM.

9. THEY MUST IN ALL CASES SPEAK THE TRUTH.

10. THEY MUST NOT QUARREL WITH, STRIKE, OR ABUSE EACH OTHER, ON ANY OCCASION.

11. THEY MUST NOT, EITHER IN SPEAKING OR WRITING, USE PROFANE, INDECENT, OR OFFENSIVE LANGUAGE.

12. THEY SHOULD BE POLITE AND RESPECTFUL IN THEIR BEHAVIOR; AND, NEITHER DO, NOR SAY, ANYTHING TO INJURE THE PERSON, FEELINGS, OR PROPERTY OF THEIR NEIGHBORS, OR ASSOCIATES.

13. NO SCHOLAR SHALL BE ADMITTED INTO THE SCHOOL ROOM, WHO DOES NOT APPEAR WITHIN FIFTEEN MINUTES OF THE APPOINTED HOUR.

14. NONE BUT THE CHILDREN OF ACTUAL RESIDENTS, SHALL BE ADMITTED INTO THE PUBLIC SCHOOLS; AND NO PUPIL SHALL BE RECEIVED, IN ANY QUARTER, AFTER THE END OF THE FIRST MONTH, UNLESS THE PARENTS HAVE RECENTLY MOVED INTO THE DISTRICT, OR THE PUPIL HAS BEEN DETAINED FROM SCHOOL BY SICKNESS, OR OTHER SUFFICIENT CAUSE.

BY ORDER OF THE BOARD OF SCHOOL COMMISSIONERS.
RUFUS KING, PRESIDENT

H. G. ABBEY, SECRETARY.
MILWAUKEE, DEC. 1846 Rules for students

A
INTRODUCTION

At the core of the "Rules For Students" is a doctrine that defines the foundation legal principle underlying the relationship between students and schools. It is entitled the doctrine of 'in loco parentis' and simply means that school authorities stand in the shoes of a reasonable and prudent parent.[487] So, under the unrefined doctrine, school authorities possessed all the rights, privileges, duties, and responsibilities that parents possessed while a child was under school supervision. Under this formulation of the student\school legal relationship children are not persons in a constitutional sense. Students are only entitled to right custody. They have no constitutional rights. The strict doctrine of in loco parentis has been modified and refined to accommodate the conclusion that children are persons in a constitutional sense in the school setting.

Exploration of the nature, scope and content of student rights and responsibilities in the school environment is the purpose of this chapter. Our exploration begins with a seminal decision of the Supreme Court.

B
STUDENT CONSTITUTIONAL RIGHTS

WHAT IS THE NATURE AND SCOPE OF A STUDENT'S RIGHT OF FREE EXPRESSION IN THE PUBLIC SCHOOL SETTING?

TINKER
v.
DES MOINES SCHOOL DISTRICT.
393 U.S. 503, 89 S.Ct. 733 (1969)

MR. JUSTICE FORTAS delivered the opinion of the Court.

Petitioner John F. Tinker, 15 years old, and petitioner Christopher Eckhardt, 16 years old, attended high schools in Des Moines, Iowa. Petitioner Mary Beth Tinker, John's sister, was a 13-year-old student in junior high school

In December 1965, a group of adults and students in Des Moines held a meeting at the Eckhardt home. The group determined to publicize their objections to the hostilities in Vietnam and their support for a truce by wearing black armbands during the holiday season and by fasting on December 16 and New Year's Eve. Petitioners and their parents had previously engaged in similar activities, and they decided to participate in the program.

The principals of the Des Moines schools became aware of the plan to wear armbands. On December 14, 1965, they met and adopted a policy that any student wearing an armband to school would be asked to remove it, and if he refused he would be suspended until he returned without the armband. Petitioners were aware of the regulation that the school authorities adopted.

On December 16, Mary Beth and Christopher wore black armbands to their schools. John Tinker wore his armband the next day. They were all sent home and suspended from school until they would come back without their armbands. They

---

[487] When children enter school, jurisdiction during school hours passes from parents to school authorities. Dual jurisdiction would mean destruction of school discipline. AGO 79 (11-22-1921, cited, AGO 684 (10-4-1948).

did not return to school until after the planned period for wearing armbands had expired—that is, until after New Year's Day.

This complaint was filed in the United States District Court by petitioners, through their fathers, under §1983 of Title 42 of the United States Code. It prayed for an injunction restraining the respondent school officials and the respondent members of the board of directors of the school district from disciplining the petitioners, and it sought nominal damages. After an evidentiary hearing the District Court dismissed the complaint. It upheld the constitutionality of the school authorities' action on the ground that it was reasonable in order to prevent disturbance of school discipline. The court referred to but expressly declined to follow the Fifth Circuit's holding in a similar case that the wearing of symbols like the armbands cannot be prohibited unless it "materially and substantially interfere[s] with the requirements of appropriate discipline in the operation of the school." Burnside v. Byars (1066).[488]

On appeal, the Court of Appeals for the Eighth Circuit considered the case en banc. The court was equally divided, and the District Court's decision was accordingly affirmed, without opinion. We granted certiorari.

I

The District Court recognized that the wearing of an armband for the purpose of expressing certain views is the type of symbolic act that is within the Free Speech Clause of the First Amendment. As we shall discuss, the wearing of armbands in the circumstances of this case was entirely divorced from actually or potentially disruptive conduct by those participating in it. It was closely akin to "pure speech" which, we have repeatedly held, is entitled to comprehensive protection under the First Amendment.

First Amendment rights, applied in light of the special characteristics of the school environment, are available to teachers and students. It can hardly be argued that either students or teachers shed their constitutional rights to freedom of speech or expression at the schoolhouse gate. This has been the unmistakable holding of this Court for almost 50 years. In Meyer v. Nebraska (1923), and Bartels v. Iowa (1923), this Court, in opinions by Mr. Justice McReynolds, held that the Due Process Clause of the Fourteenth Amendment prevents States from forbidding the teaching of a foreign language to young students. Statutes to this effect, the Court held, unconstitutionally interfere with the liberty of teacher, student, and parent.

In West Virginia v. Barnette, supra, this Court held that under the First Amendment, the student in public school may not be compelled to salute the flag. Speaking through Mr. Justice Jackson, the Court said:

> "The Fourteenth Amendment, as now applied to the States, protects the citizen against the State itself and all of its creatures—Boards of Education not excepted. These have, of course, important, delicate, and highly discretionary functions, but none that they may not perform within the limits of the Bill of Rights. That they are educating the young for citizenship is reason for scrupulous protection of Constitutional freedoms of the individual, if we are not to strangle

---

[488] In Burnside, the Fifth Circuit ordered that high school authorities be enjoined from enforcing a regulation forbidding students to wear "freedom buttons." It is instructive that in Blackwell v. Issaquena County Board of Education, 363 F. 2d 749 (1966), the same panel on the same day reached the opposite result on different facts. It declined to enjoin enforcement of such a regulation in another high school where the students wearing freedom buttons harassed students who did not wear them and created much disturbance.

the free mind at its source and teach youth to discount important principles of our government as mere platitudes."

On the other hand, the Court has repeatedly emphasized the need for affirming the comprehensive authority of the States and of school officials, consistent with fundamental constitutional safeguards, to prescribe and control conduct in the schools. Our problem lies in the area where students in the exercise of First Amendment rights collide with the rules of the school authorities.

II

The problem posed by the present case does not relate to regulation of the length of skirts or the type of clothing, to hair style, or deportment. It does not concern aggressive, disruptive action or even group demonstrations. Our problem involves direct, primary First Amendment rights akin to "pure speech."

The school officials banned and sought to punish petitioners for a silent, passive expression of opinion, unaccompanied by any disorder or disturbance on the part of petitioners There is here no evidence whatever of petitioners' interference, actual or nascent, with the schools' work or of collision with the rights of other students to be secure and to be let alone. Accordingly, this case does not concern speech or action that intrudes upon the work of the schools or the rights of other students.

Only a few of the 18,000 students in the school system wore the black armbands. Only five students were suspended for wearing them. There is no indication that the work of the schools or any class was disrupted. Outside the classrooms, a few students made hostile remarks to the children wearing armbands, but there were no threats or acts of violence on school premises

The District Court concluded that the action of the school authorities was reasonable because it was based upon their fear of a disturbance from the wearing of the armbands. But, in our system, undifferentiated fear or apprehension of disturbance is not enough to overcome the right to freedom of expression. Any departure from absolute regimentation may cause trouble. Any variation from the majority's opinion may inspire fear. Any word spoken, in class, in the lunchroom, or on the campus, that deviates from the views of another person may start an argument or cause a disturbance. But our Constitution says we must take this risk, and our history says that it is this sort of hazardous freedom—this kind of openness—that is the basis of our national strength and of the independence and vigor of Americans who grow up and live in this relatively permissive, often disputatious, society.

In order for the State in the person of school officials to justify prohibition of a particular expression of opinion, it must be able to show that its action was caused by something more than a mere desire to avoid the discomfort and unpleasantness that always accompany an unpopular viewpoint. Certainly where there is no finding and no showing that engaging in the forbidden conduct would "materially and substantially interfere with the requirements of appropriate discipline in the operation of the school," the prohibition cannot be sustained.

In the present case, the District Court made no such finding, and our independent examination of the record fails to yield evidence that the school authorities had reason to anticipate that the wearing of the armbands would substantially interfere with the work of the school or impinge upon the rights of other students. Even an official memorandum prepared after the suspension that listed the reasons for the ban on wearing the armbands made no reference to the anticipation of such disruption.[489]

On the contrary, the action of the school authorities appears to have been based upon an urgent wish to avoid the controversy which might result from the expression, even by the silent symbol of armbands, of opposition to this Nation's part in the conflagration in Vietnam.[490] It is revealing, in this respect, that the meeting at which the school principals decided to issue the contested regulation was called in response to a student's statement to the journalism teacher in one of the schools that he wanted to write an article on Vietnam and have it published in the school paper. The student was dissuaded.

It is also relevant that the school authorities did not purport to prohibit the wearing of all symbols of political or controversial significance. The record shows that students in some of the schools wore buttons relating to national political campaigns, and some even wore the Iron Cross, traditionally a symbol of Nazism. The order prohibiting the wearing of armbands did not extend to these. Instead, a particular symbol—black armbands worn to exhibit opposition to this Nation's involvement in Vietnam—was singled out for prohibition Clearly, the prohibition of expression of one particular opinion, at least without evidence that it is necessary to avoid material and substantial interference with schoolwork or discipline, is not constitutionally permissible.

In our system, state-operated schools may not be enclaves of totalitarianism. School officials do not possess absolute authority over their students. Students in school as well as out of school are "persons" under our Constitution. They are possessed of fundamental rights which the State must respect, just as they themselves must respect their obligations to the State. In our system, students may not be regarded as closed-circuit recipients of only that which the State chooses to communicate. They may not be confined to the expression of those sentiments that are officially approved. In the absence of a specific showing of constitutionally valid reasons to regulate their speech, students are entitled to freedom of expression of their views. As Judge Gewin, speaking for the Fifth Circuit, said, school officials cannot suppress ' expressions of feelings with which they do not wish to contend."

In Meyer v. Nebraska, Mr. Justice McReynolds expressed this Nation's repudiation of the principle that a State might so conduct its schools as to "foster a homogeneous people." He said:

> "In order to submerge the individual and develop ideal citizens, Sparta assembled the males at seven into barracks and intrusted their subsequent education and training to official guardians. Although such measures have been deliberately approved by men of great genius, their ideas touching the relation between individual and State were

---

[489] The only suggestions of fear of disorder in the report are these: "A former student of one of our high schools was killed in Viet Nam. Some of his friends are still in school and it was felt that if any kind of demonstration existed, it might evolve into something which would be difficult to control."

"Students at one of the high schools were heard to say they would wear arm bands of other colors if the black bands prevailed."

Moreover, the testimony of school authorities at trial indicates that it was not fear of disruption that motivated the regulation prohibiting the armbands; the regulation was directed against "the principle of the demonstration" itself. School authorities simply felt that "the schools are no place for demonstrations," and if the students "didn't like the way our elected officials were handling things, it should be handled with the ballot box and not in the halls of our public schools."

[490] The District Court found that the school authorities, in prohibiting black armbands, were influenced by the fact that "[t]he Viet Nam war and the involvement of the United States therein has been the subject of a major controversy for some time. When the arm band regulation involved herein was promulgated, debate over the Viet Nam war had become vehement in many localities. A protest march against the war had been recently held in Washington, D. C. A wave of draft card burning incidents protesting the war had swept the country. At that time two highly publicized draft card burning cases were pending in this Court. Both individuals supporting the war and those opposing it were quite vocal in expressing their views."

wholly different from those upon which our institutions rest; and it hardly will be affirmed that any legislature could impose such restrictions upon the people of a State without doing violence to both letter and spirit of the Constitution."

This principle has been repeated by this Court on numerous occasions during the intervening years. In Keyishian v. Board of Regents, MR. JUSTICE BRENNAN, speaking for the Court, said:

" 'The vigilant protection of constitutional freedoms is nowhere more vital than in the community of American schools.' Shelton v. Tucker, [364 U. S. 479,] at 487. The classroom is peculiarly the 'marketplace of ideas.' The Nation's future depends upon leaders trained through wide exposure to that robust exchange of ideas which discovers truth 'out of a multitude of tongues, [rather] than through any kind of authoritative selection.' "

The principle of these cases is not confined to the supervised and ordained discussion which takes place in the classroom. The principal use to which the schools are dedicated is to accommodate students during prescribed hours for the purpose of certain types of activities. Among those activities is personal intercommunication among the students.[491] This is not only an inevitable part of the process of attending school; it is also an important part of the educational process. A student's rights, therefore do not embrace merely the classroom hours. When he is in the cafeteria, or on the playing field, or on the campus during the authorized hours, he may express his opinions, even on controversial subjects like the conflict in Vietnam, if he does so without "materially and substantially interfer[ing] with the requirements of appropriate discipline in the operation of the school" and without colliding with the rights of others. But conduct by the student, in class or out of it, which for any reason—whether it stems from time, place, or type of behavior—materially disrupts classwork or involves substantial disorder or invasion of the rights of others is, of course, not immunized by the constitutional guarantee of freedom of speech.

Under our Constitution, free speech is not a right that is given only to be so circumscribed that it exists in principle but not in fact. Freedom of expression would not truly exist if the right could be exercised only in an area that a benevolent government has provided as a safe haven for crackpots. The Constitution says that Congress (and the States) may not abridge the right to free speech. This provision means what it says. We properly read it to permit reasonable regulation of speech-connected activities in carefully restricted circumstances. But we do not confine the permissible exercise of First Amendment rights to a telephone booth or the four corners of a pamphlet, or to supervised and ordained discussion in a school classroom.

If a regulation were adopted by school officials forbidding discussion of the Vietnam conflict or the expression by any student of opposition to it anywhere on school property except as part of a prescribed classroom exercise, it would be obvious that the regulation would violate the constitutional rights of students, at least if it could not be justified by a showing that the students' activities would

---

[491] In Hammond v. South Carolina State College, 272 F. Supp. 947 (D. C. S. C. 1967), District Judge Hemphill had before him a case involving a meeting on campus of 300 students to express their views on school practices. He pointed out that a school is not like a hospital or a jail enclosure. Cf. Cox v. Louisiana, 379 U. S. 536 (1965); Adderley v. Florida, 385 U. S. 39 (1966). It is a public place, and its dedication to specific uses does not imply that the constitutional rights of persons entitled to be there are to be gauged as if the premises were purely private property. Cf. Edwards v. South Carolina, 372 U. S. 229 (1963); Brown v. Louisiana, 383 U. S. 131 (1966).

materially and substantially disrupt the work and discipline of the school. In the circumstances of the present case, the prohibition of the silent, passive "witness of the armbands," as one of the children called it, is no less offensive to the Constitution's guarantees.

As we have discussed, the record does not demonstrate any facts which might reasonably have led school authorities to forecast substantial disruption of or material interference with school activities, and no disturbances or disorders on the school premises in fact occurred. These petitioners merely went about their ordained rounds in school. Their deviation consisted only in wearing on their sleeve a band of black cloth, not more than two inches wide. They wore it to exhibit their disapproval of the Vietnam hostilities and their advocacy of a truce, to make their views known, and, by their example, to influence others to adopt them. They neither interrupted school activities nor sought to intrude in the school affairs or the lives of others. They caused discussion outside of the classrooms, but no interference with work and no disorder. In the circumstances, our Constitution does not permit officials of the State to deny their form of expression.

We express no opinion as to the form of relief which should be granted, this being a matter for the lower courts to determine. We reverse and remand for further proceedings consistent with this opinion.

Reversed and remanded.

MR. JUSTICE BLACK, dissenting.

The Court's holding in this case ushers in what I deem to be an entirely new era in which the power to control pupils by the elected "officials of state supported public schools . . ." in the United States is in ultimate effect transferred to the Supreme Court. The Court brought this particular case here on a petition for certiorari urging that the First and Fourteenth Amendments protect the right of school pupils to express their political views all the way "from kindergarten through high school." Here the constitutional right to "political expression" asserted was a right to wear black armbands during school hours and at classes in order to demonstrate to the other students that the petitioners were mourning because of the death of United States soldiers in Vietnam and to protest that war which they were against. Ordered to refrain from wearing the armbands in school by the elected school officials and the teachers vested with state authority to do so, apparently only seven out of the school system's 18,000 pupils deliberately refused to obey the order. One defying pupil was Paul Tinker, 8 years old, who was in the second grade; another, Hope Tinker, was 11 years old and in the fifth grade; a third member of the Tinker family was 13, in the eighth grade; and a fourth member of the same family was John Tinker, 15 years old, an 11th grade high school pupil. Their father, a Methodist minister without a church, is paid a salary by the American Friends Service Committee. Another student who defied the school order and insisted on wearing an armband in school was Christopher Eckhardt, an 11th grade pupil and a petitioner in this case. His mother is an official in the Women's International League for Peace and Freedom.

****

STUDY QUESTIONS
1. What legal principle is established by the Tinker decision?
2. Does the principle improperly interfere with school discipline?

3. Do you agree with the Majority or dissenting opinion? Why?Why not?

4. Can you think of some examples where a reasonable forecast of disruption could justify interference with expression in the school setting?

****

The Supreme Court reconsidered the nature and scope of the 1st Amendment rights granted in <u>Tinker</u> in a 1986 case. In the <u>Bethel</u> case school authorities disciplined a student who delivered a speech laced with sexual innuendo at a school sponsored assembly.

<u>BETHEL</u> <u>SCHOOL</u> <u>DISTRICT</u> <u>No. 403,</u>
<u>v.</u>
<u>FRASER,</u>
478 US 675, 106 S.Ct. 3159 (1986)

CHIEF JUSTICE BURGER delivered the opinion of the court.

We granted certiorari to decide whether the First Amendment prevents a school district from disciplining a high school student for giving a lewd speech at a school assembly.

A

On April 26, 1983, respondent Matthew N. Fraser, a student at Bethel High School in Bethel, Washington, delivered a speech nominating a fellow student for student elective office. Approximately 600 high school students, many of whom were 14-year-olds, attended the assembly. Students were required to attend the assembly or to report to the study hall. The assembly was part of a school-sponsored educational program in self-government. Students who elected not to attend the assembly were required to report to study hall. During the entire speech, Fraser referred to his candidate in terms of an elaborate, graphic, and explicit sexual metaphor.

Two of Fraser's teachers, with whom he discussed the contents of his speech in advance, informed him that the speech was "inappropriate and that he probably should not deliver it," and that his delivery of the speech might have "severe consequences."

During Fraser's delivery of the speech, a school counselor observed the reaction of students to the speech. Some students hooted and yelled; some by gestures graphically simulated the sexual activities pointedly alluded to in respondent's speech. Other students appeared to be bewildered and embarrassed by the speech. One teacher reported that on the day following the speech, she found it necessary to forgo a portion of the scheduled class lesson in order to discuss the speech with the class.

A Bethel High School disciplinary rule prohibiting the use of obscene language in the school provides:

> "Conduct which materially and substantially interferes with the educational process is prohibited, including the use of obscene, profane language or gestures."

The morning after the assembly, the Assistant Principal called Fraser into her office and notified him that the school considered his speech to have been a violation of this rule. Fraser was presented with copies of five letters submitted by teachers, describing his conduct at the assembly; he was given a chance to explain his

223

conduct, and he admitted to having given the speech described and that he deliberately used sexual innuendo in the speech. Fraser was then informed that he would be suspended for three days, and that his name would be removed from the list of candidates for graduation speaker at the school's commencement exercises.

Fraser sought review of this disciplinary action through the School District's grievance procedures. The hearing officer determined that the speech given by respondent was "indecent, lewd, and offensive to the modesty and decency of many of the students and faculty in attendance at the assembly." The examiner determined that the speech fell within the ordinary meaning of "obscene," as used in the disruptive-conduct rule, and affirmed the discipline in its entirety. Fraser served two days of his suspension, and was allowed to return to school on the third day.

B

Respondent, by his father as guardian ad litem, then brought this action in the United States District Court for the Western District of Washington. Respondent alleged a violation of his First Amendment right to freedom of speech and sought both injunctive relief and monetary damages under 42 U.S.C. § 1983. The District Court held that the school's sanctions violated respondent's right to freedom of speech under the First Amendment to the United States Constitution, that the school's disruptive-conduct rule is unconstitutionally vague and overbroad, and that the removal of respondent's name from the graduation speaker's list violated the Due Process Clause of the Fourteenth Amendment because the disciplinary rule makes no mention of such removal as a possible sanction. The District Court awarded respondent $278 in damages, $12,750 in litigation costs and attorney's fees, and enjoined the School District from preventing respondent from speaking at the commencement ceremonies. Respondent, who had been elected graduation speaker by a write-in vote of his classmates, delivered a speech at the commencement ceremonies on June 8, 1983.

The Court of Appeals for the Ninth Circuit affirmed the judgment of the District Court (1985), holding that respondent's speech was indistinguishable from the protest armband in Tinker v. Des Moines Independent Community School Dist. (1969). The court explicitly rejected the School District's argument that the speech, unlike the passive conduct of wearing a black armband, had a disruptive effect on the educational process. The Court of Appeals also rejected the School District's argument that it had an interest in protecting an essentially captive audience of minors from lewd and indecent language in a setting sponsored by the school, reasoning that the school board's "unbridled discretion" to determine what discourse is "decent" would "increase the risk of cementing white, middle-class standards for determining what is acceptable and proper speech and behavior in our public schools." Finally, the Court of Appeals rejected the School District's argument that, incident to its responsibility for the school curriculum, it had the power to control the language used to express ideas during a school-sponsored activity.

We granted certiorari... We reverse.

II

This Court acknowledge in Tinker v Des Moines Independent Community School Dist., that students do not "shed their constitutional rights to freedom of speech or expression at the schoolhouse gate." The Court of Appeals read that case as precluding any discipline of Fraser for indecent speech and lewd conduct in the

224

school assembly. That court appears to have proceeded on the theory that the use of lewd and obscene speech in order to make what the speaker considered to be a point in a nominating speech for a fellow student was essentially the same as the wearing of an armband in <u>Tinker</u> as a form of protest or the expression of a political position.

The marked distinction between the political "message" of the armbands in <u>Tinker</u> and the sexual content of respondent's speech in this case seems to have been given little weight by the Court of Appeals. In upholding the students' right to engage in a nondisruptive, passive expression of a political viewpoint in <u>Tinker</u>, this Court was careful to note that the case did "not concern speech or action that intrudes upon the work of the schools or the rights of other students."

It is against this background that we turn to consider the level of First Amendment protection accorded to Fraser's utterances and actions before an official high school assembly attended by 600 students.

III

The role and purpose of the American public school system was well described by two historians, saying "public education must prepare pupils for citizenship in the Republic. . . . It must inculcate the habits and manners of civility as values in themselves conducive to happiness and as indispensable to the practice of self-government in the community and the nation." In <u>Ambach</u> <u>v.</u> <u>Norwick</u> (1979), we echoed the essence of this statement of the objectives of public education as the "inculcation of fundamental values necessary to the maintenance of a democratic political system."

These fundamental values of "habits and manners of civility" essential to a democratic society must, of course, include tolerance of divergent political and religious views, even when the views expressed may be unpopular. But these "fundamental values" must also take into account consideration of the sensibilities of others, and, in the case of a school, the sensibilities of fellow students. The undoubted freedom to advocate unpopular and controversial views in schools and classrooms must be balanced against the society's countervailing interest in teaching students the boundaries of socially appropriate behaviour. Even the most heated political discourse in a democratic society requires consideration for the personal sensibilities of the other participants and audiences.

In our nation's legislative halls, where some of the most vigorous political debates in our society are carried on, there are rules prohibiting the use of expressions offensive to other participants in the debate. The Manual of Parliamentary Practice, drafted by Thomas Jefferson and adopted by the House of Representatives to govern the proceedings in that body, prohibits the use of "impertinent" speech during debate and likewise provides that "[n]o person is to use indecent language against the proceedings of the House." The Rules of Debate applicable in the Senate likewise provide that a Senator may be called to order for imputing improper motives to another Senator or for referring offensively to any State. Senators have been censured for abusive language directed at other Senators. Can it be that what is proscribed in the halls of Congress is beyond the reach of school officials to regulate?

The First Amendment guarantees wide freedom in matters of adult public discourse. A sharply divided Court upheld the right to express an antidraft viewpoint in a public place, albeit in terms highly offensive to most citizens. It does not follow, however, that simply because the use of an offensive form of expression may not be prohibited to adults making what the speaker considers a political point, that the same latitude must be permitted to children in a public school. In <u>New Jersey</u> <u>v.</u> <u>T.L.O</u> (1985), we reaffirmed that the constitutional rights of students in public school are not automatically coextensive with the rights of adults in other settings. As cogently expressed by Judge Newman, "the First Amendment gives a high school student the classroom right to wear Tinker's armband, but not Cohen's jacket."

Surely it is a highly appropriate function of public school education to prohibit the use of vulgar and offensive terms in public discourse. Indeed, the "fundamental values necessary to the maintenance of a democratic political system" disfavor the use of terms of debate highly offensive or highly threatening to others. Nothing in the Constitution prohibits the state from insisting that certain modes of expression are inappropriate and subject to sanctions. The inculcation of these values is truly the "work of the schools." The determination of what manner of speech in the classroom or in school assembly is inappropriate properly rests with the school board.

The process of educating our youth for citizenship in public schools is not confined to books, the curriculum, and the civics class; schools must teach by example the shared values of a civilized social order. Consciously or otherwise, teachers—and indeed the older students—demonstrate the appropriate form of civil discourse and political expression by their conduct and deportment in and out of class. Inescapably, like parents, they are role models. The schools, as instruments of the state, may determine that the essential lessons of civil, mature conduct cannot be conveyed in a school that tolerates lewd, indecent, or offensive speech and conduct such as that indulged in by this confused boy.

The pervasive sexual innuendo in Fraser's speech was plainly offensive to both teachers and students—indeed to any mature person. By glorifying male sexuality, and in its verbal content, the speech was acutely insulting to teenage girl students. The speech could well be seriously damaging to its less mature audience, many of whom were only 14 years old and on the threshold of awareness of human sexuality. Some students were reported as bewildered by the speech and the reaction of mimicry it provoked.

This Court's First Amendment jurisprudence has acknowledged limitations on the otherwise absolute interest of the speaker in reaching an unlimited audience where the speech is sexually explicit and the audience may include children. In <u>Ginsberg</u> <u>v.</u> <u>New</u> <u>York</u> (1968), this Court upheld a New York statute banning the sale of sexually oriented material to minors, even though the material in question was entitled to First Amendment protection with respect to adults. And in addressing the question whether the First Amendment places any limit on the authority of public schools to remove books from a public school library, all Members of the Court, otherwise sharply divided, acknowledged that the school board has the authority to remove books that are vulgar. <u>Board</u> <u>of</u> <u>Education</u> <u>v.</u> <u>Pico</u> (1982). These cases recognize the obvious concern on the part of parents, and school authorities acting in loco parentis to protect children—especially in a captive audience—from exposure to sexually explicit, indecent, or lewd speech.

We have also recognized an interest in protecting minors from exposure to vulgar and offensive spoken language. <u>In</u> <u>FCC</u> <u>v.</u> <u>Pacifica</u> <u>Foundation</u> (1978), we dealt with the power of the Federal Communications Commission to regulate a radio broadcast described as "indecent but not obscene." There the Court reviewed an administrative condemnation of the radio broadcast of a self-styled "humorist" who described his own performance as being in "the words you couldn't say on the public, ah, airwaves, um, the ones you definitely wouldn't say ever." The commission concluded that "certain words depicted sexual and excretory activities in a patently offensive manner, [and] noted that they 'were broadcast at a time when children were undoubtedly in the audience.'" The Commission issued an order declaring that the radio station was guilty of broadcasting indecent language in violation of 18 U.S.C. § 1464. The Court of Appeals set aside the Commission's determination, and we reversed, reinstating the Commission's citation of the station. We concluded that the broadcast was properly considered "obscene." ...The plurality opinion went on to reject the radio station's assertion of a First Amendment right to broadcast vulgarity.

> "These words offend for the same reasons that obscenity offends. Their place in the hierarchy of First Amendment values was aptly sketched by Mr. Justice Murphy when he said: '[S]uch utterances are no essential part of any exposition of ideas, and are of such slight social value as a step to truth that any benefit that may be derived from them is clearly outweighed by the social interest in order and morality.'

We hold that petitioner School District acted entirely within its permissible authority in imposing sanctions upon Fraser in response to his offensively lewd and indecent speech. Unlike the sanctions imposed on the students wearing armbands in <u>Tinker</u>, the penalties imposed in this case were unrelated to any political viewpoint. The First Amendment does not prevent the school officials from determining that to permit a vulgar and lewd speech such as respondent's would undermine the school's basic educational mission. A high school assembly or classroom is no place for a sexually explicit monologue directed towards an unsuspecting audience of teenage students. Accordingly, it was perfectly appropriate for the school to disassociate itself to make the point to the pupils that vulgar speech and lewd conduct is wholly inconsistent with the "fundamental values" of public school education. Justice Black, dissenting in <u>Tinker,</u> made a point that is especially relevant in this case:

> "I wish therefore, . . . to disclaim any purpose . . . to hold that the federal Constitution compels the teachers, parents and elected school officials to surrender control of the American public school system to public school students."

IV

Respondent contends that the circumstances of his suspension violated due process because he had no way of knowing that the delivery of the speech in question would subject him to disciplinary sanctions. This argument is wholly without merit. We have recognized that "maintaining security and order in the schools requires a certain degree of flexibility in school disciplinary procedures, and we have respected the value of preserving the informality of <u>Jersey</u> v. <u>T.L.O</u>. Given the school's need to be able to impose disciplinary sanctions for a wide range of unanticipated conduct disruptive of the educational process, the school disciplinary rules need not be as detailed as a criminal code which imposes criminal sanctions. Two days' suspension from school does not rise to the level of a penal sanction calling for the full panoply of procedural due process protections applicable to a criminal prosecution. The school disciplinary rule proscribing "obscene" language and the prespeech admonitions of teachers gave adequate warning to Fraser that his lewd speech could subject him to sanctions.[492]

The judgment of the Court of Appeals for the Ninth Circuit is **Reversed.**

JUSTICE BRENNAN, concurred in the judgment.

Respondent gave the following speech at a high school assembly in support of a candidate for student government office:

> **"'I know a man who is firm—he's firm in his pants, he's firm in his shirt, his character is firm—but most . . . of all, his belief in you, the students of Bethel, is firm.**
>
> **"'Jeff Kuhlman is a man who takes his point and pounds it in. If necessary, he'll take an issue and nail it to the wall. He doesn't attack things in spurts—he drives hard, pushing and pushing until finally—he succeeds."'**
>
> **Jeff is a man who will go to the very end—even the climax, for each and every one of you.**
>
> **"'So vote for Jeff for A.S.B. vice-president—he'll never come between you and the best our high school can be."'**

The Court, referring to these remarks as "obscene," "vulgar," "lewd," and "offensively lewd," concludes that school officials properly punished respondent for uttering the speech. Having read the full text of respondent's remarks, I find it difficult to believe that it is the same speech the Court describes. To my mind, the most that can be said about respondent's speech—and all that need be said—is that in light of the discretion school officials have to teach high school students how to conduct civil and effective public discourse, and to prevent disruption of school educational activities, it was not unconstitutional for school officials to conclude, under the circumstances of this case, that respondent's remarks exceeded permissible limits. Thus, while I concur in the Court's judgment, I write separately to express my understanding of the breadth of the Court's holding.

The Court today reaffirms the unimpeachable proposition that students do not "'shed their constitutional rights to freedom of speech or expression at the schoolhouse gate.'" If respondent had given the same speech outside of the school environment, he could not have been penalized simply because government officials considered his language to be inappropriate, the Court's opinion does not suggest otherwise. Moreover, despite the Court's characterizations, the language respondent used is far removed from the very narrow class of "obscene" speech which the Court has held is not protected by the First Amendment. It is true, however, that the State has interests in teaching high school students how to conduct civil and effective public discourse and in avoiding disruption of educational school activities. Thus, the Court holds that under certain circumstances, high school students may properly be reprimanded for giving a speech at a high school assembly which school officials conclude disrupted the school's educational mission.[493] Respondent's speech may well have been protected had he given it in

---

[492] Petitioners also challenge the ruling of the District Court that the removal of Fraser's name from the ballot for graduation speaker violated his due process rights because that sanction was not indicated as a potential punishment in the school's disciplinary rules. We agree with the Court of Appeals that this issue has become moot, since the graduation ceremony has long since passed and Fraser was permitted to speak in accordance with the District Court's injunction. No part of the damage award was based upon the removal of Fraser's name from the list, since damages were based upon the loss of two days schooling.

[493] The Court speculates that the speech was "insulting" to female students, and "seriously damaging" to 14-year-olds, so that school officials could legitimately suppress such expression in order to protect these groups. Ante, at 3165. There is no evidence in the record that any

school but under different circumstances, where the school's legitimate interests in teaching and maintaining civil public discourse were less weighty.

In the present case, school officials sought only to ensure that a high school assembly proceed in an orderly manner. There is no suggestion that school officials attempted to regulate respondent's speech because they disagreed with the views he sought to express. Nor does this case involve an attempt by school officials to ban written materials they consider "inappropriate" for high school students, or to limit what students should hear, read, or learn about. Thus, the Court's holding concerns only the authority that school officials have to restrict a high school student's use of disruptive language in a speech given to a high school assembly.

The authority school officials have to regulate such speech by high school students is not limitless. See Thomas v. Board of Education, Granville Central School Dist., 607 F.2d 1043, 1057 (CA2 1979) (Newman, J., concurring in result)("[S]chool officials . . . do [not] have limitless discretion to apply their own notions of indecency. Courts have a First Amendment responsibility to insure that robust rhetoric . . . is not suppressed by prudish failures to distinguish the vigorous from the vulgar"). Under the circumstances of this case, however, I believe that school officials did not violate the First Amendment in determining that respondent should be disciplined for the disruptive language he used while addressing a high school assembly.[494] Thus, I concur in the judgment reversing the decision of the Court of Appeals.

JUSTICE MARSHALL, dissenting.

I agree with the principles that Justice BRENNAN sets out in his opinion concurring in the judgment. I dissent from the Court's decision, however, because in my view the school district failed to demonstrate that respondent's remarks were indeed disruptive.

JUSTICE STEVENS, dissenting.

"Frankly, my dear, I don't give a damn."

When I was a high school student, the use of those words in a public forum shocked the Nation. Today Clark Gable's four-letter expletive is less offensive than it was then. Nevertheless, I assume that high school administrators may prohibit the use of that word in classroom discussion and even in extracurricular activities that are sponsored by the school and held on school premises. For I believe a school faculty must regulate the content as well as the style of student speech in carrying out its educational mission. It does seem to me, however, that if a student is to be punished for using offensive speech, he is entitled to fair notice of the scope of the prohibition and the consequences of its violation. The interest in free speech protected by the First Amendment and the interest in fair procedure protected by the Due Process Clause of the Fourteenth Amendment combine to require this conclusion.

---

students, male or female, found the speech "insulting." And while it was not unreasonable to school officials to conclude that respondent's remarks were inappropriate for a school-sponsored assembly, the language respondent used does not even approach the sexually explicit speech regulated in Ginsberg v. New York, 390 U.S. 629, 88 S.Ct. 1274, 20 L.Ed.2d 195 (1968), or the indecent speech banned in FCC v. Pacifica Foundation, 438 U.S. 726, 98 S.Ct. 3026, 57 L.Ed.2d 1073 (1978). Indeed, to my mind, respondent's speech was no more "obscene," "lewd," or "sexually explicit" than the bulk of programs currently appearing on prime time television or in the local cinema. Thus, I disagree with the Court's suggestion that school officials could punish respondent's speech out of a need to protect younger students.
[494] Respondent served two days' suspension and had his name removed from the list of candidates for graduation speaker at the school's commencement exercises, although he was eventually permitted to speak at the graduation. While I find this punishment somewhat severe in light of the nature of respondent's transgression, I cannot conclude that school officials exceeded the bounds of their disciplinary authority.

This respondent was an outstanding young man with a fine academic record. The fact that he was chosen by the student body to speak at the school's commencement exercises demonstrates that he was respected by his peers. This fact is relevant for two reasons. It confirms the conclusion that the discipline imposed on him—a three-day suspension and ineligibility to speak at the school's graduation exercises—was sufficiently serious to justify invocation of the School District's grievance procedures. More importantly, it indicates that he was probably in a better position to determine whether an audience composed of 600 of his contemporaries would be offended by the use of a four-letter word—or a sexual metaphor—than is a group of judges who are at least two generations and 3,000 miles away from the scene of the crime.

****

It seems fairly obvious that respondent's speech would be inappropriate in certain classroom and formal social settings. On the other hand, in a locker room or perhaps in a school corridor the metaphor in the speech might be regarded as rather routine comment. If this be true, and if respondent's audience consisted almost entirely of young people with whom he conversed on a daily basis, can we—at this distance—confidently assert that he must have known that the school administration would punish him for delivering it?

For three reasons, I think not. First, it seems highly unlikely that he would have decided to deliver the speech if he had known that it would result in his suspension and disqualification from delivering the school commencement address. Second, I believe a strong presumption in favor of free expression should apply whenever an issue of this kind is arguable. Third, because the Court has adopted the policy of applying contemporary community standards in evaluating expression with sexual connotations, this Court should defer to the views of the district and circuit judges who are in a much better position to evaluate this speech than we are.

I would affirm the judgment of the Court of Appeals.

****

STUDY QUESTIONS

1. How has the scope of the Tinker Doctrine been modified by this decision?
2. Why do you think the Chief Justice failed to print the students speech as part of his opinion?
3. Who pays the student's attorney fees?
4. What is your view of the dissent?
5. In your view, was the speech inappropriate for the setting where it was delivered? Why? Why not?

However, the 9th Circuit Court of Appeals recently rendered a decision which suggests that there is still some vitality in the Tinker doctrine.[495] The Chandler case involved a dispute over discipline imposed because students wore buttons and stickers supporting striking school district teachers.

---

[495]For additional background see Burke, N. Denise, "Restricting Gang Clothing in the Public Schools," 80 Ed.Law Rep. [513] (April 8, 1993).

CHANDLER
v.
Mc MINNVILLE SCHOOL DISTRICT***
978 F.2d 524 (1992)

WALLACE, Chief Judge:

Chandler and Depweg appeal from a decision of the district court dismissing their action for failure to state a claim. They seek declaratory and injunctive relief and compensatory damages for violation of their First Amendment rights under the United States and Oregon Constitutions. The district court had jurisdiction pursuant to 28 U.S.C. §§ 1331, 1343. We have jurisdiction over this timely appeal pursuant to 28 U.S.C. § 1291. We reverse and remand.

I

On February 8,1990, the school teachers in McMinnville, Oregon commenced a lawful strike. In response to the strike, the school district hired replacement teachers. Chandler and Depweg were students at McMinnville High School and their fathers were among the striking teachers. On February 9, 1990, Chandler and Depweg attended school wearing various buttons and stickers on their clothing. Two of the buttons displayed the slogans "I'm not listening scab" and "Do scabs bleed?" Chandler and Depweg distributed similar buttons to some of their classmates.

During a break in the morning classes, a temporary administrator saw Depweg aiming his camera in a hallway as if to take a photograph. The administrator asserted that Depweg had no right to take his photograph without permission and instructed Depweg to accompany him to the vice principal's office. Chandler witnessed the request and followed Depweg into the office, where they were met by vice principal Whitehead Whitehead, upon noticing the buttons, asked both students to remove them because they were disruptive. Depweg told Whitehead that his morning classes had not been disrupted. A replacement teacher in one of Depweg's classes confirmed that there had been no disruption. Nonetheless, Whitehead ordered that the buttons be removed. Chandler and Depweg, in the belief that the buttons were protected as a lawful exercise of free speech, refused to comply. They also refused to be separated. Whitehead then suspended them for the remainder of the school day for willful disobedience.

Depweg and Chandler returned to school on February 13, 1990, the next regularly scheduled school day, with different buttons and stickers on their clothing. They each wore a button that read "Scabs" with a line drawn through it (i.e., "no Scabs"), and a sticker that read "Scab we will never forget." In addition, they displayed buttons with the slogans "Students united for fair settlement," and "We want our real teachers back." Approximately 1:45 p.m., assistant vice principal Hyder asked Chandler to remove those buttons and stickers containing the word

---

***"After Long, Tedious Journey Spruce Goose Has New Home", New York Times, March 1, 1993 p. 11 A.

MCMINNVILLE, Ore., Feb. 28 (AP) — After an agonizingly slow trip by ship, barge and truck from Long Beach, Calif., Howard Hughes's monster flying boat, the Spruce Goose, came on Saturday to a private airfield near this town 30 miles south of Portland, Ore.

It will be the centerpiece of the Evergreen AirVenture Museum, which is scheduled to open in 1996.

A marching band and 10,000 spectators were on hand as the disassembled aircraft traveled the final mile of its journey of more than 1,000 miles. An air show was also held for its arrival.

The journey took 138 days, for an average of just over 7 miles a day because every step required painstaking planning. Roads had to be blocked off as the convoy moved at a walking pace, and when the 200-ton wooden aircraft was moved by river, levels, tides and the weather had to be just right.

Evergreen International Aviation bought the aircraft in August.

"scab" because they were disruptive. Chandler, anticipating further disciplinary action, complied with the request.

Chandler and Depweg filed this action in district court, pursuant to 42 U.S.C. § 1983, alleging that the school officials' reasons for requesting the removal of the buttons were false and pretextual, and therefore violated their First Amendment rights to freedom of expression. They state that the buttons caused no classroom disruption. They further allege that many of their classmates wore the same buttons, but that none were asked to remove them. Chandler and Depweg charge that the school singled them out for punishment, in violation of their First Amendment rights to freedom of association, because they led the student protest against the school district's decision to hire replacement teachers.

The school district moved to dismiss the complaint for failure to state a claim pursuant to Rule 12(b)(6) of the Federal Rules of Civil Procedure. The district court granted the motion, stating that the slogans on the buttons were "offensive" and "inherently disruptive."

II

We review the dismissal of a complaint for failure to state a claim under Rule 12(b)(6) of the Federal Rules of Civil Procedure de novo. Arcade Water Dist. v. United States, 940 F.2d 1265, 1267 (9th Cir.1991). "Our review is based on the contents of the complaint, the allegations of which we accept as true and construe in the light most favorable to the plaintiff." Hoesterey v. Cathedral City, 945 F.2d 317, 318 (9th Cir.1991) (Hoesterey), cert. denied, _ U.S._, 112 S.Ct. 1941, 118 I,.Ed.2d 546 (1992). A court should not grant a motion to dismiss for failure to state a claim unless "it appears beyond doubt that the plaintiff can prove no set of facts in support of his claim which would entitle him to relief." Conley v. Gibson, 355 U.S. 41, 45-46, 78 S.Ct. 99, 102, 2 L.Ed.2d 80 (1957).

A.

We start on agreed ground: students in public schools do not "shed their constitutional rights to freedom of speech or expression at the schoolhouse gate." Tinker v. Des Moines Indep. Community School Dist., 393 U.S. 503, 506, 89 S.Ct. 733, 736, 21 L.Ed.2d 731 (1969) (Tinker). "They cannot be punished merely for expressing their personal views on the school premises . . unless school authorities have reason to believe that such expression will 'substantially interfere with the work of the school or impinge upon the rights of other students.'" Hazelwood School Dist. v. Kuhlmeier, 484 U.S. 260, 266, 108 S.Ct. 562, 567, 98 L.Ed.2d 592 (1988) (Hazelwood), quoting Tinker, 393 U.S. at 509, 512-13, 89 S.Ct. at 738, 739-40. The schoolroom prepares children for citizenship, and the proper exercise of the First Amendment is a hallmark of citizenship in our country. Nevertheless, this educational experience has its limitations. The First Amendment rights of public school students "are not automatically coextensive with the rights of adults in other settings." Bethel School Dist. No. 403 v. Fraser, 478 U.S. 675, 682, 106 S.Ct. 3159, 3163-64, 92 L.Ed.2d 549 (1986) (Fraser). Student preparation for adult experiences does not necessarily ensure adult experiences on the school campus. For example, schools need not tolerate student speech that is inconsistent with the school's "basic educational mission." Id at 685, 106 S.Ct. at 3165; Hazelwood, 484 U.S. at 266, 108 S.Ct. at 567. Despite the fact that the suppression of speech has obvious First Amendment implications, courts are not necessarily in the best position to decide whether speech restrictions are appropriate "The determination of what manner of speech in the classroom or in school assembly is inappropriate properly rests with the school board," and not with the federal courts. See Fraser, 478 U.S. at 683, 685, 106 S.Ct. at 3164, 3165; Hazelwood, 484 U.S. at 267, 108 S.Ct. at 567.

Chandler and Depweg argue that the district court applied an incorrect standard when it dismissed the complaint as a matter of law. They contend that this case is governed by Tinker. In Tinker, junior high school students were suspended for wearing black armbands in protest of the Vietnam war. The Court held that display of the armbands was a "silent, passive expression of opinion, unaccompanied by any disorder or disturbance" and that there was "no evidence whatever of [ ] interference, actual or nascent, with the schools' work or of collision with the rights of other students to be secure and to be let alone." Tinker, 393 U.S. at 508, 89 S.Ct. at 737. The Court explained that "where there is no finding and no showing that engaging in the forbidden conduct would materially and substantially interfere with the requirements of appropriate discipline in the operation of the school, the prohibition cannot be sustained." Id. at 509, 89 S.Ct. at 738 (internal quotations and citation omitted).

In this case, the district court dismissed the action although there was no allegation of disruption or interference with the rights of other students, relying primarily on Fraser. Fraser involved a speech given by a student at a high school assembly. The speech contained sexual innuendo and metaphor. Fraser, 478 U.S. at 683, 106 S.Ct. at 3164. The Court held that the school district

acted entirely within its permissible authority in imposing sanctions upon Fraser in response to his offensively lewd and indecent speech. Unlike the sanctions imposed on the students ... in Tinker, the penalties imposed in this case were unrelated to any political viewpoint. The First Amendment does not prevent the school officials from determining that to permit a vulgar and lewd speech such as [Fraser's] would undermine the school's basic educational mission.... Accordingly, it was perfectly appropriate for the school to disassociate itself to make the point to the pupils that vulgar speech and lewd conduct is wholly inconsistent with the "fundamental values" of public school education. Id. 478 U.S. at 685-86,106 S.Ct. at 3165-66.

The district court also relied upon Fraser's distinction of Cohen v. California, 403 U.S. 15, 91 S.Ct. 1780, 29 L.Ed.2d 284 (1971). In Cohen, the Court held that a man could not be criminally prosecuted for wearing a jacket bearing an obscene statement disapproving the draft. Id. at 26, 91 S.Ct. at 1788. The Court pointed out that students have "the classroom right to wear Tinker's armband, but not Cohen's jacket." Fraser, 478 U.S. at 682, 106 S.Ct. at 3164 (internal quotations and citation omitted). The district court ruled that the buttons in this case were akin to Cohen's jacket.

Chandler and Depweg argue that Fraser is distinguishable from this case on three grounds. First, they contend that the buttons constituted a "silent, passive expression of opinion" "akin to 'pure speech.' " Tinker, 393 U.S. at 508, 89 S.Ct. at 737. They contrast the silent expression of the buttons with the sexually implicit speech in Fraser. Next, the students focus on the fact that the speech in Fraser was made at a school assembly, a sanctioned school event, whereas their display of the buttons was a passive expression of personal opinion. They cite language in Hazelwood that distinguishes between suppression of "a student's personal expression that happens to occur on the school premises," and "educators' authority over school-sponsored [activities] that students, parents, and members of the public might reasonably perceive to bear the imprimatur of the school." Hazelwood, 484

U.S. at 271, 108 S.Ct. at 570. Finally, Chandler and Depweg argue that because their buttons expressed a political viewpoint they are therefore accorded greater protection. They point out that the Court in Fraser distinguished between the lewd speech in Fraser and the political speech in Tinker, thereby implying that restrictions on political speech should be governed by the more exacting Tinker test. Fraser, 478 U.S. at 685, 106 S.Ct. at 3165.

B.

We turn to Hazelwood for guidance in interpreting the meaning and scope of the earlier Tinker and Fraser cases. Hazelwood involved a dispute over the deletion of two pages of an issue of a school newspaper. The principal deleted the pages because they contained an article addressing students' experiences with pregnancy, and another article describing the impact of divorce on students at the school. The newspaper was written and edited by students in a journalism class as part of the school's curriculum. Hazelwood, 484 U.S. at 262-4, 108 S.Ct. at 565-66. The Court declined to apply Tinker, holding instead that "the standard articulated in Tinker for determining when a school may punish student expression need not also be the standard for determining when a school may refuse to lend its name and resources to the dissemination of student expression." Id. 484 U.S. at 272-73, 108 S.Ct. at 571. The Court then validated discretionary editorial control by school officials over the school-sponsored newspaper "so long as their actions are reasonably related to legitimate pedagogical concerns." Id. at 273, 108 S.Ct. at 571; see also Planned Parenthood of Southern Nevada v. Clark County School Dist., 941 F.2d 817, 828 (9th Cir.1991) (en banc) ("first amendment affords educators 'greater control' in deciding when the school will affirmatively 'promote' or 'lend its name and resources' to particular speech"), citing Hazelwood, 484 U.S. at 271-72, 108 S.Ct. at 570.

Although Hazelwood is not directly on point, it is instructive because it interpreted Tinker and Fraser together. The Court pointed out that there is a

> difference between the First Amendment analysis applied in Tinker and that applied in Fraser.... The decision in Fraser rested on the "vulgar," "lewd," and "plainly offensive" character of a speech delivered at an official school assembly rather than on any propensity of the speech to "materially disrup[t] classwork or involv[e] substantial disorder or invasion of the rights of others." Hazelwood, 484 U.S. at 271 n. 4, 108 S.Ct. at 570 n. 4, quoting Tinker, 393 U.S. at 513, 89 S.Ct. at 740.

We have discerned three distinct areas of student speech from the Supreme Court's school precedents: (1) vulgar, lewd, obscene, and plainly offensive speech, (2) school-sponsored speech, and (3) speech that falls into neither of these categories. We conclude, as discussed below, that the standard for reviewing the suppression of vulgar, lewd, obscene, and plainly offensive speech is governed by Fraser, 478 U.S. at 683-85, 106 S.Ct. at 3164-65, school-sponsored speech by Hazelwood, 484 U.S. at 273, 108 S.Ct. at 571, and all other speech by Tinker, 393 U.S. at 513-14, 89 S.Ct. at 740-41.

We first address the question of whether school officials may suppress vulgar, lewd, obscene, and plainly offensive speech, even when it is expressed outside the context of an official school program or event. Hazelwood focused on two factors that distinguish Fraser from Tinker: (1) the speech was "'vulgar,' 'lewd,' and 'plainly offensive,'" and (2) it was given at an official school assembly. Hazelwood, 484 U.S.

234

at 271 n. 4, 108 S.Ct. at 570 n. 4. Whereas both of these factors were present in Fraser, we believe the deferential <u>Fraser</u> standard applies when the first factor alone is present. "Surely it is a highly appropriate function of a public school education to prohibit the use of vulgar and offensive terms in public discourse .... " <u>Fraser</u>, 478 U.S. at 683,106 S.Ct. at 3164. "A school need not tolerate student speech that is inconsistent with its 'basic educational mission,' even though the government could not censor similar speech outside the school." <u>Hazelwood</u>, 484 U.S. at 266, 108 S.Ct. at 567, quoting <u>Fraser</u>, 478 U.S. at 685, 106 S.Ct. at 3165. Therefore, school officials may suppress speech that is vulgar, lewd, obscene, or plainly offensive without a showing that such speech occurred during a school-sponsored event or threatened to "substantially interfere with [the school's] work." <u>Tinker</u>, 393 U.S. at 509, 89 S.Ct. at 738. Such language, by definition, may well "impinge[] upon the rights of other students," id., and therefore its suppression is "reasonably related to legitimate pedagogical concerns." <u>Hazelwood,</u> 484 U.S. at 272-73, 108 S.Ct. at 570-71.

We turn next to the second category involving speech or speech-related activities that "students, parents, and members of the public might reasonably perceive to bear the imprimatur of the school." In such cases, school officials are entitled to "greater control" over student expression. Id at 271, 108 S.Ct. at 570. A school has the discretion to "disassociate itself" from an entire range of speech, including "speech that is, for example, ungrammatical, poorly written, inadequately researched, biased or prejudiced, vulgar or profane, or unsuitable for immature audiences." Id. (internal quotations omitted). According to <u>Hazelwood,</u> federal courts are to defer to a school's decision to suppress or punish vulgar, lewd, or plainly offensive speech, and to "disassociate itself" from speech that a reasonable person would view as bearing the imprimatur of the school, when the decision is "reasonably related to legitimate pedagogical concerns." Id at 271, 273, 108 S.Ct. at 570,

[4] The third category involves speech that is neither vulgar, lewd, obscene, or plainly offensive, nor bears the imprimatur of the school. To suppress speech in this category, school officials must justify their decision by showing "facts which might reasonably have led school authorities to forecast substantial disruption of or material interference with school activities." Tinker, 393 U.S. at 514, 89 S.Ct. at 740. However, the "First Amendment does not require school officials to wait until disruption actually occurs.... In fact, they have a duty to prevent the occurrence of disturbances." <u>Karp</u> v. <u>Becken,</u> 477 F.2d 171, 175 (9th Cir.1973).

C.

[5l We now turn to the facts alleged in this case. No effort was made by the school officials to suppress the buttons containing the statements "Students united for fair settlement" or "We want our real teachers back." Rather, the suppression only involved statements containing the word "scab." The word "scab," in the context most applicable to this case, is defined as "a worker who accepts employment or replaces a union worker during a strike." Webster's Third.New Int'l Dictionary 2022 (unabridged ed.) (1986). Although a dictionary definition may not be determinative in all cases, it is helpful here. "To be sure, the word is most often used as an insult or epithet." <u>Old</u> <u>Dominion</u> <u>Branch</u> <u>No.</u> <u>496,</u> <u>Nat</u> '<u>I</u> <u>Ass'n</u> of <u>Letter</u> <u>Carriers</u> v. <u>Austin,</u> 418 U.S. 264, 283, 94 S.Ct. 2770, 2780-81, 41 L.Ed.2d 745 (1974). However, the word is also "common parlance in labor disputes and has specifically been held to be entitled to the protection of § 7 of the NLRA." Id., citing <u>Linn</u> v. <u>Union</u> <u>Plant</u> <u>Guard</u>

Workers, 383 U.S. 53, 661-62, 86 S.Ct. 657, 661-62, 15 L.Ed.2d 582 (1966). Given the requirement to construe the complaint in a light most favorable to Chandler and Depweg, we are satisfied that these buttons cannot be considered per se vulgar, lewd, obscene, or plainly offensive within the meaning of Fraser. At this stage in the litigation, the school officials have made no showing that the word "scab" reasonably could be so considered.

[6] This brings us to the second category of school speech. There is nothing in the complaint alleging that Chandler and Depweg's buttons reasonably could have been viewed as bearing the imprimatur of the school. The buttons expressed the personal opinion of the students wearing them, and they were displayed in a manner commonly used to convey silently an idea, message, or political opinion to the community. See Burnside v. Byars, 363 F.2d 744, 747 (5th Cir.1966) (Burnside). In addition, they expressed a position on a local political issue that was diametrically opposed to the school district's decision to hire replacement teachers. Therefore, the complaint does not show that a reasonable person could have viewed the buttons as bearing the imprimatur of the school.

[7] We turn, therefore, to the third category of school speech and its standard: whether the "scab" buttons were properly suppressed because the school officials reasonably forecasted that they would substantially disrupt, or materially interfere with, school activities. Tinker, 393 U.S. at 514, 89 S.Ct. at 740. The district court held that the "scab" buttons were inherently disruptive, but nothing in the complaint or the analysis of the district court substantiates this conclusion. We conclude that the district court erred in holding, without more, that the "scab" buttons were inherently disruptive.

We express no opinion on the question whether, on remand, the school district may be able to meet the reasonable forecast test. We deal with a Rule 12(b)(6) dismissal of a complaint, which may be granted only if Chandler and Depweg could prove no facts to support their claim. That is not the case here because we hold that the "scab" buttons were not inherently disruptive.[496] Although some of the slogans employed by Chandler and Depweg could be interpreted as insulting, disrespectful or even threatening, we must consider the facts in the light most favorable to the students in reviewing the district court's dismissal of the complaint. Hoesterey, 915 F.2d at 318.

[8] In a case such as this one, where arguably political speech is directed against the very individuals who seek to suppress that speech, school officials do not have limitless discretion. "Courts have a First Amendment responsibility to insure that robust rhetoric ... is not suppressed by prudish failures to distinguish the vigorous from the vulgar." Thomas v. Board of Educ., Granville Cent. School Dist., 607 F.2d 1043, 1057 (2d Cir.1979) (Newman, J. concurring), cert. denied, 444 U.S. 1081, 100 S.Ct. 1034, 62 L.Ed.2d 765 (1980). Subsequent proof may show that the word "scab" can reasonably be viewed as insulting, and may show that the slogans were directed at the replacement teachers. Such evidence would bear upon the issue of whether the buttons might reasonably have led school officials to forecast substantial disruption to school activities. Mere use of the word "scab," however,

---

[496]. The concurrence suggests that we lend credence to the notion that there exists a class of "inherently disruptive" words. On the contrary, we merely respond to the district court's holding that the "scab" buttons were inherently disruptive. The district court stated in its order dismissing Chandler and Depweg's second amended complaint that: "Plaintiffs' buttons were inherently disruptive." Order dated Nov 9, 1990, at 3-4. Chandler and Depweg are appealing from the dismissal of their second amended complaint; the order dismissing that complaint thus forms the basis of this appeal. As such, we address it, and we conclude that the district court erred in holding that the "scab" buttons were inherently disruptive. we cannot simply ignore the district courts holding. To do so would be to ignore the district courts rationale for ruling the way it did. Thus, contrary to the concurrence's stated fear, we are not suggesting that "there exists a subclass of words that are inherently disruptive."

does not establish as a matter of law that the buttons could be suppressed absent the showing set forth above. Perhaps, after trial or summary judgment, the record might support the school officials' actions. On the basis of the naked complaint, however, this support is absent. The passive expression of a viewpoint in the form of a button worn on one's clothing "is certainly not in the class of those activities which inherently distract students and break down the regimentation of the classroom." Burnside, 363 F.2d at 748. The district court erred in dismissing the complaint.

****

Reversed and Remanded

GOODWIN, Circuit Judge, concurring:

While I concur in the result, I am unable to join the majority's opinion. I write separately to express my belief that the majority discusses matters unnecessary to decide the case. The majority opinion erodes important First Amendment protections.

There is no dispute that the district court erred in granting defendant's Rule 12(b)(6) motion. Chandler and Depweg have stated a claim for which relief may be granted. To reach this decision, however, we did not have to reach out and create a comprehensive three-part categorical scheme for deciding all student speech cases.[497] Unfortunately, the majority oversimplifies the case law and too readily disregards important factual distinctions. I am most troubled by the majority's conclusion that the deferential Fraser standard applies to all "vulgar, lewd, obscene, and plainly offensive speech," even if such expression occurs outside the context of an official school program or event.

The majority may have lost sight of the facts in Fraser. There, the Court held that a student delivering a vulgar, lewd and plainly offensive speech at an official school assembly could be punished by school authorities without violating his First Amendment rights. See Fraser, 478 U.S. at 683, 106 S.Ct. at 3164. Yet here, the majority concludes that the fact that the speech in Fraser was delivered at a school-sponsored event was not central to the Court's holding, and that school administrators have wide discretion in suppressing speech that they generally consider "vulgar, lewd, obscene, and plainly offensive," regardless of the context. I am not prepared to join in this conclusion.[498]

The Fraser Court was influenced, in part, by the captive nature of the audience. Id at 677, 106 S.Ct. at 3161 (student attendance at the assembly was mandatory); see also L. Tribe, American Constitutional Law § 12-10, at 852 n- 14 (2d ed. 1988) (noting that the Court employed a modified version of the captive audience theory" in Fraser). In addition, the school's interest in inculcating proper speech manners is surely higher in the context of a public speech in front of a crowded assembly than in the context of a private hallway conversation. Justice

---

[497] If lower courts need categorical guidance in determining how to approach student speech cases, they should look to the one implicitly provided by Justice White in Hazelwood rather than the one established by the majority here.

Justice White distinguished between (1) a student's personal expression that happens to occur on the school premises," and (2) "educators authority over school-sponsored [activities] that students, parents, and members of the public might reasonably perceive to bear the imprimatur of the school." 484 U.S. at 270-71, 108 S.Ct 569-70. In the first category, the more rigorous judicial scrutiny of Tinker is applied. Generally, school authorities must show that they could reasonably forecast that the student's expression would cause substantial disruption or would materially interfere with school activities in order to punish such expression without interfering with the student's First Amendment rights. In the second category, judicial scrutiny of the actions of school authorities is far more deferential since the school must be able to set "high[er] standards for the student speech that is disseminated under its auspices' Hazelwood, 484 U.S. at 271-72, 108 S.Ct. at 570. For cases falling within this second category, school authorities may limit student speech" so long as their actions are reasonably related to legitimate pedagogical concerns." Id at 273, 108 S.Ct. at 571.

[498]**Compare Sec. 392.480 NRS (1993) which outlaws using vile or indecent language within the building or grounds of a school. (Not a court Footnote)**

237

Brennan noted that Fraser's speech "may well have been protected had he given it in school but under different circumstances, where the school's legitimate interests in teaching and maintaining civil public discourse were less weighty." Id at 689, 106 S.Ct. at 3167 (Brennan, J. concurring).

Because the majority in this case concedes that the speech at issue is not within the parameters of either <u>Fraser</u> or <u>Hazelwood</u> but is instead governed by <u>Tinker</u>,[499] it was entirely unnecessary to address the issue; the majority's dicta amounts to nothing more than a preview, or worse, an advisory opinion. Therefore, I do not join in that part of the opinion.

The majority also gives credence to a mischievous notion that there exists a subclass of words that are "inherently disruptive." Rather than merely disagreeing with the district court's finding that the scab buttons were "inherently disruptive," as the majority does, I would rather have this Court clarify that there is no authoritative doctrinal support for the existence of such a category. I believe it is unwise to invite would-be censors to imagine that there may exist a category of "inherently disruptive" words. The invention of such a category would invite future courts and litigants to circumvent the <u>Tinker</u> analysis. Moreover, I doubt that it would be either workable or desirable for judges to construct a list of words that one cannot say in school.

On remand, the district court should not read the majority opinion as an invitation to disregard clear Supreme Court precedent. Rather, the court should apply the Supreme Court's <u>Tinker</u> analysis, which provides that students cannot be punished for merely expressing their views on campus unless school authorities could reasonably forecast that such expression will cause "substantial disruption of or material interference with school activities." 393 U.S. at 514, 89 S.Ct. at 740.

STUDY QUESTIONS

1. Did the 9th Circuit panel correctly interpret the <u>Bethel</u> case?
2. What test (<u>Tinker</u> or <u>Bethel</u>) do you think should be used to analyze the <u>Chandler</u> dispute? Why?
3. Do you view the decision of the court as a set back to the ability of school authorities to maintain proper decorum in school?
4. Do you agree with the majority that <u>Bethel</u> created a new catagory of student speech?
5. Do you see a difference between the armband involved in Tinker and the 'Scab' buttons worn by the students in the Chandler case? Should the difference you identify have led to a different result in the case?
6. Have you ever experienced disruption in the school setting because of what someone said or wore? What was the nature of the disruption?

****

---

[499]. Actually, the majority only concedes that Fraser does not apply "[a]t this stage in the litigation, suggesting that further development of the record may reveal that the term "scab." as
used here, was either "vulgar." "lewd," "obscene,- or "plainly offensive" within the meaning of Fraser. I cannot conceive how these facts could ever be equated with those in Fraser.

    First, this case clearly involves political speech, and Chief Justice Burger expressly relied on the "marked distinction between the political message" of the armbands in Tinker and the sexual content of Fraser's speech" in fashioning the Court's more deferential approach in Fraser. 478 U.S. at 680, 106 S.Ct. at 3162-63. Second. I object to the majority's implicit suggestion that speech need only be either "vulgar," "lewd." "obscene,-- or "plainly offensive" in order to trigger their more deferential analysis. See Opinion at———. Again the majority misreads Fraser. We must be careful not to stray from the facts of that case, lest we entirely circumvent the Court's clearly established Tinker analysis. Certainly the majority does not suggest that student political discourse which some school administrator might consider" plainly offensive" is entitled to only minimal First Amendment protection.

In 1988, The United States Supreme Court reconsidered the nature and scope of the <u>Tinker</u> principle as applied to written student expression in the context of the school curriculum?[500] The <u>Hazelwood</u> case arose when a high school principal refused to authorize student written articles concerning teen pregnancy and divorce to be run in the school newspaper.

<u>HAZELWOOD</u> <u>SCHOOL</u> <u>DISTRICT</u>
v.
<u>KUHLMEIER</u>
484 US 260, 108 S Ct . 562 (1988)

JUSTICE WHITE delivered the opinion of the Court.

This case concerns the extent to which educators may exercise editorial control over the contents of a high school newspaper produced as part of the school's journalism curriculum.

I

Petitioners are the Hazelwood School District in St. Louis County, Missouri; various school officials; Robert Eugene Reynolds, the principal of Hazelwood East High School; and Howard Emerson, a teacher in the school district. Respondents are three former Hazelwood East students who were staff members of Spectrum, the school newspaper. They contend that school officials violated their First Amendment rights by deleting two pages of articles from the May 13, 1983, issue of Spectrum.

Spectrum was written and edited by the Journalism II class at Hazelwood East. The newspaper was published every three weeks or so during the 1982-1983 school year. More than 4,500 copies of the newspaper were distributed during that year to students, school personnel, and members of the community.

The Board of Education allocated funds from its annual budget for the printing of Spectrum. These funds were supplemented by proceeds from sales of the newspaper. The printing expenses during the 1982-1983 school year totaled $4,668.50; revenue from sales was $1,166.84. The other costs associated with the newspaper—such as supplies, textbooks, and a portion of the journalism teacher's salary—were borne entirely by the Board.

The Journalism II course was taught by Robert Stergos for most of the 1982-1983 academic year. Stergos left Hazelwood East to take a job in private industry on April 29, 1983, when the May 13 edition of Spectrum was nearing completion, and petitioner Emerson took his place as newspaper adviser for the remaining weeks of the term.

The practice at Hazelwood East during the spring 1983 semester was for the journalism teacher to submit page proofs of each Spectrum issue to Principal Reynolds for his review prior to publication. On May 10, Emerson delivered the proofs of the May 13 edition to Reynolds, who objected to two of the articles scheduled to appear in that edition. One of the stories described three Hazelwood East students' experiences with pregnancy; the other discussed the impact of divorce on students at the school.

---

[500]See McCarthy, Martha M., "Post-Hazelwood Developments: A Threat to Free Inquiry in Public Schools," 81 Ed.Law Rep. [685] (June 3, 1993).

Reynolds was concerned that, although the pregnancy story used false names "to keep the identity of these girls a secret," the pregnant students still might be identifiable from the text. He also believed that the article's references to sexual activity and birth control were inappropriate for some of the younger students at the school. In addition, Reynolds was concerned that a student identified by name in the divorce story had complained that her father "wasn't spending enough time with my mom, my sister and I" prior to the divorce, "was always out of town on business or out late playing cards with the guys," and "always argued about everything" with her mother. App. to Pet. for Cert. 38. Reynolds believed that the student's parents should have been given an opportunity to respond to these remarks or to consent to their publication. He was unaware that Emerson had deleted the student's name from the final version of the article.

Reynolds believed that there was no time to make the necessary changes in the stories before the scheduled press run and that the newspaper would not appear before the end of the school year if printing were delayed to any significant extent. He concluded that his only options under the circumstances were to publish a four-page newspaper instead of the planned six-page newspaper, eliminating the two pages on which the offending stories appeared, or to publish no newspaper at all. Accordingly, he directed Emerson to withhold from publication the two pages containing the stories on pregnancy and divorce [501] He informed his superiors of the decision, and they concurred.

Respondents subsequently commenced this action in the United States District Court for the Eastern District of Missouri seeking a declaration that their First Amendment rights had been violated, injunctive relief, and monetary damages. After a bench trial, the District Court denied an injunction, holding that no First Amendment violation had occurred.

The District Court concluded that school officials may impose restraints on students' speech in activities that are "'an integral part of the school's educational function'"—including the publication of a school-sponsored newspaper by a journalism class—so long as their decision has "'a substantial and a reasonable basis.'" The court found that Principal Reynolds' concern that the pregnant students' anonymity would be lost and their privacy invaded was "legitimate and reasonable," given "the small number of pregnant students at Hazelwood East and several identifying characteristics that were disclosed in the article." The court held that Reynolds' action was also justified "to avoid the impression that [the school] endorses the sexual norms of the subjects" and to shield younger students from exposure to unsuitable material. The deletion of the article on divorce was seen by the court as a reasonable response to the invasion of privacy concerns raised by the named student's remarks. Because the article did not indicate that the student's parents had been offered an opportunity to respond to her allegations, said the court, there was cause for "serious doubt that the article complied with the rules of fairness which are standard in the field of journalism and which were covered in the textbook used in the Journalism II class." Furthermore, the court concluded that Reynolds was justified in deleting two full pages of the newspaper, instead of deleting only the pregnancy and divorce stories or requiring that those stories be modified to address his concerns, based on his "reasonable belief that he had to

---

[501] The two pages deleted from the newspaper also contained articles on teenage marriage, runaways, and juvenile delinquents, as well as a general article on teenage pregnancy. Reynolds testified that he had no objection to these articles and that they were deleted only because they appeared on the same pages as the two objectionable articles.

make an immediate decision and that there was no time to make modifications to the articles in question."

The Court of Appeals for the Eighth Circuit reversed. The court held at the outset that Spectrum was not only "a part of the school adopted curriculum," but also a public forum, because the newspaper was "intended to be and operated as a conduit for student viewpoint." The court then concluded that Spectrum's status as a public forum precluded school officials from censoring its contents except when " 'necessary to avoid material and substantial interference with school work or discipline . . . or the rights of others.' "

The Court of Appeals found "no evidence in the record that the principal could have reasonably forecast that the censored articles or any materials in the censored articles would have materially disrupted classwork or given rise to substantial disorder in the school." School officials were entitled to censor the articles on the ground that they invaded the rights of others, according to the court, only if publication of the articles could have resulted in tort liability to the school. The court concluded that no tort action for libel or invasion of privacy could have been maintained against the school by the subjects of the two articles or by their families. Accordingly, the court held that school officials had violated respondents' First Amendment rights by deleting the two pages of the newspaper.

We granted certiorari, and we now reverse.

II

Students in the public schools do not "shed their constitutional rights to freedom of speech or expression at the schoolhouse gate." They cannot be punished merely for expressing their personal views on the school premises—whether "in the cafeteria, or on the playing field, or on the campus during the authorized hours,"—unless school authorities have reason to believe that such expression will "substantially interfere with the work of the school or impinge upon the rights of other students. "

We have nonetheless recognized that the First Amendment rights of students in the public schools "are not automatically coextensive with the rights of adults in other settings," Bethel School District No. 403 v. Fraser (1986), and must be "applied in light of the special characteristics of the school environment." A school need not tolerate student speech that is inconsistent with its "basic educational mission," even though the government could not censor similar speech outside the school. Accordingly, we held in Fraser that a student could be disciplined for having delivered a speech that was "sexually explicit" but not legally obscene at an official school assembly, because the school was entitled to "disassociate itself " from the speech in a manner that would demonstrate to others that such vulgarity is "wholly inconsistent with the 'fundamental values' of public school education." We thus recognized that "[t]he determination of what manner of speech in the classroom or in school assembly is inappropriate properly rests with the school board," rather than with the federal courts. It is in this context that respondents' First Amendment claims must be considered.

A

We deal first with the question whether Spectrum may appropriately be characterized as a forum for public expression. The public schools do not possess all of the attributes of streets, parks, and other traditional public forums that "time out of mind, have been used for purposes of assembly, communicating thoughts between citizens, and discussing public questions." Hence, school facilities may be deemed to be public forums only if school authorities have "by policy or by practice" opened those facilities "for indiscriminate use by the general public," or by some segment of the public, such as student organizations. If the facilities have instead been reserved for other intended purposes, "communicative or otherwise," then no public forum has been created, and school officials may impose reasonable restrictions on the speech of students, teachers, and other members of the school community. "The government does not create a public forum by inaction or by permitting limited discourse, but only by intentionally opening a nontraditional forum for public discourse."

The policy of school officials toward Spectrum was reflected in Hazelwood School Board Policy 348.51 and the Hazelwood East Curriculum Guide. Board Policy 348.51 provided that "[s]chool sponsored publications are developed within the adopted curriculum and its educational implications in regular classroom activities." The Hazelwood East Curriculum Guide described the Journalism II course as a "laboratory situation in which the students publish the school newspaper applying skills they have learned in Journalism I." The lessons that were to be learned from the Journalism II course, according to the Curriculum Guide, included development of journalistic skills under deadline pressure, "the legal, moral, and ethical restrictions imposed upon journalists within the school community," and "responsibility and acceptance of criticism for articles of opinion." Ibid. Journalism II was taught by a faculty member during regular class hours. Students received grades and academic credit for their performance in the course.

School officials did not deviate in practice from their policy that production of Spectrum was to be part of the educational curriculum and a "regular classroom activit[y]." The District Court found that Robert Stergos, the journalism teacher during most of the 1982-1983 school year, "both had the authority to exercise and in fact exercised a great deal of control over Spectrum." For example, Stergos selected the editors of the newspaper, scheduled publication dates, decided the number of pages for each issue, assigned story ideas to class members, advised students on the development of their stories, reviewed the use of quotations, edited stories, selected and edited the letters to the editor, and dealt with the printing company. Many of these decisions were made without consultation with the Journalism II students. The District Court thus found it "clear that Mr. Stergos was the final authority with respect to almost every aspect of the production and publication of Spectrum, including its content." Ibid. Moreover, after each Spectrum issue had been finally approved by Stergos or his successor, the issue still had to be reviewed by Principal Reynolds prior to publication. Respondents' assertion that they had believed that they could publish "practically anything" in Spectrum was therefore dismissed by the District Court as simply "not credible." These factual findings are amply supported by the record, and were not rejected as clearly erroneous by the Court of Appeals.

The evidence relied upon by the Court of Appeals in finding Spectrum to be a public forum, is equivocal at best. For example, Board Policy 348.51, which stated in part that "[s]chool sponsored student publications will not restrict free expression or diverse viewpoints within the rules of responsible journalism," also stated that such publications were "developed within the adopted curriculum and its educational implications." One might reasonably infer from the full text of Policy 348.51 that school officials retained ultimate control over what constituted "responsible journalism" in a school-sponsored newspaper. Although the Statement of Policy published in the September 14, 1982, issue of Spectrum declared that "Spectrum, as a student-press publication, accepts all rights implied by the First Amendment," this statement, understood in the context of the paper's role in the school's curriculum, suggests at most that the administration will not interfere with the students' exercise of those First Amendment rights that attend the publication of a school-sponsored newspaper. It does not reflect an intent to expand those rights by converting a curricular newspaper into a public forum. Finally, that students were permitted to exercise some authority over the contents of Spectrum was fully consistent with the Curriculum Guide objective of teaching the Journalism II students "leadership responsibilities as issue and page editors." A decision to teach leadership skills in the context of a classroom activity hardly implies a decision to relinquish school control over that activity. In sum, the evidence relied upon by the Court of Appeals fails to demonstrate the "clear intent to create a public forum," that existed in cases in which we found public forums to have been created. School officials did not evince either "by policy or by practice," any intent to open the pages of Spectrum to "indiscriminate use," by its student reporters and editors, or by the student body generally. Instead, they "reserve[d] the forum for its intended purpos[e]," as a supervised learning experience for journalism students. Accordingly, school officials were entitled to regulate the contents of Spectrum in any reasonable manner. Ibid. It is this standard, rather than our decision in Tinker, that governs this case.

B

The question whether the First Amendment requires a school to tolerate particular student speech—the question that we addressed in Tinker—is different from the question whether the First Amendment requires a school affirmatively to promote particular student speech. The former question addresses educators' ability to silence a student's personal expression that happens to occur on the school premises. The latter question concerns educators' authority over school-sponsored publications, theatrical productions, and other expressive activities that students, parents, and members of the public might reasonably perceive to bear the imprimatur of the school. These activities may fairly be characterized as part of the school curriculum, whether or not they occur in a traditional classroom setting, so long as they are supervised by faculty members and designed to impart particular knowledge or skills to student participants and audiences.[502]

Educators are entitled to exercise greater control over this second form of student expression to assure that participants learn whatever lessons the activity is designed to teach, that readers or listeners are not exposed to material that may be inappropriate for their level of maturity, and that the views of the individual speaker are not erroneously attributed to the school. Hence, a school may in its capacity as publisher of a school newspaper or producer of a school play "disassociate itself," not only from speech that would "substantially interfere with [its] work . . . or impinge upon the rights of other students," but also from speech that is, for example, ungrammatical, poorly written, inadequately researched, biased or prejudiced, vulgar or profane, or unsuitable for immature audiences. A school must be able to set high standards for the student speech that is

---

[502] The distinction that we draw between speech that is sponsored by the school and speech that is not is fully consistent with Papish v. University of Missouri Board of Curators, 410 U. S. 667 (1973) (per curiam), which involved an off-campus "underground" newspaper that school officials merely had allowed to be sold on a state university campus.

disseminated under its auspices— standards that may be higher than those demanded by some newspaper publishers or theatrical producers in the "real" world—and may refuse to disseminate student speech that does not meet those standards. In addition, a school must be able to take into account the emotional maturity of the intended audience in determining whether to disseminate student speech on potentially sensitive topics, which might range from the existence of Santa Claus in an elementary school setting to the particulars of teenage sexual activity in a high school setting. A school must also retain the authority to refuse to sponsor student speech that might reasonably be perceived to advocate drug or alcohol use, irresponsible sex, or conduct otherwise inconsistent with "the shared values of a civilized social order," Fraser, supra, at 683, or to associate the school with any position other than neutrality on matters of political controversy. Otherwise, the schools would be unduly constrained from fulfilling their role as "a principal instrument in awakening the child to cultural values, in preparing him for later professional training, and in helping him to adjust normally to his environment."

Accordingly, we conclude that the standard articulated in Tinker for determining when a school may punish student expression need not also be the standard for determining when a school may refuse to lend its name and resources to the dissemination of student expression. Instead, we hold that educators do not offend the First Amendment by exercising editorial control over the style and content of student speech in school-sponsored expressive activities so long as their actions are reasonably related to legitimate pedagogical concerns.[503]

This standard is consistent with our oft-expressed view that the education of the Nation's youth is primarily the responsibility of parents, teachers, and state and local school officials, and not of federal judges. It is only when the decision to censor a school-sponsored publication, theatrical production, or other vehicle of student expression has no valid educational purpose that the First Amendment is so "directly and sharply implicate[d]," as to require judicial intervention to protect students' constitutional rights.

III

We also conclude that Principal Reynolds acted reasonably in requiring the deletion from the May 13 issue of Spectrum of the pregnancy article, the divorce article, and the remaining articles that were to appear on the same pages of the newspaper.

The initial paragraph of the pregnancy article declared that "[a]ll names have been changed to keep the identity of these girls a secret." The principal concluded that the students' anonymity was not adequately protected, however, given the other identifying information in the article and the small number of pregnant students at the school. Indeed, a teacher at the school credibly testified that she could positively identify at least one of the girls and possibly all three. It is likely that many students at Hazelwood East would have been at least as successful in identifying the girls. Reynolds therefore could reasonably have feared that the

---

[503] We reject respondents' suggestion that school officials be permitted to exercise prepublication control over school-sponsored publications only pursuant to specific written regulations. To require such regulations in the context of a curricular activity could unduly constrain the ability of educators to educate. We need not now decide whether such regulations are required before school officials may censor publications not sponsored by the school that students seek to distribute on school grounds. See Baughman v. Freienmuth, 478 F. 2d 1345 (CA4 1973); Shanley v. Northeast Independent School Dist., Bexar Cty., Tex., 462 F. 2d 960 (CA5 1972); Eisner v. Stamford Board of Education, 440 F. 2d 803 (CA2 1971).

article violated whatever pledge of anonymity had been given to the pregnant students. In addition, he could reasonably have been concerned that the article was not sufficiently sensitive to the privacy interests of the students' boyfriends and parents, who were discussed in the article but who were given no opportunity to consent to its publication or to offer a response. The article did not contain graphic accounts of sexual activity. The girls did comment in the article, however, concerning their sexual histories and their use or nonuse of birth control. It was not unreasonable for the principal to have concluded that such frank talk was inappropriate in a school-sponsored publication distributed to 14-year-old freshmen and presumably taken home to be read by students' even younger brothers and sisters.

The student who was quoted by name in the version of the divorce article seen by Principal Reynolds made comments sharply critical of her father. The principal could reasonably have concluded that an individual publicly identified as an inattentive parent—indeed, as one who chose "playing cards with the guys" over home and family—was entitled to an opportunity to defend himself as a matter of journalistic fairness. These concerns were shared by both of Spectrum's faculty advisers for the 1982-1983 school year, who testified that they would not have allowed the article to be printed without deletion of the student's name.[504]

Principal Reynolds testified credibly at trial that, at the time that he reviewed the proofs of the May 13 issue during an extended telephone conversation with Emerson, he believed that there was no time to make any changes in the articles, and that the newspaper had to be printed immediately or not at all. It is true that Reynolds did not verify whether the necessary modifications could still have been made in the articles, and that Emerson did not volunteer the information that printing could be delayed until the changes were made. We nonetheless agree with the District Court that the decision to excise the two pages containing the problematic articles was reasonable given the particular circumstances of this case. These circumstances included the very recent replacement of Stergos by Emerson, who may not have been entirely familiar with Spectrum editorial and production procedures, and the pressure felt by Reynolds to make an immediate decision so that students would not be deprived of the newspaper altogether.

In sum, we cannot reject as unreasonable Principal Reynolds' conclusion that neither the pregnancy article nor the divorce article was suitable for publication in Spectrum. Reynolds could reasonably have concluded that the students who had written and edited these articles had not sufficiently mastered those portions of the Journalism II curriculum that pertained to the treatment of controversial issues and personal attacks, the need to protect the privacy of individuals whose most intimate concerns are to be revealed in the newspaper, and "the legal, moral, and ethical restrictions imposed upon journalists within [a] school community" that includes adolescent subjects and readers. Finally, we conclude that the principal's decision to delete two pages of Spectrum, rather than to delete only the offending articles or to require that they be modified, was reasonable under the circumstances

---

[504] The reasonableness of Principal Reynolds' concerns about the two articles was further substantiated by the trial testimony of Martin Duggan, a former editorial page editor of the St. Louis Globe Democrat and a former college journalism instructor and newspaper adviser. Duggan testified that the divorce story did not meet journalistic standards of fairness and balance because the father was not given an opportunity to respond, and that the pregnancy story was not appropriate for publication in a high school newspaper because it was unduly intrusive into the privacy of the girls, their parents, and their boyfriends. The District Court found Duggan to be "an objective and independent witness" whose testimony was entitled to significant weight. 607 F. Supp. 1450, 1461 (ED Mo. 1985).

as he understood them. Accordingly, no violation of First Amendment rights occurred.

The judgment of the Court of Appeals for the Eighth Circuit is therefore

Reversed.

JUSTICE BRENNAN, with whom JUSTICE MARSHALL and JUSTICE BLACKMUN join, dissenting.

When the young men and women of Hazelwood East High School registered for Journalism II, they expected a civics lesson. Spectrum, the newspaper they were to publish, "was not just a class exercise in which students learned to prepare papers and hone writing skills, it was a . . . forum established to give students an opportunity to express their views while gaining an appreciation of their rights and responsibilities under the First Amendment to the United States Constitution. . . ." "[A]t the beginning of each school year," the student journalists published a Statement of Policy—tacitly approved each year by school authorities—announcing their expectation that "Spectrum, as a student-press publication, accepts all rights implied by the First Amendment. . . . Only speech that 'materially and substantially interferes with the requirements of appropriate discipline' can be found unacceptable and therefore prohibited." [505] The school board itself affirmatively guaranteed the students of Journalism II an atmosphere conducive to fostering such an appreciation and exercising the full panoply of rights associated with a free student press. "School sponsored student publications," it vowed, "will not restrict free expression or diverse viewpoints within the rules of responsible journalism."

This case arose when the Hazelwood East administration breached its own promise, dashing its students' expectations. The school principal, without prior consultation or explanation, excised six articles—comprising two full pages—of the May 13, 1983, issue of Spectrum. He did so not because any of the articles would "materially and substantially interfere with the requirements of appropriate discipline," but simply because he considered two of the six "inappropriate, personal, sensitive, and unsuitable" for student consumption.

In my view the principal broke more than just a promise. He violated the First Amendment's prohibitions against censorship of any student expression that neither disrupts classwork nor invades the rights of others, and against any censorship that is not narrowly tailored to serve its purpose.

****

IV

The Court opens its analysis in this case by purporting to reaffirm Tinker's time-tested proposition that public school students "do not 'shed their constitutional rights to freedom of speech or expression at the schoolhouse gate.'" That is an ironic introduction to an opinion that denudes high school students of much of the First Amendment protection that Tinker itself prescribed. Instead of "teach[ing] children to respect the diversity of ideas that is fundamental to the American system," and "that our Constitution is a living reality, not parchment preserved under glass," the Court today "teach[es] youth to discount important principles of our government as mere platitudes." The young men and women of Hazelwood East expected a civics lesson, but not the one the Court teaches them today.

----

[505]The Court suggests that the passage quoted in the text did not "exten[d] the Tinker standard to the news and feature articles contained in a school-sponsored newspaper" because the passage did not expressly mention them. Ante, at 269, n. 2. It is hard to imagine why the Court (or anyone else) might expect a passage that applies categorically to "a student-press publication," composed almost exclusively of "news and feature articles," to mention those categories expressly. Understandably, neither court below so limited the passage.

****

STUDY QUESTIONS
    1. Has the Court redefined the scope of student 1st. Amendment rights in the school setting?
    2. Could school authorities discipline a student today for wearing a black armband in protest of the gulf war?
    3. Is there a bright line defining expression in the context of school sponsored activity and expression that just happens to occur at school?

****

    The <u>Hazelwood</u> precedent also played a critical role in deciding when public access to high school newspaper advertising pages could be prohibited. The 9th circuit case involved the Clark County School District.[506]

PLANNED PARENTHOOD OF SOUTHERN NEVADA, INC.
v.
CLARK COUNTY SCHOOL DISTRICT ET.AL.
941 F.2d 817 (9th Cir. 1991)

ORIGINAL 9TH CIRCUIT PANEL DECISION FILED 10\11\89
CAN BE FOUND AT
887 F.2d 935 (9th Cir. 1989)
Before: Wallace, Chief Judge, Chambers, Goodwin, Hug,
Pregerson, Alarcon, Poole, Norris, Wiggins, Fernandez and
Rymer, Circuit Judges

Opinion by Judge RYMER; Concurrence by Judges Wallace and Chambers; Dissent by Judge Norris, with whom Judges Hug, Pregerson, and Poole, join.
OPINION
    Affirming a district court judgment, the court of appeals, en banc, held that a school district did not violate the first amendment in declining to publish planned parenthood advertisements[507] in school-sponsored publications.
    Planned Parenthood of Southern Nevada, Inc. brought a section 1983 action against The Clark County School District seeking declaratory and injunctive relief from the school district's refusal to publish a planned parenthood advertisement in school-sponsored publications. Although the school district authorizes its high schools to publish newspapers, yearbooks and athletic programs, principals are allowed to decide whether to accept advertising for these publications, establish guidelines concerning advertisements, and determine acceptability of advertisements. The school district had enacted regulations concerning "controversial issues." Pursuant to a Nevada statute, the school district adopted a

---

[506]See Walden, John C., "Ninth Circuit Again Says 'No' to Planned Parenthood," 71 Ed.Law Rep. [1] (January 30, 1992).
[507]ADVERTISEMENT
    "PLANNED PARENTHOOD
    OF SOUTHERN NEVADA, INC.
    601 South Thirteenth Street
    Las Vegas, Nevada 89101
    Routine Gynecological Exams
    Birth Control Methods
    Pregnancy Testing & Verification
    Pregnancy counseling & Referral"

regulation on sex education. Planned Parenthood's advertisement offered routine gynecologic exams, birth control methods, pregnancy testing and verification, and pregnancy counseling and referral.

The court noted that the Supreme Court decision in Hazelwood teaches that school facilities may be deemed public forums only if school authorities have by policy or by practice opened those facilities for indiscriminate use by the general public, or by some segment of the public, such as student organizations. Hazelwood established that first amendment claims must be considered in light of the special characteristics of the school environment, that the determination of what manner of speech in the classroom or in school assembly is inappropriate properly rests with the school board, rather than with the federal courts. Reviewing the factors in Planned Parenthood the Supreme Court found significant in Hazelwood led the appeals court to the same conclusion. The school district's intent was most clearly evidenced by written policies that explicitly reserved the right to control school publication content. The school districts practices were not inconsistent with these policies. There was no evidence that advertisements in newspapers or yearbooks were accepted for any purpose other than to enable the school to raise revenue to finance the publications, and at the same time impart journalistic management skills to students. Nor did the evidence suggest that the high schools were motivated by an affirmative desire to provide an open forum for advertising in athletic programs. That such activity occurs in the context of the forum created does not imply that the forum thereby becomes a public forum for first amendment purposes.

Hazelwood instructs a court to examine the nature of the government property involved in determining whether the forum was public or nonpublic. The court found that in light of the schools' limited access policy to advertising in school-sponsored publications, and their practice of retaining control and requiring prior approval, the schools' practice did not reveal the requisite clear intent to create a public forum. The court found no support for the conclusion that allowing some outside organizations to advertise converted the school-sponsored publications into public forums. Nor was the court persuaded by Planned Parenthood's argument that the nature of the speech at issue, advertisements from an outside entity rather than student speech, placed this case beyond the reach of Hazelwood. Under Hazelwood, in cases such as this where school facilities have not intentionally been opened to indiscriminate expressive use by the public or some segment of the public, school officials retain the authority reasonably to refuse to lend the schools' name and resources to speech disseminated under school auspices. The court concluded that controlling the content of school-sponsored publications so as to maintain the appearance of neutrality on a controversial issue was within the reserved mission of the Clark County School District.

The court also agreed with the district court that the school district's policy of not publishing advertisements that are controversial, offensive to some groups of persons, that cause tension and anxiety between teachers and parents, and between competing groups such as Planned Parenthood and pro-life forces was a reasonable one. Therefore, the school district did not violate the first amendment in declining to publish the material in question.

Dissenting, Judge Norris, joined by Judges Hug, Pregerson, and Poole stated that the fact that "avoidance of controversy" was the sole rationale available to the school district to justify its rejection of Planned Parenthood's advertisement was critical.

****

STUDY QUESTIONS
    1. Did the majority corrently interpret the <u>Hazelwood</u> holding?
    2. Teen pregnancy, and AIDS are issues which confront educators on a daily basis. Does the courts decision seem divorced from reality?
    3. By accepting ads in school sponsored publications is the school endorsing the products and services advertised?

    The nature and scope of the <u>Hazelwood</u> holding was assessed in a recent decision of the 9th circuit. In the <u>Burch</u> case, the court addressed the ability of school authorities to adopt rule which prevent distribution of an underground newspaper at school. The case is important since it addresses the limits of school censorship authority involving student written expression unrelated to the school curriculum.

BURCH
v.
BARKER
861 F.2d 1149 (9th Cir. 1988)

Before GOODWIN, WRIGHT and SCHROEDER, Circuit Judges.
SCHROEDER, Circuit Judge:
I. OVERVIEW
    In 1977, the Renton School District in Renton, Washington, adopted a policy requiring its high school students to submit to school officials for approval all student-written material before any such material could be distributed on school premises or at official school functions. The policy was directed at student writings that were not contained in official school publications.
    On May 20, 1983, students at Lindbergh High School distributed copies of an unauthorized student-written newspaper called Bad Astra at a school-sponsored senior class barbecue on school grounds without submitting the material for predistribution review. In addition, a parent, the president of the Lindbergh High P.T.A., placed copies of the newspaper in faculty and staff mailboxes. The school principal reprimanded the students for violating the review policy, but did not find any particular passage or article objectionable.
    The parents and the students filed this action in district court pursuant to 42 U.S.C. § 1983 claiming that the predistribution review policy violated their right to freedom of speech guaranteed by the first and fourteenth amendments. The district court held that, with procedural safeguards not relevant to this appeal, the policy of prior review of student-written materials did not invade the students' first amendment rights. The plaintiffs appeal to this court claiming that they are entitled to expungement from their records of their reprimands, and to declaratory and injunctive relief barring enforcement of policies requiring predistribution review of all non-school-sponsored student writing. The issue before us is thus whether the district court correctly held that the first amendment permitted the

school to require prior review, for possible censorship of objectionable content, of all student-written, non-school-sponsored materials distributed on school grounds.

We review the district court's decision in light of the recent Supreme Court decision in Hazelwood Sch. Dist. v. Kuhlmeier (1988) ("Kuhlmeier"). In Kuhlmeier, the Supreme Court reaffirmed the principles laid down in Tinker v. Des Moines Ind Community Sch. Dist (1969), that the first amendment protects the right of high school students to communicate with each other, and further, that school officials may interfere with such communication only in narrowly defined circumstances. The Court in Kuhlmeier held that a policy of prior review and possible censorship of student writing is justified when it is a part of educators' reasonable exercise of authority over school-sponsored publications. The Court drew a clear distinction between whether "the First Amendment requires a school to tolerate particular student speech," the issue addressed in Tinker, and "whether the First Amendment requires a school affirmatively to promote particular student speech," the issue addressed in Kuhlmeier. This case, unlike Kuhlmeier, concerns a policy aimed at curtailing communications among students, communications which no one could associate with school sponsorship or endorsement. We therefore hold this policy does violate the first amendment.

II. BACKGROUND

In 1983, five students at Lindbergh High School in Renton, Washington, wrote a four-page newspaper entitled Bad Astra. They did so at their own expense, off school property, and without the knowledge of school authorities. The content of Bad Astra included articles written by the five students and which were generally critical of school administration policies concerning student activities, student service card requirements and enforcement of student attendance. The newspaper also included a mock teacher evaluation poll, and poetry written by Stephen Crane, Edgar Lee Masters and Langston Hughes. The paper did not include any profanity, religious epithets or any material which could be considered obscene, defamatory or commercial. Students distributed approximately 350 copies of Bad Astra at a senior class barbecue; the president of the Lindbergh High School Parent Teacher Association, mother of one of the students, placed copies in school faculty and staff mailboxes.

The school principal censured the students for not submitting Bad Astra for predistribution review pursuant to existing school board policy. The principal placed letters of reprimand in the students' files, where they remain.

The five students, joined by their parents as guardians, commenced this action under 42 U.S.C. §§ 1983, 1985 and 1988. They sought injunctive and declaratory relief holding the predistribution review policy unconstitutional under the first and fourteenth amendments, and asked that the students' reprimands be expunged from their records. The defendants included Brian Barker, Principal of Lindbergh High School, Gary Kohlwes, the school superintendent, and members of the school board of Renton School District No. 403.

The policy in effect when the students were reprimanded ("old policy") was adopted by the Renton School District in 1977 and required prior approval by school officials of any material written by students enrolled in the school and which students wished to distribute on school premises. The material had to be free from "libel, slander, obscurity (sic), personal attacks or incitement to illegal action(s)," and free from "unauthorized solicitation." In addition, student authors were required to be identified on all materials. The school principal was authorized to direct the manner of distribution so as not to "interfere with or disrupt the normal educational process."

After the students' unauthorized distribution of Bad Astra, but prior to this lawsuit, the school board decided to revise its predistribution review policy. The "new policy", which included an administrative review procedure, stated that prior approval was necessary for distribution of ten or more copies of written material. While the policy stated that distribution of materials would usually be allowed, the material in order to be approved had to be written by students currently enrolled in the school district, be free from advertisements for cigarettes, liquor, drugs or drug paraphernalia, and be distributed in a manner that would not materially and substantially interfere with the normal operation of the school.

In addition, under the new policy, principals were authorized to ban distribution if the expression was "inappropriate to the maturity level of the students" or was obscene, libelous, or invaded the privacy of others. Principals could also ban materials when there was evidence "which [would reasonably support] a judgment that significant or substantial disruption of the normal operation of the school" could result. The policy provided that such evidence could include expression criticizing school officials or advocating violation of school rules, or expression attacking or promoting discrimination against ethnic, religious, social or handicapped groups or females and males as a group.

For purposes of this appeal, the parties agree the plaintiffs would have been reprimanded under either policy, and that the "new policy" has effectively superseded the old. We refer to them collectively as "the board policy." Under both versions, all student-written communications had to be submitted for prior approval before being distributed on school property; under both versions, students would be formally censured for failure to make such submission, and under neither version was this material objectionable. Also, under neither version did the school attempt to narrow or define the subject matter it wished to scrutinize in order to avoid subjecting all communication to possible censorship.

The case came before the district court for trial on plaintiffs' application for a permanent injunction enjoining enforcement of the policy. There was no evidence that Bad Astra had interfered with the operation of the high school or impinged upon other students' rights. It was distributed at a school barbecue at which a rock band was playing and at which the students were already socializing. Defendants showed that a few teachers who had been mocked in the newspaper became emotionally upset, but the distribution caused no violence or physical damage, nor did it interfere with classes. Defendants admitted that if the students had submitted Bad Astra for prior review, the defendants would have allowed distribution without change. We thus are confronted with a unique and ironic situation in which a school has punished students for distribution of material which both sides acknowledge could not be suppressed under the first amendment.

In support of its policy, the defendants offered evidence that a prior publication in a different school in the Renton School District had once harmed a student cheerleader because it contained a story concerning her alleged promiscuity. In addition, they offered evidence that other publications in another school district had caused some disruption of classes. However, only one other "underground" student publication had ever been distributed at Lindbergh High and that paper had created no disturbance.

The defendants' expert admitted that he knew of no studies nor any statistics showing that school districts without a system of predistribution review and censorship of student-written communication experience educational disruption as a result of underground newspapers. He also acknowledged that the Seattle School District, the largest in the state, does not have any requirement of prior approval. There was evidence that the distribution of student-written materials in the Seattle School District has caused no problems.

The defendants themselves testified that in their view a predistribution censorship policy was necessary for the safe operation of the school, to avoid distractions, hurt feelings and career damage to the faculty, to further parental and community expectations and to avoid potential school liability. There was, however, no evidence that anyone familiar with Bad Astra confused it with any school-sponsored publication or believed its contents reflected the view of the school administration.

Although the district court found that the distribution of Bad Astra did not disturb school discipline or harm others, it found that "uncensored student writings have been published in other high schools that did cause, or had the potential for causing, much disruption because they were distributed without prior approval." Based on its finding that student-written materials could possibly cause disruption at some time, in some school, it held that the requirement of prior school approval in this case did not offend the first amendment.[508] The court relied upon the Second Circuit's 1971 decision upholding a school policy requiring prior approval of all student-written material distributed on school premises. The district court acknowledged that its decision conflicted with the decision of the Seventh Circuit. The district court decided this case before the Supreme Court's decision in Hazelwood Sch. Dist. v. Kuhlmeier (1988).

III. DISCUSSION

The relevant history of the first amendment in American high schools began with the Vietnam War and the Supreme Court's decision in Tinker v Des Moines Ind. Community Sch. Dist. (1969).

...Tinker held that school officials may punish students for the content of their expression only in limited circumstances. In order to justify prohibiting any particular expression of opinion, they must show more than resultant discomfort or unpleasantness, but that the forbidden conduct would "materially and substantially interfere with the requirements of appropriate discipline in the operation of the school."

Tinker swept broadly in its protection of students' first amendment rights while its description of exceptional situations justifying interference was narrow. Tinker cautioned that before deciding that school interference is warranted, courts should look to concrete evidence of disturbance or disruption resulting or potentially resulting from specific expression.

---

[508] While the district court found that the policy was substantially constitutional, the court, in rulings not pertinent to this appeal, found portions of the new policy" unconstitutional because of vague terms or inadequate administrative review. First, the court held that review of material "reasonably calculated to arrive on school premises" was unconstitutional because school officials have no authority outside the school premises. In addition, the court held that a prohibition of material that encourages actions which endanger the health and safety of students" was unconstitutionally vague. Finally, the court held that the procedural due process was insufficient because it did not specify the number of days within which the school board had to answer the appeal.

The school district did not appeal these rulings. Rather, it revised its predistribution policy to include the district court's suggested modifications ("revised policy"). The "revised policy" is not formally before this court, but it contains the same ban on distribution of non approved writings which plaintiffs challenge in this appeal, and provides for censorship under essentially the same standards.

Illustrating its fact-specific test, the Court in <u>Tinker</u> cited two earlier Fifth Circuit cases, each involving students wearing and distributing "freedom buttons" depicting clasped black and white hands, each involving school prohibitions against students wearing such buttons, and each reaching the diametrically opposite result from the other. The court in <u>Burnside</u> held that the regulation infringed upon the students' right of free expression because there was no evidence that the buttons had created a disturbance. The court in <u>Blackwell</u>, however, upheld the rule because the record showed that the buttons had caused disruption of classes and a breakdown of discipline, and that students were being forced to wear the buttons against their will.

****

The record in this case shows that this policy, with its censure of students for failing to present unobjectionable material for review, is the product of just such an "undifferentiated fear" of disruption. Indeed, this policy appears to be based upon far less justification than the action of the school principals in <u>Tinker,</u> which was directed at specific expression in an atmosphere of political turmoil. The school's action in this case is contrary to the principles laid down in <u>Tinker</u>.

A decision upholding the school's actions in this case would also be contrary to circuit decisions after <u>Tinker</u> involving situations in which student expression came into conflict with school discipline. The courts of appeals after <u>Tinker</u> were sensitive to the need to examine whether interference with student expression was justified in a given case, and sensitive to the competing interests of the school in maintaining discipline and of the students in expressing their views.

****

In dealing with high school censorship policies after <u>Tinker</u>, the courts of appeals recognized that a state policy subjecting all written communications to prior review for possible censorship would be invalid outside the school context. Two key questions remained: whether the first amendment permitted prior restraints in the school context which would be impermissible outside, and if so, when.

The majority of the courts of appeals considering policies similar to the one at issue here found them violative of the first amendment because they were overly broad and inadequately focused on avoidance of disruption and interference with school discipline. While most of these opinions refrained from holding that any policy of prior review was per se a violation of the first amendment, they found constitutionally objectionable policies of blanket review designed to censor out objectionable materials that could be described in only general terms.

****

In the Court's subsequent decision in <u>Kuhlmeier</u> it dealt with a school's prepublication control of the content of a school newspaper. In <u>Kuhlmeier</u>, a school principal had banned from a school newspaper an article concerning divorce and pregnancy, and the Eighth Circuit had held that the suppression violated the first amendment. The Supreme Court disagreed with the Eighth Circuit's essentially factual determination that the school had created a public forum. The Supreme Court held that the school had reserved to itself the responsibility to regulate the conduct of the school newspaper in accordance with its perception of the proper function of education. "[E]ducators do not offend the First Amendment by exercising editorial control over the style and content of student speech in school-sponsored expressive activities so long as their actions are reasonably related to legitimate pedagogical concerns."

In initially phrasing the issue. Justice White's opinion for the Court stressed that the issue was "the extent to which educators may exercise editorial control over the contents of a high school newspaper produced as part of the school's journalism curriculum" The opinion explained that the school in its capacity, as publisher of a newspaper or producer of a school play may "disassociate" itself from speech which does not meet the school's high standards.The Court thus differentiated between pure student expression with which the Court was concerned in <u>Tinker</u> and expression to which the school has lent its name in sponsorship.

Accordingly, we conclude that the standard articulated in Tinker for determining when a school may punish student expression need not also be the standard for determining when a school may refuse to lend its name and resources to the dissemination of student expression.

Pointing to the need of educators to maintain control over the school curriculum, the Court in <u>Kuhlmeier</u> used a broad definition of curriculum, which it said encompassed "school-sponsored publications, theatrical productions, and other expressive activities that students, parents and members of the public might reasonably perceive to bear the imprimatur of the school." It expressly described the distinction it was drawing between speech protected by the standards of <u>Tinker</u> and speech which the educators could regulate as the distinction "between speech that is sponsored by the school and speech that is not." [509]

In this case the communications, like Bad Astra, which the school policy targets for review for censorship purposes are in no sense "school-sponsored." They are therefore not within the purview of the school's exercise of reasonable editorial control. The student distribution of non-school-sponsored material under the Supreme Court's decisions in <u>Tinker</u> and <u>Kuhlmeier</u> cannot be subjected to regulation on the basis of undifferentiated fears of possible disturbances or embarrassment to school officials, and no more than undifferentiated fear appears as a basis for regulation in this case. There is, therefore, no justification for this policy, which conditions all distribution of student writings on school premises upon prior school approval. Interstudent communication does not interfere with what the school teaches; it enriches the school environment for the students .

Renton's policy conditions distribution of all written materials on school premises upon prior school review for censorship purposes, and is directed at communications lacking any element of school support or endorsement. It is a blanket policy of unlimited scope and duration. For that reason, we do not need to decide under what more limited circumstances, if any, a school may impose a policy of predistribution review. We hold that Renton's policy is overbroad and violates the appellants' first amendment rights. Our holding is limited to school distribution policies which are content based, and does not pertain to regulations of time place, and manner of distribution. Nor does our holding affect the ability of the school to punish students for unacceptable or disruptive conduct after it occurs.

The judgment of the district court is reversed and the case remanded with instructions to enter an order enjoining further enforcement of the review policy and directing the school to purge the plaintiff-students' records of reprimands for violating the policy.

---

[509] <u>Kuhlmeier</u> finds resonant support in this circuit's decision in <u>Nicholson v. Bd of Educ. Torrance Unified Sch. Dist.</u>, 682 F.2d 858 (9th Cir. 1982), which also dealt with school control of what went into the newspaper the school itself published as part of the school's educational program. In <u>Nicholson.</u> this court held that "writers on a high school newspaper do not have an unfettered constitutional right to be free from prepublication review" Id at 863.

****

STUDY QUESTIONS
    1. Does the ruling in <u>Burch</u> help us understand the reach of <u>Hazelwood</u>?
    2. What is the evil underlying a rule which allows prior restraint or review of expressive activity?
    3. Should educators be insulated from student criticism?

ARE STUDENTS ENTITLED TO DUE PROCESS WHEN SCHOOL AUTHORITIES PROPOSE TO SUSPEND OR EXPEL THEM FROM SCHOOL?

<u>GOSS</u>
v.
<u>LOPEZ</u>
419 U.S. 565, 95 S.Ct. 729 (1975)

JUSTICE WHITE delivered the opinion of the Court.

    This appeal by various administrators of the Columbus, Ohio, Public School System (CPSS) challenges the judgment of a three-judge federal court, declaring that appellees—various high school students in the CPSS— were denied due process of law contrary to the command of the Fourteenth Amendment in that they were temporarily suspended from their high schools without a hearing either prior to suspension or within a reasonable time thereafter, and enjoining the administrators to remove all references to such suspensions from the students' records.

I

    Ohio law, Rev. Code Ann §3313.64 (1972), provides for free education to all children between the ages of six and 21. Section 3313.66 of the Code empowers the principal of an Ohio public school to suspend a pupil for misconduct for up to 10 days or to expel him. In either case, he must notify the student's parents within 24 hours and state the reasons for his action. A pupil who is expelled, or his parents, may appeal the decision to the Board of Education and in connection therewith shall be permitted to be heard at the board meeting. The Board may reinstate the pupil following the hearing. No similar procedure is provided in §3313.66 or any other provision of state law for a suspended student. Aside from a regulation tracking the statute, at the time of the imposition of the suspensions in this case the CPSS itself had not issued any written procedure applicable to suspensions.[510] Nor, so far as the record reflects, had any of the individual high schools involved in this case.[511]

---

[510] At the time of the events involved in this case, the only administrative regulation on this subject was §1010.04 of the Administrative Guide of the Columbus Public Schools which provided: "Pupils may be suspended or expelled from school in accordance with the provisions of Section 3313.66 of the Revised Code." Subsequent to the events involved in this lawsuit, the Department of Pupil Personnel of the CPSS issued three memoranda relating to suspension procedures, dated August 16, 1971, February 21, 1973, and July 10, 1973, respectively. The first two are substantially similar to each other and require no factfinding hearing at any time in connection with a suspension. The third, which was apparently in effect when this case was argued, places upon the principal the obligation to "investigate" "before commencing suspension procedures"; and provides as part of the procedures that the principal shall discuss the case with the pupil, so that the pupil may "be heard with respect to the alleged offense," unless the pupil is "unavailable" for such a discussion or "unwilling" to participate in it. The suspensions involved in this case occurred, and records thereof were made, prior to the effective date of these memoranda. The District Court's judgment, including its expunction order, turns on the propriety of the procedures existing at the time the suspensions were ordered and by which they were imposed.

[511] According to the testimony of Phillip Fulton, the principal of one of the high schools involved in this case, there was an informal procedure applicable at the Marion-Franklin High School. It provided that in the routine case of misconduct, occurring in the presence of a teacher, the teacher would describe the misconduct on a form provided for that purpose and would send the student, with the form, to the principal's office. There, the principal would obtain the student's version of the story, and, if it conflicted with the teacher's written version, would send for the

255

Each, however, had formally or informally described the conduct for which suspension could be imposed.

The nine named appellees, each of whom alleged that he or she had been suspended from public high school in Columbus for up to 10 days without a hearing pursuant §3313.66 filed an action under 42 U.S.C. §1983 against the Columbus Board of Education and various administrators of the CPSS. The complaint sought a declaration that §3313.66 was unconstitutional in that it permitted public school administrators to deprive plaintiffs of their rights to an education without a hearing of any kind, in violation of the procedural due process component of the Fourteenth Amendment. It also sought to enjoin the public school officials from issuing future suspensions pursuant to §3313.66 and to require them to remove references to the past suspensions from the records of the students in question.[512]

The proof below established that the suspensions arose out of a period of widespread student unrest in the CPSS during February and March 1971. Six of the named plaintiffs, Rudolph Sutton, Tyrone Washington, Susan Cooper, Deborah Fox, Clarence Byars, and Bruce Harris, were students at the Marion-Franklin High School and were each suspended for 10 days[513] on account of disruptive or disobedient conduct committed in the presence of the school administrator who ordered the suspension. One of these, Tyrone Washington, was among a group of students demonstrating in the school auditorium while a class was being conducted there. He was ordered by the school principal to leave, refused to do so, and was suspended. Rudolph Sutton, in the presence of the principal, physically attacked a police officer who was attempting to remove Tyrone Washington from the auditorium. He was immediately suspended. The other four Marion-Franklin students were suspended for similar conduct. None was given a hearing to determine the operative facts underlying the suspension, but each, together with his or her parents, was offered the opportunity to attend a conference, subsequent to the effective date of the suspension, to discuss the student's future.

Two named plaintiffs, Dwight Lopez and Betty Crome, were students at the Central High School and McGuffey Junior High School, respectively. The former was suspended in connection with a disturbance in the lunchroom which involved some physical damage to school property.[514] Lopez testified that at least 75 other students were suspended from his school on the same day. He also testified below that he was not a party to the destructive conduct but was instead an innocent bystander. Because no one from the school testified with regard to this incident, there is no evidence in the record indicating the official basis for concluding otherwise. Lopez never had a hearing.

Betty Crome was present at a demonstration at a high school other than the one she was attending. There she was arrested together with others, taken to the

---

teacher to obtain the teacher's oral version—apparently in the presence of the student. Mr. Fulton testified that, if a discrepancy still existed, the teacher's version would be believed and the principal would arrive at a disciplinary decision based on it.

[512] The plaintiffs sought to bring the action on behalf of all students of the Columbus Public Schools suspended on or after February 1971, and a class action was declared accordingly. Since the complaint sought to restrain the "enforcement" and "operation" of a state statute "by restraining the action of any officer of such state in the enforcement or execution of such statute," a three judge court was requested pursuant to 28 U. S. C. § 2281 and convened. The students also alleged that the conduct for which they could be suspended was not adequately defined by Ohio law. This vagueness and overbreadth argument was rejected by the court below and the students have not appealed from this part of the court's decision.

[513] Fox was given two separate 10-day suspensions for misconduct occurring on two separate occasions—the second following immediately upon her return to school. In addition to his suspension, Sutton was transferred to another school.

[514] Lopez was actually absent from school, following his suspension, for over 20 days. This seems to have occurred because of a misunderstanding as to the length of the suspension. A letter sent to Lopez after he had been out for over 10 days purports to assume that, being over compulsory school age, he was voluntarily staying away. Upon asserting that this was not the case, Lopez was transferred to another school.

police station, and released without being formally charged. Before she went to school on the following day, she was notified that she had been suspended for a 10-day period. Because no one from the school testified with respect to this incident, the record does not disclose how the McGuffey Junior High School principal went about making the decision to suspend Crome, nor does it disclose on what information the decision was based. It is clear from the record that no hearing was ever held.

There was no testimony with respect to the suspension of the ninth named plaintiff, Carl Smith. The school files were also silent as to his suspension, although as to some, but not all of the other named plaintiffs the files contained either direct references to their suspensions or copies of letters sent to their parents advising them of the suspension.

On the basis of this evidence, the three-judge court declared that plaintiffs were denied due process of law because they were "suspended without hearing prior to suspension or within a reasonable time thereafter," and that Ohio Rev. Code Ann. § 3313.66 (1972) and regulations issued pursuant thereto were unconstitutional in permitting such suspensions.[515] It was ordered that all references to plaintiffs' suspensions be removed from school files.

Although not imposing upon the Ohio school administrators any particular disciplinary procedures and leaving them "free to adopt regulations providing for fair suspension procedures which are consonant with the educational goals of their schools and reflective of the characteristics of their school and locality," the District Court declared that there were "minimum requirements of notice and a hearing prior to suspension, except in emergency situations." In explication, the court stated that relevant case authority would: (1) permit "[i]mmediate removal of a student whose conduct disrupts the academic atmosphere of the school, endangers fellow students, teachers or school officials, or damages property"; (2) require notice of suspension proceedings to be sent to the student's parents within 24 hours of the decision to conduct them; and (3) require a hearing to be held, with the student present, within 72 hours of his removal. Finally, the court stated that, with respect to the nature of the hearing, the relevant cases required that statements in support of the charge be produced, that the student and others be permitted to make statements in defense or mitigation, and that the school need not permit attendance by counsel.

The defendant school administrators have appealed the three-judge court's decision. Because the order below granted plaintiffs' request for an injunction—ordering defendants to expunge their records—this Court has jurisdiction of the appeal pursuant to 28 U. S. C. §1253. We affirm.

II

At the outset, appellants contend that because there is no constitutional right to an education at public expense, the Due Process Clause does not protect against expulsions from the public school system. This position misconceives the nature of the issue and is refuted by prior decisions. The Fourteenth Amendment forbids the State to deprive any person of life, liberty, or property without due process of law. Protected interests in property are normally "not created by the Constitution.

---

[515] In its judgment, the court stated that the statute is unconstitutional in that it provides "for suspension ... without first affording the student due process of law." (Emphasis supplied.) However, the language of the judgment must be read in light of the language in the opinion which expressly contemplates that under some circumstances students may properly be removed from school before the hearing is held, so long as the hearing follows promptly.

257

Rather, they are created and their dimensions are defined" by an independent source such as state statutes or rules entitling the citizen to certain benefits.

****

Here, on the basis of state law, appellees plainly had legitimate claims of entitlement to a public education. Ohio Rev. Code Ann. §§ 3313.48 and 3313.64 (1972 and Supp. 1973) direct local authorities to provide a free education to all residents between five and 21 years of age, and a compulsory-attendance law requires attendance for a school year of not less than 32 weeks. Ohio Rev. Code Ann. §3321.04 (1972). It is true that §3313.66 of the Code permits school principals to suspend students for up to 10 days; but suspensions may not be imposed without any grounds whatsoever. All of the schools had their own rules specifying the grounds for expulsion or suspension. Having chosen to extend the right to an education to people of appellees' class generally, Ohio may not withdraw that right on grounds of misconduct, absent fundamentally fair procedures to determine whether the misconduct has occurred.

Although Ohio may not be constitutionally obligated to establish and maintain a public school system, it has nevertheless done so and has required its children to attend. Those young people do not "shed their constitutional rights" at the schoolhouse door. "The Fourteenth Amendment, as now applied to the States, protects the citizen against the State itself and all of its creatures—Boards of Education not excepted." The authority possessed by the State to prescribe and enforce standards of conduct in its schools although concededly very broad, must be exercised consistently with constitutional safeguards. Among other things, the State is constrained to recognize a student's legitimate entitlement to a public education as a property interest which is protected by the Due Process Clause and which may not be taken away for misconduct without adherence to the minimum procedures required by that Clause.

The Due Process Clause also forbids arbitrary deprivations of liberty. "Where a person's good name, reputation, honor, or integrity is at stake because of what the government is doing to him," the minimal requirements of the Clause must be satisfied. School authorities here suspended appellees from school for periods of up to 10 days based on charges of misconduct. If sustained and recorded, those charges could seriously damage the students' standing with their fellow pupils and their teachers as well as interfere with later opportunities for higher education and employment.[516] It is apparent that the claimed right of the state to determine unilaterally and without process whether that misconduct has occurred immediately collides with the requirements of the Constitution.

Appellants proceed to argue that even if there is a right to a public education protected by the Due Process Clause generally, the Clause comes into play only when the State subjects a student to a "severe detriment or grievous loss." The loss of 10 days, it is said, is neither severe nor grievous and the Due Process Clause is

---

[516] Appellees assert in their brief that four of 12 randomly selected Ohio colleges specifically inquire of the high school of every applicant for admission whether the applicant has ever been suspended. Brief for Appellees 34-35 and n. 40. Appellees also contend that many employers request similar information. Ibid.

Congress has recently enacted legislation limiting access to information contained in the files of a school receiving federal funds. Section 513 of the Education Amendments of 1974, Pub. L. 93-380, 88 Stat. 571, 20 U. S. C. §1232g (1970 ed., Supp . IV), adding § 438 to the General Education Provisions Act. That section would preclude release of "verified reports; of serious; or recurrent behavior patterns" to employers without. written consent of the student's.parents. While subsection (b) (I) (B) permits release of such information to "other schools . . . in which the student intends to enroll," it does so only upon condition that the parent be advised of the release of the information and be given an opportunity at hearing to challenge the content of the information to insure against inclusion of inaccurate or misleading information. The statute does not expressly state whether the parent can contest the underlying basis for a suspension, the fact of which is contained in the student's school record.

therefore of no relevance. Appellants' argument is again refuted by our prior decisions; for in determining "whether due process requirements apply in the first place, we must look not to the 'weight' but to the nature of the interest at stake." Appellees were excluded from school only temporarily, it is true, but the length and consequent severity of a deprivation, while another factor to weigh in determining the appropriate form of hearing, "is not decisive of the basic right" to a hearing of some kind. The Court's view has been that as long as a property deprivation is not de minimis, its gravity is irrelevant to the question whether account must be taken of the Due Process Clause. A 10-day suspension from school is not de minimis in our view and may not be imposed in complete disregard of the Due Process Clause.

A short suspension is, of course, a far milder deprivation than expulsion. But, "education is perhaps the most important function of state and local governments," and the total exclusion from the educational process for more than a trivial period, and certainly if the suspension is for 10 days, is a serious event in the life of the suspended child. Neither the property interest in educational benefits temporally denied nor the liberty interest in reputation, which is also implicated, is so insubstantial that suspensions may constitutionally be imposed by any procedure the school chooses, no matter how arbitrary.[517]

III

"Once it is determined that due process applies, the question remains what process is due." We turn to that question, fully realizing as our cases regularly do that the interpretation and application of the Due Process Clause are intensely practical matters and that "[t]he very nature of due process negates any concept of inflexible procedures universally applicable to every imaginable situation." We are also mindful of our own admonition:

> "Judicial interposition in the operation of the public school system of the Nation raises problems requiring care and restraint.... By and large, public education in our Nation is committed to the control of state and local authorities."

There are certain bench marks to guide us, however. ...[A] case-often invoked by later opinions, said that "[m]any controversies have raged about the cryptic and abstract words of the Due Process Clause but there can be no doubt that at a minimum they require that deprivation of life, liberty or property by adjudication be preceded by notice and opportunity for hearing appropriate to the nature of the case." "The fundamental requisite of due process of law is the opportunity to be heard," a right that "has little reality or worth unless one is informed that the matter is pending and can choose for himself whether to . . . contest." At the very minimum, therefore, students facing suspension and the consequent interference with a protected property interest must be given some kind of notice and afforded some kind of hearing. "Parties whose rights are to be affected are entitled to be heard; and in order that they may enjoy that right they must first be notified."

It also appears from our cases that the timing and content of the notice and the nature of the hearing will depend on appropriate accommodation of the competing interests involved. The student's interest is to avoid unfair or mistaken exclusion from the educational process, with all of its unfortunate consequences.

---

[517] Since the landmark decision of the Court of Appeals for the Fifth Circuit in Dixon v. Alabama State Board of Education, 294 F. 2d 150, cert. denied, 368 U. S. 930 (1961), the lower federal courts have uniformly held the Due Process Clause applicable to decisions made by tax-supported educational institutions to remove a student from the institution long enough for the removal to be classified as an expulsion.

The Due Process Clause will not shield him from suspensions properly imposed, but it disserves both his interest and the interest of the State if his suspension is in fact unwarranted. The concern would be mostly academic if the disciplinary process were a totally accurate, unerring process, never mistaken and never unfair. Unfortunately, that is not the case, and no one suggests that it is. Disciplinarians, although proceeding in utmost good faith, frequently act on the reports and advice of others; and the controlling facts and the nature of the conduct under challenge are often disputed. The risk of error is not at all trivial, and it should be guarded against if that may be done without prohibitive cost or interference with the educational process.

The difficulty is that our schools are vast and complex. Some modicum of discipline and order is essential if the educational function is to be performed. Events calling for discipline are frequent occurrences and sometimes require immediate, effective action. Suspension is considered not only to be a necessary tool to maintain order but a valuable educational device. The prospect of imposing elaborate hearing requirements in every suspension case is viewed with great concern, and many school authorities may well prefer the untrammeled power to act unilaterally, unhampered by rules about notice and hearing. But it would be a strange disciplinary system in an educational institution if no communication was sought by the disciplinarian with the student in an effort to inform him of his dereliction and to let him tell his side of the story in order to make sure that an injustice is not done. "[F]airness can rarely be obtained by secret, one-sided determination of facts decisive of rights...." "Secrecy is not congenial to truth-seeking and self-righteousness gives too slender an assurance of rightness. No better instrument has been devised for arriving at truth than to give a person in jeopardy of serious loss notice of the case against him and opportunity to meet it."

We do not believe that school authorities must be totally free from notice and hearing requirements if their schools are to operate with acceptable efficiency. Students facing temporary suspensions have interests qualifying for protection of the Due Process Clause, and due process requires in connection with a suspension of 10 days or less that the student be given oral or written notice of the charges against him and, if he denies them, an explanation of the evidence the authorities have and an opportunity to present his side of the story. The Clause requires at least these rudimentary precautions against unfair or mistaken findings of misconduct and arbitrary exclusion from school.

There need be no delay between the time "notice" is given and the time of the hearing. In the great majority of cases the disciplinarian may informally discuss the alleged misconduct with the student minutes after it has occurred. We hold only that, in being given an opportunity to explain his version of the facts at this discussion the student first be told what he is accused of doing and what the basis of the accusation is. Lower courts which have addressed the question of the nature of the procedures required in short suspension cases have reached the same conclusion. Since the hearing may occur almost immediately following the misconduct, it follows that as a general rule notice and hearing should precede removal of the student from school. We agree with the District Court, however, that there are recurring situations in which prior notice and hearing cannot be insisted upon. Students whose presence poses a continuing danger to persons or property or an ongoing threat of disrupting the academic process may be immediately removed from school. In such cases, the necessary notice and rudimentary hearing should follow as soon as practicable, as the District Court indicated. In holding as we do, we do not believe that we have imposed procedures on school disciplinarians which are inappropriate in a classroom setting. Instead we have imposed requirements which are, if anything, less than a fair-minded school principal would impose upon himself in order to avoid unfair suspensions. Indeed, according to the testimony of the principal of Marion-Franklin High School, that school had an informal procedure, remarkably similar to that which we now require, applicable to suspensions generally but which was not followed in this case. Similarly, according to the most recent memorandum applicable to the entire CPSS, school principals in the CPSS are now required by local rule to provide at least as much as the constitutional minimum which we have described.

We stop short of construing the Due Process Clause to require, countrywide, that hearings in connection with short suspensions must afford the student the opportunity to secure counsel, to confront and cross-examine witnesses supporting the charge, or to call his own witnesses to verify his version of the incident. Brief disciplinary suspensions are almost countless. To impose in each such case even truncated trial-type procedures might well overwhelm administrative facilities in many places and, by diverting resources, cost more than it would save in educational effectiveness. Moreover, further formalizing the suspension process and escalating its formality and adversary nature may not only make it too costly as a regular disciplinary tool but also destroy its effectiveness as part of the teaching process.

On the other hand, requiring effective notice and informal hearing permitting the student to give his version of the events will provide a meaningful hedge against erroneous action. At least the disciplinarian will be alerted to the existence of disputes about facts and arguments about cause and effect. He may then determine himself to summon the accuser, permit cross-examination, and allow the student to present his own witnesses. In more difficult cases, he may permit counsel. In any event, his discretion will be more informed and we think the risk of error substantially reduced.

Requiring that there be at least an informal give-and-take between student and disciplinarian, preferably prior to the suspension, will add little to the factfinding function where the disciplinarian himself has witnessed the conduct forming the basis for the charge. But things are not always as they seem to be, and the student will at least have the opportunity to characterize his conduct and put it in what he deems the proper context.

We should also make it clear that we have addressed ourselves solely to the short suspension, not exceeding 10 days. Longer suspensions or expulsions for the remainder of the school term, or permanently, may require more formal procedures. Nor do we put aside the possibility that in unusual situations, although involving only a short suspension, something more than the rudimentary procedures will be required.

IV

The District Court found each of the suspensions involved here to have occurred without a hearing, either before or after the suspension, and that each suspension was therefore invalid and the statute unconstitutional insofar as it permits such suspensions without notice or hearing. Accordingly, the judgment is
Affirmed

MR. JUSTICE POWELL, with whom THE CHIEF JUSTICE, MR JUSTICE BLACKMUN, and MR. JUSTICE REHNQUIST join, dissenting.

The Court today invalidates an Ohio statute that permits student suspensions from school without a hearing "for not more than ten days." The decision unnecessarily opens avenues for judicial intervention in the operation of our public schools that may affect adversely the quality of education. The Court holds for the first time that the federal courts, rather than educational officials and state legislatures, have the authority to determine the rules applicable to routine classroom discipline of children and teenagers in the public schools. It justifies this unprecedented intrusion into the process of elementary and secondary education by identifying a new constitutional right: the right of a student not to be suspended for as much as a single day without notice and a due process hearing either before or promptly following the suspension.

The Court's decision rests on the premise that, under Ohio law, education is a property interest protected by the Fourteenth Amendment's Due Process Clause and therefore that any suspension requires notice and a hearing. In my view, a student's interest in education is not infringed by a suspension within the limited period prescribed by Ohio law. Moreover, to the extent that there may be some arguable infringement, it is too speculative, transitory, and insubstantial to justify imposition of a constitutional rule.

****

STUDY QUESTIONS

1. How did the Court define the students property interest involved in the case?
2. What liberty interest was infringed by suspension from school?
3. Did the Court outline the nature of the process due if a child is excluded from school longer than 10 days?
4. If a suspension is 10 days or less is the process due the same for regular and disabled children?

****

Nevada Student Discipline Statutes

The Nevada legislature has enacted a number of statutes dealing with student discipline.which reflect Supreme Court jurisprudence.[518]

Members of every board of trustees, superintendents of schools, principals and teachers are granted concurrent power with peace officers for the protection of children in school and on the way to and from school, and for the enforcement of order and discipline among such children who attend school within one school district but reside in an adjoining district or adjoining state.[519]

Each school is directed to prescribe written rules of behavior required of and prohibited for pupils attending school within their district and must prescribe appropriate punishments for violations of the rules.[520] Copies of the rules must be

---

[518] Sec. 392.460-490 NRS (1993)

[519] The legislature has further declared that the duty imposed shall not be construed to require superintendents of schools, principals and teacher to supervise the conduct of children while not on the school property. Sec. 392.460 (2) NRS (1993). Legal counsel for the state teachers association contends that teachers seek the assistance of school police or administrators instead of attempting to arrest a student. Dyer, Mike, NV Law Column, Advocate, May 1992, p. 5.; See also AGO 35 (7-26-1971) Under § 392.460 schools may promulgate and enforce rules and regulations concerning conduct of students both on and off school property, provided they are directly related ot maintenance of order and discipline for legitimate school functions.

[520] Trustees may not suspend or expel student for riding during lunch hour vehicle that student rides to school and parks off school grounds. Under former NRS 392.030 (cf. NRS 392.467), which permits boards of school trustees to discipline students who disobey reasonable rules of

distributed to each pupil at the beginning of the school year and to each new pupil who enters during the year. Copies must also be made available for inspection at each school located in the district which is open to the public.[521]

Nevada legislation also addresses specific types of behavior by students. For example, a 1993 session law prohibits students from carrying or possessing electronic devices used for paging or communications while on school grounds.[522] The law further mandates that local boards adopt and enforce measures for disciplining any pupil who is found in possession of an alcoholic beverage or a controlled substance, while on the premises of any public school in its district.

Specific punishments are also mandated by state law for certain behavior. Any pupil who commits a battery which results in bodily injury of an employee of the school or sells or distributes any controlled substance while on the premises of any public school or school sponsored activity or on any school bus must for the first occurrence be suspended or expelled from that school.[523] The period of removal from the home school is mandated to be for at least one semester. For a second occurrence the student must be permanently expelled from his\her home school.

The law also provides mandatory penalties for pupils found in possession of a dangerous weapon [524] while on school premises, at an activity sponsored by a public school or on any school bus.[525] Children who violate this statute must be suspended or expelled for a period of not less that one semester for the first offense.[526] A second offense mandates permanent expulsion for the child's home school. This provision of state law does not prohibit a pupil from having in his possession a knife or firearm with the approval of the principal of the school. Principal approval for such possession is subject to the policies and regulations adopted by the local board.[527]

In 1993 the legislature amended Chapter 392 adding a new section providing that a pupil suspended or expelled from any public school in Nevada or any school outside the state for battery on a school employee, possession of a dangerous weapon or sale or distrubution of a controlled substance is ineligible to attend any

---

order, board may not suspend or expel students who ride vehicles to school and park vehicles off school grounds, but ride vehicles during noon hour in violation of board rule. AGO 388 (2-23-1967)

Student may not be suspended for acts committed offschool property until his guilt is determined by court. Former NRS 392.030 (cf. NRS 392.467), which allows suspension or expulsion of public school pupils for failure to submit to rules of order and discipline, does not apply to acts committed off school property. Student may not be suspended, even though accused of crime, until guilt or innocence is determined by court, because to do so would be to violate common law presumption of innocence until proved guilty. AGO 625 (10-29-1969) Does this opinion prevent the school district from suspending a student who is observed damaging a teachers personal property at the teachers home?

Schools may regulate conduct of students both on and off school property when directly related to maintenance of order for school functions. Under provisions of former NRS 392.030 (cf. NRS 392.467) and NRS 392.460, schools may promulgate and enforce rules and regulations concerning conduct of students both on and off school property, provided they are directly related to maintenance of order and discipline for legitimate school functions. AGO 35 (7-26-1971)

[521] Sec. 392.463 NRS (1991).

[522]Chapter 613 Laws of Nevada (1993) amending Chapter 392 NRS. The law prohibits students from carrying beepers, portable telephones, or other similar electronic devices. However, with written approval of the principal students may be allowed to carry such devices.

[523] Sec. 392.466(1) NRS (1993) He\she may be placed in another kind of school.

[524] Chapter 21 Laws of Nevada (1993) amending Sec. 393.070 NRS (1991) enhances the penalty for certain crimes committed on school property to a gross misdemeanor. The Chapter also defines dangerous knife as a knife 2 inches or more from tip to to handle. Sec. 392.466(6)(b) NRS (1993) "Dangerous weapon" includes, without limitation, a blackjack, slung shot, billy, sand-club, sandbag, metal knuckles, explosive substance or device, dirk, dagger, pistol, revolver or other firearm, a nunchaku, switch-blade knife or trefoil, as defined in NRS 202.350, a butterfly knife or any other knife described in NRS 202.350.

[525] Sec. 392.466(2) NRS (1993). He\she may be placed in another kind of school under the law.

[526]Some 5,356 people under the age of 19 were killed by guns in 1991, or almost 15 youths a day, according to government statistics. The National Association of Children's Hospitals and Related Institutions examined discharge records from 44 acute care children's hospitals and found, in a survey that children wounded by gunfire ran up bills that averaged $14,434 in 1991. That is just about what four-year private colleges charged for tuition room and board that same year. The association counted only the hospital charges, not doctor bills or the costs of lifetime rehabilitation for the maimed. The group is now asking all of its 132 member hospitals and pediatric units to track firearms injuries and deaths to heighten public awareness of the problem. See Connell, Christopher, "Gun Violence Against Youth Costs Millions," Review Journal, Nov. 26, 1993, p. 1 A.

[527] Sec. 392.466(3) NRS (1993).

public school in Nevada during the period of the suspension or expulsion.[528] After an investigation the school district may place students declared ineligible for regular enrollment, due to current suspension or expulsion, in an alternative program for at risk pupils or court continuation school.[529]

If suspension or expulsion is used as a punishment for violating state law or school rules, the school district is required to abide by the procedures established in §392.467 NRS (1991).[530] The rules established must be and appear to be consistent with applicable judicial holdings.[531] No pupil may be suspended or expelled until he\she has been govern notice of the charges against him\her an explanation of the evidence and an opportunity for a hearing. Pupils who pose a danger to other students or property or an ongoing threat of disrupting the academic process or who is selling or distributing any controlled substance or is found in possession of a dangerous weapon may be removed immediately upon being given and explanation of the reasons for the removal. The process due under the statute and or Constitution must be conducted as soon as practicable after the removal.[532] Explusion proceedings are closed to the public.[533]

Moreover, the school board is forbidden from authorizing expulsion, suspension, or removal from the public school system solely because th pupil is declared a truant or habitual truant. [534]

Pupils in grades 1-6 may be suspended from school or permanently expelled from school only after the school board has reviewed the circumstances and approved the action in accordance with procedures adopted to address such issues.[535]

Special Education students may be suspended from school pursuant to §392.466 NRS for not more than 10 days for each occurrence of misbehavior.[536] Suspension from school for a period in excess of 10 days or permanent expulsion is subject school board review of the circumstances and a determination that the action is in compliance with the Individuals with Disabilities Education Act (IDEA).[537]

Recent school safety concerns have led the legislature to empower local school boards to employ school police officers.[538] The qualifications, training and authority

---

[528]Chapter 561 Laws of Nevada Sec. 2 (1) (1993).

[529]Chapter 561 Laws of Nevada Sec. 2 (2) (a) (b) (1993).

[530]Sec. 392.467 NRS (1993) requires that a student be given notice of the charges and an explanation of the evidence and an oppportinity for a hearing. If a student poses a continuing danger to persons and property, is selling or distributing a controlled substance, or is found in possession of a dangerous weapon they may be removed immediately pending proceedings to be conducted as soon as practicable after removal for suspension or expulsion.

[531] See Goss v. Lopez supra.

[532] Sec. 392.467(2) NRS (1993).

[533]Sec. 392.467 (3) NRS (1993). The provision that hearings upon discipline of pupils be closed to the public does not violate a pupils right equal protection of law because a rational basis exists to protect the privacy of pupils. See Davis v. Churchill County School Bd., 616 F.Supp. 1310 (D. Nev. 1985)

[534]Sec. 392.467 (4) NRS (1993).

[535] Sec. 392.466(4) NRS (1993).

[536] Sec. 392.466(5)(a) NRS (1993). Check local policy regarding suspension of special education students. Some districts have adopted adopted a policy imposing a limit on suspension days regardless of the how often a student mishaves. The Office of Civil Rights (OCR) maybe insisting on the adoption of such a policy suggesting it is required under IDEA. Ask for a citation to Federal statute, rule or judicial decision before deviating from state statute since state law was drafted to conform with Federal requirements.

[537] Sec. 392.466(5)(b) NRS (1993) As of October 1990 name changed to Individuals with Disabilities Education Act (IDEA). As to rules regarding discipline of disabled students see Honig v.Doe infra.

[538]Sec. 391.100 4 NRS (1993). Members of every board of trustees of a school district, school superintendent, principals,and teachers have concurrent power with peace officers for the protection of children in school and on the way to and from school and for the enforcement of order and discipline among such children. This concurrent power must not be construed so as to make it the duty of superintendents etc. to supervise the conduct of children while not on the school property. See Chapter 609 Laws of Nevada Sec. 6 (3) (1993) amending Chapter 281 NRS.

School custodians also have powers of a peace officer to carry out the intents and purposes of their school responsibilities. See Chapter 609 Laws of Nevada Sec. 6 (2) (1993) amending Chapter 281 NRS.

[539] of school police officers is coextensive with regular peace officers on all school property and within buildings and other facilities of the school district.[540] The jurisdiction of school police within the school community is to protect school district personnel, pupils or real and personal property. They are also charged with cooperating with local law enforcement agencies in matters relating to personnel, pupils and district property.[541]

The highly publicized [542] and problematic arrest of a Clark County Elementary School student in his classroom by three armed Clark County police officers provoked 1993 legislative action concerning school arrests.[543] Under the new legislation each school district, in conjunction with the school police officers of the school district, if any, and the local law enforcement agencies that have jurisdiction over the school district, shall establish a policy for the procedures which must be followed by a peace officer in arresting a pupil on school grounds during

---

[539] Sec. 281.275 NRS (1993) prohibits a peace officer from using the a choke hold on any on any person unless the officer has received special training and certification.

[540] See Chapter 609 Laws of Nevada Sec. 6 (1) (1993) amending Chapter 281 NRS. Chapter 609 Laws of Nevada (1993) revises and consolidates state statutes that confer the powers of a peace officer into Chapter 281 NRS. Chapter 609 Laws of Nevada Sec. 6 (1993) addresses matters related to school police.

[541] Sec. 391.275 NRS (1991).

[542] The Las Vegas Review Journal first broke the story in an article under the headline "Authorities Faulted for Nabbing Boy" on January 9 1993. The article reported that the president of the Las Vegas chapter of the NAACP, Jesse Scott, had bitterly complained about the arrest of a 10 year old boy at Lunt Elementary School on January 4, 1993.

After receiving a complaint that Stanley Johnson threatened to kill a student at a super market the previous day police officers were dispatched to Lunt elementary school. After meeting with the principal they proceeded to the childs classroom and took the student into custody. Rev. Scott explained the arrest as follows; "Three officers stand him up before his class. One puts handcuffs on him and the other two have their hands on their guns. This is so insensitive to do this in front of his peers." Stanley was then removed from the class searched in the school hallway and taken to the county's juvenile detention center. He was released Monday afternoon. "What is Metro doing?" Scott asked.

Stanley described the incident as follows; "They asked me to stand up. I thought they were going to ask me a question or something. But then one came over and put me in handcuffs and the others had their hands on their guns. I thought they were going to make a move, you know, take them out and point their guns at me." Stanley was 4 foot 6 inches tall and weighed 65 pounds at the time of the incident.

As a result of Rev. Scotts complaint the school district and Metro launched investigations into the incident. Lt Carl Fruge presented Metros initial response denying that there were any racial overtones in the incident and suggesting that police had reason for quick action. "It is normally not the district's practice to permit students to be arrested n the classroom or other public areas," said Superintendent Brian Cram in a prepared statement. See Robertson, Alonza, "Authorities Faulted for Nabbing Boy", Review Journal, January 9, 1993, p. 3 B.

On January 12, 1993 Metro reported that its investigation of the incident by the field services division concluded that the officers acted properly using their discretionary powers inthe interest of public safety. The report did not satisfy Rev. Scott or other local groups. In addition, the NAACP called for the dismissal of the principal. See "Police Cleared for Incident Involving Boy," Review Journal, January 12, 1993, p. 6 B.

More than 20 black parents and community activists attended the January 12, 1993 school board meeting. The insisted on the removal of the principal for allowing the arrest to occur in a classroom and failing to notify the parent following the arrest. School board member Dan Newburn was reported as saying "It was sad, it was stupid and we should see that it never happens again." Assemblyman Wendell williams D-Las Vegas promised the legislature would consider a bill limiting the discretion of police officers to take such action and urged the school board to support the bill. Following the meeting the superintendent explained that district policies spell out steps that should be taken during custodial action on campus. Under the district policy police are required to file a student release form, parents should be notified if possible and the arrest should be accomplished in a manner so no embarrassment to the student should result. However, Dr. Cram pointed out that no matter what school policy is in place state law gives police broad discretion and school officials must follow directions given by law enforcement authorities. He suggested that what was needed was an agreement with law enforcement agencies spelling out how and where students can be taken into custody at school. See Gallant, John, "Blacks Seek Change in School Policy", Review Journal, January 13, 1993, p. 1 B.

A Review Journal editorial labeled the arrest an "overreaction" but called upon Rev. Scott to condemn not only the police action but also the behavior of a 10 year old making threats. ("Did the Police Overreact?", Review Journal Editorial, 1-13-93, p. 6 B.)

A small group demanding dismissal of Lunt principal Ventura led by Rev. Scott began picketing at Lunt elementary school on January 22,1993. Although the pickets blamed the principal for the incident district officials noted again that police authority supersedes the districts in law enforcement matters. Dr. Cram also indicated he would not fire Ventura. See Green, Marian,"Activists Urge Principal's Firing," Review Journal, January 22, 1993, p. 6 B.

A stalemate ensued when Rev. Scott refused an invitation from the superintendent to dialog regarding the incident until the principal was removed. Then officials of the Clark County Association of School Administrators joined the dispute in support of the principal. They told the school board that the principal suggested that Stanley be brought to her office to be arrested. But the officers insisted that a safety issue was involved and that the student should be taken into custody in his classroom. They also claimed that the principal attempted to contact the mother following the arrest. Meanwhile, the student was enrolled in another school and was receiving counseling. See Green, Marian, "Bid to Oust School Principal Continuing," Review Journal, January 23, 1993, p. 4 D.

On February 22, 1993 the Review Journal reported that Stanley Johnson was doing fine in his studies at Sunrise Acres elementary school. The article also noted that even though the principal was cleared of wrongdoing she had requested a transfer which was likely to take place in March. See Gallant, John, "Fourth-Grader Doing Well," Review Journal, February 22, 1993, p. 1 B.

Chapter 290 Laws of Nevada (1993) adding a new section to Chapter 392 regarding arrests on school grounds during school hours supported by Wendell Williams was approved June 25, 1993.

[543] Chapter 290 Laws of Nevada (1993) adding a new section to Chapter 392.

school hours.[544] The policy must include the circumstances under which the chief administrative officer of a school be notified of the arrest of a pupil.[545] The legislature also directed that each law enforcement agency that has jurisdiction over any part of a schooldistrict shall adopt the policy which is established pursuant to the law.[546]

The legislature has also enacted laws which recognize the importance of civility on school premises and at school activities. It is a misdemeanor to disturb the peace of any public school by using vile or indecent language within the building or grounds of a school. The law also outlaws assaults on pupils or school employees on school grounds, on a bus, van or other motor vehicle operated by a school district or at a location where a student or school employee is involved in an activity sponsored by a public school.[547] It is also a misdemeanor to interfere with students while on their way to school.[548]

Other statutes encourage cooperation between parents and school authorities. For example, legislation has been adopted which prohibits terminating or threatening to terminate the employment of a parent or guardian who appears at a conference requested by school officials.[549] The law also prohibits such activity when a parent receives notification of an emergency regarding their child during work hours.[550] Violation of the law is a misdemeanor.[551] Civil remedies are accorded to parents discharged in violation of the law.[552]

WHEN MAY SCHOOL OFFICIALS SEARCH A STUDENT AT SCHOOL?[553]

NEW JERSEY
v.
T. L. O.
469 U. S. 325, 105 S.Ct. 733 (1985)

JUSTICE WHITE delivered the opinion of the Court.

We granted certiorari in this case to examine the appropriateness of the exclusionary rule as a remedy for searches carried out in violation of the Fourth Amendment by public school authorities. Our consideration of the proper application of the Fourth Amendment to the public schools, however, has led us to conclude that the search that gave rise to the case now before us did not violate the Fourth Amendment. Accordingly, we here address only the questions of the proper

---

[544]Chapter 290 Laws of Nevada Sec. 1 (1993). Item 16 of the Agenda of the Clark County School District meeting of October 26, 1993 reflects a recommendation for approval of an amendment to School District Policy 5140 entitled Student Discipline and Cooperation with Law Enforcement Agencies.

[545]Ibid.

[546]Chapter 290 Laws of Nevada Sec. 2 (1993).

[547] Chapter 134 Laws of Nevada (1993) amending Sec. 392.480 NRS (1991) expands the prohibition against threatening and assaulting pupils and teachers to include other school employees.

[548]Sec. 392.470 NRS (1993).

[549] Sec. 392.490 NRS (1993).

[550] Ibid.

[551]Sec. 392.490 (2) (1993).

[552]Sec. 392.490 (3) (1993). A civil action against employer for discharge in violation of law is created. Recovery of wages and benefits lost as a result of the violation, reinstatement without loss of position, seniority or benefits, damages equal to the amount of the lost wages and benefits and reasonable attorney's fees fixed by the court are also authorized for violating the statute.

[553]For additional background informantion see Rossow, Lawrence F. & Stubblefield, Brenda L., "Student Strip Search Upheld: Williams by Williams v. Ellington," 75 Ed.Law Rep. [723] (August 27, 1992), Bjorklun, Eugene C., "Drug Testing High School Athletes and the Fourth Amendment," 83 Ed.Law Rep. [913] (Sept. 9, 1993).

standard for assessing the legality of searches conducted by public school officials and the application of that standard to the facts of this case.

I

On March 7, 1980, a teacher at Piscataway High School in Middlesex County, N. J., discovered two girls smoking in a lavatory. One of the two girls was the respondent T. L. O., who at that time was a 14-year-old high school freshman. Because smoking in the lavatory was a violation of a school rule, the teacher took the two girls to the Principal's office, where they met with Assistant Vice Principal Theodore Choplick. In response to questioning by Mr. Choplick, T. L. O.'s companion admitted that she had violated the rule. T. L. O., however, denied that she had been smoking in the lavatory and claimed that she did not smoke at all.

Mr. Choplick asked T. L. O. to come into his private office and demanded to see her purse. Opening the purse, he found a pack of cigarettes, which he removed from the purse and held before T. L. O. as he accused her of having lied to him. As he reached into the purse for the cigarettes, Mr. Choplick also noticed a package of cigarette rolling papers. In his experience, possession of rolling papers by high school students was closely associated with the use of marihuana. Suspecting that a closer examination of the purse might yield further evidence of drug use, Mr. Choplick proceeded to search the purse thoroughly. The search revealed a small amount of marihuana, a pipe, a number of empty plastic bags, a substantial quantity of money in one-dollar bills, an index card that appeared to be a list of students who owed T. L. O. money, and two letters that implicated T. L. O. in marihuana dealing.

Mr. Choplick notified T. L. O.'s mother and the police, and turned the evidence of drug dealing over to the police. At the request of the police, T. L. O.'s mother took her daughter to police headquarters, where T. L. O. confessed that she had been selling marihuana at the high school. On the basis of the confession and the evidence seized by Mr. Choplick, the State brought delinquency charges against T. L. O. in the Juvenile and Domestic Relations Court of Middlesex County.[554] Contending that Mr. Choplick's search of her purse violated the Fourth Amendment, T. L. O. moved to suppress the evidence found in her purse as well as her confession, which, she argued, was tainted by the allegedly unlawful search. The Juvenile Court denied the motion to suppress. Although the court concluded that the Fourth Amendment did apply to searches carried out by school officials, it held that

> "a school official may properly conduct a search of a student's person if the official has a reasonable suspicion that a crime has been or is in the process of being committed, or reasonable cause to believe that the search is necessary to maintain school discipline or enforce school policies."

Applying this standard, the court concluded that the search conducted by Mr. Choplick was a reasonable one. The initial decision to open the purse was justified by Mr. Choplick's well-founded suspicion that T. L. O. had violated the rule forbidding smoking in the lavatory. Once the purse was open, evidence of marihuana violations was in plain view, and Mr. Choplick was entitled to conduct a thorough search to determine the nature and extent of T. L. O.'s drug-related

---

[554] T. L. O. also received a 3-day suspension from school for smoking cigarettes in a nonsmoking area and a 7-day suspension for possession of marihuana. On T. L. O.'s motion, the Superior Court of New Jersey, Chancery Division, set aside the 7-day suspension on the ground that it was based on evidence seized in violation of the Fourth Amendment. (T. L. O.) v. Pucataway Bd. of Ed., No. C.2865-79 (Super. Ct. N. J., Ch. Div., Mar. 31,1980). The Board of Education apparently did not appeal the decision of the Chancery Division.

activities. Having denied the motion to suppress, the court on March 23, 1981, found T. L. O. to be a delinquent and on January 8, 1982, sentenced her to a year's probation.

On appeal from the final judgment of the Juvenile Court, a divided Appellate Division affirmed the trial court's finding that there had been no Fourth Amendment violation, but vacated the adjudication of delinquency and remanded for a determination whether T. L. O. had knowingly and voluntarily waived her Fifth Amendment rights before confessing. State ex rel. T. L. O., 185 N. J. Super. 279, 448 A. 2d 493 (1982). T. L. O. appealed the Fourth Amendment ruling, and the Supreme Court of New Jersey reversed the judgment of the Appellate Division and ordered the suppression of the evidence found in T. L. O.'s purse.

The New Jersey Supreme Court agreed with the lower courts that the Fourth Amendment applies to searches conducted by school officials. The court also rejected the State of New Jersey's argument that the exclusionary rule should not be employed to prevent the use in juvenile proceedings of evidence unlawfully seized by school officials. Declining to consider whether applying the rule to the fruits of searches by school officials would have any deterrent value, the court held simply that the precedents of this Court establish that "if an official search violates constitutional rights, the evidence is not admissible in criminal proceedings."

With respect to the question of the legality of the search before it, the court agreed with the Juvenile Court that a warrantless search by a school official does not violate the Fourth Amendment so long as the official "has reasonable grounds to believe that a student possesses evidence of illegal activity or activity that would interfere with school discipline and order." However, the court, with two justices dissenting, sharply disagreed with the Juvenile Court's conclusion that the search of the purse was reasonable. According to the majority, the contents of T. L. O.'s purse had no bearing on the accusation against T. L. O., for possession of cigarettes (as opposed to smoking them in the lavatory) did not violate school rules, and a mere desire for evidence that would impeach T. L. O. 's claim that she did not smoke cigarettes could not justify the search. Moreover, even if a reasonable suspicion that T. L. O. had cigarettes in her purse would justify a search, Mr. Choplick had no such suspicion, as no one had furnished him with any specific information that there were cigarettes in the purse. Finally, leaving aside the question whether Mr. Choplick was justified in opening the purse, the court held that the evidence of drug use that he saw inside did not justify the extensive "rummaging" through T. L. O.'s papers and effects that followed. Id., at 347, 463 A. 2d, at 942-943.

We granted the State of New Jersey's petition for certiorari.

****

Although we originally granted certiorari to decide the issue of the appropriate remedy in juvenile court proceedings for unlawful school searches, our doubts regarding the wisdom of deciding that question in isolation from the broader question of what limits, if any, the Fourth Amendment places on the activities of school authorities prompted us to order reargument on that question.[555] Having

---

[555] State and federal courts considering these questions have struggled to accommodate the interests protected by the Fourth Amendment and the interest of the States in providing a safe environment conducive to education in the public schools. Some courts have resolved the tension between these interests by giving full force to one or the other side of the balance. Thus, in a number of cases courts have held that school officials conducting in-school searches of students are private parties acting in loco parentis and are therefore not subject to the constraints of the Fourth Amendment. At least one court has held, on the other hand, that the Fourth Amendment applies in full to in-school searches by school officials and that a search conducted without probable cause is unreasonable; others have held or suggested that the probable-cause standard is applicable at least where the police are involved in a search; or where the search is highly intrusive.

The majority of courts that have addressed the issue of the Fourth Amendment in the schools have, like the Supreme Court of New Jersey in this case, reached a middle position: the Fourth Amendment applies to searches conducted by school authorities, but the special needs

heard argument on the legality of the search of T. L. O.'s purse, we are satisfied that the search did not violate the Fourth Amendment.[556]

II

In determining whether the search at issue in this case violated the Fourth Amendment, we are faced initially with the question whether that Amendment's prohibition on unreasonable searches and seizures applies to searches conducted by public school officials. We hold that it does.

It is now beyond dispute that "the Federal Constitution, by virtue of the Fourteenth Amendment, prohibits unreasonable searches and seizures by state officers." Equally indisputable is the proposition that the Fourteenth Amendment protects the rights of students against encroachment by public school officials:

> "The Fourteenth Amendment, as now applied to the States, protects the citizen against the State itself and all of its creatures— Boards of Education not excepted. These have, of course, important, delicate, and highly discretionary functions, but none that they may

---

of the school environment require assessment of the legality of such searches against a standard less exacting than that of probable cause. These courts have, by and large, upheld warrantless searches by school authorities provided that they are supported by a reasonable suspicion that the search will uncover evidence of an infraction of school disciplinary rules or a violation of the law.

The 9th circuit case of Bilbrey v. Brown, 738 F. 2d 1462 (CA9 1984) illustrates this point. Anthony Gartner and Joseph Bilbrey, minors, appeal from a judgment which denied them relief in their civil rights action arising from an alleged unlawful search by appellees, Joseph Taylor and Gary Robinson. Gartner and Bilbrey were fifth grade students at a public school in Columbia County, Oregon. They were searched by Taylor, the school principal, and Robinson, a teacher, looking for drugs. The parents sued on behalf of the minors.

After the evidence was completed, the district court ruled that the search violated appellants' constitutional rights, but allowed the jury to decide whether appellees had immunity from monetary damages. The jury found immunity. On appeal appellants argue that, as a matter of law, appellees were not entitled to immunity, or alternatively, that the evidence was insufficient to support the jury verdict. Appellants also contend that the court erred in denying them declaratory relief, and that it abused its discretion in refusing to grant a new trial because of prejudicial misconduct of appellees' attorney and in denying attorney's fees.

FACTS

On the morning of September 3, 1978, a school bus driver, Roberta Cunningham, observed Bilbrey and Gartner exchanging something on the school playground.Although she could not identify the contents of the exchange, Cunningham suspected drugs and reported the incident to Gartner. When classes had begun, Bilbrey, and then Gartner were removed from class and taken to the locker room by Robinson, where Taylor was waiting. Taylor informed Bilbrey that they were going to search him for drugs and Robinson then patted him down. Taylor then had Bilbrey remove all clothing except his underwear, and the appellees searched his garments. When Gartner arrived appellees patted him down and searched through his pockets but did not require him to remove his clothing. Neither search produced drugs or evidence of drug use. The parties disputed whether appellants' permission to be searched had been sought. Appellees testified that they asked permission to search; the boys stated that they were simply told they were going to be searched.

Appellants, through their parents; brought this action under 42 U.S.C. § 1983 against the members of the Columbia County School Board, the Superintendent of Schools, appellees Taylor and Robinson, bus driver Cunningham, and another teacher associated with the search. Appellants sought damages and declaratory and injunctive relief for the illegal search. In addition they sought a specific declaration that the School Board guidelines, "Minimum Standards of Conduct and Discipline" (hereafter Minimum Standards), were unconstitutional on the grounds that they authorized warrantless searches of students and were unconstitutionally vague.

On cross motions for partial summary judgment the district court held that the Minimum Standards met constitutional standards. 481 F.Supp. 26 (D.Ore.1979). The court concluded that while students are entitled to the protection of the Fourth Amendment, and school administrators must have at least "reasonable cause" to search, they do not need a warrant "so long as [the] school is pursuing its legitimate interest in maintaining the order, discipline, safety, supervision, and education of students." Id at 28. The court also held that the term, "school violation," was sufficiently defined in other portions of the "Minimum Standards" to survive a vagueness challenge. Id at 29. Appellants do not appeal this ruling.

After a three-day jury trial the district court stated that (1) as a matter of law, appellants Taylor and Robinson, had had neither "reasonable cause" nor "probable cause" to believe that Bilbrey or Gartner had drugs in their possession and (2) that even if the minors were held to have agreed to the searches, "under the coercive circumstances shown" the consent was invalid as a matter of law. The court then submitted to the jury whether appellees qualified for good faith immunity under Wood v. Strickland, 420 U.S. 308, 95 S.Ct. 992 (1975). It also submitted the damage issue to the jury, advising them that the court had already found the searches to be unconstitutional under the Fourth Amendment and had ruled that there was no valid consent. The jury's verdict held that Taylor and Robinson were entitled to immunity and not subject to monetary liability for the searches of the boy. Subsequently, the court denied appellants motion for declaratory relief and their request for attorney's fees as "prevailing parties" under 42 U.S.C. § 1988.

We reverse.

Although few have considered the matter, courts have also split over whether the exclusionary rule is an appropriate remedy for Fourth Amendment violations committed by school authorities. The Georgia courts have held that although the Fourth Amendment applies to the schools, the exclusionary rule does not. See, e. g., State v. Young, supra; State v. Lamb, 137 Ga. App. 437, 224 S. E. 51(1976). Other jurisdictions have applied the rule to exclude the fruits of unlawful school searches from criminal trials and delinquency proceedings. See State v. Mora, supra; People v. D., supra.

[556] In holding that the search of T. L. 0.'s purse did not violate the Fourth Amendment, we do not implicitly determine that the exclusionary rule applies to the fruits of unlawful searches conducted by school authorities. The question whether evidence should be excluded from a criminal proceeding involves two discrete inquiries: whether the evidence was seized in violation of the Fourth Amendment, and whether the exclusionary rule is the appropriate remedy for the violation. Neither question is logically antecedent to the other, for a negative answer to either question is sufficient to dispose of the case. Thus, our determination that the search at issue in this case did not violate the Fourth Amendment implies no particular resolution of the question of the applicability of the exclusionary rule.

not perform within the limits of the Bill of Rights. That they are educating the young for citizenship is reason for scrupulous protection of Constitutional freedoms of the individual, if we are not to strangle the free mind at its source and teach youth to discount important principles of our government as mere platitudes."

These two propositions—that the Fourth Amendment applies to the States through the Fourteenth Amendment, and that the actions of public school officials are subject to the limits placed on state action by the Fourteenth Amendment— might appear sufficient to answer the suggestion that the Fourth Amendment does not proscribe unreasonable searches by school officials.

****

...But this Court has never limited the Amendment's prohibition on unreasonable searches and seizures to operations conducted by the police. Rather, the Court has long spoken of the Fourth Amendment's strictures as restraints imposed upon "governmental action"—that is, "upon the activities of sovereign authority." ... "[t]he basic purpose of this Amendment, as recognized in countless decisions of this Court, is to safeguard the privacy and security of individuals against arbitrary invasions by governmental officials." Because the individual's interest in privacy and personal security "suffers whether the government's motivation is to investigate violations of criminal laws or breaches of other statutory or regulatory standards," it would be "anomalous to say that the individual and his private property are fully protected by the Fourth Amendment only when the individual is suspected of criminal behavior."

Notwithstanding the general applicability of the Fourth Amendment to the activities of civil authorities, a few courts have concluded that school officials are exempt from the dictates of the Fourth Amendment by virtue of the special nature of their authority over schoolchildren. Teachers and school administrators, it is said, act in loco parentis in their dealings with students: their authority is that of the parent, not the State, and is, therefore, not subject to the limits of the Fourth Amendment.

...If school authorities are state actors for purposes of the constitutional guarantees of freedom of expression and due process, it is difficult to understand why they should be deemed to be exercising parental rather than public authority when conducting searches of their students. More generally, the Court has recognized that "the concept of parental delegation" as a source of school authority is not entirely "consonant with compulsory education laws." Today's public school officials do not merely exercise authority voluntarily conferred on them by individual parents; rather, they act in furtherance of publicly mandated educational and disciplinary policies. ...In carrying out searches and other disciplinary functions pursuant to such policies, school officials act as representatives of the State, not merely as surrogates for the parents, and they cannot claim the parents' immunity from the strictures of the Fourth Amendment.

III

To hold that the Fourth Amendment applies to searches conducted by school authorities is only to begin the inquiry into the standards governing such searches. Although the underlying command of the Fourth Amendment is always that searches and seizures be reasonable, what is reasonable depends on the context within which a search takes place. The determination of the standard of reasonableness governing any specific class of searches requires "balancing the need to search against the invasion which the search entails." On one side of the balance are arrayed the individual's legitimate expectations of privacy and personal security; on the other, the government's need for effective methods to deal with breaches of public order.

We have recognized that even a limited search of the person is a substantial invasion of privacy. We have also recognized that searches of closed items of personal luggage are intrusions on protected privacy interests, for "the Fourth Amendment provides protection to the owner of every container that conceals its contents from plain view." A search of a child's person or of a closed purse or other bag carried on her person,[557] no less than a similar search carried out on an adult, is undoubtedly a severe violation of subjective expectations of privacy.

Of course, the Fourth Amendment does not protect subjective expectations of privacy that are unreasonable or otherwise "illegitimate." To receive the protection of the Fourth Amendment, an expectation of privacy must be one that society is "prepared to recognize as legitimate." The State of New Jersey has argued that because of the pervasive supervision to which children in the schools are necessarily subject, a child has virtually no legitimate expectation of privacy in articles of personal property "unnecessarily" carried into a school. This argument has two factual premises: (1) the fundamental incompatibility of expectations of privacy with the maintenance of a sound educational environment; and (2) the minimal interest of the child in bringing any items of personal property into the school. Both premises are severely flawed.

Although this Court may take notice of the difficulty of maintaining discipline in the public schools today, the situation is not so dire that students in the schools may claim no legitimate expectations of privacy. We have recently recognized that the need to maintain order in a prison is such that prisoners retain no legitimate expectations of privacy in their cells, but it goes almost without saying that "[t]he prisoner and the schoolchild stand in wholly different circumstances, separated by the harsh facts of criminal conviction and incarceration." Ingraham v. Wright, supra, at 669. We are not yet ready to hold that the schools and the prisons need be equated for purposes of the Fourth Amendment.

Nor does the State's suggestion that children have no legitimate need to bring personal property into the schools seem well anchored in reality. Students at a minimum must bring to school not only the supplies needed for their studies, but also keys, money, and the necessaries of personal hygiene and grooming. In addition, students may carry on their persons or in purses or wallets such nondisruptive yet highly personal items as photographs, letters, and diaries. Finally, students may have perfectly legitimate reasons to carry with them articles of property needed in connection with extracurricular or recreational activities. In short, schoolchildren may find it necessary to carry with them a variety of legitimate, noncontraband items, and there is no reason to conclude that they have

---

[557] We do not address the question, not presented by this case, whether a schoolchild has a legitimate expectation of privacy in lockers, desks, or other school property provided for the storage of school supplies. Nor do we express any opinion on the standards (if any) governing searches of such areas by school officials or by other public authorities acting at the request of school officials. Compare Zamora v. Pomeroy, 639 F. 2d 662, 670 (CA10 1981) ("Inasmuch as the school had assumed joint control of the locker it cannot be successfully maintained that the school did not have a right to inspect it"), and People v. Overton, 24 N. Y. 2d 522, 249 N. E. 2d 366 (1969) (school administrators have power to consent to search of a student's locker), with State v. Engerud, 94 N. J. 331, 348, 463 A. 2d 934, 943 (1983) ("We are satisfied that in the context of this case the student had an expectation of privacy in the contents of his locker.... For the four years of high school, the school locker is a home away from home. In it the student stores the kind of personal 'effects' protected by the Fourth Amendment").

necessarily waived all rights to privacy in such items merely by bringing them onto school grounds.

Against the child's interest in privacy must be set the substantial interest of teachers and administrators in maintaining discipline in the classroom and on school grounds. Maintaining order in the classroom has never been easy, but in recent years, school disorder has often taken particularly ugly forms: drug use and violent crime in the schools have become major social problems. Even in schools that have been spared the most severe disciplinary problems, the preservation of order and a proper educational environment requires close supervision of schoolchildren, as well as the enforcement of rules against conduct that would be perfectly permissible if undertaken by an adult. "Events calling for discipline are frequent occurrences and sometimes require immediate, effective action." Accordingly, we have recognized that maintaining security and order in the schools requires a certain degree of flexibility in school disciplinary procedures, and we have respected the value of preserving the informality of the student-teacher relationship.

How, then, should we strike the balance between the schoolchild's legitimate expectations of privacy and the school's equally legitimate need to maintain an environment in which learning can take place? It is evident that the school setting requires some easing of the restrictions to which searches by public authorities are ordinarily subject. The warrant requirement, in particular, is unsuited to the school environment: requiring a teacher to obtain a warrant before searching a child suspected of an infraction of school rules (or of the criminal law) would unduly interfere with the maintenance of the swift and informal disciplinary procedures needed in the schools. Just as we have in other cases dispensed with the warrant requirement when "the burden of obtaining a warrant is likely to frustrate the governmental purpose behind the search," we hold today that school officials need not obtain a warrant before searching a student who is under their authority.

The school setting also requires some modification of the level of suspicion of illicit activity needed to justify a search. Ordinarily, a search-- even one that may permissibly be carried out without a warrant-- must be based upon "probable cause" to believe that a violation of the law has occurred. However, "probable cause" is not an irreducible requirement of a valid search. The fundamental command of the Fourth Amendment is that searches and seizures be reasonable, and although "both the concept of probable cause and the requirement of a warrant bear on the reasonableness of a search, . . . in certain limited circumstances neither is required." Thus, we have in a number of cases recognized the legality of searches and seizures based on suspicions that, although "reasonable," do not rise to the level of probable cause. ...Where a careful balancing of governmental and private interests suggests that the public interest is best served by a Fourth Amendment standard of reasonableness that stops short of probable cause, we have not hesitated to adopt such a standard.

We join the majority of courts that have examined this issue [558] in concluding that the accommodation of the privacy interests of schoolchildren with the substantial need of teachers and administrators for freedom to maintain order in the schools does not require strict adherence to the requirement that searches be based on probable cause to believe that the subject of the search has violated or is violating the law. Rather, the legality of a search of a student should depend simply

---

[558] See Bilbrey case supra.

272

on the reasonableness, under all the circumstances, of the search. Determining the reasonableness of any search involves a twofold inquiry: first, one must consider "whether the . . . action was justified at its inception," ; second, one must determine whether the search as actually conducted "was reasonably related in scope to the circumstances which justified the interference in the first place," Under ordinary circumstances, a search of a student by a teacher or other school official [559] will be "justified at its inception" when there are reasonable grounds for suspecting that the search will turn up evidence that the student has violated or is violating either the law or the rules of the school.[560] Such a search will be permissible in its scope when the measures adopted are reasonably related to the objectives of the search and not excessively intrusive in light of the age and sex of the student and the nature of the infraction.[561]

This standard will, we trust, neither unduly burden the efforts of school authorities to maintain order in their schools nor authorize unrestrained intrusions upon the privacy of schoolchildren. By focusing attention on the question of reasonableness, the standard will spare teachers and school administrators the necessity of schooling themselves in the niceties of probable cause and permit them to regulate their conduct according to the dictates of reason and common sense. At the same time, the reasonableness standard should ensure that the interests of students will be invaded no more than is necessary to achieve the legitimate end of preserving order in the schools.

IV

There remains the question of the legality of the search in this case. We recognize that the "reasonable grounds" standard applied by the New Jersey Supreme Court in its consideration of this question is not substantially different from the standard that we have adopted today. Nonetheless, we believe that the New Jersey court's application of that standard to strike down the search of T. L. O.'s purse reflects a somewhat crabbed notion of reasonableness. Our review of the facts surrounding the search leads us to conclude that the search was in no sense unreasonable for Fourth Amendment purposes.[562]

The incident that gave rise to this case actually involved two separate searches, with the first—the search for cigarettes—providing the suspicion that gave rise to the second—the search for marihuana. Although it is the fruits of the second search that are at issue here, the validity of the search for marihuana must

---

[559] We here consider only searches carried out by school authorities acting alone and on their own authority. This case does not present the question of the appropriate standard for assessing the legality of searches conducted by school officials in conjunction with or at the behest of law enforcement agencies, and we express no opinion on that question. Cf. Picha v. Wielgos, 410 F. Supp. 1214, 1219-1221 (ND Ill. 1976) (holding probable cause standard applicable to searches involving the police).

[560] We do not decide whether individualized suspicion is an essential element of the reasonableness standard we adopt for searches by school authorities. In other contexts, however, we have held that although "some quantum of individualized suspicion is usually a prerequisite to a constitutional search or seizure[,] . . . the Fourth Amendment imposes no irreducible requirement of such suspicion."

[561] Our reference to the nature of the infraction is not intended as an endorsement of JUSTICE STEVENS' suggestion that some rules regarding student conduct are by nature too "trivial" to justify a search based upon reasonable suspicion. See post, at 377-382. We are unwilling to adopt a standard under which the legality of a search is dependent upon a judge's evaluation of the relative importance of various school rules. The maintenance of discipline in the schools requires not only that students be restrained from assaulting one another, abusing drugs and alcohol, and committing other crimes, but also that students conform themselves to the standards of conduct prescribed by school authorities. We have "repeatedly emphasized the need for affirming the comprehensive authority of the States and of school officials, consistent with fundamental constitutional safeguards, to prescribe and control conduct in the schools." Tinker v. Des Moines Independent Community School District, 393 U. S. 503, 507 (1969). The promulgation of a rule forbidding specified conduct presumably reflects a judgment on the part of school officials that such conduct is destructive of school order or of a proper educational environment. Absent any suggestion that the rule violates some substantive constitutional guarantee, the courts should, as a general matter, defer to that judgment and refrain from attempting to distinguish between rules that are important to the preservation of order in the schools and rules that are not.

[562] Of course, New Jersey may insist on a more demanding standard under its own Constitution or statutes. In that case, its courts would not purport to be applying the Fourth Amendment when they invalidate a search.

depend on the reasonableness of the initial search for cigarettes, as there would have been no reason to suspect that T. L. O. possessed marihuana had the first search not taken place. Accordingly, it is to the search for cigarettes that we first turn our attention.

...T. L. O. had been accused of smoking, and had denied the accusation in the strongest possible terms when she stated that she did not smoke at all. Surely it cannot be said that under these circumstances, T. L. O.'s possession of cigarettes would be irrelevant to the charges against her or to her response to those charges. T. L. O.'s possession of cigarettes, once it was discovered, would both corroborate the report that she had been smoking and undermine the credibility of her defense to the charge of smoking. To be sure, the discovery of the cigarettes would not prove that T. L. O. had been smoking in the lavatory; nor would it, strictly speaking, necessarily be inconsistent with her claim that she did not smoke at all. But it is universally recognized that evidence, to be relevant to an inquiry, need not conclusively prove the ultimate fact in issue, but only have "any tendency to make the existence of any fact that is of consequence to the determination of the action more probable or less probable than it would be without the evidence." The relevance of T. L. O.'s possession of cigarettes to the question whether she had been smoking and to the credibility of her denial that she smoked supplied the necessary "nexus" between the item searched for and the infraction under investigation. Thus, if Mr. Choplick in fact had a reasonable suspicion that T. L. O. had cigarettes in her purse, the search was justified despite the fact that the cigarettes, if found, would constitute "mere evidence" of a violation.

****

Our conclusion that Mr. Choplick's decision to open T. L. O.'s purse was reasonable brings us to the question of the further search for marihuana once the pack of cigarettes was located. The suspicion upon which the search for marihuana was founded was provided when Mr. Choplick observed a package of rolling papers in the purse as he removed the pack of cigarettes. Although T. L. O. does not dispute the reasonableness of Mr. Choplick's belief that the rolling papers indicated the presence of marihuana, she does contend that the scope of the search Mr. Choplick conducted exceeded permissible bounds when he seized and read certain letters that implicated T. L. O. in drug dealing. This argument, too, is unpersuasive. The discovery of the rolling papers concededly gave rise to a reasonable suspicion that T. L. O. was carrying marihuana as well as cigarettes in her purse. This suspicion justified further exploration of T. L. O.'s purse, which turned up more evidence of drug-related activities: a pipe, a number of plastic bags of the type commonly used to store marihuana, a small quantity of marihuana, and a fairly substantial amount of money. Under these circumstances, it was not unreasonable to extend the search to a separate zippered compartment of the purse; and when a search of that compartment revealed an index card containing a list of "people who owe me money" as well as two letters, the inference that T. L. O. was involved in marihuana trafficking was substantial enough to justify Mr. Choplick in examining the letters to determine whether they contained any further evidence. In short, we cannot conclude that the search for marihuana was unreasonable in any respect.

Because the search resulting in the discovery of the evidence of marihuana dealing by T. L. O. was reasonable, the New Jersey Supreme Court's decision to exclude that evidence from T. L. O.'s juvenile delinquency proceedings on Fourth

Amendment grounds was erroneous. Accordingly, the judgment of the Supreme Court of New Jersey is
Reversed.[563]

JUSTICE BRENNAN, with whom JUSTICE MARSHALL joins, concurring in part and dissenting in part.

I fully agree with Part II of the Court's opinion. Teachers, like all other government officials, must conform their conduct to the Fourth Amendment's protections of personal privacy and personal security. As JUSTICE STEVENS points out, post, this principle is of particular importance when applied to schoolteachers, for children learn as much by example as by exposition. It would be incongruous and futile to charge teachers with the task of embuing their students with an understanding of our system of constitutional democracy, while at the same time immunizing those same teachers from the need to respect constitutional protections.

I do not, however, otherwise join the Court's opinion. Today's decision sanctions school officials to conduct full-scale searches on a "reasonableness" standard whose only definite content is that it is not the same test as the "probable cause" standard found in the text of the Fourth Amendment. In adopting this unclear, unprecedented, and unnecessary departure from generally applicable Fourth Amendment standards, the Court carves out a broad exception to standards that this Court has developed over years of considering Fourth Amendment problems. Its decision is supported neither by precedent nor even by a fair application of the "balancing test" it proclaims in this very opinion.

****

STUDY QUESTIONS

1. Can you state the test for determining when school officials may search students?
2. Should school officials ever engage in strip searches of students at school?
3. Would the same test apply if a school official performed a search of a student at the behest of a police officer?

****

DOES THE 8TH AMENDMENT RIGHT TO BE FREE FROM CRUEL AND UNUSUAL PUNISHMENT APPLY TO SCHOOLS?

Opponents of corporal punishment in schools challenged the practice before the Supreme Court arguing that its use by school authorities violated the 8th Amendment prohibition of cruel and unusual punishment and the due process clause of the 14th Amendment.

<u>**INGRAHAM**</u>
<u>**v.**</u>
<u>**WRIGHT**</u>
430 U.S. 651, 97 S.Ct. 1401 (1977)

---

[563]See also Johnson, Robert S. "Metal Detectors in Public Schools: A Policy Perspective," 80 Ed.Law Rep. [1] (March 25, 1993).

JUSTICE POWELL delivered the opinion of the Court.

This case presents questions concerning the use of corporal punishment in public schools: First, whether the paddling of students as a means of maintaining school discipline constitutes cruel and unusual punishment in violation of the Eighth Amendment; and second, to the extent that paddling is constitutionally permissible, whether the Due Process Clause of the Fourteenth Amendment requires prior notice and an opportunity to be heard.

I

Petitioners James Ingraham and Roosevelt Andrews filed the complaint in this case on January 7,1971, in the United States District Court for the Southern District of Florida. At the time both were enrolled in the Charles R. Drew Junior High School in Dade County, Fla., Ingraham in the eighth grade and Andrews in the ninth. The complaint contained three counts, each alleging a separate cause of action for deprivation of constitutional rights, under 42 U. S. C. §§1981-1988. Counts one and two were individual actions for damages by Ingraham and Andrews based on paddling incidents that allegedly occurred in October 1970 at Drew Junior High School. Count three was a class action for declaratory and injunctive relief filed on behalf of all students in the Dade County schools. Named as defendants in all counts were respondents Willie J. Wright (principal at Drew Junior High School), Lemmie Deliford (an assistant principal), Solomon Barnes (an assistant to the principal), and Edward L. Whigham (superintendent of the Dade County School System) .

Petitioners presented their evidence at a week-long trial before the District Court. At the close of petitioners' case, respondents moved for dismissal of count three "on the ground that upon the facts and the law the plaintiff has shown no right to relief," Fed. Rule Civ. Proc. 41 (b), and for a ruling that the evidence would be insufficient to go to a jury on counts one and two.[564] The District Court granted the motion as to all three counts, and dismissed the complaint without hearing evidence on behalf of the school authorities.

Petitioners' evidence may be summarized briefly. In the 1970-1971 school year many of the 237 schools in Dade County used corporal punishment as a means of maintaining discipline pursuant to Florida legislation and a local School Board regulation.[565] The statute then in effect authorized limited corporal punishment by negative inference, proscribing punishment which was "degrading or unduly severe" or which was inflicted without prior consultation with the principal or the teacher in charge of the school. Fla Stat. Ann. § 232.27 (1961).[566] The regulation, Dade County

---

[564] Petitioners had waived their right to jury trial on the claims for damages in counts one and two, but respondents had not. The District Court proceeded initially to hear evidence only on count three, the claim for injunctive relief. At the close of petitioners' case, however, the parties agreed that the evidence offered on count three (together with certain stipulated testimony) would be considered, for purposes of a motion for directed verdict, as if it had also been offered on counts one and two. It was understood that respondents could reassert a right to jury trial if the motion were denied. App. 142.

[565] The evidence does not show how many of the schools actually employed corporal punishment as a means of maintaining discipline. The authorization of the practice by the School Board extended to 231 of the schools in the 1970-1971 school year, but at least 10 of those schools did not administrator corporal punishment as a matter of school policy.

[566] In the 1970-1971 school year, § 232.27 provided:

"Each teacher or other member of the staff of any school shall assume such authority for the control of pupils as may be assigned to him by the principal and shall keep good order in the classroom and in other places in which he is assigned to be in charge of pupils, but he shall not inflict corporal punishment before consulting the principal or teacher in charge of the school, and in no case shall such punishment be degrading or unduly severe in its nature...."

Effective July 1, 1976, the Florida Legislature amended the law governing corporal punishment. Section 232.27 now reads:

"Subject to law and to the rules of the district school board, each teacher or other member of the staff of any school shall have such authority for the control and discipline of students as may be assigned to him by the principal or his designated representative and shall keep good order in the classroom and in other places in which he is assigned to be in charge of students. If a teacher feels that corporal punishment is necessary, at least the following procedures shall be followed:

School Board Policy 5144, contained explicit directions and limitations.[567] The authorized punishment consisted of paddling the recalcitrant student on the buttocks with a flat wooden paddle measuring less than two feet long, three to four inches wide, and about one-half inch thick. The normal punishment was limited to one to five "licks" or blows with the paddle and resulted in no apparent physical injury to the student. School authorities viewed corporal punishment as a less drastic means of discipline than suspension or expulsion. Contrary to the procedural requirements of the statute and regulation, teachers often paddled students on their own authority without first consulting the principal.

Petitioners focused on Drew Junior High School, the school in which both Ingraham and Andrews were enrolled in the fall of 1970. In an apparent reference to Drew, the District Court found that "[t]he instances of punishment which could be characterized as severe, accepting the students' testimony as credible, took place in one junior high school." The evidence, consisting mainly of the testimony of 16 students, suggests that the regime at Drew was exceptionally harsh. The testimony of Ingraham and Andrews, in support of their individual claims for damages, is illustrative. Because he was slow to respond to his teacher's instructions, Ingraham was subjected to more than 20 licks with a paddle while being held over a table in the principal's office. The paddling was so severe that he suffered a hematoma[568] requiring medical attention and keeping him out of school for several days. Andrews was paddled several times for minor infractions. On two occasions he was struck on his arms, once depriving him of the full use of his arm for a week.

The District Court made no findings on the credibility of the students' testimony. Rather, assuming their testimony to be credible, the court found no constitutional basis for relief. With respect to count three, the class action, the court concluded that the punishment authorized and practiced generally in the county schools violated no constitutional right. With respect to counts one and two, the individual damages actions, the court concluded that while corporal punishment could in some cases violate the Eighth Amendment, in this case a jury could not lawfully find "the elements of severity, arbitrary infliction, unacceptability in terms of contemporary standards, or gross disproportion which are necessary to bring 'punishment' to the constitutional level of 'cruel and unusual punishment.'"

"(1) The use of corporal punishment shall be approved in principle by the principal before it is used, but approval is not necessary for each specific instance in which it is used.

"(2) A teacher or principal may administer corporal punishment only in the presence of another adult who is informed beforehand, and in the student's presence, of the reason for the punishment.

"(3) A teacher or principal who has administered punishment shall, upon request, provide the pupil's parent or guardian with a written explanation of the reason for the punishment and the name of the other [adult] who was present." Fla. Stat. Ann. § 232.27 (1977) (codifier's notation omitted).

Corporal punishment is now defined as "the moderate use of physical force or physical contact by a teacher or principal as may be necessary to maintain discipline or to enforce school rules." §228.041 (28). The local school boards are expressly authorized to adopt rules governing student conduct and discipline and are directed to make available codes of student conduct. § 230.23 (6). Teachers and principals are given immunity from civil and criminal liability for enforcing disciplinary rules, "[e]xcept in the case of excessive force or cruel and unusual punishment ...." § 232.275.

[567] In the 1970-1971 school year, Policy 5144 authorized corporal punishment where the failure of other means of seeking cooperation from the student made its use necessary. The regulation specified that the principal should determine the necessity for corporal punishment, that the student should understand the seriousness of the offense and the reason for the punishment, and that the punishment should be administered in the presence of another adult in circumstances not calculated to hold the student up to shame or ridicule. The regulation cautioned against using corporal punishment against a student under psychological or medical treatment, and warned that the person administering the punishment "must realize his own personal liabilities" in any case of physical injury. App. 15.

While this litigation was pending in the District Court, the Dade County School Board amended Policy 5144 to standardize the size of the paddles used in accordance with the description in the text, to proscribe striking a child with a paddle elsewhere than on the buttocks, to limit the permissible number of "licks" (five for elementary and intermediate grades and seven for junior and senior grades), and to require a contemporaneous explanation of the need for the punishment to the student and a subsequent notification to the parents.

[568] Stedman's Medical Dictionary (23d ed. 1976) defines "hematoma" as "[a] localized mass of extravasated blood that is relatively or completely confined within an organ or tissue . . .; the blood is usually clotted (or partly clotted), and, depending on how long it has been there, may manifest various degrees of organization and decolorization."

A panel of the Court of Appeals voted to reverse. The panel concluded that the punishment was so severe and oppressive as to violate the Eighth and Fourteenth Amendments, and that the procedures outlined in Policy 5144 failed to satisfy the requirements of the Due Process Clause. Upon rehearing, the en banc court rejected these conclusions and affirmed the judgment of the District Court. The full court held that the Due Process Clause did not require notice or an opportunity to be heard:

> "In essence, we refuse to set forth, as constitutionally mandated, procedural standards for an activity which is not substantial enough, on a constitutional level, to justify the time and effort which would have to be expended by the school in adhering to those procedures or to justify further interference by federal courts into the internal affairs of public schools." Id., at 919.

The court also rejected the petitioners' substantive contentions. The Eighth Amendment, in the court's view, was simply inapplicable to corporal punishment in public schools.

****

We granted certiorari, limited to the questions of cruel and unusual punishment and procedural due process.

II

In addressing the scope of the Eighth Amendment's prohibition on cruel and unusual punishment, this Court has found it useful to refer to "[t]raditional common-law concepts," and to the "attitude[s] which our society has traditionally taken." So, too, in defining the requirements of procedural due process under the Fifth and Fourteenth Amendments, the Court has been attuned to what "has always been the law of the land," and to "traditional ideas of fair procedure." We therefore begin by examining the way in which our traditions and our laws have responded to the use of corporal punishment in public schools.

The use of corporal punishment in this country as a means of disciplining schoolchildren dates back to the colonial period. It has survived the transformation of primary and secondary education from the colonials' reliance on optional private arrangements to our present system of compulsory education and dependence on public schools. Despite the general abandonment of corporal punishment as a means of punishing criminal offenders, the practice continues to play a role in the public education of schoolchildren in most parts of the country. Professional and public opinion is sharply divided on the practice,[569] and has been for more than a century. Yet we can discern no trend toward its elimination.

At common law a single principle has governed the use of corporal punishment since before the American Revolution: Teachers may impose reasonable but not excessive force to discipline a child. Blackstone catalogued among the "absolute rights of individuals" the right "to security from the corporal insults of menaces, assaults, beating, and wounding," but he did not regard it a "corporal insult" for a teacher to inflict "moderate correction" on a child in his care. To the

---

[569] For samplings of scholarly opinion on the use of corporal punishment in the schools, see F. Reardon & R. Reynolds, Corporal Punishment in Pennsylvania 1-2, 34 (1975); National Education Association, Report of the Task Force on Corporal Punishment (1972); K. James, Corporal Punishment in the Public Schools 8-16 (1963). Opinion surveys taken since 1970 have consistently shown a majority of teachers and of the general public favoring moderate use of corporal punishment in the lower grades. See Reardon & Reynolds, supra, at 2, 23-26; Delaware Department of Public Instruction, Report on the Corporal Punishment Survey 48 (1974); Reitman, Follman, & Ladd, supra, at 34-35; National Education Association, supra, at 7.

extent that force was "necessary to answer the purposes for which [the teacher] is employed," Blackstone viewed it as "justifiable or lawful." The basic doctrine has not changed. The prevalent rule in this country today privileges such force as a teacher or administrator "reasonably believes to be necessary for [the child's] proper control, training, or education." To the extent that the force is excessive or unreasonable, the educator in virtually all States is subject to possible civil and criminal liability.[570]

Although the early cases viewed the authority of the teacher as deriving from the parents, the concept of parental delegation has been replaced by the view—more consonant with compulsory education laws—that the State itself may impose such corporal punishment as is reasonably necessary "for the proper education of the child and for the maintenance of group discipline." [571] All of the circumstances are to be taken into account in determining whether the punishment is reasonable in a particular case. Among the most important considerations are the seriousness of the offense, the attitude and past behavior of the child, the nature and severity of the punishment, the age and strength of the child, and the availability of less severe but equally effective means of discipline. Id., at 290-291; Restatement (Second) of Torts § 150, Comments c-e, p. 268 (1965).

Of the 23 States that have addressed the problem through legislation, 21 have authorized the moderate use of corporal punishment in public schools.[572] Of these States only a few have elaborated on the common-law test of reasonableness, typically providing for approval or notification of the child's parents,[573] or for infliction of punishment only by the principal or in the presence of an adult witness. Only two States, Massachusetts and New Jersey, have prohibited all corporal punishment in their public schools. Where the legislatures have not acted, the state courts have uniformly preserved the common-law rule permitting teachers to use reasonable force in disciplining children in their charge.

Against this background of historical and contemporary approval of reasonable corporal punishment, we turn to the constitutional questions before us.

III

The Eighth Amendment provides: "Excessive bail shall not be required, nor excessive fines imposed, nor cruel and unusual punishments inflicted." Bail, fines, and punishment traditionally have been associated with the criminal process, and by subjecting the three to parallel limitations the text of the Amendment suggests an intention to limit the power of those entrusted with the criminal-law function of government. An examination of the history of the Amendment and the decisions of this Court construing the proscription against cruel and unusual punishment confirms that it was designed to protect those convicted of crimes. We adhere to this

[570] See cases cited n. 28, infra. The criminal codes of many States include provisions explicitly recognizing the teacher's common-law privilege to inflict reasonable corporal punishment. E. g., Ariz Rev. Stat. Ann. §13-246 (A) (1) (1956); Conn. Gen. Stat. § 53a-18 (1977); Neb. Rev. Stat.. § 28-840 (2) (1975); N. Y. Penal Law § 35.10 (McKinney 1975 and Supp. 1976); Ore. Rev. Stat. §161.205 (1) (1975).

[571] Today, corporal punishment in school is conditioned on parental approval only in California. Cal. Educ. Code § 49001 (West Supp. 1977). Cf. Morrow v. Wood, 35 Wis. 59 (1874). This Court has held in a summary affirmance that parental approval of corporal punishment is not constitutionally-required. Baker v. Owen, 423 U. S. 907 (1975), aff'g 395 F. Supp. 294 (MDNC).

[572] Cal. Educ. Code §§ 49000-49001 (West Supp. 1977); Del. Code Ann., Tit. 14, §701 (Supp. 1976); Fla. Stat. Ann. §232.27 (1977); Ga. Code Ann. §§32-835, 32-836 (1976); Haw. Rev. Stat. §§298-16 (1975 Supp.), 703-309(2) (Spec. Pamphlet 1975); Ill. Ann. Stat., c. 122, §§ 24-24, 34-84a (1977 Supp.); Ind. Code Ann. § 20-8.1-5-2 (1975); Md. Ann. Code, Art. 77, § 98B (1975) (in specified counties); Mich. Comp. Laws Ann., § 340.756 (1970); Mont. Rev. Codes Ann. § 75-6109 (1971) ; Nev. Rev. Stat. § 392.465 (1973); N. C. Gen. Stat. § 115-146 (1975) ; Ohio Rev. Code Ann. § 3319.41 (1972); Okla. Stat Ann., Tit. 70, § 6-114 (1972); Pa. Stat. Ann., Tit. 24, §13-1317 (Supp. 1976); S. C. Code § 59-63-260 (1977); S. D. Compiled Laws Ann. §13-32-2 (1975); Vt. Stat. Ann., Tit. 16, §1161 (Supp. 1976); Va. Code Ann. § 22-231.1 (1973); W. Va. Code, §18A-5-1 (1977); Wyo. Stat. § 21.1-64 (Supp. 1975).

[573] Cal. Educ. Code § 49001 (West Supp. 1977) (requiring prior parental approval in writing); Fla. Stat. Ann. §232.27 (3) (1977) (requiring a written explanation on request); Mont. Rev. Codes Ann. § 75-6109 (1971) (requiring prior parental notification).

long-standing limitation and hold that the Eighth Amendment does not apply to the paddling of children as a means of maintaining discipline in public schools.

****

IV

The Fourteenth Amendment prohibits any state deprivation of life, liberty, or property without due process of law. Application of this prohibition requires the familiar two-stage analysis: We must first ask whether the asserted individual interests are encompassed within the Fourteenth Amendment's protection of "life, liberty or property"; if protected interests are implicated, we then must decide what procedures constitute "due process of law." Following that analysis here, we find that corporal punishment in public schools implicates a constitutionally protected liberty interest, but we hold that the traditional common-law remedies are fully adequate to afford due process

A

"[T]he range of interests protected by procedural due process is not infinite." We have repeatedly rejected "the notion that any grievous loss visited upon a person by the State is sufficient to invoke the procedural protections of the Due Process Clause." Due process is required only when a decision of the State implicates an interest within the protection of the Fourteenth Amendment. And "to determine whether due process requirements apply in the first place, we must look not to the 'weight' but to the nature of the interest at stake."

The Due Process Clause of the Fifth Amendment, later incorporated into the Fourteenth, was intended to give Americans at least the protection against governmental power that they had enjoyed as Englishmen against the power of the Crown. The liberty preserved from deprivation without due process included the right "generally to enjoy those privileges long recognized at common law as essential to the orderly pursuit of happiness by free men." Among the historic liberties so protected was a right to be free from, and to obtain judicial relief for, unjustified intrusions on personal security.[574]

While the contours of this historic liberty interest in the context of our federal system of government have not been defined precisely,[575] they always have been thought to encompass freedom from bodily restraint and punishment. It is fundamental that the state cannot hold and physically punish an individual except in accordance with due process of law.

This constitutionally protected liberty interest is at stake in this case. There is, of course, a de minimus level of imposition with which the Constitution is not concerned. But at least where school authorities, acting under color of state law, deliberately decide to punish a child for misconduct by restraining the child and

---

[574]See 1 W. Blackstone, Commentaries 134. Under the 39th Article of the Magna Carta, an individual could not be deprived of this right of personal security "except by the legal judgment of his peers or by the law of the land." Perry & Cooper, supra, n. 33, at 17. By subsequent enactments of Parliament during the time of Edward III, the right. was protected from deprivation except "by due process of law." See Shattuck, The True Meaning of the Term "Liberty," 4 Harv. L. Rev 365, 372-373 (1891).

[575] See, e. g., Skinner v. Oklahoma, 316 U. S. 535, 541 (1942) (sterilization); Jacobson v. Massachusetts, 197 U. S. 11 (1905) (vaccination); Union Pacific R. Co. v. Botsford, 141 U. S. 250, 251-252 (1891) (physical examinations); cf. ICC v. Brimson, 154 U. S. 447, 479 (1894).

   The right of personal security is also protected by the Fourth Amendment, which was made applicable to the States through the Fourteenth because its protection was viewed as "implicit in 'the concept of ordered liberty' . . . enshrined in the history and the basic constitutional documents of English-speaking peoples." Wolf v. Colorado, 338 U. S. 25, 27-28 (1949). It has been said of the Fourth Amendment that its "over- riding function . . . is to protect personal privacy and dignity against unwarranted intrusion by the State." Schmerber v. California, 384 U. S. 757, 767 (1966). But the principle concern of that Amendment's prohibition against unreasonable searches and seizures is with intrusions on privacy in the course of criminal investigations. See Whalen v. Roe, 429 U. S. 589, 604 n. 32 (1977). Petitioners do not contend that the Fourth Amendment applies, according to its terms, to corporal punishment in public school.

inflicting appreciable physical pain, we hold that Fourteenth Amendment liberty interests are implicated.[576]

B

"[T]he question remains what process is due." Were it not for the common-law privilege permitting teachers to inflict reasonable corporal punishment on children in their care, and the availability of the traditional remedies for abuse, the case for requiring advance procedural safeguards would be strong indeed. But here we deal with a punishment ---paddling---within that tradition, and the question is whether the common-law remedies are adequate to afford due process.

> " '[D]ue process,' unlike some legal rules, is not a technical conception with a fixed content unrelated to time, place and circumstances.... Representing a profound attitude of fairness . . . 'due process' is compounded of history, reason, the past course of decisions, and stout confidence in the strength of the democratic faith which we profess...."

Whether in this case the common-law remedies for excessive corporal punishment constitute due process of law must turn on an analysis of the competing interests at stake, viewed against the background of "history, reason, [and] the past course of decisions." The analysis requires consideration of three distinct factors: "First, the private interest that will be affected . . .; second, the risk of an erroneous deprivation of such interest . . . and the probable value, if any, of additional or substitute procedural safeguards; and finally, the [state] interest, including the function involved and the fiscal and administrative burdens that the additional or substitute procedural requirement would entail."

1

Because it is rooted in history, the child's liberty interest in avoiding corporal punishment while in the care of public school authorities is subject to historical limitations. Under the common law, an invasion of personal security gave rise to a right to recover damages in a subsequent judicial proceeding. But the right of recovery was qualified by the concept of justification. Thus, there could be no recovery against a teacher who gave only "moderate correction" to a child. To the extent that the force used was reasonable in light of its purpose, it was not wrongful, but rather "justifiable or lawful."

The concept that reasonable corporal punishment in school is justifiable continues to be recognized in the laws of most States. It represents "the balance struck by this country," between the child's interest in personal security and the traditional view that some limited corporal punishment may be necessary in the course of a child's education. Under that longstanding accommodation of interests, there can be no deprivation of substantive rights as long as disciplinary corporal punishment is within the limits of the common-law privilege.

This is not to say that the child's interest in procedural safeguards is insubstantial. The school disciplinary process is not "a totally accurate, unerring

---

[576] Unlike Goss v. Lopez, 419 U. S. 565 (1975), this case does not involve the state-created property interest in public education. The purpose of corporal punishment is to correct a child's behavior without interrupting his education. That corporal punishment may, in a rare case, have the unintended effect of temporarily removing a child from school affords no basis for concluding that the practice itself deprives students of property protected by the Fourteenth Amendment.

Nor does this case involve any state-created interest in liberty going beyond the Fourteenth Amendment's protection of freedom from bodily restraint and corporal punishment. Cf. Meachum v. Fano, 427 U. S. 215, 225-227 (1976).

281

process, never mistaken and never unfair...." In any deliberate infliction of corporal punishment on a child who is restrained for that purpose, there is some risk that the intrusion on the child's liberty will be unjustified and therefore unlawful. In these circumstances the child has a strong interest in procedural safeguards that minimize the risk of wrongful punishment and provide for the resolution of disputed questions of justification.

We turn now to a consideration of the safeguards that are available under applicable Florida law.

2

Florida has continued to recognize, and indeed has strengthened by statute, the common-law right of a child not to be subjected to excessive corporal punishment in school. Under Florida law the teacher and principal of the school decide in the first instance whether corporal punishment is reasonably necessary under the circumstances in order to discipline a child who has misbehaved. But they must exercise prudence and restraint. For Florida has preserved the traditional judicial proceedings for determining whether the punishment was justified. If the punishment inflicted is later found to have been excessive—not reasonably believed at the time to be necessary for the child's discipline or training—the school authorities inflicting it may be held liable in damages to the child and, if malice is shown, they may be subject to criminal penalties.

Although students have testified in this case to specific instances of abuse, there is every reason to believe that such mistreatment is an aberration. The uncontradicted evidence suggests that corporal punishment in the Dade County schools was, "[w]ith the exception of a few cases, . . . unremarkable in physical severity." Moreover, because paddlings are usually inflicted in response to conduct directly observed by teachers in their presence, the risk that a child will be paddled without cause is typically insignificant. In the ordinary case, a disciplinary paddling neither threatens seriously to violate any substantive rights nor condemns the child "to suffer grievous loss of any kind."

In those cases where severe punishment is contemplated, the available civil and criminal sanctions for abuse considered in light of the openness of the school environment ---afford significant protection against unjustified corporal punishment. See supra, at 670. Teachers and school authorities are unlikely to inflict corporal punishment unnecessarily or excessively when a possible consequence of doing so is the institution of civil or criminal proceedings against them.

It still may be argued, of course, that the child's liberty interest would be better protected if the common-law remedies were supplemented by the administrative safeguards of prior notice and a hearing. We have found frequently that some kind of prior hearing is necessary to guard against arbitrary impositions on interests protected by the Fourteenth Amendment. But where the State has preserved what "has always been the law of the land," the case for administrative safeguards is significantly less compelling.

There is a relevant analogy in the criminal law. Although the Fourth Amendment specifically proscribes "seizure" of a person without probable cause, the risk that police will act unreasonably in arresting a suspect is not thought to require an advance determination of the facts. In United States v. Watson (1976), we reaffirmed the traditional common-law rule that police officers may make warrantless public arrests on probable cause. Although we observed that an advance determination of probable cause by a magistrate would be desirable, we declined "to transform this judicial preference into a constitutional rule when the judgment of the Nation and Congress has for so long been to authorize warrantless public arrests on probable cause ...." Despite the distinct possibility that a police officer may improperly assess the facts and thus unconstitutionally deprive an individual of liberty, we declined to depart from the traditional rule by which the officer's perception is subjected to judicial scrutiny only after the fact. There is no more reason to depart from tradition and require advance procedural safeguards for intrusions on personal security to which the Fourth Amendment does not apply.

3

But even if the need for advance procedural safeguards were clear, the question would remain whether the incremental benefit could justify the cost. Acceptance of petitioners' claims would work a transformation in the law concerning corporal punishment in Florida and most other States. Given the impracticability of formulating a rule of procedural due process that varies with the severity of the particular imposition,[577] the prior hearing petitioners seek would have to precede any paddling, however moderate or trivial.

Such a universal constitutional requirement would significantly burden the use of corporal punishment as a disciplinary measure. Hearings—even informal hearings—require time, personnel, and a diversion of attention from normal school pursuits. School authorities may well choose to abandon corporal punishment rather than incur the burdens of complying with the procedural requirements. Teachers, properly concerned with maintaining authority in the classroom, may well prefer to rely on other disciplinary measures—which they may view as less effective rather than confront the possible disruption that prior notice and a hearing may entail.[578] Paradoxically, such an alteration of disciplinary policy is most likely to occur in the ordinary case where the contemplated punishment is well within the common-law privilege.[579]

Elimination or curtailment of corporal punishment would be welcomed by many as a societal advance. But when such a policy choice may result from this Court's determination of an asserted right to due process, rather than from the normal processes of community debate and legislative action, the societal costs cannot be dismissed as insubstantial. We are reviewing here a legislative judgment, rooted in history and reaffirmed in the laws of many States, that corporal punishment serves important educational interests. This judgment must be viewed in light of the disciplinary problems commonplace in the schools. As noted in <u>Goss</u> v. <u>Lopez</u>, "Events calling for discipline are frequent occurrences and sometimes require immediate, effective action." Assessment of the need for, and the appropriate means of maintaining, school discipline is committed generally to the discretion of school authorities subject to state law. "[T]he Court has repeatedly emphasized the need for affirming the comprehensive authority of the States and of

---

[577] "[P]rocedural due process rules are shaped by the risk of error inherent in the truthfinding process as applied to the generality of cases, not the rare exceptions...." <u>Mathews</u> v. <u>Eldridge</u>, 424 U. S. 319, 344 (1976).

[578] If a prior hearing, with the inevitable attendant publicity within the school, resulted in rejection of the teacher's recommendation, the consequent impairment of the teacher's ability to maintain discipline in the classroom would not be insubstantial.

[579] The effect of interposing prior procedural safeguards may well be to make the punishment more severe by increasing the anxiety of the child. For this reason, the school authorities in Dade County found it desirable that the punishment be inflicted as soon as possible after the infraction. App. 48 49.

school officials, consistent with fundamental constitutional safeguards, to prescribe and control conduct in the schools."

"At some point the benefit of an additional safeguard to the individual affected . . . and to society in terms of increased assurance that the action is just, may be outweighed by the cost." We think that point has been reached in this case. In view of the low incidence of abuse, the openness of our schools, and the common-law safeguards that already exist, the risk of error that may result in violation of a schoolchild's substantive rights can only be regarded as minimal. Imposing additional administrative safeguards as a constitutional requirement might reduce that risk marginally, but would also entail a significant intrusion into an area of primary educational responsibility. We conclude that the Due Process Clause does not require notice and a hearing prior to the imposition of corporal punishment in the public schools, as that practice is authorized and limited by the common law.

V

Petitioners cannot prevail on either of the theories before us in this case. The Eighth Amendment's prohibition against cruel and unusual punishment is inapplicable to school paddlings, and the Fourteenth Amendment's requirement of procedural due process is satisfied by Florida's preservation of common-law constraints and remedies. We therefore agree with the Court of Appeals that petitioners' evidence affords no basis for injunctive relief, and that petitioners cannot recover damages on the basis of any Eighth Amendment or procedural due process violation.

Affirmed.

MR. JUSTICE WHITE, with whom MR. JUSTICE BRENNAN, MR. JUSTICE MARSHALL, and MR. JUSTICE STEVENS join, dissenting.

Today the Court holds that corporal punishment in public schools, no matter how severe, can never be the subject of the protections afforded by the Eighth Amendment. It also holds that students in the public school systems are not constitutionally entitled to a hearing of any sort before beatings can be inflicted on them. Because I believe that these holdings are inconsistent with the prior decisions of this Court and are contrary to a reasoned analysis of the constitutional provisions involved, I respectfully dissent.

****

Nevada Corporal Punishment Statute

Therefore, the regulation of corporal punishment remains a matter to be addressed by the courts and legislatures of the various states. The Nevada legislature has enacted a statute regulating the use of corporal punishment in schools.[580] The law was originally adopted in 1960.[581] It was amended in 1979,[582] 1987[583] and 1993.[584]

The 1993 amendment repealed and recreated the Nevada corporal punishment law. The new law initially declares that corporal punishment may <u>not be administered</u> upon a pupil in any public school.[585] The law also provides that

---

[580] Sec. 392.465 NRS (1993).

[581] Chapter 60 Laws of Nevada (1960).

[582] Chapter 1616 Laws of Nevada (1979).

[583] Chapter 1013 Laws of Nevada (1987).

[584].Chapter 625 Laws of Nevada (1993).

[585]Sec. 392.465 1 NRS (1993).

barring the use of corporal punishment does not prohibit a teacher, principal, or other licensed person from defending themselves if attacked by a pupil.[586]

The new legislation includes a definition of corporal punishment. Under the amendment "corporal punishment" means the intentional infliction of physical pain upon or the physical restraint of a pupil for disciplinary purposes.[587] However, the law goes on to state that the term does not include the use of reasonable and necessary force: (a) to quell a disturbance that threatens physical injury to any person or the destruction of property;[588] (b) to obtain possession of a weapon or other dangerous object within a pupil's control;[589] (c) for the purpose of self-defense or the defense of another person;[590] or (d) to escort a disruptive pupil who refuses to go voluntarily with the proper authorities.[591]

****

STUDY QUESTIONS

1. Does the law give sufficient guidance to educators regarding use of physical force involving students?
2. What are the risks if any entailed in using physical force under the new law?
3. Does the law conflict with an educators resposnibility to maintain a safe school setting for all pupils?

****

C
SPECIAL EDUCATION LEGISLATION

As we know litigation in the middle 70's successfully challenged the constitutionality of excluding disabled children from the regular school setting.[592] Partially as a result of these court precedents Congress enacted the Vocational Rehabilitation Act in 1973 [593]and The .i.Education for All Handicapped Children Act (EAHCA) P.L. 94-142 in 1975.[594] Since its enactment in 1975 the law has been amended a number of times.[595]

The 1978 amendments stressed the importance of applied research and related activities to improve educational opportunities for the handicapped and reinforced the importance of the states role in improving existing programs. In 1983, the law was amended to clarify the term "special education" as services designated "to meet the unique, educational needs of the handicapped child" and specifically expanded services for the deaf-blind children. The 1986 amendments extended the age groups covered, mandating that all preschool handicapped children aged three to five years be entitled to public education, and establishing a

---

[586]Sec. 392.465 2 NRS (1993).

[587]Sec. 392.465 3 NRS (1993).

[588]Sec. 392.465 3 (a) NRS (1993).

[589]Sec. 392.465 3 (b) NRS (1993).

[590]Sec. 392.465 3 (c) NRS (1993).

[591]Sec. 392.465 3 (d) NRS (1993).

[592]Two cases, Mills v. Board of Education of District of Columbia, 348 F. Supp. 866 (DC 1972), and Pennsylvania Assn. for Retarded Children v. Commonwealth, 334 F. Supp. 1257 (ED Pa. 1971) and 343 F. Supp. 279 (1972).

[593] Sec. 504 of the Rehabilitation Act prohibits discrimination against otherwise qualified persons as a result of a handicap.

[594] The law has been amended a number of times since 1975. As of October 1990 the law was retitled Individuals With Disabilities Education Act (IDEA) 20 U.S.C.A. 1400 et seq.

[595]Public Law 95-561, 92 Stat. 2364 (1978), Public Law 98-199, 97 Stat 1357 (1983); Public Law 99-372,100 Stat. 796(1986); and Public Law 99-457,100 Stat. 1145 (1986).

new federal education program for handicapped babies from birth through age two. In addition, the Handicapped Children's Protection Act (HCPA) was adopted in 1986. The HCPA enables handicapped children, parents or guardians to receive attorney's fees if they are successful in litigation against state or local agencies. Finally, the name of the legislation was changed to Individuals with Disabilities Education Act (IDEA) [596] effective October 1990.[597]

Nevada statutes, addressing the education of children with disabilities cannot deviate from federal legal mandates.[598]

On July 26, 1990 the Americans with Disabilities Act (ADA) was signed into law.[599] The Act will have its greatest impact on the private sector since the provisions are patterened after the provisions of Section 504 of the Rehabilitation Act of 1973, which prohibits discrimination against the disabled by agencies receiving federal financial assistance. The main impact will be in the employment area. It does not appear that ADA will affect the requirements imposed upon school districts by IDEA.[600]

IDEA contains six key concepts. (1) Zero Reject, (2) Free 'Appropriate' Public Education (FAPE)[601] , (3) Individualized Educational Program (IEP), (4) Least Restrictive Environment (LRE) [602] and (5) Due Process Procedures[603] and (6) Attorney fees payable to parents who prevail in due process proceedings.[604]

The following landmark cases give meaning to the concepts and define the nature of the obligations imposed by the law.

---

[596]Osborne, Allan G., "Parental Rights Under the IDEA," 80 Ed.Law Rep. [771] (April 22, 1993).

[597]Zirkel, Perry A. "Special Education Law Update III," 83 Ed.Law Rep. [543] (Aug. 26,1993).

[598]Sec. 388. 440-520 NRS (1991). Nevada statutes concerning education of disabled children also include provisions relating to programs for gifted and talented children. Chapter 521 Laws of Nevada (1993) amends Nevada statutes changing the designation of handicapped minors to 'pupils with disabilities.' In addition, Chapter 521 Laws of Nevada Sec. 11 (1993) requires that the state board of education prescribe minimum standards for pupils with disabilities and gifted and talented pupils. Pursuant to Chapter 521 minimum standards are required for children with autism, traumatic brain injury and those who are developmentally delayed.

[599]Public Law 101-336, 42 U.S.C. Sections 12101-12213.

[600]Wenkart, Ronald D., "The Americans with Disabilities Act and Its Impact on Public Education," 82 Ed.Law Rep. [291] at [291] (July 1, 1993).

[601]There are two components to a Free Appropriate Public Education: 1 Special Education and 2. Related Services. Recent 9th Circuit cases include Hoeft v. Tucson Unified School District, 967 F.2d 1298 (9th Cir. 1992) holding parents are required to exhaust their administrative remedies in order to mount a class action challenging the school district's extended education policies, Hacienda La Puente Unified Sch. Dist. of L.A. v. Honig, 967 F.2d 487 (9th Cir. 1992) holding that a special education hearing officer has jurisdiction to determine whether a child is eligible for special education and related services even though the student had not been identified by the school district as "disabled," Ash v. Lake Oswego School Dist. No. 7J, 980 F.2d 585 (9th Cir. 1992) holding that failure of the school district to provide a residential placement for an autistic child violated IDEA. Ojai Unified School Dist. v. Jackson, 4 F.3d 1467 (9th Cir. 1993) holding that evidence supported a hearing officer's decision that the appropriate educational placement was not at a public school but in a private school and requiring the school district to pay for the student to reside with his grandparents while he attended the private school day program pending availability of a placement in a residential program.

[602]See Bartlett, Larry D., "Mainstreaming: On the Road to Clarification," 76 Ed.Law Rep. [17] (September 24, 1992), & Osborne Jr., Allan G., "The IDEA's Least Restrictive Environment Mandate: Implications for Public Policy," 71 Ed.Law Rep. [369] (February 13, 1992).
The term 'Full Inclusion' is also being used to describe a school districts obligation to serve disabled students in the Least Restrictive Environment. See Rogers, Joy "The Inclusion Revolution" Research Bulletin Phi Delta Kappa Center for Evaluation, Development, and Research, May 1993, Bloomington, IN. Two recent Federal district court cases have also been cited as precedent for a 'Full Inclusion' definition of Least Restrictive Environment. See Bd. of Ed..Sacramento City School Dist.. v. Holland, 786 F. Supp. 874 (E.D.Cal. 1992) & Oberti v. Bd.of Ed.Borough of Clementon Sch. Dist., 789 F.Supp. 1322 (D.N.J. 1992). See also Mawdsley, Ralph D. "Supervisory Standard of Care for Students with Disabilities," 80 Ed.Law Rep. [779] (April 22, 1993).

[603]See Menacker, Julius, "The 'Due Weight' Standard for Special Education Hearing Appeals," 73 Ed.Law Rep. [11] (May 7, 1992), Zirkel, Perry A., "A Special Education Case of Parental Hostility," 73 Ed.Law Rep. [1] (May 7, 1992) and Zirkel, Perry A. & Collins, Leslie A., "To What Extent, If Any, May Cost Be A Factor In Special Education Cases?," 71 Ed.Law Rep. [11] (January 30, 1992).

[604]Barlow-Gresham Union H.S. Dist. v. Mitchell, 940 F.2d 1280 (9th Cir. 1991). Fees awarded even though settlement reached before full due process hearing.

WHO MUST BE SERVED UNDER THE CONCEPT OF "ZERO REJECT"?

TIMOTHY W
v.
ROCHESTER NEW HAMPSHIRE SCHOOL DISTRICT
875 F.2d 954 (1st Cir. 1989)
cert. denied
___ U.S.___,110 S.Ct. 519 (1989)

Before BOWNES, ALDRICH, and BREYER, Circuit Judges.
BOWNES, Circuit Judge.

Plaintiff-appellant Timothy W. appeals an order of the district court which held that under the Education for All Handicapped Children Act, a handicapped child is not eligible for special education if he cannot benefit from that education, and that Timothy W., a severely retarded and multiply handicapped child was not eligible under that standard. We reverse.

I. BACKGROUND

Timothy W. was born two months prematurely on December 8, 1975 with severe respiratory problems, and shortly thereafter experienced an intracranial hemorrhage, subdural effusions, seizures, hydrocephalus, and meningitis. As a result, Timothy is multiply handicapped and profoundly mentally retarded. He suffers from complex developmental disabilities, spastic quadriplegia, cerebral palsy, seizure disorder and cortical blindness. His mother attempted to obtain appropriate services for him, and while he did receive some services from the Rochester Child Development Center, he did not receive any educational program from the Rochester School District when he became of school age.

On February 19, 1980, the Rochester School District convened a meeting to decide if Timothy was considered educationally handicapped under the state and federal statutes, thereby entitling him to special education and related services. The school district heard testimony from Dr. Robert Mackey, Timothy's pediatrician and Medical Consultant for SSI (Supplemental Security Income Program), to the effect that Timothy was severely handicapped. Dr. Mackey recommended the establishment of an educational program for Timothy, which emphasized physical therapy and stimulation. Reports by Susan Curtis, M.S., and Mary Bamford, O.T.R., an occupational therapist, also recommended an educational program consisting of occupational therapy and increasing Timothy's responses to his environment. Testimony of Timothy's mother indicated that he responded to sounds. Carrie Foss, director of the Rochester Child Development Center, testified that Timothy localized sound, responded to his name, and responded to his mother. On the other hand, Dr. Alan Rozycki, a pediatrician at the Hitchcock Medical Center, reported that Timothy had no educational potential, and Dr. Patricia Andrews, a developmental pediatrician, stated that hydrocephalus had destroyed part of Timothy's brain. The school district adjourned without making a finding. In a meeting on March 7, 1980, the school district decided that Timothy was not educationally handicapped—that since his handicap was so severe he was not "capable of benefitting" from an education and, therefore, was not entitled to one. During 1981 and 1982 the school district did not provide Timothy with any educational program.

In May, 1982, the New Hampshire Department of Education reviewed the Rochester School District's special education programs and made a finding of non-compliance, stating that the school district was not allowed to use "capable of benefitting" as a criterion for eligibility. No action was taken in response to this finding until one year later, on June 20, 1983, when the school district met to discuss Timothy's case. Ruth Keans, from the Rochester Child Development Center, reported that Timothy responded to bells and his mother's voice, and recommended frequent handling and positioning. Brenda Clough, Program Director at the Rochester Child Development Center, also concluded that Timothy could respond to positioning and handling, and recommended a physical therapy program that included a tactile component. The school district, however, continued its refusal to provide Timothy with any educational program or services.

In response to a letter from Timothy's attorney, on January 17, 1984, the school district's placement team met. In addition to the previously listed reports, it had available a report from Lynn Miller, an expert in physical therapy for handicapped children, who had seen Timothy seven times, and concluded that he responded to motion and handling and enjoyed loud music. She determined that his educational needs included postural drainage, motion exercises, sensory stimulation, positioning, and stimulation of head control. The placement team recommended that Timothy be placed at the Child Development Center so that he could be provided with a special education program. The Rochester School Board,[605] however, refused to authorize the placement team's recommendation to provide educational services for Timothy, contending that it still needed more information. The school district's request to have Timothy be given a neurological evaluation, including a CAT Scan, was refused by his mother.

On April 24, 1984, Timothy filed a complaint with the New Hampshire Department of Education requesting that he be placed in an educational program immediately. On October 9,1984, the Department of Education issued an order requiring the school district to place him, within five days, in an educational program, until the appeals process on the issue of whether Timothy was educationally handicapped was completed. The school district, however, refused to make any such educational placement. On October 31, 1984, the school district filed an appeal of the order. There was also a meeting on November 8, 1984, in which the Rochester School Board reviewed Timothy's case and concluded he was not eligible for special education.

On November 17, 1984, Timothy filed a complaint in the United States District Court, pursuant to 42 U.S.C. § 1983, alleging that his rights under the Education for All Handicapped Children Act (20 U.S.C. § 1400 et seq.), the corresponding New Hampshire state law (RSA 186-C), §504 of the Rehabilitation Act of 1973 (29 U.S.C. §794), and the equal protection and due process clauses of the United States and New Hampshire Constitutions, had been violated by the Rochester School District. The complaint sought preliminary and permanent injunctions directing the school district to provide him with special education, and $175,000 in damages.

A hearing was held in the district court on December 21, 1984. Timothy's mother testified that he hears somewhat, sees bright light, smiles when happy, cries when sad, listens to television and music, and responds to touching and talking.

---

[605] The School Board has the final decision-making authority for the school district.

Lynn Miller, who had been providing physical therapy to Timothy for over a year, testified that Timothy responded to movement, touch, music, and other sounds, and that his educational needs included postural drainage, range of motion, sensory stimulation of all kinds, correct positioning, proper sitting equipment, and work with his head control. Mariane Riggio, an expert in services for severely handicapped deaf-blind children, testified that Timothy was severely retarded but that he had definite light perception and could differentiate between sounds. She concluded that Timothy would be harmed if he was not given the benefit of an educational program. Dr. William Schofield, an expert in special education for the severely handicapped, testified that he had evaluated Timothy and that his educational needs included occupational therapy, development of some kind of communication program, a toileting program, a feeding program, and tactile stimulation discrimination which might be the basis for a communication process. Dr. Patricia Andrews, a developmental pediatrician, was the only person who testified that Timothy did not have educational needs and could not benefit from education. Her only contact with Timothy had been during an evaluation when he was two months old. While she testified that Timothy was profoundly mentally retarded and that an X-ray study of his brain showed he had virtually no cortex present, she also stated that such a study alone could not predict how much functioning was going to develop. On January 3, 1985, the district court denied Timothy's motion for a preliminary injunction, and on January 8, stated it would abstain on the damage claim pending exhaustion of the state administrative procedures.

On December 7, 1984, the State Commissioner of Education had ordered a diagnostic prescriptive program for Timothy: that he receive three hours of tutoring per week and that an evaluation be made concerning his capacity to benefit. Timothy's attorney, not the school district, made the necessary arrangements, and Timothy entered the school district's ABLE program in May, 1985. The ABLE reports on Timothy indicate that he is handicapped, has educational needs, and would benefit from an educational program. An Evaluation Summary prepared on August 2, 1985 by Susan Keefe, a teacher who worked with Timothy in the ABLE program, concluded that he demonstrated abilities in visual development (could see shadows), auditory development (recognizes familiar voices, responds with smiles, extension of limbs, and turns head) tactile development (responds to stimulation), cognition communication, language (uses different facial expressions to show emotions), and social development (resists changes in his immediate environment). Keefe noted that Timothy had made particular progress in learning to move his head towards a person speaking his name and in learning to activate a switch. Subsequently, Timothy was allowed to attend the ABLE program intermittently: from October 29, 1985 to November 18, 1985, from December 2 to December 22, 1985, and from May 8, 1986 through June 3, 1986. Keefe reiterated her previous recommendation of a long-term uninterrupted program.

In September, 1986, Timothy again requested a special education program. In October, 1986, the school district continued to refuse to provide him with such a program, claiming it still needed more information. Various evaluations were done at the behest of the school district. On December 30, 1985, Dr. Cecilia Pinto-Lord, a neurologist, had given Timothy a negative prognosis for learning, but did indicate he had some awareness of his environment; on October 10, 1986, Dr. Pinto-Lord stated that acquisition of new skills by Timothy was very unlikely. On May 19,

1986, Mary-Margaret Windsor, an occupational therapist, conducted an occupational therapy evaluation and concluded that Timothy might respond to an oral-motor program, and that without consistent management strategies there was great potential for increased deformities and contractures (a condition of fixed high resistance to passive stretch of a muscle). A psychological evaluation conducted by Dr. John Morse, a psychologist, on June 23, 1986, concluded that Timothy demonstrates behavioral awareness of strangers, recognizes familiar voices, positively responds to handling by a familiar person, recognizes familiar sounds, and demonstrates a selective response to sound. He recommended physical and occupational therapy, and cognitive programming efforts to continue in the areas of consistently responding to sound, anticipating feeding, and operating an electronic device to operate a sound source. And on January 9, 1987, Ruth Keans, a physical therapist at the Child Development Center, performed a physical therapy evaluation and concluded that she did not see any voluntary movements, but that Timothy did respond to his mother's voice. She recommended physical therapy.

The school district, on January 12, 1987, arranged another diagnostic placement at the Rochester Child Development Center. A report of March 13, 1987 by Dr. Schofield, an expert in special education for the severely handicapped, indicated that Timothy was aware of his environment, could locate to different sounds made by a busy box, and that he attempted to reach for the box himself. He recommended the establishment of specific teaching/learning strategies for Timothy. On June 23,1987, Rose Bradder, Program Coordinator at the Center, also recommended that Timothy continue to receive educational services. Experts in the field of special education retained on behalf of Timothy all concluded that he responded to certain stimuli and was capable of learning. For example, Dr. Robert Kugel, a physician specializing in developmental disabilities, found that Timothy responded to light, familiar voices, touch, taste, smell, pain, and temperature, that he made purposeful movements with his head, and that he showed evidence of retaining some higher cortical functioning which indicated that he could learn in certain areas.

On May 20,1987, the district court found that Timothy had not exhausted his state administrative remedies before the New Hampshire Department of Education, and precluded pretrial discovery until this had been done. On September 15, 1987, the hearing officer in the administrative hearings ruled that Timothy's capacity to benefit was not a legally permissible standard for determining his eligibility to receive a public education, and that the Rochester School District must provide him with an education. The Rochester School District, on November 12, 1987, appealed this decision to the United States District Court by filing a counterclaim, and on March 29, 1988, moved for summary judgment. Timothy filed a cross motion for summary judgment.

Hearings were held on June 16 and 27, 1988, pursuant to Fed.R.Civ.P. 65(a)(2), relating "solely to the issue of whether or not Timothy W. qualifie[d] as an educationally handicapped individual." In addition to the large record containing the reports described above, additional testimony was obtained from various experts. Timothy's experts, Kathy Schwaninger, consultant to United Cerebral Palsy, and Rose Bradder, Program Coordinator at the Child Development Center, testified that Timothy would benefit from a special educational program including physical and occupational therapy, with emphasis on functional skills. The school district presented Carrie Foss, Executive Director of the Child Development Center, who disagreed with her own staff and testified that Timothy had shown no progress. The district court relied heavily on another school district witness, Dr. Patricia Andrews, a developmental pediatrician, who testified that Timothy probably does not have the capacity to learn educational skills and activities. She also testified: that she was not an expert in the education of handicapped children; that her only contact with Timothy was when he was two months old; that he might have the capacity to respond to his environment and change in some ways; that the X-ray bubble test performed on Timothy in 1976, which she was using as a basis for concluding that Timothy had virtually no brain cortex and therefore no capacity to learn, was not the most sophisticated and accurate technology currently available; and that even a CAT scan could not predict Timothy's ability to learn.

On July 15, 1988, the district court rendered its opinion entitled "Order on Motion for Judgment on the Pleadings or in the Alternative, Summary Judgment." The record shows that the court had before it all the materials and reports submitted in the course of the administrative hearings, and the testimony from the two-day hearing. The court made rulings of law and findings of fact. It first ruled that "under EAHCA [the Education for All Handicapped Children Act], an initial determination as to the child's ability to benefit from special education, must be made in order for a handicapped child to qualify for education under the Act." After noting that the New Hampshire statute (RSA 186-C) was intended to implement the EAHCA, the court held: "Under New Hampshire law, an initial decision must be made concerning the ability of a handicapped child to benefit from special education before an entitlement to the education can exist." The court then reviewed the materials, reports and testimony and found that "Timothy W. is not capable of benefitting from special education.... As a result, the defendant [school district] is not obligated to provide special education under either EAHCA [the federal statute] or RSA 186-C [the New Hampshire statute]." Timothy W. has appealed this order. Neither party objected to the procedure followed by the court.

The primary issue is whether the district court erred in its rulings of law.

II. THE LANGUAGE OF THE ACT
A. The Plain Meaning of the Act Mandates a Public Education for All Handicapped Children
****

The language of the Act could not be more unequivocal. The statute is permeated with the words "all handicapped children" whenever it refers to the target population. It never speaks of any exceptions for severely handicapped children. Indeed, as indicated supra, the Act gives priority to the most severely handicapped. Nor is there any language whatsoever which requires as a prerequisite to being covered by the Act, that a handicapped child must demonstrate that he or she will "benefit" from the educational program. Rather, the Act speaks of the state's responsibility to design a special education and related services program that will meet the unique "needs" of all handicapped children. The language of the Act in its entirety makes clear that a "zero-reject" policy is at the core of the Act, and that no child, regardless of the severity of his or her handicap, is to ever again be subjected to the deplorable state of affairs which existed at the time of the Act's passage, in which millions of handicapped children received inadequate education or none at all. In summary, the Act mandates an appropriate public education for all handicapped children, regardless of the level of achievement that such children might attain.

B. Timothy W.: A Handicapped Child Entitled to An Appropriate Education
****

There is no question that Timothy W. fits within the Act's definition of a handicapped child: he is multiply handicapped and profoundly mentally retarded. He has been described as suffering from severe spasticity, cerebral palsy, brain damage, joint contractures, cortical blindness, is not ambulatory, and is quadriplegic.

****

The record shows that Timothy W. is a severely handicapped and profoundly retarded child in need of special education and related services. Much of the expert testimony was to the effect that he is aware of his surrounding environment, makes or attempts to make purposeful movements, responds to tactile stimulation, responds to his mother's voice and touch, recognizes familiar voices, responds to noises, and parts his lips when spoon fed. The record contains testimony that Timothy W.'s needs include sensory stimulation, physical therapy, improved head control, socialization, consistency in responding to sound sources, and partial participation in eating. The educational consultants who drafted Timothy's individualized education program recommended that Timothy's special education program should include goals and objectives in the areas of motor control, communication, socialization, daily living skills, and recreation. The special education and related services that have been recommended to meet Timothy W.'s needs fit well within the statutory and regulatory definitions of the Act.

We conclude that the Act's language dictates the holding that Timothy W. is a handicapped child who is in need of special education and related services because of his handicaps. He must, therefore, according to the Act, be provided with such an educational program. There is nothing in the Act's language which even remotely supports the district court's conclusion that "under [the Act], an initial determination as to a child's ability to benefit from special education, must be made in order for a handicapped child to qualify for education under the Act." The language of the Act is directly to the contrary: a school district has a duty to provide an educational program for every handicapped child in the district, regardless of the severity of the handicap.

III. LEGISLATIVE HISTORY
An examination of the legislative history reveals that Congress intended the Act to provide a public education for all handicapped children, without exception; that the most severely handicapped were in fact to be given priority attention; and that an educational benefit was neither guaranteed nor required as a prerequisite for a child to receive such education. These factors were central, and were repeated over and over again, in the more than three years of congressional hearings and debates, which culminated in passage of the 1975 Act.
****

C. Guarantees of Educational Benefit Are Not A Requirement For Child Eligibility
We sum up. In the more than three years of legislative history leading to passage of the 1975 Act, covering House and Senate floor debates, hearings, and

Congressional reports, the Congressional intention is unequivocal: Public education is to be provided to all handicapped children, unconditionally and without exception. It encompasses a universal right, and is not predicated upon any type of guarantees that the child will benefit from the special education and services before he or she is considered eligible to receive such education. Congress explicitly recognized the particular plight and special needs of the severely handicapped, and rather than excluding them from the Act's coverage, gave them priority status. The district court's holding is directly contradicted by the Act's legislative history, as well as the statutory language.

D. Subsequent Amendments to the Act

In the 14 years since passage of the Act, it has been amended four times. Congress thus has had ample opportunity to clarify any language originally used, or to make any modifications that it chose. Congress has not only repeatedly reaffirmed the original intent of the Act, to educate all handicapped children regardless of the severity of their handicap, and to give priority attention to the most severely handicapped, it has in fact expanded the provisions covering the most severely handicapped children. Most significantly, Congress has never intimated that a benefit/eligibility requirement was to be instituted.

****

In summary, the Congressional reaffirmation of its intent to educate all handicapped children could not be any clearer. It was unequivocal at the time of passage of the Act in 1975, and it has been equally unequivocal during the intervening years. The school district's attempt in the instant case to "roll back" the entire thrust of this legislation completely ignores the overwhelming congressional consensus on this issue.

****

E. Proof of Benefit is Not Required

The district court relied heavily on Board of Education of Hendrick Hudson Central School District v. Rowley, 458 U.S. 176, 102 S.Ct. 3034 (1982), in concluding that as a matter of law a child is not entitled to a public education unless he or she can benefit from it. The district court, however, has misconstrued Rowley. In that case, the Supreme Court held that a deaf child, who was an above average student and was advancing from grade to grade in a regular public school classroom, and who was already receiving substantial specialized instruction and related services, was not entitled, in addition, to a full time sign-language interpreter, because she was already benefitting from the special education and services she was receiving. The Court held that the school district was not required to maximize her educational achievement. It stated, "if personalized instruction is being provided with sufficient supportive services to permit the child to benefit from the instruction, .. the child is receiving a 'free appropriate public education' as defined by the Act," and that "certainly the language of the statute contains no requirement ... that States maximize the potential of handicapped children."

Rowley focused on the level of services and the quality of programs that a state must provide, not the criteria for access to those programs. The Court's use of "benefit" in Rowley was a substantive limitation placed on the state's choice of an educational program; it was not a license for the state to exclude certain handicapped children.

The district court in the instant case, is, as far as we know, the only court in the 14 years subsequent to passage of the Act, to hold that a handicapped child was not entitled to a public education under the Act because he could not benefit from the education. This holding is contrary to the language of the Act, its legislative history, and the case law.

V. CONCLUSION

The statutory language of the Act, its legislative history, and the case law construing it, mandate that all handicapped children, regardless of the severity of their handicap, are entitled to a public education. The district court erred in requiring a benefit/eligibility test as a prerequisite to implicating the Act. School districts cannot avoid the provisions of the Act by returning to the practices that were widespread prior to the Act's passage, and which indeed were the impetus for the Act's passage, of unilaterally excluding certain handicapped children from a public education on the ground that they are uneducable.

The law explicitly recognizes that education for the severely handicapped is to be broadly defined, to include not only traditional academic skills, but also basic functional life skills, and that educational methodologies in these areas are not static, but are constantly evolving and improving. It is the school district's responsibility to avail itself of these new approaches in providing an education program geared to each child's individual needs. The only question for the school district to determine, in conjunction with the child's parents, is what constitutes an appropriate individualized education program (IEP) for the handicapped child. We emphasize that the phrase "appropriate individualized education program" cannot be interpreted, as the school district has done, to mean "no educational program."

We agree with the district court that the Special Education Act of New Hampshire, N.H. Rev.Stat.Ann. 186-C, implements the federal statute. Its policy and purpose is as unequivocal as that of the federal Act:

> It is hereby declared to be the policy of the state that all children in New Hampshire be provided with equal educational opportunities. It is the purpose of this chapter to insure that the state board of education and the school districts of the state provide a free and appropriate public education for all educationally handicapped children.

N.H.Rev.Stat.Ann. 186-C:l (emphasis added).

For the reasons already stated, we hold that the New Hampshire statute is not subject to a benefit/eligibility test.

The judgment of the district court is reversed, judgment shall issue for Timothy W. The case is remanded to the district court which shall retain jurisdiction until a suitable individualized education program (IEP) for Timothy W. is effectuated by the school district. Timothy W. is entitled to an interim special educational placement until a final IEP is developed and agreed upon by the parties. The district court shall also determine the question of damages.

Costs are assessed against the school district.

****

294

WHAT DOES THE WORD "APPROPRIATE" MEAN IN THE PHRASE FREE APPROPRIATE PUBLIC EDUCATION?

HENDRICK HUDSON DIST. BD. OF ED.
v.
ROWLEY
458 U.S. 176, 102 S.Ct. 3034 (1982)

JUSTICE REHNQUIST delivered the opinion of the Court.

This case presents a question of statutory interpretation. Petitioners contend that the Court of Appeals and the District Court misconstrued the requirements imposed by Congress upon States which receive federal funds under the Education of the Handicapped Act. We agree and reverse the judgment of the Court of Appeals.

I

The Education of the Handicapped Act (Act), 84 Stat. 175, as amended, 20 U. S. C. §1401 et seq. provides federal money to assist state and local agencies in educating handicapped children, and conditions such funding upon a State's compliance with extensive goals and procedures. The Act represents an ambitious federal effort to promote the education of handicapped children, and was passed in response to Congress' perception that a majority of handicapped children in the United States "were either totally excluded from schools or [were] sitting idly in regular classrooms awaiting the time when they were old enough to 'drop out.'" The Act's evolution and major provisions shed light on the question of statutory interpretation which is at the heart of this case.

Congress first addressed the problem of educating the handicapped in 1966 when it amended the Elementary and Secondary Education Act of 1965 to establish a grant program "for the purpose of assisting the States in the initiation, expansion, and improvement of programs and projects . . . for the education of handicapped children." Pub. L. 89-750, §161, 80 Stat. 1204. That program was repealed in 1970 by the Education of the Handicapped Act, Part B of which established a grant program similar in purpose to the repealed legislation. Neither the 1966 nor the 1970 legislation contained specific guidelines for state use of the grant money; both were aimed primarily at stimulating the States to develop educational resources and to train personnel for educating the handicapped.

Dissatisfied with the progress being made under these earlier enactments, and spurred by two District Court decisions holding that handicapped children should be given access to a public education,[606] Congress in 1974 greatly increased federal funding for education of the handicapped and for the first time required recipient States to adopt "a goal of providing full educational opportunities to all handicapped children." The 1974 statute was recognized as an interim measure only, adopted "in order to give the Congress an additional year in which to study what if any additional Federal assistance [was] required to enable the States to

---

[606] Two cases, Mills v. Board of Education of District of Columbia, 348 F. Supp. 866 (DC 1972), and Pennsylvania Assn. for Retarded Children v. Commonwealth, 334 F. Supp. 1257 (ED Pa. 1971) and 343 F. Supp. 279 (1972). were later identified as the most prominent of the cases contributing to Congress' enactment of the Act and the statutes which preceded it. H. R. Rep., at 3-4. Both decisions are discussed in Part III of this opinion.

meet the needs of handicapped children." The ensuing year of study produced the Education for All Handicapped Children Act of 1975.

In order to qualify for federal financial assistance under the Act, a State must demonstrate that it "has in effect a policy that assures all handicapped children the right to a free appropriate public education." That policy must be reflected in a state plan submitted to and approved by the Secretary of Education. §1413, which describes in detail the goals, programs, and timetables under which the State intends to educate handicapped children within its borders. States receiving money under the Act must provide education to the handicapped by priority, first "to handicapped children who are not receiving an education" and second "to handicapped children . . . with the most severe handicaps who are receiving an inadequate education," and "to the maximum extent appropriate" must educate handicapped children "with children who are not handicapped.".[607] The Act broadly defines "handicapped children" to include "mentally retarded, hard of hearing, deaf, speech impaired, visually handicapped, seriously emotionally disturbed, orthopedically impaired, [and] other health impaired children, [and] children with specific learning disabilities."[608]

The "free appropriate public education" required by the Act is tailored to the unique needs of the handicapped child by means of an "individualized educational program" (IEP). The IEP, which is prepared at a meeting between a qualified representative of the local educational agency, the child's teacher, the child's parents or guardian, and, where appropriate, the child, consists of a written document containing

> "(A) a statement of the present levels of educational performance
> of such child, (B) a statement of annual goals, including short-
> term instructional objectives, (C) a statement of the specific
> educational services to be provided to such child, and the extent to
> which such child will be able to participate in regular educational
> programs, (D) the projected date for initiation and anticipated duration
> of such services, and (E) appropriate objective criteria and evaluation
> procedures and schedules for determining, on at least an annual basis,
> whether instructional objectives are being achieved." §1401(19).

Local or regional educational agencies must review and, where appropriate, revise each child's IEP at least annually.

In addition to the state plan and the IEP already described, the Act imposes extensive procedural requirements upon States receiving federal funds under its provisions. Parents or guardians of handicapped children must be notified of any proposed change in "the identification, evaluation, or educational placement of the child or the provision of a free appropriate public education to such child," and must be permitted to bring a complaint about "any matter relating to" such evaluation and education. [609]

---

[607] Despite this preference for "mainstreaming" handicapped children— educating them with nonhandicapped children—Congress recognized that regular classrooms simply would not be a suitable setting for the education of many handicapped children. The Act expressly acknowledges that "the nature or severity of the handicap [may be] such that education in regular classes with the use of supplementary aids and services cannot be achieved satisfactorily." §1412(5). The Act thus provides for the education of some handicapped children in separate classes or institutional settings See ibid; §1413(a)(4).

[608] In addition to covering a wide variety of handicapping conditions, the Act requires special educational services for children "regardless of the severity of their handicap." §§1412(2)(C), 1414(a)(1)(A).

[609] The requirements that parents be permitted to file complaints regarding their child's education, and be present when the child's IEP is formulated, represent only two examples of Congress' effort to maximize parental involvement in the education of each handicapped child. In addition the Act requires that parents be permitted "to examine all relevant records with respect to the identification, evaluation, and educational placement of the child, and . . . to obtain an independent educational evaluation of the child." §1415(b)(1)(A). See also

Complaints brought by parents or guardians must be resolved at "an impartial due process hearing," and appeal to the state educational agency must be provided if the initial hearing is held at the local or regional level. [610] Thereafter, "[a]ny party aggrieved by the findings and decision" of the state administrative hearing has "the right to bring a civil action with respect to the complaint . . . in any State court of competent jurisdiction or in a district court of the United States without regard to the amount in controversy."

Thus, although the Act leaves to the States the primary responsibility for developing and executing educational programs for handicapped children, it imposes significant requirements to be followed in the discharge of that responsibility. Compliance is assured by provisions permitting the withholding of federal funds upon determination that a participating state or local agency has failed to satisfy the requirements of the Act, §§1414(b)(2)(A), 1416, and by the provision for judicial review. At present, all States except New Mexico [611] receive federal funds under the portions of the Act at issue today. Brief for United States as Amicus Curiae 2, n. 2.

II

This case arose in connection with the education of Amy Rowley, a deaf student at the Furnace Woods School in the Hendrick Hudson Central School District, Peekskill, N. Y. Amy has minimal residual hearing and is an excellent lipreader. During the year before she began attending Furnace Woods, a meeting between her parents and school administrators resulted in a decision to place her in a regular kindergarten class in order to determine what supplemental services would be necessary to her education. Several members of the school administration prepared for Amy's arrival by attending a course in sign-language interpretation, and a teletype machine was installed in the principal's office to facilitate communication with her parents who are also deaf. At the end of the trial period it was determined that Amy should remain in the kindergarten class, but that she should be provided with an FM hearing aid which would amplify words spoken into a wireless receiver by the teacher or fellow students during certain classroom activities. Amy successfully completed her kindergarten year.

As required by the Act, an IEP was prepared for Amy during the fall of her first-grade year. The IEP provided that Amy should be educated in a regular classroom at Furnace Woods, should continue to use the FM hearing aid, and should receive instruction from a tutor for the deaf for one hour each day and from a speech therapist for three hours each week. The Rowleys agreed with parts of the IEP but insisted that Amy also be provided a qualified sign-language interpreter in all her academic classes in lieu of the assistance proposed in other parts of the IEP. Such an interpreter had been placed in Amy's kindergarten class for a 2-week experimental period, but the interpreter had reported that Amy did not need his

---

§§1412(4),1414(a)(4). State educational policies and the state plan submitted to the Secretary of Education must be formulated in "consultation with individuals involved in or concerned with the education of handicapped children, including handicapped individuals and parents or guardians of handicapped children." §1412(7). See also §1412(2)(E). Local agencies, which receive funds under the Act by applying to the state agency, must submit applications which assure that they have developed procedures for "the participation and consultation of the parents or guardian[s] of [handicapped] children" in local educational programs, §1414(a)(1)(C)(iii), and the application itself, along with "all pertinent documents related to such application," must be made "available to parents, guardians, and other members of the general public." §1414(a)(4)

[610] "Any party" to a state or local administrative hearing must "be accorded (1) the right to be accompanied and advised by counsel and by individuals with special knowledge or training with respect to the problems of handicapped children, (2) the right to present evidence and confront, cross examine, and compel the attendance of witnesses, (3) the right to a written or electronic verbatim record of such hearing, and (4) the right to written findings of fact and decisions." §1415(d).

[611] New Mexico entered the program subsequent to the decision of the Court.

services at that time. The school administrators likewise concluded that Amy did not need such an interpreter in her first-grade classroom. They reached this conclusion after consulting the school district's Committee on the Handicapped, which had received expert evidence from Amy's parents on the importance of a sign-language interpreter, received testimony from Amy's teacher and other persons familiar with her academic and social progress, and visited a class for the deaf.

When their request for an interpreter was denied, the Rowleys demanded and received a hearing before an independent examiner. After receiving evidence from both sides, the examiner agreed with the administrators' determination that an interpreter was not necessary because "Amy was achieving educationally, academically, and socially" without such assistance. The examiner's decision was affirmed on appeal by the New York Commissioner of Education on the basis of substantial evidence in the record. Pursuant to the Act's provision for judicial review, the Rowleys then brought an action in the United States District Court for the Southern District of New York, claiming that the administrators' denial of the sign-language interpreter constituted a denial of the "free appropriate public education" guaranteed by the Act.

The District Court found that Amy "is a remarkably well-adjusted child" who interacts and communicates well with her classmates and has "developed an extraordinary rapport" with her teachers. It also found that "she performs better than the average child in her class and is advancing easily from grade to grade," but "that she understands considerably less of what goes on in class than she could if she were not deaf" and thus "is not learning as much, or performing as well academically, as she would without her handicap," This disparity between Amy's achievement and her potential led the court to decide that she was not receiving a "free appropriate public education," which the court defined as "an opportunity to achieve [her] full potential commensurate with the opportunity provided to other children." According to the District Court, such a standard "requires that the potential of the handicapped child be measured and compared to his or her performance, and that the resulting differential or 'shortfall' be compared to the shortfall experienced by non- handicapped children." Ibid. The District Court's definition arose from its assumption that the responsibility for "giv[ing] content to the requirement of an 'appropriate education'" had "been left entirely to the [federal] courts and the hearing officers."

A divided panel of the United States Court of Appeals for the Second Circuit affirmed. The Court of Appeals "agree[d] with the [D]istrict [C]ourt's conclusions of law," and held that its "findings of fact [were] not clearly erroneous."

We granted certiorari to review the lower courts' interpretation of the Act. Such review requires us to consider two questions: What is meant by the Act's requirement of a "free appropriate public education"? And what is the role of state and federal courts in exercising the review granted.

III
A

This is the first case in which this Court has been called upon to interpret any provision of the Act. As noted previously, the District Court and the Court of Appeals concluded that "[t]he Act itself does not define 'appropriate education,'" but leaves "to the courts and the hearing officers" the responsibility of "giv[ing] content to the requirement of an 'appropriate education.'" Petitioners contend that the definition of the phrase "free appropriate public education" used by the courts below overlooks the definition of that phrase actually found in the Act. Respondents agree that the Act defines "free appropriate public education," but contend that the statutory definition is not "functional" and thus "offers judges no guidance in their consideration of controversies involving 'the identification, evaluation, or educational placement of the child or the provision of a free appropriate public education.'" The United States, appearing as amicus curiae on behalf of respondents, states that "[a]lthough the Act includes definitions of a 'free appropriate public education' and other related terms, the statutory definitions do not adequately explain what is meant by 'appropriate.'"

We are loath to conclude that Congress failed to offer any assistance in defining the meaning of the principal substantive phrase used in the Act. It is beyond dispute that, contrary to the conclusions of the courts below, the Act does expressly define "free appropriate public education":

> "The term 'free appropriate public education' means special education and related services which (A) have been provided at public expense, under public supervision and direction, and without charge, (B) meet the standards of the State educational agency, (C) include an appropriate preschool, elementary, or secondary school education in the State involved, and (D) are provided in conformity with the individualized education program required under section 1414(a)(5) of this title." §1401(18) (emphasis added).

"Special education," as referred to in this definition, means "specially designed instruction, at no cost to parents or guardians, to meet the unique needs of a handicapped child, including classroom instruction, instruction in physical education, home instruction, and instruction in hospitals and institutions." §1401(16). "Related services" are defined as "transportation, and such developmental, corrective, and other supportive services . . . as may be required to assist a handicapped child to benefit from special education." § 1401(17).[612]

Like many statutory definitions, this one tends toward the cryptic rather than the comprehensive, but that is scarcely a reason for abandoning the quest for legislative intent. Whether or not the definition is a "functional" one, as respondents contend it is not, it is the principal tool which Congress has given us for parsing the critical phrase of the Act. We think more must be made of it than either respondents or the United States seems willing to admit.

According to the definitions contained in the Act, a "free appropriate public education" consists of educational instruction specially designed to meet the unique needs of the handicapped child, supported by such services as are necessary to permit the child "to benefit" from the instruction. Almost as a checklist for adequacy under the Act, the definition also requires that such instruction and services be provided at public expense and under public supervision, meet the State's educational standards, approximate the grade levels used in he State's regular education, and comport with the child's IEP. Thus, if personalized instruction is being provided with sufficient supportive services to permit the child to benefit from the instruction, and the other items on the definitional checklist are satisfied, the child is receiving a "free appropriate public education" as defined by the Act.

---

[612] Examples of "related services" identified in the Act are "speech pathology and audiology, psychological services, physical and occupational therapy, recreation, and medical and counseling services, except that such medical services shall be for diagnostic and evaluation purposes only." § 1401(17).

Other portions of the statute also shed light upon congressional intent. Congress found that of the roughly eight million handicapped children in the United States at the time of enactment, one million were "excluded entirely from the public school system" and more than half were receiving an inappropriate education. In addition, as mentioned in Part I, the Act requires States to extend educational services first to those children who are receiving no education and second to those children who are receiving an "inadequate education." When these express statutory findings and priorities are read together with the Act's extensive procedural requirements and its definition of "free appropriate public education," the face of the statute evinces a congressional intent to bring previously excluded handicapped children into the public education systems of the States and to require the States to adopt procedures which would result in individualized consideration of and instruction for each child.

Noticeably absent from the language of the statute is any substantive standard prescribing the level of education to be accorded handicapped children. Certainly the language of the statute contains no requirement like the one imposed by the lower courts—that States maximize the potential of handicapped children "commensurate with the opportunity provided to other children." That standard was expounded by the District Court without reference to the statutory definitions or even to the legislative history of the Act. Although we find the statutory definition of "free appropriate public education" to be helpful in our interpretation of the Act, there remains the question of whether the legislative history indicates a congressional intent that such education meet some additional substantive standard. For an answer, we turn to that history.

B
(i)

As suggested in Part I, federal support for education of the handicapped is a fairly recent development. Before passage of the Act some States had passed laws to improve the educational services afforded handicapped children, but many of these children were excluded completely from any form of public education or were left to fend for themselves in classrooms designed for education of their nonhandicapped peers. As previously noted, the House Report begins by emphasizing this exclusion and misplacement, noting that millions of handicapped children "were either totally excluded from schools or [were] sitting idly in regular classrooms awaiting the time when they were old enough to 'drop out.'" One of the Act's two principal sponsors in the Senate urged its passage in similar terms:

> "While much progress has been made in the last few years, we can take no solace in that progress until all handicapped children are, in fact, receiving an education. The most recent statistics provided by the Bureau of Education for the Handicapped estimate that . . . 1.75 million handicapped children do not receive any educational services, and 2.5 million handicapped children are not receiving an appropriate education."

This concern, stressed repeatedly throughout the legislative history, confirms the impression conveyed by the language of the statute: By passing the Act, Congress sought primarily to make public education available to handicapped children. But in seeking to provide such access to public education, Congress did not impose upon the States any greater substantive educational standard than would be necessary to make such access meaningful. Indeed, Congress expressly "recognize[d] that in many instances the process of providing special education and related services to handicapped children is not guaranteed to produce any particular outcome." Thus, the intent of the Act was more to open the door of public education to handicapped children on appropriate terms than to guarantee any particular level of education once inside.

Both the House and the Senate Reports attribute the impetus for the Act and its predecessors to two federal-court judgments rendered in 1971 and 1972. As the Senate Report states, passage of the Act "followed a series of landmark court cases establishing in law the right to education for all handicapped children." The first case, Pennsylvania Assn. for Retarded Children v. Commonwealth, 334 F. Supp. 1257 (ED Pa. 1971) and 343 F. Supp. 279 (1972) (PARC), was a suit on behalf of retarded children challenging the constitutionality of a Pennsylvania statute which acted to exclude them from public education and training. The case ended in a consent decree which enjoined the State from "deny[ing] to any mentally retarded child access to a free public program of education and training."

PARC was followed by Mills v. Board of Education of District of Columbia (DC 1972), a case in which the plaintiff handicapped children had been excluded from the District of Columbia public schools. The court's judgment, quoted in S. Rep., at 6, provided that

"no [handicapped] child eligible for a publicly supported education in the District of Columbia public schools shall be excluded from a regular school assignment by a Rule, policy, or practice of the Board of Education of the District of Columbia or its agents unless such child is provided (a) adequate alternative educational services suited to the child's needs, which may include special education or tuition grants, and (b) a constitutionally adequate prior hearing and periodic review of the child's status, progress, and the adequacy of any educational alternative." 348 F. Supp., at 878 (emphasis added).

Mills and PARC both held that handicapped children must be given access to an adequate, publicly supported education. Neither case purports to require any particular substantive level of education. Rather, like the language of the Act, the cases set forth extensive procedures to be followed in formulating ,personalized educational programs for handicapped children. The fact that both PARC and Mills are discussed at length in the legislative Reports suggests that the principles which they established are the principles which, to a significant extent, guided the drafters of the Act. Indeed, immediately after discussing these cases the Senate Report describes the 1974 statute as having "incorporated the major principles of the right to education cases." Those principles in turn became the basis of the Act, which itself was designed to effectuate the purposes of the 1974 statute.

That the Act imposes no clear obligation upon recipient States beyond the requirement that handicapped children receive some form of specialized education is perhaps best demonstrated by the fact that Congress, in explaining the need for the Act, equated an "appropriate education" to the receipt of some specialized educational services. The Senate Report states: "[T]he most recent statistics provided by the Bureau of Education for the Handicapped estimate that of the more than 8 million children . . . with handicapping conditions requiring special education and related services, only 3.9 million such children are receiving an appropriate education." This statement, which reveals Congress' view that 3.9

million handicapped children were "receiving an appropriate education" in 1975, is followed immediately in the Senate Report by a table showing that 3.9 million handicapped children were "served" in 1975 and a slightly larger number were "unserved." A similar statement and table appear in the House Report.

It is evident from the legislative history that the characterization of handicapped children as "served" referred to children who were receiving some form of specialized educational services from the States, and that the characterization of children as "unserved" referred to those who were receiving no specialized educational services. For example, a letter sent to the United States Commissioner of Education by the House Committee on Education and Labor, signed by two key sponsors of the Act in the House, asked the Commissioner to identify the number of handicapped "children served" in each State. The letter asked for statistics on the number of children "being served" in various types of "special education program[s]" and the number of children who were not "receiving educational services." Similarly, Senator Randolph, one of the Act's principal sponsors in the Senate, noted that roughly one-half of the handicapped children in the United States "are receiving special educational services." By characterizing the 3.9 million handicapped children who were "served" as children who were "receiving an appropriate education," the Senate and House Reports unmistakably disclose Congress' perception of the type of education required by the Act: an "appropriate education" is provided when personalized educational services are provided.[613]

(ii)

Respondents contend that "the goal of the Act is to provide each handicapped child with an equal educational opportunity." We think, however, that the requirement that a State provide specialized educational services to handicapped children generates no additional requirement that the services so provided be sufficient to maximize each child's potential "commensurate with the opportunity provided other children." Respondents and the United States correctly note that Congress sought "to provide assistance to the States in carrying out their responsibilities under . . . the Constitution of the United States to provide equal protection of the laws." But we do not think that such statements imply a congressional intent to achieve strict equality of opportunity or services.

The educational opportunities provided by our public school systems undoubtedly differ from student to student, depending upon a myriad of factors that might affect a particular student's ability to assimilate information presented in the classroom. The requirement that States provide "equal" educational opportunities would thus seem to present an entirely unworkable standard requiring impossible measurements and comparisons. Similarly, furnishing handicapped children with only such services as are available to nonhandicapped children would in all probability fall short of the statutory requirement of "free appropriate public education"; to require, on the other hand, the furnishing of every special service necessary to maximize each handicapped child's potential is, we think, further than Congress intended to go. Thus to speak in terms of "equal" services in one instance gives less than what is required by the Act and in another instance more. The theme of the Act is "free appropriate public education," a phrase which is too

---

[613] In seeking to read more into the Act than its language or legislative history will permit, the United States focuses upon the word "appropriate," arguing that "the statutory definitions do not adequately explain what [it means]." Brief for United States as Amicus Curiae 13. Whatever Congress meant by an "appropriate" education, it is clear that it did not mean a potential-maximizing education.

complex to be captured by the word "equal" whether one is speaking of opportunities or services.

The legislative conception of the requirements of equal protection was undoubtedly informed by the two District Court decisions referred to above. But cases such as Mills and PARC held simply that handicapped children may not be excluded entirely from public education. In Mills, the District Court said:

> "If sufficient funds are not available to finance all of the services and programs that are needed and desirable in the system then the available funds must be expended equitably in such a manner that no child is entirely excluded from a publicly supported education consistent with his needs and ability to benefit therefrom."

The PARC court used similar language, saying "[i]t is the commonwealth's obligation to place each mentally retarded child in a free, public program of education and training appropriate to the child's capacity ...." The right of access to free public education enunciated by these cases is significantly different from any notion of absolute equality of opportunity regardless of capacity. To the extent that Congress might have looked further than these cases which are mentioned in the legislative history, at the time of enactment of the Act this Court had held at least twice that the Equal Protection Clause of the Fourteenth Amendment does not require States to expend equal financial resources on the education of each child.

In explaining the need for federal legislation, the House Report noted that "no congressional legislation has required a precise guarantee for handicapped children, i. e. a basic floor of opportunity that would bring into compliance all school districts with the constitutional right of equal protection with respect to handicapped children." H. R. Rep., at 14. Assuming that the Act was designed to fill the need identified in the House Report—that is, to provide a "basic floor of opportunity" consistent with equal protection—neither the Act nor its history persuasively demonstrates that Congress thought that equal protection required anything more than equal access. Therefore, Congress' desire to provide specialized educational services, even in furtherance of "equality," cannot be read as imposing any particular substantive educational standard upon the States.

The District Court and the Court of Appeals thus erred when they held that the Act requires New York to maximize the potential of each handicapped child commensurate with the opportunity provided nonhandicapped children. Desirable though that goal might be, it is not the standard that Congress imposed upon States which receive funding under the Act. Rather, Congress sought primarily to identify and evaluate handicapped children, and to provide them with access to a free public education.

(iii)

Implicit in the congressional purpose of providing access to a "free appropriate public education" is the requirement that the education to which access is provided be sufficient to confer some educational benefit upon the handicapped child. It would do little good for Congress to spend millions of dollars in providing access to a public education only to have the handicapped child receive no benefit from that education. The statutory definition of "free appropriate public education," in addition to requiring that States provide each child with "specially designed instruction," expressly requires the provision of "such . . . supportive services . . . as may be required to assist a handicapped child to benefit from special education." We therefore conclude that the "basic floor of opportunity" provided by the Act consists of access to specialized instruction and related services which are individually designed to provide educational benefit to the handicapped child.

The determination of when handicapped children are receiving sufficient educational benefits to satisfy the requirements of the Act presents a more difficult problem. The Act requires participating States to educate a wide spectrum of handicapped children, from the marginally hearing-impaired to the profoundly retarded and palsied. It is clear that the benefits obtainable by children at one end of the spectrum will differ dramatically from those obtainable by children at the other end, with infinite variations in between. One child may have little difficulty competing successfully in an academic setting with nonhandicapped children while another child may encounter great difficulty in acquiring even the most basic of self-maintenance skills. We do not attempt today to establish any one test for determining the adequacy of educational benefits conferred upon all children covered by the Act. Because in this case we are presented with a handicapped child who is receiving substantial specialized instruction and related services, and who is performing above average in the regular classrooms of a public school system, we confine our analysis to that situation.

The Act requires participating States to educate handicapped children with nonhandicapped children whenever possible.[614] When that "mainstreaming" preference of the Act has been met and a child is being educated in the regular classrooms of a public school system, the system itself monitors the educational progress of the child. Regular examinations are administered, grades are awarded, and yearly advancement to higher grade levels is permitted for those children who attain an adequate knowledge of the course material. The grading and advancement system thus constitutes an important factor in determining educational benefit. Children who graduate from our public school systems are considered by our society to have been "educated" at least to the grade level they have completed, and access to an "education" for handicapped children is precisely what Congress sought to provide in the Act.[615]

C

When the language of the Act and its legislative history are considered together, the requirements imposed by Congress become tolerably clear. Insofar as a State is required to provide a handicapped child with a "free appropriate public education," we hold that it satisfies this requirement by providing personalized instruction with sufficient support services to permit the child to benefit educationally from that instruction. Such instruction and services must be provided at public expense, must meet the State's educational standards, must approximate the grade levels used in the State's regular education, and must comport with the child's IEP. In addition, the IEP, and therefore the personalized instruction should be formulated in accordance with the requirements of the Act and, if the child is being educated in the regular classrooms of the public education system, should be

---

[614] "Title 20 U. S. C. §1412(5) requires that participating States establish "procedures to assure that, to the maximum extent appropriate, handicapped children, including children in public or private institutions or other care facilities, are educated with children who are not handicapped, and that special classes, separate schooling, or other removal of handicapped children from the regular educational environment occurs only when the nature or severity of the handicap is such that education in regular classes with the use of supplementary aids and services cannot be achieved satisfactorily. "

[615] We do not hold today that every handicapped child who is advancing from grade to grade in a regular public school system is automatically receiving a "free appropriate public education." In this case, however, we find Amy's academic progress, when considered with the special services and professional consideration accorded by the Furnace Woods school administrators, to be dispositive.

reasonably calculated to enable the child to achieve passing marks and advance from grade to grade.

IV
A

As mentioned in Part I, the Act permits "[a]ny party aggrieved by the findings and decision" of the state administrative hearings "to bring a civil action" in "any State court of competent jurisdiction or in a district court of the United States without regard to the amount in controversy." The complaint, and therefore the civil action, may concern "any matter relating to the identification, evaluation, or educational placement of the child, or the provision of a free appropriate public education to such child." In reviewing the complaint, the Act provides that a court "shall receive the record of the [state] administrative proceedings, shall hear additional evidence at the request of a party, and, basing its decision on the preponderance of the evidence, shall grant such relief as the court determines is appropriate."

The parties disagree sharply over the meaning of these provisions, petitioners contending that courts are given only limited authority to review for state compliance with the Act's procedural requirements and no power to review the substance of the state program, and respondents contending that the Act requires courts to exercise de novo review over state educational decisions and policies. We find petitioners' contention unpersuasive, for Congress expressly rejected provisions that would have so severely restricted the role of reviewing courts. In substituting the current language of the statute for language that would have made state administrative findings conclusive if supported by substantial evidence, the Conference Committee explained that courts were to make "independent decision[s] based on a preponderance of the evidence."

But although we find that this grant of authority is broader than claimed by petitioners, we think the fact that it is found in §1415, which is entitled "Procedural Safeguards," is not without significance. When the elaborate and highly specific procedural safeguards embodied in §1415 are contrasted with the general and somewhat imprecise substantive admonitions contained in the Act, we think that the importance Congress attached to these procedural safeguards cannot be gainsaid. It seems to us no exaggeration to say that Congress placed every bit as much emphasis upon compliance with procedures giving parents and guardians a large measure of participation at every stage of the administrative process, see, as it did upon the measurement of the resulting IEP against a substantive standard. We think that the congressional emphasis upon full participation of concerned parties throughout the development of the IEP, as well as the requirements that state and local plans be submitted to the Secretary for approval, demonstrates the legislative conviction that adequate compliance with the procedures prescribed would in most cases assure much if not all of what Congress wished in the way of substantive content in an IEP.

Thus the provision that a reviewing court base its decision on the "preponderance of the evidence" is by no means an invitation to the courts to substitute their own notions of sound educational policy for those of the school authorities which they review. The very importance which Congress has attached to compliance with certain procedures in the preparation of an IEP would be frustrated if a court were permitted simply to set state decisions at nought. The fact that §1415(e) requires that the reviewing court "receive the records of the [state] administrative proceedings" carries with it the implied requirement that due weight shall be given to these proceedings. And we find nothing in the Act to suggest that merely because Congress was rather sketchy in establishing substantive requirements, as opposed to procedural requirements for the preparation of an IEP, it intended that reviewing courts should have a free hand to impose substantive standards of review which cannot be derived from the Act itself. In short, the statutory authorization to grant "such relief as the court determines is appropriate" cannot be read without reference to the obligations, largely procedural in nature, which are imposed upon recipient States by Congress.

Therefore, a court's inquiry in suits brought under §1415(e)(2) is twofold. First, has the State complied with the procedures set forth in the Act?[616] And second, is the individualized educational program developed through the Act's procedures reasonably calculated to enable the child to receive educational benefits?[617] If these requirements are met, the State has complied with the obligations imposed by Congress and the courts can require no more.

B

In assuring that the requirements of the Act have been met, courts must be careful to avoid imposing their view of preferable educational methods upon the States. The primary responsibility for formulating the education to be accorded a handicapped child, and for choosing the educational method most suitable to the child's needs, was left by the Act to state and local educational agencies in cooperation with the parents or guardian of the child. The Act expressly charges States with the responsibility of "acquiring and disseminating to teachers and administrators of programs for handicapped children significant information derived from educational research, demonstration, and similar projects, and [of] adopting, where appropriate, promising educational practices and materials." In the face of such a clear statutory directive, it seems highly unlikely that Congress intended courts to overturn a State's choice of appropriate educational theories in a proceeding conducted pursuant to § 1415(e)(2).[618]

We previously have cautioned that courts lack the "specialized knowledge and experience" necessary to resolve "persistent and difficult questions of educational policy." We think that Congress shared that view when it passed the Act. As already demonstrated, Congress' intention was not that the Act displace the primacy of States in the field of education, but that States receive funds to assist them in extending their educational systems to the handicapped. Therefore, once a court determines that the requirements of the Act have been met, questions of methodology are for resolution by the States.

V

Entrusting a child's education to state and local agencies does not leave the child without protection. Congress sought to protect individual children by

---

[616] This inquiry will require a court not only to satisfy itself that the State has adopted the state plan, policies, and assurances required by the Act, but also to determine that the State has created an IEP for the child in question which conforms with the requirements of §1401(19).

[617] When the handicapped child is being educated in the regular classrooms of a public school system, the achievement of passing marks and advancement from grade to grade will be one important factor in determining educational benefit. See Part III, supra.

[618] It is clear that Congress was aware of the States' traditional role in the formulation and execution of educational policy. "Historically, the States have had the primary responsibility for the education of children at the elementary and secondary level." 121 Cong. Rec. 19498 (1975) (remarks of Sen. Dole). See also Epperson v. Arkansas, 393 U. S. 97,104 (1968) ("By and large, public education in our Nation is committed to the control of state and local authorities").

providing for parental involvement in the development of state plans and policies, and in the formulation of the child's individual educational program. As the Senate Report states:

> "The Committee recognizes that in many instances the process of providing special education and related services to handicapped children is not guaranteed to produce any particular outcome. By changing the language [of the provision relating to individualized educational programs] to emphasize the process of parent and child involvement and to provide a written record of reasonable expectations, the Committee intends to clarify that such individualized planning conferences are a way to provide parent involvement and protection to assure that appropriate services are provided to a handicapped child."

As this very case demonstrates, parents and guardians will not lack ardor in seeking to ensure that handicapped children receive all of the benefits to which they are entitled by the Act.[619]

VI

Applying these principles to the facts of this case, we conclude that the Court of Appeals erred in affirming the decision of the District Court. Neither the District Court nor the Court of Appeals found that petitioners had failed to comply with the procedures of the Act, and the findings of neither court would support a conclusion that Amy's educational program failed to comply with the substantive requirements of the Act. On the contrary, the District Court found that the "evidence firmly establishes that Amy is receiving an 'adequate' education, since she performs better than the average child in her class and is advancing easily from grade to grade." In light of this finding, and of the fact that Amy was receiving personalized instruction and related services calculated by the Furnace Woods school administrators to meet her educational needs, the lower courts should not have concluded that the Act requires the provision of a sign-language interpreter. Accordingly, the decision of the Court of Appeals is reversed, and the case is remanded for further proceedings consistent with this opinion.

So ordered.

JUSTICE WHITE, with whom JUSTICE BRENNAN and JUSTICE MARSHALL join, dissented.

****

---

[619] In addition to providing for extensive parental involvement in the formulation of state and local policies, as well as the preparation of individual educational programs, the Act ensures that States will receive the advice of experts in the field of educating handicapped children. As a condition tor receiving federal funds under the Act, States must create "an advisory panel, appointed by the Governor or any other official authorized under State law to make such appointments, composed of individuals involved in or concerned with the education of handicapped children, including handicapped individuals, teachers, parents or guardians of handicapped children, State and local education officials, and administrators of programs for handicapped children, which (A) advises the State educational agency of unmet needs within the State in the education of handicapped children, [and] (B) comments publicly on any rules or regulations proposed for issuance by the State regarding the education of handicapped children." 1413(a)(12).

The implications of failing to meet the education program standard established in the Rowley case were explained in a recent decision of the Supreme Court involving a dispute which arose in South Carolina.

FLORENCE COUNTY SCHOOL DISTRICT
v.
CARTER
__ U.S.__, 62 L.W. 4001 (1993)

JUSTICE O'CONNOR delivered the opinion of the Court.

The Individuals with Disabilities Education Act (IDEA), 84 Stat. 175, as amended, 20 U. S. C. §1400 et seq. (1988 ed. and Supp. IV), requires States to provide disabled children with a "free appropriate public education," §1401(a)(18). This case presents the question whether a court may order reimbursement for parents who unilaterally withdraw their child from a public school that provides an inappropriate education under IDEA and put the child in a private school that provides an education that is otherwise proper under IDEA, but does not meet all the requirements of §1401(a)(18). We hold that the court may order such reimbursement, and therefore affirm the judgment of the Court of Appeals.

I

Respondent Shannon Carter was classified as learning disabled in 1985, while a ninth grade student in a school operated by petitioner Florence County School District Four. School officials met with Shannon's parents to formulate an individualized education program (IEP) for Shannon, as required under IDEA. 20 U. S. C. §§ 1401(a)(18) and (20), 1414(a)(5) (1988 ed. and Supp. IV). The IEP provided that Shannon would stay in regular classes except for three periods of individualized instruction per week, and established specific goals in reading and mathematics of four months' progress for the entire school year. Shannon's parents were dissatisfied, and requested a hearing to challenge the appropriateness of the IEP. See §1415(b)(2). Both the local educational officer and the state educational agency hearing officer rejected Shannon's parents' claim and concluded that the IEP was adequate. In the meantime, Shannon's parents had placed her in Trident Academy, a private school specializing in educating children with disabilities. Shannon began at Trident in September 1985 and graduated in the spring of 1988.

Shannon's parents filed this suit in July 1986, claiming that the school district had breached its duty under IDEA to provide Shannon with a "free appropriate public education," §1401(a)(18), and seeking reimbursement for tuition and other costs incurred at Trident. After a bench trial, the District Court ruled in the parents' favor. The court held that the school district's proposed educational program and the achievement goals of the IEP "were wholly inadequate" and failed to satisfy the requirements of the Act. App. to Pet. for Cert 27a. The court further held that "[a]lthough [Trident Academy] did not comply with all of the procedures outlined in [IDEA]," the school "provided Shannon an excellent education in substantial compliance with all the substantive requirements' of the statute. Id., at 37a. The court found that Trident "evaluated Shannon quarterly, not yearly as mandated in [IDEA], it provided Shannon with low teacher-student ratios, and it developed a plan which allowed Shannon to receive passing marks and progress from grade to grade." Ibid. The court also credited the findings of its own expert, who determined that Shannon had made "significant progress" at Trident and that her reading comprehension had risen three grade levels in her three years at the school. Id., at 29a. The District Court concluded that Shannon's education was "appropriate" under IDEA, and that Shannon's parents were entitled to reimbursement of tuition and other costs. Id., at 37a.

The Court of Appeals for the Fourth Circuit affirmed. 950 F. 2d 156 (1991). The court agreed that the IEP proposed by the school district was inappropriate under IDEA. It also rejected the school district's argument that reimbursement is never proper when the parents choose a private school that is not approved by the State or that does not comply with all the terms of IDEA. According to the Court of Appeals, neither the text of the Act nor its legislative history imposes a "requirement that the private school be approved by the state in parent-placement reimbursement cases." Id., at 162. To the contrary, the Court of Appeals concluded, IDEA's state-approval requirement applies only when a child is placed in a private school by public school officials. Accordingly, when a public school system has defaulted on its obligations under the Act, a private school placement is 'proper under the Act' if the education provided by the private school is 'reasonably calculated to enable the child to receive educational benefits.'" Id., at 163, quoting Board of Ed. of Hendrick Hudson Central School Dist. v. Rowley, 458 U. S. 176, 207 (1982).

The court below recognized that its holding conflicted with Tucker v. Bay Shore Union Free School Dist., 873 F. 2d 563, 568 (1989), in which the Court of Appeals for the Second Circuit held that parental placement in a private school cannot be proper under the Act unless the private school in question meets the standards of the state education agency. We granted certiorari, 507 U. S. ___(1993), to resolve this conflict among the Courts of Appeals.

II

In School Comm. of Burlington v. Department of Ed. of Mass., 471 U. S. 359, 369 (1985), we held that IDEA's grant of equitable authority empowers a court "to order school authorities to reimburse parents for their expenditures on private special education for a child if the court ultimately determines that such placement, rather than a proposed IEP, is proper under the Act." Congress intended that IDEA's promise of a "free appropriate public education" for disabled children would normally be met by an IEP's provision for education in the regular public schools or in private schools chosen jointly by school officials and parents. In cases where cooperation fails, however, parents who disagree with the proposed IEP are faced with a choice: go along with the IEP to the detriment of their child if it turns out to be inappropriate or pay for what they consider to be the appropriate placement." Id., at 370. For parents willing and able to make the latter choice, "it would be an empty victory to have a court tell them several years later that they were right but that these expenditures could not in a proper case be reimbursed by the school officials" Ibid. Because such a result would be contrary to IDEA's guarantee of a "free appropriate public education" we held that "Congress meant to include retroactive reimbursement to parents as an available remedy in a proper case." Ibid.

As this case comes to us, two issues are settled: 1) the school district's proposed IEP was inappropriate under IDEA, and 2) although Trident did not meet the §1401(a)(18) requirements, it provided an education otherwise proper under

309

IDEA. This case presents the narrow question whether Shannon's parents are barred from reimbursement because the private school in which Shannon enrolled did not meet the §1401(a)(18) definition of a "free appropriate public education." We hold that they are not, because §1401(a)(18)'s requirements cannot be read as applying to parental placements.

Section §1401(a)(18)(A) requires that the education be "provided at public expense, under public supervision and direction." Similarly, §1401(a)(18)(D) requires schools to provide an IEP, which must be designed by "a representative of the local educational agency," 20 U. S. C. §1401(a)(20) (1988 ed., Supp. IV), and must be "establish[ed]," revise[d]," and "review[ed]" by the agency, §1414(a)(5). These requirements do not make sense in the context of a parental placement. In this case, as in all Burlington reimbursement cases, the parents' rejection of the school district's proposed IEP is the very reason for the parents' decision to put their child in a private school. In such cases, where the private placement has necessarily been made over the school district's objection, the private school education will not be under "public supervision and direction." Accordingly, to read the §1401(a)(18) requirements as applying to parental placements would effectively eliminate the right of unilateral withdrawal recognized in Burlington. Moreover, IDEA was intended to ensure that children with disabilities receive an education that is both appropriate and free. Burlington, supra, at 373. To read the provisions of §1401(a)(18) to bar reimbursement in the circumstances of this case would defeat this statutory purpose.

Nor do we believe that reimbursement is necessarily barred by a private school's failure to meet state education standards. Trident's deficiencies, according to the school district, were that it employed at least two faculty members who were not state-certified and that it did not develop. As we have noted, however, the §1401(a)(18) requirements—including the requirement that the school meet the standards of the state educational agency §1401(a)(18)(B) do not apply to private parental placements. Indeed, the school district's emphasis on state standards is somewhat ironic. As the Court of Appeals noted, "it hardly seems consistent with the Act's goals to forbid parents from educating their child at a school that provides an appropriate education simply because that school lacks the stamp of approval of the same public school system that failed to meet the child's needs in the first place." 950 F. 2d, at 164. Accordingly, we disagree with the Second Circuit's theory that "a parent may not obtain reimbursement for a unilateral placement if that placement was in a school that was not on [the State's] approved list of private" schools. Tucker, 873 F. 2d, at 568 (internal quotation marks omitted). Parents' failure to select a program known to be approved by the State in favor of an unapproved option is not itself a bar to reimbursement.

Furthermore, although the absence of an approved list of private schools is not essential to our holding, we note that parents in the position of Shannon's have no way of knowing at the time they select a private school whether the school meets state standards. South Carolina keeps no publicly available list of approved private schools, but instead approves private school placements on a case-by-case basis. In fact, although public school officials had previously placed three children with disabilities at Trident, see App. to Pet. for Cert. 28a, Trident had not received blanket approval from the State. South Carolina's case-by-case approval system meant that Shannon's parents needed the cooperation of state officials before they could know whether Trident was state-approved. As we recognized in Burlington, such cooperation is unlikely in cases where the school officials disagree with the need for the private placement. 471 U. S., at 372.

III

The school district also claims that allowing reimbursement for parents such as Shannon's puts an unreasonable burden on financially strapped local educational authorities. The school district argues that requiring parents to choose a state-approved private school if they want reimbursement is the only meaningful way to allow States to control costs; otherwise States will have to reimburse dissatisfied parents for any private school that provides an education that is proper under the Act no matter how expensive it may be.

There is no doubt that Congress has imposed a significant financial burden on States and school districts that participate in IDEA. Yet public educational authorities who want to avoid reimbursing parents for the private education of a disabled child can do one of two things: give the child a free appropriate public education in a public setting, or place the child in an appropriate private setting of the State's choice. This is IDEA's mandate, and school officials who conform to it need not worry about reimbursement claims.

Moreover, parents who, like Shannon's, "unilaterally change their child's placement during the pendency of review proceedings, without the consent of the state or local school officials, do so at their own financial risk." Burlington, supra, at 373-374. They are entitled to reimbursement only if a federal court concludes both that the public placement violated IDEA, and that the private school placement was proper under the Act.

Finally, we note that once a court holds that the public placement violated IDEA, it is authorized to "grant such relief as the court determines is appropriate." 20 U. S. C. §1415(e)(2). Under this provision, "equitable considerations are relevant in fashioning relief," Burlington, 471 U. S., at 374, and the court enjoys "broad discretion" in so doing, id., at 369. Courts fashioning discretionary equitable relief under IDEA must consider all relevant factors, including the appropriate and reasonable level of reimbursement that should be required. Total reimbursement will not be appropriate if the court determines that the cost of the private education was unreasonable.

Accordingly, we **affirm** the judgment of the Court of Appeals .

So ordered.

STUDY QUESTIONS

1. Should local school districts be concerned that parents will be anxious to sue because of the Court's decision?
2. Is it likely that parents will remove their children from public schools as a result of the Court's ruling?

HOW IS THE TERM "MEDICAL SERVICES" DEFINED WITHIN THE SCHOOL'S RESPONSIBILITY TO PROVIDE RELATED SERVICES [620] UNDER THE ACT?

IRVING INDEPENDENT SCHOOL DISTRICT
v.
TATRO
468 U.S. 883, 104 S.Ct. 3371 (1984)

CHIEF JUSTICE BURGER delivered the opinion of the Court.

We granted certiorari to determine whether the Education of the Handicapped Act or the Rehabilitation Act of 1973 requires a school district to provide a handicapped child with clean intermittent catheterization during school hours.

I

Amber Tatro is an 8-year-old girl born with a defect known as spina bifida. As a result, she suffers from orthopedic and speech impairments and a neurogenic bladder, which prevents her from emptying her bladder voluntarily. Consequently, she must be catheterized every three or four hours to avoid injury to her kidneys. In accordance with accepted medical practice, clean intermittent catheterization (CIC), a procedure involving the insertion of a catheter into the urethra to drain the bladder, has been prescribed. The procedure is a simple one that may be performed in a few minutes by a layperson with less than an hour's training. Amber's parents, babysitter, and teenage brother are all qualified to administer CIC, and Amber soon will be able to perform this procedure herself.

In 1979 petitioner Irving Independent School District agreed to provide special education for Amber, who was then three and one-half years old. In consultation with her parents, who are respondents here, petitioner developed an individualized education program for Amber under the requirements of the Education of the Handicapped Act, 84 Stat. 175, as amended significantly by the Education for All Handicapped Children Act of 1975, 89 Stat. 773, 20 U. S. C. §§1401(19), 1414(a)(5). The individualized education program provided that Amber would attend early childhood development classes and receive special services such as physical and occupational therapy. That program, however, made no provision for school personnel to administer CIC.

Respondents unsuccessfully pursued administrative remedies to secure CIC services for Amber during school hours. In October 1979 respondents brought the present action in District Court against petitioner, the State Board of Education, and others. They sought an injunction ordering petitioner to provide Amber with CIC and sought damages and attorney's fees. First, respondents invoked the Education of the Handicapped Act. Because Texas received funding under that statute, petitioner was required to provide Amber with a "free appropriate public education," §§1412(1), 1414(a)(1)(C)(ii), which is defined to include "related

---

[620]Julnes, Ralph E., Brown, Sharan E., "The Legal Mandate to Provide Assistive Technology in Special Education Programing," 82 Ed.Law Rep. [737] (July 15, 1993).

services," §1401(18). Respondents argued that CIC is one such "related service."[621] Second, respondents invoked §504 of the Rehabilitation Act of 1973, 87 Stat. 394, as amended, 29 U. S. C. §794, which forbids an individual, by reason of a handicap, to be "excluded from the participation in, be denied the benefits of, or be subjected to discrimination under" any program receiving federal aid.

The District Court denied respondents' request for a preliminary injunction. That court concluded that CIC was not a "related service" under the Education of the Handicapped Act because it did not serve a need arising from the effort to educate. It also held that § 504 of the Rehabilitation Act did not require "the setting up of governmental health care for people seeking to participate" in federally funded programs. Id., at 1229.

The Court of Appeals reversed. (Tatro I). First, it held that CIC was a "related service" under the Education of the Handicapped Act, 20 U. S. C. §1401(17), because without the procedure Amber could not attend classes and benefit from special education. Second, it held that petitioner's refusal to provide CIC effectively excluded her from a federally funded educational program in violation of § 504 of the Rehabilitation Act. The Court of Appeals remanded for the District Court to develop a factual record and apply these legal principles.

On remand petitioner stressed the Education of the Handicapped Act's explicit provision that "medical services" could qualify as "related services' only when they served the purpose of diagnosis or evaluation. The District Court held that under Texas law a nurse or other qualified person may administer CIC without engaging in the unauthorized practice of medicine, provided that a doctor prescribes and supervises the procedure. The District Court then held that, because a doctor was not needed to administer CIC, provision of the procedure was not a "medical service" for purposes of the Education of the Handicapped Act. Finding CIC to be a "related service" under that Act, the District Court ordered petitioner and the State Board of Education to modify Amber's individualized education program to include provision of CIC during school hours. It also awarded compensatory damages against petitioner.

On the authority of Tatro I, the District Court then held that respondents had proved a violation of § 504 of the Rehabilitation Act. Although the District Court did not rely on this holding to authorize any greater injunctive or compensatory relief, it did invoke the holding to award attorney's fees against petitioner and the State Board of Education.[622] 516 F. Supp., at 968; App. to Pet. for Cert. 55a-63a. The Rehabilitation Act, unlike the Education of the Handicapped Act, authorizes prevailing parties to recover attorney's fees. See 29 U. S. C. §794a.

The Court of Appeals affirmed. (Tatro II). That court accepted the District Court's conclusion that state law permitted qualified persons to administer CIC without the physical presence of a doctor, and it affirmed the award of relief under the Education of the Handicapped Act.

We granted certiorari and we affirm in part.

---

[621] As discussed more fully later, the Education of the Handicapped Act defines "related services" to include "supportive services (including . . . medical and counseling services, except that such medical services shall be for diagnostic and evaluation purposes only) as may be required to assist a handicapped child to benefit from special education." 20 U. S. C. §1401(17).

[622] The District Court held that § 505 of the Rehabilitation Act, 29 U. S. C. § 794a, which authorizes attorney's fees as a part of a prevailing party's costs, abrogated the State Board's immunity under the Eleventh Amendment. See App. to Pet. for Cert. 56a-60a. The State Board did not petition for certiorari, and the Eleventh Amendment issue is not before us.

II

This case poses two separate issues. The first is whether the Education of the Handicapped Act requires petitioner to provide CIC services to Amber. The second is whether §504 of the Rehabilitation Act creates such an obligation. We first turn to the claim presented under the Education of the Handicapped Act.

States receiving funds under the Act are obliged to satisfy certain conditions. A primary condition is that the state implement a policy "that assures all handicapped children the right to a free appropriate public education." 20 U. S. C. §1412(1). Each educational agency applying to a state for funding must provide assurances in turn that its program aims to provide "a free appropriate public education to all handicapped children." §1414(a)(1)(C)(ii).

A "free appropriate public education" is explicitly defined as "special education and related services." §1401(18).[623] The term "special education" means

> "specially designed instruction, at no cost to parents or guardians, to meet the unique needs of a handicapped child, including classroom instruction, instruction in physical education, home instruction, and instruction in hospitals and institutions." §1401(16).

"Related services" are defined as

> "transportation, and such developmental, corrective, and other supportive services (including speech pathology and audiology, psychological services, physical and occupational therapy, recreation, and medical and counseling services, except that such medical services shall be for diagnostic and evaluation purposes only) as may be required to assist a handicapped child to benefit from special education, and includes the early identification and assessment of handicapping conditions in children." §1401(17) (emphasis added).

The issue in this case is whether CIC is a "related service" that petitioner is obliged to provide to Amber. We must answer two questions: first, whether CIC is a "supportive servic[e] . . . required to assist a handicapped child to benefit from special education"; and second, whether CIC is excluded from this definition as a "medical servic[e]" serving purposes other than diagnosis or evaluation.

A

The Court of Appeals was clearly correct in holding that CIC is a "supportive servic[e] . . . required to assist a handicapped child to benefit from special education." It is clear on this record that, without having CIC services available during the school day, Amber cannot attend school and thereby "benefit from special education." CIC services, therefore, fall squarely within the definition of a "supportive service."

As we have stated before, "Congress sought primarily to make public education available to handicapped children" and "to make such access meaningful." A service that enables a handicapped child to remain at school during the day is an important means of providing the child with the meaningful access to education that Congress envisioned. The Act makes specific provision for services, like transportation, for example, that do no more than enable a child to be physically

---

[623] Specifically, the "special education and related services" must "(A) have been provided at public expense, under public supervision and direction, and without charge, (B) meet the standards of the State educational agency, (C) include an appropriate preschool, elementary, or secondary school education in the State involved, and (D) [be] provided in conformity with the individualized education program required under section 1414(a)(5) of this title." §1401(18).

present in class, and the Act specifically authorizes grants for schools to alter buildings and equipment to make them accessible to the handicapped. Services like CIC that permit a child to remain at school during the day are no less related to the effort to educate than are services that enable the child to reach, enter, or exit the school.

We hold that CIC services in this case qualify as a "supportive servic[e] . . . required to assist a handicapped child to benefit from special education."

B

We also agree with the Court of Appeals that provision of CIC is not a "medical servic[e]," which a school is required to provide only for purposes of diagnosis or evaluation. See 20 U. S. C. §1401(17). We begin with the regulations of the Department of Education, which are entitled to deference.[624] The regulations define "related services" for handicapped children to include "school health services," 34 CFR §300.13(a) (1983), which are defined in turn as "services provided by a qualified school nurse or other qualified person," §300.13(b) (10). "Medical services" are defined as "services provided by a licensed physician." §300.13(b)(4).[625] Thus, the Secretary has determined that the services of a school nurse otherwise qualifying as a "related service" are not subject to exclusion as a "medical service," but that the services of a physician are excludable as such.

This definition of "medical services" is a reasonable interpretation of congressional intent. Although Congress devoted little discussion to the "medical services" exclusion, the Secretary could reasonably have concluded that it was designed to spare schools from an obligation to provide a service that might well prove unduly expensive and beyond the range of their competence.[626] From this understanding of congressional purpose, the Secretary could reasonably have concluded that Congress intended to impose the obligation to provide school nursing services.

Congress plainly required schools to hire various specially trained personnel to help handicapped children, such as "trained occupational therapists, speech therapists, psychologists, social workers and other appropriately trained personnel." S. Rep. No. 94-168, supra, at 33. School nurses have long been a part of the educational system, and the Secretary could, therefore, reasonably conclude that school nursing services are not the sort of burden that Congress intended to exclude as a "medical service." By limiting the "medical services" exclusion to the services of a physician or hospital, both far more expensive, the Secretary has given a permissible construction to the provision.

Petitioner's contrary interpretation of the "medical services" exclusion is unconvincing. In petitioner's view, CIC is a "medical service," even though it may be provided by a nurse or trained layperson; that conclusion rests on its reading of Texas law that confines CIC to uses in accordance with a physician's prescription and under a physician's ultimate supervision. Aside from conflicting with the

---

[624] The Secretary of Education is empowered to issue such regulations as may be necessary to carry out the provisions of the Act. 20 U. S. C. §1417(b). This function was initially vested in the Commissioner of Education of the Department of Health, Education, and Welfare, who promulgated the regulations in question. This function was transferred to the Secretary of Education when Congress created that position, see Department of Education Organization Act, §§ 301(a)(1), (2)(H), 93 Stat. 677, 20 U. S. C. §§3441(a)(1), (2)(H).

[625] The regulations actually define only those "medical services" that are owed to handicapped children: "services provided by a licensed physician to determine a child's medically related handicapping condition which results in the child's need for special education and related services." 34 CFR §300.13(b)(4) (1983). Presumably this means that "medical services" not owed under the statute are those "services by a licensed physician" that serve other purposes.

[626] Children with serious medical needs are still entitled to an education. For example, the Act specifically includes instruction in hospitals and home within the definition of "special education." See 20 U. S. C. § 1401(16).

Secretary's reasonable interpretation of congressional intent, however, such a rule would be anomalous. Nurses in petitioner School District are authorized to dispense oral medications and administer emergency injections in accordance with a physician's prescription. This kind of service for nonhandicapped children is difficult to distinguish from the provision of CIC to the handicapped. It would be strange indeed if Congress, in attempting to extend special services to handicapped children, were unwilling to guarantee them services of a kind that are routinely provided to the nonhandicapped.

To keep in perspective the obligation to provide services that relate to both the health and educational needs of handicapped students, we note several limitations that should minimize the burden petitioner fears. First, to be entitled to related services, a child must be handicapped so as to require special education. See 20 U. S. C. §1401(1); 34 CFR §300.5 (1983). In the absence of a handicap that requires special education, the need for what otherwise might qualify as a related service does not create an obligation under the Act. See 34 CFR §300.14, Comment (1) (1983).

Second, only those services necessary to aid a handicapped child to benefit from special education must be provided, regardless how easily a school nurse or layperson could furnish them. For example, if a particular medication or treatment may appropriately be administered to a handicapped child other than during the school day, a school is not required to provide nursing services to administer it.

Third, the regulations state that school nursing services must be provided only if they can be performed by a nurse or other qualified person, not if they must be performed by a physician. See 34 CFR §§300.13(a), (b)(4), (b)(10) (1983). It bears mentioning that here not even the services of a nurse are required; as is conceded, a layperson with minimal training is qualified to provide CIC. See also, e. g., Department of Education of Hawaii v. Katherine D., 727 F. 2d 809 (CA9 1983).

Finally, we note that respondents are not asking petitioner to provide equipment that Amber needs for CIC. Tr. of Oral Arg. 18-19. They seek only the services of a qualified person at the school.

We conclude that provision of CIC to Amber is not subject to exclusion as a "medical service," and we affirm the Court of Appeals' holding that CIC is a "related service" under the Education of the Handicapped Act.[627]

III

[T]he judgment of the Court of Appeals is affirmed [on the issue of the proper definition of "medical services" under the EAHCA].

****

STUDY QUESTIONS
1. Does the Court address who will perform CIC at school?
2. Where might such issues be discussed?
3. Why do you think the Court outlines the limited nature of its ruling?

---

[627] We need not address respondents' claim that CIC, in addition to being a "related service," is a "supplementary ai[d] and servic[e]" that petitioner must provide to enable Amber to attend classes with nonhandicapped students under the Act's "mainstreaming" directive. See 20 U. S. C. §1412(5)(B). Respondents have not sought an order prohibiting petitioner from educating Amber with handicapped children alone. Indeed, any request for such an order might not present a live controversy. Amber's present individualized education program provides for regular public school classes with nonhandicapped children. And petitioner has admitted that it would be far more costly to pay for Amber's instruction and CIC services at a private school, or to arrange for home tutoring, than to provide CIC at the regular public school placement provided in her current individualized education program. Tr. of Oral Arg. 12.

The duty of public school districts to provide related services for a disabled children who enroll in parochial schools was decided by the Supreme Court on June 18, 1993.[628] In the <u>Zobrest</u> case, an Arizona school district refused to provide a sign language interpreter for a student who enrolled at a Catholic school citing the 1st Amendment Establishment Clause.

ZOBREST
v.
CATALINA FOOTHILLS SCHOOL DISTRICT
___ U.S. ___, 113 S.Ct. 2462 (1993)

CHIEF JUSTICE REHNQUIST delivered the opinion of the Court.

Petitioner James Zobrest, who has been deaf since birth, asked respondent school district to provide a sign-language interpreter to accompany him to classes at a Roman Catholic high school in Tucson, Arizona, pursuant to the Individuals with Disabilities Education Act (IDEA), 20 U. S. C. §1400 et seq., and its Arizona counterpart, Ariz. Rev. Stat. Ann. §15-761 et seq.(1991 and Supp. 1992). The United States Court of Appeals for the Ninth Circuit decided, however, that provision of such a publicly employed interpreter would violate the Establishment Clause of the First Amendment. We hold that the Establishment Clause does not bar the school district from providing the requested interpreter.

James Zobrest attended grades one through five in a school for the deaf, and grades six through eight in a public school operated by respondent. While he attended public school, respondent furnished him with a sign-language interpreter. For religious reasons, James' parents (also petitioners here) enrolled him for the ninth grade in Salpointe Catholic High School, a sectarian institution.[629] When petitioners requested that respondent supply James with an interpreter at Salpointe, respondent referred the matter to the County Attorney, who concluded that providing an interpreter on the school's premises would violate the United States Constitution. App. 10-18. Pursuant to Ariz. Rev. Stat. Ann. §15-253(B) (1991), the question next was referred to the Arizona Attorney General, who concurred in the County Attorney's opinion. App. to Pet. for Cert. A-137. Respondent accordingly declined to provide the requested interpreter.

Petitioners then instituted this action in the United States District Court for the District of Arizona under 20 U. S. C. §1415(e)(4)(A), which grants the district courts jurisdiction over disputes regarding the services due disabled children under the IDEA.[630] Petitioners asserted that the IDEA and the Free Exercise Clause of the First Amendment require respondent to provide James with an interpreter at Salpointe, and that the Establishment Clause does not bar such relief. The complaint sought a preliminary injunction and "such other and further relief as the

---

[628]Two comments written before the decision was rendered can be found in Wests Educational Law Reporter. See Osborne, Allan G., "Special Education and Related Services for Parochial School Students," 81 Ed.Law Rep. [1] (May 6, 1993) and Johnson, T. Page, "Zobrest v. Catalina Foothills School District: Does the Establishment Clause Bar Sending Public School Employees into Religious Schools?," 82 Ed.Law Rep. [5] (1993).

[629]The parties have stipulated: "The two functions of secular education and advancement of religious values or beliefs are inextricably intertwined throughout the operations of Salpointe." App. 92.

[630]The parties agreed that exhaustion of administrative remedies would be futile here. Id., at 94-95.

Court deems just and proper." App. 25.[631] The District Court denied petitioners' request for a preliminary injunction, finding that the provision of an interpreter at Salpointe would likely offend the Establishment Clause. Id at 52-53. The court thereafter granted respondent summary judgment, on the ground that "[t]he interpreter would act as a conduit for the religious inculcation of James --thereby, promoting James' religious development at government expense." App. to Pet. for Cert. A-:35. "That kind of entanglement of church and state," the District Court concluded, "is not allowed." Ibid.

The Court of Appeals affirmed by a divided vote, 963 F. 2d 1190 (CA9 1992), applying the three-part test announced in Lemon v. Kurtzman, 403 U. S. 602, 613 (1971). It first found that the IDEA has a clear secular purpose: "'to assist States and Localities to provide for the education of all handicapped children.'" 963 F. 2d, at 1193 (quoting 20 U. S. C. §1400(c)).[632] Turning to the second prong of the Lemon inquiry, though, the Court of Appeals determined that the IDEA, if applied as petitioners proposed, would have the primary effect of advancing religion and thus would run afoul of the Establishment Clause. "By placing its employee in the sectarian school," the Court of Appeals reasoned, "the government would create the appearance that it was a 'joint sponsor' of the school's activities." 963 F. 2d at 1194-1195. This, the court held, would create the 'symbolic union of government and religion" found impermissible in School Dist. of Grand Rapids v. Ball, 473 U. S. 373, 392 (1985).[633] In contrast, the dissenting judge argued that "[g]eneral welfare programs neutrally available to all children," such as the IDEA, pass constitutional muster, "because their benefits diffuse over the entire population." 963 F 2d, at 1199 (Tang, J., dissenting). We granted certiorari, 506 U. S.___ (1992), and now reverse.

Respondent has raised in its brief in opposition to certiorari and in isolated passages in its brief on the merits several issues unrelated to the Establishment Clause question.[634] Respondent first argues that 34 CFR §76.532(a)(1), a regulation promulgated under the IDEA precludes it from using federal funds to provide an interpreter to James at Salpointe. Brief in Opposition 13[635] In the alternative, respondent claims that even if there is no affirmative bar to the relief, it is not required by statute or regulation to furnish interpreters to students at sectarian schools. Brief for Respondent 4, n. 4.[636] And respondent adds that providing such a service would offend Art. II, §12, of the Arizona Constitution. Tr. of Oral Arg. 28.

---

[631]During the pendency of this litigation, James completed his high school studies and graduated from Salpointe on May 16, 1992. This case nonetheless presents a continuing controversy, since petitioners seek reimbursement for the cost they incurred in hiring their own interpreter, more than $7,000 per year. Id., at 65.

[632]Respondent now concedes that "the IDEA has an appropriate secular purpose.'" Brief for Respondent 16.

[633]The Court of Appeals also rejected petitioners' Free Exercise Clause claim. 963 F. 2d 1190, 1196-1197 (CA9 1992). Petitioners have not challenged that part of the decision below. Pet. for Cert. 10, n. 9.

[634]Respondent may well have waived these other defenses. For in response to an interrogatory asking why it had refused to provide the requested service, respondent referred only to the putative Establishment Clause bar. App. 59-60.

[635]That regulation prohibits the use of federal funds to pay for "[r]eligious worship, instruction, or proselytization. 34 CFR §76.532(a)(l) (1992). The United States asserts that the regulation merely implements the Secretary of Education's understanding of (and thus is coextensive with) the requirements of the Establishment Clause. Brief for United States as Amicus Curiae 23; see also Brief for United States as Amicus. Curiae in Witters v. Dept. of Services for Blind, O. T. 1985, No. 84-1070, p. 21, n. 11 ("These regulations are based on the Departments interpretation of constitutional requirements"). This interpretation seems persuasive to us. The only authority cited by the Secretary for issuance of the regulation is his general rulemaking power. See 34 CFR §76.532 citing 20 U. S. C. §§122le-3(a)(l), 2831(a), and 2974(b)). Though the Fourth Circuit placed a different interpretation on §76.532 in Goodall v. Stafford County School Board, 930 F.2d 363, 369 (holding that the regulation prohibits the provision of an interpreter to a student in a sectarian school), cert.denied, 502 U.S. ___(1991), that court did not have the benefit of the United States' views.

[636]In our view, this belated contention is entitled to little, if any , weight here given respondent's repeated concession that, but for the perceived federal constitutional bar, it would have willingly provided James with an interpreter at Salpointe as a matter of local policy. See, e.g., TR. of Oral Arg. 31 ("We don't deny that...we would have voluntarily done that. The only concern that came up at the time was the Establishment Clause concern").

It is a familiar principle of our jurisprudence that federal courts will not pass on the constitutionality of an Act of Congress if a construction of the Act is fairly possible by which the constitutional question can be avoided. See, e.g., United States v. Locke, 471 U. S. 84, 92 (1985), and cases cited therein. In Locke, a case coming here by appeal under 28 U. S. C.,§1252 (1982 ed.), we said that such an appeal "brings before this Court not merely the constitutional question decided below, but the entire case." 471 U. S., at 92. "The entire case," we explained, "includes nonconstitutional questions actually decided by the lower court as well as nonconstitutional grounds presented to, but not passed on, by the lower court." Ibid. Therefore, in that case, we turned "first to the nonconstitutional questions pressed below." Ibid.

Here, in contrast to Locke, and other cases applying the prudential rule of avoiding constitutional questions, only First Amendment questions were pressed in the Court of Appeals. In the opening paragraph of its opinion, the Court of Appeals noted that petitioners' appeal raised only First Amendment issues:

"The Zobrests appeal the district court's ruling that provision of a state-paid sign language interpreter to James Zobrest while he attends a sectarian high school would violate the Establishment Clause. The Zobrests also argue that denial of such assistance violates the Free Exercise Clause." 963 F. 2d, at 1191.

Respondent did not urge any statutory grounds for affirmance upon the Court of Appeals, and thus the Court of Appeals decided only the federal constitutional claims raised by petitioners. In the District Court too, the parties chose to litigate the case on the federal constitutional issues alone. "Both parties' motions for summary judgment raised only federal constitutional issues." Brief for Respondent 4, n. 4. Accordingly, the District Court's order granting respondent summary judgment addressed only the Establishment Clause question. App. to Pet. for Cert. A-35.

Given this posture of the case, we think the prudential rule of avoiding constitutional questions has no application. The fact that there may be buried in the record a nonconstitutional ground for decision is not by itself enough to invoke this rule. See, e.g., Board of Airport Comm'rs of Las Angeles v. Jews for Jesus, Inc., 482 U. S. 569, 572 (1987). "Where issues are neither raised before nor considered by the Court of Appeals, this Court will not ordinarily consider them." Adickes v. S. H. Kress & Co., 398 U. S. 144, 147, n. 2 (1970). We therefore turn to the merits of the constitutional claim.

We have never said that "religious institutions are disabled by the First Amendment from participating in publicly sponsored social welfare programs." Bowen v. Kendrick, 487 U. S. 589, 609 (1988). For if the Establishment Clause did bar religious groups from receiving general government benefits, then "a church could not be protected by the police and fire departments, or have its public sidewalk kept in repair." Widmar v. Vincent, 454 U. S. 263, 274-275 (1981) (internal quotation marks omitted). Given that a contrary rule would lead to such absurd results, we have consistently held that government programs that neutrally provide benefits to a broad class of citizens defined without reference to religion are not readily subject to an Establishment Clause challenge just because sectarian institutions may also receive an attenuated financial benefit. Nowhere have we stated this principle more clearly than in Mueller v Allen, 463 U. S. 388 (1983), and Witters v. Washington Dept of Services for Blind, 474 U. S. 481(1986), two cases dealing specifically with government programs offering general educational assistance.

In <u>Mueller</u>, we rejected an Establishment Clause challenge to a Minnesota law allowing taxpayers to deduct certain educational expenses in computing their state income tax, even though the vast majority of those deductions (perhaps over 90%) went to parents whose children attended sectarian schools. See 463 U. S., at 401; id., at 405 (Marshall, J., dissenting). Two factors, aside from States' traditionally broad taxing authority, informed our decision. See <u>Witters,</u> supra, at 491 (Powell, J., concurring) (discussing <u>Mueller</u>). We noted that the law "permits all parents—whether their children attend public school or private—to deduct their children's educational expenses." 463 U. S., at 398 (emphasis in original). See also <u>Widmar</u>, supra, at 274 ("The provision of benefits to so broad a spectrum of groups is an important index of secular effect"); <u>Board of Ed. of Westside Community Schools (Dist. 66) v. Mergens,</u> 496 U. S. 226, 248 (1990) (plurality opinion) (same). We also pointed out that under Minnesota's scheme, public funds become available to sectarian schools "only as a result of numerous private choices of individual parents of school-age children," thus distinguishing <u>Mueller</u> from our other cases involving "the direct transmission of assistance from the State to the schools themselves." 463 U. S., at 399.

<u>Witters</u> was premised on virtually identical reasoning. In that case, we upheld against an Establishment Clause challenge the State of Washington's extension of vocational assistance, as part of a general state program, to a blind person studying at a private Christian college to become a pastor, missionary, or youth director. Looking at the statute as a whole, we observed that "[a]ny aid provided religious institutions does so only as a result of the genuinely independent and private choices of aid recipients." 474 U.S., at 487. The program, we said, "creates no financial incentive for students to undertake sectarian education." Id., at 488. We also remarked that like the law in Mueller, Washington's program is 'made available generally without regard to the sectarian-nonsectarian, or public-nonpublic nature of the institution benefited.'" <u>Witters</u>, supra. at 487 (quoting <u>Committee for Public Education and Religious Liberty v. Nyquist,</u> 413 U. S. 756, 782-783, n. 38 (1973)). In light of these factors, we held that Washington's program—even as applied to a student who sought state assistance so that he could become a pastor—would not advance religion in a manner inconsistent with the Establishment Clause Witters, supra, at 489.

That same reasoning applies with equal force here. The service at issue in this case is part of a general government program that distributes benefits neutrally to any child qualifying as "handicapped" under the IDEA, without regard to the "sectarian-nonsectarian, or public-nonpublic nature" of the school the child attends. By according parents freedom to select a school of their choice, the statute ensures that a government-paid interpreter will be present in a sectarian school only as a result of the private decision of individual parents. In other words, because the IDEA creates no financial incentive for parents to choose a sectarian school, an interpreter's presence there cannot be attributed to state decision making. Viewed against the backdrop of Mueller and Witters, then, the Court of Appeals erred in its decision. When the government offers a neutral service on the premises of a sectarian school as part of a general program that "is in no way skewed towards religion," <u>Witters</u>, supra, at 488, it follows under our prior decisions that provision of that service does not offend the Establishment Clause. See <u>Wolman v. Walter,</u>

433 U. S. 229, 244 (1977). Indeed, this is an even easier case than Mueller and Witters in the sense that, under the IDEA, no funds traceable to the government ever find their way into sectarian schools' coffers. The only indirect economic benefit a sectarian school might receive by dint of the IDEA is the handicapped child's tuition—and that is, of course, assuming that the school makes a profit on each student; that, without an IDEA interpreter, the child would have gone to school elsewhere; and that the school, then, would have been unable to fill that child's spot.

Respondent contends, however, that this case differs from Mueller and Witters, in that petitioners seek to have a public employee physically present in a sectarian school to assist in James' religious education. In light of this distinction, respondent argues that this case more closely resembles Meek v. Pittenger, 421 U. S. 349 (1975), and School Dist. of Grand Rapids v. Ball, 473 U. S. 373 (1985). In Meek, we struck down a statute that, inter alia, provided "massive aid" to private schools—more than 75% of which were church related—through a direct loan of teaching material and equipment. 421 U. S., at 364- 365. The material and equipment covered by the statute included maps, charts, and tape recorders. Id., at 355. According to respondent, if the government could not place a tape recorder in a sectarian school in Meek, then it surely cannot place an interpreter in Salpointe. The statute in Meek also authorized state-paid personnel to furnish "auxiliary services"—which included remedial and accelerated instruction and guidance counseling—on the premises of religious schools. We determined that this part of the statute offended the First Amendment as well. Id., at 372. Ball similarly involved two public programs that provided services on private school premises; there, public employees taught classes to students in private school classrooms.[637] 473 U. S., at 375. We found that those programs likewise violated the Constitution relying largely on Meek. 473 U.S. at 386-389. According to respondent, if the government could not provide educational services on the premises of sectarian school in Meek and Ball, then it surely cannot provide James an interpreter on the premises of Salpointe.

Respondent's reliance on Meek and BalI is misplaced for two reasons. First. the programs in Meek and Ball—through direct grants of government aid—relieved sectarian schools of costs they otherwise would have borne in educating their students. See Witters, supra, at 487. "[T]he State may not grant aid to a religious school whether cash or in kind, where the effect of the aid is 'that of a direct subsidy to the religious school' from the State") (quoting Ball, supra, at 394). For example, the religious schools in Meek received teaching material and equipment from the State, relieving them of an otherwise necessary cost of performing their educational function. 421 U. S., at 365-366 "Substantial aid to the educational function of such schools," we explained, "necessarily results in aid to the sectarian school enterprise as a whole," and therefore brings about "the direct and substantial advancement of religious activity." Id., at 366. So, too, was the case in Ball: The programs challenged there, which provided teachers in addition to instructional equipment and material, "in effect subsidize[d] the religious functions of the parochial schools by taking over a substantial portion of their responsibility for teaching secular subjects." 473 U. S., at 397. "This kind of direct aid," we determined, "is indistinguishable from the provision of a direct cash subsidy to the religious school." Id., at 395. The extension of aid to petitioners, however, does not amount to "an

---

[637]Forty of the forty-one private schools involved in Ball were pervasively sectarian. 473 U. S., at 384-385.

impermissible 'direct subsidy'" of Salpointe. <u>Witters</u>. 474 U. S., at 487. For Salpointe is not relieved of an expense that it otherwise would have assumed in educating its students. And, as we noted above, any attenuated financial benefit that parochial schools do ultimately receive from the lDEA is attributable to "the private choices of individual parents." <u>Mueller</u>, 463 U. S., at 400. Handicapped children, not sectarian schools, are the primary beneficiaries of the IDEA; to the extent sectarian schools benefit at all from the IDEA, they are only incidental beneficiaries. Thus, the function of the IDEA is hardly "'to provide desired financial support for nonpublic, sectarian institutions.'" Id., at 488 (quoting Nyquist, 413 U. S.. at 783).

Second, the task of a sign-language interpreter seems to us quite different from that of a teacher or guidance counselor. notwithstanding the Court of Appeals' intimations to the contrary, see 963 F. 2d. at 1195, the Establishment Clause lays down no absolute bar to the placing of a public employee in a sectarian school.[638] Such a flat rule, smacking of antiquated notions of "taint," would indeed exalt form over substance.[639] Nothing in this record suggests that a sign-language interpreter would do more than accurately interpret whatever material is presented to the class as a whole. In fact, ethical guidelines require interpreters to "transmit everything that is said in exactly the same way it was intended." App. 73. James' parents have chosen of their own free will to place him in a pervasively sectarian environment. The sign-language interpreter they have requested will neither add to nor subtract from that environment, and hence the provision of such assistance is not barred by the Establishment Clause.

The IDEA creates a neutral government program dispensing aid not to schools but to individual handicapped children. If a handicapped child chooses to enroll in a sectarian school, we hold that the Establishment Clause does not prevent the school district from furnishing him with a sign-language interpreter there in order to facilitate his education. The judgment of the Court of Appeals is therefore
Reversed.

JUSTICE BLACKMUN, with whom JUSTICE SOUTER joins, and with whom JUSTICE STEVENS and JUSTICE O'CONNOR join as to Part I, dissenting.

Today, the Court unnecessarily addresses an important constitutional issue, disregarding long-standing principles of constitutional adjudication. In so doing, the Court holds that placement in a parochial school classroom of a public employee whose duty consists of relaying religious messages does not violate the Establishment Clause of the First Amendment. I disagree both with the Court's decision to reach this question and with its disposition on the merits. I therefore dissent.

I

"If there is one doctrine more deeply rooted than any other in the process of constitutional adjudication, it is that we ought not to pass on questions of constitutionality . . . unless such adjudication is unavoidable." <u>Specter</u> <u>Motor</u>

---

[638]For instance, In Wolman v. Walter. 433 U S. 229. 242 (1977), we made clear that "the provision of health services to all school children—public and nonpublic-does not have the primary effect aiding religion," even when those services are provided within sectarian schools. We accordingly rejected a First Amendment challenge to the State's providing diagnostic speech and hearing services on sectarian school premises. Id. at 244; see also; Meek v. Pittenger, 421 U. S. 349, 371, n. 21 (1975).

[639]Indeed, respondent readily admits, as it must, that there would be no problem under the Establishment Clause if the IDEA funds instead went directly to James' parents, who, in turn, hired the interpreter themselves. Brief for Respondent 11 ("If such were the case, then the sign language interpreter would be the student's employee not the school District's and governmental involvement in the enterprise would end with the disbursement of funds").

Service, Inc., v. McLaughlin, 323 U. S. 101, 105 (1944)(cites omitted) This is a "fundamental rule of judicial restraint," which has received the sanction of time and experience. It has been described as a "corollary" to the Article III case or controversy requirement, and is grounded in basic principles regarding the institution of judicial review and this Court's proper role in our federal system. Ibid.

Respondent School District makes two arguments that could provide grounds for affirmance, rendering consideration of the constitutional question unnecessary. First, respondent maintains that the Individuals with Disabilities Education Act (IDEA), 20 U. S. C. §1400 et ,seq, does not require it to furnish petitioner with an interpreter at any private school so long as special education services are made available at a public school. The United States endorses this interpretation of the statute, explaining that "the IDEA itself does not establish an individual entitlement to services for students placed in private schools at their parents' option." Brief for United States as Amicus Curiae 13. And several courts have reached the same conclusion. (cites omitted) Second, respondent contends that 34 CFR §76.532(a)(1) (1992), a regulation promulgated under the IDEA, which forbids the use of federal funds to pay for"[r]eligious worship, instruction, or proselytization," prohibits provision of a sign-language interpreter at a sectarian school. The United States asserts that this regulation does not preclude the relief petitioners seek, Brief for United States as Amicus Curiae 23, but at least one federal court has concluded otherwise. See Goodall, supra. This Court could easily refrain from deciding the constitutional claim by vacating and remanding the case for consideration of the statutory and regulatory issues. Indeed, the majority's decision does not eliminate the need to resolve these remaining questions. For, regardless of the Court's views on the Establishment Clause, petitioners will not obtain what they seek if the federal statute does not require or the federal regulations prohibit provision of a sign-language interpreter in a sectarian school.[640]

The majority does not deny the existence of these alternative grounds, nor does it dispute the venerable principle that constitutional questions should be avoided when there are nonconstitutional grounds for a decision in the case. Instead, in its zeal to address the constitutional question, the majority casts aside this "time-honored canon of constitutional adjudication," with the cursory observation that "the prudential rule of avoiding constitutional questions has no application" in light of the "posture" of this case. Ante, at 6. Because the parties chose not to litigate the federal statutory issues in the District Court and in the Court of Appeals, the majority blithely proceeds to the merits of their constitutional claim.

But the majority's statements are a non .sequitur. From the rule against deciding issues not raised or considered below, it does not follow that the Court should consider constitutional issues needlessly. The obligation to avoid unnecessary adjudication of constitutional questions does not depend upon the parties' litigation strategy, but rather is a "self-imposed limitation on the exercise of this Court's jurisdiction [that] has an importance to the institution that transcends the significance of particular controversies." City of Mesquite v. Aladdin's Castle, Inc., 455 U. S. 283, 294 (1982). It is a rule whose aim is to protect not parties but

---

[640]Respondent also argues that public provision of a sign-language interpreter would violate the Arizona Constitution. Article II § 12 of the Arizona Constitution provides: "No public money or property shall be appropriated for or applied to any religious worship, exercise, or instruction, or to the support of any religious establishment." The Arizona Attorney General concluded that, under this provision, the interpreter services could not be furnished to petitioner. See App. 9.

the law and the adjudicatory process. Indeed, just a few days ago, we expressed concern that "litigants, by agreeing on the legal issue presented, could extract the opinion of a court on hypothetical Acts of Congress or dubious constitutional principles, an opinion that would be difficult to characterize as anything but advisory." (cite omitted).

That the federal statutory and regulatory issues have not been properly briefed or argued does not justify the Court's decision to reach the constitutional claim. The very posture of this case should have alerted the courts that the parties were seeking what amounts to an advisory opinion. After the Arizona Attorney General concluded that provision of a sign-language interpreter would violate the Federal and State Constitutions, the parties bypassed the federal statutes and regulations and proceeded directly to litigate the constitutional issue. Under such circumstances, the weighty nonconstitutional questions that were left unresolved are hardly to be described as "buried in the record." Ante, at 6. When federal and state law questions similarly remained open in Wheeler v. Barrera, 417 U. S. 402 (1974), this Court refused to pass upon the scope or constitutionality of a federal statute that might have required publicly employed teachers to provide remedial instruction on the premises of sectarian schools. Prudence counsels that the Court follow a similar practice here by vacating and remanding this case for consideration of the nonconstitutional questions, rather than proceeding directly to the merits of the constitutional claim. (cites omitted)

II

Despite my disagreement with the majority's decision to reach the constitutional question, its arguments on the merits deserve a response. Until now, the Court never has authorized a public employee to participate directly in religious indoctrination. Yet that is the consequence of today's decision.

Let us be clear about exactly what is going on here. The parties have stipulated to the following facts. Petitioner requested the State to supply him with a sign-language interpreter at Salpointe High School, a private Roman Catholic school operated by the Carmelite Order of the Catholic Church. App. 90. Salpointe is a "pervasively religious" institution where "[t]he two functions of secular education and advancement of religious values or beliefs are inextricably intertwined." Id., at 92. Salpointe's overriding "objective" is to "instill a sense of Christian values." Id., at 90. Its "distinguishing purpose" is "the inculcation in its students of the faith and morals of the Roman Catholic Church." Religion is a required subject at Salpointe, and Catholic students are "strongly encouraged" to attend daily Mass each morning. Ibid. Salpointe's teachers must sign a Faculty Employment Agreement which requires them to promote the relationship among the religious, the academic, and the extracurricular.[641] They are encouraged to do so by "assist[ing] students in experiencing how the presence of God is manifest in nature, human history, in the struggles for economic and political justice, and other secular areas of the curriculum." Id., at 92. The Agreement also sets forth detailed rules of conduct teachers must follow in order to advance the school's Christian mission.[642]

---

[641]The Faculty Employment Agreement provides: "Religious programs are of primary importance in Catholic educational institutions. They are not separate from the academic and extracurricular programs, but are instead interwoven with them and each is believed to promote the other." App. 90-91.
[642]The Faculty Employment Agreement sets forth the following detailed rules of conduct:

At Salpointe. where the secular and the sectarian are "inextricably intertwined," governmental assistance to the educational function of the school necessarily entails governmental participation in the school's inculcation of religion. A state-employed sign-language interpreter would be required to communicate the material covered in religion class, the nominally secular subjects that are taught from a religious perspective, and the daily Masses at which Salpointe encourages attendance for Catholic students. In an environment so pervaded by discussions of the divine, the interpreter's every gesture would be infused with religious significance. Indeed. petitioners willingly concede this point: "That the interpreter conveys religious messages is a given in the case." Brief for Petitioners 22. By this concession, petitioners would seem to surrender their constitutional claim.

The majority attempts to elude the impact of the record by offering three reasons why this sort of aid to petitioners survives Establishment Clause scrutiny. First, the majority observes that provision of a sign-language interpreter occurs as "part of a general government program that distributes benefits neutrally to any child qualifying as 'handicapped' under the IDEA, without regard to the 'sectarian-nonsectarian, or public-nonpublic' nature of the school the child attends." Ante, at 8. Second, the majority finds significant the fact that aid is provided to pupils and their parents, rather than directly to sectarian schools. As a result, "'[a]ny aid . . . that ultimately flows to religious institutions does so only as a result of the genuinely independent and private choices of aid recipients.'" Ante, at 7, quoting Witters v. Washington Department of Services for the Blind, 474 U. S. 481, 487 (1986). And, finally, the majority opines that "the task of a sign-language interpreter seems to us quite different from that of a teacher or guidance counselor." Ante, at 11.

But the majority's arguments are unavailing. As to the first two, even a general welfare program may have specific applications that are constitutionally forbidden under the Establishment Clause. See Bowen v. Kendrick 487 U. S. 589 (1988) (holding that Adolescent Family Life Act on its face did not violate the Establishment Clause, but remanding for examination of the constitutionality of particular applications). For example, a general program granting remedial assistance to disadvantaged schoolchildren attending public and private, secular and sectarian , schools alike would clearly offend the Establishment Clause insofar as it authorized the provision of teachers. See Aguilar v. Felton, 473 U. S. 402, 410 (1985); Grand Rapids School District v. Ball, 473 U. S. 373, 385 11985); Meek v. Pittenger, 421 U. S. 349, 371 (1975). Such a program would not be saved simply because it supplied teachers to secular as well as sectarian schools. Nor would the fact that teachers were furnished to pupils and their parents, rather than directly to sectarian schools, immunize such a program from Establishment Clause scrutiny. See Witters, 474 U. S., at 487 ("Aid may have unconstitutional effect even though it takes the form of aid to students or parents"); Wolman v. Walter, 433 U. S. 229, 250 (1977) (it would "exalt form over substance if this distinction [between equipment loaned to the pupil or his parent, and equipment loaded directly to the school] were found to justify a . . . different" result); Grand. Rapids, 473 U. S., at 395 (rejecting

---

"1. Teacher shall at all times present a Christian image to the students by promoting and living the school philosophy stated herein, in the School's Faculty Handbook, the School Catalog and other published statements of this School. In this role the teacher shall support all aspects of the School from its religious programs to its academic and social functions. It is through these areas that a teacher administers to mind, body and spirit of the young men and women who attend Salpointe Catholic High School.

"3. The School believes that faithful adherence to its philosophical principles by its teachers is essential to the School's mission and purpose. Teachers will therefore be expected to assist in the implementation of the philosophical policies of the School, and to compel proper conduct on the part of the students in the areas of general behavior, language, dress and attitude toward the Christian ideal." Id., at 91.

"fiction that a . . program could be saved by masking it as aid to individual students"). The majority's decision must turn, then, upon the distinction between a teacher and a sign-language interpreter.

"Although Establishment Clause jurisprudence is characterized by few absolutes," at a minimum the Clause does absolutely prohibit government-financed or government-sponsored indoctrination into the beliefs of a particular religious faith." Grand Rapids, 473 U. S. at 335. See Bowen v. Kendrick, 487 U S, at 623 (O'CONNOR, J. concurring) ("[A]ny use of public funds to promote religious doctrines violates the Establishment Clause") (emphasis in original); Meek, 421 U. S. at 371 ("'The State must be certain, given the Religion Clauses, that subsidized teachers do not inculcate religion,'" quoting Lemon v. Kurtzman, 403 U. S. 602, 619 (1971)); Levitt v. Committee for Public Education and Religious Liberty, 413 U. S. 472, 480 (1973) ("[T]he State is constitutionally compelled to assure that the state-supported activity is not being used for religious indoctrination"). In keeping with this restriction, our cases consistently have rejected the provision by government of any resource capable of advancing a school's religious mission. Although the Court generally has permitted the provision of "secular and nonideological services unrelated to the primary, religion-oriented educational function of the sectarian school," Meek, 421 U. S. at 364, it has always proscribed the provision of benefits that afford even the opportunity for the transmission of sectarian view," Wolman, 433 U. S., at 244.

Thus, the Court has upheld the use of public school buses to transport children to and from school, Everson v. Board of Education, 330 U. S. 1 (1947), while striking down the employment of publicly funded buses for field trips controlled by parochial school teachers, Wolman, 433 U. S., at 254. Similarly, the Court has permitted the provision of secular textbooks whose content is immutable and can be ascertained in advance, Board of Education v. Allen, 392 U. S. 236 (1968), while prohibiting the provision of any instructional materials or equipment that could be used to convey a religious message, such as slide projectors, tape recorders, record players, and the like, Wolman, 433 U. S., at 249. State-paid speech and hearing therapists have been allowed to administer diagnostic testing on the premises of parochial schools, Wolman, 433 U. S., at 241-242, whereas state-paid remedial teachers and counselors have not been authorized to offer their services because of the risk that they may inculcate religious beliefs, Meek, 421 U. S., at 371.

These distinctions perhaps are somewhat fine, but "'lines must be drawn.'" Grand Rapids, 473 U. S., at 398 (citation omitted). And our cases make clear that government crosses the boundary when it furnishes the medium for communication of a religious message. If petitioners receive the relief they seek, it is beyond question that a state employed sign-language interpreter would serve as the conduit for petitioner's religious education, thereby assisting Salpointe in its mission of religious indoctrination. But the Establishment Clause is violated when a sectarian school enlists "the machinery of the State to enforce a religious orthodoxy." Lee v. Weisman, __ U. S ___,___(1992).

Witters, supra, and Mueller v Allen, 463 U. S. 388 (1983) are not to the contrary. Those cases dealt with the payment of cash or a tax deduction, where governmental involvement ended with the disbursement of funds or lessening of tax. This case, on the other hand, involves ongoing, daily, and intimate governmental participation in the teaching and propagation of religious doctrine. When government dispenses public funds to individuals who employ them to finance private choices, it is difficult to argue that government is actually endorsing religion. But the graphic symbol of the concert of church and state that results when a public employee or instrumentality mouths a religious message is likely to "enlis[t]—at least in the eyes of impressionable youngsters—the powers of government to the support of the religious denomination operating the school " Grand Rapids, 473 U. S., at 385. And the union of church and state in pursuit of a common enterprise is likely to place the imprimatur of governmental approval upon the favored religion, conveying a message of exclusion to all those who do not adhere to its tenets.

Moreover, this distinction between the provision of funds and the provision of a human being is not merely one of form. It goes to the heart of the principles animating the Establishment Clause. As Amicus Council on Religious Freedom points out, the provision of a state-paid sign-language interpreter may pose serious problems for the church as well as for the state. Many sectarian schools impose religiously based rules of conduct, as Salpointe has in this case. A traditional Hindu school would be likely to instruct its students and staff to dress modestly, avoiding any display of their bodies. And an orthodox Jewish yeshiva might well forbid all but kosher food upon its premises. To require public employees to obey such rules would impermissibly threaten individual liberty, but to fail to do so might endanger religious autonomy. For such reasons, it long has been feared that "a union of government and religion tends to destroy government and to degrade religion." Engel v. Vitale, 370 U. S. 421, 431 (1962). The Establishment Clause was designed to avert exactly this sort of conflict.

III

The Establishment Clause "rests upon the premise that both religion and government can best work to achieve their lofty aims if each is left free from the other within its respective sphere." McCollum v. Board of Education, 333 U. S. 203, 212 (1948). To this end, our cases have strived to "chart a course that preserve[s] the autonomy and freedom of religious bodies while avoiding any semblance of established religion." Walz v. Tax Commission, 397 U. S. 664, 672 (1970). I would not stray, as the Court does today, from the course set by nearly five decades of Establishment Clause jurisprudence. Accordingly, I dissent.

JUSTICE O CONNOR, with whom JUSTICE STEVENS joins, dissenting.

*****

DO DISCIPLINARY PROCEDURES APPLICABLE TO DISABLED CHILDREN DIFFER FROM THOSE CHILDREN INELIGIBLE FOR SPECIAL EDUCATION SERVICES?[643]

HONIG[644]
v.
DOE
484 U.S. 305,108 S.Ct. 592(1988)

JUSTICE BRENNAN delivered the opinion of the Court.

As a condition of federal financial assistance, the Education of the Handicapped Act requires States to ensure a "free appropriate public education" for all disabled children within their jurisdictions. In aid of this goal, the Act establishes a comprehensive system of procedural safeguards designed to ensure parental participation in decisions concerning the education of their disabled children and to provide administrative and judicial review of any decisions with which those parents disagree. Among these safeguards is the so-called "stay-put" provision, which directs that a disabled child "shall remain in [his or her] then current educational placement" pending completion of any review proceedings, unless the parents and state or local educational agencies otherwise agree. 20 U. S. C. §1415(e)(3). Today we must decide whether, in the face of this statutory proscription, state or local school authorities may nevertheless unilaterally exclude disabled children from the classroom for dangerous or disruptive conduct growing out of their disabilities. In addition, we are called upon to decide whether a district court may, in the exercise of its equitable powers, order a State to provide educational services directly to a disabled child when the local agency fails to do so.

In the Education of the Handicapped Act (EHA or the Act), 84 Stat. 175, as amended, 20 U. S. C. §1400 et seq., Congress sought "to assure that all handicapped children have available to them . . . a free appropriate public education which emphasizes special education and related services designed to meet their unique needs, [and] to assure that the rights of handicapped children and their parents or guardians are protected." §1400(c). When the law was passed in 1975, Congress had before it ample evidence that such legislative assurances were sorely needed: 21 years after this Court declared education to be "perhaps the most important function of state and local governments, "congressional studies revealed that better than half of the nation's eight million disabled children were not receiving appropriate educational services. §1400(b)(3). Indeed, one out of every eight of these children was excluded from the public school system altogether, §1400(b)(4); many others were simply "warehoused" in special classes or were neglectfully shepherded through the system until they were old enough to drop out. Among the most poorly served of disabled students were emotionally disturbed children: Congressional

---

[643]See Sorenson, Gail, "Update on Legal Issues in Special Education Discipline," 81 Ed.Law Rep. [399] (May 20, 1993).

See also Metropolitan School Dist. of Wayne Tp. v. Davila, 969 F.2d 485 (7th Cir. 1992) dismissing a preemptive challenge to The Office of Special Education and Rehabilitative Services of the United States Department of Education (OSERS) rule requiring states to provide educational services to disabled children who are expelled or suspended for an extended period for reasons unrelated to their disability. The rule was announced by Robert Davila, the Assistant Secretary for Special Education and Rehabilitative Services, in a letter responding to an inquiry from Frank E. New, the Director of Special Education for Ohio. Davila stated OSERS interpreted the IDEA to require states to continue services in these circumstances.

[644] Nevada law dealing with the discipline of disabled children was amended during the 1991 legislative session. See Sec 392.466(5) & 392.467(5) NRS (1991). The amendments declare the legislature's intent to follow federal rules regarding discipline of disabled children.

statistics revealed that for the school year immediately preceding passage of the Act, the educational needs of 82 percent of all children with emotional disabilities went unmet.

Although these educational failings resulted in part from funding constraints, Congress recognized that the problem reflected more than a lack of financial resources at the state and local levels. Two federal-court decisions, which the Senate Report characterized as "landmark," see id., at 6, demonstrated that many disabled children were excluded pursuant to state statutes or local rules and policies, typically without any consultation with, or even notice to, their parents. Indeed, by the time of the EHA's enactment, parents had brought legal challenges to similar exclusionary practices in 27 other States.

In responding to these problems, Congress did not content itself with passage of a simple funding statute. Rather, the EHA confers upon disabled students an enforceable substantive right to public education in participating States and conditions federal financial assistance upon a State's compliance with the substantive and procedural goals of the Act. Accordingly, States seeking to qualify for federal funds must develop policies assuring all disabled children the "right to a free appropriate public education," and must file with the Secretary of Education formal plans mapping out in detail the programs, procedures, and timetables under which they will effectuate these policies. 20 U. S. C. §§1412(1), 1413(a). Such plans must assure that, "to the maximum extent appropriate," States will "mainstream" disabled children, i. e., that they will educate them with children who are not disabled, and that they will segregate or otherwise remove such children from the regular classroom setting "only when the nature or severity of the handicap is such that education in regular classes . . . cannot be achieved satisfactorily. " § 1412(5) .

The primary vehicle for implementing these congressional goals is the "individualized educational program" (IEP), which the EHA mandates for each disabled child. Prepared at meetings between a representative of the local school district, the child's teacher, the parents or guardians, and, whenever appropriate, the disabled child, the IEP sets out the child's present educational performance, establishes annual and short-term objectives for improvements in that performance, and describes the specially designed instruction and services that will enable the child to meet those objectives. §1401(19). The IEP must be reviewed and, where necessary, revised at least once a year in order to ensure that local agencies tailor the statutorily required "free appropriate public education" to each child's unique needs. §1414(a)(5).

Envisioning the IEP as the centerpiece of the statute's education delivery system for disabled children, and aware that schools had all too often denied such children appropriate educations without in any way consulting their parents, Congress repeatedly emphasized throughout the Act the importance and, indeed, the necessity of parental participation in both the development of the IEP and any subsequent assessments of its effectiveness. See §§1400(c), 1401(19), 1412(7) 1415(b)(1)(A), (C), (D), (E), and 1415(b)(2). Accordingly the Act establishes various procedural safeguards that guarantee parents both an opportunity for meaningful input into all decisions affecting their child's education and the right to seek review of any decisions they think inappropriate. These safeguards include the right to examine all relevant records pertaining to the identification, evaluation, and educational placement of their child; prior written notice whenever the responsible educational agency proposes (or refuses) to change the child's placement or program; an opportunity to present complaints concerning any aspect of the local agency's provision of a free appropriate public education; and an opportunity for "an impartial due process hearing" with respect to any such complaints. §1415(b)(1), (2).

At the conclusion of any such hearing, both the parents and the local educational agency may seek further administrative review and, where that proves unsatisfactory, may file a civil action in any state or federal court. §1415(c), (e)(2). In addition to reviewing the administrative record, courts are empowered to take additional evidence at the request of either party and to "grant such relief as [they] determine[] is appropriate." §1415(e)(2). **The "stay-put" provision at issue in this case governs the placement of a child while these often lengthy review procedures run their course**. It directs that:

> "During the pendency of any proceedings conducted pursuant to [§ 1415], unless the State or local educational agency and the parents or guardian otherwise agree, the child shall remain in the then current educational placement of such child ...." §1415(e)(3).

The present dispute grows out of the efforts of certain officials of the San Francisco Unified School District (SFUSD) to expel two emotionally disturbed children from school indefinitely for violent and disruptive conduct related to their disabilities. In November 1980, respondent John Doe assaulted another student at the Louise Lombard School, a developmental center for disabled children. Doe's April 1980 IEP identified him as a socially and physically awkward 17-year-old who experienced considerable difficulty controlling his impulses and anger. Among the goals set out in his IEP was "[i]mprovement in [his] ability to relate to [his] peers [and to] cope with frustrating situations without resorting to aggressive acts." App. 17. Frustrating situations, however, were an unfortunately prominent feature of Doe's school career: physical abnormalities, speech difficulties, and poor grooming habits had made him the target of teasing and ridicule as early as the first grade, id., at 23; his 1980 IEP reflected his continuing difficulties with peers, noting that his social skills had deteriorated and that he could tolerate only minor frustration before exploding. Id., at 15-16.

On November 6, 1980, Doe responded to the taunts of a fellow student in precisely the explosive manner anticipated by his IEP: he choked the student with sufficient force to leave abrasions on the child's neck, and kicked out a school window while being escorted to the principal's office afterwards. Id., at 208. Doe admitted his misconduct and the school subsequently suspended him for five days. Thereafter, his principal referred the matter to the SFUSD Student Placement Committee (SPC or Committee) with the recommendation that Doe be expelled. On the day the suspension was to end, the SPC notified Doe's mother that it was proposing to exclude her child permanently from SFUSD and was, therefore, extending his suspension until such time as the expulsion proceedings were completed.[645] The Committee further advised her that she was entitled to attend the November 25 hearing at which it planned to discuss the proposed expulsion.

After unsuccessfully protesting these actions by letter, Doe brought this suit against a host of local school officials and the State Superintendent of Public

---

[645] California law at the time empowered school principals to suspend students for no more than five consecutive schooldays, Cal. Educ. Code Ann. §48903(a) (West 1978), but permitted school districts seeking to expel a suspended student to "extend the suspension until such time as [expulsion proceedings were completed]; provided, that [it] has determined that the presence of the pupil at the school or in an alternative school placement would cause a danger to persons or property or a threat of disrupting the instructional process." § 48903(h). The State subsequently amended the law to permit school districts to impose longer initial periods of suspension. See n. 3, infra.

Instruction. Alleging that the suspension and proposed expulsion violated the EHA, he sought a temporary restraining order canceling the SPC hearing and requiring school officials to convene an IEP meeting. The District Judge granted the requested injunctive relief and further ordered defendants to provide home tutoring for Doe on an interim basis; shortly thereafter, she issued a preliminary injunction directing defendants to return Doe to his then current educational placement at Louise Lombard School pending completion of the IEP review process. Doe reentered school on December 15, 5-1/2 weeks, and 24 schooldays, after his initial suspension.

Respondent Jack Smith was identified as an emotionally disturbed child by the time he entered the second grade in 1976. School records prepared that year indicated that he was unable "to control verbal or physical outburst[s]" and exhibited a "[s]evere disturbance in relationships with peers and adults." Id., at 123. Further evaluations subsequently revealed that he had been physically and emotionally abused as an infant and young child and that, despite above average intelligence, he experienced academic and social difficulties as a result of extreme hyperactivity and low self-esteem. Id., at 136, 139, 155, 176. Of particular concern was Smith's propensity for verbal hostility; one evaluator noted that the child reacted to stress by "attempt[ing] to cover his feelings of low self worth through aggressive behavior[,] . . . primarily verbal provocations."

Based on these evaluations, SFUSD placed Smith in a learning center for emotionally disturbed children. His grandparents, however, believed that his needs would be better served in the public school setting and in September, 1979, the school district acceded to their requests and enrolled him at A. P. Giannini Middle School. His February 1980 IEP recommended placement in a Learning Disability Group, stressing the need for close supervision and a highly structured environment. Like earlier evaluations, the February 1980 IEP noted that Smith was easily distracted, impulsive, and anxious; it, therefore, proposed a half-day schedule and suggested that the placement be undertaken on a trial basis.

At the beginning of the next school year, Smith was assigned to a full-day program; almost immediately thereafter he began misbehaving. School officials met twice with his grandparents in October 1980 to discuss returning him to half-day program; although the grandparents agreed to the reduction, they apparently were never apprised of their right to challenge the decision through EHA procedures. The school officials also warned them that if the child continue his disruptive behavior—which included stealing, extorting money from fellow students, and making sexual comments to female classmates—they would seek to expel him. On November 14, they made good on this threat, suspending Smith for five days after he made further lewd comments. His principal referred the matter to the SPC, which recommended exclusion from SFUSD. As it did in John Doe's case, the Committee scheduled a hearing and extended the suspension indefinitely pending a final disposition in the matter. On November 28, Smith's counsel protested these actions on grounds essentially identical to those raised by Doe, and the SPC agreed to cancel the hearing and to return Smith to a half-day program at A. P. Giannini or to provide home tutoring. Smith's grandparents chose the latter option and the school began home instruction on December 10; on January 6, 1981, an IEP team convened to discuss alternative placements.

After learning of Doe's action, Smith sought and obtained leave to intervene in the suit. The District Court subsequently entered summary judgment in favor of respondents on their EHA claims and issued a permanent injunction. In a series of decisions, the District Judge found that the proposed expulsions and indefinite suspensions of respondents for conduct attributable to their disabilities deprived them of their congressionally mandated right to a free appropriate public education, as well as their right to have that education provided in accordance with the procedures set out in the EHA. The District Judge, therefore, permanently enjoined the school district from taking any disciplinary action other than a 2- or 5-day suspension against any disabled child for disability-related misconduct, or from effecting any other change in the educational placement of any such child without parental consent pending completion of any EHA proceedings. In addition, the judge barred the State from authorizing **unilateral** placement changes and directed it to establish an EHA compliance-monitoring system or, alternatively, to enact guidelines governing local school responses to disability-related misconduct. Finally, the judge ordered the State to provide services directly to disabled children when, in any individual case, the State determined that the local educational agency was unable or unwilling to do so.

On appeal, the Court of Appeals for the Ninth Circuit affirmed the orders with slight modifications. Agreeing with the District Court that an indefinite suspension in aid of expulsion constitutes a prohibited "change in placement" under §1415(e)(3), the Court of Appeals held that the stay-put provision admitted of no "dangerousness" exception and that the statute therefore rendered invalid those provisions of the California Education Code permitting the indefinite suspension or expulsion of disabled children for misconduct arising out of their disabilities. The court concluded, however, that fixed suspensions of up to 30 schooldays did not fall within the reach of §1415(e)(3) and, therefore, upheld recent amendments to the state Education Code authorizing such suspensions.[646] Lastly, the court affirmed that portion of the injunction requiring the State to provide services directly to a disabled child when the local educational agency fails to do so.

Petitioner Bill Honig, California Superintendent of Public Instruction, sought review in this Court, claiming that the Court of Appeals' construction of the stay-put provision conflicted with that of several other Courts of Appeals which had recognized a dangerousness exception and that the direct services ruling placed an intolerable burden on the State. We granted certiorari to resolve these questions, and now affirm.

At the outset, we address the suggestion, raised for the first time during oral argument, that this case is moot. Under Article III of the Constitution this Court may only adjudicate actual, ongoing controversies. That the dispute between the parties was very much alive when suit was filed, or at the time the Court of Appeals rendered its judgment, cannot substitute for the actual case or controversy that an exercise of this Court's jurisdiction requires. In the present case, we have jurisdiction if there is a reasonable likelihood that respondents will again suffer the deprivation of EHA-mandated rights that gave rise to this suit. We believe that, at least with respect to respondent Smith, such a possibility does in fact exist and that the case therefore remains justiciable.

****

---

[646] In 1983, the State amended its Education Code to permit school districts to impose initial suspensions of 20, and in certain circumstances, 30 schooldays. Cal. Educ. Code Ann. § 48912(a), 48903 (West Supp. 1988). The legislature did not alter the indefinite suspension authority which the SPC exercised in this case, but simply incorporated the.earlier provision into a new section. See § 48911(g).

We have previously noted that administrative and judicial review under the EHA is often "ponderous," Burlington School Committee v. Massachusetts Dept. of Education, 471 U. S. 359, 370 (1985), and this case, which has taken seven years to reach us, amply confirms that observation. For obvious reasons, the misconduct of an emotionally disturbed or otherwise disabled child who has not yet reached adolescence typically will not pose such a serious threat to the well-being of other students that school officials can only ensure classroom safety by excluding the child. Yet, the adolescent student improperly disciplined for misconduct that does pose such a threat will often be finished with school or otherwise ineligible for EHA protections by the time review can be had in this Court. Because we believe that respondent Smith has demonstrated both "a sufficient likelihood that he will again be wronged in a similar way," Los Angeles v. Lyons, 461 U. S., at 111, and that any resulting claim he may have for relief will surely evade our review, we turn to the merits of his case.

III

The language of §1415(e)(3) is unequivocal. It states plainly that during the pendency of any proceedings initiated under the Act, unless the state or local educational agency and the parents or guardian of a disabled child otherwise agree, "the child shall remain in the then current educational placement." §1415(e)(3) (emphasis added). Faced with this clear directive, petitioner asks us to read a "dangerousness" exception into the stay-put provision on the basis of either of two essentially inconsistent assumptions: first, that Congress thought the residual authority of school officials to exclude dangerous students from the classroom too obvious for comment; or second, that Congress inadvertently failed to provide such authority and this Court must therefore remedy the oversight. Because we cannot accept either premise, we decline petitioner's invitation to rewrite the statute.

Petitioner's arguments proceed, he suggests, from a simple, common-sense proposition: Congress could not have intended the stay-put provision to be read literally, for such a construction leads to the clearly unintended, and untenable, result that school districts must return violent or dangerous students to school while the often lengthy EHA proceedings run their course. We think it clear, however, that Congress very much meant to strip schools of the **unilateral** authority they had traditionally employed to exclude disabled students, particularly emotionally disturbed students, from school. In so doing, Congress did not leave school administrators powerless to deal with dangerous students; it did, however, deny school officials their former right to "self-help," and directed that in the future the removal of disabled students could be accomplished only with the permission of the parents or, as a last resort, the courts.

As noted above, Congress passed the EHA after finding that school systems across the country had excluded one out of every eight disabled children from classes. In drafting the law, Congress was largely guided by the recent decisions in Mills v. Board of Education of District of Columbia, 348 F. Supp. 866 (1972), and PARC, 343 F. Supp. 279 (1972), both of which involved the exclusion of hard-to-handle disabled students. Mills in particular demonstrated the extent to which schools used disciplinary measures to bar children from the classroom. There, school officials had labeled four of the seven minor plaintiffs "behavioral problems," and had excluded them from classes without providing any alternative education to them or any notice to their parents. 348 F. Supp., at 869-870. After finding that this practice was not limited to the named plaintiffs but affected in one way or another an estimated class of 12,000 to 18,000 disabled students, id., at 868-869, 875, the District Court enjoined future exclusions, suspensions, or expulsions "on grounds of discipline." Id., at 880.

Congress attacked such exclusionary practices in a variety of ways. It required participating States to educate all disabled children, regardless of the severity of their disabilities, 20 U. S. C. §1412(2)(C), and included within the definition of "handicapped" those children with serious emotional disturbances. §1401(1). It further provided for meaningful parental participation in all aspects of a child's educational placement, and barred schools, through the stay-put provision, from changing that placement over the parent's objection until all review proceedings were completed. Recognizing that those proceedings might prove long and tedious, the Act's drafters did not intend §1415(e)(3) to operate inflexibly, see 121 Cong. Rec. 37412 (1975) (remarks of Sen. Stafford); and they, therefore, allowed for interim placements where parents and school officials are able to agree on one. Conspicuously absent from §1415(e)(3), however, is any emergency exception for dangerous students. This absence is all the more telling in light of the injunctive decree issued in PARC, which permitted school officials unilaterally to remove students in "'extraordinary circumstances.'" 343 F. Supp., at 301. Given the lack of any similar exception in Mills, and the close attention Congress devoted to these "landmark" decisions, see S. Rep., at 6, we can only conclude that the omission was intentional; we are therefore not at liberty to engraft onto the statute an exception Congress chose not to create.

Our conclusion that §1415(e)(3) means what it says does not leave educators hamstrung. The Department of Education has observed that, "[w]hile the [child's] placement may not be changed [during any complaint proceeding], this does not preclude the agency from using its normal procedures for dealing with children who are endangering themselves or others." Comment following 34 CFR §300.513 (1987). Such procedures may include the use of study carrels, time-outs, detention, or the restriction of privileges. More drastically, where a student poses an immediate threat to the safety of others, officials may temporarily suspend him or her for up to 10 schooldays.[647] This authority, which respondent in no way disputes, not only ensures that school administrators can protect the safety of others by promptly removing the most dangerous of students, it also provides a "cooling down" period during which officials can initiate IEP review and seek to persuade the child's parents to agree to an interim placement. And in those cases in which the parents of a truly dangerous child adamantly refuse to permit any change in placement, the 10-day respite gives school officials an opportunity to invoke the aid of the courts under §1415(e)(2), which empowers courts to grant any appropriate relief.

---

[647] The Department of Education has adopted the position first espoused in 1980 by its Office of Civil Rights that a suspension of up to 10 schooldays does not amount to a "change in placement" prohibited by §1415(e)(3). U. S. Dept. of Education, Office of Special Education Programs, Policy Letter (Feb. 26, 1987), Ed. for Handicapped L. Rep. 211:437 (1987). The EHA nowhere defines the phrase "change in placement," nor does the statute's structure or legislative history provide any guidance as to how the term applies to fixed suspensions. Given this ambiguity, we defer to the construction adopted by the agency charged with monitoring and enforcing the statute. See INS v. Cardoza-Forseca, 480 U. S. 421, 448 (1987). Moreover, the agency's position comports fully with the purposes of the statute: Congress sought to prevent schools from permanently and unilaterally excluding disabled children by means of indefinite suspensions and expulsions; the power to impose fixed suspensions of short duration does not carry the potential for total exclusion that Congress found so objectionable. Indeed, despite its broad injunction, the District Court in Mills v. Board of Education of District of Columbia, 348 F. Supp. 866 (DC 1972), recognized that school officials could suspend disabled children on a short- term, temporary basis. See id, at 880. Cf. Goss v. Lopez, 419 U. S. 565, 574-576 (1975) (suspension of 10 schooldays or more works a sufficient deprivation of property and liberty interests to trigger the protections of the Due Process Clause). Because we believe the agency correctly determined that a suspension in excess of 10 days does constitute a prohibited "change in placement," we conclude that the Court of Appeals erred to the extent it approved suspensions of 20 and 30 days' duration.

Petitioner contends, however, that the availability of judicial relief is more illusory than real, because a party seeking review under §1415(e)(2) must exhaust time-consuming administrative remedies, and because under the Court of Appeals' construction of §1415(e)(3), courts are as bound by the stay-put provision's "automatic injunction," 793 F. 2d, at 1486, as are schools.[648] It is true that judicial review is normally not available under §1415(e)(2) until all administrative proceedings are completed, but as we have previously noted, parents may bypass the administrative process where exhaustion would be futile or inadequate. See Smith v. Robinson, 468 U. S. 992, 1014, n. 17 (1984) (citing cases); see also 121 Cong. Rec. 37416 (1975) (remarks of Sen. Williams) ("[E]xhaustion . . . should not be required . . . in cases where such exhaustion would be futile either as a legal or practical matter"). While many of the EHA's procedural safeguards protect the rights of parents and children, schools can and do seek redress through the administrative review process, and we have no reason to believe that Congress meant to require schools alone to exhaust in all cases, no matter how exigent the circumstances. The burden in such cases, of course, rests with the school to demonstrate the futility or inadequacy of administrative review, but nothing in §1415(e)(2) suggests that schools are completely barred from attempting to make such a showing. Nor do we think that §1415(e)(3) operates to limit the equitable powers of district courts such that they cannot, in appropriate cases, temporarily enjoin a dangerous disabled child from attending school. As the EHA's legislative history makes clear, one of the evils Congress sought to remedy was the unilateral exclusion of disabled children by schools, not courts, and one of the purposes of §1415(e)(3), therefore, was "to prevent school officials from removing a child from the regular public school classroom over the parents' objection pending completion of the review proceedings." Burlington School Committee v. Massachusetts Dept. of Education, 471 U. S., at 373 (emphasis added). The stay-put provision in no way purports to limit or pre-empt the authority conferred on courts by §1415(e)(2), see Doe v. Brookline School Committee, 722 F. 2d 910, 917 (CA1 1983); indeed, it says nothing whatever about judicial power.

In short, then, we believe that school officials are entitled to seek injunctive relief under §1415(e)(2) in appropriate cases. In any such action, §1415(e)(3) effectively creates a presumption in favor of the child's current educational placement which school officials can overcome only by showing that maintaining the child in his or her current placement is substantially likely to result in injury either to himself or herself, or to others. In the present case, we are satisfied that the District Court, in enjoining the state and local defendants from indefinitely suspending respondent or otherwise unilaterally altering his then current placement, properly balanced respondent's interest in receiving a free appropriate public education in accordance with the procedures and requirements of the EHA against the interests of the state and local school officials in maintaining a safe learning environment for all their students.[649]

---

[648] Petitioner also notes that in California, schools may not suspend any given student for more than a total of 20, and in certain special circumstances 30, schooldays in a single year, see Cal. Educ. Code Ann. § 48903 (West Supp. 1988); he argues, therefore, that a school district may not have the option of imposing a 10-day suspension when dealing with an obstreperous child whose previous suspensions for the year total 18 or 19 days. The fact remains, however, that state law does not define the scope of §1415(e)(3). There may be cases in which a suspension that is otherwise valid under the stay-put provision would violate local law. The effect of such a violation, however, is a question of state law upon which we express no view.

[649] We, therefore, reject the United States' contention that the District Judge abused her discretion in enjoining the local school officials from indefinitely suspending respondent pending completion of the expulsion proceedings. Contrary to the Government's suggestion, the District Judge did not view herself bound to enjoin any and all violations of the stay-put provision, but rather, consistent with the analysis we set out above, weighed the relative harms to the parties and found that the balance tipped decidedly in favor of respondent. App. 222-223. We of course

IV

We believe the courts below properly construed and applied §1415(e)(3), except insofar as the Court of Appeals held that a suspension in excess of 10 schooldays does not constitute a "change in placement." We, therefore, affirm the Court of Appeals' judgment on this issue as modified herein. Because we are equally divided on the question whether a court may order a State to provide services directly to a disabled child where the local agency has failed to do so, we affirm the Court of Appeals' judgment on this issue as well.

Affirmed.[650]

****

STUDY QUESTIONS

    1. Does the Courts holding mean that schools must keep dangerous students in the school setting?

    2. Why was the Court worried about the school officials unilateral decisions to exclude disabled students from their educational placements?

    3. Is the remedy outlined by the Court fair to teachers and students ineligible for coverage under IDEA?

    4. How do the discipline procedures differ between regular education and special education students?

    5. What practical problems are posed by implementation of special education laws in the school setting?

****

D
DISCRIMINATION

TITLE VI FORBIDS RACE DISCRIMINATION IN EDUCATION PROGRAMS

The Supreme Court rendered its landmark decision interpreting Title VI in a case dealing with a school districts bilingual education efforts.

LAU
v.
NICHOLS
414 U.S. 563, 94 S.Ct. 786 (1974)

MR. JUSTICE DOUGLAS delivered the opinion of the Court.

    The San Francisco, California, school system was integrated in 1971 as a result of a federal court decree. The District Court found that there are 2,856 students of Chinese ancestry in the school system who do not speak English. Of those who have that language deficiency, about 1,000 are given supplemental

---

do not sit to review the factual determinations underlying that conclusion. We do note, however, that in balancing the parties' respective interests, the District Judge gave proper consideration to respondent's rights under the EHA. While the Government complains that the District Court indulged an improper presumption of irreparable harm to respondent, we do not believe that school officials can escape the presumptive effect of the stay-put provision simply by violating it and forcing parents to petition for relief. In any suit brought by parents seeking injunctive relief for a violation of §1415(e)(3), the burden rests with the school district to demonstrate that the educational status quo must be altered.

[650] Courts have issued injunctions excluding disabled children from school pending the outcome of a placement reconsideration. See <u>Barlow-Gresham Union High School Dist. 2 v. Mitchell</u>, 940 F.2d 1280 (9th Cir. 1991).

336

courses in the English language. About 1,800, however, do not receive that instruction.

This class suit brought by non-English-speaking Chinese students against officials responsible for the operation of the San Francisco Unified School District seeks relief against the unequal educational opportunities, which are alleged to violate, inter alia, the Fourteenth Amendment. No specific remedy is urged upon us. Teaching English to the students of Chinese ancestry who do not speak the language is one choice. Giving instructions to this group in Chinese is another. There may be others. Petitioners ask only that the Board of Education be directed to apply its expertise to the problem and rectify the situation.

The District Court denied relief. The Court of Appeals affirmed, holding that there was no violation of the Equal Protection Clause of the Fourteenth Amendment or of § 601 of the Civil Rights Act of 1964, 42 U. S. C. § 2000d, which excludes from participation in federal financial assistance, recipients of aid which discriminate against racial groups, 483 F. 2d 791. One judge dissented. A hearing en banc was denied, two judges dissenting. Id., at 805.

We granted the petition for certiorari because of the public importance of the question presented.

The Court of Appeals reasoned that "[e]very student brings to the starting line of his educational career different advantages and disadvantages caused in part by social, economic and cultural background, created and continued completely apart from any contribution by the school system,". Yet in our view the case may not be so easily decided. This is a public school system of California and § 71 of the California Education Code states that "English shall be the basic language of instruction in all schools." That section permits a school district to determine "when and under what circumstances instruction may be given bilingually." That section also states as "the policy of the state" to insure "the mastery of English by all pupils in the schools." And bilingual instruction is authorized "to the extent that it does not interfere with the systematic, sequential, and regular instruction of all pupils in the English language." Moreover, §8573 of the Education Code provides that no pupil shall receive a diploma of graduation from grade 12 who has not met the standards of proficiency in "English," as well as other prescribed subjects. Moreover, by §12101 of the Education Code (Supp. 1973) children between the ages of six and 16 years are (with exceptions not material here) "subject to compulsory full-time education ."

Under these state-imposed standards there is no equality of treatment merely by providing students with the same facilities, textbooks, teachers, and curriculum; for students who do not understand English are effectively foreclosed from any meaningful education.

Basic English skills are at the very core of what these public schools teach. Imposition of a requirement that, before a child can effectively participate in the educational program, he must already have acquired those basic skills is to make a mockery of public education. We know that those who do not understand English are certain to find their classroom experiences wholly incomprehensible and in no way meaningful.

We do not reach the Equal Protection Clause argument which has been advanced but rely solely on § 601 of the Civil Rights Act of 1964, 42 U. S. C. § 2000d, to reverse the Court of Appeals.

That section bans discrimination based "on the ground of Race Color, or national origin," in "any program or activity receiving Federal financial assistance." The school district involved in this litigation receives large amounts of federal financial assistance. The Department of Health, Education, and Welfare (HEW), which has authority to promulgate regulations prohibiting discrimination in federally assisted school systems, 42 U. S. C. § 2000d-1, in 1968 issued one guideline that "[s]chool systems are responsible for assuring that students of a particular race, color, or national origin are not denied the opportunity to obtain the education generally obtained by other students in the system." 33 Fed. Reg. 4956. In 1970 HEW made the guidelines more specific, requiring school districts that were federally funded "to rectify the language deficiency in order to open" the instruction to students who had "linguistic deficiencies," 35 Fed. Reg. 11595.

By § 602 of the Act HEW is authorized to issue rules, regulations, and orders [651] to make sure that recipients of federal aid under its jurisdiction conduct any federally financed projects consistently with § 601. HEW's regulations, 45 CFR § 80.3 (b) (1), specify that the recipients may not

> "(ii) Provide any service, financial aid, or other benefit to an individual which is different, or is provided in a different manner, from that provided to others under the program;

****

> "   (iv) Restrict an individual in any way in the enjoyment of any advantage or privilege enjoyed by others receiving any service, financial aid, or other benefit under the program."

Discrimination among students on account of race or national origin that is prohibited includes "discrimination . . . in the availability or use of any academic . . . or other facilities of the grantee or other recipient." Id., § 80.5 (b).

Discrimination is barred which has that effect even though no purposeful design is present: a recipient "may not . . . utilize criteria or methods of administration which have the effect of subjecting individuals to discrimination" or have "the effect of defeating or substantially impairing accomplishment of the objectives of the program as respect individuals of a particular race, color, or national origin." Id., § 80.3 (b) (2) .

It seems obvious that the Chinese-speaking minority receive fewer benefits than the English-speaking majority from respondents' school system which denies them a meaningful opportunity to participate in the educational program—all earmarks of the discrimination banned by the regulations.[652] In 1970 HEW issued clarifying guidelines, 35 Fed. Reg. 11595, which include the following:

> "Where inability to speak and understand the English language excludes national origin-minority group children from effective participation in the educational program offered by a school district, the district must take affirmative steps to rectify the language deficiency in order to open its instructional program to these students."

> "Any ability grouping or tracking system employed by the school system to deal with the special language skill needs of national origin-

---

[651] Section 602 provides:

"Each Federal department and agency which is empowered to extend Federal financial assistance to any program or activity, by way of grant, loan, or contract other than a contract of insurance or guaranty, is authorized and directed to effectuate the provision of section 2000d of this title with respect to such program or activity by issuing rules, regulations, or orders of general applicability which shall be consistent with achievement of the objectives of the statute authorizing the financial assistance in connection with which the action is taken...." 42 U. S. C. §2000d-1.

[652] And see Report of the Human Rights Commission of San Francisco, Bilingual Education in the San Francisco Public Schools, Aug. 9, 1973.

minority group children must be designed to meet such language skill needs as soon as possible and must not operate as an educational deadend or permanent track."

Respondent school district contractually agreed to "comply with title VI of the Civil Rights Act of 1964 . . . and all requirements imposed by or pursuant to the Regulation" of HEW (45 CFR pt. 80) which are "issued pursuant to that title . . ." and also immediately to "take any measures necessary to effectuate this agreement." The Federal Government has power to fix the terms on which its money allotments to the States shall be disbursed. Oklahoma v. CSC, 330 U. S. 127,142-143. Whatever may be the limits of that power, Steward Machine Co. v. Davis, 301 U. S. 548, 590 et seq., they have not been reached here. Senator Humphrey, during the floor debates on the Civil Rights Act of 1964, said:[653]

" Simple justice requires that public funds, to which all taxpayers of all races contribute, not be spent in any fashion which encourages, entrenches, subsidizes, or results in racial discrimination."

We accordingly reverse the judgment of the Court of Appeals and remand the case for the fashioning of appropriate relief.

Reversed and remanded.

JUSTICE BLACKMUN join, concurring in the result

It is uncontested that more than 2,800 schoolchildren of Chinese ancestry attend school in the San Francisco Unified School District system even though they do not speak, understand, read, or write the English language, and that as to some 1,800 of these pupils the respondent school authorities have taken no significant steps to deal with this language' deficiency. The petitioners do not contend, however, that the respondents have affirmatively or intentionally contributed to this inadequacy, but only that they have failed to act in the face of changing social and linguistic patterns. Because of this laissez-faire attitude on the part of the school administrators, it is not entirely clear that § 601 of the Civil Rights Act of 1964, 42 U. S. C. § 2000d, standing alone, would render illegal the expenditure of federal funds on these schools. For that section provides that "[n]o person in the United States shall, on the ground of race, color, or national origin, be excluded from participation in, be denied the benefits of, or be subjected to discrimination under any program or activity receiving Federal financial assistance."

On the other hand, the interpretive guidelines published by the Office for Civil Rights of the Department of Health, Education, and Welfare in 1970, 35 Fed. Reg. 11595, clearly indicate that affirmative efforts to give special training for non-English-speaking pupils are required by Tit. VI ,as a condition to receipt of federal aid to public schools:

"Where inability to speak and understand the English language excludes national origin-minority group children from effective participation in the educational program offered by a school district, the district must take affirmative steps to rectify the language deficiency in order to open its instructional program to these students.[654]

---

[653] 110 Cong. Rec. 6543 (Sen. Humphrey, quoting from President Kennedy's message to Congress, June 19, 1963).

[654] These guidelines were issued in further clarification of the Department's position as stated in its regulations issued to implement Tit. VI, 45 CFR pt. 80. The regulations provide in part that no recipient of federal financial assistance administered by HEW may

"Provide any service, financial aid, or other benefit to an individual which is different, or is provided in a different manner, from that provided to others under the program; [or]

339

The critical question is, therefore, whether the regulations and guidelines promulgated by HEW go beyond the authority of § 601.[655] Last Term, in Mourning v. Family Publications Service, Inc., 411 U. S. 356, 369, we held that the validity of a regulation promulgated under a general authorization provision such as § 602 of Tit. VI [656] "will be sustained so long as it is 'reasonably related to the purposes of the enabling legislation.'." I think the guidelines here fairly meet that test. Moreover, in assessing the purposes of remedial legislation we have found that departmental regulations and "consistent administrative construction" are "entitled to great weight.". The Department has reasonably and consistently interpreted § 601 to require affirmative remedial efforts to give special attention to linguistically deprived children.

For these reasons I concur in the result reached by the Court.

MR. JUSTICE BLACKMUN, with whom THE CHIEF JUSTICE joins, concurring in the result.

I join MR. JUSTICE STEWART's opinion and thus I, too, concur in the result. Against the possibility that the Court's judgment may be interpreted too broadly, I stress the fact that the children with whom we are concerned here number about 1,800. This is a very substantial group that is being deprived of any meaningful schooling because the children cannot understand the language of the classroom. We may only guess as to why they have had no exposure to English in their preschool years. earlier generations of American ethnic groups have overcome the language barrier by earnest parental endeavor or by the hard fact of being pushed out of the family or community nest and into the realities of broader experience.

I merely wish to make plain that when, in another case, we are concerned with a very few youngsters, or with just a single child who speaks only German or Polish or Spanish or any language other than English, I would not regard today's decision, or the separate concurrence, as conclusive upon the issue whether the statute and the guidelines require the funded school district to provide special instruction. For me, numbers are at the heart of this case and my concurrence is to be understood accordingly.

****

STUDY QUESTIONS

1. Has the Court given specific enough guidance to school districts faced with serving pupil populations from diverse language backgrounds?
2. Does the Court address the professional questions of methods to be employed to deal with pupil population with diverse language skills?
3. Why did the Court dodge the constitutional question in favor of statutory interpretation?

****

Restrict an individual in any way in the enjoyment of any advantage or privilege enjoyed by others receiving any service, financial aid, or other benefit under the program." 45 CFR § 80.3 (b) (1) (ii), (iv).

[655] The respondents do not contest the standing of the petitioners to sue as beneficiaries of the federal funding contract between the Department of Health, Education, and Welfare and the San Francisco Unified School District.

[656] Section 602, 42 U. S. C. §2000d-1, provides in pertinent part:

"Each Federal department and agency which is empowered to extend Federal financial assistance to any program or activity, by way of grant, loan, or contract other than a contract of insurance or guaranty, is authorized and directed to effectuate the provisions of section 2000d of this title with respect to such program or activity by issuing rules, regulations, or orders of general applicability which shall be consistent with achievement of the objectives of the statute authorizing the financial assistance in connection with which the action is taken...."
The United States as amicus curiae asserts in its brief, and the respondents appear to concede, that the guidelines were issued pursuant to § 602.

TITLE IX (20 U.S.C.A. §1681) FORBIDS DISCRIMINATION ON THE BASIS OF SEX IN EDUCATION PROGRAMS.[657]

Recently, the Court issued a unanimous concluding that victims of sex discrimination may recover damages from school districts. The urgency of dealing with gender differences in the school setting has been heightened by this holding because legal counsel for students may be more willing to take such cases and because the disputes may now be presented to a jury instead of a judge for resolution.

FRANKLIN
v.
GWINNETT COUNTY PUBLIC SCHOOLS[658]
____U.S.___, 112 S.Ct. (1992)

JUSTICE WHITE delivered the opinion of the Court.

This case presents the question whether the implied right of action under Title IX of the Education Amendments of 1972, 20 U.S.C. §1681-1688 (Title IX),[659] which this Court recognized in <u>Cannon</u> v. <u>University of Chicago</u>, 441 U.S. 677 (1979), supports a claim for monetary damages.

I

Petitioner Christine Franklin was a student at North Gwinnett High School in Gwinnett County Georgia between September 1985 and August 1989. Respondent Gwinnett County School District operates the high school and receives federal funds. According to the complaint filed on December 29, 1988 in the United States District Court for the Northern District of Georgia, Franklin was subjected to continual sexual harassment beginning in the autumn of her tenth grade year (1986) from Andrew Hill, a sports coach and teacher employed by the district. Among other allegations, Franklin avers that Hill engaged her in sexually-oriented conversations in which he asked about her sexual experiences with her boyfriend and whether she would consider having sexual intercourse with an older man,[660] that Hill forcibly kissed her on the mouth in the school parking lot, that he telephoned her at her home and asked if she would meet him socially, and that, on three occasions in her junior year, Hill interrupted a class, requested that the teacher excuse Franklin, and took her to a private office where he subjected her to coercive intercourse. The complaint further alleges that though they became aware of and investigated Hill's sexual harassment of Franklin and other female students, teachers and administrators took no action to halt it and discouraged Franklin from

---

[657]Assembly Concurrent Resolution (ACR) No. 23 File No. 151 (1993) urges the state board of education, the board of regents and the board of trustees of each school district in Nevada to take actions to end gender bias in the educational system, foster the equitable treatment of girls and boys, including the manner in which they are disciplined and create an educational environment which is gender equitable. The Resolution also suggests that the recommendations of the American Association of University Women Educational Foundation be considered when taking action and developing regulations.

[658]See Mawdsley, Ralph D., "Compensation for the Sexually Abused Student," 84 Ed.Law Rep. [13] (Sept. 23, 1993), Russo, Charles J., Nordin, Virginia D. & Leas, Terrence, "Sexual Harrassment and Student Rights: The Supreme Court Expands Title IX Remedies, 75 Ed.Law Rep. [733] (August 27, 1992), Valente, William D., "Liability for Teacher's Sexual Misconduct with Students-Closing and Opening New Vistas," 74 Ed.Law Rep. [1021] (July 30, 1992).

[659] This statute provides in pertinent part that "No person in the United States shall, on the basis of sex, be excluded from participation in, be denied the benefit, of, or be subjected to discrimination under any education program or activity receiving Federal financial assistance." 20 U.S.C. §1681(a).

[660] This exhibit is the report of the United States Department of Education's Office of Civil Rights based on that office's investigation of this case. Franklin incorporated this exhibit into her amended complaint,

pressing charges against Hill. Hill resigned on the condition that all matters pending against him be dropped. The school thereupon closed its investigation.

In this action,[661] the District Court dismissed the complaint on the ground that Title IX does not authorize an award of damages. The Court of Appeals affirmed. Franklin v. Gwinnett Cty. Public Schools, 911 F. 2d 617 (CA11 1990). The court noted that analysis of Title IX and Title VI of the Civil Rights Act of 1964, 42 U.S.C. §2000d et .seq. (Title VI), has developed along similar lines. Citing as binding precedent Drayden v. Needville Independent School Dist., 642 F. 2d 129 (CA5 1981), a decision rendered prior to the division of the Fifth Circuit, the court concluded that Title VI did not support a claim for monetary damages. The court then analyzed this Court's decision in Guardians.Assn. v. Civil Service Comm'n of New York City, 463 U.S. 582 (1983), to determine whether it implicitly overruled Drayden. The court stated that the absence of a majority opinion left unresolved the question whether a court could award such relief upon a showing of intentional discrimination. As a second basis for its holding that monetary damages were unavailable, the court reasoned that Title IX was enacted under Congress' Spending Clause powers and that "[u]nder such statutes, relief may frequently be limited to that which is equitable in nature, with the recipient of federal funds thus retaining the option of terminating such receipt in order to rid itself of an injunction." Franklin, 911 F. 2d, at 621. The court closed by observing it would "proceed with extreme care" to afford compensatory relief absent express provision by Congress or clear direction from this Court. Id., at 622. Accordingly, it held that an action for monetary damages could not be sustained for an alleged intentional violation of Title IX and affirmed the District Court's ruling to that effect; Ibid.   Because this opinion conflicts with a decision of the Court of Appeals for the Third Circuit, see Pfeiffer v. Marion Center Area School Dist.,917 F. 2d 779, 787-789 (1990), we granted certiorari. 501 U.S.._ (1991). We reverse.

II

In Cannon v. University of Chicago, 441 U.S. 677 (1979), the Court held that Title.IX is enforceable through an implied right of action. We have no occasion here to reconsider that decision. Rather, in this case we must decide what remedies are.available in a suit brought pursuant to this implied right. As we have often stated, the question of what remedies are available under a statute that provides a private right of action is "analytically distinct" from the issue of whether such a right exists in the first place. Davis v. Passman, 442 U.S. 228, 239 (1979). Thus, although we examine the text and history of a statute to determine whether Congress intended to create a right of action, Touche Ross & Co. v. Redington, 442 U.S. 560, 575-576 (1979), we presume the availability of all appropriate remedies unless Congress has expressly indicated otherwise. Davis, supra, at 246-247. This principle has deep roots in our jurisprudence.

---

[661] Prior to bringing this lawsuit, Franklin filed a complaint with the Office of Civil Rights of the United States Department of Education (OCR) in August 1988. After investigating these charges for several months, OCR concluded that the school district had violated Franklin's rights by subjecting her to physical and verbal sexual harassment and by interfering with her right to complain about conduct proscribed by Title IX. OCR determined, however, that because of the resignations of Hill and respondent William Prescott and the implementation of a school grievance procedure, the district had come into compliance with Title IX. It then terminated its investigation. First Amended Complaint, Exh. A.,. pp. 7-9.

A

"[W]here legal rights have been invaded, and a federal statute provides for a general right to sue for such invasion, federal courts may use any available remedy to make good the wrong done."

****

III

We now address whether Congress intended to limit application of this general principle in the enforcement of Title IX.

****

In the years after the announcement of <u>Cannon</u>, on the other hand, a more traditional method of statutory analysis is possible, because Congress was legislating with full cognizance of that decision. Our reading of the two amendments to Title IX enacted after <u>Cannon</u> leads us to conclude that Congress did not intend to limit the remedies available in a suit brought under Title IX

IV

In sum, we conclude that a damages remedy is available for an action brought to enforce Title IX. The judgment of the court of appeals, therefore, is reversed and the case is remanded for further proceedings consistent with this opinion.

JUSTICE SCALIA, with whom the CHIEF JUSTICE and JUSTICE THOMAS join, concurring in the judgment.

****

E
STUDENT RECORDS

Federal law also addresses the manner in which school districts maintain student records.[662] The law came about because various groups including the Sage Foundation discovered abuses in school record keeping. Concern centered on issues of record content, accuracy, and access. The pressures led to the enactment of the Family Educational Rights and Privacy Act.[663] Nevada schools are obligated to comply with its provisions.

Relevant portions of the statute are printed below:

---

[662]Johnson, T. Page, "Managing Student Records: The Courts and the Family Educational Rights and Privacy Act of 1974," 79 Ed.Law Rep. [1] (February 11, 1993)

[663] 20 U.S.C.A. § 1232g-i. Regulations of the Family Educational Rights and Privacy Act of 1974, 45 C.F.R. § 99.1-99.67 (1979) Note "The Buckley Amendment: Opening School Files for Student and Parental Review," 24 Cath. U.L.Rev. 588 (1975) The Hatch amendment adopted in 1978 gives parents the right to inspect instructional material.
"Inspection by parents or guardians of instructional material
(a) All instructional material, including teacher's manuals, films, tapes, or other supplementary instructional material which will be used in connection with any research or experimentation program or project shall be available for inspection by the parents or guardians of the children engaged in such program or project. For the purpose of this section "research or experimentation program or project" means any program or project in any applicable program designed to explore or develop new or unproven teaching methods or techniques.
Psychiatric or psychological examinations, testing, or treatment
(b) No student shall be required, as part of any applicable program, to submit to psychiatric examination, testing, or treatment, or psychological examination, testing, or treatment, in which the primary purpose is to reveal information concerning:
(1) political affiliations;
(2) mental and psychological problems potentially embarrassing to the student or his family;
(3) sex behavior and attitudes;
(4) illegal, anti-social, self-incriminating, and demeaning behavior;
(5) critical appraisals of other individuals with whom respondents have close family relationships;
(6) legally recognized privileged and analogous relationships, such as those of lawyers, physicians, and ministers; or
(7) income (other than that required by law to determine eligibility for participation in a program or for receiving financial assistance under such program), without the prior consent of the student (if the student is an adult or emancipated minor), or in the case of unemancipated minor, without the prior written consent of the parent. "

20 U.S.C.A. §1232G

§1232G Family Educational and Privacy Rights
Conditions for availability of funds to educational agencies or institutions; inspection and review of education records; specific information to be made available procedure for access to education records; reasonableness of time for such access; hearings; written explanations by parents; definitions

(a)(1)(A) No funds shall be made available under any applicable program to any educational agency or institution which has a policy of denying, or which effectively prevents, the parents of students who are or have been in attendance at a school of such agency or at such institution, as the case may be, the right to inspect and review the education records of their children. If any material or document in the education record of a student includes information on more than one student, the parents of one of such students shall have the right to inspect and review only such part of such material or document as relates to such student or to be informed of the specific information contained in such part of such material. Each educational agency or institution shall establish appropriate procedures for the granting of a request by parents for access to the education records of their children within a reasonable period of time, but in no case more than forty-five days after the request has been made.

(2) No funds shall be made available under any applicable program to any educational agency or institution unless the parents of students who are or have been in attendance at a school of such agency or at such institution are provided an opportunity for a hearing by such agency or institution, in accordance with regulations of the Secretary, to challenge the content of such student's education records, in order to insure that the records are not inaccurate, misleading, or otherwise in violation of the privacy or other rights of students, and to provide an opportunity for the correction or deletion of any such inaccurate, misleading, or otherwise inappropriate data contained therein and to insert into such records a written explanation of the parents respecting the content of such records.

Release of education records; parental consent requirement; exceptions; compliance with judicial orders and subpoenas; audit and evaluation of Federally-supported education programs; record-keeping

(b)(1) No funds shall be made available under any applicable program to any educational agency or institution which has a policy or practice of permitting the release of education records (or personally identifiable information contained therein other than directory information[664], as defined in paragraph (5) of subsection (a) of this section) of students without the written consent of their parents to any individual, agency, or organization, other than to the following—
(A) other school officials, including teachers within the educational institution determined by such agency or institution to have legitimate educational interests;

---

[664] (P.L. 93-568) amending the act defines "directory information" to include the following: students name, address, telephone listing, date and place of birth, major field of study, participation in officially recognized activities and sports, weight and height of members of athletic teams, dates of attendance, degrees and awards of attendance, degrees and awards, dates of attendance, degrees and awards of attendance, degrees and awards received, and the most recent previous educational agency or institution attended by the student.

(B) officials of other schools or school systems in which the student seeks or intends to enroll, upon condition that the student's parents be notified of the transfer, receive a copy of the record if desired, and have an opportunity for a hearing to challenge the content of the record;

(C) authorized representatives of (i) the Comptroller General of the United States, (ii) the Secretary, (iii) an administrative head of an education agency (as defined in section 1221e-3(c) of this title), or (iv) State educational authorities, under the conditions set forth in paragraph (3) of this subsection;

(D) in connection with a student's application for, or receipt of, financial aid;

(E) State and local officials or authorities to whom such information is specifically required to be reported or disclosed pursuant to State statute adopted prior to November 19, 1974;

(F) organizations conducting studies for, or on behalf of, educational agencies or institutions for the purpose of developing, validating, or administering predictive tests, administering student aid programs, and improving instruction, if such studies are conducted in such a manner as will not permit the personal identification of students and their parents by persons other than representatives of such organizations and such information will be destroyed when no longer needed for the purpose for which it is conducted;

(G) accrediting organizations in order to carry out their accrediting functions;

(H) parents of a dependent student of such parents, as defined in section 152 of Title 26; and

(I) subject to regulations of the Secretary, in connection with an emergency, appropriate persons if the knowledge of such information is necessary to protect the health or safety of the student or other persons. Nothing in clause (E) of this paragraph shall prevent a State from further limiting the number or type of State or local officials who will continue to have access thereunder

(2) No funds shall be made available under any applicable program to any educational agency or institution which has a policy or practice of releasing, or providing access to, any personally identifiable information in education records other than directory information, or as is permitted under paragraph (1) of this subsection unless—

(A) there is written consent from the student's parents specifying records to be released, the reasons for such release, and to whom, and with a copy of the records to be released to the student's parents and the student if desired by the parents, or

(B) such information is furnished in compliance with judicial order, or pursuant to any lawfully issued subpoena, upon condition that parents and the students are notified of all such orders or subpoenas in advance of the compliance therewith by the educational institution or agency

(C) With respect to this subsection, personal information shall only be transferred to a third party on the condition that such party will not permit any other party to have access to such information without the written consent of the parents of the student.

****

STUDY QUESTIONS

    1. Are noncustodial parents entitled to see their child's records under the law?

    2. What is the obligation of a school district that receives notice of enrollment in another school district regarding transfer of a students records.

    3. Suppose you believe your child's record is inaccurate. What are your rights under the statute?

    4. Are there any restrictions on teacher access to student records?

****

F

CHAPTER SUMMARY

    The student\school legal relationship has been restructured. The "in loco parentis" doctrine has been amended to incorporate limited constitutional protections for children in the school setting. As a result of successful constitutional litigation the Congress enacted the Education for All Handicapped Children Act.(IDEA) requiring that disabled children be served in the regular school setting. Moreover, schools are also required to refrain from discriminating against children based on race and sex. The new legal framework for the student\school relationship also obligates schools to adopt record keeping practices which restrict access to student records and assure their accuracy. One conclusion seems abundantly clear from our consideration of the law of the student\school relationship. Nevada school law dealing with students is grounded primarily in pronouncements by Congress and the Federal courts.

CHAPTER VI

HEALTH & SAFETY ISSUES

Schools are presented with various health issues.[665] Health issues are not new in the school setting.[666] In the past educators have had to contend with immunization, spread of disease, child nutrition, use of controlled substances, the need for health services at schools, the identification of abused and neglected children and teen pregnancy.[667] Today, the problems are even more diverse and complex.[668]

A complete discussion of the legal aspects of school health and safety issues cannot be accomplished within the confines of a general school law treatise.[669] Therefore, this chapter will focus on specific Nevada statutes which impact directly on school health and safety, recent case law and Nevada's statutes regarding child abuse and neglect.

---

[665]The legislature recognized the serious nature of the health problems presented in the school setting and the critical role education plays in attending to those issues when it adopted Assembly Concurrent Resolution No. 10 File Number 41 (1993) designating October as Child Health Care Month. In the resolution the legislature urged educators to observe the month by reminding children and their parents of the importance of preventative health care and providing information concerning all locally available programs, providers and facilities that provide such care.

The U.S. Department of Education and the U.S. Department of Health and Human Services have recently released (April 1993) a book to help communities improve coordination of education, health and human services for at-risk children and families. The book entitled "Together We Can: A Guide for Crafting a Profamily System of Education and Human Services" presents a five-stage collaborative process to assist communities with the difficult task of creating a more responsive education and human service delivery system. The work is the product of the School-Linked Integrated Services Study Group. The document is available from the U.S. Government Printing Office, Superintendent of Documents Mail Stop: SSOP. Washington, DC 20402-9328 ISBN 0-16-041721-X.

[666] See Rules for Students supra. See also Thomas, Steven B. "Health Related Legal Issues in Education", NOLPE, Topeka, Ka. (1987). This publication describes the diseases most often found in the school setting. applicable statutes and constitutional provisions and the legal aspects regarding admission, continued attendance and employment issues.

[667] It has been reported that Nevada has the highest teen pregnancy rate nationwide. Pappa, Erik, "Lusk: School birth control clinics set", Las Vegas Sun, November 28, 1989. The establishment of school health clinics is a controversial issue. Papinchak, Steve, "Official: School Clinics Essential," Review Journal, September 21, 1991, p. 1 B.

[668] Thomas, supra.

[669]On June 25, 1992 the State Superintendent of Public Instruction, Eugene Paslov, released a report entitled "Nevada's Children." Written by Mary Horner, a research assistant at the University of Nevada, Reno, the report consists of 350 different statistical observations of children from a variety ofsources. Findings include:

—15.2 percent of Nevada children live in poverty, a 54 percent increase during the 1980s.

—Reports of child abuse in Nevada increased from 5,054 in 1983 to 12,286 in 1990. More than a third of the abuse cases had alcohol or drugs as a contributing factor.

—About 80 percent of the girls and 70 percent of the boys at the Caliente Youth Training Center had been sexually abused prior to entering the facility.

—There were 1,300 known homeless youths in Nevada in 1990.

—Nevada ranked first in per-capita alcohol consumption and second for hard-core cocaine consumption in 1992.

—In Nevada in 1991, about 20 percent of high school seniors used marijuana regularly. Half reported it was easy to obtain cocaine.

—Children nationally watch three hours to five hours of television a night, while spending less than an hour on homework. Half of all children have a television in their bedrooms.

—Nevada has one of the highest teen-age pregnancy rates in the country. The number of births to Nevada teens increased by 20 percent during the 1970s and 1980s, compared with a 26 percent decrease nationally.

—Of every 10 Nevada teen pregnancies, four end in abortion, one ends with adoption and five babies are kept by their mothers.

—Twenty-two percent of sexually active girls 15 to 19 use condoms.

-Surveys show that 49 percent of Nevada teachers report misbehavior in their classrooms interferes with their teaching.

—Nevada has the highest per-capita female labor force in the country. Women head 50 percent of the families living in poverty.

To acquire the report, call Kevin Crowe at the Department of Education in Carson City, at 1 (702) 687-3130. See Vogel, Ed, "Report Details Perils Facing Schoolchildren," Review Journal, June 6, 1992, p. 3 B.

A
NEVADA SCHOOL HEALTH AND SAFETY LAWS

School Nurses

Recognizing the importance of health issues presented in the school setting local school boards are empowered by law to employ school nurses.[670] A person must hold an license endorsement to serve as a school nurse issued pursuant to regulations adopted by the Commission on Professional Standards.[671]

The duties of the school nurse are also outlined in state law.[672] They include ensuring that each pupil enrolled in the school has been immunized in accordance with Nevada law,[673] assessing and evaluating the general health and physical development of pupils enrolled in the school to identify those pupils who have physical or mental conditions that impede their ability to learn and reporting the results their evaluation to 1) parents and guardians, 2) each administrator or teacher directly involved with the education of the pupil and 3) other professional personnel within the school district who need the information to assist the pupil with his health or education.[674] The school nurse is also responsible for designing and carrying out a plan of nursing care for a pupil with special needs which incorporates any plan specified by the students physician and which is approved by the pupils parent or guardian.[675] When appropriate the school nurse should refer the student and his parent or guardian to other sources in the community to obtain health services.[676] Moreover, a school nurse is charged with interpreting medical and nursing information that relates to a students individual educational plan and making recommendations to professional personnel directly involved with that student and the parents or guardian of that student.[677]

Nevada Student Immunization Requirements

Unless excused because of religious belief or medical condition, a child may not be enrolled in a public school in Nevada unless his parents or guardian submit

---

[670] The Clark County School District has 60 nurses serving approximately 129,000 students over an area of 8000 square miles. Typical assignments are three schools per nurse. Clark County School District Hotline, Public Information Office, January 13, 1992, p. 1. Chapter 535, Stats. 1991 contains the following provision not included in the NRS:

"1. Each school district shall:

    (a) Develop a plan for the school district to achieve and maintain a ratio of one school nurse for every 1,000 pupils enrolled in the school district and submit that plan to the state board of education.

    (b) By January 1, 1993, and January 1, 1995 report to the state board of education the progress made in achieving a ratio of one school nurse for every 1,000 pupils enrolled in the school district.

2. The state board of education shall report to the 67th and 68th sessions of the Nevada legislature:

    (a) The progress made by the school districts in achieving a ratio of one school nurse for every 1,000 pupils enrolled in a school district.

    (b) The need for and the estimated cost of maintaining a ratio of one school nurse for every 1,000 pupils enrolled in a school district. "

"See LCB Bulletin No. 91-9, Legislative Committee on Health Care, which recommended the development of a plan to achieve a ratio of one school nurse for every 1,000 pupils. "

[671] Sec. 391.207 NRS (1993).

[672] Sec. 391.208 NRS (1993). See also 392.420 NRS (1993). This section of the statutes outlines the nature of the general plan to be carried out in each school regarding observation and examination of students. For example, the law requires that a special examination for possible visual or auditory problems be accomplished for any child who is repeating a grade. Sec. 392.420(3)(b) NRS (1993). However, any child must be exempted from the examinations provided by the law if parents or guardian file with a teacher a written statement objecting to the examination. See Sec. 392.430(6) NRS (1993)

See also Alexander, Suzanne, "School Nurse Job Responsibilities Increase", Wall Street Journal, June 21, 1991, p. 1 B. The article reports that California school districts employ 3,300 nurses for their 5 million students. However, budget problems may reduce that total by 20%.

[673] Sec. 392.435-448 NRS (1993).

[674] Sec. 391.208(2) & (3) NRS (1993).

[675] Sec. 391.208(4) NRS (1993).

[676] Sec. 391.208 (5) NRS (1993).

[677] Sec. 391.208 (6) NRS (1993).

to the school board of residence a certificate stating that the child has been immunized and has received proper boosters for that immunization for a number of diseases.[678] The diseases listed in the statute are Diphtheria, Tetanus, Pertussis if the child is under 6 years of age, Polio, Rubella, Rubeola and such other diseases as the local board of health or the state board of health may determine. A child may be admitted conditionally if the parent or guardian of the child submits a certificate from a physician or local health officer that the student is receiving the required immunizations.[679] If a completed certificate is not submitted with 90 school days after the child is admitted he\she must be excluded until the requirements have been met.

A child who is excluded from school under the law is a neglected child and the provisions of Nevada's Child Abuse and Neglect Law [680] become applicable to the matter.[681]

After enrollment if additional immunization requirements are enacted certificates must be provided prior to registration for subsequent school years.[682]

Public schools cannot refuse to enroll a child because they have not been immunized if the parents or guardian of the child have submitted to the school board a written statement indicating that their religious beliefs prohibit immunization.[683] However, whenever the state board of health or a local board of health determines that there is a contagious disease in a public school attended by a child for whom exemption has been granted the school board must require that the child be immunized or remain outside the school environment and the local health officer be notified.[684]

Any parent who refuses to remove a child from school when the immunization law requires exclusion is guilty a misdemeanor.[685]

Nevada Legislative Response to AIDS in School Setting[686]

Not all contagious diseases present in the school setting are subject to immunization medicine. The common cold is the most recognizable example. However, a new lethal contagious disease is also present. Acquired Immune Deficiency Syndrome (AIDS) was first recognized in 1979 and established as a separate disease entity in 1981.[687]

Nevada policymakers have responded to this problem in two principal ways which have a direct impact on schools.

---

[678] Sec. 392.435 (5) & (6) NRS (1993) These sections require that the school district report to the health division of the department of human resources the 'exact' number of pupils who have completed the immunization schedule required by the law. The certificate of immunization must be included in the pupil's academic or cumulative record and transferred as part of that record upon request.

[679] Sec. 392.435 (4) NRS (1993).

[680] Chapter 432B NRS (1993).

[681] Ibid. See also Sec. 432.100 to 432.130 NRS (1993).

[682] Sec. 392.443 NRS (1993).

[683] Sec. 392.437 NRS (1993).

[684] Sec. 392.446 NRS (1993).

[685] Sec. 392.448 NRS (1993).

[686] Related statutes dealing with health issues. See Sec 389.060 NRS (1993) requiring instruction in physiology, hygiene and caardiopulmonary resuscitation. However, a student may be excused from instruction in the basic emergency care of a person in cardiac arrest if their parent or guardian submits a written statement that such instruction is not in conformity with the religious beliefs of the parent or guardian. Chapter 385 Laws of Nevada (1993) adding a new section to Chapter 389 requiring the state board to establish a program of instruction in the prevention of suicide. The instruction must be provided to each pupil by the completion of grade 12 as a part of a required course of study.

[687] See Thomas supra. See also Kirp, David L. & Epstein, Steven, "AIDS in America's Schoolhouses: Learning the Hard Lessons," Phi Delta Kappan, Vol. 70 No. 8 April 1989, p. 585-93. In addition, monthly reports of Clark County Health District indicate the extent of the disease in the County. For example, the number of AIDS deaths in Clark County stood at 374 as of August 1991. About 600 cases of AIDS had been diagnosed in the county since the early 1980s. Papinchak, Steve, "Clark County AIDS Cases Set Record," Review Journal, September 24, 1991, p. 1 B.

Most recently, the legislature enacted Senate Bill 492 amending § 441A.190 of the Nevada statutes. This law requires that a health authority who knows of the presence of the AIDS within a school shall notify the superintendent of the school district of that fact and direct what action, if any, must be taken to prevent the spread of the virus. The amendment further directs that the principal of a school who knows or suspects the presence of a communicable disease or knows of the presence of AIDS within the school must notify the superintendent of the school district of that fact. Once notified by a principal or having received such information by other means the superintendent obligated to notify the state health authority.[688] It is then the responsibility of the health authority to investigate the matter and direct what action, if any, must be taken.

The legislature has also responded to the issue by mandating the development of school curriculum and instruction on interrelated health issues including AIDS.

A specific provision of Nevada school law addresses instruction on Acquired Immune Deficiency Syndrome, human reproductive system, related communicable diseases and sexual responsibility.[689] The statute reads as follows:

1. The board of trustees of a school district shall establish a course or unit of a course of:

(a) Factual instruction concerning Acquired Immune Deficiency Syndrome;

(b) Instruction on the human reproductive system, related communicable diseases and sexual responsibility.

2. Each board of trustees shall appoint an advisory committee consisting

a) Five parents of children who attend schools in the district; and

b) Four representatives, one from each of four of the following professions or occupations:

(1) Medicine or nursing;

(2) Counseling;

(3) Religion;

(4) Pupils who attend schools in the district; or

(5) Teaching.

This committee shall advise the district concerning the content of and materials to be used in a course of instruction established pursuant to this section, and the recommended ages of the pupils to whom the course is offered. The final   decision on these matters must be that of the board of trustees.

3. The subjects of the courses may be taught only by a teacher or school nurse whose qualifications have been previously approved by the board of trustees.

4. The parent or guardian of each pupil to whom a course is offered must first be furnished written notice that the course will be offered. The notice must be given in the usual manner used by the local district to transmit written material to parents, and must contain a form for the signature of the parent or guardian of the pupil consenting to his attendance. Upon receipt of the written consent of the parent or guardian, the pupil may attend the course. If the written consent of the parent or guardian is not received, he must be excused from such attendance without any penalty as to credits or academic

---

[688] Sec. 441A.190 (2) NRS (1993).
[689] Sec. 389.065 NRS (1993).

350

standing. Any course offered pursuant to this section is not a requirement for graduation.

5. All instructional materials to be used in a course must be available for inspection by parents or guardians of pupils at reasonable times and locations before the course is taught, and appropriate written notice of the availability of the material must be furnished to all parents and guardians.[690]

Judicial Response to AIDS in the School Setting.[691]

The <u>Chalk</u> case (supra) involved the school employment setting. Three published opinions address the legal aspects of the problem from the perspective of the student school relationship. They all involve complaints of discrimination under section 504.

In <u>Thomas v. Atascadero Unified School Dist.</u>,662 F.Supp 376 (C.D.Cal. 1987), the court granted a preliminary injunction prohibiting the school district from excluding a child with AIDS from the classroom, despite the child's involvement in a biting incident. The court found that:

> The overwhelming weight of medical evidence is that the AIDS virus is not transmitted by human bites, even bites that break the skin. Based upon the abundant medical and scientific evidence before the Court, Ryan poses no risk of harm to his classmates and teachers. Any theoretical risk if transmission of the AIDS virus by Ryan in connection with his attendance in regular kindergarten class is so remote that it cannot form the basis for any exclusionary action by the School District. (<u>Thomas</u> at 380) Following the entry of the preliminary injunction, the parties in that case stipulated to the entry of a permanent injunction.

In <u>Ray v. School Dist. of DeSoto County</u>, 666 F. Supp. 1524 (M.D.Fla. 1987), the court followed Thomas and granted a preliminary injunction prohibiting the district from excluding three seropositive [692] brothers from the classroom. The court rejected the "future theoretical harm" of transmission of the AIDS virus in the classroom as unsupported by the weight of medical evidence.

The Third case, <u>District 27 Community School Bd. v. Board of Educ.</u>, 130 Misc.2d 398 (Sup. Ct. 1986), concerned the New York City Board of Education's policy of determining on a case-by case basis whether the health and development of children with AIDS permitted them to attend school in an unrestricted setting. Two school districts challenged the policy, seeking an injunction prohibiting the Board from admitting any child with AIDS into the classroom. After a five-week trial, the court upheld the policy in an exhaustive opinion. One of the central conclusions was that the transmission of the AIDS virus in the classroom setting was "a mere theoretical possibility" and that exclusion of AIDS victims on that bases would violate section 504.

Courts have also reached this conclusion regarding hepatitis B. In <u>New York State v. Carey</u>, 612 F.2d 644, 650 (2d Cir. 1979), the Second Circuit affirmed a district court ruling that the segregation of carriers of hepatitis B by the New York City Board of Education violated section 504. The court said:

---

[690] Sec. Ibid., Compare this approach to the policy recently adopted by the school board of New York City which allows condoms to be distributed upon student request. Parent wishes are disregarded under the New York policy.

[691] The seminal case regarding the definition of handicap as including contagious diseases is <u>School Board v. Arline</u> 480 U.S. 273, 107 S.Ct. 1123 (1987).

[692] "Seropositive" denotes persons who have tested positive for the HIV virus, but who have not yet exhibited symptoms of AIDS.

[T]he Board was unable to demonstrate that the health hazard posed by the hepatitis B carrier children was anything more that a remote possibility. There has never been any definite proof that the disease can be communicated by nonparenteral routes such as saliva. Even assuming there were, the activities that occur in classroom settings were not shown to pose any significant risk that the disease would be transmitted from one child to another.

Nevada Legislation Regarding Other School Health and Safety Issues

School board power to provide programs for nutrition for children and adults are authorized under the Nevada statutes dealing with financial support of school systems.[693]

Nevada lawmakers have specifically empowered school board trustees to make and enforce regulations for sanitation in the public schools and to prevent the spread of contagious and infectious diseases.[694] The legislature also vested the school district with authority to expend district funds to enforce the regulations among indigent children.[695] A new Nevada statute forbids placement of cigarette vending machines in a public area if minors are permitted access to that area and creates a health education account funded by penalties for violations of the law.[696] The account may only be used for health education and is administered by the state superintendent of public instruction.

Nevada law also requires that school districts provide drills at least once a month to instruct students in the appropriate procedures to be followed in the event of a fire or other emergency.[697] The 1993 legislature amended the fire drill requirement to provide that not more than three of the monthly drills may include instruction in appropriate procedures to be followed in the event of a chemical explosion, related emergencies and other natural disasters.[698] The person in charge of each school building is charged with causing the provisions of safety drill statute to be enforced.[699] Violation of the safety drill statute is a misdemeanor.[700]

Nevada policy makers have also passed laws dealing with eye safety.[701] If a school district has established classes in occupational education, teachers and pupils in those classes must wear devices provided by the school district that are designed to protect their eyes while using power tools, torches or other dangerous equipment or machinery.[702] The law further mandates that teachers and pupils in science classes must wear devices designed to protect their eyes , provided by the school district, when chemicals or other toxic substances are used in those classes.[703]

---

[693]Sec. 387.070-105 NRS (1993). Chapter 659 Laws of Nevada (1993) amends Chapter 387 expanding eligible participants in progams of nutrition provided through school to adults. Major funding for the program is provided by the Federal government.

[694] Sec. 392.430 NRS (1993).

[695] Sec. 392.430(2) NRS (1993).

[696]Chapter 651 Laws of Nevada (1993) amending Chapter 202 NRS. Violations of the statute entail both criminal and civil penalties. A health authority where the violation occurs may commence a civil proceeding to collect the penalty. Money collected is deposited with the state treasurer for credit to the account for health education for minors. The superintendent of public instruction is empowered to adiminister the account and may expend money in the account only for programs of health education for minors.

[697]Sec. 392.450 NRS (1993). See also Sec. 394.170 NRS (1993) Law requiring private schools to conduct safety drills.

[698]Chapter 68 Laws of Nevada (1993).

[699]Sec. 392.450 (4) NRS (1993).

[700]Sec. 392.450 (5) NRS (1993).

[701]Sec. 392.455 NRS (1993).

[702]Sec. 392.455 (1) NRS (1993).

[703]Sec. 392.455 (2) NRS (1993).

Transportation of school children by the school district is also the subject of extensive safety regulations.[704] Most recently, the legislature adopted an amemdment to the school bus safety lighting law requiring school buses to be equipped with mechanical devices that mandate persons walk at a certain distance in front of buses being loaded and unloaded. The law is intended to prevent children from being hidden in driver blind spots during the loading and unloading process.[705]

State law also addresses streets used to walk to and from school and streets adjacent to school property.[706] 'School zones' are those sections of streets which are adjacent to school property.[707] Traffic speed is limited to 15 miles per hour in school zones during the period one half hour before school begins to one half hour after school ends.[708] 'School crossing zones' are those sections of streets not adjacent to school property that pupils cross while following a designated walking route to school.[709] Traffic speed is limited to 25 miles per hour in 'school crossing zones' during the same period of time applicable to 'school zones'.[710] If the zones are designated by an operational speed limit beacon the zone limit is in effect only when the beacon is operating.[711]

B
NEVADA CHILD ABUSE LEGISLATION[712]

The National Committee for Prevention of Child Abuse released a study in April 1991 stating that 2.5 million cases of child abuse and neglect were reported to authorities in 1990, a four percent increase from the previous year.[713] The study also indicated that more than 1200 children died from abuse-related incidents in 1990. Another group concerned with child welfare claimed that since 1981 child abuse had increased 80%, child sexual abuse was up 277% and fatalities from abuse up 36%.[714] Clark county 1991 child abuse statistics were released in April 1992. The

---

[704]Sec. 392.300 NRS (1993). Transportation authority, power to eatablish bus routes, districts over 100,000 population may transport private school students, school trustee authority to regulate student conduct while being transported; Sec. 392.320 NRS (1993) Authority to procure appropriate insurance coverage; Sec. 392.360 NRS (1993) Transportation purposes limitation, Driver operation limitations; Sec. 392.375 NRS (1993) Evacuation drill requirements; Sec. 392.380 NRS (1993) Driver qualifications; Sec. 392.390 NRS (1993) Employment of unlicensed driver misdemeanor; Sec. 392.400 NRS (1993) Vehicle specifications, condition, inspection and penality; Sec. 392.410 NRS (1993) School bus lighing system.

[705]Chapter 101 Laws of Nevada (1993) amending Sec. 392.410 (1) NRS (1993)

[706]Assembly Concurrent Resolution No. 31 File No. 102 (1993) urges local governments to identify those school zones in congested areas that would benefit from the installation of flashing yellow lights, post school zone speed limit signs that exceed minimum size requirements and establish advisory committees of parents and other interested persons to work in cooperation with the Department of Transportation regarding school traffic safety.

[707]Chapter 618 Laws of Nevada Sec. 3 (1993).

[708]Sec. 484.366 1 NRS (1993).

[709]Chapter 618 Laws of Nevada Sec. 2 (1993).

[710]Sec. 484.366 2 NRS (1993).

[711]Chapter 618 Laws of Nevada Sec. 5 (1993).

[712]In 1993 the legislature adopted a statute requiring local boards to establish a program of instruction relating to child abuse for pupils in kindergarten and grades 1 to 6 inclusive. The law provides that the program must include, without limitation, instruction relating to the types of child abuse and the methods used to recognize, report, prevent and stop child abuse. Chapter 223 Laws of Nevada (1993) adds a new section to Chapter 389 NRS (1991). Implementation of this statute poses some difficult questions for local boards. What process should the board use to develop the program? Should a committee composed of diverse interests professional expertise and experience be established to make recommendations to the board? What interests should be represented on such a committee; law enforcement experts, juvenile authorities, medical professionals, mental health workers, educators, child psychologists, religious leaders, parents, others? How do you instruct kindergarten, first and second students to recognize, report, prevent and stop child abuse? How much school time should be devoted to the issue? What staff development should precede implementation of the program? Unlike instruction in AIDS, the human reproductive system and related communicable diseases (see Sec. 389.065 (1991) the legislature has not required parental notice or consent prior to instruction. Should the board make an effort to share the nature and content of the curriculum with parents prior to all children (K-6) receiving the instruction? Note the legislature has not appropriated any financial assistance for local boards to accomplish the statutory directive.

[713] "U.S. Child-Abuse Cases at 2.5 Million." Review Journal, April 17, 1991.

[714] The Childrens Campaign, New York Times, February 7, 1990, p. 15 A. The comment indicates that the fatality increase figure covers the period 1985-88.

sexual abuse investigative team of the county reported that it looked into 171 reports in 1991.

Chapter 432B entitled **PROTECTION OF CHILDREN FROM ABUSE AND NEGLECT** was added to the Nevada Revised Statutes in 1985.[715]

The statute defines abuse and neglect [716] of a child[717] as 1) physical or mental injury [718] of a non accidental nature, 2) sexual abuse [719] or sexual exploitation [720] or 3) negligent treatment or maltreatment [721] of a child caused or allowed by a person responsible for his welfare [722] under circumstances which indicate that the child's health or welfare is harmed or threatened with harm.[723] As used in the definition the word 'allow' means to do nothing to prevent or stop the abuse or neglect of a child in circumstances where the person knows or has reason to know that a child is abused or neglected.[724]

Reports must be made by persons who in their professional or occupational capacities, know or have reason to believe [725] that a child has been abused or neglected.[726] Occupations specifically named in the law relevant to the school setting include, professional or practical nurse, psychologist, alcohol or drug abuse counselor and social worker. Moreover, the law also requires that a social worker and an administrator, teacher, librarian, or counselor of a school to make reports.[727] Other persons not specifically named in the law may make reports.

---

[715] The preamble to the legislation reads as follows: Ch. 455, Stats. 1985,
WHEREAS, The legislature finds that there are abused or neglected children within this state who need protection; and
WHEREAS, The legislature finds that there is a need for the prevention, identification and treatment of abuse or neglect of children; and
WHEREAS, It is the purpose of this act to establish judicial procedures to protect the rights of parents and children and to provide a system for the services necessary to protect the welfare and development of abused or neglected children and, if appropriate, to preserve and stabilize the family;

[716] A chart of indicators of abuse and neglect follows the discussion. Herbert, Myra, "What Principals Should Know About Child Abuse, Principal, November, 1985 p. 12.

[717] Child means a person under the age of 18 Sec. 432.040 NRS (1993).

[718] Physical injury is defined as 1. Permanent or temporary disfigurement or 2. Impairment of any bodily function or organ of the body See Sec. 432B.090 NRS (1993); Mental injury is defined as injury to the intellectual or psychological capacity or the emotional condition of a child as evidenced by an observable and substantial impairment of his ability to function within his normal range of performance. See Sec. 432B.070 NRS (1993) Excessive corporal punishment may constitute child abuse or neglect. See Sec. 432B.150 NRS (1993)

[719] Sexual abuse is defined as acts upon a child constituting: Incest, lewdness with a child, Annoyance or molestation of a child, Sado-masochistic abuse, Sexual assault, Statutory sexual seduction, and Open and gross lewdness. See Sec. 432B.100 NRS (1993).

[720] Sexual exploitation is defined as forcing, allowing or encouraging a child 1) to solicit for or engage in prostitution, 2) to view a pornographic film or literature and 3) to engage in a) filming, photographing or recording or video tape or b) posing, modeling, depiction or a live performance before an audience, which involves the exhibition of a child' genitals or any sexual conduct with a child. See Sec. 432B.110 NRS (1993).

[721] Negligent treatment or maltreatment is defined as occurring if a child has been abandoned, is without proper care, control and supervision or lacks the subsistence, education, shelter, medical care or other care necessary for the well-being of the child because of the faults or habits of the person responsible for his\her welfare or his\her neglect or refusal to provide them when able to do so. See Sec. 432B.140 NRS (1993) See also August H. v. State, 105 Nev. 441, 777 P.2d 901 (1989) which found evidence sufficient to show that children were neglected where their parents were unable to protect the them from each other and failed to teach their children basic social skills or to provide any guidance to their children regarding basic toilet functions and hygiene.

[722] The phrase is defined as a child's parent, guardian or foster parent, a stepparent with whom the child lives,an adult person continually or regularly found in the same household as the child, or a person directly responsible or serving as a volunteer for or employed in a public or private home, institution or facility where the child actually resides or is receiving child care outside of his home for a portion of the day. See Sec. 432B.130 NRS (1993).

[723] Sec. 432B.020 NRS (1993).

[724] The law also states that a child is not abused or neglected, nor is his\her health or welfare harmed or threatened for the sole reason that his parent of guardian, in good faith, selects and depends upon nonmedical remedial treatment for such child, if such treatment is recognized and permitted under the laws of this state in lieu of medical treatment. However, this exception to the abuse definition does not limit a court in ensuring a child receive a medical examination and treatment under § 62.231 NRS (1993).

[725] See Fossey, Richard, "Child Abuse Investigations in the Public Schools: A Practical Guide for School Administrators," 69 Ed.Law Rep. [991] (November 21, 1991).

[726] Sec. 432B.220(2) NRS (1993).

[727] Sec. 432B.220(2)(e) NRS (1993).

Reports are made to an agency which provides protective services or to a law enforcement agency.[728] The law requires that the report be made immediately [729], but in no event later than 24 hours after there is reason to believe that a child has been abused or neglected. Notice that the amount of evidence required for the reporting duty to arise to is very low. A clear preponderance of evidence or proof beyond a reasonable doubt would impose a much higher threshold for the duty to report to arise. The statute is clearly drafted in a manner to encourage reporting of suspected child abuse.[730] School personnel do not have the responsibility or authority to determine whether protective care is needed. It is also important to note that the duty to report is a personal responsibility.[731] The report triggers an investigation. It is not a finding of abuse or neglect.

The statute outlines the method for making a report and its contents.[732] The report may be made verbally, by telephone of otherwise. If the information is obtainable the report should include; the name, address, age and sex of the child; the name and address of the child's parents or other person responsible for the child's care; the nature and extent of the abuse or neglect of the child; any evidence of previously known or suspected abuse or neglect of the child or the child's siblings; the name, address and relationship, if known, of the person who is alleged to have abused or neglected the child; and any other information known to the person making the report that the agency which provides protective services considers necessary.[733]

Reports of suspected child abuse and neglect as well as all records concerning the reports and investigations thereof are confidential.[734]

Immunity from civil and criminal liability extends to every person who, in good faith, makes a report of suspected child abuse or neglect pursuant to Chapter 432B.[735]
Furthermore, in any proceeding to impose liability against a person for making a report there is a presumption that the person acted in good faith.[736]

Any person who knowingly and willfully fails to make a report is guilty of a misdemeanor.[737]

---

[728] Sec. 432B.220(1) NRS (1993). The Welfare Division is required to establish and maintain a center with a toll-free telephone number to receive reports of abuse or neglect of children in Nevada 24 hours a day 7 days a week. Reports made to the center are promptly transmitted to the agency providing protective services in the community where the child is located. Sec. 432B.200 NRS (1993).

[729] Former provisions of section which required 'immediate' reports were found unconstitutionally vague in Sheriff, Washoe County v. Sferrazza, 104 Nev. 747, 766 P.2d 896 (1988).

[730] Although the belief threshold is designed to encourage reporting such a report should not be taken lightly. See Brannigan, Martha, "Child Abuse Charges Ensnare Some Parents In Baseless Proceedings," Wall Street Journal, August 23,1989, p. 1 A.

[731] For example, the statute requires teachers who have reason to believe that a child has been abused or neglected, to make a report to protective services or a law enforcement agency. The law does not state that a teachers supervisor must be informed prior to a report, nor that the teacher's supervisor can order a teacher who has reason to believe that abuse or neglect has occurred refrain from reporting. Further, the teacher's duty to report is not fulfilled by reporting the matter to his\her supervisor. Enlightened practice would entail communication with the teachers supervisor indicating the teachers intention to make a report. But it would be contrary to the letter and the spirit of the law for the teacher's supervisor to order that the teacher to refrain from reporting when the teacher has reason to believe abuse or neglect has occurred. The conceptual framework of the law is simple. It is written in a manner that encourages reporting. A report merely triggers an investigation. A report is not a finding.

[732] Sec. 432B.230 NRS (1993).

[733] Ibid.

[734] 432B.280 NRS (1993). Names of persons making reports and names of children concerned remain confidential and protected from general dissemination to the public even after the death of the abused. AGO 88-15 (12-14-1988)

[735] Sec. 432B.160 NRS (1993).

[736] Sec. 432B.160 NRS (1993). Absent actual malice reporters have immunity from liability. See Davis v. Durham City Schools 372 S.E.2d 318 (N.C. 1989).

[737] Sec. 432B.240 NRS (1993). State mandated reporters can be held liable for failure to report. See Landeros v. Flood, 551 P.2d 389 (Cal. 1976) and Sowers v Bradford Area School District, 869 F.2d 591 (3rd Cir. 1989).

In 1993 the legislature adopted a statute requiring local boards to establish a program of instruction relating to child abuse for pupils in kindergarten and grades 1 to 6 inclusive.[738] (See Specific Board Duties) The law provides that the program must include, with limitation, instruction relating to the types of child abuse and the methods used to recognize, report, prevent and stop child abuse.[739]

STUDY QUESTIONS

1. Is a certificate of immunization always required in order to enroll a child in school in Nevada?

2. Where would you expect to find Nevada school district regulations concerning school district sex education curriculum?

3. Compare and contrast the policy response adopted in New York City school board and Nevada schools regarding the AIDS epidemic.

4. When is an educator obligated to report child abuse or neglect?

C
CHAPTER SUMMARY

Health issues are not new to the school setting. Now, however, the health problems present in schools impose new legal duties and responsibilities on educators. Further, the new legal duties and responsibilities are mandated by both federal and state authorities. So our limited consideration of the legal aspects of health issues presented in the school setting reaffirms the diversity of individuals and entities exerting legal authority over the governance of education.

---

[738]Chapter 223 Laws of Nevada (1993) adds a new section to Chapter 389. Chapter 223 Laws of Nevada Sec. 1 (1993).

[739]Chapter 223 Laws of Nevada Sec. 2 (1993). Implementation of this statute poses some difficult questions for local boards. What process should the board use to develop the program? Should a committee composed of diverse interests professional expertise and experience be established to make recommendations to the board? What interests should be represented on such a committee; law enforcement experts, juvenile authorities, medical professionals, mental health workers, educators, child psychologists, religious leaders, parents, others? How do you instruct kindergarten, first and second students to recognize, report, prevent and stop child abuse? How much school time should be devoted to the issue? What staff development should precede implementation of the program? Unlike instruction in AIDS, the human reproductive system and related communicable diseases (see Sec. 389.065 (1991) the legislature has not required parental notice or consent prior to instruction. Should the board make an effort to share the nature and content of the curriculum with parents prior to all children (K-6) receiving the instruction? Note the legislature has not appropriated any financial assistance for local boards to accomplish the statutory directive.

INDICATORS OF CHILD ABUSE

TYPE OF ABUSE	PHYSICAL INDICATORS	BEHAVIORAL INDICATORS
PHYSICAL	Unexplained bruises and welts • on face, lips, or mouth • on torso, back, buttocks, or thighs • in various stages of healing • clustered or forming patterns • shaped like recognizable object (e.g., belt buckle) • appearing regularly after absences, weekends, or vacation periods Unexplained burns • by cigars or cigarettes, especially on soles, palms, back, or buttocks • by immersion in hot liquid, especially on hands, feet, buttocks, or genitalia • shaped in a recognizable form (e.g., electric range coils, electric iron) • by rope on arms, legs, neck, or torso Unexplained fractures • of skull, nose, or facial bones • in various stages of healing • in multiple locations Unexplained lacerations or abrasions • on mouth, lips, gums, or eyes • on external genitalia	Wary of adult contacts Apprehensive when other children cry Extreme aggressiveness or extreme withdrawal Fear of parents Fear of going home Reporting of injury by parents or others
SEXUAL	Difficulty in walking or sitting Torn, stained, or bloody underclothes Pain or itching in genital area Bruises or bleeding in external genitalia, vaginal, or anal areas Venereal disease symptoms, especially in pre-teens Pregnancy	Unwillingness to change clothing or to participate in physical education classes Withdrawal, fantasy, or infantile behavior Bizarre, sophisticated, or unusual sexual behavior or knowledge Poor peer relationships Chronic delinquency Reporting of sexual assaults
EMOTIONAL	Speech disorders Lag in physical development Severe allergies, asthma, or ulcers Alcohol or drug abuse	Habit disorders (e.g., thumb sucking, lip biting, rocking) Antisocial or destructive conduct Psychoneurotic traits (e.g., hysteria, obsessions, compulsions, phobias, hypochondria) Behavior extremes of compliance or aggression Inappropriate adult or infantile behavior Mental and emotional developmental lags Suicide threats or attempts

NEGLECT	Consistent hunger	Begging or stealing food
	Poor hygiene	Early arrivals and late departures
	Inappropriate dress	Constant fatigue or listlessness
	Unattended physical problems or medical needs	Chronic delinquency, especially thefts
	Alcohol or drug abuse	Reporting of no caretaker at home

Source: Myra Herbert, *What Principals Should Know About Child Abuse*, Principal (November, 1985), at 12

CHAPTER VII

EDUCATOR LIABILITY

A
INTRODUCTION

Our discussion of educator liability involves exploration of the law of torts. Tort is a French word meaning civil wrong. A person who commits a civil wrong is called a tortfeasor. Under our system of jurisprudence a tort committed by citizen against another citizen is remedied through a lawsuit in which the injured party attempts to win compensation for the injuries suffered.

B
CONCEPTUAL FRAMEWORK

There are basically two types of civil wrongs. Intentional torts include trepass, assault, battery and defamation. Unintentional torts are the result of negligence. The overwhelming majority of tort cases involving educators concern allegations that they committed an unintentional or negligent tort which resulted in injury.

A civil wrong is defined as a violation of a duty causing harm. Thus, understanding the conceptual framework for educator liability requires exploration of the four elements of a tort. Specifically, 1) what duty educators owe students in the school setting 2) what standard is used to determine whether the duty has been violated 3) what the nature of the causal connection must be between the breach of duty and the injury and 4) how harm is determined. The plaintiff or injured person must be able to establish all four elements of the conceptual framework by a preponderance of the evidence in order to prevail.[740]

Duty

Our discussion of the concept of duty begins with a doctrine we have considered earlier. The doctrine of 'in loco parentis' is the key to our understanding as to the nature of the duty owed by educators to children under their supervision. Remember, under the doctrine a educator stands in the shoes of a reasonable and prudent parent. He/she possesses all the duties, responsibilities, rights and privileges that a reasonable and prudent parent possesses with regard to supervision of the child. As a result of prior study we know that the strict doctrine has been modified in the school setting. Children have constitutional rights in the school setting that do not impact on parental authority.

---

[740] **BURDEN OF PROOF is defined in Nevada law as follows:**
    The party who has the burden of proof in a civil action **must prove every essential element** of that claim by a "preponderance of the evidence." A preponderance of the evidence means such evidence as , when considered and compared with that opposed to it, has more convincing force and produces in jurors minds a belief that what is sought to be proved is more likely true than not true. In other words, to establish a claim by a "preponderance of the evidence" merely means to prove that the claim is more likely so than not so.
    The plaintiff has the burden to prove duty, violation of duty, proximate cause and harm.
    The defendant has the burden of proving, as an affirmative defense, that some contributory negligence on the part of the plaintiff, himself, was a cause of any damage plaintiff may have sustained. See "Nevada Tort Law Principles From Nevada Jury Instructions Prepared By Chief Judge Donald Mosley Clark Count District Court," September 1989. See also Joynt v. California Hotel & Casino, 108 Nev. Advance Opinion 95 (1992).

A teacher is liable for injury to the pupils under his/her supervision caused by his/her negligenceor failure to use reasonable care.[741] It is extremely important to remember that educators do not insure or guarantee the safety of pupils at school. Judge Donald Mosley of the Clark County District Court has drafted jury instructions which present the current status of Nevada tort law regarding the concept duty.[742]

Reasonable supervision is the primary duty educators owe to children under their care. Courts have also found that educator's have a duty to instruct and warn pupils in their care of any dangers which they know or in the exercise of ordinary care ought to know are present. The duty to instruct includes teaching methods which will protect students form the dangers present. Courts have also alluded to a duty to inspect equipment and locations which children may encounter while under the educators care.

Educators also have a duty to recognize and respect the Federal constitutional rights of students.[743]

A statute may establish a duty.[744] For example, Nevada statutes require that if a school district has established classes in occupational education that teacher and pupils in those classes must wear devices provided by the district which are designed to protect their eyes while they are using power tools, torches, or other dangerous equipment or machinery.[745] Teachers and pupils in classes in science must wear devices provided by the school district which are designed to protect their eyes when chemicals or toxic substances are used in those classes.[746] Another example involves fire safety. School boards must provide fire drills for pupils in the schools at least once per month during the school year.[747] Copies of fire escape route diagrams and fire drill information as approved by the chief of the fire department

---

[741]**NEGLIGENCE DEFINITION**

Negligence is the failure to exercise that degree of care which an ordinarily careful and prudent person would exercise under the same or similar circumstances.

Ordinary care is that care which persons of ordinary prudence exercise in the management of their own affairs in order to avoid injury to themselves or to others.

Note that the person whose conduct is set up as a standard is not the extraordinary cautious individual, not the exceptionally skillful one, but a person of reasonable and ordinary prudence. While exceptional skill is an admirable characteristic and encouraged, the law does not demand it as a general standard of conduct. See Nevada Tort Law Principles From Nevada Jury Instructions Prepared By Chief Judge Donald Mosley Clark Count District Court, September 1989. See also Joynt v. California Hotel & Casino, 108 Nev. Advance Opinion 95 (1992).

CONTRIBUTORY NEGLIGENCE

Contributory negligence is negligence (failure to exercise reasonable care) on the part of the plaintiff (injured party) which, cooperating to some degree with the negligence of another, helps in proximately causing an injury to the plaintiff.

The plaintiff may not recover damages if his contributory negligence has contributed more to his injury than the negligence of the defendant.

The defendant bears the burden of proving that some contributory negligence on the part of the complainant was a cause of the damage he/she sustained. The injured person may not recover damages if his/her contributory negligence has contributed more to his/her injury than the lack of due care of the defendant. However, if the plaintiff is negligent, the plaintiff may still recover a reduced sum so long as his contributory negligence is not greater than the negligence of the defendant.

[742] See Nevada Tort Law Principles From Nevada Jury Instructions Prepared By Chief Judge Donald Mosley Clark Count District Court, September 1989. See also Joynt v. California Hotel & Casino, 108 Nev. Advance Opinion 95 (1992).

[743]See Sorenson, Gail Paulus, "School District Liability for Federal Civil Rights Violations Under Section 1983," 76 Ed.Law Rep. [313] (October 8, 1992), Horner, Jeffrey J. & Lopez, Vianei G., "Collins v. City of Harker Heights- The Liability of Public Entity for 'Constitutional Torts'" 74 Ed.Law Rep. [441] (July 16, 1992). See also Doe v. Taylor Independent School Dist., 975 F.2d 137 (5th Cir 1992). In the Doe case the 5th Circuit held that a student had a firmly established constitutional right under the due process and equal protection clauses of the Fourteenth Amendment to be free from sexual molestation by a state-employed school teacher. The court further held that the principal and superintendent had an affirmative constitutionally based duty to protect students from such intrusion into bodily integrity.

Prevailing parties in civil rights litigation (Sec.1983 lawsuits) are entitled to attorney fees. The Supreme Court addressed the standard to be applied by lower courts when considering attorney fee applications in Farrar v. Hobby, __U.S. __, 113 S.Ct. 566 (1992). "When a plaintiff recovers only nominal damages because of his failure to prove an essential element of his claim for monetary relief ... the only reasonable fee is usually no fee at all.".

[744]Federal Statutes as well as Nevada law may create a duty of care. For example, Title IX of the Educational Amendments of 1972, 20 U.S.C. §1681-1688 (Title IX) forbids sex discrimination in educational programs, Title VI Civil Rights Act 1964, 42 U.S.C. §2000d bans discrimination based on the ground of Race, Color or national origin in any program or activity receiving federal financial assistance.

[745] Sec. 392.455(1) NRS (1993).

[746] Sec. 392.455(2) NRS (1993).

[747] Sec. 392.450(1) NRS (1993).

or state fire marshall must be posted in every classroom of every public school by the principal or teacher in charge.[748] Most recently, during the 1991 legislative session the lawmakers responded to teacher safety concerns by requiring each school district to inform certain school employees of pupils who may be violent when the employee may have consistent contact with the student.[749]

Furthermore, students have attempted to persuade the courts that new duties should be recognized. They have argued that schools and educators have a duty to educate [750] and may, therefore, be held liable for educationalEducator liability:Malpracticemalpractice. The duty to educate students who are not eligible for special education services has not been recognized in Nevada [751]or any other

---

[748] Sec. 392.450(3) NRS (1993).

[749] The statue reads as follows:

392.468 Provision of information to certain employees regard unlawful conduct of pupil.

1. The board of trustees of a county school district, or its designee, shall inform each employee of the district, including teachers, other licensed employees, drivers of school buses, instructional aides and office managers who may have consistent contact with a pupil if that pupil has, within the preceding 3 years, unlawfully caused or attempted to cause serious bodily jury to any person. The district shall provide this information based upon any written records that the district maintains or which it receives from a Iaw enforcement agency. The district need not initiate a request for such information from any source.

2. A school district and the members of its board of trustees are not liable for failure strictly to comply with this section if a good faith effort to comply is made

3. Any information received by an employee pursuant to this section is confidential and must not be further disseminated by the employee.

[750] See Jurenas, Albert C., "Will Educational Malpractice Be Revived?," 74 Ed.Law Rep. [449] (July 16, 1992) and Brown, Sharan E. & Cannon, Kim, "Educational Malpractice Actions: A Remedy for What Ails Our Schools?," 78 Ed.Law Rep. [643] (January 28, 1993).

[751]The Nevada supreme court recently considered a tort case brought against a private school involving (among others) a claim of educational malpractive. The court reinstated the lawsuit dismissed by the district court. The problem with the courts treatment of the issue was its failure to discuss the educational malpractice claim thereby suggesting an unwillingness to declare the legal theory dead in Nevada in cases involving regular education. The case opinion follows.

Squires v. Sierra Nevada Educational Foundation Inc., DBA Cambridge School, 107 Nev. 902, 823 P.2d 256 (1991).

By the Court, ROSE, J.:

Brandon Squires (Brandon) attended Cambridge School from pre-kindergarten through second grade. Brandon's parents, Bon- nie and Burke Squires (the Squires), chose to send him to Cambridge because they suspected that he might experience difficulties learning to read, based upon his difficulties in articulating words and the difficulties his father had experienced in learning to read. In her affidavit, Bonnie Squires states that she expressed this concern to the principal of Cambridge, Linda Fisher, when she was choosing a school for Brandon. Ms. Fisher specifically advised her that Cambridge had the capabilities and the facilities to diagnose and remediate any reading difficulties which might develop. In addition, Bonnie states that Ms. Fisher told her that Cambridge could provide an education superior to that provided by public schools because of smaller classes, individualized instruction, and a highly qualified staff.

The Squires contend that, in reliance upon Ms. Fisher's statements, they elected to send Brandon to Cambridge, foregoing a public school education. Brandon appeared to be progressing normally at Cambridge. All of his progress reports were positive, except his second grade fourth quarter report, which noted that his reading ability was significantly below grade level and recommended that he repeat the second grade. The school had not provided the Squires with any previous indication that Brandon was having difficulties. The Squires failed to detect this problem at home, in part because Brandon was capable of memorizing stories and reciting them back to people, and in part because of Burke Squires' own reading diffIculties.

During part of the time that Brandon was attending Cambridge, Bonnie worked as a secretary at the school. During this time, she personally observed Brandon's first grade teacher, Betty Weiser, who was also the school's administrator, spending a great deal of time on administrative duties. Consequently, many of Brandon's first grade classes were taught by inexperienced teaching interns.

The Squires obtained an affidavit from Verlinda Thompson, an expert in the teaching of reading, stating that Brandon's reading deficiencies were more likely than not the result of inappropriate instruction and intervention, or lack thereof, during Brandon's four years at Cambridge School. Ms. Thompson based her conclusion on the fact that the standardized tests given to Brandon indicated that he is an extremely bright boy with language comprehension skills far in advance of his chronological age, and that none of the documents she reviewed indicated any evidence of an organic component to Brandon's reading disability.

After Brandon's second grade year at Cambridge, the Squires transferred him to a public school where, as a result of his reading deficiencies, he was required to repeat the second grade. As of last February, Brandon was twelve years old and in the fourth grade, and he had been identified as a special education student. Brandon alleges injuries consisting of permanent injury to his mental and emotional development and the pain, frustration, and shame associated with being held back. Furthermore, according to Verlinda Thompson's affidavit, Brandon is likely to suffer future harm because, as a very bright older child with markedly discrepant reading skills, he possesses traits which would characterize him as being at a high risk of dropping out of school. Brandon's parents also allege monetary damages in the form of wasted tuition expenses, the cost of remediation services at the University of Nevada at Reno's Reading Clinic, and three years of private tutoring.

Appellants brought several claims for relief before the district court, alleging primarily (1) educational malpractice, (2) misrepresentation, and (3) breach of contract. Cambridge submitted a motion to dismiss for failure to state a claim upon which relief can be granted, pursuant to NRCP 12(b)(5). The district judge granted this motion, because he was persuaded that there is no standard for instructing or testing students and because he concluded that as a matter of policy, teachers should not be confined to a limited number of teaching methods. We reverse and remand.

The standard of review for dismissals under NRCP 12(b)5) is rigorous. The court "must construe the pleading liberally and draw every fair intendment in favor of the [appellant]." Merluzzi v. Larson, 96 Nev. 409, 411, 610 P.2d 739, 741 (1980) (citing San Diego Prestressed Concrete Co. v. Chicago Title Ins. Corp., 92 Nev. 569, 573, 555 P.2d 484, 487 (1976)). However, the appellant must have presented some relevant legal authority in support of his contention. Plankinton v. Nye County, 95 Nev. 12, 588 P.2d 1025 (1979). In addition, all factual allegations of the complaint must be accepted as true. Hynds Plumbing v. Clark Co. Sch. Dist., 94 Nev. 776, 777, 587 P.2d 1331, 1332 (1978). Under this standard of review, the Squires have clearly alleged claims of breach of contract and negligent and intentional misrepresentation upon which relief may be granted.

This case presents issues of first impression to this court. A cause of action in contract for educational claims was recognized in dicta in Paladino v. Adelphi University, 454 N.Y.S.2d 868, 873 (N.Y.App.Div. 1982), which held that a cause of action in contract can exist against a

361

state.[752] What do you think is the primary reason that courts have refused to find a duty to educate students in the regular education program? What is it about the system set up for students served in special education programs that could convince courts to look more favorably upon claims lodged on a theory of educational malpractice?[753]

A statute may grant a privilege to one person which creates a duty on the part of another. The Nevada legislature has enacted laws creating a Teacher Pupil Privilege [754] and a Counselor Pupil Privilege.[755] The privilege accorded by the law, in the sense used here, creates a duty of nondisclosure as to communications received from the person (in this case pupil) who holds the privilege. In this case then, pupils are given the privilege to hold or release a Teacher or Counselor from their duty of nondisclosure.[756]

The statutes read as follows:

TEACHER AND PUPIL 49.291

1.   *As used in this section, "teacher" means a person who is regularly employed by a public or private school in this state as a teacher or administrator and who holds a valid license issued by the superintendent of public instruction authorizing the holder to teach or perform administrative functions in schools.*

2.   *Communications by a pupil to a teacher concerning the pupil's possession or use of drugs or alcoholic beverages made while the teacher was counseling or attempting to counsel the pupil are privileged communications and the teacher must not, without the consent of the pupil, be examined as a witness concerning any such communication in any civil ar criminal action to which the pupil is a party.*

COUNSELOR AND PUPIL 49.290

1.   *As used in this section,"counselor" means a person who is regularly employed by a public or private school in this state as a counselor, psychologist or*

---

private educational institution when that institution provides no services or does not provide certain specified services, such as an agreed upon number of hours of instruction. In <u>Paladino</u>, parents sued a private elementary school because their fifth grader failed to perform at grade level and had to repeat the fifth grade. Id at 870. The court ruled in favor of the school, but only because the parents' claim of misrepresentation based upon misleading progress reports was contradicted by the record, which overwhelmingly demonstrated that the parents were in fact aware of their child's academic deficiencies. Id at 874. In addition, the parents' claim that the school failed to provide necessary tutorial services was contradicted by the record, which showed that the child had received tutoring in the fourth and fifth grades. Id at 875.

The claims presented by appellants in the instant case are similar to those presented in <u>Paladino</u>. The Squires allege that a contract existed, whereby they promised to pay tuition in exchange for Cambridge's promise to provide Brandon with a quality elementary education. Unlike the contract alleged in Paladino, the quality education for which the Squires contracted was to include certain specified services, such as appropriate individualized reading instruction and adequate diagnostic and remediation services should reading problems develop. Thus, in the instant case, the contract is alleged to contain sufficiently particularized services to support a claim for breach of contract.

The allegations of misrepresentation in the instant case are also similar to those in <u>Paladino</u>. The Squires allege that Ms. Fisher made specific representations as to the quality of Cambridge's educational offerings in response to the Squires' specific questions concerning Brandon's potential reading problems. As in Paladino, the Squires allege that Brandon's teachers sent progress reports which negligently or knowingly misrepresented that he was not having academic difficulties.** In Paladino, however, these claims of misrepresentation were rejected because there was evidence suggesting the parents had actual knowledge of their child's problems in school. In the instant case, interpreting the facts favorably to appellants, there is no evidence contradicting appellants' claim. Therefore, appellants' claim of misrepresentation is also valid.

Because we conclude that appellants have successfully articulated claims of breach of contract and misrepresentation upon which relief may be granted, we decline to address the justiciability of the claim for educational malpractice at this time. Accordingly, we reverse and remand for trial.

MOWBRAY, C. J., SPRINGER, STEFFEN and YOUNG, JJ., concur.

** The allegations of misrepresentation sound in negligence, except for the claim that the statements made by Cambridge were known to be false. For the purposes of this appeal, we will treat this cause of action as one for negligent misrepresentation. If the appellants choose to proceed on the theory of intentional misrepresentation as well as negligent misrepresentation and they believe they have stated a cause of action upon which to base such relief, that matter can be resolved by the district court.

[752] See <u>Peter W. v. San Francisco Unified School District</u>, 60 Cal. App3d 814, 131 Cal. Rptr 854 (1976) and <u>Donohue v. Copiague Union Free School District</u>, 47 N.Y.S. 2d 440, 391 N.E. 2d 1352 (1979).

[753] <u>Hunter v. Board of Education of Montgomery County</u>, 292 Md. 481, 439 A.2d 582 (1982); <u>Brosnan v. Livonia Public Schools</u>, 123 Mich. App. 377, 333 N.W.2d 288 (1983); <u>B.M. v. Montana</u>, 649 P.2d 425 (Mont. 1982).

[754] Sec. 49.291 NRS (1991).

[755] Sec. 49.290 NRS (1991).

[756] Does the duty of nondisclosure only apply to court proceedings? Can a teacher or counselor refuse to disclose the principal or the parents of the child information received in a counseling sessions? See <u>Eisel v. Board of Educ. of Montgomery County</u>, 597 A.2d 447 (Md.1991) Comment on case Zirkel, Perry, "Confident About Confidences?," Phi Delta Kappan, May 1992, p. 732.

psychological examiner for the purpose of counseling pupils, and who holds a valid certificate issued by the superintendent of public instruction authorizing the holder to engage in pupil counseling.

2.   Except for communications relating to any criminal offense the punishment for which ls death or life imprisonment,[757] communications by a pupil to a counselor in the course of counseling or psychologlcal examination are privileged communications, and a counselor shall not, without the consent of the pupil, be examined as a witness concerning any such communication in any civil or criminal action to which such pupils a party.[758]

---

[757]Sec. 432B.250 NRS (1993) specifically provides that counselors may not invoke the privilege granted by Chapter 49 for his/her failure to report child abuse, in cooperating with an agency which provides protective services or a guardian ad litem for a child or any proceeding to enforce the child abuse statutes.

[758] LEGISLATIVE HISTORY COUNSELOR \ TEACHER PRIVILEGE
§ 49.290 NRS COUNSELOR & PUPIL PRIVILEGE ADDED NRS 1973, 1840, A 1979, 1639; § 49.291 NRS TEACHER & PUPIL PRIVILEGE ADDED 1973, 1840 A 1979, 1987, 1014.
COMMITTEE ON JUDICIARY
COMMITTEE MINUTES
SENATE BILL NO. 316.APPROVED MAY 3, 1973
Minutes of the meeting of March 12, 1973
　　　SB 316
　　　　　　　Present-Senators. Foley, Bryan, Dodge, Swobe, Hecht, Wilson and also
　　　　　　　Richard Morgan, NEA
　　　　　　　Madeline Rutherford, Sparks JHS Counselor
　　　　　　　Jack Clark, Counselor University of Nevada
　　　　　　　John Bailey, Counselor University of Nevada
　　　　　　　Fred Doctor, School Psychologist and President of Washoe County Counselors Association
　　　　　　　Robert Groves, Deputy Attorney General Rep. State Bd. of Pharmacy
　　　　　　　Vern Calhoun, State Narcotics Division
　　　　　　　Carroll Nevin, Crime Commission
　　　S.B. 316---Grant privilege against disclosure for certain communications between students, counselors, and teachers.
　　　P. 242 of minutes Senate judiciary committee
　　　Mr. Morgan testified that the bill is necessary to increase the credibility of student confidence on their counselors and teachers. Senator Wilson felt that the bill should not encompass the iron bound language of privileged communications since the child would then be the only one who could waive that privilege. If one of the purposes of counseling is to protect the child, the counselors should have more flexibility to divulge any information they receive if it would help the child. Senator Wilson suggested deleting the traditional language of privilege and giving counselors immunity from testifying in court.
　　　Madeline Rutherford testified that students are reluctant to confide in counselors and ask them if what they confide would be revealed in court. Presently the counselors can be subpoenaed and must divulge testimony received from students. Chairman Close asked Mrs Rutherford if she shouldn't be compelled to reveal information relative to drugs. Mrs Rutherford repeated that information given by one student about another is hearsay and commented further that most information that students reveal in confidence is not drug related but abnormal sexual behavior.
　　　P. 243 cont.
　　　Jack Clark testified that this bill would conform the privilege procedure with the professional code of ethics.
　　　The code states that in order to have successful counseling, the first interest is the well-being of the student; therefore, confidentiality is necessary. Considering the welfare to the individual counseled, the counselor must recognize that his ability might not be adequate and, therefore, would request help from other qualified persons.
　　　Counselors mist recognize that some individuals are no longer responsible for their own behavior and the counselor must be willing to assume responsibility for them. These individuals usually give their permission for the counselors to do this.
　　　Mr. Clark stated that he is not interested in a bill which would limit him beyond the code or ethics of lock him into a situation where he could not communicate with a third party unless he got a waiver or consent from the person he is counseling.
　　　Chairman Close remarked that he would be willing to give more confidentiality to a university counselor than grammar or middle school counselors. He feels very protective toward the family and child in lower grades because students are involved. Mr Clark felt that the junior or high school counselor should have the same consideration since in most cases the student is the healthiest member of the family.
　　　Mr. John Bailey testified that the goal of counseling is to increase the individual's responsibility for making his own decisions. This is sometimes tested out in fantasy. The counselor's purpose is not to seek truth, but to understand the counselee from his changing perceptions of truth. Relating to the drug problem, quite a few junior high school students admit to taking drugs so that they can be popular with other students.
　　　Mr Fred Doctor stated that counselors in Washoe County School District are in full support of this bill and they would be in agreement to take out the traditional privilege language. The counselors want to be able to use their own individual judgment.
Minutes March 13, 1973 Committee on the Judiciary
　　　Present
　　　　　　　Chairman　　　　Close
　　　　　　　　　　　　　　　　Foley
　　　　　　　　　　　　　　　　Bryan
　　　　　　　　　　　　　　　　Dodge
　　　　　　　　　　　　　　　　Hecht
　　　　　　　　　　　　　　　　Swobe
　　　　　　　　　　　　　　　　Wilson
　　　　　　　Sharon Green
　　　　　　　Howard Hill Director DMV
　　　　　　　Frank Daykin Legislative Counsel Bureau
　　S.B. 316
　　P. 253

Breach of Duty

When an educator by some action or inaction fails to use reasonable care in supervising students under his/her control he/she is said to have breached a duty. An educator who violates the well known constitutional rights of students under his/her control is also said to have breached his/her duty.

Bound up in a determination of this element of a civil wrong is the doctrine of foreseeability.[759] Courts have often stated that harm must be reasonably foreseen as probable by a person of ordinary prudence under the circumstances if the conduct resulting in such harm is to constitute negligence. There is no necessity, however, that the actual harm that resulted from the conduct be foreseen.The importance of this concept to liability analysis will become apparent as we consider various cases.

Proximate Cause

The breach of an educator's duty of reasonable care must be the proximate cause of the injury to another person or property. Judge Mosley's jury instruction provides the legal definition of proximate cause in Nevada tort litigation.

> A proximate cause of an injury is a cause which, in natural and continuous sequence, produces the injury, and without which the injury would not have occurred.[760]

Damages

The final element of proof in a negligence action is damages (harm). The injured party must prove that he was actually harmed in order to recover money damages. In determining the amount of damages juries may take into consideration the nature, extent and duration of the injuries they believe from the evidence have been sustained and decide on a sum of money sufficient to reasonably and fairly compensate the plaintiff for the following items:

1. The reasonable medical expenses the complainant has necessarily incurred as a result of the accident.

2. The medical expenses which the jury believes the plaintiff is reasonably certain to incur in the future as a result of the accident.

3. Plaintiff's loss of earnings from the date of the accident to the present.

Senator Dodge objected to the bill stating that the legislatures should not extend privileged communications beyond the present concept because other groups will come in and ask for the same privilege.

Senator Wilson objected that the amendment he suggested would remove the thrust of the bull from the common law privilege concept and limit it to a counselor not being obligated to testify.

Senator Hecht stated that he does not agree with the concept of the bill. Senator Close stated he didn't feel the bill would accomplish as much as the counselors expected to accomplish, but on the other hand did not feel it would do any harm to exempt them from testifying n court.

March 15, 1973 Committee on the Judiciary
P. 263

Senator Close read the amendments which would limit the bill to be applicable only to counselors being exempted from testifying in court.

Senator Dodge objected to the bill on the grounds that the legislature would be setting a precedent and would have then to honor all requests from other groups.

Senator Bryan moved to amend amend and Do Pass Seconded by Senator Wilson

Yeas	4 Close, Foley, Bryan, Swobe
Nays	3 Dodge, Hecht, Wilson

April 18 1973 Committee on Judiciary
P. 460
S.B. 316

Mr Morgan (NEA) explained that the assembly had amended (S.B. 316) the bill further and by so doing reinserted the common law privilege which was removed by Senate Committee) this committee. Senator Bryan moved not to concur in the amendment and go to conference committee to restore the bill to the form of the first reprint, Motion seconded by Senator Wilson. Motion carried.

[759] One of the practical problems inherent with application of the forseeability doctrine is that it is applied by courts using 20/20 hindsight.

[760] Mosley supra.

4. The loss of earnings which the jury believes plaintiff is reasonably certain to experience in the future as a result of the accident.

5. The physical and mental pain, suffering, anguish and disability endured by the plaintiff from the date of the accident to the present.

6. The physical and mental pain, suffering, anguish and disability which the jury believes plaintiff is reasonably certain to experience in the future as a result of the accident.

Whether any of these elements of damage been by the evidence is for the jury to determine. Neither sympathy nor speculation is a proper basis for determining damages. However, absolute certainty as to the damages is not required. It is only required that the injured person prove each item if damage by a preponderance of the evidence.[761]

Application of the Conceptual Framework

Liability is determined on a case by case basis through application of the conceptual framework outlined above. As a result, the outcome of each case depends on the facts of the case. There are not many bright lines which define whether a person acted as a reasonable person under all the circumstances or violated their duty of reasonable care. Jurors charged with determining the issue of liability are not only instructed to consider only the evidence presented at the trial but also to bring to the consideration of the evidence their everyday common sense and judgment as 'reasonable men and women.' They may also draw reasonable inferences from the evidence which they feel is justified in the light of common experience, keeping in mind that such inferences should not be based on speculation or guess. In addition, jurors are admonished that their verdict may never be influenced by sympathy, prejudice or public opinion.

So the risk of liability is reduced to the extent that an educators actions or inaction regarding a child meet or exceed those of a reasonable and prudent person.

Now let us apply the conceptual framework. The scene is a high school gym class with 50 students. The students range in age from 14 to 16 years old. The teacher convened the class, checked attendance and told the boys to "shoot around" with basketballs. He then left the class unattended for 25 minutes while he went to the teachers lounge for a cup of coffee. While he was gone the game of basketball deteriorated into a game of keep-away in 10 minutes. Subsequently, it got rougher including tripping and pushing. A student was pushed into another student, fell to the floor and sustained a severe head injury. The student sues the teacher. What duty was involved? Did the teacher violate the duty? Was the breach of duty the proximate cause of the students injury? Was the student harmed? What is your decision and why?

There are many cases where students sustained injury during a teachers absence from the classroom. If an injury occurs in the teacher's absence should the teacher always be found responsible for the injury and required to compensate the injured student? Courts and juries have not always found educators liable under those circumstances. Can you think of circumstances where absence from class would be the action of a reasonable and prudent person under the circumstances?

Courts have indicated a number of relevant considerations in determining whether the absent teacher was negligent:

---

[761] Moaley supra.

1. What activity were the students engaged in during the absence?
2. What instrumentalities were the students working with at the time of the absence? (band saws, dangerous chemicals, scissors)
3. What was the age and composition of the class?
4. What had been the teachers past experience with the class and its propensities?
5. What was the reason for and the duration of the teacher's absence?

Now suppose you wish to be absent from your classroom. What steps can and should you take to reduce your risk of liability if an accident occurs in your absence?

Although there are few bright lines defining liability issues, an educator can reduce his/her risk of negligent action simply by pausing before a proposed action and asking him/herself silently whether the proposed action would be taken by a reasonable and prudent person.

C
CONSTITUTIONAL TORTS

We know that educators can be held liable for violating the constitutional rights of students. The principle was established in the landmark case entitled **Wood v. Strickland.**[762]

WOOD
v.
STRICKLAND
420 U.S. 308, 95 S.Ct. 992 (1975)

MR. JUSTICE WHITE delivered the opinion of the Court.

Respondents Peggy Strickland and Virginia Crain brought this lawsuit against petitioners, who were members of the school board at the time in question, two school administrators, and the Special School District of Mena, Ark., purporting to assert a cause of action under 42 U. S. C. §1983, and claiming that their federal constitutional rights to due process were infringed under color of state law by their expulsion from the Mena Public High School on the grounds of their violation of a school regulation prohibiting the use or possession of intoxicating beverages at school or school activities. ...After the declaration of a mistrial arising from the jury's failure to reach a verdict, the District Court directed verdicts in favor of petitioners on the ground that petitioners were immune from damages suits absent proof of malice in the sense of ill will toward respondents. The Court of Appeals, finding that the facts showed a violation of respondents' rights to "substantive due process," reversed and remanded for appropriate injunctive relief [763] and a new trial on the question of damages. A petition for rehearing en banc was denied with three judges dissenting. See id., at 191. Certiorari was granted to consider whether this application of due process by the Court of Appeals was warranted and whether that court's expression of a standard governing immunity for school board members from liability for compensatory damages under 42 U. S. C. 1983 was the correct one.

---

[762] 420 U.S. 308, 95 S.Ct. 992 (1975).

[763] The Court of Appeals noted that reinstatement was no longer possible since the term of expulsion had ended, but that the respondents were entitled to have the records of the expulsions expunged and to be relieved of any other continuing punishment, if any.

I

The violation of the school regulation [764] prohibiting the use or possession of intoxicating beverages at school or school activities with which respondents were charged concerned their "spiking" of the punch served at a meeting of an extracurricular school organization attended by parents and students. At the time in question, respondents were 16 years old and were in the 10th grade. The relevant facts begin with their discovery that the punch had not been prepared for the meeting as previously planned. The girls then agreed to "spike" it. Since the county in which the school is located is "dry," respondents and a third girl drove across the state border into Oklahoma and purchased two 12-ounce bottles of "Right Time," a malt liquor. They then bought six 10-ounce bottles of a soft drink, and, after having mixed the contents of the eight bottles in an empty milk carton, returned to school. Prior to the meeting, the girls experienced second thoughts about the wisdom of their prank, but by then they were caught up in the force of events and the intervention of other girls prevented them from disposing of the illicit punch. The punch was served at the meeting, without apparent effect.

Ten days later, the teacher in charge of the extracurricular group and meeting, Mrs. Curtis Powell, having heard something about the "spiking," questioned the girls about it. Although first denying any knowledge, the girls admitted their involvement after the teacher said that she would handle the punishment herself. The next day, however, she told the girls that the incident was becoming increasingly the subject of talk in the school and that the principal, P. T. Waller, would probably hear about it. She told them that her job was in jeopardy but that she would not force them to admit to Waller what they had done. If they did not go to him then, however, she would not be able to help them if the incident became "distorted." The three girls then went to Waller and admitted their role in the affair. He suspended them from school for a maximum two-week period, subject to the decision of the school board. Waller also told them that the board would meet that night, that the girls could tell their parents about the meeting, but that the parents should not contact any members of the board .

Neither the girls nor their parents attended the school board meeting that night. Both Mrs. Powell and Waller, after making their reports concerning the incident, recommended leniency. At this point, a telephone call was received by S. L. Inlow, then the superintendent of schools from Mrs. Powell's husband, also a teacher at the high school, who reported that he had heard that the third girl involved had been in a fight that evening at a basketball game. Inlow informed the meeting of the news, although he did not mention the name of the girl involved. Mrs. Powell and Waller then withdrew their recommendations of leniency, and the board voted to expel the girls from school for the remainder of the semester, a period of approximately three months.

The board subsequently agreed to hold another meeting on the matter, and one was held approximately two weeks after the first meeting. The girls, their parents, and their counsel attended this session. The board began with a reading of

---

[764] "3. Suspension
"b. Valid causes for suspension from school on first offense: Pupils found to be guilty of any of the following shall be suspended from school on the first offense for the balance of the semester and such suspension will be noted on the permanent record of the student along with reason for suspension
"(4) The use of intoxicating beverage or possession of same at school or at school sponsored activity." App. 102.

a written statement of facts as it had found them.[765] The girls admitted mixing the malt liquor into the punch with the intent of "spiking" it, but asked the board to forgo its rule punishing such violations by such substantial suspensions. Neither Mrs. Powell nor Waller was present at this meeting. The board voted not to change its policy and, as before, to expel the girls for the remainder of the semester.[766]

II

The District Court instructed the jury that a decision for respondents had to be premised upon a finding that petitioners acted with malice in expelling them and defined "malice" as meaning "ill will against a person— a wrongful act done intentionally without just cause or excuse." In ruling for petitioners after the jury had been unable to agree, the District Court found "as a matter of law" that there was no evidence from which malice could be inferred.

The Court of Appeals, however, viewed both the instruction and the decision of the District Court as being erroneous. Specific intent to harm wrongfully, it held, was not a requirement for the recovery of damages. Instead, "[i]t need only be established that the defendants did not, in the light of all the circumstances, act in good faith. The test is an objective, rather than a subjective, one."

Petitioners as members of the school board assert here, as they did below, an absolute immunity from liability under §1983 and at the very least seek to reinstate the judgment of the District Court. If they are correct and the District Court's dismissal should be sustained, we need go no further in this case. Moreover, the immunity question involves the construction of a federal statute, and our practice is to deal with possibly dispositive statutory issues before reaching questions turning on the construction of the Constitution. We essentially sustain the position of the Court of Appeals with respect to the immunity issue.

****

Common-law tradition, recognized in our prior decisions and strong public-policy reasons also lead to a construction of §1983 extending a qualified good-faith immunity to school board members from liability for damages under that section. Although there have been differing emphases and formulations of the common-law immunity of public school officials in cases of student expulsion or suspension, state courts have generally recognized that such officers should be protected from tort liability under state law for all good-faith, nonmalicious action taken to fulfill their official duties.

As the facts of this case reveal, school board members function at different times in the nature of legislators and adjudicators in the school disciplinary process. Each of these functions necessarily involves the exercise of discretion, the weighing of many factors, and the formulation of long-term policy. "Like legislators and judges, these officers are entitled to rely on traditional sources for the factual

---

[765] "FACTS FOUND BY SCHOOL BOARD
"1. That Virginia Crain, Peggy Strickland and Jo Wall are students of Mena High School and subject to the governing rules and policies of Mena High School.
"2. That on or about February 7, 1972 these three girls were charged with the responsibility of providing refreshments for a school function, being a gathering of students of the Home Economic class and some of their parents, on school premises, being the auditorium building of Mena High School, and being under the direction of Mrs. Curtis Powell.
"3. That the three girls in question traveled to Oklahoma, purchased a number of bottles of malt liquor, a beer type beverage, and put two or more of the bottles of the drink into the punch or liquid refreshment which was to be served to members of the class and parents"App. 137.
        The Court of Appeals in its statement of the facts observed that the malt liquor and ,soft drinks were mixed by the girls prior to their return to school, 485 F. 2d, at 187, and petitioners in their brief recite the facts in this manner. Brief for Petitioners 5. This discrepancy in the board's findings of fact is not material to any issue now before the Court.
[766] By taking a correspondence course and an extra course later, the girls were able to graduate with their class. Tr. of Oral Arg. 38-39.

information on which they decide and act." As with executive officers faced with instances of civil disorder, school officials, confronted with student behavior causing or threatening disruption. also have an "obvious need for prompt action, and decisions must be made in reliance on factual information supplied by others."

Liability for damages for every action which is found subsequently to have been violative of a student's constitutional rights and to have caused compensable injury would unfairly impose upon the school decisionmaker the burden of mistakes made in good faith in the course of exercising his discretion within the scope of his official duties. School board members, among other duties, must judge whether there have been violations of school regulations and, if so, the appropriate sanctions for the violations. Denying any measure of immunity in these circumstances "would contribute not to principled and fearless decisionmaking but to intimidation." The imposition of monetary costs for mistakes which were not unreasonable in the light of all the circumstances would undoubtedly deter even the most conscientious school decisionmaker from exercising his judgment independently, forcefully, and in a manner best serving the long-term interest of the school and the students. The most capable candidates for school board positions might be deterred from seeking office if heavy burdens upon their private resources from monetary liability were a likely prospect during their tenure.

These considerations have undoubtedly played a prime role in the development by state courts of a qualified immunity protecting school officials from liability for damages in lawsuits claiming improper suspensions or expulsions. But at the same time, the judgment implicit in this common-law development is that absolute immunity would not be justified since it would not sufficiently increase the ability of school officials to exercise their discretion in a forthright manner to warrant the absence of a remedy for students subjected to intentional or other-wise inexcusable deprivations.

...We think there must be a degree of immunity if the work of the schools is to go forward; and however worded the immunity must be such that public school officials understand that action taken in the good-faith fulfillment of their responsibilities and within the bounds of reason under all the circumstances will not be punished and that they need not exercise their discretion with undue timidity.

> "Public officials whether governors, mayors, or police, legislators, or judges who fail to make decisions when they are needed or who do not act to implement decisions when they are made do not fully and faithfully perform the duties of their offices. Implicit in the idea that officials have some immunity— absolute or qualified—for their acts is a recognition that they may err. The concept of immunity assumes this and goes on to assume that it is better to risk some error and possible injury from such error than not to decide or act at all."
> Scheuer v. Rhodes, 416 U. S. at 241-242 (footnote omitted).

The disagreement between the Court of Appeals and the District Court over the immunity standard in this case has been put in terms of an "objective" versus a "subjective" test of good faith. As we see it the appropriate standard necessarily contains elements of both. The official himself must be acting sincerely and with a belief that he is doing right but an act violating a student's constitutional rights can be no more justified by ignorance or disregard of settled, indisputable law on the part of one entrusted with supervision of students' daily lives than by the presence of actual malice. To be entitled to a special exemption from the categorical remedial language of §1983 in a case in which his action violated a student's constitutional rights, a school board member, who has voluntarily undertaken the task of supervising the operation of the school and the activities of the students, must be held to a standard of conduct based not only on permissible intentions, but also on knowledge of the basic, unquestioned constitutional rights of his charges. Such a standard imposes neither an unfair burden upon a person assuming a responsible public office requiring a high degree of intelligence and judgment for the proper fulfillment of its duties, nor an unwarranted burden in light of the value which civil rights have in our legal system. Any lesser standard would deny much of the promise of §1983. Therefore, in the specific context of school discipline, we hold that a school board member is not immune from liability for damages under §1983 if he knew or reasonably should have known that the action he took within his sphere of official responsibility would violate the constitutional rights of the student affected, or if he took the action with the malicious intention to cause a deprivation of constitutional rights or other injury to the student. That is not to say that school board members are "charged with predicting the future course of constitutional law." A compensatory award will be appropriate only if the school board member has acted with such an impermissible motivation or with such disregard of the student's clearly established constitutional rights that his action cannot reasonable be characterized as being in good faith.

III

The Court of Appeals, based upon its review of the facts but without the benefit of the transcript of the testimony given at the four-day trial to the jury in the District Court, found that the board had made its decision to expel the girls on the basis of no evidence that the school regulation had been violated:

> "To justify the suspension, it was necessary for the Board to establish that the students possessed or used an 'intoxicating' beverage at a school-sponsored activity. No evidence was presented at either meeting to establish the alcoholic content of the liquid brought to the campus. Moreover, the Board made no finding that the liquid was intoxicating. The only evidence as to the nature of the drink was that supplied by the girls, and it is clear that they did not know whether the beverage was intoxicating or not."

****

When the regulation is construed to prohibit the use and possession of beverages containing alcohol there was no absence of evidence before the school board to prove the charge against respondents. The girls had admitted that they intended to "spike" the punch and that they had mixed malt liquor into the punch that was served. The third girl estimated at the time of their admissions to Waller that the malt liquor had an alcohol content of 20%. After the expulsion decision had been made and this litigation had begun, it was conclusively determined that the malt liquor in fact had an alcohol content not exceeding 3.2% by weight. Testimony at trial put the alcohol content of the punch served at 0.91%.

Given the fact that there was evidence supporting the charge against respondents, the contrary judgment of the Court of Appeals is improvident. It is not the role of the federal courts to set aside decisions of school administrators which the court may view as lacking a basis in wisdom or compassion. Public high school students do have substantive and procedural rights while at school. But §1983 does not extend the right to reliquidate in federal court evidentiary questions arising in school disciplinary proceedings or the proper construction of school regulations. The system of public education that has evolved in this Nation relies necessarily upon the discretion and judgment of school administrators and school board members, and §1983 was not intended to be a vehicle for federal-court corrections of errors in the exercise of that discretion which do not rise to the level of violations of specific constitutional guarantees.

IV

The judgment of the Court of Appeals is vacated and the case remanded for further proceedings consistent with this opinion. So ordered.

MR. JUSTICE POWELL, with whom THE CHIEF JUSTICE, MR. JUSTICE BLACKMUN and MR. JUSTICE REHNQUIST join, concurring in part and dissenting in part.

The holding of the Court on the immunity issue is set forth in the margin. It would impose personal liability on a school official who acted sincerely and in the utmost good faith, but who was found—after the fact—to have acted in "ignorance . . . of settled, indisputable law ." Or, as the Court also puts it, the school official must be held to a standard of conduct based not only on good faith "but also on knowledge of the basic, unquestioned constitutional rights of his charges. Moreover, ignorance of the law is explicitly equated with "actual malice."

This harsh standard, requiring knowledge of what is characterized as "settled, indisputable law," leaves little substance to the doctrine of qualified immunity. The Court's decision appears to rest on an unwarranted assumption as to what lay school officials know or can know about the law and constitutional rights. These officials will now act at the peril of some judge or jury subsequently finding that a good-faith belief as to the applicable law was mistaken and hence actionable.[767]

The Court states the standard of required knowledge in two cryptic phrases: "settled, indisputable law" and "unquestioned constitutional rights." Presumably these are intended to mean the same thing, although the meaning of neither phrase is likely to be self-evident to constitutional law scholars much less the average school board member. One need only look to the decisions of this Court---to our reversals, our recognition of evolving concepts, and our five-to-four splits—to recognize the hazard of even informed prophecy as to what are "unquestioned constitutional rights." Consider, for example, the recent five-to-four decision in Goss v. Lopez, 419 U. S. 565 (1975), holding that a junior high school pupil routinely suspended for as much as a single day is entitled to due process. I suggest that most lawyers and judges would have thought, prior to that decision, that the law to the contrary was settled, indisputable, and unquestioned.

****

---

[767] The opinion indicates that actual malice is presumed where one acts in ignorance of the law; thus it would appear that even good-faith reliance on the advice of counsel is of no avail.

STUDY QUESTIONS

    1. What is the test for determining whether educators have qualified immunity from liability for constitutional torts?

    2. How does the holding of the Court impact on professional practice?

****

    The test for determining qualified immunity for school officials was modified in **Harlow v. Fitzgerald** 457 U.S. 800, 102 S.Ct. 272 (1982). In that case the Court eliminated the subjective aspect of the <u>Wood</u> test (good faith) and determined that officials conduct that violates the clearly established statutory or constitutional rights of which a reasonable person would have known will subject the official to liability.

    After <u>Wood,</u> school board members, administrators and teachers could be held personally liable for violations of students constitutional rights.[768] But what standard would the courts apply to assess damage issues in constitutional cases? Many argued that if a school official violated the well known constitutional rights of students substantial damages should be awarded even in the absence of harm being established. That issue was resolved the the case of **Cary v. Piphus.**[769]

CARY

v.

PIPHUS

435 U.S. 247, 98 S.Ct. 1042 (1978)

MR. JUSTICE POWELL delivered the opinion of the Court.

    In this case, brought under 42 U. S. C §1983, we consider the elements and prerequisites for recovery of damages by students who were suspended from public elementary and secondary schools without procedural due process. The Court of Appeals for the Seventh Circuit held that the students are entitled to recover substantial nonpunitive damages even if their suspensions were justified, and even if they do not prove that any other actual injury was caused by the denial of procedural due process. We disagree, and hold that in the absence of proof of actual injury, the students are entitled to recover only nominal damages.

I

Respondent, Jarius Piphus was a freshman at Chicago Vocational High School during the 1973-1974 school year. On January 23,1974, during school hours, the school principal saw Piphus and another student standing outdoors on school property passing back and forth what the principal described as an irregularly shaped cigarette. The principal approached the students unnoticed and smelled what he believed was the strong odor of burning marihuana. He also saw Piphus try to pass a packet of cigarette papers to the other student. When the students became aware of the principal's presence, they threw the cigarette into a nearby hedge.

    The principal took the students to the school's disciplinary office and directed the assistant principal to impose the "usual" 20-day suspension for violation of the school rule against the use of drugs. The students protested that they had not been smoking marihuana, but to no avail. Piphus was allowed to remain at school,

---

[768]Dagley, David L. & Oldaker, Lawrence Lee, "Are School Districts State Actors (Alter Egos)?," 79 Ed.Law Rep. [367] (February 25, 1993).

[769] 435 U.S. 247, 98 S.Ct. 1042 (1978)

although not in class, for the remainder of the school day while the assistant principal tried, without success, to reach his mother.

A suspension notice was sent to Piphus' mother, and a few days after two meetings were arranged among Piphus, his mother, his sister, school officials, and representatives from a legal aid clinic. The purpose of the meetings was not to determine whether Piphus had been smoking marihuana, but rather to explain the reasons for the suspension. Following an unfruitful exchange of views, Piphus and his mother, as guardian ad litem, filed suit against petitioners in Federal District Court under 42 U. S. C. §1983 ...charging that Piphus had been suspended without due process of law in violation of the Fourteenth Amendment. The complaint sought declaratory and injunctive relief, together with actual and punitive damages in the amount of $3,000. Piphus was readmitted to school under a temporary restraining order after eight days of his suspension.

Respondent Silas Brisco was in the sixth grade at Clara Barton Elementary School in Chicago during the 1973-1974 school year. On September 11, 1973, Brisco came to school wearing one small earring. The previous school year the school principal had issued a rule against the wearing of earrings by male students because he believed that this practice denoted membership in certain street gangs and increased the likelihood that gang members would terrorize other students. Brisco was reminded of this rule, but he refused to remove the earring, asserting that it was a symbol of black pride, not of gang membership.

The assistant principal talked to Brisco's mother, advising her that her son would be suspended for 20 days if he did not remove the earring. Brisco's mother supported her son's position, and a 20-day suspension was imposed. Brisco and his mothers guardian ad litem, filed suit in Federal District Court under 42 U. S. C. §1983 charging that Brisco had been suspended without due process of law in violation of the Fourteenth Amendment. The complaint sought declaratory and injunctive relief, together with actual and punitive damages in the amount of $5,000. Brisco was readmitted to school during the pendency of proceedings for a preliminary injunction after 17 days of his suspension.

Piphus' and Brisco's cases were consolidated for trial and submitted on stipulated records. The District Court held that both students had been suspended without procedural due process.[770] It also held that petitioners were not entitled to qualified immunity from damages under the second branch of Wood v. Strickland, 420 U. S. 308 (1975), because they "should have known that a lengthy suspension without any adjudicative hearing of any type" would violate procedural due process. App. to Pet. for Cert. A14.[771] Despite these holdings, the District Court declined to award damages because:

> "Plaintiffs put no evidence in the record to quantify their damages, and the record is completely devoid of any evidence which could even form the basis of a speculative inference measuring the

---

[770] The District Court read Goss v. Lopez, supra, as requiring "more formal procedures" for suspensions of more than 10 days than for suspensions of less than 10 days, and it. set forth a detailed list of procedural requirements. See App. to Pet. for Cert. A11-A12. Petitioners have not challenged either the holding that respondents were denied procedural due process, or the listing of rights that must be granted.

[771] Although respondents' suspensions occurred before Goss v. Lopez was decided, the District Court thought that petitioners should have been placed on notice that the suspensions violated procedural due process by Linwood v. Board of Ed. of City of Peoria, 463 F. 2d 763 (CA7), cert. denied, 409 U . S. 1027 (1972) . Petitioners have not challenged this holding.

The District Court expressly held that petitioners did not lose their immunity under the first branch of Wood v. Strickland, i. e., that they did not act "with the malicious intention to cause a deprivation of constitutional rights or other injury to the student," 420 U. S., at 322: "Here the record is barren of evidence suggesting that any of the defendants acted maliciously in enforcing disciplinary policies against the plaintiffs. Undoubtedly defendants believed that they were protecting the integrity of the educational process." App. to Pet. for Cert. A13.

extent of their injuries. Plaintiffs' claims for damages, therefore, fail for complete lack of proof." Ibid.

The court also stated that the students were entitled to declaratory relief and to deletion of the suspensions from their school records, but for reasons that are not apparent the court failed to enter an order to that effect. Instead, it simply dismissed the complaints. No finding was made as to whether respondents could have been suspended if they had received procedural due process.

****

So the Court held that in an action under §1983 for the deprivation of procedural due process, a plaintiff must prove that he actually was injured by the deprivation before he may recover substantial "non-punitive" damages.

****

STUDY QUESTIONS

1. Why should educators keep informed of the nature of student constitutional rights?

2. Does the holding of the Court in the Cary case give license to educators to violate students' constitutional rights? Why? Why not?

3. In your judgment will the test for determining liability discourage individuals   from serving on school boards, as school administrators or teachers?

****

D

NEVADA 'PEACE OF MIND' STATUTES!!!

Nevada has enacted a limited waiver of its sovereign immunity from suit. This waiver means that school boards and educators may be held to account for their negligent conduct.

The waiver of immunity was accompanied by another important change in Nevada laws. I call the change the Nevada 'Peace of Mind' statutes.[772] In general

---

[772] Sec. 41.031--41.039 NRS (1993). The Nevada supreme court has recently decided a case involving the Clark County School District which explains the nature and scope of the protection offered by the **'Peace of Mind' statutes**

Nardozzi v. Clark County School District, 108 Nev. Advance Opinion 2 (1992)

By the Court, Rose

Appellant Linda Nardozzi (Nardozzi) slipped and fell at the entrance of Tomiyasu Elementary School, the property of respondent Clark County School District (CCSD). As a result of the fall, Nardozzi broke her ankle in several places. She filed suit against CCSD, alleging that it negligently failed to take safety precautions by keeping the floor dry on a rainy day. CCSD denied any knowledge of the alleged hazardous condition and claimed total immunity under NRS 41.033. The district court granted CCSD's motion for summary judgment. Nardozzi argues that the court erred because there are disputed issues of material fact and because implied knowledge is sufficient to circumvent the governmental immunity established in NRS 41.033.** See NRCP 56(e).

Based on her contention that implied notice is sufficient to circumvent the governmental immunity established by NRS 41.033, Nardozzi argues that material facts remain in dispute as to whether CCSD had implied notice of the hazardous condition. NRS 41.033 provides:

Conditions and limitations on actions: Failure to inspect or discover. No action may be brought under NRS 41.031 or against an officer or employee of the state or any of its agencies or political subdivisions which is based upon:

1. Failure to inspect any building, structure or vehicle, or to inspect the construction of any street, public highway or other public work to determine any hazards, deficiencies or other matters, whether or not there is a duty to inspect; or

2. Failure to discover such hazard, deficiency or other matter, whether or not an inspection is made.

This court has held that immunity will not bar actions based upon a public entity's failure to act reasonably when the entity has express knowledge of a hazard. Lotter v. Clark Co. Bd. of Commissioners, 106 Nev. 366, 368, 793 P.2d 1320, 1322 (1990) (where county inspectors had knowledge of house's framing defects and approved framing despite those defects, NRS 41.033 providing immunity to county from liability to purchaser for negligent inspection or failure to inspect did not apply). Nardozzi argues that the Lotter holding applies to implied knowledge of the defect, because Mr. Lotter's complaint alleged that any inspection of the premises would have led to the immediate discovery of the defects. Lotter is distinguishable from the case at bar, however, because the basis of our decision was that there were sufficient facts presented to show that the inspection was actually made, and in so doing, it would have been impossible to have avoided actual knowledge of the defects. See also Crucil v. Carson City, 95 Nev. 583, 585, 600 P.2d 216, 217 (1979) (where automobile accident victims alleged that city had actual knowledge of downed condition of stop sign, complaint satisfied requirements of NRCP 8). In Crucil, the complaint alleged that the city had either actual and/or constructive knowledge of the hazardous condition. The court found that although NRS 41.033 grants immunity when the State has failed to inspect or discover a hazard, the statute does not apply in cases where the complaint alleges actual knowledge of the hazard. Despite

374

terms the legislation requires that public employers offer protection when their employees are named as defendants in lawsuits based on allegations of negligent conduct.

There are four preconditions which must be present for the statutory protection to become operative.

First, the action which resulted in the claimed injury must have occurred in the course of employment. Second, the action must have been taken in 'good faith.' Third, the court papers delivered to the employee (served on the employee) must be promptly delivered to the official attorney of the school district with a written demand that the school district defend the employee or pay reasonable attorney fees. Fourth, the employee must cooperate in defending against the allegations.

Following a trial if the court determines that the employee was acting in good faith in the course of their employment any damages awarded against them up to the statutory maximum that can be awarded becomes the responsibility of the public employer. In addition, the attorney fees expended in the defense of the employee are the responsibility of the employer win or lose if the findings of good faith and acting in the course of employment accompany the damage award.

There is good reason to label these provisions of Nevada law as 'Peace of Mind' statutes.[773]

Finally, Nevada lawmakers expanded legal defense protections for employees charged with certain crimes committed within the scope of their employment during the 1989 legislative session.[774]

Nardozzi's interpretations of the relevant cases, the express knowledge exception to NRS 41.033 has not been extended to include situations in which the government had only implied knowledge of the condition. Therefore, we conclude that Nardozzi's argument lacks merit.

Nardozzi further argues that even if CCSD is immune from liability for implied knowledge, CCSD had actual notice of the hazardous condition. She asserts that a Clark County employee acknowledged that he had seen water on the floor of the entryway shortly before Nardozzi fell. That individual, however, was employed by the Clark County Parks and Recreation Program not CCSD, and there is no evidence that he informed a CCSD employee of the hazardous condition. The school district and the county are separate entities with different governing boards. See Walsh v. Clark County School District, 82 Nev. 414, 419 P.2d 774 (1966). Therefore the knowledge of the Clark County employee cannot be imputed to CCSD. We hereby affirm the decision of the district court.
SPRINGER, STEFFEN and YOUNG, JJ., concur.
MOWBRAY, C. J., dissenting:
    Respectfully, I dissent.
    One purpose of NRS 41.031, Nevada s waiver of immunity statute, is to compensate victims of governmental negligence in circumstances like those in which victims of private negligence would be compensated. Harrigan v. City of Reno, 86 Nev. 678, 475 P.2d 94 (1970). Another purpose, often overlooked though equally important, is to encourage officers and employees of the state, state agencies and political subdivisions of the state to perform their duties using reasonable care. The majority today defeats both of these public policies. Not only does the majority deny appellant the opportunity to obtain compensation from the state for injuries that may well have resulted from governmental negligence, but in doing so, the majority unwittingly promotes "willful blindness" as a means by which the state can avoid tort liability. Officers and employees will now be encouraged to close their eyes to hazardous conditions they confront while performing their duties.
    Appellant has alleged that respondent school district had actual knowledge of the hazardous pool of water inside the school building. Construing the pleadings and documentary evidence in favor of appellant, I perceive a genuine issue of material fact concerning the school district's knowledge of the pool of water. See Wiltsie v. Baby Grand Corp., 105 Nev. 291, 774 P.2d 432 (1989). Moreover, a summary judgment motion should not be granted if there is any possibility that the factual aspects of the case will look different at trial from the evidence tendered in support of and against the motion. See Adickes v. S.H. Kress & Co., 398 U.S. 144 (1970). Here, discovery and other pretrial procedures may well disclose additional evidence sufficient to persuade a trier of fact of the truth of appellant's allegation. Summary judgment was thus improper.
**CCSD argues that this court does not have jurisdiction to consider this appeal because Nardozzi filed notice of appeal before the district court entered its order denying rehearing. According to CCSD, a motion for rehearing is the functional equivalent to a motion under NRCP 59, which provides that an appeal is void when notice is filed before the formal disposition of any timely postjudgment motion filed under Rule 50(b), Rule 52(b) or Rule 59. A motion for rehearing cannot reasonably be construed as a motion to alter or amend the judgment pursuant to Rule 59(e). Alvis v. State Gaming Control Bd., 99 Nev. 184, 186 n.l, 660 P.2d 980, 981 n.l (1983). We therefore conclude that CCSD's argument lacks merit.
[773] The 'Peace of Mind' statutes are applicable to students at the University assigned for training as student teachers See Sec. 391.095 NRS (1991)
[774] Sec. 391.271 NRS (1993) reads as follows:
School district to provide for legal defense of employee charged with certain crimes committed within scope of employment; exceptions .
1. If a person who is or was employed by a school district is charged by criminal complaint with assault, battery or a similar crime as a result of his actions in attempting to maintain a safe or peaceful school environment, the school district shall, as soon as practicable, provide for the legal defense of the employee in that case. The school district shall not require a waiver of the attorney-client privilege as a condition of providing the defense.
2. In any case in which the school district is required to provide for an employee's legal defense pursuant to subsection 1, the court shall include in its judgment a finding as to whether the conduct of the defendant which was alleged to be criminal was within the scope of his employment and whether the conduct was malicious or wanton.

CHAPTER SUMMARY

Educator liability is determined pursuant to state tort law principles. School employees owe a duty of reasonable care to the children they supervise. Educators do not guarantee the safety of students while under school supervision. In order to establish liability an injured party must prove by a preponderance of the evidence the existence of a duty, violation of that duty, proximate cause and damages. The reasonableness of an action is based on consideration of all the facts.

Public educators may be sued for constitutional violations. Real harm must be established before substantial damages can be awarded. Educators are held accountable for recognizing and respecting the clearly established constitutional rights of students.

Nevada has enacted a limited waiver of its sovereign immunity. It has also enacted a law which offers protection to those employees who act in good faith in the course of their duties.

---

3. If the court finds that the conduct of the defendant was not within the scope of his employment or was wanton or malicious, the employee or former employee is liable to the school district for the amount expended by the school district for his defense.

CHAPTER VIII

CONCLUSION

Our journey began with a reminder of the key concepts of governance which form the foundation of our system of representative democracy. They are of major importance to our understanding of education law in general and Nevada school law in particular. Our grounding in the Nevada school legal setting has entailed consideration of all the sources of school law explained in the opening chapter.

One theme that has emerged from our study is captured in the word "change." Traditional legal relationships have undergone profound change, modification and refinement. The phrase "Local layperson control of schools" no longer adequately explains how Nevada schools are governed. School governance is now a complex mix of local, state and federal control. Moreover, the power to control schools is more widely disbursed than ever before among laypersons, elected officials, and a varied array of professionals.

The realignment of the school legal setting will continue as Nevada and national policy makers struggle to find solutions to Nevada's and the nation's education challenges.

The school employment framework has also witnessed structural realignment. A Nevada teacher's license is still a precondition to employment in the public schools of the state. However, the responsibility for development of standards for licensure (competence and character) is now vested with the Commission on Professional Standards in Education. A teaching license is subject to revocation. However, revocations are unusual.

The school employment process is subject to equal employment opportunity laws. Nevada teachers are still employed on an annual basis under an individual contract and new teachers serve a minimum one year probationary period (short by national standards).

In the not so distant past the employment relationship could be properly characterized as Master/Servant. School boards were vested with broad discretion to determine the worthiness of teacher candidates and teacher employees. This discretion allowed unfettered scrutiny of a teachers personal as well as professional behavior.

Today, the teacher/school district employment relationship is regulated by a complex set of substantive and procedural state statutes. Moreover, the Nevada Local Government Employee-Management Relations Act (EMRA) authorized public sector collective bargaining in 1969. Now 16 of 17 Nevada school districts have collective bargaining agreements regulating the wages, hours and conditions of employment of teachers. Furthermore, resolution of disputes over the interpretation and application of the collective bargaining agreements now rests with an impartial arbitrator instead of the local school board. Moreover, during the 1991 legislative session Nevada lawmakers amended the state labor statutes to require "last best offer" binding arbitration as the final step in the negotiation dispute resolution process. So now in the absence of a voluntary settlement the contract terms of the employment relationship are determined by a person not responsible to the school district electorate.

The U.S. Constitution also impacts on the school employment setting. Public school teachers have 1st, 4th and 14th Amendment rights at school. Teachers may speak out on matters of public concern related to schools as long as their expression does not undermine the efficiency with which the work of the schools is accomplished. Teachers are entitled to due process (fundamental fairness) if the school board wishes to discharge them for their position. Public school teachers are also protected from unreasonable searches and seizures at the workplace. Finally, equal employment opportunity laws mandate that school districts refrain from discriminatory employment practices. In short, the school employment setting can no longer be fairly characterized as Master/Servant. At the heart of the new laws regulating the education employment setting appears to be the desire to promote professional excellence and fairness in the employment process. The challenge is to recognize and resist policy initiatives which give lip service to excellence and fairness but are truly grounded in self interest.

The student/school legal relationship has also changed dramatically. The traditional doctrine of "in loco parentis" has been eroded, modified and refined. Children are now persons in a constitutional sense while under the supervision of school authorities. StudentFirst Amendment1st, 4th and 14thFourteenth AmendmentAmendment rights are limited, but, teachers are obligated to recognize and respect the nature of the new relationship these rights create. The decisions explaining the new legal environment appear to be searching for a proper balance between the schools' duty to inculcate on the one hand and refrain from imposing a pall of orthodoxy on the other. The new legal environment recognizes the importance of education by requiring fair procedure before a child can be excluded from school. The new rules also appear to be struggling to find the right balance between school safety and student privacy. School doors are no longer closed to disabled students. Education programs must be provided on a nondiscriminatory basis. Student records are accessible to parents and those with a legitimate educational interest and confidential to others.

The school/student legal relationship is infinitely more complex than a setting dominated by "in loco parentis." This new and still evolving legal setting has frustrated some educators who pine at the erosion of their absolute authority over students while celebrating the erosion of school board power over the employment relationship. Here the challenge is to champion policy which 1)encourages educators to celebrate the strengths present in our diverse student population, 2) promotes fair treatment for all and 3) promptly removes those who would destroy a school's ability to provide a safe place for teaching and learning.

Health issues are not new to schools. However, these issues have taken on a new urgency. Health problems faced by our society are reflected in the school environment. How should the school react to the presence of children or teachers with a lethal contagious disease which evidence suggests is not transmitted by casual contact. What should children be taught about human sexuality and when? What responsibility do educators bear for developing and implementing curriculum which will equip students with the knowledge to make wise decisions regarding their own health and the health of others? School health challenges still include immunization. But some issues involve controversial and very delicate matters which strike at the core of the responsibility and integrity of the family unit.

Nevada law empowers schools to employ nurses to assist with health issues faced by its schools. Furthermore, Nevada statutes impose responsibility for immunization, health screening, curriculum development, health classes and reporting suspected child abuse. The challenge here is to retain a professional approach to the problems and demand thoughtful responses instead of succumbing to emotional argument and panic when facing health issues in the school setting.

Student injuries at school are inevitable. Educators do not insure student safety. However, teachers are obligated to act in a reasonable and prudent manner when they are supervising children. Nevada has recognized the wisdom of compensating victims for injury do to negligence and protecting educators, acting in good faith, from the risk of financial ruin as they carry out their professional responsibilities. Nevada's 'peace of mind' statutes protect educators whose good faith actions in the course of their employment, unfortunately, result in a student injury. Teachers who comply with the procedural and substantive requirements of the law are entitled to have damages awarded against them paid by the school district. In addition, they are entitled to be defended by the school district or be reimbursed for reasonable attorney fees expended in their own defense.

Nevada school law is a reflection of it's citizens' struggle to achieve safe, fair and excellent schools. The struggle will continue. New rules, roles and relationships governing the school legal setting will emerge. Educators must be committed to effective participation in the ongoing search for school excellence. This is essential because they are professionally bound to seek the best means and methods for addressing the educational needs of Nevada's most precious resource-it's children!

APPENDIX A
GLOSSARY OF TERMS[775]

Ab initio: From the beginning.

Ad valorem: According to the value, e.g., a duty or tax.

Allegation: A statement of fact made in a legal proceeding.

Annotation: A remark, note, or commentary on some law or case, intended to illustrate its meaning.

Appeal: An application by an appellant to a higher court to rectify the order of the court below.

Appellant: One who appeals from a judicial decision.

Appellate court: A higher court which hears a case from a lower court on appeal.

Appellee: The person against whom an appeal is taken; the respondent to an appeal.

Arbitrary: Means in an "arbitrary" manner, as fixed or done capriciously or at pleasure, Without adequate determining principle; not founded in the nature of things; nonrational; not done or acting according to reason or judgment; depending on the will alone; absolutely in power;capriciously; tyrannical; despotic.

Assault: Threatening to strike or harm

Battery: Beating and wounding, including every touching or laying hold, however trifling, of another's person or clothes in an angry, insolent, or hostile manner.

Bona fide: With good faith, honestly, openly.

Breach: A breaking; either the invasion of a right, or the violation of a duty.

Certiorari: (To be more fully informed) An original writ or action whereby a cause is removed from an inferior to a superior court for trial. The record of proceedings is then transmitted to the superior court. The term is most commonly used when requesting the U.S. Supreme Court to hear a case from a lower court.

Civil action: An action which has for its object the recovery of private or civil rights, or compensation for their infraction.

Code: A compilation of statutes, scientifically separated into chapters, subheadings, and sections with a table of contents and an index. A collection or system of laws.

Common law: Legal principles derived from usage and custom, or from court decisions affirming such usages and custom, or from the acts of Parliament in force at the time of the American Revolution, as distinguished from law created by enactment of American legislatures.

Concurring opinion: An opinion, separate from that which embodies the views and decision of the majority of the court, prepared and filed by a judge who agrees in the general result of the decision, and which either reinforces the majority opinion by the expression of the particular judge's own views or reasoning, or (more commonly) voices his disapproval of the grounds of the decision or the arguments on which it was based, though approving the final result.

Contract: A promissory agreement between two or more persons that creates, modifies, or destroys a legal relation.

Court of record: A court that keeps a permanent record of its proceedings. (Nevada district court, Federal district court). Frequently appellate courts are called courts of record since their decisions are published.

---

[775]These definitions were selected from Black's Law Dictionary by Henry Campbell Black, West Publishing Co. , St. Paul, Minn.

Declaratory relief: The opinion of a court on a question of law that, without ordering anything to be done, simply declares the rights of the parties.

De facto: (In fact) A de facto officer is in actual possession of an office without lawful title. A de facto corporation may be reorganized as legally effective even though defective in some particular.

Defamation: Scandalous words written or spoken concerning another, tending to the injury of his reputation, for which an action on the case for damages would lie.

Defendant: One required to make answer in a suit—the one against whom the suit is brought.

De jure: (By right or law) A de jure officer has just claim and rightful title to an office, though not necessarily in actual possession thereof; a legal or true corporation or officer as opposed to one that is de facto.

De minimus: A matter that is insignificant or not worthy of judicial attention

Dictum: The expression by a judge of an opinion on a point of law not necessary to the decision on the case; not binding on lower courts.

Dissenting opinion: An opinion disagreeing with that of the majority, handed down by one or more members of the court.

Due process: Law in the regular course of administration through courts of justice, according to those rules and forms that have been established for the protection of private rights

En banc In the bench, all judges sitting.

Enjoin: To require, command, positively direct. To require a person, by **Estop:** To stop, bar, or impede; to prevent, to preclude.

Estoppel: A man's own act or acceptance stops or closes his mouth to allege or plead the truth.

Et al: And others.

Ex rel: (ex relation) At the instance of; on behalf of; on relation of information.

Executory: That which is yet to be performed or accomplished.

Hearsay evidence: Evidence not proceeding from the personal knowledge of the witness, but from the mere repetition of what he has heard others say.

In loco parentis: In place of the parent; charged with some of the parents' rights, duties, and responsibilities.

Injunction: A prohibitive writ issued by a court of equity forbidding the defendant to do some act he is threatening, or forbidding him to continue doing some act that is injurious to the plaintiff and cannot be adequately redressed by an action at law.

Malfeasance: The commission of an unlawful act.

Malice: Hatred, ill will; a formed design of doing an unlawful act.

Mandamus: A writ of mandamus is a command from a court of law directed to an inferior court, officer, corporate body, or person regarding him or them to do some particular thing.

Ministerial: Belonging to a minister or sub- ordinate who is bound to follow instructions; opposed to judicial or discretionary.

Misfeasance: A wrongful act, negligence, or the improper performance of some lawful act.

Negligence: Want of care.

Nominal damages: A trifling sum awarded to a plaintiff when no substantial loss or injury has occurred.

Nuisance: Anything that unlawfully results in harm, inconvenience, or damage.

Original jurisdiction: The jurisdiction of a court to entertain a case in its inception, as contrasted with the appellate jurisdiction.

Per curiam: By the court, opinion written by the whole court as opposed to an opinion written by any one judge. Per se: By itself, alone.

Petition: Written application or prayer to the court for the redress of a wrong or the grant of a privilege or license.

Plaintiff: Person who brings an action, the one who sues by filing a complaint.

Plenary: Full; conclusive.

Police power: Inherent or plenary legislative power to enact laws for the comfort, health, and prosperity of the state. The right to modify for the common good. In short, the right of the sovereign to govern.

Precedent: A decision considered as furnishing an example or authority for an identical or similar case afterward arising on a similar question of law.

Prima facie: At first view; on the first aspect. Prima facie evidence, presumptions, etc., are such as will prevail, if not rebutted or disproved.

Quasi: As if; almost.

Quid pro quo "Something for something"; a consideration

Remand a case: An action by an appellate court to send the case back to the court from which it came for further proceedings there.

Res judicata A matter judicially decided.

Respondeat superior: The responsibility of a master for the acts of his servants.

Respondent: The one making an answer— the defendant.

Restrain To prohibit from action; to enjoin.

Restraining order: An injunction.

Stare decisis: Adherence to precedent. When the court has made a declaration of legal principle it is the law until changed by a competent authority.

Statute: Law enacted by the legislative power of a country or state.

Subpoena duces tecum: A process by which a court commands a witness to produce some document or paper that is pertinent to the controversy being litigated.

Substantive law: The positive law of rights and duties.

Tenure: Right to perform duties and receive emoluments thereof.

Tort: Legal injury or wrong committed upon the person or property of another independent of contract.

Trespass: The unauthorized entry upon taking, or interfering with the property of another. Also, common law form of action brought to obtain damages for unlawful injury.

Ultra vires: An ultra vires contract is one beyond the powers of the corporation to make. In other words, it is one the corporation had no authority to make.

Void: Null; ineffectual; nugatory, having no legal force or binding effect; unable, in law, to support the purpose for which it was intended.

Voidable: That may be avoided, or declared void; not absolutely void, or void in itself.

INDEX

A

D

E

K

L

M

N

Nevada teachers license 110
Ninth (9th) Circuit 2, 89, 132, 230, 247

O-P-Q

Prime 6 Educational Proposal 89
Public schools 14

R

Real property 32
Reserved Powers Doctrine 7
Rules for students 216
Rules for teachers 109

S

School curriculum 16-17, 52-54, 90-107, 350-354
School Districts 10, 13, 16, 17, 19, 21, 23, 24, 32-56, 115, 116, 117, 128, 132, 214, 215, 266, 317, 336, 341
    Duties 51
        Class size reduction 54
        School Curriculum 52-54
            Achievement/proficiency tests 53
            AIDS instruction 52
            Textbooks 53
    General powers 27
    Specific powers 27-50
        School property 28-49
            Kennedy, Justice
                concurring on use of school facilities by community sectarian groups 47
                on prayer at public school graduation ceremony 28
            O'Connor, Justice, on Equal Access Act 33
            Scalia, Justice
                concurring on use of school facilities by community sectarian groups 47
                dissent on prayer at public school graduation ceremony 32
            Stevens, Justice, dissent on Equal Access Act 41
            White, Justice, on use of school facilities for community sectarian groups 42
School Finance 21
    Ad Valorem Tax 22
    Adult high school diploma program 23
    Basic per Student Support 22
    Basic per Student Support Rate 22, 23
    Distributive School Account 21
    Educational foundations 23
    Local school support tax 22
    Security Tax Authorization Law 23
    Special Education 22